GENERAL CORRESPONDENCE

VOLUME I

CRITICAL EDITION OF THE COMPLETE WORKS

(Texts and Words)

OF

SAINT THÉRÈSE OF LISIEUX

Centenary Edition

(1873-1973)

SAINT THÉRÈSE OF LISIEUX

GENERAL CORRESPONDENCE

VOLUME I

1877–1890

Translated by

John Clarke, O.C.D.

ICS Publications
Institute of Carmelite Studies
Washington, D.C.

A critical edition of all the letters written by St. Thérèse according to the autographs, and, for the letters that are lost, according to copies; these are accompanied by all the letters from her correspondents and by letters shedding light upon her life and thought.

This edition was prepared by Sister Cécile, Lisieux Carmel, with the assistance of Sister Marie-Ange, Lisieux Carmel, Sister Geneviève, O.P., Clairefontaine monastery, Sister Anne, Boulogne Carmel, Pères Albert Patfoort, O.P., Bernard Bro, O.P., Guy Gaucher, O.C.D., Jeanne and Jacques Lonchampt.

ST. THÉRÈSE OF LISIEUX GENERAL CORRESPONDENCE I
is a translation of *Correspondance Générale I*
(Les Editions du Cerf - Desclée De Brouwer, 1972)

ICS Publications
2131 Lincoln Road, N.E.
Washington, D.C. 20002
U.S.A.

Typeset by the Carmelites of Indianapolis

Library of Congress Cataloging in Publication Data

Thérèse, de Lisiuex, Saint, 1873-1897.
General correspondence.

Translation of: Correspondance générale.
Includes bibliographical references.
Contents: v. 1. 1877-1890.
1. Thérèse, de Lisieux, Saint, 1873-1897. 2. Christian saints—France—Lisieux—Correspondence. 3. Lisieux (France)—Biography. I. Title.
BX4700.T5A4 1982 282'.092'4 [B] 81-6474
ISBN 0-9600876-9-9 (v. 1) AACR2

CONTENTS

THE TEXTS

First Period

CHILDHOOD

(April 1877 - November 1886)

Second Period

ADOLESCENCE

(Christmas 1886 - April 1888)

Third Period

THE POSTULANCY

(April 9, 1888 - January 10, 1889)

Fourth Period

THE NOVITIATE

(January 1889 - September 1890)

FOREWORD

Many readers of books are not sufficiently patient to struggle through long introductory pages. However, I would urge the readers of this volume to devote enough time to its "Introduction" (pp. 19-95), for this will prove to be very rewarding. I have translated the work done on it by the French editors of *General Correspondence*, and from it we learn not only the long history of Thérèse's letters but also why these letters were not published in their entirety for so many years. We are given a detailed explanation of the three periods of this history:

1) the period of the "fragments" when only some of these letters were published, and then only as a note of interest annexed to the various editions of the *Story of a Soul* (1898-1946);
2) the period of preparation for publishing the first edition of the letters (1946-1948);
3) the period of preparation for publishing all Thérèse's extant letters, along with those from her correspondents, and a large number of documents concerning the Saint directly or indirectly (1962-1972).

The first period explains, among other matters, a difficult problem: how to deal with a young girl's letters when that girl has suddenly become the center of attention shortly after her death, September 30, 1897. The publication of her simple *Story of a Soul* (1898) had attracted many to her, and now they wanted to read more from her pen. However, her letters to her father, four sisters, uncle, aunt, and two cousins (all of whom were still living with the exception of her father) were judged to be too intimate, some of them even too trite, to be published indiscriminately. Thérèse had also attracted the attention of the Church authorities because of the innumerable favors granted through her intercession, and as early as 1909 there was talk of introducing her "cause." This would necessitate, of course, an examination into all her writings. Her sisters—three Carmelites at Lisieux and one Visitandine at Caen—were concerned about handing over all this correspondence to the scrutiny of examiners appointed for this task; their concern was shared by some of the Carmelite nuns, especially the novices who had received personal notes from Thérèse (she had been assistant mistress of novices). The advice given by Msgr. Roger de Teil, vice postulator for the "cause," led to slight alterations in some of the autographs and to the destruction of others. However, a volume of 184 pages of Thérèse's letters was assembled, and it was sent to Rome to be studied by theologians. These letters received the *nihil obstat* on December 12, 1912. What is interesting in this context is the fact that the Saint's sisters did not consent to publish these letters *in toto*; they continued to release them only as "fragments," and only fifty-one letters appeared in the editions of the *Story of a Soul*. Even as late as March 9, 1932, seven years after St. Thérèse's canonization (1925), Mother Agnes of Jesus (Pauline) expressed her reluctance at seeing her sister's letters read by others:

> At certain times, I consider it as a trial that we are so known here below, including our little Thérèse. If it were not for her mission, I would prefer to keep so many unspeakable memories in a deep silence.

The second period of this history opens in 1945. The fiftieth anniversary of St. Thérèse's death (1947) and her recent designation as Patroness of France (1944) gave rise to a renewal of devotion to her. An historian appeared on the scene, Abbé André Combes,* who was eager to draw out the doctrinal significance of this devotion. I shall not go into the rather lengthy discussion this theologian had with Sister Geneviève (Céline), who was appointed by Mother Agnes of Jesus (Pauline) to work with him (see Introduction, pp. 41-55). Abbé Combes was convinced that the time had come for a serious study of St. Thérèse's letters, for a study which would lead to a proper understanding of her spiritual development from childhood to death. He was about to conduct a course on her spiritual doctrine at the *Institut catholique de Paris* in 1946, and he intended to proceed according to the same method he had employed in his courses on the great Doctors of the Church. In other words, Abbé Combes considered Thérèse on a level with these great teachers of the past. We can readily understand, then, his line of reasoning: only the original copies of her letters would make this study possible. We can understand, too, the reluctance on the part of the Saint's sister to release them in a published edition. She was still faced with the same difficulty mentioned above: What to do with a canonized Saint's correspondence when some of it (especially her childhood letters) was so trite and unimportant? She was a little disturbed, too, about these letters because some of them contained errors in spelling and punctuation. To help her overcome her fears, Abbé Combes wrote:

> In the case of a Saint, nothing is trite. Even in Sacred Scripture, how many parts we would have deleted had the Lord consulted us! We would have been mistaken! We have to take God's work as it is and meditate on it insofar as we are capable of understanding it and drawing out suitable lessons from it.

*André Combes (October 29, 1899-December 8, 1969), doctor of theology (Toulouse), doctor of letters (Sorbonne), professor of ascetic and mystical theology at the *Institut catholique de Paris*, professor of research at the *Centre national de la Recherche scientifique*.

> As for Thérèse, we must be careful. What seems trite (especially to Céline, who knows all, who knows much more than all that has been written!) can be filled with usefulness for history and for the edification of simple souls, who will be responsive to what they find 'within their reach.' Through this, they will immediately see that Thérèse lived just as they do, that she was not always soaring on the wings of the Eagle, and, little by little, they will allow themselves to be carried along.

His powers of persuasion finally won the battle, and, after two years of work, the first edition of the letters was published in 1948. (This was translated into English in 1949; see p. 13.) This volume contained almost all of St. Thérèse's extant letters, and it was arranged according to the two main divisions of her life:

1) *before her entrance into Carmel,* twenty-four letters (thirty-three, if we include the notes written in her early childhood, which appear in the Prologue);
2) *after her entrance into Carmel,* 214 letters.

We come, finally, to the third period of this history, the most interesting and fruitful of all. With the subsequent deaths of Mother Agnes of Jesus (1951) and Sister Geneviève (1959), the way was cleared for a new edition of the letters. This work was begun in 1962 when the 1948 edition was out of print. At first, it was decided that the new edition would contain only St. Thérèse's correspondence, with possibly some additional footnotes. However, the new editors now had access to all the Saint's autographs, those of her correspondents, and a large number of documents concerning her, all of which were in the archives of the Lisieux Carmel. These editors decided to release all this material to the public, with the exception of those things not relating to Thérèse. After ten years of hard work, they published *General Correspondence,* a work in two volumes which came out in 1972, commemorating the first centenary of St. Thérèse's birth, January 2, 1873.

These volumes contain 266 letters from Thérèse, 202 from her correspondents, and a large number of other letters concerning St. Thérèse directly (in which she is a co-recipient of a letter) or indirectly (in which she is mentioned in passing or at length).

When I was translating the first volume of *General Correspondence,* I was surprised by the amount of additional information it contained. Since we now have the opportunity of reading not only Thérèse's letters but those of her correspondents, we can learn something about the characters and spiritual ideals of these correspondents. We see how she looked up to her older sisters, seeking their help and advice; we learn, too, how her older sisters frequently sought out Thérèse's own wise counsel, especially Céline, who was left at home to take care of her father during his long illness (1888-1894). The letters from Marie Guérin, Thérèse's younger cousin, contain requests for a word of encouragement from the young Carmelite in the spiritual struggles Marie was experiencing at times.

This volume supplies us, too, with much additional information on various events in the life of the future St. Thérèse. Many of us have come to know her through the reading of her *Story of a Soul,* that famous little book which has been read by millions throughout the world. However, there are many "gaps" in this Autobiography, and I am referring here to Ms. A, the account of her "childhood memories." This account was written by her in 1895 when she had reached a very high peak in her spiritual itinerary. We must keep in mind, however, that Thérèse was writing exclusively for her sisters and that she had no idea her account would be read by others. We can understand, then, how Thérèse recalled many of the important events in her life by merely making a reference to them. Many of these "gaps" are filled out by the reading of *General Correspondence.*

In the first volume, the editors have arranged the texts of Thérèse's letters according to the following four stages of her life:

1) *childhood* (April 1877 - November 1886)
2) *adolescence* (Christmas 1886 - April 1888)
3) *postulancy* (April 9, 1888 - January 10, 1889)
4) *novitiate* (January 1889 - September 1890)

After providing the reader with a short introduction to each of these stages, the editors have been very helpful in referring him to the pages of the *Story of a Soul* which correspond with these stages. In this way, the reader will find that much of what he already knows about Thérèse is greatly amplified by the reading of *General Correspondence.*

Many of us are aware of the fact that over these many years the popes have called our attention to the importance of St. Thérèse's providential "mission" in the Church. I will quote a few words of two of these popes: John Paul I and John Paul II. We know that John Paul I lived only thirty-four days after his election as pope, and he did not have time to give us any specific teaching on Thérèse. However, when he was Patriarch of Venice, he wrote a delightful letter to her on the occasion of the first centenary of her birth (1973), which begins as follows:

> Dear little Thérèse,
>
> I was seventeen years old when I read your Autobiography. For me it was like a bolt from the blue. 'Story of a little flower' you called it. To me it seemed like the story of a 'steel bar' because of the will power, the courage, and the decision that shone from it. Once you had chosen the path of complete devotion to God, nothing then could stand in your way: no illness, no external contradictions, no inner shadows or uncertainty.*

On June 2, 1980, Pope John Paul II, in his homily at St. Thérèse's basilica, stated:

*Albino Luciani, *Illustrissimi, Letters from Pope John Paul I* (Boston: Little, Brown and Company, 1978), p. 146.

> I am happy that it has been possible for me to come to Lisieux on the occasion of my visit to the French capital. I am here on pilgrimage, dear Brothers and Sisters, who have come, you too, from many regions of France, to the one whom we love so much, 'little Thérèse,' whose way of holiness is closely linked with the Carmelite convent of Lisieux. If those versed in asceticism and mysticism, and those who love the Saints, have acquired the habit of calling this way of Sister Thérèse of the Child Jesus 'the little way,' it is beyond all doubt that the Spirit of God, who guided her along this way, did so with the same generosity as when He guided her Patroness, the 'great Teresa' of Avila, and as when He guided—and continues to guide—so many saints in His Church. So glory be to Him forever!

May all of us find in this same "little Thérèse" a sure guide on the road of life, and, like her, may we learn to love God as she loved Him, for this was a desire she expressed on her deathbed:

> I feel that I am about to enter into my rest. But I feel especially that my mission is about to begin, my mission of making God loved as I love Him, of giving my little way to souls. If God answers my requests, my heaven will be spent on earth until the end of the world. Yes, I want to spend my heaven in doing good on earth. This is not impossible since from the bosom of the Beatific Vision the angels watch over us.*

I would like to express my deep appreciation to all those who, in one way or another, helped me in the preparation of this volume. I want to thank Father Kieran Kavanaugh, O.C.D. and Father Emmanuel Sullivan, O.C.D. for their expert advice when reading my manuscript; Mother Marie-Therese (Morristown Carmel) for her helpful suggestions when comparing my transla-

**Thérèse of Lisieux, St., Her Last Conversations,* trans. by John Clarke, O.C.D. (Washington, D.C: ICS Publications, Institute of Carmelite Studies, 1977), p. 102.

tion with the French edition; Sister Agnes (Morristown Carmel) for her excellent work in typing the final copy of the manuscript; the Sisters of the Indianapolis Carmel for their careful work in typesetting in which they followed closely the format of the French edition; the Sisters of Danvers Carmel for so kindly doing the proofreading; Sister Romaine (Barre Carmel) and Father Adrian Cooney, O.C.D. for their artistic work on the Cover.

John Clarke, O.C.D.
Carmelite Monastery
Brookline, Massachusetts

November 1980

ABBREVIATIONS*

ACL	Archives du Carmel de Lisieux. (Lisieux Carmel Archives).
AL	*Annales de sainte Thérèse de Lisieux* (revue). (Annals of St. Thérèse of Lisieux).
CE I, etc.	Copie des Ecrits, 1910 (CE I, II, III, IV). (Copy of the Writings, 1910).
CF	*Correspondance familiale,* Lettres de Zélie Martin (1863-1877) (Family Correspondence, Letters from Zélie Martin, 1863-1877).
ChrIG	Cahier de M. Isidore Guérin, contenant des généalogies et chronologies de sa famille. (Copybook of M. Isidore Guérin, containing his family genealogy and chronology).
CJ	"Carnet jaune" de Mère Agnès de Jesus.* ("Yellow Notebook" of Mother Agnes of Jesus).

* Most of these references do not appear in English translation. Any work that has already been translated is indicated by an asterisk, and it will be given at the end of the list of abbreviations.

CMG I, etc.	Carnets manuscrits de soeur Geneviève (CMG I, II, III, IV). (Manuscript Notebooks of Sister Geneviève).
CSG	*Conseils et Souvenirs,* publiés par soeur Geneviève, 1952.* (Counsels and Reminiscences, published by Sister Geneviève, 1952).
DCL	Documentation du Carmel de Lisieux. (Lisieux Carmel's Documentation).
DE	Sainte Thérèse de l'Enfant-Jésus et de la Sainte-Face, *Derniers Entretiens,* 1971. (Saint Thérèse of the Child Jesus and the Holy Face, *Last Conversations,* 1971).
DE/G	Derniers Entretiens recueillis par soeur Geneviève. (Last Conversations set down by Sister Geneviève).
DE/Meu	Derniers Entretiens recueillis par soeur Marie de l'Eucharistie. (Last Conversations set down by Sister Marie of the Eucharist).
DE/MSC	Derniers Entretiens recueillis par soeur Marie du Sacré-Coeur. (Last Conversations set down by Sister Marie of the Sacred Heart).
G/NPHF	Soeur *Geneviève, Notes préparatoires à l'Histoire d'une Famille.* (Sister Geneviève, Preparatory Notes for the *Story of a Family.*)
HA 98, etc.	*Histoire d'une âme,* édition 1898 (07 = 1907; 53 = 1953).* (Story of a Soul, 1898 edition).
Im	*Imitation de Jésus-Christ.* (Imitation of Christ).

LC	Lettres des correspondants de Thérèse. (Letters from Thérèse's correspondents).
LD	Lettres diverses des correspondants entre eux. (Diverse letters from the correspondents).
LT	Lettres de Thérèse. (Letters from Thérèse).
LT 1948	*Lettres de sainte Thérèse de l'Enfant-Jésus,* édition 1948.* (Letters of St. Thérèse of the Child Jesus, 1948 edition).
LTS	Lettres supplémentaires de Thérèse (devoirs de style). (Supplementary letters from Thérèse—composition homework).
Ms. A	Manuscrit autobiographique dédié à Mère Agnès de Jésus (1895)* (Autobiographical manuscript dedicated to Mother Agnes of Jesus, 1895).
Ms. B	Lettre à soeur Marie du Sacré-Coeur, manuscrit autobiographique (1896)* (Letter to Sister Marie of the Sacred Heart, autobiographical manuscript, 1896).
Ms. C	Manuscrit autobiographique dedié a Mère Marie de Gonzague (1897). (Autobiographical manuscript dedicated to Mother Marie de Gonzague).
Mss. I	Trois volumes du P. François de Sainte-Marie, accompagnant l'édition en fac-similé (1956) des *Manuscrits Autobiographiques* (Mss. I, II, III). (Three volumes of P. François de Sainte-Marie, accompanying the facsimile edition (1956) of the Autobiographical Manuscripts).

NPPA	Notes préparatoires au Procès Apostolique. (Preparatory notes for the Apostolic Process).
NPPO	Notes préparatoires au Procès de l'Ordinaire. (Preparatory notes for the Bishop's Process).
OCL	Office Central de Lisieux (maison d'éditions). (Lisieux' Central Office, publishing house).
P	Poésies de sainte Thérèse de l'Enfant-Jésus (numérotage de Mss. I). (Poems of St. Thérèse of the Child Jesus, according to the Mss. I numbering).
PA	Procès Apostolique, 1915-1916 (d'après Sum. II). (Apostolic Process, 1915-1916, according to the second volume of the Summary).
PO	Procès de l'Ordinaire, 1910-1911 (ibid.). The Bishop's Process, 1910-1911 (ibid.).
RP	"Récréations pieuses" de sainte Thérèse de l'Enfant-Jésus (numérotation de Mss. I). ("Pious Recreations" of St. Thérèse of the Child Jesus, according to the Mss. I numbering).
VT	*Vie Thérésienne,* Lisieux (revue). (Theresian Life, Lisieux).
VTL	*Visage de Thérèse de Lisieux* (1961), en deux *volumes.** (Face of Thérèse of Lisieux (1961), in two volumes).

Works already translated:

1. *"Carnet jaune" de Mère Agnès de Jésus: St. Thérèse of Lisieux, Her Last Conversations,* trans. by John Clarke O.C.D. (Washington, D.C: ICS Publications, Institute of Carmelite Studies, 1975), "Yellow Notebook," pp. 35-207.
2. *Conseils et Souvenirs,* 1952: Sister Geneviève of the Holy Face (Céline Martin), *A Memoir of my Sister, St. Thérèse,* authorized translation by the Carmelite Sisters of New York (New York: P.J. Kenedy & Sons, 1959).
3. *Histoire d'une Ame,* édition 1898: *Soeur Thérèse of Lisieux, An Autobiography,* edited by T.N. Taylor (London: Burns & Oates, Ltd., 1912). Also: *Saint Thérèse of Lisieux, The Little Flower of Jesus,* revised translation by Rev. Thomas N. Taylor (New York: P.J. Kenedy & Sons, 1927).
4. *Lettres de sainte Thérèse de l'Enfant-Jésus,* édition 1948: *Collected Letters of Saint Thérèse of Lisieux,* trans. by F.J. Sheed (New York: Sheed & Ward, 1949).
5. *Manuscrit autobiographique dédié à Mère Agnès de Jésus* (1895): *Story of a Soul, The Autobiography of St. Thérèse of Lisieux,* a new translation from the original manuscripts by John Clarke, O.C.D. (Washington, D.C: ICS Publications, Institute of Carmelite Studies, 1972); see Ms. A, pp. 13-182.
6. *Lettre à soeur Marie du Sacré-Coeur, manuscrit autobiographique* (1896): see *Story of a Soul, The Autobiography of St. Thérèse of Lisieux,* Ms. B, pp. 183-200.
7. *Manuscrit autobiographique dédié à Mère Marie de Gonzague* (1897): see *Story of a Soul, The Autobiography of St. Thérèse of Lisieux,* Ms. C, pp. 201-259.
8. *Visage de Thérèse de Lisieux* (1961): *Photo Album of St. Thérèse de Lisieux,* trans. by Peter-Thomas Rohrbach, O.C.D. (New York: P.J. Kenedy & Sons, 1962).

PRESENTATION
CONVENTIONAL SIGNS AND GUIDE FOR USING THIS VOLUME

General Correspondence is presented in two volumes, following a continuous pagination:

Volume I: Introduction. Correspondence from April 4, 1877 to September 24, 1890 (the day Thérèse received the Veil).

Volume II: Correspondence from September 28, 1890 to September 30, 1897 (the day of Thérèse's death). Appendices and Charts.

The texts of the letters (LT, LC, LD) are clarified by introductions, captions, and footnotes.

THE TEXTS OF THE LETTERS

1. *Letters from Thérèse* (*LT*)

The text of Thérèse's letters was transcribed according to the entire content of the autograph. The French editors scrupulously respected her spelling, use of capital letters, and abbreviations. Surprising irregularities resulted from this, but this is to be expected in a critical edition. In cases of doubt (for example, when certain words in the autograph were almost illegible), they gave

Thérèse the benefit of the doubt. It was impossible, of course, to duplicate Thérèse's occasional errors in spelling; however, I did capitalize the words she capitalized, such as Divine, Heavenly, Sun, etc.

The editors applied the same rigor to Thérèse's punctuation, although her use of the "period" and "comma" was difficult to distinguish at times. Her marks of suspension and exclamation were also introduced by them into the printed text. Here, again, it was not possible to observe Thérèse's punctuation, but I did duplicate her marks of suspension and exclamation.

Very frequently when writing, Thérèse emphasized her point by underlining certain words. These underlinings were interpreted in the following way: a single underlining: *italics*; a double underlining: SMALL CAPITALS; a triple underlining: LARGE CAPITALS; anything beyond this: LARGE CAPITALS and a footnote to indicate their exact number.

2. *Letters from correspondents* (*LC, LD*)

The original text was followed as closely as possible. Since these letters were not the main object of the critical edition, the editors corrected the spelling errors and a *minimum* of the errors in punctuation in order to facilitate the reading.

INTRODUCTIONS

The "introductions," printed in italics, which accompany these letters, replace, for each period or stage of Thérèse's life, the chronological notes given year by year in Abbé Combes' first edition of the Letters (1948).

These "introductions" divide the text in a very free manner, making no attempt to point out the minor incidents in the Saint's life but simply its important stages. Volume I, then, will deal with:

1) childhood
2) adolescence
3) postulancy
4) novitiate

These "introductions" encourage the reader to make a comparison between the event actually written about in the letters (LT, LC, LD) and the rereading of this same event as it was explained years later by Thérèse in her *Story of a Soul* (Ms. A, B, C). For if the letters by their very nature serve to complete and confirm the *Story of a Soul,* inversely, the *Story of a Soul* is indispensable for completing the letters. (For this reason, at the end of these "introductions" the editors have carefully pointed out the corresponding passage in Ms. A, B, and C.)

In spite of their appearance, these "introductions" make no attempt to fill in the normal "gaps" in any correspondence. They are simply rough outlines, "guideposts," and they have no other purpose but that of aiding the reader to situate Thérèse's letters within their historical and psychological context, as well as within the context of the Saint's spiritual development.

CAPTIONS AND FOOTNOTES

The "captions" (beneath the heading of some of the letters) and the "footnotes" are mainly historical and documentary in nature. Biographical accounts are rare and not developed at length: a "Biographical Guide to Proper Names" will be provided in the Appendix (volume II) and will complete this information, especially with regard to the letters of St. Thérèse.

The sources, certain or probable, of thoughts expressed by Thérèse were indicated whenever it was possible to trace these sources. The editors were conscious of the fact that St. Teresa's influence on Thérèse would call for a deeper study, especially since the Carmelite nuns at Lisieux at this time (1888-1897) were very much imbued with St. Teresa's spirit and writings. Likewise,

a systematic reading of the expressions that Thérèse borrowed from the "Conferences" of Abbé Arminjon could also be the object of a special study.

Some important themes are explained in the "footnotes": the little toy (LT 34, note 2), the grain of sand (LT 45, note 4), the prayer for priests (LT 94, note 7), etc.

CONVENTIONAL SIGNS

The following "conventional signs" will aid the reader to know precisely where he is in the correspondence. At the top of each page, along with the date, the reader will see the abbreviations LT and LC. An abbreviation in Roman type corresponds to the letter which appears on the page; an abbreviation in *italics* points to the last letter of this category that has been read. For example, on page 447: *LT 56*/LC 86 means that LT 56 is the *last* letter from Thérèse read hitherto, which appears on a former page, and that LC 86 is on the present page (in text or footnotes). Two abbreviations in Roman type naturally indicate that there is one or several letters of each category on the page; for example, on page 446: LT 56/LC 86.

The *title* of each letter (bold-faced for LT and *italics* for LC, LD) makes mention of the sender and the recipient: the family name for the five Martin sisters before their entrance into religion was omitted, as well as the words "of the Child Jesus and the Holy Face" for Thérèse in Carmel.

The *title* is sometimes followed by the words: "Fragments" or "Extracts" in parentheses. In the first case, it must be understood that the editors found only an incomplete document but that they cited it integrally. In the second case, *and this has reference to the LD exclusively,* curtailments were made in order to prevent developments which were of no interest for this edition.

The *date*, at the beginning of each letter, sometimes has a question mark. Depending on its position, uncertainty has reference to the day, the month, or the year.

Immediately under the date, the arrow (→) indicates a direct link between two documents. Thus, LT 79 is an immediate response to LC 101 which was cited some ten pages before. The reader may be interested in going back to this document before reading the response, especially when these two documents are far apart. This will be the case, for example, regarding exchanges between Thérèse and P. Roulland after his departure for China.

The words "LT *lost*" (or LC) means that the letter in question has certainly been destroyed by its recipient (P. Pichon, for example), or letters have disappeared, been destroyed (we often don't know by whom), or that letters have not been found up to this day.

Immediately after the text of the letters, and before the "footnotes," the *source of the document* is indicated (preceded by an asterisk).

GENERAL INTRODUCTION

PLAN OF THE INTRODUCTION

First Part

THE FORMER EDITIONS

Second Part

THE GENERAL CORRESPONDENCE

Unlike the *Histoire d'une Ame* (published in 1898), which sold close to 200,000 copies in fifteen years, Thérèse's *Letters* were not known in their entirety until fifty years later (1948). Up to that time, the public had access to a very restricted number of these letters.

The critical edition of the *Complete Works of Thérèse of Lisieux,* entitled the *Centenary Edition,* now presents the *General Correspondence* in two volumes. This does not mean the simple republication of the 1948 *Letters.* The purpose of this publication is to give the reader a critical and documentary collection comprising:

1) all letters from Thérèse (LT);
2) all letters addressed to her by her correspondents (LC);
3) all diverse letters (*lettres diverses*) written during her lifetime, concerning her directly or indirectly (LD).

These documents, then, are finally being published seventy-five years after Thérèse's death. They had a checkered history from 1897 to 1972, and this, of course, conditions the character of the present publication. We shall divide this history into the following three periods:

1897-1946: Thérèse's letters appeared in fragmentary form in the *Histoire d'une Ame*;

1946-1948: preparation was underway for an *exact and complete* publication of the *Letters*;

1962-1972: preparation for and publication of the *General Correspondence,* in two volumes.

FIRST PART

THE FORMER EDITIONS

FIRST CHAPTER

THE PERIOD OF THE FRAGMENTS

(1897 - 1946)

1. First Editions of the "Histoire d'une Ame" (1898-1910)

"When the Lisieux Carmel consented to give the public extracts from the letters, it had no intention of compiling a critical edition. Considering these texts simply as useful additions to the basic book which was—and remains—the *Histoire d'une Ame,* the Saint's sisters treated these letters as a rich mine of edifying thoughts from which it seemed to them permissible to extract various passages that would serve to clarify and render more exact the essential positions established by the Autobiography. From this point of view, the chronology, the original content, or the strict integrity of each letter presented no importance. Nothing seemed to be wrong with bringing together, sometimes under the same date, sentences coming from different letters but totally relative to the same subject."[1]

We see, here, the process of amalgamation, current at the time.[2] Thanks to this "method," eighteen fragments of letters to

[1] A. Combes, *Lettres* (1948), Preface, p. xxii.

[2] See DE, pp. 63-64, 78, 124.

Céline were published in 1898. The collection was enriched in later editions. It reached forty-seven in 1907,[3] and fifty-one in 1910.

New extracts from Thérèse's letters came in chance ways. In the 1907 edition of *Histoire d'une Ame*, we read this note: "We regret being unable to publish at least some of the many charming letters addressed to Léonie; these were unfortunately burned by mistake."[4] However, the following year, Sister Marie of the Sacred Heart wrote to Léonie:

> What a surprise when I read in your last letter that you had found fourteen letters from Thérèse.... We are sorry we did not know that you still had some letters. I beg you, don't refuse to copy them for me. A woman from Belgium has already written to us: "What a pity that Léonie's letters were burned, for one word from this Little Saint is a real treasure we would not want to lose."[5] Mother Agnes of Jesus realizes better than anyone else the value of Thérèse's *smallest word*; a short time ago, she arranged a collection of her last conversations, which was as complete as she could possibly make it.[6] She is insisting, then, with Léonie: "Don't omit one word, I entreat you."[7]

Sister Marie was granted her request:

> You gave me great joy this morning; you sent me a treasure. I didn't think you were so rich. We will draw from this treasure some of the beautiful passages for a future edition. What a pity we published this time that these letters were burned. However, we will make up for this by saying that these pearls escaped the flames.[8]

[3] HA 1907, twenty letters to Céline, eight to Mother Agnes of Jesus, six to Sister Marie of the Sacred Heart, two to Marie Guérin, one to Jeanne Guérin, ten to her brother missionaries.

[4] HA 1910, p. 353. The assumption is likely: between 1900 and 1905, Sister Françoise-Thérèse (Léonie), recently professed at the Visitation, Caen, had been encouraged to destroy her family correspondence; see Mss. I, p. 35.

[5] Letter of June 7, 1908.

[6] Her "black notebook" (1904)? See DE, pp. 65-66, 119-120.

[7] August 22, 1908.

[8] September 23, 1908.

To Sister Marie of the Sacred Heart fell the task of recasting the letters she received from Léonie:

> During these past few days, I have worked at arranging the letters that Thérèse wrote you in order to place them in the next edition. I think this will please you, and we, too, will be happy to see our little Léonie appear in her turn. Several people wrote us and said they did not want to believe your letters from Thérèse were lost. We can't put all of them in, however, because we should not repeat the same thoughts expressed in other letters. This was a recommendation made some time ago by R. P. Godefroy when he was working on Thérèse's manuscript. So we made a choice of the most beautiful passages, and there will be four very nice little letters that don't repeat others.[9]

These four mosaics appeared in the March 1910 edition of *Histoire d'une Ame*.

2. Sister Genevieve's Notebooks (1903-1907?)

Leaving to her older sisters the task of preparing these anthologies of her sister's letters, Sister Geneviève (Céline) gathered together some documents for her personal use, and these were to prove of great interest in the future.

In a heavily bound notebook (CMG III), Céline gathered together the elements of a biography of her sister. She distributed into five periods[10] extracts from the first manuscript (Ms. A), letters from Thérèse or from her family, and various documents

[9] December 28, 1909

[10] The notebook begins on p. 32. The first pages could have been written about her parents. The first period extends from 1873 to 1877, from Thérèse's birth to her mother's death; the second period, 1877-1882, from Mme. Martin's death to Pauline's entrance into Carmel, pp. 40-63; the third period, 1882-1886, from Pauline's entrance to the "Christmas grace," pp. 64-112; the fourth period, 1886-1888, from the "Christmas grace" to Thérèse's entrance into Carmel, pp. 113-168; the fifth period, 1888-1897, in Carmel, pp. 171-269.

(homework exercises, retreat notes, etc.). The first four periods regrouped twenty-six letters from Thérèse as a child and an adolescent. The fifth period was made up exclusively of forty-five letters from Thérèse as a Carmelite nun.[11]

At this same time, Sister Geneviève began a second notebook (CMG IV), identical in form, in which she copied forty-four letters that she had received from Thérèse between the years 1888 and 1894.[12]

What was the *precise* date on which these copies were made? She has left us no clue whatsoever. In 1910, this transcription was already considered as having been done long ago: "done before," "done a long time ago."[13] This is a subjective appraisal which internal criticism should attempt to make more definite.

An examination of Sister Geneviève's handwriting favors its being done a long time ago. But this estimate—by comparing the handwriting with other documents spread out over several years—is approximate, with a fluctuating margin of ten years.

The inventory of the recopied texts furnishes us with the most interesting clues. Thus, from the total absence of letters from Thérèse to Léonie, we may infer that the CMG copy was made before 1908;[14] from the copying out, in an independent appendix, of the letters to l'abbé Bellière, we may infer that the copy of the years 1896-1897 was terminated when this collection was returned to the Carmel after l'abbé Bellière's death, July 14, 1907. On the other hand, we note that the letters to the Guérin family furnish an important part of the material of CMG III and that they are classified chronologically in the very first pages.[15] If

[11] We should add here ten letters to Abbé Bellière, pp. 271-307. Then we have the "health reports" on Thérèse's illness, pp. 309-338; see DE, p. 837.

[12] We must mention a copy, anterior to this one, of Thérèse's letters to Céline, May 8, 1888 to October 20, 1891, in CMG I, pp. 1-76. It is difficult to suggest a date: either around 1893, before Céline's entrance into Carmel, or, more likely, a short time after Thérèse's death (1897-1898).

[13] See following page.

[14] The year when fourteen letters were found; see note 7.

[15] We number forty-six of them among the seventy-one letters that CMG III arranged from 1876 to 1897.

M. Guérin waited until 1905 to give his Carmelite nieces his most intimate *dossiers,* namely, the correspondence received from his sister, Mme. Martin,[16] he could have given them, before 1905, the letters from Thérèse, which were somewhat less important.

A final question, and this is only conjecture: could not Sister Marie of the Sacred Heart's urgent intervention with Mother Agnes of Jesus, in 1904, to copy out Thérèse's last conversations,[17] have been inspired by Sister Geneviève's own work on Thérèse's correspondence?

It seems, then, reasonable to place Sister Geneviève's composition of her notebooks around the year 1905.[18]

What credence can we give to this copy with regard to its *authenticity*? The question is important insofar as Sister Geneviève's notebooks are the sole source of some of Thérèse's letters.[19] This *dossier,* let us remember, was not destined for future publication. We would like to hope, then, that its "intimate" nature enabled it to enjoy a much greater literal fidelity. Nothing is less certain, however. Examinations made regarding citations from the Autobiography show that Sister Geneviève exercised here a compromise between the authentic text of the *Manuscripts* and the official version of the *Histoire d'une Ame*: and so we have words which are not from Thérèse, nor from Mother Agnes of Jesus but from Céline! The same can be said with regard to the letters, the autographs of which still exist.

And Sister Geneviève makes no mystery about these variations in form. Witness, for example, this consultation with the vice postulator of the Cause, Msgr. de Teil, in 1910:

[16] Judging by Sister Geneviève's letter to P. Piat, January 2, 1958; see also CF, pp. 9-10 and 47. Another statement relating to this correspondence: "St. Thérèse never had any knowledge of the letters [of Mme. Martin], addressed to Uncle, but only of those sent to Pauline. I asked for and obtained the letters of the Guérin family only after her death [read: Thérèse's death]." (Letter of Sister Geneviève to P. Piat, December 26, 1957.)

[17] See note of May 2, 1904, cited in DE, p. 64.

[18] CMG IV has other sections written much later, for example, Céline's letters to her sisters, the last conversations (copied around 1924?), extracts from Ms. A, transcribed in 1941, souvenirs of her golden jubilee (1946), etc.

[19] See, p. 73.

> Sister Geneviève would like to know, Monseigneur, whether the copies of the little childish letters which she made some time ago of Sister Thérèse's letters (now cut up into pieces to make little relics) must be recopied to be presented with the writings. She would not be able to declare under oath that her copy is authentic; it is too long ago since this was done. These letters said absolutely nothing of interest except for the family. This is the only matter that is troubling her.[20]

We shall be reading, in a moment, the reassuring answer from Msgr. de Teil. However, two statements in this letter hold our attention: 1) Sister Geneviève cannot answer for the authenticity of her copies; 2) and, more seriously, some of the autographs were cut into pieces to be given out as "relics." This mutilation of the autographs, unusual up to this date, took on disconcerting proportions in the spring of 1910 when the Process concerning the Servant of God's "writings" began.

3. The Copy of the Writings (1910)

In his first visit to the Carmel, January 26, 1909, Msgr. de Teil began preparing the Carmelite nuns for the necessary stage of the examination into the "writings" of Sister Thérèse. The date for this examination was still rather remote, for the examiners first had to proceed to the testimonies regarding the Servant of God's virtues and her reputation for sanctity. However, the copyists preferred to set to work immediately. Sister Geneviève wrote to Léonie:

> You would be very kind to copy out the letters she wrote to you, an integral copy; the copy done in this way and given under oath has the same value as the original in the eyes of the Church, and you don't have to part with her relics (Msgr. de Teil told us this). An integral copy does not mean copying out the mistakes in spelling or the erasures; you may correct it. When you have copied

[20] Mother Agnes of Jesus to Msgr. de Teil, May 1, 1910.

them, you may send them here, and we will give them in along with our own."[21]

On March 5, 1910, contrary to Roman usage or custom, the *Sacred Congregation of Rites* took the initiative to invite the bishop of Bayeux, Bishop Lemonnier, to undertake the examination into the "writings."

This "examination" was to comprise three stages: 1) a copy of the originals by the holders of the autographs (March-May 1910); 2) a comparison of these copies with the originals by two reviewers and the appearance of the witnesses before a special ecclesiastical Commission (May); and 3) the sending of these copies to Rome for examination by a theologian (1910-1912). We are interested in the first two stages only.

The directives given to the Carmelite nuns for setting up the copies were, one day, to become the cause of much trouble to the editors of the *Letters*. The treatment to which the autographs were subjected (scrapings, mutilations, or total destruction)[22] is rather disturbing. The line of reasoning employed at the time to justify all this is even more distressing. Let us try to enter into the viewpoint of the 1910 examiners. It was the Servant of God's virtues that held their attention, not her opinions or even her spiritual doctrine. In a Process held so close to the facts, in which a number of eyewitnesses were involved, the testimonies of contemporaries obtained more credence than the writings of the interested party. What the Church was seeking was not "the sentiments of a fertile imagination but realities actually lived."[23] That is why, according to the court procedure, "the writings are

[21] To Sister Françoise-Thérèse (Léonie), February 16, 1909. Because of a failure to use the prescribed format, the copies made in 1909 were null and void. We have found no trace of them whatsoever.

[22] See, pp. 63-66.

[23] Msgr. de Teil to Mother Agnes of Jesus, June 14, 1910; the context differs slightly; in fact, in this letter, he is encouraging the citing of the "writings." But on June 20, he puts them on their guard against an abusive usage of texts: "If the whole time is spent dictating from documents, we would lose what the Process is seeking, namely, *information furnished by eyewitnesses* who say: 'I know that . . . because I saw her; I state it under oath.' Otherwise, if we were to take only written pieces, we could just as well have the Process in fifty years and in a Carmel in China."

examined [at Rome] by a special commission, independent of the other [which is examining the virtues], and then only to testify as to whether there is anything against faith and morals."[24]

The first instructions to the copyists were given by word of mouth, in the Carmel's speakroom, on May 17, 1910. Sister Geneviève transmitted these instructions to Léonie, the Visitandine:

> Now, little Léonie, I am going to say a word about the letters you have from Thérèse. Very soon, Bishop Lemonnier will publish a letter to be read from the pulpit on three consecutive Sundays;[25] he will ask for the *Servant of God's* writings, and we shall be *obliged* to send them to the bishop's residence, either our original or a true *copy*. Msgr. de Teil told us not to part with the originals but to copy them and to have the courage to make disappear what we do not want to hand in, such as family secrets, intimate conversations, etc. As for ourselves, we are hurrying up to rectify the autographs *before* the appeal from Monseigneur. I have destroyed all the letters she wrote to Papa.[26] As for your own, if there are any expressions like 'Baby' or others, erase them and put in another word instead. Have no scruples, for we have the right, and, besides, Thérèse told us prophetically before she died that she entrusted herself to us in this matter[27] and that she would be doing all that we did when making the changes."[28]

Most fortunately, Léonie made no use whatsoever of this "prophetic" permission granted by Thérèse. Sister Marie of the Sacred Heart was very careful. Sister Geneviève and Mother Agnes, too, contrary to what we could have feared, proved relatively moderate in the rectification of the originals. However, it is not possible

[24]Sister Geneviève to Sister Françoise-Thérèse, April 16, 1910.

[25]The bishop's mandate was dated April 4, 1910, and sets down May 20, 1910, as the last date for handing in the "writings" at the bishop's residence.

[26]Theoretical "destruction." See, p. 64.

[27]See DE, *volume d'Annexes*, pp. 164-165 (*Novissima Verba*, July 16, no. 2).

[28]To Sister Françoise-Thérèse, March 27, 1910.

to form any judgment, with any kind of certitude, concerning the number of autographs that were destroyed at this time.

Some further directives confirmed the Carmelite nuns in their right:

> To calm your conscience with reference to the examination into the writings, you may consider as NONEXISTENT the passages already crossed out which you will testify as being puerile passages dealing, for example, with the games of children or things like that, which cannot be really qualified as "Letters" in the elevated sense of the term, but that, in your eyes, these autographs are real relics and that you preferred to destroy the passages in question by *erasing* them rather than by burning this little relic; that this had been done *before* ecclesiastical authority had claimed these writings . . . . You will see that all this will be accepted *with understanding* . . . . As for all the difficulties of detail, it will be good for me to come to an understanding with you *viva voce.*[29]

After this interview (April 16), there arose the problem of Sister Geneviève's notebooks and those "little childish letters which said absolutely nothing of interest."[30] Msgr. de Teil gives new reassurances:

> As for this child's letters in which there is question only of family matters or feast-day wishes, if I were you I would keep them; I would read them to the Commission, declaring myself ready and disposed to copy them if the Commission judged it *à propos*; I would say that, attaching no special importance to them, you cut them in pieces as fragments of relics and that you cannot, neither can Sister Geneviève, state, under oath, anything else except their childish character; that you would reconstruct them as well as you can if they so desire. I would then await their decision.[31]

[29] Msgr. de Teil to Mother Agnes, April 8, 1910.

[30] See, p. 30, note 20.

[31] Msgr. de Teil to Mother Agnes, May 2, 1910.

The work of copying was not entirely finished when two examiners came to the Carmel, May 9, 1910, for a first comparison of the texts. These were Canon E. Deslandes from Bayeux, diocesan scholar,[32] and l'abbé Ch. Marie from St. Jacques, Lisieux.[33] They approached their task very seriously, in fact, even too seriously according to Mother Agnes' opinion:

> Since yesterday, in the afternoon, Monsieur le Chanoine Deslandes and M. l'abbé Marie have been in the speakroom, examining the writings. But how slow they are!!! I can hardly keep from laughing. I noticed that M. le Chanoine, when he arrived, believed it would take a day or two, but should he continue at this pace, I am afraid the 'Last Judgment' will surprise him at his copybooks. He is making M. l'abbé Marie put in as many periods, commas, and underlinings as the autographs before him already have.[34] Meanwhile, he admires and he speaks joyfully at having to do this work; this consoles me very much, for, really, he puts great fervor into his work in spite of his scruples and his slowness. I was going to say he puts a real enthusiasm into it.[35]

Msgr. de Teil was quick to pick up that last word "enthusiasm":

[32] Eucher Deslandes (February 13, 1849 - November 13, 1922) gave early signs of "his calling as research expert and archivist." He had to his credit several publications which won academic degrees for him and the distinction of *Officier de l'Instruction Publique.* His death notice pointed out the very important part he played "as *notary* in the preparation and writing of the material required for the various canonical processes set up for the beatification of little Sister Thérèse of the Child Jesus. He collated these with such a scrupulous care, with such a clear and precise methodology, that we can attribute, in part, the rapidity with which the Cause advanced at Rome to the perfection of his voluminous *dossier.*" (*Semaine Religieuse de Bayeux*, December 3, 1922, pp. 488-493.)

[33] Charles-Louis-Auguste Marie (1849-1912), deputy notary at the diocesan Process (Procès de l'Ordinaire, 1910).

[34] We can still see these changes in punctuation, especially wavy underlinings, in a different ink, for several pages of the copy of Thérèse's letters to Céline (CE II, pp. 62 to 71).

[35] Mother Agnes to Msgr. de Teil, May 10, 1910.

> M. Deslandes' enthusiasm will exert a great influence on the bishop and his *entourage*, for they consider M. Deslandes as a real scholar and not a dreamer, and so they will attach all the more credibility to my own affirmations which surprised them; I have really experienced this.[36]

However, time was limited, and the rigor of their examination relented: "These gentlemen ended up by abandoning the underlinings and the textual punctuation."[37] For the little time that they spent with the autographs, especially Thérèse's letters to Céline, which they examined first, we have no touble in excusing these readers whose eyes were no longer those of a twenty-year-old. Never drawn herself to any kind of precision, Sister Marie of the Sacred Heart was amazed at them: "Never would I have believed that anyone would give these writings such meticulous care. It was necessary to copy not only the manuscript but all the letters, even those addressed to Uncle and Aunt."[38]

These "letters to Aunt": we shall talk about them often!

From May 23-26, 1910, the diocesan Commission presided over by M. Dubosq, vicar general,[39] questioned the persons in possession of Thérèse's letters.[40] The witnesses had to furnish a detailed explanation as to the names on the autographs, clarifications on their preservation, examination, publication, and, eventually, the destruction of the writings.[41] On the last point, the an-

[36] To Mother Agnes of Jesus, May 10, 1910.

[37] From Mother Agnes to Msgr. de Teil, May 11, 1910.

[38] To Sister Françoise-Thérèse, May 19, 1910.

[39] Pierre-Théophile Dubosq (1860-1932), priest of St. Sulpice, doctor of theology and canon law, superior of the major seminary at Bayeux; he was promoter of the faith at the Beatification and Canonization Process. This "devil's advocate" was, along with Msgr. de Teil, Mother Agnes of Jesus' faithful adviser throughout the "Cause."

[40] Doctor and Mme. La Néele, Thérèse's four sisters, Marie, Pauline, Léonie, and Céline, Sisters Marie of the Trinity, Martha of Jesus, and Marie-Madeleine of the Blessed Sacrament; Marceline Husé, former servant of the Guérin family (in religion: Sister Marie-Joseph of the Cross, a Benedictine at Bayeux).

[41] These testimonies were recorded in the "*Processiculus de scriptis*, 1910." The Commission held seven sessions (March 24 to June 12, 1910).

swers were very cautious. Léonie's response was striking because of its frankness:

> I received, either when I was in the world or after my entrance into the Visitation convent, a certain number of letters which I burned, attaching no importance to them, and I regret this today. A certain number written to her father, relatives, and others, were also destroyed for the same motivation: that we attached no importance to them or because they contained intimate details of family life; their destruction, however, took place before the ordinance of Monseigneur the bishop, relative to the examination into the "writings" of the Servant of God, and this does not imply any bad intention.[42]

Sister Marie-Madeleine's statement is even more picturesque! The examiners had asked her: "Have they searched well? Is there any risk of finding some writings?" Her answer was filled with conviction: "I know that the Sisters have searched well, that is certain, throughout the whole monastery, especially our Reverend Mother Prioress and Sister Geneviève; it is certain that they will find nothing else."[43]

And we found some letters fifty years later!

The official *Copy of the Writings* makes up four volumes (28 x 21 cms.), a total of 491 pages. The *Letters* (volume 2) fill 184 pages. The examination into the writings was terminated at the last session, June 12, 1910. Delegated by Bishop Lemonnier, Canon Deslandes arrived at Rome the following week to deliver his manuscript, "not without some justified pride."[44] The "writings" received the *Nihil obstat* from Rome, December 10, 1912.

[42] Session IV, May 25, 1910, p. 32, according to the Bayeux copy.

[43] Session III, May 24, 1910, p. 29.

[44] Msgr. de Teil to Mother Agnes, June 21, 1910. The documents were brought to the *Sacred Congregation of Rites*, February 6, 1912, at the same time as those of the "Acts" of the diocesan Process.

4. Status Quo (1910-1946)

Monseigneur de Teil had advised the witnesses to bring into their testimonies "the most typical sentences" from the Servant of God's letters. He wrote to Mother Agnes: "*I add that the collection of Writings does not make up a part of the diocesan process which is concerned with the reputation for sanctity.* Not being aware of this, you and yours would deprive the proof of sanctity of one of its most precious elements."[45] He recommended that they make these citations according to the autographs, and not according to the fragments published in *Histoire d'une Ame.* He added: "And take care to inform the judges that you are doing this, for this is an important point in citations at a Process."[46]

As a matter of fact, Mother Agnes of Jesus and Sister Marie of the Sacred Heart quoted few of Thérèse's letters in their testimonies; on the other hand, Sister Geneviève drew generously from her rich collection: marginal notes written in pencil on the autographs are proof of this.[47] Léonie, following Sister Geneviève's advice, acted in the same way but made no marginal notes.

The diocesan Process finally came to an end, and each of Thérèse's sisters locked her treasures within her archives. The "fragments" of the letters, annexed to *Histoire d'une Ame*, remained practically the same for the next thirty years.

The correspondence suffered much more than Thérèse's other writings because of the defensive attitude of her sisters, who were faced with the first demands of a critical inquiry at the time of the Beatification (1923) and the Canonization (1925). The investigations and publications, however well-intentioned, of l'abbé Ruel[48]

[45] June 14, 1910.

[46] To Mother Agnes of Jesus, June 30, 1910.

[47] See p. 66.

[48] Pierre Ruel (1892-1944), Bayeux diocese, author of three articles on Thérèse in *Cahiers catholiques* (May 2, 10, and June 25, 1923); these articles were later published in a booklet: *La Bienheureuse Thérèse de l'Enfant-Jésus, Sa valeur humaine* (Mamers, July 1923, 36 pages). This study displeased Mother Agnes; see DE, p. 108.

and P. Lepetit,[49] and P. Ubald's[50] attacks very probably brought about the destruction of the family papers by the Carmelite nuns. Although Thérèse's letters were spared, they were withheld from the public, and there arose the problem of the "seekers after the unpublished," those interested in reading every word from the pen of the Saint.

Mother Agnes of Jesus explained her conduct to Léonie: on May 16, 1926, she had a complaint to make with one of these investigators:

> Jeanne had written me that he "*had coaxed her*" into copying out all the letters that she has from Thérèse!! She was sorry about this, for this good priest has a mania for wanting to publish all that comes from Thérèse, without changing anything or passing over a word.... I have spoken about this to Msgr. de Teil and M. Dubosq.... We agreed that in order to "cut the ground from under the feet" of all these seekers after the unpublished, for he is not the only one, we should publish some extracts from the letters of our Saint to the Guérin family in the next edition of Msgr. Laveille. I made the choice myself. It will take up seven or eight pages in the appendix.[51]
>
> Above all, give nothing to *anyone* of what you have. I have read in these unpublished letters of our Thérèse things which the public has no right to know and to exploit; we should be able to keep certain family secrets.... M. Lepetit is going to calm down, especially when he sees the beautiful passages from the published letters. Will he be surprised and bored! We must excuse this need to say *everything*. It's a sickness, a mania, but just the same we must protect ourselves from people who have this sickness as we would from a fire.

[49] The "good priest" of the following paragraph. *Missionnaire de La Délivrande,* he was interested, among other things, in Thérèse's sojourns at Trouville. Author of a booklet: *Sur les pas d'une Sainte* (Téqui, 1932), a revised publication of articles that appeared in 1923 in *Le petit Trouvillais.*

[50] A Franciscan from Alençon, author of an article: "*Sainte Thérèse de l'Enfant-Jésus comme je la connais*" (*Estudis Franciscans,* no. 220, January 1926, Barcelone), which unleashed passionate controversies. See DE, p. 93.

[51] *Sainte Thérèse de l'Enfant-Jésus,* 2nd. ed., 1926 (there were two editions that year), pp. 445-453.

And her letter concludes with the following delightful recommendation: "Give me a *textual* copy of all you have from Thérèse."[52]

In private conversations, Mother Agnes said: "At certain times, I consider it as a trial that we are so known here below, including our little Thérèse. If it were not for her mission, I would prefer to keep so many unspeakable memories in a deep silence."[53]

Mother Agnes was the first to understand this mission and to be totally committed to it: "I shall be your little herald . . . . I will take care that God is loved and served through all the lights He has given to you and which will never be extinguished."[54] However, Thérèse had paid dearly for her position as a "child of light."[55] In spite of her tenderness for the "fearful little bird,"[56] she had too much of a "horror for pretense"[57] not to draw her sisters "to the whole truth." This was her own conviction: "Truth always triumphs."[58]

[52] To Sister Françoise-Thérèse, June 3, 1926. The paragraph begins in this way: "You tell me that it was P. Lepetit, who preached at your convent on May 17. On the 16th, I had it out with him because Jeanne had written me, etc."

[53] March 9, 1932, last page of "*Souvenirs intimes*" written for her two Carmelite sisters.

[54] Note to Thérèse, LC 185, June 4, 1897.

[55] Ms. B, p. 195.

[56] CJ 10.7.8: "You are like a fearful little bird that has never lived among men; you have always feared being taken. I have never been afraid of anyone; I always went wherever I wanted to go."

[57] CJ 7.7.4.

[58] Ms. C, p. 240.

SECOND CHAPTER

THE FIRST EDITION OF THE LETTERS

(1946 - 1948)

The fiftieth anniversary of Thérèse's death (1947) and her recent designation as patroness of France (1944) gave rise to a renewed fervor regarding her. An historian appeared on the scene, l'abbé André Combes,[1] who was eager to draw out the doctrinal import of this devotion. However, not doctrine separated from her life, not theology cut off from her history. He expressed the desire that this anniversary "rise from the advances of a technical order which will conduct her history beyond the limits in which it is still confined."[2] Circumstances made him the promoter of this "technical advance" at Lisieux and the collaborator of the first edition of the *Letters of Saint Thérèse of the Child Jesus.*

1. Preliminary Steps (1946 - 1947)

Abbé Combes entered into a letter-writing relationship with Mother Agnes of Jesus on August 15, 1945. He told her of his in-

[1] André Combes (October 29, 1899 - December 8, 1969), doctor of theology (Toulouse), doctor of letters (Sorbonne), professor of ascetic and mystical theology at the *Institut catholique de Paris*, professor of research at the *Centre national de la Recherche scientifique*; domestic prelate, 1960.

[2] *Introduction à la spiritualité de sainte Thérèse de l'Enfant-Jésus,* 1st ed. (Paris: Vrin, 1946), p. 28.

tention to dedicate his course, during the next year at the university, to Saint Thérèse of the Child Jesus' spiritual doctrine. He intended to proceed ". . . with the strict historical method and exact analysis of the texts which he had hitherto applied to the doctors of the past."[3]

He was seeking, therefore, from the Carmel a suitable documentation, and, furthermore, the personal collaboration of Mother Agnes of Jesus, the privileged witness of the Saint's life and thought. Too old to assume such an undertaking,[4] Mother Agnes entrusted her correspondent to certain secretaries.[5] Among these secretaries, Sister Geneviève of the Holy Face became the main person to speak with Abbé Combes.

We have, then, face to face, the Carmelite nun, who was soon to be eighty years old,[6] in whom the intrepid Céline still survived, and the professor, in full vigor—he was forty-five—the indefatigable dialectician. They were to carry out together this important stage of the edition, their progress being frequently difficult but always fruitful; they had the same love of truth and of Thérèse, although the truth concerning Thérèse was perceived differently by each.

Abbé Combes had examined all the literature on Thérèse when he was preparing his own course at the university. This literature was quite extensive. In his study, however, one thing became evident:

> In the mind of the greater part of Saint Thérèse's admirers there reigns an extreme lack of precision concerning the order of events and the relationship between her life and her works, whereas the published texts permit a tightening up of this relationship, making it closer than they think . . . . If I were not to attempt this chronological fusion between her life and her works, I would never be able

[3] Msgr. Beaussart, *op. cit.*, Preface, p. 12.

[4] She was eighty-four on September 7, 1945.

[5] Principally Sister Marie-Henriette (1890-1968), archivist.

[6] She was seventy-seven on April 28, 1946.

> to accomplish my plan, namely, to discover her doctrine in her life and her life in her doctrine by following the development of her thought in its evolution.[7]

He expresses here the prime necessity of a chronology, the foundation of every spiritual itinerary. The correspondence is of the utmost importance in the establishment of this chronology, and this historian was aware of it. Its integral publication appeared to him as a preamble to all future progress, and, especially, to the writing of a more complete work he was planning because of the success of his lectures on Thérèse at the *Institut catholique.*[8]

To ensure first-hand information for his new book, Abbé Combes took up residence at Lisieux for a few months. In a written declaration, September 30, 1946, he stated his goal and his method. This statement goes beyond the matter of the *Letters.* Nevertheless, it merits a long quotation here, for it explains the type of cooperation which will make the publication of his work possible:

> What I am seeking to attain is the very movement of Thérèse's thought in its vital reactions, either in contact with influences coming from the outside, or in the intimate experience of her natural development, her own graces, her trials.
>
> This is the only way, it seems to me, to discover Thérèse *in herself,* how she realized in time the idea that God had of her in eternity . . . . The only means of succeeding in this, insofar as one can hope to succeed, is to take up all the documentation in order to analyze it from this point of view.
>
> All she writes. All that was written about her. Seeing her as she is in herself. Seeing her as she was seen. Complementing these two sources, one with the other. Respecting all the shades of meaning.

[7] To Sister Marie-Henriette, January 25, 1946.

[8] See Msgr. Beaussart, *op. cit.*, pp. 12-13. These were his courses (March-May 1946), which appeared as *Introduction à la spiritualité de sainte Thérèse de l'Enfant-Jésus.*

Keeping the sharp sense of the *gaps* and the imprecisions. Counting on her help!

In the first stage, any information whatsoever, nothing is unimportant. A detail which may seem insignificant in other respects may open up a trail, the importance of which only the future will reveal.[9]

The fundamental question relating to the *Letters* was approached in the speakroom of the Carmel on October 22, 1946, with Sister Geneviève. She had already made up her mind on the eventual publication of the *Letters* in a collection independent of the *Histoire d'une Ame.* In this first meeting, did these two come to an agreement upon the content and the character of this publication? We can doubt it, judging by the sequence of events. With his formation as a scholar, Abbé Combes could picture no other form but that of an "exact and complete" edition, based on a chronological structure. Sister Geneviève was also interested in a chronological structure. But as for certain other matters, her mental habits of half a century could not be eradicated in one day. She no doubt had in mind a very extended anthology which would not exclude alterations in the form of the letters. Were they conscious of the difference in their viewpoints? Or, better still, did each of them hope to bring the other in line with his or her views? The important thing was to make a beginning, and it was agreed that the copies of the letters be prepared by two secretaries. Sister Geneviève gave the texts; she helped in determining the dates; she drew from her archives and from her prodigious memory the material for notes, the writing of which was

[9] To Sister Marie-Henriette, October 2, 1946. This letter began in this way: "I don't want to write a new biography. I am not undertaking a new doctrinal study on Theresian work, which I consider a closed entity. I don't want to consider Thérèse in her life as a child or a religious, asking her questions valid for all: 'What were your virtues? What was your faith, your hope, your fortitude? etc.'" Abbé Combes did not realize that his statement was to preface twenty-three years of work for Thérèse; its fruitfulness is all the more surprising when we remember that he pursued his other research work as a medievalist. He worked fifteen hours a day at Lisieux.

done by the two secretaries. L'abbé Combes became technical adviser and typist.[10]

For the next three months, the documents[11] made their rounds between the cloister and the speakroom. On February 2, 1947, Abbé Combes was able to express his satisfaction:

> With reference to the letters and the notes properly so-called, the *Summarium* lists 168;[12] the edition, though it is not complete, will give 196.[13] This is already an admirable result. I offer my warm, respectful, and fraternal congratulations to the diligent workers to whom this is due.

Abbé Combes insistently requested that Thérèse's first notes as a little girl be ranked on a level with the letters and included in the general numbering of the letters:

> I believe that no one, among the publishers of the correspondence, will understand why you have isolated them as unworthy. I had occasion to tell several persons that the first text of Thérèse which has been preserved was from 1877. They were filled with admiration, saying these should be assigned a place of prominence, that a precocity like this is rare . . . . No doubt it is a question of a few lines. But were it only a word, this would be a saint's first word accessible to history, and we should not lose it among our sentences

[10] "I am making five copies, keeping the fifth for myself; the other four are for you" (October 25, 1946, to Sister Marie-Henriette). Abbé Combes was able to use these fresh texts for his own work: *Introduction à la spiritualité de sainte Thérèse de l'Enfant-Jésus,* 2nd ed., revised and enlarged. (Paris: Vrin, 1948).

[11] Certainly not the autographs, nor the *Copy of the Writings,* nor Sister Geneviève's notebooks, but "copies" the source of which is impossible to determine today for want of any trace of them; altered copies, as we shall see.

[12] In fact, 170, on pp. 11-12 of the "*Summarium ex Officio,*" which followed the testimonies of the witnesses in *Summarium* II (1919). These pages reproduce the nomenclature of Volume II of the *Copy of the Writings* but with some ambiguities and errors; see note 44 in LT.

[13] The edition will be completed, in fact. It contained 238 letters and nine notes of Thérèse as a child.

in a prologue or an introduction. And then, from a different point of view, what a striking contrast between these little notes of this predestined child and the little notes at the end! From the first to the last stammerings, what an itinerary! We should leave it on paper just as it was in reality . . . .[14]

Abbé Combes did not win his case: nine notes from Thérèse as a child were placed in the Prologue (LT 1948, pp. 1–6).

The work seemed to have reached its term. Sister Geneviève then asked for a Preface.[15] The author brought up the question of confidence:

> It is necessary to foresee what is going to happen. If I give you this Preface, hardly will the edition appear when I shall receive this question from all sides: 'You are covering this edition with all your scientific authority, *but have you seen the autographs*?' Since I shall not be able to answer: yes, the goal at which we should have aimed would not be attained, and my intervention would be more harmful than useful . . . . *Will you* push your confidence to the point of giving me, in the speakroom, *understood*, these very precious relics? From the moment when I have been able to examine them, I shall be all the stronger against critics because it will be possible for me to forestall them.[16]

On Easter Monday, April 7, 1947, Abbé Combes was finally able to examine the autographs.[17] An examination of a few hours was evidently insufficient for any kind of methodical verification. However, to the experienced eye of the scholar, a few probings were enough to convince him of what he suspected he would find: the typewritten text up to this moment was not authentic.

After a close discussion, Sister Geneviève gave in to Abbé Combes' reasoning. He recalled later: ". . . that memorable visit

[14] To Sister Marie-Henriette, February 4, 1947.

[15] Request deduced from Abbé Combes' answer.

[16] To Sister Geneviève, April 3, 1947.

[17] See his *Preface*, p. xxiv.

in which the liberating decision was taken of returning scrupulously to the autographs."[18] On the strength of this promise, Abbé Combes wrote his *Preface*.[19]

2. Certain Matters Called into Question (1947-1948)

The copies duly revised by the Carmelite nuns[20] were sent off to Abbé Combes at Paris. All went well until he found an extract from Thérèse's letter to Sister Marie of the Sacred Heart, September 1896 (Ms. B). In 1898, this letter had become Chapter XI of *Histoire d'une Ame*. At this time, ". . . different reasons had led to the condensing, in a noteworthy way, of the passage close to the end, and of practically reducing to infinitesimal proportions the "little bird" that played an important role in Thérèse's line of reasoning."[21]

The preceding winter, Abbé Combes had persuaded the workers on the *Letters* to introduce the parable of the "little bird" into the collection of the *Letters*, reestablishing it in its original words. The text they were now offering did not carry out this agreement. He called this to the attention of his Carmelite correspondent:

> The text at which we stopped constituted an immense progress, but there remains a certain number of differences with the original. When you had prepared it, the decision to respect the autographs scrupulously had not been made. Now that this decision has been made and the other texts have been brought in line with the original copies,[22] is only this one going to be left lagging behind? This would be all the more regrettable since I cite it in my *Preface*.[23]

[18] To Sister Marie-Henriette, June 2, 1947.

[19] Dated April 9, 1947.

[20] According to the version of the Process (CE II) for the greater part of the texts. We don't doubt, then, the authenticity of this copy.

[21] *Preface*, p. xx.

[22] Not exactly, as we shall see later on.

[23] Letter of May 31, 1947.

This was a normal request. But in 1947, this incident, though mild in appearance, took on dramatic proportions: if one is not careful—the Carmelite nuns, especially—one just goes from the problem of the *Letters* to that of the *Histoire d'une Ame*. To concede this passage of the "*little bird*"would be the same thing as initiating the edition of the original text of the *Manuscrits autobiographiques* (something that was not done until some years later). It would be tantamount to calling Mother Agnes of Jesus' work into question; it would be striking at her in her most cherished possession. The Carmelite nuns resisted because of their attachment to their "little Mother." In spite of his veneration for Mother Agnes, however, Abbé Combes, the historian, because of his own attachment to the truth, refused to make any concessions:[24]

> What to do? The matter is getting out of hand . . . . I am extremely unhappy to come to this *impasse* with you, without seeing any favorable solution . . . . If the "little bird" is sacrificed, my *Nihil obstat,* my Preface, and myself, we shall all undergo the same fate. My whole Preface sparkles with enthusiasm for the truth: my wings clipped, all falls apart.[25]

Once again, the "intrepid Céline" makes her choice in favor of the truth: so be it, the "little bird" will appear among the *Letters* in its original form.

The work continued. In July 1947, there was a total of 220 documents. The manuscript copy was taken to the publishers. Then came the first trials. Sister Geneviève experienced a shock

[24] Paradoxically, the positions were reversed in 1949-1950. Sister Geneviève, supported by P. Marie-Eugène, O.C.D. (d. 1967), and advisers, fought for the publication of the *Manuscrits autobiographiques.* Abbé Combes upheld Mother Agnes of Jesus in his fidelity to her version of *Histoire d'une Ame,* and he defended the thesis of the "two originals" in *Le Problème de l'histoire d'une Ame et des oeuvres complètes de sainte Thérèse de Lisieux* (Ed. Saint-Paul, 1950). It is in this atmosphere that we should read again pp. 87-89 of the *Introduction* of P. François de Sainte-Marie, *Manuscrits autobiographiques,* ed. in *facsimile,* volume I.

[25] To Sister Marie-Henriette, June 5, 1947.

on September 11, expressing her anxiety at being the *one in charge* of this publication. An anthology, such as Mother Agnes of Jesus had in mind at one time, this was all well and good! That would be worthy of a *canonized Saint*. But was there any necessity of digging up all these letters of this child, of this young girl, even of this Carmelite nun, letters that were so trite?

Abbé Combes answered her objections one by one:

> It is exactly because she is *Saint* Thérèse and because she is about to hold, from this jubilee year (1947) onward, a higher and higher place in the history of spirituality that what has happened to all outstanding persons has happened to her, too. History is interested in all the phases of her life and her works, and history may publish all that comes from her pen . . . . This is inevitable and we understand it fully. Since we are dealing with a Saint, her whole life has exemplary value, and, in order to be assured of understanding her whole life, we must be acquainted with all its details. Hence the necessity of all these publications of the *complete* works. Hence my insistence to have all the letters make their appearance, all the notes (*billets*) of your saintly little sister. We had to treat her just as we do the greatest Saints.
>
> However, you are shocked at the thought of seeing her trite letters being published. But I will answer you by what I say to myself:
>
> 1. In the case of a Saint, nothing is trite. Even in Sacred Scripture, how many parts we would have eliminated had the Lord consulted us! We would have been mistaken! We have to take God's work as it is and to meditate on it insofar as we are capable of understanding it and drawing out suitable lessons.
>
> 2. As for Thérèse, we must be careful. What seems trite (especially to Céline, who knows all, who knows much more than all that has been written!) can be filled with usefulness for history and for the edification of simple souls, who will be responsive to what they find "within their reach." Through this, they will see immediately that Thérèse lived just as they do, that she was *not* always soaring on the wings of the Eagle, and, little by little, they will allow themselves to be carried along.
>
> 3. History, furthermore, will be able to make a use of these let-

ters that we do not foresee, these letters which distress you because they say "nothing." I have in mind, particularly, that series of letters from Italy or Rome,[26] containing nothing lively or picturesque about the trip and the personages of distinction whom she met. Must you regret this? Much to the contrary! It is a document of extreme importance for the refuting of the old thesis of P. Ubald, which Van der Meersch[27] has just brought to life. Thérèse appears, here, so detached from all that is accidental, so concentrated on her one main interest, on her vocation and her audience with the pope, that I am going to be able to reply with much force to all these amateurs: ". . . the author of such letters was certainly not the little, feather-brained girl, the runaway horse whom you don't hesitate to describe. She was a recollected and deep soul, whom no distraction could seriously affect." Since the account in *Histoire d'une Ame* is much more colorful and picturesque, we shall be able to build up a proper balance, and the truth will be vindicated.

4. As for the letters to her aunt and her cousins, I will show with what fidelity, even when she was climbing with such joy and swiftness to the summit of the Mount of Love, she still remains attentive to family duties, loving and simple, delicate and affectionate, without ever "preaching," adapting herself to each person's taste, equally capable of writing to Marie Guérin a letter that will astound Pius X by the soundness of her eucharistic doctrine[28] and, at the same time, being capable of joking with her about "Pott's disease," on the tip of her [Marie Guérin's] tongue.[29]

This is very, very important for *many* souls who are frightened by sustained sublimities of thought, and for psychiatrists who will be in admiration at the subtle ease with which Thérèse moved within all these levels of life.

5. And this letter, set aside to the end as the most 'insignificant' of all,[30] and which supplies us with such a good argument against

[26] See LT 30 to 37.

[27] In *La petite Sainte Thérèse* (Paris, 1947). See the fifth point in this same letter.

[28] See LT 92.

[29] See LT 50.

[30] See LT 69.

Van der Meersch! Since Divine Providence permitted all these letters to be preserved, are we not serving the designs of Providence when we publish all of them?

6. Really, must we linger on the effect produced by only these first pages of the book? I don't believe so. We have hardly reached Carmel! What is so surprising if a child writes the letters of a child? The opposite would be serious! The marvel is that these letters of a child overflow with love! Let us wait! You will see that, when all is done, the pearls will come into their splendor. Were I to dare do so, I would answer your comparison with another. This book puts me in mind of a symphony. If we cut a symphony off after its first bars, we are confused, we don't understand where the composer wants to go . . . .

But, if we wait until the end, if we allow the composer to introduce and to develop his entire theme right to the *end*, then we understand, we are delighted, and we are filled with admiration.

The author of the Theresian symphony is Thérèse, but it is principally Jesus Himself. We must give Him time to prepare His little "lyre," to allow it to warm up to His Heart's vibrations . . . . When the lyre is ready, what tones!

But what is more touching, what is even more divine than the introductions! The more humble they appear, the *truer* they are!

7. Let us, finally, not forget that the *Letters* form part of a whole. We must fill them out with the *Histoire d'une Ame* and her *Poems*. Then, I assure you, all will fall into place. I assure you, I am not running the risk of being in error about the splendor of this incomparable soul.[31]

Nothing less than this long letter was needed to convince and *console* Sister Geneviève. It attained its purpose: the restrictions were lifted, and the book proceeded on its course.

However, at the beginning of 1948, there was another sudden change. On January 19, after an interview with Monseigneur Picaud,[32] Abbé Combes wrote this little sentence in a letter: "He

[31] To Sister Geneviève, September 11, 1947.

[32] François-Marie Picaud (1878-1960), bishop of Bayeux and Lisieux from 1931 to 1954, and, at this time, superior of the Carmel. He had already advised on the edition in the process of being prepared, in a letter dated July 12, 1947; see LT 1948, pp. v-viii.

told me, and he also told you, I think, that not *a single* alteration was necessary, even in the style. I believe, then, all goes well."[33] All was going well, as a matter of fact, but now a distinction had to be made. Sister Geneviève conceded that for the letters handed in at the 1910 Process it was necessary to be faithful to that source. As for the texts that owe their conservation to the only copy of her private notebook, they remain her property. She thinks, therefore, that she has the right to make cuttings and alterations according to what she will judge necessary.

The "great Doctor"[34] was forced once again to resume his ministry of persuasion:

> In my opinion, you remain the exlusive owners of *all* the *Letters*, including those of the Process. Nobody, it seems to me, has the right to force you to publish them, nor, if you publish them, to oblige you to publish them integrally.
>
> However, the integral text of the *Letters* handed in at the Process is no longer exclusively in your possession. There is at least one authentic copy at Rome.[35] When your edition of the *Letters* appears, anyone will be able to compare it with that copy. If there were the slightest difference, this would be—considering the state of mind of your adversaries—a real catastrophe for you and for me, unless you can give proof that your edition reproduces the autograph, and that the 'authentic copy' is in error. So, for this side of the question, the most important of many, no hesitation whatsoever is permitted: you must respect the autograph with an absolute fidelity.[36]

[33] To Sister Marie-Henriette, January 19, 1948.

[34] For the feast of St. Andrew, November 29, 1947, the Carmel had given to André Combes a fragment of an autograph (LT 136), containing these words from the hand of Thérèse.

[35] As a favor, these four volumes of the *Copy of the Writings* brought to Rome in 1910 had been returned to Mother Agnes of Jesus, June 14, 1928. "These volumes made up the only official collection of the Theresian *corpus*, the judges not having deemed it necessary to make a double copy" (Mss. I, p. 25, note 1). Only the text of the *Manuscrits autobiographiques* had been transcribed in each of the copies of the diocesan Process (*Bayeux, Rites, Postulation de la Cause*).

[36] Even on this point he was not entirely heeded.

But the difficulty begins with the other side of the question. In my opinion, the reasons which inspired M. Dubosq [read: Msgr. de Teil] to give you this advice[37] no longer exist. There is no longer any question of avoiding the handing in to the *dossier* some unimportant or incorrect texts. Thérèse is a canonized Saint. The least word written by her hand is a relic. Her spelling mistakes themselves are venerable. They form part of the Little Way! If, at age four, she had written: '*Jemeu bocoux ma chaire peutite Séline,*' I would consider this sentence a treasure which I would be infinitely happy to possess .... When her pen, still unskillful, stumbles over a difficult word or hesitates in its syntax, you think she is still the pupil at the Abbey whom one mistake in French runs the risk of dishonoring: no, she is the universal Saint ... who is able to fire the most learned with enthusiasm through the elevation of her doctrine, while bringing consolation to the most humble through the banalities which life imposed on her at times.

Having said this, you can see that, personally, I would be of the opinion to extend to *all* the letters the rule which must be respected regarding the *Letters of the Process.* And I can guarantee that, in certain awkward expressions that seem to you worthy of oblivion, there are graces of attraction and conversion for certain types of souls, who will remain untouched by the sublimities of the letters which used to come to you from the Carmel. If God permitted all her letters to be preserved, should we believe this was without any purpose?

It is, above all, absolutely certain that you are free to give or not to give these preserved portions to the public. Since my Preface speaks of an edition without alterations, the thing you should not do is to change the sentences that don't please you.

Believe me, I am very sorry for imposing this restriction on you, but this is the result of the honor you gave me by asking me for this Preface .... If we were to be unfortunate enough to write the word *alterations* in the Preface, we would be opening the door to confusion and endless controversies. But in order not to write the word *alterations* in the Preface, it is absolutely necessary before God that not a single one be in the text.

If, then, you judge that there are, in Thérèse's *Letters* as a child, some sentences unworthy of publication, then it is better to omit

[37] See above, The *Copy of the Writings.*

them simply, since the Preface admits of some *omissions.* Nothing will have to be said.[38]

From this line of reasoning, Sister Geneviève seems to have retained especially what sanctioned her freedom of choice. As justified as were the Teacher's opinions, he was not forcing them upon her. Abbé Combes' courageous tenacity was always blended with respect for and deference to Thérèse's sisters. In the last resort, then, Céline remained the "one in charge."[39] She was upholding not so much her right of ownership as her right of being Thérèse's older sister, a right which was equivalent in her eyes to the *duty* of protecting her little sister just as she had done at the Abbey;[40] she had not missed the point of Abbé Combes' reference. And Céline did not fail in her "mission." This was a sisterly reflex, we might even say "a gut reaction," which no scientific conclusion ever counterbalanced.

Sister Geneviève boldly made use of her right of omission,[41] and she was not resigned to allowing the "venerable" errors in spelling to be published. As for the rest, she had gone from concession to concession, much beyond what she had foreseen in October 1946, thus realizing more "progress of a technical order" in two years than she was to realize all through the remainder of her life. L'Abbé Combes was witness to this himself, and he paid homage to her "generous detachment which, yielding to the entreaties of history,"[42] had surrendered such treasures to it.

To sum up: conditions were still not ripe for permitting the strictly authentic edition Abbé Combes was dreaming about. The

[38] To Sister Geneviève, January 20, 1948.

[39] See LT 182, resuming an expression of Céline as a child. (CF, July 9, 1873, p. 174).

[40] See Ms. A, p. 55.

[41] See end of volume 2, the concordance of the 1948 and 1972 editions. Certain omissions were fortuitous: they did not come from a decision of the editors but from the state of the documents in 1948. Since then the mutilated autographs have been put together, the erasures deciphered, etc.

[42] *Preface*, pp. xii-xiii.

imperfections, then, in the first edition of the *Letters* are not to be blamed on him. On the other hand, we can understand his joy when the publication appeared on the eve of September 30, 1948, exactly fifty years after the publishing of *Histoire d'une Ame*:

> I view with an indescribable emotion this book, the publication of which I so much desired; it is going to spread so many graces in our poor world . . . . At last, it is here! All the delays had but one purpose: to exercise our patient trust and to have its birth coincide with these great days. *Dominus regit me*! . . . What an honor and what a divine joy to be chosen by the Good Shepherd of Thérèse and her sisters to help in this much needed publication![43]

[43] To Mother Agnes of Jesus and Sister Geneviève, September 27, 1948, with a citation from psalm 22.

SECOND PART

THE GENERAL CORRESPONDENCE

Preparation for the "General Correspondence" (1962-1972)

When the republication of the *Letters* became necessary in 1962 – the first edition being out of print – the principle of a literal fidelity to the originals was no longer a difficulty.

For the past eight years, the Lisieux Carmel had been engaged in the work of a critical and integral publication of all Thérèse's writings. P. François de Sainte-Marie[1] was placed in charge of this undertaking in 1953.[2] He published successively: the *Manuscrits autobiographiques*[3] and the authentic photographs, *Visage de Thérèse de Lisieux.*[4] Research was begun for the edition of *Derniers Entretiens* (Last Conversations).[5] The way was open for work on the *Letters*.

The initial plan was modest: a simple "revised and corrected edition." At first, we thought it would suffice to compare the texts with the autographs,[6] to make a more exact chronology, and to

[1] François Liffort de Buffévent (1910-1961), Carmelite of the Paris Province, founder of *Vigne du Carmel* (Seuil) in 1943.

[2] He succeeded P. Gabriel of Saint Mary Magdalene, Carmelite; P. Gabriel died on March 15, 1953, only a few months after he had been asked to undertake this task; see Mss. I, p. 89.

[3] *Office Central de Lisieux*, 1956; *facsimile* edition in four volumes; it was followed by a printed edition in 1957.

[4] *Office Central de Lisieux*, 1961; forty-seven original photographs, edition in two volumes.

[5] In 1958, this undertaking was interrupted by the accidental death of P. François, August 30, 1961; it was resumed in 1962 by P. Bernard Delalande, O.C.D.

[6] The Lisieux Carmel expresses its gratitude to the Carmelite Institute of *Notre-Dame de Vie*, some of whose members took on the first reading of the autographs in 1962.

enlarge the footnotes. Perhaps, too, a short "foreword" would inform the readers of these improvements.

However, when we were carrying out these plans, various factors arose which made it necessary to modify them. On the one hand, an examination into the sources brought to light, with regard to Thérèse's letters, a problem as complex as that of the text of the *Manuscrits autobiographiques* (Thérèse's Autobiography). The preceding pages have already made this clear. On the other hand, an easy access to a very rich family documentation, brought about by the death of Mother Agnes (1951) and Sister Geneviève (1959), presented the problem of Thérèse's correspondents.

After the first spadework was done (1963-1966), the work had to be laid aside (1966-1969) in order to ensure priority to *Derniers Entretiens.* When it was resumed later, this work ended up in what we call today *Correspondance générale* (General Correspondence).

CHAPTER ONE

THE LETTERS FROM THÉRÈSE (LT)

Let us lay down the following directive: we consider as a "letter" from Thérèse every text in prose (letter, note, inscription on a holy picture, etc.) directed to some person,[1] and we make no distinction as to the text's length or interest. We list 266 letters (LT), from April 4, 1877 to August 24, 1897,[2] and these have been given a new numbering.[3]

These texts come from the following sources: autographs for

[1] We [the editors] excluded the *prayers*; these will be presented in another volume of the *Edition du Centenaire* (*Poésies, Récréations pieuses, écrits divers*); for this reason, we excluded letters CLXII and CCXXXVIII of the first edition (1948, pp. 305 and 438-439).

Partly excluded are letters to fictitious persons, contained in her school copybooks; two only are cited as documentary material (LTS 18a and 18b).

We did not retain the poems (P 33 and 34) to Mme. La Néele (see LC 168), recorded with the letters in the *Copy of Writings* (CE II, p. 25).

Finally, we eliminated letter CLXIX (LT 1948, p. 319): this postscript was written in Sister Marie of the Sacred Heart's hand, not that of Thérèse.

[2] The last true letter is dated August 10 (LT 263). The last three documents are inscribed holy pictures. To these 266 LT are added the documents: LT 167 *bis* and LT 221 *bis*. The first is a postscript of Thérèse, July 19, 1894 (date changed), to a letter of Sister Marie of the Sacred Heart to Mme. Guérin (former LT CLX); the second is composed of annotations of Thérèse, April 3, 1897, to a letter of Sister Marie of the Eucharist (Marie Guérin) to M. Guérin (see DE, p. 670).

[3] A concordance of these two numberings is made at the end of volume 2.

227; partial autographs completed by copies for twenty-five others; different copies for the last fourteen.

These were addressed to twenty-six recipients, nine of whom were members of the Martin and Guérin families.

I. Sources

A) Autographs

Unlike the Autobiography, which was made up of three somewhat similar copybooks (Mss. A,B,C), the collection of the *Letters* brings together the most dissimilar sheets of paper. Though much could be said about these sheets, we are limiting ourselves here to information of a general interest: the appearance of the manuscripts (format, type of paper, ink), accidents they underwent (cuttings, scrapings, words written over words), and observations relative to the handwriting.

Description

From a folded sheet, 15.5 x 21.5 centimeters (LT 165, for example), to tiny sheets, 2.5 x 4 cms. (LT 227), there is place for all *formats,* from the triangular reverse side of an envelope, a scrap of paper torn hastily, having no specific shape (LT 219).

Paper of a slightly ribbed surface or squared paper predominates; however, we come across, too, fancy pale blue or gray paper, with a gold "T" stamping, or tint on tint (LT 23, 25, 26), imitation parchment (LT 183) taken from a box of almonds, the margin taken from the cover of a copybook (LT 210), the reverse side of a wedding card (LT 95) or a death notice (LT 76), etc. In Carmel, and especially during her novitiate year, Thérèse used very poor paper on which to write notes to her sisters.

A variety of inks: at Les Buissonnets, black, blue, red, purple, green; black in Carmel, except for a few months in the year 1892, when Thérèse was using a purple ink; this gives us a chronological

reference mark for the dating of these documents. A family note has recourse to colored pencils: a different color for each word! (See LT 179). When outside her cell, Thérèse scribbled her message in pencil (LT 174). In July 1897, when she was in the infirmary, she used the pencil as a substitute for the pen.

The simple declaration of these facts gives us an idea of the difficulties of a practical order which a facsimile edition of the letters would raise. There are difficulties, too, on the critical level.

Accidents

Few of the autographs have come through unscathed by the operations mentioned above. The most serious alterations came from *cutting*. Sister Geneviève seems to have excelled in this art.[4] In 1910, she announced to Léonie the destruction of all Thérèse's letters to her father.[5] Two autographs were spared (LT 18 and 68); a third is extant in three quarters (LT 77). For the remaining ten, copied in her notebook,[6] we may be sure they have disappeared.

After the death of Sister Geneviève, however, the archivist in the Carmel gathered together Thérèse's writings, even to the

[4] She was even doing this at the age of six! "Céline, who is not satisfied unless she is cutting everything that falls into her hands, has taken two St. Joseph Bulletins and cut them into pieces" (Mme. Martin to Pauline, CF 143, October 1875).

[5] See *above*, letter of March 27, 1910, under *The Copy of the Writings*.

[6] It was the CMG III copy which was used as the source for the letters to M. Martin at the time the first edition (1948) was published. The letter of July 31, 1888 (LT 58) merits special mention. Cut up at the time of the Process, glued together, and even borrowing a sentence from an autograph of a different date (LT 52), it was placed in the collection in this composite form as an extract (CE II, p. 16). The text published in 1948 represents an intermediate writing between the copy of the Process and the original text. Between 1948 and her death in 1959, Sister Geneviève cut the page of her notebook (CMG III, pp. 177-179) on which she had transcribed this letter around the year 1905 (an undoubtedly authentic copy . . . or almost). With the exception of a sentence (lines 16 and 17, absent from the autograph, cited according to LT 1948), the original content was finally restored here. No less curious is the case of a note to Sister Agnes of Jesus (LT 104), reconstructed with the aid of three sources; see LT 104.

smallest fragment of the autographs.[7] In January 1963, we decided to make a systematic inventory of these fragments. There were 346 which could be identified as coming from her correspondence.[8] These fragments contained one or several lines, at times even one single word. We sorted them out by the color of the ink, the paper, or by the movement of the handwriting, and we succeeded in piecing together, after the manner of a puzzle, as many as twenty-five letters, in whole or in part; among these, there were ten letters addressed to her father, M. Martin.[9]

The *scrapings* are numerous. Their attribution is a delicate matter as far as spelling corrections are concerned. Expert evaluation of the autobiographical manuscripts[10] revealed that in 1895-1897 Thérèse made use of a scraper. Her last letters in pencil still retain the traces of frequent erasings with her hand. Above all, up to 1894-1895, an examination of her writings suggests that she rarely reread her material. The greater part of the scrapings, then, are to be ascribed to her sisters, and to Mother Agnes especially because she was always careful about formal correctness.[11]

There was no hesitation whatsoever about scraping away an

[7] Up to the time of their death, Thérèse's sisters kept their respective collections in their possession. We have a list from the box of Mother Agnes of Jesus' autographs which was made by Sister Madelaine of St. Joseph (d. 1967) around 1948-1950. Besides the letters and poems written to her, Mother Agnes kept, for example, the "red notebook" of the poems copied by Thérèse for Sister Marie of the Trinity, the notes to Sister Marie of St. Joseph, the letter to Mother Marie de Gonzague (LT 190), an envelope of "autographs to be cut up," etc. After Mother Agnes' death (1951), Sister Geneviève came into possession of all these.

[8] The rest of the fragments came from rough drafts of poems, pious recreations.

[9] The others are divided as follows: three to Pauline or Sister Agnes (LT 6, 7, 104), one to Céline (LT 8), one to Mme. Guérin (LT 84), ten to Marie Guérin (LT 19, 20, 23, 25, 37, 50, 62, 69, 88, 136). These fragments, placed between two pieces of glass, were photographed on a black background to bring out the gaps. See plate LT 69.

[10] See Mss. II, pp. 83-117.

[11] See, for example, LT 197, in which are many changes in punctuation and spelling. There was the same doctoring up for LT 140, which Mother Agnes loved to reread for her consolation.

entire sentence. Their content says enough about the reason for their suppression during the time of the Process: "Be careful not to put in things that would appear childish to others but not to us who know our little Thérèse."[12] For example, what would critics have thought of this reflection, charming in its simplicity: "The good Pope is so old that one would say he is dead; I would never have pictured him like this."[13] (LT 36)? . . . And would not the critics take this confession literally: ". . . from day to day, I am getting more wicked" (LT 202)? And how would they interpret this "if": "If there is *a heaven, it is for me*" (LT 216)?

Furthermore, did not certain statements go beyond Thérèse's thought? Better still, was not Thérèse herself a little excessive in the occasional statement? Thus, with regard to sanctity: "Sanctity does not consist in saying beautiful things; it does not consist in even thinking them, feeling them! . . . It consists in *suffering* and suffering from *everything*." (LT 89.) Sister Geneviève corrected the last statement: "Sanctity . . . consists in being willing to suffer."[14]

A long time after the examination into the Writings (1910), the originals still underwent some alterations in details.

More serious is Sister Geneviève's faultfinding around 1930. The preceding year, the retreat master[15] was speaking about "Di-

[12] Sister Marie of the Sacred Heart to Sister Françoise-Thérèse (Léonie), Easter 1910, cited in DE, pp. 442-443. Sister Marie erased the nickname "Lion" (see LT 75, note 1).

[13] Letter written after the audience with Leo XIII, November 20, 1887.

[14] The text was recorded under this form at the Process (CE II, p. 71) and in the first edition (LT LXV). Another example: in LT 143, July 18, 1893, Thérèse wrote: "I thought at times that now since Jesus was asking nothing from me, I had to go along gently in peace and love, doing only what He was asking . . . ." To remove the apparent contradiction, Sister Geneviève added after the last word: "formerly" (1st. ed., LT CXXII; addition recorded at the Process). We do not know if these alterations and interpolations were the result of later conversations between Thérèse and Céline, as was the case for certain interpolations attributable to Mother Agnes of Jesus in *Histoire d'une Ame*. In any case, their close daily relationship went very much beyond the *writings*, with which we must be satisfied today. An appreciation of these strange interventions must, then, be treated very prudently by us.

[15] P. Desbuquois, S.J. (d. 1959).

vine Providence" in terms that set her on fire instantly.[16] However, upon reflection, she judged his statements too exaggerated, and she went against them. Temptation crept in: if the smallest things in our lives are not only permitted but *willed* by God, then what about suffering? Would God, then, be pleased with tormenting us?[17] Deeply moved by her reflections, Sister Geneviève gasped when reading some statements from Thérèse's pen which were just as provocative: "Jesus is a Spouse of *blood*. He wants all my heart's blood for Himself . . . ." (LT 82); "If you only knew how I look upon the sorrow I have today as being willed by Jesus, for He is pleased to sow little sorrows in our life in this way . . . ." (LT 98); "Jesus is happy to see her [Céline] suffering" (LT 144), etc. In order to remove responsibility from God in this formidable problem of evil, Céline, who rejected such sentences, crossed them out on the autographs and in her own notebooks.[18]

Finally, we see some *annotations* on the originals: explanatory notes by the hand of Mother Agnes of Jesus (for example, LT 46, 114, 160); a virtue marked in a paragraph which Sister Geneviève wants to cite in her testimonies (LT 142, 143, 149, 165, 167, etc.); dates in pencil or practical annotations, contemporaneous with the first edition (1946-1948).

16 "What struck me especially was his insistence in always seeing God in the smallest things, in the minutest incidents of life. We can say to ourselves: Surely, it is God who *wills* this trouble for me, this little lack of attention, and how can I not face up joyfully to all that happens to us since it is the expression of God's will for me?" (Letter to Sister Françoise-Thérèse, November 26, 1929).

17 "However, Father went too far, telling us, for example, that if a fire were to break out, we could say to ourselves: It is God who WILLS that the house burn down. A great uneasiness invaded me little by little and I suffered extremely because of it for two years" (Sister Geneviève's note, after Léonie's death in 1941). In fact, she was haunted for the rest of her life by this mystery. But in January 1959, a month before her death, she whispered in her sufferings—and the Sisters were struck by this—: "God has done this." "Jesus wills it." (See Piat, *Céline, soeur et témoin de sainte Thérèse de l'Enfant-Jésus*, pp. 185-188 and 203-204).

18 The authentic text was recorded at the Process.

Handwriting Peculiarities

One fact is quite evident in our first contact with the autographs: there are two types of handwriting. Up to January 1894,[19] Thérèse's handwriting was slanted to the right, and then her writing takes on a vertical position after this date.[20] Mother Agnes of Jesus revealed the reason for this change.[21] From February 1896, Thérèse combined both types of writing in a skillful manner.

In the first type (slanted writing), its legibility leaves much to be desired. However, Thérèse is aware of this, and she begs pardon from her correspondents for her "ugly handwriting" (LT 62, 136, 221),[22] her "spidery handwriting"—"*écriture de chat*" (LT 155) or her "scribbling" (LT 37, 201, 224). Legibility becomes increasingly difficult when she decides at times to cross over her written lines in an upward direction.[23] (LT 26, 31, 62, etc.)

More than in her Autobiography, Thérèse's correspondence is bedecked with "venerable" errors in spelling.[24] Some of these errors are constant, at least for several years;[25] others are only occa-

[19] With some exceptions; for example, LT 69, 87, and the Isaian texts in LT 108 in which the handwriting is vertical.

[20] The first sample for the correspondence is LT 156.

[21] Which came in the very month when Thérèse was twenty-one! See below, note 43, and Mother Agnes' letter to Msgr. de Teil.

[22] On the envelope containing fragments of cut-up letters, Sister Geneviève had written: "Her autographs, but with the ugly handwriting of her childhood, or before they permitted her to write vertically." In private conversations, however, Sister Geneviève admitted she perferred her sister's former handwriting.

[23] A custom of the time which was quite widespread in convents but not exclusively. Thérèse realizes that "it is not respectful to end up like this, across a letter" (LT 146, August 10, 1893). We should note that she never crossed her lines when writing to her father.

[24] See P. François de Sainte-Marie: "Thérèse was never at ease in spelling; she admits this openly, and the evidence proves it" (Mss. I, p. 55). Reference to Ms. A, p. 82: ". . . my spelling which was nothing less than original."

[25] For example: "*jentil*," "*reçevoir*," "*j'usqu'à*"; she never doubled the "r" in the future and conditional tenses of the verb "pouvoir," etc.

sional mistakes.[26] The greater part comes from an incorrect accentuation[27] or simply a phonetic transcription of the Norman accent.[28] In Carmel, the malformation of certain words could be due, in part, to the precarious writing conditions, to say nothing of the cold which in winter stiffened her hand; there was no heating whatsoever in her cell.

Thérèse enjoyed a great independence regarding the use of the capital letters. We could even call these "theresian": *Amour, Aimer, Divin,*[29] *Céleste*. Some imply revealing nuances: King (M. Martin, her father),[30] Sun (either the material sun or Jesus),[31] etc. It even happens that the game of capitals supplies for a mistake of syntax, as in this paragraph: "*Oui celui qui aime Jésus est toute sa famille, Il trouve dans ce coeur unique qui n'a pas son semblable, tout ce qu'il désire, Il y trouve son Ciel!*"[32] (LT 130).

[26] At times, pleasant: "*alletante*" (LT 75), "*annéantir*" (LT 96), "*fraguement*" (LT 108). The error: "*allouette*" (LT 103) was inherited from her sister Pauline (Mother Agnes) as we can verify in several writings: see CJ, July 13, no. 16. We find, too, "*dommaine*" (LT 88), "*tirroir*" (LT 88), "*blacard*" (ibid.), "*orizon*" (LT 81), "*ennivrantes*" (LT 94), etc.

[27] Frequent confusion between: "ou" and "où"; between "a" and "à," in spite of a penalty imposed by Mme. Papinau, her teacher, after a dictation exercise, February 16, 1888: "The pupil, Thérèse Martin, will copy ten times: 'The verb *avoir* never takes the *grave* accent'." We find, too, these persistent errors: "*déja*," "*celà*," "*bientot*"; and often: "*Jesus*," "*repondre*," "*rejouir*," etc.

[28] Thus: "*chôse*," "*rôse*," "*gâgner*"; but, at times, "*ame*." She used to say: "Pôline," someone at the Abbey recalled in 1927 (Mère Saint-Léon; see LT 24, note 2).

[29] She uses the capital letter twice out of forty-four times before 1894; twenty-seven times out of fifty from 1894 on.

[30] She uses the capital letter thirty-seven times out of thirty-eight for M. Martin; the last time (LT 142, July 6, 1893). M. Martin was then in a very bad state of health. Thérèse was content to enlarge the small letter "r" (as in Ms. A, p. 37).

[31] A difficult distinction, at times, as in LT 134, April 26, 1892; the capital letter is used twenty times out of thirty-four.

[32] The three "Il" (with or without the capital letter "I") designate "Jesus." The first edition (p. 193), taking up CMG IV, p. 71, has this version: "*Oui, celui qui aime Jésus est toute sa famille, il trouve dans ce Coeur unique qui n'a pas son semblable tout ce qu'il désire, il y trouve son Ciel*! . . ." The reversal of perspective is, then, radical: for Thérèse, it is not a question of "being pleased *with*" Jesus alone but of pleasing *Him* by welcoming Him. She shows she is instinctively in agreement with "the humanity of God our Savior" (Titus 3:4) whose "delights are to be with the children of men" (Proverbs 8:31). CE II, p. 87, places a capital "I" on the three "Il."

FACSIMILES OF LETTERS
FROM THÉRÈSE

First page

LT 6, December 1, 1880.
This letter is the first (of those we have) which Thérèse wrote by herself. She was seven and a half.
The autograph was cut into seven fragments.
Reproduced according to the size.

Second page

LT 24, June 27, 1887.
Thérèse was fourteen and a half.
Someone else dated the letter.
Reproduced according to the size.

Third page

LT 69, November (?) 1888.
Nineteen fragments (the twentieth does not appear on the photo).
Size of the original: 10.5 x 21.2 cms.

Fourth page

LT 96, October 15, 1889.
Size of the original: 13.2 x 20.6 cms.

Ma chère Pauline

Je suis bien contente de técrire,
je l'ai demandé à ma tante. je fais bauc
oup de fautes, mais tu conais bien ta petite
Thérèse et tu sait bien que je ne suis gere
abile. tu vas bien embrasser Papa pour
moi. j'ai eus quatre bons-points le premier
jours et le segon cinc cienc.

7

Juillet 15[illegible]

Ma chère petite Jeanne
n'ayant pas l'artiste Darel
pour me dessiner un bateau
et voulant cependant en
mettre un au haut de ma
lettre j'ai été obligée de me
mettre moi-même à en griffonner
un. Je viens, ma chère Jeanne
t'amuser pendant quelques instants
j'espère que ta migraine est
entièrement passée, maintenant
que la grande Anglaise est
partie tu seras moins tourmentée
et bien sûr que tout le monde
se portera beaucoup mieux.
Je pense que tu es bien contente
de ne plus entendre mes sermons
sur la [illegible] & de ne plus voir
mes yeux qui te faisaient ~~et~~ de me

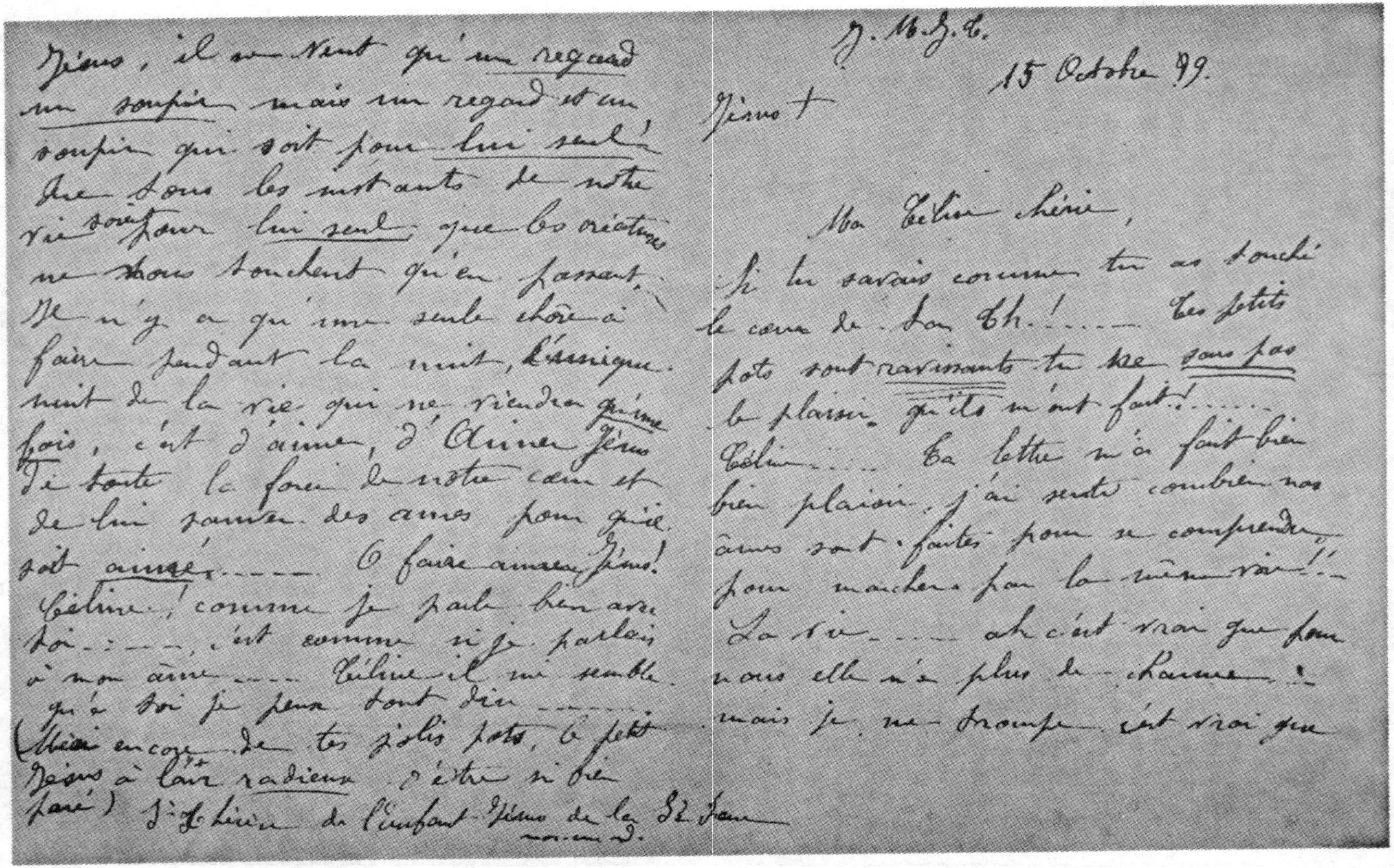

J.M.J.T.

15 Octobre 89.

Jésus †

Ma Céline chérie,

Si tu savais comme tu as touché le cœur de ton Th!..... tes petits pots sont ravissants tu ne sais pas le plaisir qu'ils m'ont fait!.....

Céline.... Ta lettre m'a fait bien bien plaisir, j'ai senti combien nos âmes sont faites pour se comprendre, pour marcher par la même voie!..

La vie.... ah c'est vrai que pour nous elle n'a plus de charmes..? mais je me trompe c'est vrai que

Jésus, il ne veut qu'un regard un soupir mais un regard et un soupir qui soit pour lui seul!.. que tous les instants de notre vie soient pour lui seul, que les créatures ne nous touchent qu'en passant. Il n'y a qu'une seule chose à faire pendant la nuit, l'unique nuit de la vie qui ne viendra qu'une fois, c'est d'aimer, d'aimer Jésus de toute la force de notre cœur et de lui sauver des âmes pour qu'il soit aimé.... O faire aimer Jésus! Céline, comme je parle bien avec toi...., c'est comme si je parlais à mon âme.... Céline il me semble qu'à toi je peux tout dire......

(Merci encore de tes jolis pots, le petit Jésus a l'air radieux d'être si bien paré)

Sr Thérèse de l'Enfant-Jésus de la Ste Face

nov. ind.

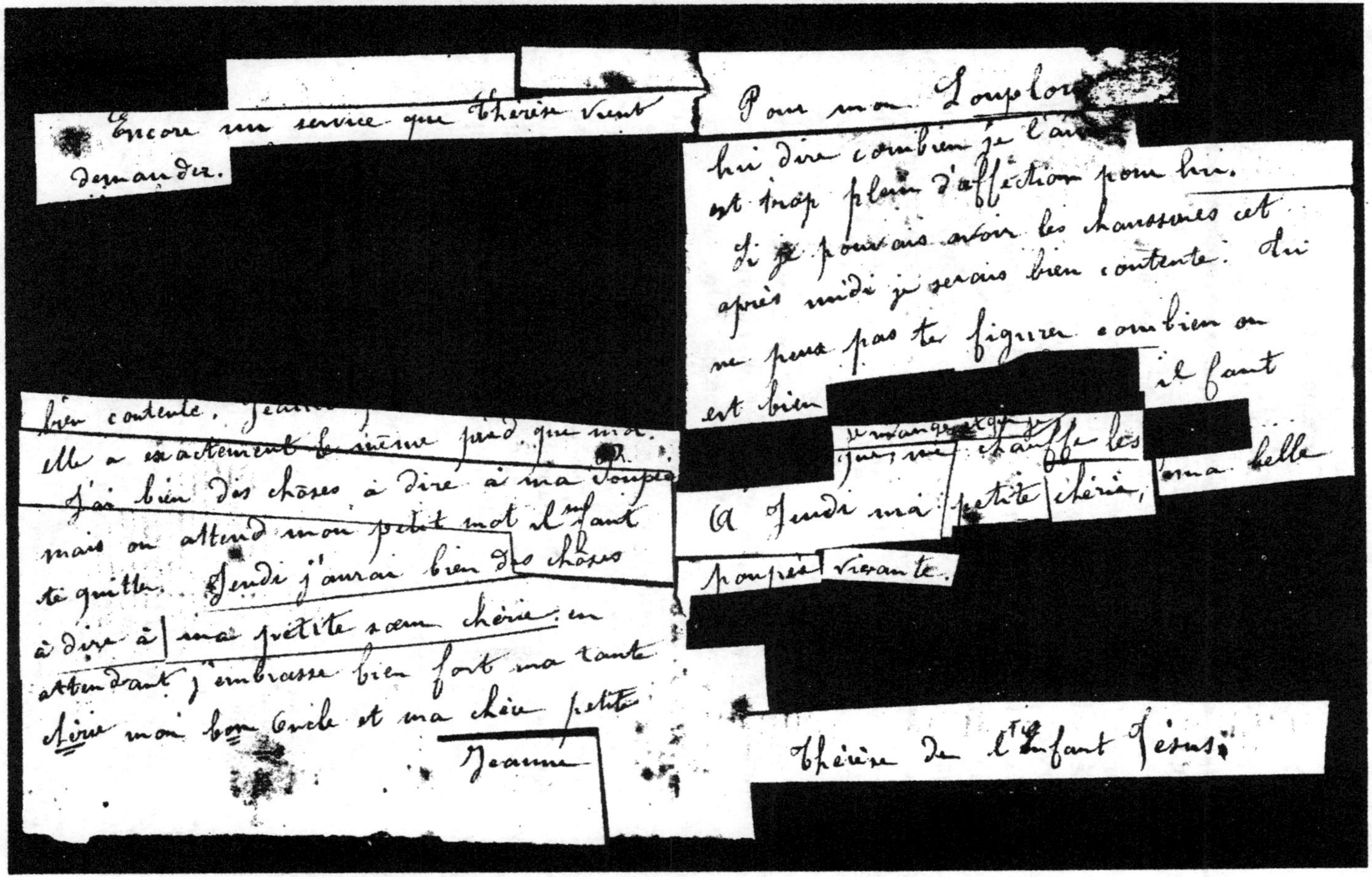

Encore un service que Thérèse vient
demander.

bien contente, Jeanne
elle a exactement le même pied que moi.
J'ai bien des choses à dire à ma Soupla
mais on attend mon petit mot il faut
te quitter. Jeudi j'aurai bien des choses
à dire à ma petite sœur chérie; en
attendant j'embrasse bien fort ma tante
Aimée mon bon Oncle et ma chère petite
Jeanne

Pour ma Souplou
lui dire combien je l'ai
est trop plein d'affection pour lui.
Si je pouvais avoir les chaussures cet
après midi je serais bien contente. On
ne peut pas te figurer combien on
est bien il faut
je mange et je
jusqu'au chauffe les
ma belle
A Jeudi ma petite chérie,
poupée vivante.

Thérèse de l'Enfant Jésus.

Her punctuation is frequently disconcerting. At one time, her sentences are linked together without periods or commas in a burning flow of words; at another time, the whole text of a letter is studded with marks of suspension[33] or exclamation.[34] For a long time,[35] Thérèse was unaware of the use of quotation marks, and she used parentheses instead.

We should take note, too, of her underlinings, at times replaced by the enlargement of a word.[36] Frequently without any justification, even whimsical during 1888-1890, these underlinings revealed subtle shades of meaning later on! There are underlinings to emphasize a point, but there are also some indicating a sort of conniving wink at the recipient; then we have to enter into her game to detect the fact, the reference, etc., well known to the two interested parties.[37]

As a matter of fact, a number of these peculiarities simply reflect certain family mannerisms,[38] characteristic of the time.

This enumeration makes no pretense at being complete. However, we should not pass over in silence her faculty of adapting herself to the other person, a faculty which gave Thérèse the freedom to change her handwriting according to the person who was to receive her letter. Thus, letters to the Guérin family show more application in the handwriting; the same may be said regarding those addressed to Léonie at the Visitation convent, no doubt because of the possibility of their being read by the superi-

[33] See especially the year 1889: under the pressure of moral suffering (her father's illness), Thérèse revealed her emotional upset in her handwriting.

[34] Especially in 1896-1897 (LT 202, 215, 230; P.S. to M. Guérin, April 3, 1897, etc.)

[35] Up to 1894.

[36] Thus in LT 45: "I *want* to become perfect"; in LT 165, the trinitarian "notre," etc. But Thérèse never writes it in capital letters.

[37] Perceptible shades of meaning, especially from 1896 onward.

[38] "We were in the habit of underlining words and putting in exclamation marks. After Thérèse's death, Uncle Guérin brought this to our attention, and we gave up the marks of exclamation" (Sister Geneviève's note, 1958). M. Guérin's remark could have been made when he was proofreading *Histoire d'une Ame*, for he was the "technical adviser" for this publication.

or! On the other hand, there is more spontaneity in her notes to her sisters in Carmel, and even more in her letters to Céline.[39]

These few remarks tell us enough about the exceptional field of investigation opened up to handwriting experts by Thérèse's letters. An *Histoire d'une Ame* in its spontaneity—in its mode of *expression* rather than in its *story*—is inscribed in the handwriting of twenty years (1877-1897), with the advances, the regressions, the sufferings, the crises, and finally in the total liberation of a woman's and a saint's existence, transfigured by the Spirit of Love.

In 1911, Msgr. de Teil spoke for a graphologist,[40] who was interested in the project of making a complete study of Thérèse's handwriting. He explained to Mother Agnes, in the terminology of the time, that this study would focus "on the work of Sister Thérèse, ON HER DETERMINATION *to transform* her CHARACTER. M. Eloy glimpses traces of this work in the modification of her handwriting which thus becomes a kind of moral photograph. If it be true that it takes less time than will power to make a saint,[41] this study will be of great interest."[42] Not in favor of this type of intrusion, Mother Agnes wrote in reply:

> We have thought over the matter of Thérèse's handwriting, but it seems to me that there is nothing to be done here. Sister Thérèse did not use her last type of handwriting—slightly upward—until the end of her life. I had never wanted to allow her to write in this way even though she had requested this because her ordinary penmanship, slanted to the right, was tiring her hand. It was, then, an act of obedience that she performed when writing—but very badly, I must admit—in this type of penmanship which is taught in the

[39] Interesting in this regard is the comparison between LT 147 and LT 148, August 13, 1893, addressed respectively to Céline and Léonie.

[40] M. Eloy. "He is a serious and very competent man. His beard is white, and he has been studying handwriting for a long time already" (Msgr. de Teil to Mother Agnes, April 15, 1911).

[41] P. Olivaint, S.J.

[42] April 15, 1911.

schools. All the letters to Céline were written in this way [slanted to the right]. Finally, I did allow her (during the last three years of her life) to write in the way that was easiest for her, and it was thus that she wrote her *Histoire d'une Ame*, her letters to the missionaries, her poems, etc., facsimiles of which are in the book.

So you see, Monseigneur, it would be difficult to make a sustained study of her handwriting. If we had left her free from her childhood to write in her own way, all well and good! But this was not the case. The facsimiles of the book are not a reduction in her writing; she used to write in small penmanship in order to use up less paper out of a spirit of poverty.[43]

We can see better today the value of these "moral photographs": free from any kind of posing, they offer just as much interest as do the pictures taken by Céline's lens, bringing to life the real Thérèse.

B) Other sources

Not having the autographs, we had recourse to the following sources for fourteen documents:

1) *Copy of the Writings*[44] (CE), contemporaneous with the

[43] April 14, 1911. Mother Agnes did not have Msgr. de Teil's letter of April 15 but only that of M. Eloy. We have found no trace of this document in the Carmel's archives. On April 16, she discouraged any further insistence: "I am less and less inclined to have a study made of Thérèse's handwriting. What good would it be? And, then, Monseigneur, as I have explained to you it is impossible to make a sustained study of it."

[44] A volume, 27.5 x 21 cms., in leather binding, entitled: *Baiocen. Beatificationis et Canonizationis Servae Die Theresiae a Puero Jesu et Sacro Vultu. Exemplar scriptorum Servae Dei.* II. *Lettres.* This volume has 189 pages and a collection of 189 letters. The discrepancy with the figure 170 given by the *Summarium* comes from errors in the latter: the *Summarium* itemizes thirteen letters instead of thirty-three for part "B" (to the family, after Thérèse's entrance into Carmel) and twenty-six letters instead of thirty for Part "C" (to Mother Agnes of Jesus and Sister Marie of the Sacred Heart, after her entrance into Carmel); finally, five documents (prayers, poems) are listed as letters by mistake. The synoptic chart of the sources (volume 2 of the *General Correspondence*) will give details of the letters recorded at the Process. Each document is marked with three

Process (1910). This copy supplies us with four texts:

a) two notes to Sister Marie of St. Joseph[45] (LT 199 and 206);
b) a note to Sister Martha of Jesus[46] (LT 241);
c) a letter to Sister Agnes of Jesus (LT 11).

This Copy supplies us, too, with sentences or paragraphs in those cases where there are "gaps" in the autographs, and some information, such as chronology, explanatory notes.

2) *Sister Geneviève's notebooks* (CMG):

CMG III[47] supplies us with LT 209; CMG IV,[48] with LT 260. Moreover, CMG III is frequently the only source of complementary passages of the mutilated autographs when these were not handed in at the Process.[49]

---

stamps: that of the Lisieux Carmel, that of Bishop Lemonnier († *Sigillum Thomae Episcopi Baiocen. et Lexovien*, with his coat of arms), that of the reviewer (*E. Deslandes, Chanoine Titulaire*, and his academic degrees). He signs each document by hand: "*Ita est*. E. Deslandes, *not. deput*." This was to signify their conformity with the originals.

[45] This religious left the Carmel on June 29, 1909. Perhaps the autographs were returned to her after the *Process of the Writings*, and she kept them up to her death on November 26, 1936. The date and the reason for the disappearance of the two missing notes (given away? destroyed?) are unknown.

[46] The original must have been burned along with the greater part of this Sister's private papers, among which were other autographs of Thérèse, not handed in at the Process. Sister Martha of Jesus died in 1916 from a contagious form of consumption, hence the need to burn these papers.

[47] Notebook, 16.5 x 11 cms., quadrilled paper, leather binding, 340 written pages, plus 212 blank pages.

[48] Identical in appearance to the preceding notebook; 463 pages. We find here: pp. 1-140, letters of Thérèse to Céline, before the latter's entrance into Carmel; pp. 313-338, in a much later handwriting, contain letters and holy pictures concerning Sister Geneviève's Profession (February 24, 1896); pp. 369-376, contain letters and notes in Carmel; pp. 337-382, contain family notes before and after Céline's entrance into Carmel; on a loose sheet, four notes or holy pictures from Thérèse to Céline.

[49] In particular, the letters to M. Martin and Marie Guérin. We present here Sister Geneviève's written declaration on January 17, 1954, prefacing this notebook; she sums up forty years of history in two pages (1905-1948):

"When there was question of opening the *Informative Process* for the Cause of the Servant of God, Sister Thérèse of the Child Jesus, the vice postulator,

3) *Different copies:*

a) an abridged facsimile (LT 70);
b) loose sheets (LT 41, 221, 226, 254);
c) separate notebooks (LT 38 C and 204); a total of seven letters.[50]

4) *Edition of 1948*: this is the only source of LT 16 and of a paragraph of LT 104.

Msgr. de Teil, interviewed us on several occasions concerning the examination of the Writings which the bishop of Bayeux and Lisieux was to announce.

"We were very much perplexed regarding certain letters of our saintly sister which seemed too insignificant to present.

"It was then, and before the *Examination of the Writings* was begun, that we were advised by a higher authority to cut these letters into pieces, and we did this. This partial destruction made it possible later on for us to give out fragments of the autographs, such as, detached words, signatures of our Saint.

"Because of my innate attraction for keeping records, however, I had copied down beforehand these insignificant little letters in this bound notebook given to me and in which I entered my memories. I conscientiously believed that it was sufficient, at the time of the official *Examination of the Writings,* to cross out in pencil as nonexistent all the letters not handed in at the Process. (A long time afterward, some of the pencil marks were rubbed out by mistake.)

"We have evidence of this on pp. 160 and 161 [see CMG III] in the letters from Thérèse to Marie Guérin where the paragraph: 'I am not speaking to you . . . .' (p. 161) is enclosed in pencil because it was handed in at the Process, whereas all the rest of the letter not recorded is crossed out. The same thing applies to p. 204, the beginning of the letter to M. Martin is crossed out because it was not presented at the Process.

"If some are not crossed out, though not handed in, it is because I had returned them to the Guérin family after having copied them, not knowing that they had forgotten to include them in the collection presented at the Process by the Guérin family.

"When we were preparing the integral edition of the *Letters* of St. Thérèse of the Child Jesus in 1947, M. l'abbé Combes, then professor of history of Christian spirituality at the *Institut catholique de Paris,* Doctor of Theology, and professor of research at the *Centre National de la Recherche Scientifique,* persuaded us to insert in this publication all the letters and notes that were not handed in at the Process, and we did this in good faith. Sister Geneviève of the Holy Face and St. Teresa, O.C.D. Sunday, January 17, 1954."

[50] These documents will be described in the Appendix, volume 2.

II. Recipients of Thérèse's Letters

Thérèse of Lisieux became acquainted with very few persons during her lifetime. She had been reared in a family that was very much closed to outsiders; at the age of fifteen, she entered a religious Order that strongly encouraged "separation from the world"; she died at the age of twenty-four. However, she was soon to be called "the beloved child of the whole world."[51] Her correspondence reflects this state of affairs. Her immediate family—father, sisters, uncle, aunt, cousins—absorbs seventy-eight percent of her letters; her Carmelite family—excluding her three sisters in Carmel—received hardly ten percent; the remainder of her letters is divided among twelve correspondents: seven ecclesiastics, three religious, and two friends.[52]

The charts on pp. 82-83 and 86-87 give some information concerning the recipients and the flow of Thérèse's correspondence. It will be sufficient here to accompany these charts with a few notations about Thérèse and those who received her letters.

Thérèse, the writer

Encouraged by the example of her mother and her older sisters, even Céline, all of whom were adept at letter-writing, Thérèse, at a very early age, manifested the desire to communicate through letters. She even begged for help from her sisters (LT 3, 6, and 7).

With Pauline's entrance into Carmel on October 2, 1882, and Thérèse's subsequent withdrawal into herself, this form of communication seems to have been hampered. When she writes, Thérèse has to "rack her brains for words" (LD, May 4, 1885); she usually has to have recourse to an outline, even when writing to her little cousin, Marie Guérin (LT 19).

[51] Pius XI.

[52] These numbers have reference to the correspondence preserved. See the remarks below concerning the correspondence that has *disappeared*.

This difficulty in writing letters was to persist even after the liberation of the "Christmas grace" of 1886 whenever there was a question of expressing her intimate thoughts (LT 28, 36).

When she was in Carmel, during the years 1888-1889, she welcomed an "outline" at times drawn up by Pauline (Sister Agnes of Jesus) for difficult matters (LT 70, 112).

Thérèse manifests a real ease when writing to her Sister Céline (see LT 96; and also during the years 1891-1892). However, she had to wait until the year 1893 to arrive at that gift of expression which was to continue to improve right up to her death in 1897.[53] Then she writes with real ease[54] and at great length.

One final remark: with the exception of the notes exchanged inside the Carmel—the prioress' permission was required—few of Thérèse's letters were to be read by the recipient only. At her home in Les Buissonnets, letters were not private matters. In Carmel, each message destined for the outside was read by the prioress according to the existing custom, and, in more than one case, by her older sisters, Sister Agnes of Jesus and Sister Marie of the Sacred Heart. Did this kind of interference have any influence on the composition of these letters? Perhaps it did at the beginning of her religious life: we see it in such notes as the following to Sister Agnes (LT 54, 55, 76, 78, 95, etc.). But very soon, no doubt because she walked in the truth of God's presence, Thérèse attained such an independence of thought that her freedom of expression seems to have been unhampered by the intrusion of a third person, that is, someone other than the recipient reading her letters.

[53] In February 1893, Thérèse composed her first poem; in December 1893-January 1894, her first play (pious recreation) on Joan of Arc. In autumn 1895, she wrote: ". . . now I can express my thoughts with great ease" (Ms. A, p. 151).

[54] Within the limits imposed by the Rule of Carmel and the commands of her prioress. See Ms. C, p. 252.

The recipients

At a time when the use of the telephone was still not very widespread,[55] letter-writing played an important role in such families as those of the Guérins and Martins. Short vacations in the country or at the seashore,[56] and, *a fortiori*, the exceptional trip to Italy in 1887, gave rise to much letter-writing. Thérèse followed the example of her family in this matter.

But it was especially the cloister of Carmel that traced out the line of demarcation among the correspondents in accordance with the successive entrances into the Carmel of the four Martin sisters and their cousin, Marie Guérin. These entrances either separated or reunited the members of the family.

Thus, from April 9, 1888, Thérèse no longer had to write to *her two older* sisters, Marie and Pauline, whom she had rejoined in Carmel. She was authorized by Mother Marie de Gonzague, her prioress, to write notes to them during her retreat for the reception of the Habit (January 10, 1889), and of Profession (September 8, 1890), or during their own private retreats (1888-1889).[57] Afterward, Thérèse enters into an almost total silence until the end of 1896.[58] She makes an attempt to inform her sisters of the change in her physical condition through notes written to them.

The situation is different regarding her father, *M. Martin*. If the letters from Thérèse as a Carmelite to her father are all contemporaneous with her postulancy, this is because the mental state of her "dear King" has cut off dialogue sharply. From 1888, her letters are being sent out to a man who is already seriously ill.[59]

[55] Invented in 1876, the telephone became a state service in 1899.

[56] At *Saint-Ouen-le-Pin* or at Trouville.

[57] This permission was an exception; it was customary during retreats for the religious to write twice to their prioress when she was on retreat, and the novices, twice to their novice-mistress.

[58] It is true that in 1895 Thérèse wrote at length to Mother Agnes when addressing her "childhood memories" to her. In fact, all three of her manuscripts (Mss. A, B, C) are in the form of "letters."

[59] Did Thérèse perceive intuitively what she was to say in May 1889: "Papa is God's little child" (LT 91)? The letters of Sister Agnes of Jesus and Sister Marie of the Sacred Heart to their father in 1888 have the same emphasis.

Céline remained Thérèse's privileged correspondent during the six years of the former's "exile," before her own entrance into Carmel on September 14, 1894, after M. Martin's death. At the approach of feast days or birthdays, Céline abstained from her weekly visit to the Carmel in order to ensure her right to receive a letter. The critical months, February-May 1889, and the summer of 1893, when Mother Agnes (then prioress) had recourse to the "player of the lyre" (Thérèse) to aid Céline in overcoming certain seductions of the world (see LT 143), are times strong in this correspondence between Thérèse and Céline.

Until the two years of her stay in the Visitation convent (1893-1895) when she received eleven letters from Thérèse, *Léonie* could appear to have been forgotten by Thérèse; however, Léonie tells us herself that she received letters both when she was in the world and after she had entered the convent.[60] During the years 1896-1897, Thérèse treated Léonie as an equal, looking upon her as an ideal client of her "little way."

The traditional greetings for a happy feast or a happy New Year to the *Guérin family* don't contain much inspiraton from the pen of Thérèse.[61] On the other hand, Marie Guérin's spiritual

[60] It is true, however, that Thérèse did not have the time to write Léonie (LT 105, 122), sometimes giving Léonie advice through intermediaries (LT 85).

[61] This is how Abbé Combes explained himself in 1947:

> Regarding the letters to Mme. Guérin and Marie Guérin, it is quite true that Thérèse says nothing startling. If we take them one by one, in isolation, they appear negligible, but, once set in proper perspective, they take on new meaning. . . . The marvel is that when we consider them in this way, in their chronological background, we discover in them things that Thérèse did not actually write: a very profound humility, a self-forgetfulness, fraternal charity, a zeal for souls, and a tenderness of heart, which appear to me as extraordinarily touching. I shall go even further. Thérèse was always kept in the background at her uncle's home. Well, what I find admirable in these letters from the Saint is that she never tried to depart from this position, to shine in her turn, to say to her uncle: "You can see how wrong you were to judge me as insignificant, don't you?" Now she had really felt this!. . . This is the triumph of the rarest humility. (To Sister Geneviève, September 12, 1947.)

needs render Thérèse eloquent (1889-1890). After Marie's entrance into Carmel (August 15, 1895), Thérèse's letters to her uncle and aunt are reduced in number.

In 1896-1897, moreover, the family circle is doubled by her spiritual family: the *novices* entrusted to her care by Mother Marie de Gonzague, and the two *missionaries*, P. Roulland and P. Bellière, to whom the prioress also wrote. For them, especially for the seminarian Bellière, Thérèse's devotedness will reach heroic proportions in her last weeks on earth.[62]

Dating the letters

A few remarks regarding the dating of the letters are needful for a fruitful reading of the following charts.

Thérèse had a love for history (Ms. A, p. 82). Later on, she wrote her *Story of a Soul* with very few chronological errors. The whole of her writings prove that she gave a certain attention to dates. She was only nine years old when she gave evidence of this attention in a note to Céline (LT 8). As a young girl, she writes down even the day of the week (LT 19, 20, 21, 23, 27, etc.). At the beginning of her life in Carmel, she loses her notion of time somewhat because of her eremitical life (LT 98). Nevertheless, she customarily dated letters destined for the outside, and about sixty percent of her correspondence is dated by her hand. There is no indication, or almost none, for the remainder, especially for notes written within the Carmel. The recipients supply these dates for six percent of the autographs.[63] Some sixty documents

[62] See DE, pp. 508-510. The two correspondents expressed their sentiments about her letters. "These letters are a precious treasure, a complement to her story" (P. Bellière to Mother Marie de Gonzague, November 24, 1898). "The few letters you allowed her to write to me made me admire her beautiful soul. Her letters did me some good; they made me love God and souls. Love of God was the goal of her actions, and I tried to imitate her example" (P. Roulland to Mother Marie de Gonzague, October 13, 1897).

[63] Especially Mother Agnes of Jesus in May-June 1897 (LT 229 to 233). She was collecting, and very often dating, the last conversations of Thérèse; see DE, p. 123.

were dated through cross-reference. For about thirty documents, the date is approximate or uncertain.

With reference to the first edition of the *Letters*, the chronology is confirmed most of the time, made more precise on certain points, especially for the retreat notes, and at times it has been changed.[64]

Missing letters

Precious as is this collection of 266 letters, it does not match Thérèse's actual output. The number of missing letters can now be estimated at about one third: this estimate comes from actual evidence, oral tradition, and conjecture.

We note, especially, the absence, pure and simple, of her letters to P. Pichon,[65] to Mother Marie de Gonzague,[66] to Sister Marie of the Angels, the novice-mistress.[67] This is a serious loss not only on the quantitative level but also for a knowledge of Thérèse's soul: had she not always tried to be "an *open book*" to her superiors? (Ms. A, p. 150).

Mention is made in her letters or in answers from her correspondents of pieces of mail which have not been discovered thus far.[68]

Some recipients have revealed and have regretted the destruction of letters because they did not suspect at the time their real value.[69]

[64] For example, LT 24, 54, 55, 56, 95, etc.

[65] With the exception of a rough outline; see LT 28, note 6. Thérèse must have addressed *at least* fifty letters to Père Pichon; see VT, April 1968, p. 137, no. 19.

[66] With two exceptions (LT 9 and 190). Judging by the number of answers, we would say there must have been some fifteen notes or more.

[67] Some ten notes according to the same criterion.

[68] Some fifteen for volume 1; see the recapitulation at the end of volume 2.

[69] For example, besides Léonie, at the *Process of the Writings*: Sister Marie Joseph of the Cross (PA, 49) or even Louise Marais (d. 1923), the former maid at Alençon (testimony of her nurse, 1964).

Others suppressed them more or less intentionally because, no doubt, these notes were too personal. Such would be the case with Thérèse's novices: according to an oral tradition, some received many more notes from Thérèse than they handed in at the *Examination of the Writings*.

We know, too, from oral tradition that Thérèse communicated occasionally with some of the other Carmels: Saigon, Jerusalem, etc. Was she not going to write to Diana Vaughan, whose "conversion" had fired her with enthusiasm and who even answered her . . . by the hand, of course, of Leo Taxil, the great impostor?[70]

Finally, it is very likely that her companions at the Abbey, some friends, for example, the Maudelondes, the Primois, the Colombes, etc., received a few lines from her, even if it were on the back of a holy picture, May 8, 1884 (the day of her First Communion) and on other important events in her life.

The collection of the letters presented here, then, is not complete. It would be presumptuous to repeat, after the passage of sixty years, Sister Marie-Madelaine's words: "Certainly they will not find anything else!" At least, we have done our best to collect even the smallest fragment of her correspondence, left to history by the Saint's sisters.

[70] See Mss. I, p. 19; there is no trace of this answer in the archives of the Carmel.

Volume I RECIPIENTS*	Childhood Apr. 4, 1877	Adolescence Dec. 25, 1886	Postulancy Apr. 9, 1888	Novitiate Jan. 10, 1889	Total
M. Martin	1	—	12	—	13
Marie	4	2(+1)	3	5	14
Pauline	4	6	6	8	24
Léonie	—	1	—	—	1
Céline	4	1	4	17	26
M. Guérin	—	—	1	1	2
Mme. Guérin	1	1	4	3(+1)	9
Jeanne	1	1	—	—	2
Marie	4(+1)	6	3	4	17
L. Magdelaine	1	—	—	—	1
Mother M. de Gonzague	1	—	—	—	1
Bishop Hugonin	—	3	—	—	3
M. Révérony	—	1	—	—	1
M. Delatroëtte	—	1	—	—	1
P. Pichon	—	1	—	—	1
Mother St. Placide	—	—	1	—	1
Sister Martha	—	—	1	1	2
"to all"	—	—	—	1	1
Total of LT,	21	24	35	40	120
including holy pictures	6	0	1	2	9

* The sign (+1) means that a letter is common to this recipient and another; for example: letters to Jeanne and Marie Guérin, M. and Mme. Guérin, Marie and Pauline, etc.

Volume II RECIPIENTS	Novitiate Sept. 24, 1890	before Céline's entrance Feb. 20, 1894	after Céline's entrance Sept. 14, 1894	Mar. 21, 1896	period of *Last Conversations* Apr. 4, 1897	Total
Sr. Marie of Sacred Heart	1	—	—	3	(1)	4
Mother Agnes of Jesus	—	2	—	5	10	17
Léonie	—	7	4	2	3	16
Céline (Sr. Geneviève)	10	14	6	6	5(+1)	41
M. Guérin	1	2	—	—	2	5
Mme. Guérin	4(+1)	2(+1)	3	2	(2)	11
Mme. La Néele	1	1	1	—	—	3
Marie Guérin	1	—	1	—	3	5
Sr. M. Joseph of the Cross	1	—	—	—	—	1
Céline Maudelonde	—	2	—	—	—	2
Sr. M. Aloysia Vallée	—	1	—	—	—	1
Sr. M. of the Trinity	—	—	—	3	6	9
Sr. M. of St. Joseph	—	—	—	7	1	8
Sr. Martha	—	—	—	—	3	3
Sr. Anne of Sacred Heart	—	—	—	—	1	1
Mother M. de Gonzague	—	—	—	1	—	1
P. Roulland	—	—	—	4	2	6
Abbé Bellière	—	—	—	3	8	11
Brother Siméon	—	—	—	—	1	1
Total of LT,	19	31	15	36	45	146
including holy pictures	1	1	1	1	7	11

SECOND CHAPTER

THE LETTERS FROM HER CORRESPONDENTS (LC)

A complete and critical republication of Thérèse's letters would appear sufficient. Such was the original objective in 1962, and such, even today, is our principal objective in this present edition. However, in order to place her letters in their historical context, a critical study of all contemporaneous documents preserved in the Carmel's archives became indispensable, especially those addressed to Thérèse.

1. The Documents

The words "letters from her correspondents" (LC) mean the letters and notes addressed to Thérèse personally, i.e., alone, excluding those in which she is a co-recipient.[1] The two hundred letters thus collected are spread out from January 8, 1880 to October 4, 1897.[2] We shall divide these into the following three categories:

[1] This section is given in the "diverse letters" (*lettres diverses*) (LD); see below.

[2] The last three, coming from China (P. Roulland), from Algeria (P. Bellière), from Canada (P. Pichon), arrived after her death, and these are to be found in the Appendix, volume 2.

a) about fifty are directly in dialogue with letters from Thérèse, that is, they call for a response from her;

b) a second group, sixty or seventy letters, are answers to letters from Thérèse, lost today;

c) the remainder of the collection, about eighty letters, belong to one or the other category, either the correspondent is answering Thérèse or the correspondent's initiative did not receive an answer.

Sources

These texts are published according to the following sources: 183 complete autographs; seven partial autographs, completed by copies when there are any;[3] twelve texts coming from copies.[4]

We shall not spend any time in the *description* of these manuscripts since this does not constitute the main objective of this critical edition. The greater part of them, however, appear as normal correspondence. The notes exchanged within the Carmel are written on paper just as poor as that of Thérèse's own notes. The "beautiful little letter"[5] sent each week by Sister Agnes of Jesus to Thérèse, who was preparing for her First Communion in 1884, really merits the description "little." The average size is 6.5 x 5 cms.

[3] LC 71, 105, 185, from Sister Agnes of Jesus; LC 110, 121, 125, 159, from Céline.

[4] LC 86, 88, 96, 129, 149, 152, 154, 155, from Céline (eight letters), cited according to the copybook and annotated by Sister Geneviève around 1950; LC 50, 56, and 156, from Léonie, cited according to a manuscript copy of Sister Marie of the Sacred Heart (described in the *Sources*, volume 2); LC 148 from Mme. Guérin: manuscript copy of Sister Geneviève.

[5] Ms. A, p. 74.

Volume I SENDERS	Childhood Apr. 4, 1877	Adolescence Dec. 25, 1886	Postulancy Apr. 9, 1888	Novitiate Jan. 10, 1889	Total
Marie Martin	4	7	6	9	26
"Pauline" (Sr. Agnes)	30	14	6	3	53
Léonie	—	2	—	—	2
Céline	—	—	3	5	8
Mme. Guérin	—	1	—	1	2
Marie Guérin	3	4	—	3	10
Sr. M. A. Vallée	2	—	—	—	2
Mother M. de Gonzague	5	2	4	1	12
Sr. M. of the Angels	—	—	4	3	7
Mother Hermance	1	—	—	—	1
Bishop Hugonin	—	1	1	—	2
M. Révérony	—	1	1	1	3
M. Delatroëtte	—	1	1	1	3
P. Pichon	1	—	4	5	10
Brother Siméon	—	—	—	1	1
Total	46	33	30	33	142

Volume II SENDERS	Novitiate Sept. 24, 1890	before Céline's entrance Feb. 20, 1894	after Céline's entrance Sept. 14, 1894	after Mar. 21, 1896	period of *Last Conversations* Apr. 4, 1897	Total
Sr. Marie of Sacred Heart	1	—	—	2	—	3
Mother Agnes of Jesus	—	—	—	—	7	7
Léonie	—	1	—	1	1	3
Céline (Sr. Geneviève)	1	5	—	—	1	7
M. Guérin	—	—	—	—	2	2
Mme. Guérin	1	—	1	—	1	3
Mme. La Néele	—	—	—	1	2	3
Marie Guérin	—	—	—	—	—	0
Mother M. de Gonzague	2	—	1	—	—	3
Sr. M. of the Angels	1	—	—	—	—	1
Sr. Th. of St. Augustine	—	1	—	—	—	1
P. Pichon	2	2	1	—	1	6
Abbé Bellière	—	—	—	2	9	11
P. Roulland	—	—	—	6	2	8
Brother Siméon	1	—	—	—	—	1
Brother Salutaire	—	—	—	1	—	1
Total	9	9	3	13	26	60

There are no *alterations* or almost none on the originals. It would not enter into Thérèse's mind to interfere in the writings of another person.[6] Her sisters, on their part, did not foresee the integral publication of their own letters.[7] Mother Agnes of Jesus signed some of her notes which had not been signed; she seems to have wanted these notes destroyed on the day of her death.[8] We can see some annotations on the autographs, made by Sister Geneviève.

Dating

One of the best services provided by the last living member of the Martin family, Sister Geneviève, was the dating of letters. During the last twenty years of her life, she was always revising, classifying, copying or having copies made, dating, annotating this documentation.[9] The chronology left much to be desired in this present collection (LC). A little more than one third bears the date written by the correspondent.[10] On the basis of Sister Gene-

[6] One exception: a careful alteration in pencil on a letter from P. Roulland (LC 171). The word "Mother" is substituted twice for the word "Sister"; a sentence is placed in parenthesis. We may deduce that it was read in the Community as addressed to the prioress: the Sisters were unaware of the relationship between Thérèse and "our Mother's missionary" (LT 221); see CJ 1.5.2.

[7] Except Sister Geneviève; she either destroyed or rewrote a part of Thérèse's letters addressed to her.

[8] On an envelope, today empty, Mother Agnes wrote around 1940: "Our little Thérèse carefully kept these little outlines that I wrote for her; I did not think I should destroy them. They are not even dated, but one can guess quite closely the time when one reads them. They are not even signed. Put them in the fire after my death. Sister Agnes of Jesus, c.d.i." (c.d.i. means *carmélite déchausée indigne.*)

[9] When Sister Geneviève was helping in the preparation for the publication of *Histoire d'une Famille* (research done in 1943), the first edition of the *Letters* (1946-1948), and finally, in the publication of *Manuscrits autobiographiques* (1953-1956).

[10] The following rarely omitted the date: the priests, even P. Pichon, who reduced the date to a minimum; the Guérins, Céline and Léonie. These omit it most frequently: Marie and Pauline, especially after their entrance into Carmel; Mother Marie de Gonzague (notes within the cloister), and Sister Marie of the Angels (novice-mistress).

viève's notations, we were able to date about twenty-six percent of the whole with some kind of certitude and to give an approximate date for almost twenty-four percent. As for the rest, some thirty letters, we were reduced to conjectures.

Preservation and usage by Thérèse

How do we explain the preservation of all these documents down to this day? Undoubtedly, it was a characteristic of the times, which benefited from a greater stability in habitat. Undoubtedly, too, it was a family characteristic: who does not know families like those of the Martins and Guérins, who carefully preserve correspondence, holy pictures, dried flowers, photos, hair, etc.? Finally, this preservation came about through chance circumstances: of the seven cousins, six chose the religious life. The only one who married was Jeanne Guérin, and she did not have any children. Thus all the documents went to the Carmel.

Thérèse, on her part, did not break with family habits. When she was about to enter Carmel in 1888, she arranged her treasures in the drawers of a chest in her study. Céline was careful not to touch them: ". . . they have remained all intact, all is arranged just as you put them, your copybooks, your books . . . ." (LC 86). We might add without any risk of error: "your correspondence."

In 1894, Céline also joined her sisters in the cloister. Very likely, she brought all the family documents with her. Thérèse thus came into possession of her belongings. The letters which were the delight of her childhood were placed on her writing table, along with the notes of her mothers and sisters in Carmel, accumulated over a period of six years. This was a development of no small importance for the study of her "writings": she was able to consult this correspondence in 1895 in order to recall her *memories* when she was writing her autobiography.[11]

[11] We say this even though she wrote by inspiration and not by compilation. One fact is certain: Mother Agnes gave her Mme. Martin's correspondence to supply for the absence of memories regarding her first three years of life; see Ms. A, pp. 17ff.

In 1897, finally, when she realized she was failing, she put all her affiars in order: her workbasket, painting equipment, various compositions. She classified her correspondence under marked wrappers.[12]

II. The Correspondents

With scarcely any difference in names, the list of twenty-two correspondents covers that of the recipients of Thérèse's letters already mentioned.

The Martin and Guérin families supply forty-six percent of the documents. Eight out of nine names appear, with the exception of *M. Martin's* name. He never liked writing letters, those of 1885 from Constantinople being the only exception.[13] After his daugh-

---

Three other facts are somewhat certain: Thérèse must have read over the letters of 1889 from Céline since she writes in the present tense: "All the letters she wrote at this time *are* stamped with resignation and love . . . ." (Ms. A, p. 157). She seems to have recopied "the invitation" of Ms. A, p. 168, according to the version preserved by Sister Geneviève; see LT 118, note 2. Finally, she could have paged through the *Journal du Pèlerinage à Rome* of Abbé Huet to recall the memories of November 1887 (Ms. A, p. 119).

Internal criticism allows us to detect many similarities of expression between passages of the *Manuscript* and letters from her sisters which were contemporaneous with the events.

[12] We have five of these wrappers cut from obituary notices on which Thérèse wrote in pencil: "Mother Agnes of Jesus and Sister Marie of the Sacred Heart to Sister Thérèse of the Child Jesus"; "Letters from Céline to Thérèse"; "Letters from Aunt and from Jeanne to Sister Geneviève and Sister Thérèse of the Child Jesus"; "Marie Guérin to Mother Marie de Gonzague and Sister Marie of the Angels" (this on the back of a note from Sister Thérèse of St. Augustine, LC 153).

There is no trace of the letters of Marie Guérin to Mother Marie de Gonzague. We know neither the time nor the reason for their destruction, either by Sister Marie of the Eucharist (Marie Guérin) or by the sisters of Thérèse. Marie Guérin died in the Carmel in 1905.

[13] Regarding this correspondence, Sister Marie of the Sacred Heart said: "Sister Geneviève read me the letters that Papa had sent from Constantinople. Mother Agnes of Jesus was telling me that it was good he had made the trip because now we had these letters; when he was with us, he never spoke much about his feelings, whereas when he wrote this was not the same." (Conversation of April 8, 1935, written down by Sister Marie of the Incarnation in her notebook, p. 158.)

ters' entrance into Carmel, his weekly visit to them dispensed him from any writing communication. From 1889, his mental state made all writing impossible for him right up until his death in 1894. This complete silence does not help us in unravelling the mystery of this personage with the "veiled" countenance (Ms. A, p. 46).

The letters from Thérèse's "little mother" (Pauline) total close to thirty percent of the "LC" collection. A study of the texts confirms what we already know: Pauline's tremendous influence on Thérèse, on both the human and spiritual levels.

To the seven priests already mentioned, we must add the name of a Brother Salutaire, who appears nowhere else. It is not certain whether Thérèse answered his request (LC 176).

The five other correspondents make up Thérèse's ordinary world: Mother Marie de Gonzague (fifteen), Sister Marie of the Angels (eight), Mother Heart of Jesus (one), Sister Thérèse of St. Augustine (one), all of whom were Carmelite nuns at Lisieux; and Sister Marie-Aloysia Valée (two), a Visitandine at Le Mans.

The preceding charts show us the flow of this correspondence.

THIRD CHAPTER

DIVERSE LETTERS (LD)

The correspondence addressed directly to Thérèse (which is still in the Carmel's archives) represents hardly one tenth of the family letters and those of her close relatives. In this collection of some two thousand documents,[1] a great number have reference to her more or less directly. And the whole furnishes us much information on the persons, the events, the psychological and spiritual atmosphere of the years 1887-1897. Establishing any kind of chronological and definitive *dossier* from these old papers – at times, real scribblings! – meant engaging ourselves in a long and exacting work. However, we had to dare to open this vast shambles if we wanted to set the *Centenary Edition* on firm foundations.[2]

From all this work, undertaken without any preconceived notions, there soon emerged the outline of a *biography* which was startling in its truthfulness. When we discovered their original soil, the letters of Thérèse and her correspondents ceased to be merely a collection of faded flowers and became a living plant. What were we to give the reader from this rich documentation?

[1] See Mss. I, pp. 34-36. Sister Geneviève's correspondence is not in this collection.

[2] *Dernier Entretiens* (Last Conversations) had already benefited from this research done during 1963-1966.

I. Options

Among the possible options, one choice became clear: around the letters from Thérèse—the main objective of this publication—the restructuring in an organic body not only of the letters addressed to her but the communications exchanged regarding her by a third party.

Every choice has its risks. Would not the important proportion of letters *to* Thérèse or *on* Thérèse as a child and an adolescent (1877-1888) have as a consequence the hiding of Thérèse's own correspondence, for it was not too extensive—which is normal—during those same years? However, this "disproportion" was considered less as an inconvenience than as an historic fact. The human and spiritual itinerary of Thérèse consisted of a prolonged immersion in her family *milieu*: this is a fact. It appeared necessary to "leave that [itinerary] on paper just as it was in reality."[3] Thus the publication of the diverse letters allows for, among other things, the taking of the first manifestations of Thérèse's personality by surprise. Since her childhood has remained unknown up to this day, the return to the sources can be only beneficial to history.[4] Getting into contact with this documentation—free from any kind of adulteration—makes for a balanced judgment on the different persons who were called upon to fashion the countenance of a Saint.

This indispensable conditioning on the part of the reader once realized, he will be ready to listen to Thérèse alone.[5]

II. Documents

The "diverse letters" (LD) are divided into three groups:

[3] Msgr. André Combes, letter of February 4, 1947; see above.

[4] See Msgr. Combes, *Introduction*: "Such is the general law of every historical advancement: to pass from commentators to origins."

[5] The text of Thérèse's Letters alone will be the object of a future publication.

1. Letters destined for two or more co-recipients, *one of whom is Thérèse*. Volume 1 contains twenty of these, half of which are addressed to both Céline and Thérèse before the latter's entrance into Carmel.[6] We have counted seven others from Céline to her Carmelite sisters during M. Martin's illness in 1889-1890. Volume 2 presents a dozen of these documents which come from the pens of Céline, P. Pichon, and l'abbé Bellière.

These letters are published in whole or in part depending on whether Thérèse is the principal or the secondary recipient of them. Céline's collection to her sisters was the object of a more rigorous selection because of the doubt as to its authenticity.[7] We gathered from this collection the elements which could shed light on the "painful passion" of M. Martin which had been thus far concealed from historical research,[8] elements, too, which could unveil at the same time the unsuspected depths in the soul of his "little queen."

2. Letters of correspondents, making mention of Thérèse; this is the most important section of the diverse letters, comprising close to 150 fragments. Only the most significant are retained in the *corpus* of the work (some fifty in volume 1), the remainder being reported in the Appendix, volume 2.

These documents bring to light unknown or little known aspects of Thérèse's life: vacations in the country or at the seashore (1884-1887), sudden changes postponing her entrance into Carmel (October-December 1887), the trip to Rome which we can now follow as though it were on film (November 1887), small incidents at Carmel (see July 8, 1888), etc. From the collection

[6] Four from Sister Marie of the Sacred Heart, three from Sister Agnes of Jesus, two from Mme. Guérin, one from Mother Marie de Gonzague; about eleven are addressed to the "three pilgrims" at Rome.

[7] See note 12, below.

[8] We did not set up an exhaustive *dossier* on M. Martin's illness. The documentation was severely censored by Thérèse's sisters and even destroyed in part. It was necessary, however, to be more precise on the trial which served as a background to Thérèse's life for almost six years of its duration (1888-1894).

entitled "the illness," already cited in *Last Conversations,*[9] we took only those extracts which explained the major stages of Thérèse's last six months on earth.

3. Letters from correspondents among themselves, without any mention of Thérèse, published for various reasons: either because they aided in establishing chronological information, dispensing with any proof on this point;[10] or because they recreated the context of events which had important bearing on Thérèse.[11]

The greater part of these documents is cited according to the originals. For the others, the sources are pointed out in their proper place.[12]

The dating followed the same directives as those of the "LC" series.

With rare exceptions, these letters come from the immediate family.

[9] Seventy-five letters from April 3 to September 30, 1897; see DE, pp. 665-774.

[10] For example, Céline's letters of April 12-17, 1877 and June 10-17, 1877; Marie of the Sacred Heart's of August 14, 1887, etc.

[11] Thus M. Isidore Guérin's letter of October 15, 1886 or the unpublished document of February 18, 1889.

[12] Appendix, volume II. It may be useful, however, to point out the source of Céline's letters to her sisters (1889-1890). These fragments were copied in 1924 by Sister Geneviève (Céline) in one of her notebooks (CMG IV). She divided them into two sections:

1. Céline's sentiments during this trial (CMG IV, pp. 159-176), with this foreword, p. 158: "Before we destroyed this correspondence, Mother Agnes of Jesus told me to copy the passages which revealed my sentiments at that time." Our edition has borrowed little from this, the assumption of a rewriting not being excluded..
2. Details on the state of M. Martin's health (pp. 177-226), preceded by this introduction, p. 177: "Some information on '*Papa's trial,*' but many things and the most painful which crushed our hearts 'will never be known on earth . . . .'" Circumstances permitted us to discover some of these mysterious data; see LD, February 18, 1889.

At times, we find extracts from the same letter in the two sections. In some cases, it is difficut to reconstruct the line of thought.

FIRST PERIOD

CHILDHOOD

(April 1877 - November 1886)

ALENÇON

Through her family roots, Thérèse of Lisieux was first Thérèse of Alençon.

When she first saw the light of day, January 2, 1873, this peaceful county town of 16,037 persons[1] *was known only for its lace, its linens, and its horses.*

The unforgettable witness of the "sunny years" of her early childhood (Ms. A, p. 29) and the setting of a delightful vacation when she was ten: ("joy," "happiness," "flowers," see Ms. A, p. 73), Alençon was identified especially for her with the image of her parents —neither of whom was born there.

When, in January 1895, Thérèse placed a duke of Alençon, a very attractive personality, by the side of Joan of Arc,[2] *she was no doubt conforming herself to the facts of history. But it must not have displeased her thus to exalt the name of her native town side by side with that of her favorite heroine.*

Louis Martin was approaching his fifties at Thérèse's birth, his ninth child. At twenty, knightly in bearing —he was a soldier's son—and naturally religious, he had sought admission among the monks of the great Saint Bernard (Swiss Alps). But in vain. He was to retain, however, throughout his life, his attraction for the "silence and peace of a deep solitude."[3] *At the age of thirty-five he chose the married state (1858). He was*

then working at his profession as watchmaker and jeweler (1850-1870), but not so much as a merchant as an artist. In his home, his great goodness was shown in his tenderness for his children. There was no weakness, however: no one ever challenged his authority.

Zélie Martin, at the age of forty-one, was looking forward to this new birth: "I love children to the point of folly; I was born to have them." But she thinks: ". . . it will soon be time for all this to end. . . . I'm at an age when I should be a grandmother!"[4] Besides, this woman, tender as she was energetic, was already carrying the marks of a great physical fatigue and, especially, a deep moral suffering: her handwriting and her photograph give proof of this. The loss of four very young children and the long evenings spent on her cobweb-like work (point d'Alençon) had worn her out prematurely. However, she always maintained a surprising buoyancy. Far from becoming engrossed in her own family worries, she discreetly took charge of the worries of others—faithful to her first vocation as a "Sister of Charity." "How many times," her maid was to say later on, "was I in the homes of poor families, with a hot meal, bottles of wine, coins worth forty sous, and nobody knew it except us two."[5]

Engaged in temporal affairs, the Martins were not shut up within them. Faith, the key to their whole existence, invited them to see in the "goods" of earth the shadow of the "goods" to come: how could these Normans drop the substance for the shadow? The search for a "goal" beyond earthy horizons was expressed in him by his attraction for making pilgrimages, and in her by a nostalgic longing for heaven. Attracted, in their turn, by the image of the "Homeland," their five daughters advanced joyfully to the conquest of this "new world."

"Even from my childhood," Thérèse was to write later, "I heard these marvels spoken about. I know that the country in which I am is not my homeland, that there is another, after which I must aspire without ceasing." (Ms. C, p. 212.) This great aspiration raises the Correspondence *to a high level.*

For the present moment, however, Thérèse is revealing to us her native town. It is easy to determine the four cardinal points of her child's universe: the prefecture, which she was able to contemplate from the balcony of her home, rue Saint-Blaise. In her eyes, the marvel of this former hôtel de Guise resided not in its Louis XIII architectural style but... in the beautiful toys of the "little prefect," with whom she played at times. As she walked along the sidewalk to the left of her home, she reached Notre-Dame church where she was baptized, January 4, 1873. Here she had received her first religious impressions, coming in contact with the liturgy which she loved instinctively. Another goal of her walks: the train station! What a joy for her to see Pauline reappear there at the time of her vacations! But the favor she most desired was the visit to the pavilion, her father's little piece of property, south of a bend in the river Sarthe. She would not exchange its bizarre, hexagonal tower for the castle of the Dukes or the Maison d'Oze....

Another delight was the Sunday walks out into the countryside: the wildflowers, the gold of ripened corn, the "distances" in half-tint filled with poetry.

1. Archives of the Orne department, 1873.
2. "*Jeanne d'Arc accomplissant sa mission*" (RP 3, January 21, 1895.)
3. Mother Agnes of Jesus, *Histoire d'une Ame*, 1898, Introduction, p. xvii.
4. Letter to Mme. Guérin, December 15, 1872.
5. Testimony of Louise Marais, July 22, 1923.

"I was beginning to enjoy life" (*Ms. A, p. 29*)
(April-June 1877)
Age four

"All my life God was pleased to surround me with love. My first memories are stamped with smiles and the most tender caresses!. . . Oh! truly, everything smiled at me on earth. I found flowers under each of my steps, and my happy disposition contributed much to make life pleasant" (Ms. A, p. 30).

Thérèse's statements sum up the fifteen pages of her Autobiography, dealing with her early childhood memories (Ms. A, pp. 16–30). Mme. Martin's letters confirm her words.[1]

A "little four-year-old rascal" (Ms. A, p. 28): this is how Thérèse appears at the beginning of the Correspondence. *Four older sisters bestowed their attention and gifts on her. The two oldest—seventeen and fifteen and a half—were ecstatic over their Benjamin's deeds. Marie was not a little proud of her goddaughter and her pupil (LD, May 9, 1877). Pauline (le petit Paulin), still a boarder at Le Mans, received the "little angel's" first confidences during the Easter vacation (LD, April 4, 1877). Pauline had already become the child's "ideal" (Ms. A, p. 20).*

Léonie, a fourteen-year-old adolescent, undergoing a

deep psychological change (see CF, March–July 1877), holds a "large place" in Thérèse's affection, though she does not enjoy it in the present Correspondence.

As for Céline, three and a half years older than Thérèse, she is the companion in her games. Thérèse would rather be deprived of her dessert than to be separated from Céline (Ms. A, p. 26). But the little one is "...more lively and much less naive" than her sister (Ms. A, p. 22). It is because of her desire to be like her in all things (Ms. A, p. 20) that we have two of Thérèse's first letters (LT 2 and 3).

Overflowing with vitality, the little child passes from an expressive pantomime—she "gesticulates," her older sisters tell us—to an interiority which reveals her "pensive nature" (LD, April 4, May 9, 1877).

This is truly that portrait in contrasts, depicted in her Autobiography: "a very expressive child" (Ms. A, p. 17) but capable of "thinking seriously" (Ms. A, p. 25).

1. *Correspondance familiale*, 1863-1877 (OCL, 1958). Two hundred and seventeen letters of Mme. Martin, one hundred and thirty-four of which were written after Thérèse's birth.

LD — *From Pauline to Louise Magdelaine.*
April 4, 1877 — (Extracts.)

Wednesday, April 4, 1877

Dear little Louise,[1]

...Thérèse and Céline are in the garden, enjoying themselves blowing soap bubbles. Mamma is occupied remonstrating with Léonie; Marie went out this instant to go and work downstairs with little Mother; Papa is at the Pavilion;[2] finally I'm in com-

plete solitude and I'm hearing nothing but my pen running on my paper. I'm going to be able, then, to think of my dear Visitation at my ease and to speak to my little Louise.

. . .How are you spending your days? I hope you're seeing Sister Marie de Sales[3] often. I want you to tell her that in a few years she will have a new novice, guess whom? Like Madame de Sévigné, I'm going to give you ten, thirty, and even one hundred guesses. . . . Marie? No. . . . Léonie? No. . . . Me, you, then who?. . . Any more. . . Well, this new postulant is, is, is. . . Mademoiselle. . . Thérèse Martin. . . . These are the motives that will guide her. Yesterday evening, she made her confession to me, and it was enough to make me die laughing. "I will be a religious in a cloister because Céline wants to go there, and, then, also, Pauline, I must learn how to read to children, don't you see? But I will not conduct class for them because this would bore me too much. Céline will do it. I will be Mother; I'll walk all day in the cloister, and then I'll go with Céline; we'll play in the sand and with our dolls. . . ." I quickly broke down her "castles in the air": "You think, then, dear Thérèse, that you'll talk all day long; do you know you will have to keep silent?" "True. . . . Ah! what a pity! I will say nothing. . . ." "What will you do then?" "That's no problem; I'll pray to good Jesus. But what can I do to pray to Him without saying anything? I don't know, and who will show me since I'll be Mother? Tell me!" I had a frightful desire to laugh. However, I remained serious. She was gazing at me thoughtfully. Her little face had such a candid expression; all she was saying was coming from the bottom of her heart, so much so that it was impossible not to take any interest. Finally, after reflecting for a few moments, she fixed her big blue eyes on me, and smiling mischievously, she gesticulated with her little arms like a grown person, saying: "After all, *mon petit Paulin*, it's not worth tormenting myself already, I'm too little, don't you see, and when I'll be big like you and Marie, I will be told what to do before entering the cloister. . . ." "That's it, dear baby," I answered, covering her with kisses. "Now it's late; let's go to bed; I'll undress you. . . .

Spend a few good nights before calling yourself Sister Marie Aolysia[4] (this is the name she has chosen), you still have time to think it over." At that, both of us went upstairs. I put her to bed, and, no longer remembering what she had told me, she fell asleep peacefully, thinking no more about it. . . . How I'd like this little angel not to grow up. A little soul who has never offended God is so beautiful. . . . So I love very much having Thérèse close to me; it seems to me that with her no misfortune can befall me. . . .

Your friend,

Pauline, *enf. de Marie*

. . . Thérèse is sending you a little letter; she is delighted with it and thinks herself *quite learned.*

* Autograph.

1. Louise Magdelaine, boarder at the Visitation like Pauline, was unable to go home for the Easter vacation because of her father's illness.
2. A little piece of property bought by M. Martin, April 24, 1857, in the *Sénatorerie* quarter (*rue des Lavoirs*), south of Alençon. It was made up of a hexagonal tower, two stories, surrounded by a spacious garden.
3. Mother Marie-Françoise de Sales Guyas (1843-1909), directress of the boarding school, 1875-1876; mistress of novices since the summer 1876.
4. Childish mispronunciation of Marie-Aloysia Vallée, mistress of the boarding school, to whom Pauline was attached. See letter of Céline to Marie, LD, October 13, 1877. We still have traces of an occasional correspondence between Thérèse and this Visitandine (see LC 1 and 2, 1880 and 1881; LT 160).

LT 1 — From Thérèse to Louise Magdelaine.

April 4, 1877

This first "letter" owes its inspiration to Pauline, who was guiding the little child's hand. Same date as preceding LD.

Dear little Louise,

I don't know you, but I love you very much just the same. Pauline told me to write you; she is holding me on her knees because I don't know how to hold a pen. She wants me to tell you that I'm a lazy little girl, but this isn't true because I work all day long playing tricks on my poor little sisters. So I'm a little rascal who is always laughing.[1] *Adieu*, little Louise. I'm sending you a big kiss. Kiss the Visitation for me, that is, Sister Marie Aolysia[2] and Sister Louise de Bonzague,[3] for I don't know anyone else.

Thérèse

* Autograph.

1. Pauline wrote, during this same vacation or at the beginning of August 1877, on the inside cover of a *Petite Géographie*: "The second course (held at home by Marie) is comprised of a charming little pupil named Thérèse, who laughs and plays from morning to night.... However, the devoted care that Mlle. Marie Martin is giving her will end up, I hope, in developing her intelligence which, after producing nothing but child's pranks, will be adorned with all the qualities proper to a *superior mind*.
2. See preceding LD, note 4.
3. Sister Marie-Louise de Gonzague Vétillart (1849-1884), directress of the boarding school.

LD *From Céline to Jeanne Guérin.*
April 12-17, 1877 Date deduced from the content; see notes 1 and 5.

Dear little Jeanne,[1]

I'm very happy to write you, for it has been a long time since I've written. Your portrait pleased me very much because it was very good.

We had lots of fun during Pauline's vacation.[2] I'd have loved to have you with us. We were in the country at the home of Thérèse's nurse.[3] When we arrived in the country, a woman was waiting for us and she took us along a very dirty road.[4] Finally, we arrived at the home of Thérèse's nurse. We drank some milk, and we were in her field. We played "wolf," we climbed trees and we made a swing.

Dear little Jeanne, I'm telling you about this outing only because it was one when we had a lot of fun and many disagreements as well.

I'm going to tell you about some trouble we had. When we were going there, it was raining, but we were in a wagon, fortunately. However, we did get wet just the same.[5]

Au revoir, dear little Jeanne. I'm kissing you with all my heart, also, little Marie,[6] Uncle and Aunt.

Your little cousin, who loves you very much.

Céline

* Autograph.

1. First cousin of the Martin children; daughter of M. Isidore Guérin, Mme. Martin's brother; pharmacist at Lisieux. Jeanne was nine years old at this time.
2. From April 7 to 17, according to CF, April 12, 1877.
3. Mme. Moise Taillé, *née* Rosalie Cosnard (1863-1908), called "little Rose," Thérèse's nurse (1873-1874).
4. The road (three hundred meters) undoubtedly belonged to the La Fontaine house of the Taillé farm, which was at Semallé (seven kilometers from Alençon). The woman was Mme. Royer.

5. See Mme. Martin: "On Monday, April 9, we went to the country. The day was good from noon to six o'clock. But then a terrible storm broke out. We had an uncovered wagon and we were drenched in spite of our umbrellas. The children didn't have a dry stitch on them when we returned." (Letter to Mme. Guérin, CF, April 12, 1877). Céline wrote the same day, no doubt, as her mother.
6. Marie Guérin, not yet seven years old.

LT 2 — **From Thérèse to Jeanne and Marie Guérin.**

April 12-17, 1877 — This letter, written with Marie's help, could be dated the same as Céline's to Jeanne; see preceding LD.

Dear little Cousins,

Since Céline is writing to you, I want to write you also to tell you that I love you with all my heart. I'd like to see and kiss you.

Adieu, dear little cousins. Marie doesn't want to guide my hand any longer, and I can't write by myself.

Thérèse

* Autograph.

LD — *From Marie to Pauline.* (Fragments.)

May 9, 1877

Alençon, May 9, 1877

I'm going to leave you soon, dear Pauline, for I am doing nothing but letters this morning,[1] and so Louise,[2] who just came in, was saying: "This room is soon going to be like a notary's office!"

As for myself, I think it looks like a chapel instead; my May-altar is so pretty it's running competition to the one at *Notre-Dame*. It's really something to arrange a May-altar in this house, Mamma is too difficult, more difficult than the Blessed Virgin! It has to have hawthorn branches reaching up to the ceiling, walls covered in greens, etc., etc....

Thérèse is filled with admiration. Each morning, she comes here to make her prayer, leaping with joy. If you only knew how full of mischief she is, and yet not silly. I am full of admiration for this little "bouquet."[3] All at home devour her with kisses; she's just a poor little martyr! However, she's so accustomed to caresses that she hardly pays any attention to them; and so when Céline sees how indifferent she is, she tells her in a tone of reproach: "One would say that all these caresses are *Mademoiselle's* due." You should see Thérèse's face!

On Sunday, she was reciting a little fable she knows by heart. It is incredible the facility she has for learning. But most interesting of all is when she gives you, with gestures, the sermon of "*pov'mère Na*!"...when she tells us, with a hopeless gesture, her "*ni son ni motte*,"[4] which never comes to an end.

Sometimes she attends Céline's classes[5] and she grasps immediately the explanations I'm giving. You can see her little imagination constantly at work. She has a remarkable intelligence. The other day, I was saying to her: "Poor little *Patira*." Céline, who is always asking questions even when she knows things well, asked what *Patira* meant, and Thérèse answered immediately: "It's a little girl who isn't happy."

Just now she was on the balcony and was looking very pensively at the street leading to the train station. I asked her what she was thinking about: "Ah! I'm thinking it is this way that *petit Paulin*[6] returns from Le Mans!" So you see the little baby isn't forgetting you either.

Last week, she was playing with a little friend and when the latter asked her in fun for news about her mother, her father, the whole family, the poor little girl thought she had to answer, and

do you know what she said? "Mamma has a bruise here (meaning her illness),[7] and Papa has a bruise on his ear."[8] I told this to Mamma in front of Thérèse, and the poor little darling began to sob. She is very sensitive; when she's said a word too many, or when she's made a mistake, she notices it immediately and, to make up for it, the poor baby has recourse to tears, and she asks for pardons which never end.[9] We tell her she's forgiven but in vain. She goes on crying just the same.

How innocent is a little child, how darling, how good! I'm not surprised that God loves them more than adults; they're much more lovable!

* ACL copy.

1. No other letter of this date has been found.
2. Louise Marais, a maid in the Martin family since 1865.
3. See Mme. Martin: "Thérèse is the joy, the happiness of Marie, and her glory; it is incredible how proud she is of her." (Letter to Pauline, CF, May 10, 1877.)
4. For: "*ni son ni moute*," read: *ni son ni mouture* (neither grain nor the leavings after grinding); which means the "poor woman" got nothing at all.
5. Since her completion of studies at the boarding school (August 1875), Marie was helping her mother in the making of lace and in Céline's instructions. Concerning these "classes," see Ms. A, p. 20.
6. A diminutive of Pauline's name given her by her father. It will be given her for a long time; see, for example, M. Guérin's letter, August 2, 1897 (L/DE, 43). Pauline soon did the same thing with Céline's name, nicknaming her: "*le petit Célin.*"
7. Mme. Martin had a cancerous tumor on her breast. The first symptoms appeared in 1865 (CF, April 23, 1865). After a remission of eleven years, the tumor appeared again (see CF, October 20, 1876), leaving her no longer with any hope of a cure (see CF, December 17, 1876). On Mme. Martin's state of health in May, 1877, see CF, May 10, 1877.
8. A sting from an insect, which, according to Sister Geneviève, will develop into an epithelioma (a benign or malignant tumor derived

from epithelial tissue); see *Le Père de sainte Thérèse de L'Enfant-Jésus*, p. 73.

9. Conduct already pointed out by Mme. Martin in CF, May 21, 1876.

LD *From Céline to Marie.*

June 10-17, 1877 Date deduced from content; see note 3.

Dear little Marie,

Thérèse is bothering me to write you a little letter; I'm going to have her write one to please you.[1]

I forgot to give you any news about the garden in my letter.[2] But, first, Louise wants me to tell you she wishes you a "good day," and to tell Pauline she will be happy when she returns.[3] There are six geraniums and the dahlias have really grown; they're longer than my finger.

* Autograph.

1. See LT 3.
2. Letter is lost.
3. Documents from this period make mention of two absences of Marie, from June 26 to July 3, 1876, and June 10 to 17, 1877, when she was with Pauline at Le Mans, on the retreat being conducted at the closing of the school year. Céline, no doubt, wrote this letter during the second absence. That same year, Mme. Martin, Pauline, and Léonie went on pilgrimage to Lourdes, seeking Mme. Martin's cure from the cancerous tumor. See LD, May 9, 1877, note 7.

LT 3 **From Thérèse to Marie.**

June 10-17, 1877

Letter written on second page of Céline's letter (see LD, same day). The page is decorated with a white geranium.

Dear little Marie,

I am kissing you with all my heart, and Pauline too.

Thérèse[1]

* Autograph.

1. The signature is followed by a formless scribble. This "letter" is difficult to decipher. Céline's handwriting is still unsteady. And Thérèse must not have allowed herself to be guided easily by her sister's hand.

"Pauline will be my Mamma!" (*Ms. A, p. 34*)
(July - November 1877)
Age four

After the Lourdes pilgrimage, made under painful circumstances (see CF, June 24, 1877), Mme. Martin's state of health rapidly grew worse. "What do you expect? If the Blessed Virgin does not want to cure me, it's because my time has come, and God wants me to take my rest elsewhere than on earth. . . ." Last letter of Mme. Martin (CF, August 16, 1877). She knew that her oldest daughter Marie had the qualifications for running the house and wielding an influence over the two youngest children (see CF, December 17, 1876). She was able to trust her. Mme. Martin's main concern, however, was for Léonie (see LD, November 16, 1877, note 3).

Mme. Martin died at dawn, August 28, 1877, after much suffering. She was only forty-six. "I do not remember having cried very much," Thérèse was to write later. "I spoke to no one about the profound feelings I was experiencing. . . . I looked and listened in silence." (Ms. A, p. 33.)

On the day of the burial, Céline threw herself into Marie's arms, saying: "Well, you will be my Mamma!" (ibid.). Thérèse broke with her habit of always following Céline's example. In an instant, she noticed "that Pauline was going to be sad and to feel cast aside, not having a little girl."[1] *And Thérèse "chose freely": "Well! Pauline will be my Mamma!" (Ms. A, pp. 34–35.)*

The dying mother's last look was given to her sister-in-law, Mme. Guérin, who was not to fail in her mission. "I believed I understood that look, and nothing will ever make me forget it. It is engraved on my heart. Since that day, I tried to take the place of her whom

God had taken from you." (*Letter to Thérèse, LC 148, November 16, 1891.*)

To bring his daughters into closer contact with their aunt, M. Martin was willing to sever all his ties with Alençon, even at the age of fifty-four. At his request, M. Guérin, Mme. Martin's brother, found, near his own home, the "delightful house" which he described with great enthusiasm (LD, September 10, 1877).[2] *The orphans were delighted with the solution, especially Thérèse (LT 4, September 16, 1877). The latter had already resumed her child's games (LD, October 13, 1877). Time was needed for her to show the signs of the shock she suffered at her mother's death.*

On November 15, 1877, accompanied by their uncle, the five Martin children left forever the house on rue Saint-Blaise. Thérèse was not to see Alençon again until six years later. She "chose" her second home, having no regrets at leaving Alençon. "I did not feel sad when leaving Alençon; children love change, and it was with pleasure that I came to Lisieux" (Ms. A, p. 35)

→Read: Ms. A, pp. 30-35

1. *Histoire d'une Ame*, 1898; passage inserted by Mother Agnes of Jesus; Thérèse did not write this in her Ms. A, p. 34.
2. Letter cited on pp. 167-169.

LT 4 **From Thérèse to Marie Guérin.**

September 16, 1877

Date obtained through cross-references. A family council brought M. Guérin to Alençon, September 16 (ChrIG, p. 31). M. Martin was named guardian of the five children and M. Guérin, deputy guardian. Pauline gave her uncle a letter for Jeanne and Marie; Thérèse added her personal message on the fourth page. Pauline noted in the margin: "Thérèse composed this letter herself, and I guided her hand in writing it."

Dear little Marie,

I kiss you with all my heart. Your letter pleased me very much. I am very much pleased to go to Lisieux.

Your little cousin,
Thérèse

* Autograph.

LD *From Céline to Marie.*

October 13, 1877

Date deduced from the content; see note 2.

Dear little Marie,

I'm very happy to write you.[1] Today, I'm going to attend little Jeanne Charon's burial.[2] I'm sorry she died, for she was a darling.

Thérèse is here at my back, talking to me about Sister Aolysia,[3] but I told her to be silent. She's not playing with shells any longer. I just lent her my top, and so she's really enjoying herself. If I have time, I'll make you a little copy to please you, so my letter will not be long. Now that I lent my top to Thérèse she's no longer bothering me.

Au revoir, dear little Marie. I'm kissing you with all my heart.

Your little pupil,[4] who loves you very much.

A person, Céline[5]

* Autograph.

1. A fictitious letter, it seems. Written on a piece of school paper, after mention of a homework in Bible History. On the back, there is a fragment of a "Diary"; see note 5.
2. Jeanne Charon (December 5, 1870 - October 11, 1877), lived at 16, *rue Saint-Blaise*; buried on Saturday, October 13, 1877.
3. See LD, April 4, 1877, note 4.
4. See LD, May 9, 1877, note 5.
5. Immediately after the signature, we read: "DIARY. Céline. Friday. I was very sad yesterday. Louise left (that is, my maid). Thérèse cried a little; I did not cry, but I was very sad just the same, and when saying this, I am still sad. We leave for Lisieux after "All Saints." Papa already brought some things by train yesterday. I forgot to say that the day before yesterday I played with the little prefect; she has a beautiful swing. We used the swing, and I was also in the bedroom of the lady; the little prefect" (The end is missing.)

   The Friday referred to at the beginning of the diary is undoubtedly October 19.

LISIEUX

Since the August vacation of 1875, Lisieux had ceased to be merely a name for the Martin children; it had taken on a form for them. Their mother had accompanied them on this vacation.[1] *Sixty years later, Marie recalled that event: "Recently I was looking at the Basilica, and I was thinking of Mamma; when she came to Lisieux, Aunt always used to take her to the cemetery. It was on a beautiful site, and she had members of her family who were buried there. Mamma loved to go there. If any one, at that time, had said to her: 'Do you see this beautiful hill where we are? Well! in fifty years, a superb Basilica will be built here. . . and this Basilica will be in honor of your little Thérèse.' Poor little Mother! She would have said: 'You're losing your mind!!' Certainly, she wouldn't have believed it, she who had so many troubles!. . . "*[2]

From this restful site, one can look down upon the red and gray town, surrounded by its green hills. It's an old town, indeed! Founded by the Gauls, it had undergone the Roman occupation, the pillaging of Saxon pirates, then, after being conquered by the Normans, all the vicissitudes of the second millenium. Comic or grimacing gargoyles, from their carved beams on the façades of fourteenth and sixteenth century manors, had observed the passing events of history: English troops during the

Hundred Years' War; the funeral procession of Pierre Cauchon, Joan of Arc's judge, interred in the cathedral of Saint-Pierre; the wars of religion; the upheaval of the French Revolution. Little Thérèse Martin walked its streets for a few short years (1877–1888). Little did she know that she would be followed by crowds from all nations, attracted there by her, between the two world wars. The bombings of the 1944 Normandy invasion reduced its old houses to heaps of ashes.

In that autumn of 1877, the Martin children took note, above all, of the dismal appearance of the town. From the valleys of Orbiquet, the Touques, and the Cirieux, there arose a thick fog, which quickly formed the low ceiling in its encounter with the smoke from the factories. Lisieux (eighteen thousand population), the second largest town of the Calvados department, led all the other towns in its industrial output. "Its tanneries could supply its markets each year with fourteen thousand hides; its spinning mills, with seven hundred thousand kilograms of thread; its linen factories, with twenty-six thousand pieces of manufactured goods; and its cloth factories, with seventy-four thousand pieces."[3] One of the most flourishing factories, that of Orival, had been established in 1860, at the gates of the town, by a relative of Mme. Guérin, Jean Fournet. At one time a peddler in the streets of Lisieux, this man died a millionaire in 1871. It was, however, a crumbling prosperity. The town of Lisieux underwent, as did the whole Calvados department, a decrease in population, which was the cause or the consequence of the textile failure. "Calvados is not only walking on the road of depopulation, it is rushing headlong on it."[4]

The countryside was more stable. Each Saturday, the pastures of the Pays d'Auge poured out on the Saint-

Pierre square their rich produce. On such a day, the pharmacist (M. Guérin) could hardly keep up with his clientele.

When the Martin family arrived in Lisieux, M. Guérin was not yet the important person he was to become in the 1890's, when a sizeable inheritance changed his way of life. Freeing him from the servitude of business, this new way of life gave him the opportunity to give free rein to the flights of his poetic imagination and to devote himself passionately to political journalism. For the time being, however, Thérèse's uncle was an active, methodical, and exact man, who was improving his situation through hard work. His gifts as an organizer made him much appreciated in parish projects.

At her fiery husband's side, the gentle and discreet Mme. Guérin maintained an atmosphere of peace, which spread its influence even over the household at Les Buissonnets.

In this secluded little home, close to the "jardin de l'Étoile," and not far from the Delauney barracks constructed in 1875 to accommodate six hundred soldiers, the Martin family recreated their own universe, on the margin of the town's political and social life. M. Martin administered his affairs, cultivated his garden, and fed his mind by serious reading. In the evenings, it was not the newspaper but Guéranger's "Liturgical Year" or some other educative book that was read aloud. The younger children will pursue their studies at the Benedictine Abbey (Thérèse began her studies there on October 3, 1881), and, very soon, the older ones, Pauline and Marie, will begin to show an interest in the Carmelite monastery at Lisieux.

1. Concerning this trip, see CF 137, 138, and 212. Thérèse was not on the trip.
2. Conversation of Sister Marie of the Sacred Heart, written down by Sister Marie of the Incarnation, January 1939; from the latter's notebook, p. 228.
3. Levasseur, *Géographie du département du Calvados*, Caen, 1874, p. 57.
4. Ibid., p. 127.

A life "tranquil and happy" (*Ms. A, p. 49*)
(November 1877 - October 1881)
Age four to eight

On November 16, 1877, not waiting for M. Martin's arrival (he was detained on business at Alençon), the five daughters settled in at "Les Buissonnets." This "charming house, cheerful and gay" (LD, November 16, 1877), immediately won their hearts. Thérèse spent more than ten years in this peaceful atmosphere.

The twenty or so letters of this period—three from Thérèse to Pauline—give the same tone as do the pages of her Autobiography, recalling these first years at Lisieux, until her entrance into the boarding school. "My life flowed by tranquilly and happily; the affection with which I was surrounded at Les Buissonnets made me grow, so to speak." (Ms. A, p. 49.)

The older sisters, Marie and Pauline, who had now become her little mothers, lavished their little "baby" with tokens of affection; she received these from her father, too, her "little king," who gave proof of a "truly maternal love!" (Ms. A, p. 35). The Guérin family was most gracious.

Undoubtedly the little girl showed more timidity and sensitiveness than she did at Alençon, but this was especially with regard to strangers (Ms. A, p. 34). But few

were the strangers who climbed the steep road up to "Les Buissonnets."

At the reopening of school in January 1878, Léonie and Céline were entrusted to the Benedictines of the town, the older one as a boarder, the younger one as a day-boarder. "Mamma Pauline" (Ms. A, p. 41) doubled for little Thérèse as a firm and affectionate school-teacher. Her pupil was so diligent that she knew how to write by herself before she was seven (LC 1).

Certain events stand out in her life, though we find no trace of them in the correspondence: her first confession (winter 1879–1880), which made her "happy and light-hearted" as never before (Ms. A, p. 41); Céline's First Communion (May 13, 1880), one of the most beautiful days in Thérèse's life (Ms. A, p. 57); and the most dramatic event, the strange vision of her father, then on a trip to Alençon (summer 1879 or 1880), whom she saw before her, bowed, aged, and with veiled head, walking along the side of her garden (Ms. A. pp. 45–47).

We shall have to wait for the Autobiography to know something of the "profound thoughts" of the little girl, whom the correspondence shows us as so joyful in her contact with nature: flowers, birds, and "this great sea" which filled her with wonder.

→ Read: Ms. A, pp. 34–49; 53–57.

LD *From M. Guérin to M. Martin.*

September 10, 1877

Lisieux, September 10, 1877

Dear Louis,

Taking my stand on your word, I set out in search of a house capable of lodging seven. We searched as much as possible in our own vicinity[1] and in a healthful section for a house with a garden or, at least, a little flower bed for the children. This was a recommendation made to me by my poor sister.[2]

Of the twenty-five houses for rent, having as much space as yours, we weren't able to find one which didn't have a redhibitory defect.

Finally, we discovered one such as I'd desire to have if I were retired from business:

A beautiful gate facing the public thoroughfare.

You then enter a little, landscape garden. Shrubs on each side. A delightful house topped by a belvedere.

On the ground floor, four rooms, one of which is a beautiful dining room panelled in oak. Behind this room, a cellar divided into a wine cellar and a storeroom for fruit.

Above the ground floor, a first floor level with a large garden situated behind the house; three magnificent bedrooms and a smaller one; two dressing rooms.

Above: a belvedere with a fireplace and three attics well-lighted and papered. The whole in perfect condition, newly painted and papered.

At the side of the house, a beautiful well, a water pump. At the rear of the house, a spacious garden, at least as large as M. Vital's;[3] a beautiful cistern; a carriage gateway for bringing in provisions (wood, cider), opening onto another road; a shed; a laundry; a greenhouse; a very comfortable shelter for poultry and

rabbits; an enclosure with a shelter and bath for ducks, etc., etc. All is surrounded by walls and overlooks part of the town; it is set behind the "*jardin de l'Etoile.*"

Distance from the church,[4] seven hundred paces, and from my house, seven hundred and sixty-four, which is almost equivalent to the distance from your house to that of M. Tifenne.[5]

But there is a difficulty and a big one, it's the access: from the entrance of the "*jardin de l'Etoile,*"[6] which is on the boulevard, there are one hundred paces to reach the house, on a narrow and steep road but clean, well-lighted, for a lamppost is right in front of the door.

From the house, you are not seen from any direction, and you see no road but simply a delightful panorama of the town.

I prayed to my poor sister to guide me, and I was so happy with my find that I wasn't able to sleep all night. In such a pretty property, you will forget the Pavilion[7] and all Alençon's attractions; however, I'm told that the trout and the eels have begun to take flight at the news of your arrival.[8]

The proprietor of the house promised me not to enter into any contract with anyone else until the end of next week. That is why you and Marie would do well to return there with me[9] in order to know what you should do.

This in short is all I have to tell you; I'll give you *viva voce* more ample details.

Adieu, dear Louis. We embrace you with all our heart, as well as your children.

Your devoted brother,
I. Guérin

* G. Copy.

1. The Guérins were living above their pharmacy, at the corner of *Place Thiers* and *Grande-Rue,* Lisieux.
2. On the occasion of a trip to Alençon, during the first two weeks of August 1877 (see CF, July 27 and August 16, 1877). M. Guérin had, then, advised his sister to encourage M. Martin to settle later at

Lisieux (that is, after Mme. Martin's death). "But she answered that she'd never do that, that she knew only too well that to please her he wouldn't hesitate, that she feared very much he would be unhappy afterward when seeing his life completely changed. Good little Father, having learned from Uncle about these details after Mamma's death, did not hesitate, in fact, to change his life for the good of his children." (Sister Marie of the Sacred Heart, *Souvenirs autobiographiques,* p. 61).

3. Vital Romet, a friend of M. Martin's and Céline's godfather. He lived at Alençon, *rue du Mans.*
4. *Saint-Jacques* church. In fact, the Martin family attended Mass at the cathedral of *Saint-Pierre.*
5. Friend of both M. Martin and M. Guérin. He lived at Alençon, *place de Plénître.*
6. A park made by a private individual in 1778 on *route de Pont-Evêque;* it was bought in 1824 by a group of forty shareholders, who rented its access to some travelers. The "*jardin de l'Etoile*" became one of Thérèse's favorite spots. See LD, June 4, 1879.
7. See LD, April 4, 1877, note 2.
8. M. Martin was an expert fisherman.
9. Undoubtedly after a family meeting, which was to take place at Alençon, September 16; see LT 4, this date. Pauline answered on September 11: "Papa finds it useless for us to go to Lisieux to see the house; it's understood that we are in agreement with his wishes which are certainly our own." (Letter to Mme. Guérin, September 11, 1877.) An inventory was made on September 17 and 18 (according to a deed authorized by M. Racinet), and so M. Martin's trip to Lisieux must have been made on September 19, the day on which he signed the lease for the *Maison Le Valois aux Bissonnets* (ChrIG, p. 31). The Martin children baptized their new home "Les Buissonnets," in this way restoring the original name of their district. According to M. E. Deville, the name "Bissonnets" was an incorrect spelling of "Buissonnets," a mistake which was made during a commune survey at the beginning of the nineteenth century. (See *Journal de Rouen,* April 29, 1924.)

LD *From Marie to M. Martin.* (Extracts.)

November 16, 1877

Lisieux, November 16, 1877

Dear little Father,

We are settled at Les Buissonnets.[1] It is a charming house, cheerful and gay, with a large garden in which Céline and Thérèse will be able to play. There is only one staircase which leaves something to be desired, and also the road, "road to Paradise," as you called it, for, in fact, it is narrow. It is not the "wide and spacious road." What does it matter? All this is a very little thing. . . .

In the meanwhile, dear little Father, we would love to have you in our midst; your absence already appears long to us. When, then, will your business at Alençon be terminated?[2] I'm constantly thinking about you. It seems to me you will be happy here, surrounded by your little family. Oh! yes, we will take care to be very good, to make your life very sweet in order to thank you for the great sacrifice you made for our happiness. This happiness will also be yours, for we shall do everything to make you happy.

Uncle and Aunt are very much worried about our becoming accustomed to this place. And so Aunt is inviting us tomorrow to go to her house in the afternoon; she's going to prepare apple tart for lunch. The little ones are delighted to go and play with their cousins. Léonie, especially, is delighted.

I notice she is changing from day to day for some time; haven't you noticed it, little Father? Uncle and Aunt are already aware of it. I am sure it is our dear Mother, who is obtaining this grace for us,[3] and I am convinced that one day our Léonie will give us some consolation.

Au revoir, dear little Father; see you soon. We kiss you with all our heart.

Your oldest daughter,
Marie

* G copy.

1. The trip to Lisieux from Alençon was made on November 15 (ChrIG, p. 31). The Martin children spent the first night at the home of their uncle and aunt.
2. M. Martin "is urging the workers to finish the *Point d'Alençon,*" which remained to be done at the assemblers (letter to his daughters, November 25, 1877). He did not rejoin his daughters at *Les Buissonnets* until November 30 (letter from the same, November 29, 1877).
3. Worry over Léonie's future is one of the greatest worries in Mme. Martin's correspondence during her last months. See, for example, CF, May 13, 1877, p. 396; June 25, 1877, etc. A few days before her death, she confided her worries to Marie: " 'Ah! when I no longer will be here, who will be interested in my poor Léonie? Who will love her?' Then I reassured her, telling her: 'I! Mamma, I promise you.' And I'm holding to my promise; I've always had for her a very special affection; I've always protected her." (Sister Marie of the Sacred Heart, *Souvenirs autobiographiques*, p. 63.)

LD *From Mme. Guérin to Pauline.*

June 26, 1878

On the occasion of an "Exposition," M. Martin visited Paris with his two oldest daughters, from June 17 to July 2, 1878 (ChrIG, p. 43). Léonie and Céline stayed at the Benedictine Abbey where they were making their studies, and Thérèse was entrusted to care of her aunt.

Dear Pauline,

I received your good little letter this afternoon.[1] It pleased us very much. You're using your time well and you are right, but how I pity you for the excessive heat we're having these days. You must be really suffering. We are frequently thinking of you, even very frequently. Thérèse isn't in the least bit bored, and she seems to be very much at home with her aunt; there is a wisdom about

her that delights me. You don't know that Marie is at the country since Monday; she'll return tomorrow with Grandmamma.[2] Well! would you believe it? Thérèse isn't at all bored with me. She will, however, be delighted to see her Papa and her sisters again, but she's happy, very happy; she laughs so heartily that her good laugh wins me over. Just now I was saying to her, must I write Pauline that you're bored? Oh! no, Aunt, oh! no. We've hardly gone out these days because of the great heat. I put her into a light skirt, with a little blue blouse of Marie's,[3] and this way she'll not suffer so much from the heat as she would with her dress, and she's very delighted with this arrangement.

Your uncle told me to ask you if you've visited *Parc Monceau* and, right next to it, St. Augustine's church, which is magnificent, and if you've seen the *Chaumont* mounds? But it is especially *Parc Monceau* that he recommends.

We're always getting beautiful strawberries from your garden. We're like real proprietors. Victoire[4] supplies us with some every day. I went the day before yesterday to your house, and I took the liberty of picking two bouquets of roses. Thérèse wanted to give me, at all costs, her Thélaspie[5] and so I took some. The geranium patch is beginning to bloom fairly well, and I hope it will be still more beautiful to hail your arrival.

Adieu, dear Pauline. Your uncle and I kiss you with all our heart; kiss Marie for us and give our best regards to your good father.

I carried out your message to all our little girls; they kiss you with all their heart.

Don't fail to write us about the day and hour of your arrival.

Your very devoted aunt,
C. Guérin

Thérèse wanted very much to write you, so you will receive a beautiful letter *from her hand.*[6]

* Autograph.

1. Letter of June 25, 1878; an enthusiastic account given of the excur-

sions at Paris (visit to the *Palais de l'Industrie*), to Versailles, etc.

2. Mme. Fournet, mother of Mme. Guérin, owner of a house in the country at *Saint-Ouen-le-Pin*, some ten kilometers from Lisieux; regarding this property, see p. 207. On June 25, Mme. Guérin wrote her mother: "Little Thérèse keeps me faithful company. She's not difficult to take care of and amuses herself with nothings while I'm working."
3. Marie Guérin, who was two and a half years older than Thérèse.
4. Victoire Pasquier, maid of the Martin family; see Ms. A, p. 38.
5. Childish mispronunciation of "thlaspi" (rock-alyssum).
6. Mme. Guérin had saved the first page of her letter for Thérèse; it is this page that has the date.

LT 5 From Thérèse to Pauline.

June 26, 1878

Thérèse was five and a half and was not able to write alone. Mme. Guérin was guiding her hand.

Lisieux, June 26, 1878

My dear Pauline,

Marie Guérin is at the country[1] since Monday, but I'm enjoying myself all alone with Aunt. I bought some gray stockings with Aunt, and the lady gave me some pearls. I'm going to make a ring with them.

Adieu, little Pauline. Kiss Papa and Marie for me. I kiss you with all my heart.

Your little sister, Thérèse

* Autograph.

1. At *Saint-Ouen-le-Pin*, note 2, in preceding LD.

LD

August 9, 1878

From Mme. Guérin to M. Guérin. (Extracts.)

In 1878 the Guérin family rented a villa at Trouville for the month of August (*Maison Leroux, Grande-Rue*, according to ChrIG, p. 32). The Martin nieces were invited there by turn on Sunday or even for several days. On Thursday, the 8th (date obtained by cross-references, see note 2), Thérèse discovered the sea for the first time. "Never will I forget the impression the sea made on me; I wasn't able to refrain from looking at it ceaselessly. Its majesty, the roaring of its waves, everything spoke to my soul of the grandeur and power of God" (Ms. A, p. 48).

My dear Friend,

I received your good letter yesterday and it pleased me. I had mail. . . . I was very happy because of all this loving correspondence, and also to see good little Thérèse's beaming face at the sight of the great sea. M. Martin hardly enjoyed the spectacle of the sea, for he was busy the whole time fishing in the river.[1] He caught an eel for us as big as my little finger and two crabs (one of which escaped last night in the kitchen, and we haven't been able to find it this morning). Marie[2] was very quick to tell him he used to do better than that at Lisieux. . . . I have lost, then, my charming companion Marie. . . . I'm waiting with much impatience for Sunday to see you, and then I'll have another little companion in Pauline.[3]

* Autograph.

1. The Touques, which flows into the English Channel, between Trouville and Deauville.
2. Marie Martin. According to letters from Mme. Guérin, August 2 and 9, and a letter from Pauline, August 9 (dates obtained through cross-references), Marie arrived at Trouville on Sunday, August 4, with her uncle. Her father came to get her, Thursday, August 8, with Thérèse, *perhaps* accompanied also by Céline and Léonie.

3. She arrived on Sunday, August 11, for a few days. She wasn't at Trouville, then, on August 8, the day of Thérèse's first trip to the sea. In her manuscript (Ms. A, pp. 48-49), Thérèse combined, in the same account, several memories separated in time. We don't know exactly the date of her meditation "all alone on a rock with Pauline," facing the setting sun. Sister Geneviève wrote: "Independently of these stays with Aunt Guérin, we used to go together to Trouville with Papa to spend some nice days and we returned in the evening to Les Buissonnets" (G/ NPHF, p. 551).

LD *From Pauline to Mme. Guérin.* (Extracts.)

June 4, 1879 The Guérin family was at *Saint-Ouen-le-Pin.*

Dear Aunt,

It appears you want a short note from your big nieces, and they are going to satisfy you[1].... Mademoiselle Pigeon[2] left just this instant.... Would you believe, dear Aunt, that she came to look for us in order to take us to the *"jardin de l'Etoile"*?[3] It was very good on her part; we weren't able to go with her as you well know because of the above-mentioned workers. Thérèse went alone, very happy at the opportunity. This baby loves flowers so much...to listen to her, she's very soon going to pick all there are of lilies of the valley in the *"jardin de l'Etoile."*... Is Monsieur Fournet there?[4] Keep the secret, good Aunt, please.... Papa and the little ones are well. Céline and Thérèse send a thousand kisses to Jeanne and Marie.

* Autograph.

1. Marie's letter, mentioned several times in her own, hasn't been preserved. Before destroying it, Sister Geneviève could have taken the date "June 4, 1879," which she writes down in pencil.
2. Joséphine and Clémence Pigeon. Friends of the Guérin family who were in their mid-forties.

3. See letter from M. Guérin, LD, September 10, 1877, note 5.
4. No doubt at *Saint-Ouen-le-Pin*. At this time, M. Fournet was president of the society in charge of the *"jardin de l'Etoile."* Was there possibly a restriction on picking flowers from the park? However, Thérèse made generous use of the permission; see Ms. A, p. 54.

LC 1 *From Sister Marie-Aloysia Vallée to Thérèse.*

January 8, 1880
→ LT lost

V. + J.[1]

January 8, 1880

Your letter gave us real pleasure, good little Thérèse, and all the more because we didn't need glasses to read it![2] How proud your teacher[3] must be of her pupil. Although your little fingers move so skillfully, and *all alone*, your heart is also able to find many pretty things!

This should really merit a beautiful reward, and this poor aunt,[4] presenting herself with empty hands, will surely not be well received. We would be very happy, however, Thérèse, to bring you some nice gifts, but I am so poor I can't even find a pretty picture to offer you. While you are waiting for us to make one, dear little one, we're going to send you a very little seal of the Sacred Heart, provided our letter doesn't weigh too much. We're sure it will please you, for you love the Heart of Jesus very much, don't you? And He loves "His child" even more because she is so good and obedient.

Thank you for your good prayers. Please continue them for an aunt who loves her little Thérèse very much.

Sister M. Aloysia

D.S.B.[5]

* Autograph.

1. Abbreviation for "*Vive Jésus*!" (Long live Jesus!), in usage in the Visitation Order.
2. Thérèse, who was seven on January 2, 1880, wrote in a large handwriting. The oldest sample of her writing (a homework exercise, June 5, 1880) is written in large characters.
3. Pauline, although Marie was giving Thérèse her lessons in penmanship (MS. A, p. 36).
4. Pauline gave this title "aunt" to her former teacher in memory of her Visitandine aunt, Sister Marie-Dosithée Guérin (d.February 2, 1877). Following Pauline's wishes, Thérèse did the same; see LT 160, April 3, 1894.
5. Abbreviation for "*Dieu soit béni*!" (Blessed be God!), an expression in use at the Visitation.

LD *From Pauline to Mme. Guérin.* (Extracts.)

August 9, 1880

The Guérin family was at *Saint-Ouen-le-Pin* since the preceding day.

I'll tell you, dear little Aunt, that your big niece[1] has set her hand to spade and rake today; the paths of the landscape garden have had their cleaning done for at least a month. As for the lazy *little dwarf*[2] as her naughty big sister calls her, her brush is once again in use. . . the famous work is progressing but very slowly; I'm about at the end of my patience! My two rascals[3] came bothering me this morning to get permission to spend the morning with me. I gave in to them, and, in return, they read a pretty story to distract me: *la Soeur de Gribouille* by the *Ctesse de Ségur*; it's written in the same style as the two *Niquads*,[4] so I had something to laugh about! *L'Oncle Boni*[5] has arrived; I saw it on the table yesterday. This will be a good pastime for our two little girls.

Léonie spent the whole day in her little bedroom with Thérèse alone as company; she loves her new dwelling[6] so much that we'll soon be obliged to serve her meals there. . . . Léonie, Céline, Thérèse tell me to give you their love.

* Autograph.
1. Marie.
2. Pauline, almost nineteen (September 7), was about five feet tall.
3. Céline and Thérèse
4. Likewise by the *Comtesse de Ségur* (published in 1862). We know through a note of Sister Geneviève (Céline) that "Thérèse as a child used to read with pleasure books from the *Bibliothèque rose - Mme Ségur*, Canon Schmidt." In the *Bibliothèque rose illustrée* are a hundred stories for children (between four and eight) by the German Canon von Schmidt (1768 - 1854), author of many books for children.
5. Another volume of the *Bibliothèque rose illustrée*, by *Mademoiselle de Martignat*, for children eight to fourteen; published in 1879 - 1880.
6. Concerning the distribution of rooms at *Les Buissonnets*, see below, LD, December 1, 1880, note 3.

LD — *From Marie to Pauline.* (Extracts.)

December 1, 1880 — Pauline was traveling with her father. Marie and Thérèse spent part of their time at the Guérin home.

Lisieux, December 2, 1880[1]

Dear Pauline,

I was very happy to receive news from you; I see you were welcomed with open arms at your dear Alençon, and I hope it was the same at Le Mans. . . . Well, it seems strange, especially in the evenings, not having you; for the rest of the time I'm at Aunt's as you know, and this distracts me a little and prevents me from thinking that I am without you.

There is nothing new at Les Buissonnets, except that Louise

isn't getting brave. In fact, we are both taking so many precautions against thieves and robbers[2]...that we have changed the little girls from the bedroom so that they may be in a safer place[3] and can also lock their door. I've put them in Papa's room, much to their joy.

Marie Guérin just came up behind me, and I feel I'll not be too calm just now with this little ferret at my side. She's returned from the Abbey, and since tomorrow, Thursday, is a holiday, I have to wait this evening until seven o'clock for Léonie.[4] And so I'm writing you, seated at the drug cabinet in the midst of a continual coming and going....

It's time for me to leave you, dear little Pauline, for Léonie is going to arrive immediately. Pardon me for this scribbling; I've not been writing you for a half hour, and Thérèse has been disturbing me often for her letter. She wanted, at all costs, to send you a short note. She's been pestering poor Aunt for three quarters of an hour to get some paper....

Your little sister, who is waiting for you with great impatience,

Marie

...Uncle is well this week; he's even very happy during the meals. He has played all sorts of tricks on poor Thérèse.[5]

* Autograph.

1. Inexact date: Marie spoke of the next day, Thursday, a holiday. She was writing, then, the evening of Wednesday, December 1.
2. We should recall here a statement of Thérèse as a little girl, perhaps before this date? "Oh! as for me, if a thief comes, I'll pinch his nose with a nutcracker!" (Oral tradition; the statement is as close as possible to Thérèse's childish jargon; a gesture accompanied the words.)
3. First writing: "closer to me." Marie shared with Pauline one of the two bedrooms at the front of the house. M. Martin occupied the other bedroom. For a few days, Marie gave M. Martin's room to Céline and Thérèse, who slept usually in the larger of the two bedrooms in the back of the house, almost on a level with the

garden; see the description by M. Guérin, LD, September 10, 1877. Léonie occupied the little bedroom also in the back. Certain improvements modified the layout of some rooms at the time of the restoration of Les Buissonnets in 1912-1913.

4. The school year of 1880-1881 was the last for Léonie, who was seventeen and a half.
5. Provided one of her sisters was present, Thérèse loved the evenings at her uncle's house, and she listened to him with great pleasure (Ms. A, p. 42), while, at the same time, being a little afraid of him (see LT 27, October 8, 1887; LT 139, December 31, 1892).

LT 6 From Thérèse to Pauline.

December 1, 1880

Same date as Marie's (see LD, preceding, note 1); written at the Guérins. This letter is the first of those preserved that Thérèse wrote by herself.

Dear Pauline,

I am very happy to write you. I asked Aunt. I'm making many mistakes, but you know your little Thérèse well, and you know that I'm not smart.[1] You're going to kiss Papa for me. I had four good marks on the first day, and five on the second.

Kiss *Mademoiselle* Pauline[2] for me. I have a lot of fun, for you know that we are at Aunt's house. While Marie is taking care of the accounts,[3] I am enjoying myself painting[4] the pretty pictures Aunt has given me.

Au revoir, dear little Pauline, your little Thérèse, who loves you.

* Autograph in fragments. See plate.

1. Thérèse was at this time Pauline's pupil, and she will never be at ease in spelling; see Ms. A, p. 82.

2. Pauline Romet, who lived with her brother Vital Romet. It was at their home (or at Mme. Tifenne's) that the Martins stayed most frequently on their trips to Alençon.
3. The accounts at the end of the year for the Guérin pharmacy; Thérèse spelled "*comptes*" as "*conte.*"
4. Thérèse wrote "*pendre*" instead of "*peindre.*"

LC 2 *From Sister Marie-Aloysia Vallée to Thérèse.*

January 10, 1881
→ LT lost

V. + J.

From our monastery of Le Mans
January 10, 1881

If little Thérèse is happy to write to her aunt at Le Mans,[1] the latter is no less happy to answer her, and she would be still happier to be able to send her some pretty gifts. Pauline must have told you, dear little one, that this aunt was very poor and was able only to pray for her nieces, and this all the more because she loves you very much.

It is, then, from Jesus that I will ask, not so much for pretty toys and candy, since you wouldn't know where to put them, your two slippers are already filled, but for very special graces which will make you grow "in age and wisdom" like the divine Child.

I know, besides, from Pauline, that Thérèse is very good and very obedient, and that she loves God and the Blessed Virgin with all her heart. I can only want her, then, to continue and to remain, even while growing up, a good little girl for the consolation of her worthy father and her dear big sisters.

In the meantime, Thérèse, I entrust you with my love for Marie, Pauline, Léonie, and Céline. You'll give them a kiss for me.

Continue also, dear child, to speak a little word to God for this aunt, whom you don't know[2] and for her other little nephews. She'll be very grateful to you.

Sister M. Aloysia

* Autograph.

1. See LC 1, note 4, January 8, 1880.
2. On the occasion of her trip to Le Mans, March 29, 1875 (see Ms. A, p. 23), Thérèse met only her Aunt Guérin and the superior of the monastery. (See CF, April 29, 1875; and VT, April 1972, letter of Sister Marie-Dosithée, April 4, 1875.)

LD *From Marie to Pauline.* (Fragment.)

July 4 (?), 1881

Pauline is on vacation at Houlgate (Calvados), at the home of a friend from the boarding school; see LT 7, the same date.

Yesterday was the feast of St. Domitia and Mass was very early; Céline had to be at the Abbey for 6:30. You can well imagine the trouble I had dressing my two girls for that hour. The celebration was charming; the crowd filled the chapel like last year.

Thérèse has advised me to leave room for her, so I'll leave you; she has very many things to tell you, it seems. I suppose she's going to make a long confession to you.

* CMG.

LT 7 **From Thérèse to Pauline.**

July 4 (?), 1881

Approximate date; see preceding LD; and below, notes 1 and 3.

Dear Pauline,

I'm very happy to write to you. I wish you a happy feast, for you know I wasn't able to wish you one on Wednesday, the day of your feast.[1]

I hope you're enjoying yourself at Houlgate. I would really like to know if you got up on a donkey?

I thank you for giving me holidays while you're at Houlgate. It would please me very much if you were to write Marie, and if you would write me also a short note.[2]

If you only knew about St. Domitia's Day.[3] Aunt put a pink cincture on me, and I threw roses to St. Domitia. Don't show my letter to anyone.

Au revoir, dear little Pauline. I'm kissing you with all my heart. Kiss Marie-Thérèse[4] and little Marguerite[5] for me.

Your little Thérèse, who loves you.

* Autograph.

1. Wednesday, June 29, feast of Sts. Peter and Paul.
2. See LC 3, Pauline's answer to Thérèse.
3. A young Roman martyr whose relics the Benedictine Abbey had received in 1879 (*Semaine religieuse de Bayeux*, July 13, 1879). Her shrine was dedicated on June 27, 1880 (*Semaine religieuse*, July 11, 1880). The feast of 1881 was to be the last: the authenticity of the relics was called into question. They were replaced by a relic of St. Amata. A photograph of St. Domitia's shrine shows an honor ribbon of Léonie's for the third trimester, 1880-1881. According to an oral tradition, Thérèse as a child served as model for the making of clothing for the wax effigy.

4. Marie-Thérèse Pallu of Bellay, Pauline's companion at the boarding school of Le Mans.
5. Sister of Marie-Thérèse.

LC 3 *From Pauline to Thérèse.*

July 5-11 (?),
1881
→LT 7

My dear little Thérèse,

I thank you for your nice little letter and for your feast-day wishes. I hope you were happy on St. Domitia's feast!

Always be very good and very diligent, my little darling; don't give Marie any trouble. Enjoy yourself and take advantage of these beautiful holidays.

Kiss little Céline and my little cousins for me.

Adieu, Thérèse. I'm sending you a great big kiss, and I'll be delighted to see you again.

Your teacher,
Pauline
Child of Mary

Tell Céline to kiss little Léonie tenderly for me.

Marguerite would like to meet you both; she's a nice little girl, well-mannered and very darling. She kisses you from her heart.

* Autograph.

LD *From Marie to Pauline.* (Fragment.)

July 11-12 (?),
1881

Papa arrived Saturday morning.[1] Do you know what he brought Thérèse from her little foster brother?[2] Guess if you

can.... A magpie! which is being cared for each moment as a child in a cradle. This is Thérèse's sole occupation; she remains whole hours contemplating it in a squirrel cage which Papa bought for her. I'd say it's a doll's house; never have I seen a cage like it.[3]

* CMG.

1. From Alençon; on July 10? CMG III separates this text from the other fragment which we set down for July 4 (LD), and transcribes it after Thérèse's letter (LT 7). If the magpie had arrived on the 3rd, Thérèse would not have failed to speak of it to Pauline.
2. Eugène Taillé, born December 14, 1871, fourth child of "little Rose." M. Martin undoubtedly went to the Taillés, who lived then at Valframbert, to visit his own mother. In 1877, his mother had been unable to make up her mind to follow her relatives to Lisieux. M. Martin had entrusted her to Rose Taillé's care.
3. "We taught it to talk," adds Sister Geneviève. "Then Papa gave it its freedom. This is when our terrors began. If we were seated, the magpie used to come clandestinely, pulling at the buttons on our boots. If we were standing up, it bit at the calves of our legs.... At this time, Thérèse and Céline, having calculated that it took forty turns around the garden to make one league, set out courageously on the road like the wandering Jew. Like him, too, they provided themselves with sticks, a supply of which was placed at the entrance to the garden, to defend themselves from the magpie, which followed them tirelessly, calling out: Thérèse! And this cry was repeated by a superb parrot owned by a neighbor. It used to say in clear and strident language: Thérèse! Thérèse!... We closed the magpie within the greenhouse to withdraw ourselves from its persecution. One day, it found the door open and, out of despair, undoubtedly, took advantage of its freedom only by drowning itself in a bucket which was close by." (CMG III, pp. 61-62).

From a "choice soil" to a "common soil" (*Ms. A, p. 53*)
(School year 1881 - 1882)
Age eight and nine

Thérèse was now eight and a half. In October 1881, she entered the Benedictine Abbey as a day boarder. Placed in the fourth class,[1] *with children her own age, she easily took first place.*

The family correspondence contains no information on Thérèse's encounter with her school milieu. And the only note of the little girl to Céline (LT 8) is insignificant in this regard. Her Autobiography tells us that the shock was severe: "The poor little flower had been accustomed to plunging its fragile roots into a choice soil, made expressly for it, so it seemed very hard for it. . . to be obliged to find in a common soil the necessary nourishment for its subsistence!. . . " (Ms. A, p. 53). In spite of the affection of "all the religious" (p. 53), Thérèse will describe her five years at the boarding school as "the saddest years of my life"[2] *(p. 53). This hermit, the fondled child at Les Buissonnets, was not able to relate to the group. Her favorite distraction consisted precisely in playing "at hermits" with her cousin Marie Guérin (Ms. A, p. 54). Her great dream was to go with Pauline "into a far-distant desert" (Ms. A, p. 57).*

→ *Read Ms. A, pp. 48-55.*

1. In the "green class" (named for the color "green" of the cincture of the uniform). For Thérèse's entire school period, see *La Petite Thérèse à l'Abbaye. Souvenirs inédits recueillis par une ancienne maîtresse (Mère Saint-Léon), Notre Dame du Pré,* 1930.
2. Thérèse has the "second period" of her life (see Ms. A, p.

34) begin with her mother's death, but "especially" with Pauline's entrance into Carmel, October 2, 1882. She tells us this was the saddest period of her life. However, this period could have started in October 1881 with the hidden griefs about which the correspondence reveals nothing. These griefs came from her difficulty in relating to the other pupils.

LT 8 — From Thérèse to Céline. (Fragments.)

April 23, 1882

At the Abbey, Céline bravely defended Thérèse, who had become her "little girl" (see Ms. A, p. 55).

April 23, 1882[1]
Sunday

My dear little Céline,

I love you very much. You know it[2]...
Adieu, dear little Céline.
Your little Thérèse, who loves you with all her heart.

Thérèse Martin

* Three fragments of the autograph.

1. Not having this date (it has been found since then), the first edition of the 1948 Letters suggested the year 1879, taking its stand on a note from Sister Geneviève (loose sheet): "She was perhaps six years old." (See LT 1948, p. 12; the description is also erroneous.)
2. End of the second fragment on which we can read this syllable partly effaced: *pau-(pauvre).*

"Pauline is lost to me!!!" (*Ms. A, p. 60*)
(October 1882 - March 1883)
Age nine and ten

On October 2, 1882, with death in her soul, Thérèse received "the last kiss from Pauline" (Ms. A, p. 59). That day, her second mother left her to enter the Lisieux Carmel. She would be henceforth Sister Agnes of Jesus.

Unexpectedly, this young woman had heard the call to the cloistered life on the preceding February 16. Since then she was trying to accustom herself to total renunciation: to leaving all, ". . . my white-haired Father . . . my little sisters . . . my little jewel Thérèse! . . . her childish caresses . . . her little soul that I was carrying to God!" (Meditation, May 6, 1882; CMG III, p. 64).

During the summer of 1882, the child learned by chance of the plan, which they were trying to hide from her. The blow was brutal: "It was as though a sword had been plunged into my heart . . . a trial which seemed to be above my strength!" (Ms. A, p. 58).

Pauline explained the life of Carmel to her. The little girl felt that her own vocation was being described. The "far-off desert" about which she was dreaming was Carmel. But she chose it "not for Pauline but for Jesus alone. . . . " (Ms. A, p. 58). In the meanwhile, since they were not receiving nine-year-old postulants (Ms. A, 59), Thérèse went off to school on October 2.

She skipped a class and passed into the third class, the "violet class." The pupils were older than she. Her success continued. An older pupil made her pay dearly for this "in a thousand ways" (Ms A, p. 53). Her companions, for the greater part, were preparing for their First Communion at the end of the school year. Thérèse

missed the required age by two days; her hope for a dispensation was shattered (see LT 9, note 7, November – December 1882).

To whom was she going to confide her little troubles? Marie did not possess Pauline's tact. At the beginning, Thérèse took Marie's authority badly (see LT 9, note 4). Undoubtedly, the prioress, Mother Marie de Gonzague, was most kind to her "angelic child" (LC 6), her "Thérèsita" (LT 9, LC 9). There was especially the weekly interview with Sister Agnes at the Carmel. However, to say nothing of the austere grilles, this meeting was simply a keen disappointment for the little girl: "Ah! how I suffered during this visit to Carmel! . . . Every Thursday, we used to go together as a family to Carmel, and I, accustomed to speaking heart to heart with Pauline, I obtained with great trouble two or three minutes at the end of the visit; it is understood that I spent them in tears and left with a broken heart . . . ." (Ms. A, p. 60).

The postulant, whose attention was held by the conversation of the grownups, seemed no longer even to see her little sister. Thérèse tried in vain to capture her attention: "Look, Pauline, I'm wearing the little skirt that you made for me!" Her prattling fell on deaf ears (see LC 4, note 2, November 1882). "If I had only known!" each of the two older sisters said later on (ibid.). For the moment, however, it was too late. Thérèse's health deteriorated.

In the seven letters of this winter of 1882 – 1883, we can see the warning symptoms of the severe attack which was to come at Easter.

→*Read: Ms. A, pp. 57–60.*

LC 4 *From Sister Agnes of Jesus (Pauline) to Thérèse.*

November, 1882 (?) Approximate date; see note 1.

My dear little Thérèse,

You distressed me this morning when you were crying like *a baby!*[1] But since I've already preached to you and *scolded* you, I must now act as the indulgent sister, isn't that so?

I'm coming to say "good day" on paper since it's so nice, so much desired by you! As for me, if I were a little Thérèse and if I had a Pauline in Carmel, it seems to me I would prefer to hear and see my Pauline[2] than to read, with great difficulty, a word from her heart. Well, my darling, since you want both joys, here they are. I'm becoming weak in my convent, weak like a good old grandmother. This is the result of my affection for my two well-loved little girls. Oh! I think often about them. I'm praying to good Jesus to make my little Thérèse another little St. Teresa, except that she's not to go seeking martyrdom in the streets![3] Oh! no, what I'm asking is that she seek each day the means of pleasing the Child Jesus and, to do this, that she offer Him *all the flowers on her path!*

Adieu, my little Benjamin. Yes, gather always these hidden little flowers about which we used to speak so much in the past; these won't fade like earth's flowers but will be preserved by the angels to perfume heaven's gardens and to form your crown one day.

Your little sister
Agnes of Jesus

* Autograph.

1. In spite of Sister Geneviève's note on the autograph, giving 1884 as the year this letter was written, it seems it was written shortly after Pauline's entrance into Carmel.

2. Thérèse wanted especially *to speak* to her "Mamma." But Marie, the oldest, took up the greater part of the visit: "Each week, I used to return to the Carmel as to the spring of all my happiness. Ah! how sorry I am today for not having shared with my little sisters this visit, which I found, however, too short for me. If I had only known that my poor little Thérèse had suffered so much from this! I was far from suspecting it. However, I remember one day how she said to you: 'Look, Pauline, I'm wearing the little skirt that you made for me.' We hardly paid any attention to her childish prattle, and, afterward, I saw tears in her eyes. Poor little thing! She was thinking much more seriously than I believed!" (Sister Marie of the Sacred Heart, *Souvenirs autobiographiques,* p. 74.)

Mother Agnes of Jesus had the same regrets: "I used to be very sad when Thérèse cried at the end of Marie's visits. But how was I to console her! I was unaware of the abyss of sadness that formed in her soul at my departure. I understand very well now how the five minutes given to her with me could only cause her more anguish. And, then, I was so foolish with all my politeness to my aunt when she came with my cousins! Céline and Thérèse no longer counted; all my attention was centered on the other side, and if I said a word to my little sisters, to Thérèse it was to [two lines and a half are erased] and other reflections of this kind. That is all she had from me in these family visits!

"And yet I believed I was acting well, and that Marie was going to understand me and have my poor little Thérèse understand me, in whose eyes I always used to see tears forming! And a little pout which would show whenever she tried to refrain from crying any more. Ah! once again, If I had only known!" (Mother Agnes of Jesus, *Souvenirs intimes,* pp. 59-60.)

3. Reference to St. Teresa of Avila, who, at the age of seven, convinced her brother Rodrigo to go with her to the country of the Moors, seeking martyrdom.

LT 9 **From Thérèse to Mother Marie de Gonzague.**

November-December, 1882 (?)

Approximate date; see notes 1, 2, 3.

Dear Mother,

It has been a long time since I saw you,[1] so I am very happy to write[2] you to tell you about my little affairs. Pauline told me you were on retreat,[3] and I'm coming to ask you to pray to little Jesus for me because I have many faults and want to correct them.

I have to make my confession to you. For some time, I am always answering Marie back when she tells me to do something.[4] It seems when Pauline was little and when she made excuses to Aunt at Le Mans,[5] Aunt used to say to her: So many holes, so many pegs! But with me it's even worse. So I want to correct myself, and, into each little hole, put a pretty little flower[6] which I'll offer to little Jesus to prepare myself for my First Communion. Won't you, dear Mother, pray for this? Oh! yes, this beautiful moment will come quickly,[7] and how happy I shall be to have so many flowers to offer Him when the little Jesus comes into my heart.

Au revoir, dear Mother. I kiss you tenderly; how I love you.

Your little daughter
Thérésita[8]

* Autograph.

1. Thérèse was introduced to the prioress of the Carmel during the summer of 1882, but the exact date is not known; see Ms. A, p. 58. She saw her again "shortly after Pauline's entrance" (Ms. A. p. 66).
2. Her exceptional application to the writing of this letter makes its exact dating difficult through the simple examination of the handwriting.
3. According to the documents of the period, Mother Marie de Gonzague made her private retreat preferably at the end of the year; we have no precise information for the years 1882-83.

4. Marie testified that she had never seen her sister "commit the smallest act of disobedience," even in her childhood (Sister Marie of the Sacred Heart, PO, 1671 and PA, 875). This testimony, like many others, calls for a correction. According to an oral tradition preserved in the Maudelonde family, Marguerite-Marie, at the age of fifteen, had judged it useful to advise Thérèse to be more submissive to Marie, who was henceforth taking Pauline's place. We must say, however, in the child's defense, that Marie's cantankerous character was a severe trial to the patience of her younger sisters, Céline and Thérèse.
5. Sister Marie-Dosithée Guérin (d. 1877).
6. Under Pauline's influence, the symbolism of the flower—an act of virtue or love of God—was part of the little girl's piety for a long time. See LC 4, last paragraph.
7. In 1875, a diocesan synod, the acts of which came into effect in 1877, had set age ten completed before January 1 as the age for receiving First Communion. Thérèse was born on January 2, and M. Guérin tried in vain to obtain from Bishop Hugonin a dispensation of a year in his niece's favor; see *La Petite Thérèse à l'Abbaye, op. cit.*, p. 30. (The truth of this episode was contested by Sister Geneviève but was upheld by Mother Saint-Lèon, in a letter of October 21, 1931. For the sake of peace, the Abbey suppressed it in the second edition.)
8. A diminutive given to Thérèse by the Carmelites in memory of Teresita de Jesus, niece of St. Teresa of Avila, who entered the cloister at the age of nine.

LC 5 *From Sister Agnes of Jesus to Thérèse.*

Around
December 20,
1882

J. M. J. T.

Jesus

For Thérèse

My dear little child,

I'm coming to you to ask for your two little babies,[1] the little and the big. We need them for representing the Child Jesus in a pretty little crib we're making. I'll choose which one of the two is more suitable; I thought at first the little one, but the big one pleases me too. However, I'll see.

This will be for only one day; don't fear that we'll keep your dear children for the whole month of the Christmas season. Ah! I would be sorry to make your motherly heart accept such a trial!

The two dolls will come back to you safe and sound on Tuesday morning[2] . . . and I'll entrust them with all my caresses for my beloved little patient. . . .

How naughty of you, Mademoiselle, to aim at being sick like this! Wait till I scold you. . . .

Your poor little Pauline, here in her cloister, is dreaming at night about the pains in your side, your head, your heart, your pimples, and your ointments[3] . . . . Ah! naughty child!

However, it doesn't matter; if little Pauline is annoyed, Agnes knows only how to love and caress her Benjamin.

Darling, I love you more than I can express; you're the little rosebud of the rosebush of my affections. . . .

So how I watch over it; how eager I am to see it open up to the very gentle Sun of the Child Jesus' Love! . . .

And, then, I have my secrets, my own inner hopes! . . . When the bud has become a rose, I know where I'll place it, my dear rose. . . .

But, *adieu,* little bud; cure yourself quickly in order to come and see

Your Agnes

Ask Marie whether she can send me, at the same time as the babies, a few shepherdesses' kerchiefs and aprons, the ones we had in my little plays.[4] But I think they are at Aunt's house.

These will be used for the singing of the "*petit Noël.*" Sister Isabelle of the Angels[5] and I would like to dress up as shepherdesses.

* Autograph.

1. Her dolls.
2. December 26.
3. See Ms. A, p. 60: "Toward the end of the year, I began to have a constant headache, which didn't cause me to suffer much; I was able to pursue my studies, and no one was worried about me." In fact, they were worried at the Carmel; see LC 6, and, around February 7, 1883, LC 8.
4. Plays composed by Pauline for the "distribution of prizes" at Les Buissonnets (Ms. A, p. 45). The participants were Céline and Thérèse, Jeanne and Marie Guérin.
5. A companion of Sister Agnes in the postulancy. She left the Carmel without having received the Habit.

LC 6 *From Mother Marie de Gonzague to Thérèse.*

End of December 1882 or January 1883 — Approximate date; see note 4.

J. M. J. T.

Sunday evening

I learned that my little daughter, Thérèse of the Child Jesus,[1] was not sleeping much and that she is ailing.[2] I'm coming to tell my angelic child that she mustn't be thinking all day long about Agnes of Jesus; this would tire out our little heart and could harm our health!...

I allow my future little daughter to think only of her holy little Carmelite sister in the presence of the Jesus of her heart but never

during the night. *Thérèse is to sleep all night, and she is to eat everything her beloved sister Marie wants her to eat;* and from this moment, to prepare herself for First Communion she is going to be very *obedient.*[3]

If my dear little daughter follows what I advise her to do, she will strengthen her health and will be able to come and see her Agnes of Jesus again, and, like her, she will become a good and fervent *Spouse of Jesus*!

I kiss you with all my heart, little angel, and I'm praying to Jesus to bless His little fiancée.

I am entrusting you with only one message for your dear sisters: kiss them for me.

You have a big place in my heart.

Thérèse, let us love Jesus very much.

Sister Marie de Gonzague
r.c.ind.[4]

* Autograph.

1. Religious name desired by Thérèse and chosen for her by the Carmelite nuns at the beginning of October 1882; see Ms. A, p. 71.
2. See LC 5, note 3.
3. See LT 9, note 4 and 7.
4. Abbreviation for *"religieuse carmélite indigne"* (unworthy Carmelite religious), formula used at this time. The general tone of the letter gives the impression that Mother Marie de Gonzague was still prioress. She was no longer prioress as of January 31, 1883.

LC 7 *From Sister Agnes of Jesus to Thérèse.*

End of December 1882 or January 1883 — Approximate date; see note 1.

J. M. J. T.

Long live Jesus.

My poor little Patient,

How are you today? Has your headache eased up a little? Say "yes," I beg you. Dear baby, don't be sick anymore like that.

Don't you know you are distressing me, that you are causing me worries. And worry is such an ugly flower! Little one, you would be more lovable by showing me some beautiful roses on your face, always so pale. Do you understand? To make up for the bouquet of worries you will have to come and offer me soon a bouquet of roses.

And now what should I say to you, my dear little child? I know nothing, nothing but one thing, we must love God more and more. Oh! don't you see, in that is life's only joy, even for little children. I don't think there ever could have been more joyful children than those who were formerly caressed by the gentle hand of Jesus. Well, I still think that for little girls, very good, very sweet, very diligent today, the Holy Child in the crib[1] reserves all kinds of divine caresses. They won't see Him, undoubtedly, but they feel His sweet kisses at the bottom of their heart when He tells them: I am pleased!

Adieu, my dear Thérèse; I trust little Jesus will caress you very often in this way, and, as a consequence, that you may merit these caresses by very many efforts and by love.

But get well at the same time.

Your Agnes

* Autograph.

1. It is Christmas time then? In December 1882, P. Pichon had invited Marie to meet him at Vimoutiers, not far from Lisieux, a plan compromised by Thérèse's illness. In January, the Jesuit inquired: "Is your dear Thérèse well? I'm praying much for this intention." (Letter to Marie, without any date: the heading of the letter is missing; January 1883, according to the content.)

LC 8 *From Sister Agnes of Jesus to Thérèse.*

About February 7, 1883 Approximate date; see note 1.

J. M. J. T.

Long Live Jesus!

My dear little Benjamin,

I'm sending you my most tender kisses before burying myself up to my neck in the retreat for Lent.[1]

Little darling, you must pray a little to Jesus for me because, you see, when one is big, one must be good in a *big way,* and I'm good only in a little way.

See how much confidence I have in you! I'm almost making my confession to you!

Dear little one, you must also be very good during this Lent. Each day, you will have to offer to the Child Jesus a pretty bouquet made up of acts of virtue. I desire, above all, that your flowers be gathered in the very beautiful garden of gentleness, for I am thinking at this moment of the little fights with Céline.[2] Oh! you will work to correct this, won't you, my dear little child?

And you will love to pray to God very much and the Blessed Virgin. These are very beautiful flowers, too, and well-perfumed, these flowers that bloom in the garden of prayer.

Finally, little child, you will draw profit from everything, just as the bee gathers honey from the tiniest flowers.

Adieu. I am kissing you just as I used to do, pressing you tightly in my arms and on my heart.

Your Agnes

Embrace little Léonie very tightly for me, and tell her I love her with all my heart, that I am thinking of her very often, very often. Kiss, too, little Father for me.

* Autograph.

1. During Lent, visits and correspondence were suspended at the Carmel. This "farewell" letter was, then, written shortly before Ash Wednesday (February 7, 1883). Pauline will break her silence, March 13, to tell her family that she has been approved by the Community Chapter to receive the Habit. She wrote her father: "I have been accepted! My dear Carmel wants to keep me and lead me to heaven! What happiness and how express it? . . . Come quickly to see me, you and all my own, for my pen can't express the feelings in my heart, and, nevertheless, I have to express them." (To M. Martin, March 13, 1883.) That same day, the day for the reception of the Habit was set for Friday, April 6.
2. Thérèse had never disguised these "little arguments" with Céline (Ms. A. p. 56). Sister Agnes of Jesus' correspondence gives us a sample of these childish tiffs: "There is a Chinese picture for you, and the other is for Thérèse; don't argue over the choice. Let my little Céline make a sacrifice rather, if there is any necessity for one" (Letter to Céline, November 21, 1883). Céline will later on claim responsibility for these disputes; she'll push self-criticism to the point of even denying their very existence; "I used to hoard everything; she had to ask permission to use my toys, make insistent requests to obtain a piece of castoff silk for her dolls, and there were always very many conditions laid down for my generosity; well! never did I see her start an argument with me. . . . Because of her exceptional character, we understood each other perfectly, and we never argued. So we were cited as models for other children." (Sister Geneviève, NPPO 1908, pp. 75-76, Virtue of Fortitude.)

LC 9 *From Mother Marie de Gonzague to Thérèse.*

February 7–
March 25, 1883
→ LT lost?

Approximate date; see notes 1 and 2.

†

J. M. J. T.

Jesus!

My dear little Thérésita,

I kiss you with all my heart, which loves you very much; after Easter,[1] I'll see you and give you a good answer, *according to your desires*.

Trust and confidence!

The holy time of penance[2] forces me to silence today; you may write me as often as your little heart desires. Our very good Mother[3] is totally happy over our union, dear angel. . . .

Your Mother,
Sister Marie de Gonzague
r.c.ind.

I'm writing you with the eyes of faith; I can't see anything. It's 5:30, and I am without any light.

Let us sleep well and eat very much![4]

* Autograph.

1. March 25, that year.
2. Lent had begun on February 7; see LC 8, note 1.
3. Mother Geneviève of St. Teresa, one of the foundresses of the Lisieux Carmel in 1838; she was elected prioress the preceding January 31, 1883. Mother Marie de Gonzague was mistress of novices.
4. Advice given to Thérèse before; see LC 6.

A "strange sickness" (*Ms. A, p. 60*)
(March–May 1883)
Age ten

M. Martin took Marie and Léonie to Paris, March 23, 1883 (ChrIG, p. 99) for the services of Holy Week. Already weakened in health through sadness, Thérèse, placed in charge of her aunt and uncle, was unable to sustain this short separation.

M. Guérin, March 25, Easter night, succeeded, without being aware of it, in disturbing Thérèse by recalling certain memories of her mother (Ms. A, p. 60). A few hours later, the little girl was seized ". . . with a nervous trembling, followed by seizures of fright and hallucinations, which were repeated several times a day. In the intervals, she was left in a debilitated condition and could not be left all alone. It seems to me that she retained her reason even during these seizures; and when they were over, she could remember what had happened." (Testimony of Marcelline, the Guérin family's maid, who later on became Sister Marie-Joseph of the Cross, PO, 296.)

Doctor Notta considered her condition to be very serious. M. Martin and his daughters were called back home immediately.[1] *The child could not be taken back to Les Buissonnets, so Marie took her place at her sister's bedside in the Guérin home (Ms. A. p. 61).*

Thérèse's great desire to embrace Pauline once again on the occasion of her reception of the Habit gave her a burst of energy for the day of April 6. The following day, however, she suffered a relapse at Les Buissonnets; heart-rending manifestations of her illness were multiplied.

The child believed she was surrounded by steep precipices and, from her raised bed, she allowed herself to fall heavily to the floor. Marie stated later: "Frequently

I succeeded in stopping her but with great difficulty, for I felt an extraordinary force which carried her off in spite of me. Seeing this, I used to play tricks, making believe I had no fear whatsoever of seeing her fall, and then she would keep quiet; but if I were to show the least bit of fear, she would begin again with renewed vigor." (Sister Marie of the Sacred Heart, NPPO 1908, p. 4.)

She wanted to speak, to articulate words, but she did not emit a single sound. (Same source.) She wanted to open her eyes but in vain. She succeeded in doing this when she was alone (Ms. A, p. 62). She clenched her teeth and refused to eat. "Fortunately," Marie recounted, "she was missing a tooth, and I said, always having recourse to my tricks: 'It doesn't bother me that your teeth are clenched; I'll be able to feed you some bouillon through that little hole. Aren't you fortunate, little Thérèse, that you're missing a tooth!' Immediately her teeth were unclenched" (NPPO 1908, p. 5). Jeanne Guérin made mention of ". . . propulsive seizures during which she made wheel-like movements that she would have been absolutely incapable of making in a state of health" (Mme. La Néele, PA, 208).

Doctor Notta spoke at one time of "St. Vitus' dance," but formally excluded hysteria (Sister Marie of the Sacred Heart, PA, 143). To tell the truth, ". . . he appeared to be hesitant in his diagnosis and allowed one to think it was something else; but what?. . . He did not know himself, for certainly he would have told my father" (Mme. La Néele, PO, 321).

Thérèse stated later on the general opinion of her family: "I believe the devil had received an exterior power over me" (Ms. A, p. 63).

The faith of the Martin family finally obtained, after five weeks of agony, the cure which science was incapable of effecting, "A miracle was necessary, and it was

Our Lady of Victories who performed it." (Ms. A, p. 65). Sunday, May 13, feast of Pentecost, the child felt suddenly liberated by "...the ravishing smile of the Blessed Virgin" (ibid.).

We have eight letters contemporaneous with this sickness.

→Read: Ms. A, pp. 60–66.

1. The return must have taken place on March 28 or 29. See M. Martin: "Last Easter, I was in Paris with my two older daughters and we spent five very pleasant days." (Letter to his friend, M. Nogrix, 1883.)

LC 10 *From Sister Agnes of Jesus to Thérèse.*

Around April 2, 1883 Approximate date; see note 1.

J. M. J. T.

Long live Jesus!

My poor little Patient,

How naughty of you to put me into this state of penance and suffering like this for a whole week already.[1] I am a little angry with you, almost very angry; and the proof is that if I were holding you in my arms, I would have to watch over myself to refrain from choking you. Come now, *Mademoiselle la baigneuse,*[2] *mademoiselle la trembleuse, mademoiselle la fiévreuse, mademoiselle la dormeuse, mademoiselle la beuveuse,* you must not plan on carrying all these titles of a grubby and fishy nobility here on Friday.[3]... You must get well quickly[4] in order to come and kiss this poor sad one and restore her to joy, for, you know, she can no longer laugh but only dreams about you and cries over you ever since the beginning of your sickness.

Yes, my darling little baby, I want to see you all better on the day of my espousals,[5] and this wish I shall obtain from God's goodness, from the Blessed Virgin, and also from your own good will. *Eat much, much;* this is how you can get well. Mother Marie de Gonzague's little niece[6] was sick like you, exactly like you, and it was good slices of roast beef which cured her and made her fresh like a rose.

Adieu, little white rose. I am praying to the good Jesus to take up His palette and His brush to color with a heavenly and lasting ruby the pallor of your darling cheeks.

Your Agnes who kisses you with all her heart.

* Autograph.

1. Thérèse fell sick on the evening of Easter, March 25.
2. Doctor Notta had prescribed hydrotherapy for Thérèse's nervous condition. [Sister Agnes' playful French titles were: ". . . Miss Bather, Miss Trembler, Miss Feverish, Miss Sleepyhead, Miss Drinker."]
3. Sister Agnes of Jesus was to receive the Habit on Friday, April 6.
4. See these lines to Céline, shortly after the above letter: "I am delighted with Friday in order to kiss you; I hope you will be happy also and that this day will be spent without any tears and regrets since our Thérèse is going to be better. How lovable on the part of God, then, to cure her for me these days." (From Sister Agnes of Jesus, April 3-4?, 1883.)
5. At this time, the postulant used to go out of the cloister, dressed as a bride, assisted at part of the ceremony in the outside chapel, and entered again the choir of the religious for the clothing in the Habit. Thérèse kissed and hugged Pauline only in the outside speakroom (Ms. A, p. 61).
6. Probably Marie-Thérèse de Liesville, granddaughter of Thérèse Davy de Virville (Mme. de Bouillon).
7. We should call attention here to the existence of three fragments of very small envelopes, the pompous wording of which was an attempt to distract Thérèse. Sister Agnes' handwriting dates from 1883-1884. We read:
   i. Mademoiselle Thérèse Martin in her chateau at Les Buissonnets - Boulevard Pont l'Evêque - near the Jardin de l'Etoile - Lisieux - Calvados - France - Europe.

ii. To her Royal Highness, Mademoiselle Thérèse Martin - Queen of France and Navarre - in her Palace at Les Buissonnets - Lisieux.

iii. Mademoiselle Thérésita E. V. - care of Mademoiselle Marie Martin.

LD *From Sister Agnes of Jesus to Marie.*
April (?), 1883 (Extracts.)

J. M. J. T.

Sursum corda!

My dear little Sister,

It appears that Thérèse isn't better, that you have a lot of trouble;[1] I was very sad this morning when thinking of you.... I have an idea that very often you are suffering from my absence and that discouragement is very close to this suffering.... When you can come to see me, I shall be very happy, but you must wait, if possible, until Thérèse is much better. Poor little thing. I'm suffering, seeing her like this. Well, we must resign ourselves and love God much, much in order to love the Cross a little bit....

* Autograph.

1. Thérèse had become tyrannical with Marie: "I used to give her much trouble, not allowing her to be far away from me" (Ms. A, p. 63), never ceasing to call her even during her meals. "When Marie wanted to go out, it had to be either to go to Mass or else to see *Pauline*, and then I said nothing" (ibid.).

LC 11 *From Sister Agnes of Jesus to Thérèse.*

April (?), 1883

J. M. J. T.

Long live Jesus!

My beloved little Thérésita,

It has been a long time since I had any news about you, so send me quickly Papa or Marie[1] and have them tell me you are cured, cured for good. Oh! how happy this would make me!...

Dear little pet, I'm sending you a real means of giving me this joy. Here is a little miraculous scapular[2] that you are to wear with much confidence while we are making a novena here. I intend to explain this to Marie during her next visit, but I want you to know immediately, my little darling, that this scapular has already worked very many miracles, cured little girls as sick as you and even sicker...this gives us hope, doesn't it? Yes, I myself want to believe that my poor baby will soon leave her bed. All Paradise is in a flutter, the Powers on high, the Virtues are shaken...and we're on the verge of the great moment.... And one of these fine days, my Thérésita's good angel will give one last flap of his wings, and her ugly sickness will fly away forever very far, very far.

Adieu, my dear little patient, the dearest of all little patients here below. There is always by your side a little Agnes, the most loving of all Agneses, who covers you with kisses which are all the more tender as they are silent.... Do you know her? Indeed, you do, always in your heart.

Your *petit Paulin*, your poor little teacher, both a little bit a Mother and very much a sister,

Agnes of Jesus

* Autograph.

1. See preceding LD, note 1.
2. This scapular is unidentified; it is either the Mount Carmel scapular or that of some other confraternity.

LD *From Père Almire Pichon to Marie. (Extracts.)*

April 17,
1883

† Nantes, April 17, '83

Dear true and good child in Christ Jesus,

. . . I am with you on your painful Calvary, at your little Thérèse's bedside. Tell her I'm praying for her as though I were her grandfather.[1] Teach her, above all, to kiss the adorable Hand that places her upon the Cross.

How grateful I am to my good Master for having been so solicitous in your regard. I recognize His Heart in this. He did not want to darken your happy Pauline's espousals by a mourning[2] or by the absence of her dear Benjamin[3] . . . . I am praying as well as I can for your dearly departed, for your little patient, and for all your intentions.

Share with your Thérèse all the blessings I am drawing for you from the Heart of Jesus.

A.P.[4]

* Autograph.

1. See LD, May 21, 1883. On his behavior as "grandfather" with regard to Thérèse, whom he had not seen up to that time, see DCL, *Le Père Pichon et la famille Martin,* 1882-1897, VT, October 1967, p. 193.
2. The death of M. Martin's mother on April 8, 1883 (two days after Sister Agnes received the Habit) at Valframbert (Orne). See LD, July 11-12, 1881, note 2.
3. Thérèse was able to kiss Pauline on April 6; see LC 10, note 5.
4. Except on rare occasions, P. Pichon always signed with his initials.

LT 10 April 29, 1883

From Thérèse to Céline.

Lines in pencil on the back of a piece of paper on which Thérèse had painted a Sacred-Heart, surrounded with these words: "Behold this Heart which has so loved men."

To my dear little Céline from her little sister, who loves her tenderly.

Thérèse

Sunday, April 29, 1883[1]

* Autograph.

1. Céline had just reached age fourteen on the preceding day.

LC 12 Beginning of May (?), 1883

From Sister Agnes of Jesus to Thérèse.

Approximate date, see note 5.

J. M. J. T.

Long live Jesus!

Dear little Thérèse,

Since you've scolded me through Marie for not having written you at all,[1] here is a large sheet of paper which I'm going to fill to the end in order to make up for my fault.

Poor little Benjamin of my heart, if you only knew how much I love you, with what tenderness I think of you each day, at each moment of the day! Do you recall the little stanzas you used to recite for Papa's feast, two or three years ago?[2] Well, I'm going to say to you today what you used to say to him then:

In the morning when I awake
After God, I think of you.
In the evening when I sleep
In my dreams I see you once again!*

Oh, yes, my little darling, you are always in my mind. At each moment, I send you my good angel to carry my caresses; is he carrying out my assignment well?

Darling, from time to time, send me your angel, after you have placed the very sweet kisses of your heart under his wings.

Mother Marie de Gonzague was very happy, the other day, with the pretty bouquet; she kisses her dear little daughter and is keeping her in her heart close to *petit Paulin*. . . . In Carmel, we love Thérèse just as they do at *Les Buissonnets*, we pray for her, we're concerned about her, and we talk about her incessantly. I myself am waiting the beautiful day of her cure with great impatience; I've already made all my plans for making it a day of real celebration. Our Mother[3] has promised me that I'll see the *cured little one* in the very delightful speakroom which she so much loves, the speakroom of her confidences! We'll stay there, the two of us, as long as we want. Oh! I'm the one who will have things to tell you, poor darling, since the time we've said nothing to each other except in our heart. . . . I'm going to provide myself with all kinds of beautiful Carmelite stories in order not to be destitute of things to say for even one instant. We'll babble and babble and laugh, and it will be a case of who outdoes the other! . . .

Come, then, good Saint Gorgonius,[4] touch quickly and speed up that sweet moment! What does all this contemplating mean for an endless time without doing anything at all! . . . Hurry up or

**Le Matin quand je me réveille*
Après Dieu je pense à toi
Et puis le soir quand je sommeille
Dans mes rêves je te revois!

the both of us will not remain good friends.... Behold the spring which is passing away and the summer which is coming with its beautiful days of blue skies;[5] make my poor Thérésita benefit by them.... And the little birds are coming to build their nests. Papa has even told me that he had seen several of them in the garden. I would not want one little bird to fly away from its little house without having you as a witness, my dear little girl!

There are many of them at Carmel in the morning; I hear them singing and I think of you, poor little bird, plunged up to your neck in feathers for such a long time. There are also beautiful flowers here, especially at this very moment: shepherd's purse, primroses, daisies, gilliflowers, and my dear little flower, the forget-me-not. It's showing me its blue eye[6] and seems to be saying: "Think of your dear child with the blue eyes, who is smiling at you from afar."

Well, little child, the flowers of Carmel are lovable, aren't they? We can see and feel them blooming under the angels' wings and in the shadow of the Tabernacle where Thérèse's little Jesus always dwells and rests.

Adieu, my darling; my tenderest kisses are for you. Without your realizing it, I'm always at your side, taking care of you in my heart. I can see you, kiss you, love you.... Whenever I go to see Mother Marie de Gonzague, we both talk about you as a much-loved and spoiled little girl.... She loves you very much, this gentle Mamma of your soul....

Little Benjamin, everybody loves you, but above us there is a Heart that surpasses us in its tenderness, it is the Heart of the Holy Child Jesus!... Oh! how He constantly looks lovingly at His little Thérèse! How He smiles at her...how He blesses her.

Adieu, Baby. Get well quickly. I am always,

Your Agnes, your *petit Paulin.*

* Autograph.

1. "My greatest consolation when I was sick was to receive a letter from *Pauline*. . . . I read it and read it over again until I knew it by heart. . . ." (Ms. A, p. 64).
2. August 25, 1881. We still have the copy done in Thérèse's hand; the poem was composed by Pauline; see LT 18, note 1, August 25, 1885.
3. Mother Geneviève of St. Teresa.
4. Perhaps St. Gorgonius, one of the old "fourteen auxiliary Saints "?
5. It is because of this reference that we suggest "May" as the date for this letter.
6. See LT 240.

LC 13 *From Sister Agnes of Jesus to Thérèse.*

May 14-15 (?), 1883

J. M. J. T.

Long live Jesus!

Little Thérésita,

What a joy to see you well! How good the Blessed Virgin really is![1] I offered her your beautiful bouquet, and she seemed to be all radiant with her little daughter's flowers. . . . Along with the flowers, I expressed a big "thanks," which was as tender as it was big, and I begged her to continue her work and to complete it soon.

Poor darling, how eager I am to see your little face so dear to my heart. I can see it from here, that's true, but for sometime my telescope is no longer any good; when you were so sick, I let a tear fall on the lens and suddenly it became blurred.

Well, the Blessed Virgin keeps us together under her mantle; she is watching over us in her heart, blessing us, loving us and caressing us with the same hand!

How can you say that Thérésita is far from Agnes, and Agnes far from Thérésita?

How beautiful the weather is today! Look, how blue the sky is! From time to time, I see little swallows passing by, gay and light, just like a little girl in good health, and I think of my Benjamin, and I pray to the dwellers of this very blue heaven to have a little pair of wings fall down from on high for my own swallow. With this pair of wings she would run through the fields, she would play in the beautiful sun, she would come and rest from time to time in her Agnes' very sweet nest, up there high on the mount of Carmel where the weather is so good, so good! and where one breathes in heaven's air and is always able to see, even during the winter, the sun and flowers. . . .

Little child, let us ask our dear Mother not to allow her month to pass by without reuniting us.[2]

Adieu! Let us love the Blessed Virgin, let us love her; she is a Mother, and beneath her glance, beneath her hand, the little bark of her heart is safe and is sailing peacefully toward heaven.

I kiss your little bark, my cherub; always keep at the bottom of its hold the love I know you have for me. I need it just as a little mother needs to be paid in return for the love she has for her child,

Your Agnes

* Autograph.

1. See Ms. A, pp. 64-65, which gives the account of Thérèse's cure on Sunday, May 13. See, too, the letter which follows: LD, May 21, 1882.
2. According to this statement, a delay seemed necessary before the convalescent's first outing. The assumption of "Thursday, May 17" (Mss. II, p. 20) seems very weak. In a letter from Sister Agnes of Jesus to Céline, the first days of June 1883, we read: "I was counting on seeing you on Thursday and making my visit an answer [to your letter]. And so, as you see, here's a short note which would not be at Les Buissonnets without your sacrifice of Thursday." That Thursday was May 31. Was it in favor of Thérèse that Céline was deprived of

this visit? Nothing in the rest of the letter supports arguments for or against this assumption. Later on, Mother Agnes described as "... a very pleasant visit the one when Thérèse came after her cure; I remember she was still in mourning for Grandmamma and her black clothing made her look even prettier" (*Souvenirs intimes*, p. 16). Concerning this grandmother, see LD, April 17, 1883, note 2.

LD *From P. Pichon to Marie. (Extracts.)*

May 21, 1883

†Laval, May 21

My good Child in Christ Jesus,

... With you and with all my heart I call it a miracle.[1] Do you know I have a very warm affection for your dear little Thérèse? A grandpapa[2] is subject to weaknesses for his grandchildren. I love everything in this very candid soul, even her demands for your presence.[3] Since she loves you so much, she is very deeply in my heart. I rejoice to think that God is reserving for her a very privileged future and that the Blessed Virgin is watching over her with a motherly affection....

... Tell your Thérèse that I bless her with Mamma[4] just as one blesses the best of his children.... The enclosed holy picture[5] is for our risen one....

A.P.

* Autograph.

1. From the very first moment, Marie believed in Thérèse's miraculous cure: "I saw Thérèse all of a sudden staring at the statue; her look was radiant. I understood she was restored, that she was looking not at the image of Mary but at the Blessed Virgin herself. She remained in ecstasy for four or five minutes." (Sister Marie of the Sacred Heart, NPPO 1908, p. 5.) See DE, pp. 455-456, July 6, no. 5, note 1.

2. See LD, April 17, 1883, note 1.
3. See Sister Agnes of Jesus to Marie, LD, April 1883, note 1.
4. Marie; see Ms. A, p. 63: "My dear 'Mamma' as I was calling her. . . ." And it was her sister Marie, whom she was calling during the last attack of May 13, even though she had her at her side and did not recognize her; see Ms. A, p. 65.
5. This picture has not been identified.

"My first entrance into the world" (*Ms. A, p. 73*)
(August 1883 - February 1884)
Age ten and eleven

Restored to health, Thérèse was able to enjoy a special vacation M. Martin provided for his daughters the last two weeks of August 1883. She had not seen Alençon since November 15, 1877. The Romet and Tifenne families brought their visitors from chateau to chateau: Pierre Romet's home at Saint-Denis-sur-Sarthon, Mme. Monnier's at Grogny; the Rabinel's at the Lanchal manor, at Semallé. "I could say it was during my stay at Alençon that I made my first entrance into the world. Everything was joy and happiness around me; I was fêted, coddled, and admired. . . . I admit this life had its attractions for me. . . . At the age of ten, the heart allows itself to be easily dazzled" (*Ms. A, p. 73*). *Thérèse needed this experience, she tells us, in order to choose "more freely" the path of renunciation which will soon be hers* (*ibid.*).

One of the historic events of this trip took place at Alençon, undoubtedly on August 22. P. Pichon, an inhabitant of Orne, was traveling in the district. He arranged a meeting with Marie, telling her: "Above all, bring my little Thérèse and your charming imp [*Céline*]

to me." (Card from Vitré, August 20–21, 1883.) In this way, he got acquainted with the whole family (with the exception of the Carmelite, Sister Agnes) since Marie had already introduced him to her father and Léonie at Paris, at Easter 1883. They felt very quickly at ease with this kind religious. And the little girl of ten, without any embarrassment, complied when her father told her to kiss P. Pichon.[1]

In October 1883, Thérèse passed into the second division of the "purple class." She applied herself more carefully than ever to the study of catechism, even during recreation (Ms. A, p. 81). Was it at this time or before that the pupil "contested" the current teaching on the lot of children dying without baptism? "But they haven't sinned! But not to see God, that is unfortunate! Well, since God can do all things, if I were in His place, I would show myself." (La Petite Thérèse à l'Abbaye, op. cit., pp. 28–29.)

As background, at this time (and for a long time to come), Thérèse was acquainted with "spiritual trials": fear of having pretended her illness during the spring 1883 (see Ms. A, p. 62 and 67), fear of having lied when giving the account of a "smile of the Queen of heaven," May 13 (Ms. A, p. 65–66). She was not freed from these trials until November 1887 (see LT 30, note 2), and in May 1888 (LC 82, note 3).

Sister Agnes of Jesus has unfortunately not preserved the few letters she received during these months from her "little Benjamin" (see LC 14, 15, 16, 18, 19).

1. Incident reported by Boncompain, *Un directeur d'âmes, le P. Almire Pichon de la Compagnie de Jésus. Notes et Souvenirs*, Montréal, 1921, p. 30; cited in VT, October 1967, p. 203, no. 32.

LC 14 *From Sister Agnes of Jesus to Thérèse.*

August 24-28 (?), 1883 Approximate date; see notes 1 and 2.

→ LT lost

J. M. J. T.

Long live Jesus!

My little Benjamin,

Thanks for your nice letter; I see that both far away and close by you are thinking of your former teacher, that you love her and always see her through your heart.

And I, too, think of my dear little pupil. I love her and I'm happy to see her in the midst of the pleasures of this incomparable trip.[1] Enjoy yourself, little baby; God wills it and from heaven He blesses Thérèse and her joys.

Your Agnes

Kiss Papa with all your heart for his little Carmelite, who does nothing but think of him.[2]

* Autograph.

1. See the letter to Céline, the same day: "I'm very happy you're having so much pleasure at Alençon; see how spoiled you are, you and Thérèse!... Take advantage of these happy days, my darling...and next week you will tell me at the grille about the thousand joys seasoned by a thousand virtues." (Sister Agnes of Jesus; no date. August 24-28)? The Martin family returned to Lisieux on Saturday, September 1, or Monday, September 3.

   Did the trip include a visit to Valframbert? The documents make no mention of it, but the assumption has some likelihood: M. Martin could have taken his daughters to their grandmother's grave; she had died four months before. In this case, a visit to Rose Taillé would appear quite logical.

2. Sister Agnes wrote him on August 24, the eve of St. Louis' feast; she also wrote to Marie. The letters to Céline and Thérèse were perhaps included in the same mail.

LC 15 *From Sister Agnes of Jesus to Thérèse.*
October 14, 1883 or 1884 (?) Date uncertain.

J. M. J. T.

Happy feast, little Benjamin. Oh! how pleased St. Teresa is going to be, then, to bless her little Thérèse. You will have to pray very much to her tomorrow, very much for yourself, but also a little for her naughty daughter Agnes, who hasn't finished being converted.

I'm sending you a little picture, little and darling like you;[1] I think it will please you.

Adieu, my dear. I haven't the time to fill the four pages, but you know that my heart has the time to be filled with love and kisses for you.

Your Agnes

Mother Marie de Gonzague kisses her dear little daughter. Our Mother sends her this pretty little basket, filled with all the affection of the Carmel for Thérésita.

* Autograph.

1. The picture has not been identified.

LC 16 *From Sister Agnes of Jesus to Thérèse.*
December 1883 (?)
→ LT lost

J. M. J. T.
Jesus

My dear little Baby,

I kiss you in order to thank you for your nice (and *very well written*)[1] little letter. I am content with you, my darling; you are always my little consolation and my Benjamin.

"Virgin most pure" fell to your lot, then, for the procession.[2] This is a sign that the Blessed Virgin, your Mother, wants her little daughter to resemble her and become like her a beautiful lily of purity and innocence.

To do this, my darling, and also to prepare yourself for the great and very sweet feast of Christmas, you will have to be very good, very obedient, very diligent, and, above all, put forth many efforts to live always in peace with Céline. It is so good when two little sisters understand one another, never finding fault with one another.[3] . . .

Oh! how the little Jesus will caress you and speak sweet things to you from His blessed crib if you follow my advice. He will perhaps allow you to come and adore Him before the shepherds, at the same time as the Blessed Virgin and St. Joseph! And how beautiful it would be to receive the first blessings of the Divine Baby!

Adieu. I kiss you with all the tenderness of my heart.

Your Agnes

Little Benjamin, I entrust you with all my love for Papa and my little Léonie, whom I always love.

* Autograph.

1. The same compliment in LC 19.
2. We don't know the date (perhaps December 8?) and the ceremony of this feast. It seems that each pupil drew one of the invocations of the Litany of Loreto by lot.
3. See LC 8, note 2, February 7, 1883.

LC 17 *From Mother Hermance of the Sacred Heart to Thérèse.*

1883-1884 Inscription on a sheet of paper used to wrap a holy picture (which has disappeared and has not been identified). Approximate date; see note 1.

J. M. J. T.

For our dear little sister Térésita, sister of our little lamb, all white.[1]

Sister C. de J. de l'I.C., et St. J.[2]
r.c.i.

* Autograph.

1. Probable reference to Sister Agnes of Jesus' white veil. She was wearing it from April 6, 1883 to July 16, 1884. Another assumption: a reference to the wedding dress on the day of her clothing (April 6, 1883)?
2. Abbreviation for "*Soeur Coeur de Jésus de l'Immaculée Conception et de Saint Joseph.*" She was simply called: Mother Heart of Jesus.

LC 18 *From Sister Agnes of Jesus to Thérèse.*

January 1884 (?) Date uncertain; see note 1.

J. M. J. T.

May the Blessed Virgin always keep my little Thérèse
under her virginal mantle.

My little Benjamin,

Since my last letter is *all worn out*, here is another to replace it. But I haven't the time to make a long discourse, poor little one. Always be very good, very gentle, very diligent, and very studious. Don't forget to carry each day your little collection to the Child

Jesus. Oh! how happy the Child Jesus must be when His little Thérèse places on His crib[1] the perfumed harvest of her efforts and her little acts of love!... How beautiful must His smile be! and how His little arms must press the dear bouquet of virtues and the little flower girl also gently to His Heart.

You see, dear Thérèse, there are so many bad people who make the Child Jesus' tears flow immediately...there are so many, so many! that you must console Him a little and dry our Jesus' little tears as much as possible!

Adieu, my dear little child. I love you, I love you *big as the world*, and I kiss you with my best kiss.

Your Agnes

* Autograph.

1. A time index: close to Christmas. However, we don't know with any certainty if it is the Christmas of 1883 or 1884. The Marian invocation at the beginning *could be* a reminder of the invocation: "Virgin most pure" of LC 16.

LC 19 *From Sister Agnes of Jesus to Thérèse.*

January 1884 (?) Approximate date; see note 1.

→ LT lost

J. M. J. T.

Love for the Child Jesus![1]

My little Benjamin,

I have only time to place a good kiss here for you.

Your little letter pleased me, and I found it especially VERY WELL WRITTEN.[2] I recognized in it my Thérèse's good heart, her good will, her desire to please her *petit Paulin*, in a word, all sorts of delightful things which gave me very much joy.

But before all else, little Baby, you must try to please little

Jesus, isn't that true? Little Jesus must come before *petit Paulin*, that's understood. Oh! my darling, here is what must occupy us both: we must please the Child Jesus, console Him, dry His *little tears*. You remember that, don't you?[3]

Adieu, my baby. I kiss you tenderly. Give all those dear to me a little hug for me.

Your Agnes

* Autograph.

1. This invocation would suggest that we place this letter during the Christmas season, which ended, then, on February 2. In January 1883, Sister Agnes of Jesus would have made a reference undoubtedly to Thérèse's illness; see LC 7, note 1.
2. See LC 16, note 1.
3. Possible reference to the preceding letter, LC 18, par. 2. As a Carmelite, Thérèse still wanted "to dry the little tears" of the Child Jesus; see LT 74, January 6, 1889.

"A new thrust" (*Ms. A, p. 73*)
(February-May 1884)
Age eleven

The three months which immediately preceded Thérèse's First Communion mark one of the periods strong in spiritual dialogue between the child and her "little Mother." Pauline presents the ideal, and Thérèse carries it out. Such will be, for years to come, the essence of the relationship between the two sisters.

"Each week," Thérèse wrote, "you used to write me a pretty little letter which filled my soul with profound thoughts and aided me to practice virtue" (Ms. A, p. 73). Twelve of these miniature letters are preserved.

They are undated, and so we have tried our best to place them in chronological order. In them, Sister Agnes of Jesus plays the role of spiritual guide, exhorting, tirelessly stimulating, in proportion to her ambition for her little daughter.

Only one of several answers from Thérèse has been preserved (LT 11).[1] *In fact, her true response was her extraordinary generosity. Each day she gathered tens of "flowers"—sacrifices, acts of virtue—for the Child Jesus and she "perfumed" these with her aspirations of love. In the evening, she entered the total in the illuminated "little copybook" prepared for this purpose by the Carmelite artist, Sister Agnes of Jesus.*

Marie took an active part in her little sister's preparation; Thérèse wrote: "I used to sit on her knees and there I listened avidly to what she was telling me. It seemed to me that her whole heart, so big, so generous, passed into me.... She pointed out the way to become a saint through fidelity to the littlest things; she gave me the little leaflet: 'Renunciation,' which I meditated upon with delight...." (Ms. A, p. 74).

This child of eleven was being encouraged to practice a meticulous form of asceticism. Marie formed the ideas (see LC 20, note 5), and Thérèse applied them literally, and Pauline adorned them with delightful symbols: roses, violets, daisies, hawthorns, lilies of the valley, forget-me-nots, etc. Thus the symbolism of the flower entered into the vocabulary, or better into the spirituality of Thérèse. This language will remain for a long time a kind of secret code between her and Sister Agnes of Jesus (see Manuscript A, dedicated to her "little Mother," in which the theme of the flower predominates).

In 1896, in the full bloom of her mystical genius, the Saint found no better expression of her passionate love for Jesus than the gesture of the little girl at Les Buisson-

nets: strewing flowers (see P. 30, June 28, 1896, and Ms. B, p. 196). And this was to last up until the day when the symbol became a reality: on her bed in the infirmary, the flower she was unpetalling was her very life. (See DE, pp. 414, 439, 543, etc.)

→Read: Ms. A, pp. 72–77.

1. This is Letter I of the 1948 edition of the *Letters*; the letters of her childhood were not considered as the "correspondence" properly so-called; see Introduction, p. 43, 1948 edition.

LC 20 *From Sister Agnes of Jesus to Thérèse.*

February 7 (?), 1884

J. M. J. T.

Long live Thérèse's Jesus!

My dear little Pet,

I'm very much pleased with you; Marie has shared your good resolutions with me, and I find you very reasonable, very good. Little Jesus will be the first one to reward you for your sacrifice,[1] I haven't any doubt. As for myself, my darling, I promise to be faithful to the little letter you're asking from me each week; it will come to tell you how much I'm thinking about you and your First Communion. At this very moment, I am making up the famous little copybook. I've already spent a great amount of time on it, but I'm not tired, and I count on making it as beautiful as possible.[2] Céline, I'm sure, will not be jealous;[3] she's much too big in soul and size!

I recommend, my darling, that you be very confiding in your big sister Marie. You should tell her about all your efforts; she's so good; remember your sickness![4] I'm entrusting her with explaining the little copybook and with helping you bring to bloom this whole garden of flowers for the great day.[5]

We shall begin on March 1.

Adieu, Thérésita. I am pressing you to my heart.

Your Agnes

Kiss everybody for me, especially dear little Céline. I love little Céline very much! She's also my little girl. I have two little girls: Céline and Thérésita.

Mother Marie de Gonzague embraces her dear little daughter very tightly.

* Autograph.

1. See Ms. A, p. 74: "...your poor little girl...was making such a *great sacrifice* in accepting the fact that she was not being prepared each evening on your knees as her dear Céline had been...." Far from benefiting from the additional visits to the Carmel, Thérèse was soon deprived of these because of Lent (February 27-April 13). See LC 26, note 4.
2. See her description in LC 23, note 2, February 28, 1884.
3. In 1880, Pauline had prepared a similar notebook for Céline, but it was much less ornate than that of Thérèse.
4. Her sickness during March-May 1883.
5. Concerning Marie's help, see Ms. A, p. 74, referred to above. In the Appendix, *Various Documents*, we shall see the text of the leaflet about which Thérèse is speaking: "Way of holy renunciation or Maxims of the Saints."

LC 21 *From Sister Agnes of Jesus to Thérèse.*
February 14 (?), 1884

J. M. J. T.

Long live Jesus!

My Thérésita,

This morning, I promised Marie I'd give you the little copybook for the beginning of March.[1] I'm working on it all the time. I hope my Benjamin will work very hard, too, in order to cultivate her little garden. To plant flowers in this garden which are just as beautiful as those in the little copybook, she must not allow one single weed in it.

Oh! when I think that in three months[2] Jesus will come to rest in this little child's heart, in my Thérésita's heart!...

You must, darling, spare yourself nothing to make your soul a little heaven where the Child Jesus will want to dwell forever!...

Ah! may this gentle Child already be the King, the love of your heart. What is there on earth more delightful than Jesus? Jesus in His cradle, Jesus in Thérésita's heart on May 29...sleeping among flowers!

Adieu, darling. I love you.

Your Agnes

Kiss my *beloved* little Céline for me.

Your Mother[3] is sending you some kisses.

* Autograph.

1. See Sister Agnes of Jesus to Marie: "I shall send the little notebook for March 1, or, perhaps, you will want to take it along with her little Friday letter." (Undated; a little after February 24, 1884.) The final clause seems to suggest Thursday for the writing of the "little letter," each week.

2. The First Communion was then set for May 29; see paragraph four. However, we should undoubtedly take the three months roughly.
3. Mother Marie de Gonzague.

LC 22 *From Sister Agnes of Jesus to Thérèse.*
February 21 (?), 1884

J. M. J. T.

Long live Thérésita's little Jesus.

My little darling,

I think you are always busily cultivating the little garden of your heart. . . . You must, for in a few days the planting of the flowers will begin.[1]

Oh, Thérèse, just think! in hardly[2] three months little Jesus will come to rest in your heart for the very first time! And who is this little Jesus? He is the same, yes, the same one whom the Blessed Virgin held in her arms, whom she wrapped in swaddling clothes, laid in the manger, and rocked on her knees! It is this little Child, so beautiful, so ravishing, who today makes up heaven's delights! It is He! . . .

Oh, my darling, the day of First Communion is the most beautiful day in our life; it is a heavenly day! Ask Céline![3] . . . But to taste its infinite charms, we must turn our heart into a little angel's heart. Don't forget this, my little Benjamin.

Adieu. How blessed you are! I love and kiss you.

Your Agnes

Your Mother, Marie de Gonzague loves and kisses you also.

* Autograph.

1. On February 27 and 28, 1884, Thérèse drew, at the end of her diary (a beige diary described in Mss. I, p. 22), a little plot with little flowers in all colors.
2. It seems, according to this letter and the following, that the First Communion date, first set for May 29 (see LC 21) had just been changed to mid-May? It was a matter of conjecture for almost a whole month (see LC 28).
3. Céline's First Communion (May 13, 1880) had been a very fervent one (see Ms. A, p. 57). See Mother Agnes of Jesus: "I was also tending to Céline, and I prepared her for her First Communion. I was well rewarded for it, for on that day Céline was like a lily of innocence. Everybody was struck by this. Uncle told me, in the evening, when we returned to Les Buissonnets: 'What a good First Communion this child made! Pauline, it's your work.' I've always kept this compliment; I took it as coming from God." (*Souvenirs intimes,* pp. 47-48.) In her correspondence with Céline, before 1894, Sister Agnes frequently reminded her of this fervent preparation.

LC 23 *From Sister Agnes of Jesus to Thérèse.*

February 28, 1884

J. M. J. T.

My little darling,

I don't know if it's you who will come tomorrow morning[1] to get this short note. In any case, I'm informing you about the famous copybook[2] for this evening. When I think that my Thérésita will begin her great preparation on Saturday morning! Only two months and a half and little Jesus will come down for the first time into her heart! Oh! how necessary it is to use these two months and a half well! How much work to do and how many

flowers to sow in so little time! But, my dear, look at nature. It is beginning to repair its dress almost on the same day as yourself. We already see buds on the trees in gardens, and very soon the flowers will appear. Certainly during the month of May everything will charm the eyes. Well, what nature is doing just to give joy to our eyes, will you not do also, Thérésita of the Child Jesus, to receive and give joy to the beloved little Child at His first awakening in your heart?

However, I hear your answer, and I feel it's almost useless to encourage you when one possesses a good little heart like yours, my darling!

I feel that from a distance Jesus Himself is inviting and encouraging His little sister to work for Him, and so what are your poor Agnes' incentives compared to little Jesus' gentle words?

Adieu, Thérésita. If your little garden is in bloom, if all is ready when the great day arrives, believe that Jesus will not come with empty hands! Ah! If you only knew the delightful treasures hidden in this little Host of a well-prepared First Communion!

I kiss you a thousand times.

Your Agnes

Kiss little Céline for me, and tell her that I love her as much as is possible for a little Mother to love her daughter. Kiss *Marie* also, tell her *that my heart is filled with memories of her.* A big kiss for Léonie and all possible tokens of affection for dear little Father.

Mother Marie de Gonzague kisses her little daughter and loves her with all her heart.

* Autograph.

1. Friday, May 29 (leap year), and it is this same day that Sister Agnes meant when she wrote "this evening," putting herself in Thérèse's place, who would be reading the note on Friday. See LC 24.
2. It was made up of ninety-six pages; one page for each day. Each page was decorated with a border, rays in each of the corners, the

date in Gothic illumination, the name of a flower and a short invocation which the scent of the flower symbolized; it was all done in black and red ink. The flyleaf was particularly well done. Prayers to the Child Jesus, the Blessed Virgin, Saint Joseph, the guardian angel preface each of the four months. Preparation was to begin on March 1.

After some alterations, for example, additional drawings and the revision of some prayers, simpler in the original, this collection was published under the title: *Deux mois et neuf jours de préparation à ma première communion* (Boumard Fils, 1909, lst edition).

LC 24 *From Sister Agnes of Jesus to Thérèse.*

February 29, 1884

My Darling,

Here is the copybook or rather the *little book* of preparation. Are you satisfied? Oh! how I'd like to be a witness of your joy!

Madame Leroyer[1] gave me this pretty cover and Sister Thérèse of St. Augustine[2] embroidered it.[3] You must really pray for them on the day of your First Communion.

Adieu, baby. Be a little angel, yes, nothing less than an angel; the Eucharistic Jesus wants to find heaven in your child's heart.

I see Him smiling at you from the Tabernacle; oh! what a smile that is, the smile of little Jesus!...

I am sending you all my kisses and my dear Mother's blessings to encourage you in the planting of the flowers.

Sister Thérèse of St. Augustine gave me this little chaplet of practices[4] for you, and Marie will explain how you are to use it.

Your Agnes

Thank dear little Father for his excellent fish this morning.

* Autograph.
1. Sister Thérèse of St. Augustine's mother. She was living at Lisieux.
2. The Carmelite who had openly complimented Thérèse on her first visit to the Carmel; see Ms. A, p. 59. She was twenty-eight years old, seven years professed.
3. The cover was in blue velvet, embroidered with the initials T M in white.
4. This was a small chaplet with movable beads, and it was used to count one's acts of sacrifice; it was undoubtedly different in form from the one Thérèse used as early as the age of three and a half. See Ms. A, p. 25. Ten years later, she resumed this practice with a companion in the novitiate. See LT 144, July 23, 1893.

LT 11 From Thérèse to Sister Agnes of Jesus

March 1-6,
1884
→ LC 24

February 1884[1]

My dear little Pauline,

I had really thought about writing you to thank you for your delightful little book, but I believed it was not permitted during lent.[2] However, now that I know it is permitted, I thank you with all my heart.

You don't know the joy I felt when Marie showed me your pretty little book. I found it delightful. I had never seen anything so beautiful, and I was unable to grow tired looking at it. What nice prayers there were at the beginning! I recited them to little Jesus with all my heart. Every day, I try to perform as many practices[3] as I can, and I do all in my power not to let a single occasion pass by. I am saying at the bottom of my heart the little prayers which form the perfume of roses,[4] as often as I can.

What a beautiful picture it has at the beginning![5] It's a little

dove giving its heart to little Jesus. Well! I, too, want to adorn my heart with all the beautiful flowers I will meet in order to offer it to little Jesus on the day of my First Communion, and I desire, in fact, just as it says in the little prayer at the beginning of the book, that little Jesus be so pleased in my heart that He will not think of going back to heaven. . . .

Thank Sister Thérèse of St. Augustine for me for her pretty little chaplet of practices and for having embroidered the beautiful cover of my book. Kiss Mother Marie de Gonzague for me and tell her that her little daughter loves her with all her heart.

Léonie and Céline kiss you.

Au revoir, dear little Pauline. I kiss you with all my heart.

Your little girl, who loves you very much.

Thérésita

* CE

1. Incorrect date; it could have been offered as an approximate date at the time of the *Process of the Writings* (1910). The autograph (now lost) had undoubtedly not been dated.
2. Lent had begun on February 27; concerning this regulation, see LC 8, note 1, 1883. In her answer (LC 25), Sister Agnes of Jesus justifies the "favor" granted to Thérèse that year.
3. These are little acts of mortification and acts of virtue. Within sixty-eight days (March 1 - May 7), Thérèse had totaled 1,949 (this count is from the original notebook; the number 818, given by Mother Agnes of Jesus in PO, 224 and PA, 634, is not exact).
4. We find "white roses" on March 1 (first day), and "Christmas roses" on March 10. The name of the flower varied each day, but Thérèse includes them all under the category of rose, which to her was the flower *par excellence.* On May 7, she had repeated 2,773 times the invocations suggested by Sister Agnes. Here are the first five invocations: "Little Jesus, I love You" (fifty times); "Little Jesus, don't let me be proud anymore" (thirty times); "Little Jesus, may I always be simple and docile" (thirty-five times); "My whole heart is Yours, Jesus" (thirty times); "Little Jesus, I kiss You" (fifty times).
5. A pasted picture, delicately colored and illuminated by Sister Agnes of Jesus.

LC 25 *From Sister Agnes of Jesus to Thérèse.*

March 6 (?), 1884
→LT 11

J. M. J. T.

My Darling,

Your little letter pleased me very much. I see that Thérésita is preparing her heart well for the great day. You must continue and not stop for an instant, for one instant lost is a flower less in the little garden.

Yes, my darling, you will really be the little dove that carries its heart to good Jesus. It's you I thought of when placing this picture at the beginning of the book.[1]

However, do you realize what Jesus will give you in return? He will bring you His Heart also! We could think, undoubtedly, that Thérésita's heart should not expect anything else but a little place in the Heart of Jesus, but not at all. It is the little Host, it is the Heart of Jesus that is claiming an entrance into Thérèse's heart. Oh! what a marvel! Are these two months and a half too long to think of this and to spread flowers on the path of this sweet Host that holds up the heavens?

Adieu, my Benjamin. Oh! don't grow tired of your gardening; the days are passing by quickly and Jesus is approaching!

I kiss you, little angel.

Your Agnes

You realize, my darling, that it's a great favor our Mother[2] is granting you when allowing you to write me during Lent. It's really true that this isn't permitted, but the circumstance of your First Communion gives you the right for this year. Thanks for the pretty bouquets and the fish from dear Father. I'm praying for all of you. *I think very often of little Marie.* A big kiss for Céline and Léonie.

Mother Marie de Gonzague kisses her little daughter.

* Autograph.

1. The symbol of the dove, frequently used in Sister Agnes' miniatures, retained a place of importance in her artistic productions right up to her old age (in poems, various sculptures done under her inspiration, etc.). Thérèse rarely used this symbol.
2. Mother Geneviève of St. Teresa.

LC 26 *From Sister Agnes of Jesus to Thérèse.*

March 13, 1884

J. M. J. T.

Long live Jesus! Thursday evening

My darling,

Thank Papa for yesterday's excellent fish and also for the delightful little reeds. Tell him his little daughter loves him more and more, and she would like to be worthy of such a father!

And you, Baby, how are you? Is your little garden getting covered over with flowers? I think so. . . . When will you return the book to me so that I can add to it what remains for the month of May?[1] I'd like so much to know what day Thérésita will receive her little Jesus.[2] Oh! how fervent her heart will have to be at that moment! For the eyes of the angels, I would like flames to be coming out of her heart. . . . Do you know, my darling, that your flowers need warmth in order to bloom? Well, your love will be the sweet Sun that will make them bloom under the feet of Jesus.

Adieu, my Benjamin. Jesus is very little for you. He is a brother in His cradle, but for me He has grown up. Ask Him to accept me soon for His little Spouse and that I will love Him only.

Your Agnes

Kiss my beloved little Marie for me and tell her to pray for

Sister Marie-Henriette,[3] who has just died. I'll have many things to talk to her about in mid-Lent.[4] A big kiss for little Céline and Léonie.

* Autograph.
1. Uncertain about the date of the First Communion, Sister Agnes of Jesus had prepared only the months of March and April. And on pages six and nine, she left the exact date blank: "for May 1884" and "May the Child Jesus, on May , find only perfumed flowers," etc. The numeral "8" was added after the event, and the color of ink is different.
2. Sister Agnes of Jesus was eager to know the date of Thérèse's First Communion because she wanted to make her Profession on the same day. See the prioress' letter to M. Martin after Sister Agnes had been approved for Profession by the Community: "Her desire is that this day of her Profession be the same day as your angel's First Communion. We hope, Monsieur, that we can carry out her wishes." (Mother Geneviève of St. Teresa to M. Martin, March 28, 1884.)
3. Sister Marie-Henriette Pouriau (October 29, 1843 - March 7, 1884), Visitandine at Le Mans. She was professed in 1868, and she had taught grammar, arithmetic, and music at the boarding school to which Marie and Pauline went for their education.
4. Thursday, March 20. Thérèse undoubtedly shared in this visit, at least for the last few minutes. That is why there is no weekly letter for this date of March 20.

LC 27 *From Sister Agnes of Jesus to Thérèse.*

March 27 (?), 1884

J. M. J. T.

Long live Jesus!

My dear little girl,

When are you going to send me the little copybook so that I can finally finish what remains for the month of May? I'd really like to

know what day will be the *great day*? As soon as it has been decided upon, write me, and then I'll be happy about it.[1]

I hope you're continuing to adorn your little heart for the *sweet visit* you're preparing for. My darling, don't let a single flower escape. It would be bad to see in your garden a little corner of soil not in bloom. Time is passing; be courageous! Oh! if you could see the beautiful reward awaiting you! If you only knew, dear baby, what joy it is to have Jesus in one's heart for the first time!

I'm thinking much about you and the great day!

Adieu, Thérésita. Kiss Papa for me, and give him a big thanks for his beautiful fish. Kiss also Marie and little Céline and good little Léonie.

Mother Marie de Gonzague kisses you.

* Autograph.
1. See LC 26, note 2.

LC 28 *From Sister Agnes of Jesus to Thérèse.*

April 3 (?), 1884

J. M. J. T.

What a joy, my little darling, that your First Communion is on May 8.[1] Oh! how sweet it will be for me to give myself to God on the same day as yourself. You will really have to pray for your Agnes, for, you see, my Benjamin, it's such a great grace to become the Spouse of Jesus, and I'm not worthy of it!

And so, listen, I'm going to confide in you. Jesus will give Himself as very little to you who are still very little. He will be the divine Child whom Mary rocked and warmed on her heart on Christmas night. He will smile at you, and His little hands will be filled with roses for you, and the angels will remove the thorns

from them. Nothing will wound you, and everything will be bright and beautiful. That morning will become a heavenly morning!

Ah! for me, too, undoubtedly, this day will be a heavenly day, but to me who am a grown-up Jesus will give Himself as a *grown-up*, that is, I will not see Him in His crib, as you will, my darling, but on the Cross, and not with roses but with the love of His thorns, not with His smile but with His tears[2].... You must, then, beg from your little Jesus the grace for me to love Him as a *grown-up*, to live and die in the shadow of His Cross, refusing Him no sacrifices His love must ask from me. As for me, I'll ask the *grown-up* Jesus that Thérésita may love Him *so much, so much, so much* very little in His crib that she may merit one day to love Him as a *grown-up* on His Cross just as her Agnes does.

Adieu, my darling. I love you!...

* Autograph.

1. The choice of the date must have either preceded or followed a short time after the children's final examination in school. On that occasion, Thérèse wrote on the first page of her catechism: "April 2, 1844 (*sic*), T. Martin was approved for First Communion at 4:00 in the afternoon." On April 20, P. Pichon wrote to Marie: "I have just inscribed May 8 among my family dates. You'll not be an orphan at the altar between Pauline and Thérèse....I am praying with May 8 in mind. You should have your two angels pray for my apostolate."
2. If the suggested date is correct, it was Thursday of Passion Week. This liturgical season may have influenced Sister Agnes' reflections.

LC 29 *From Sister Agnes of Jesus to Thérèse.*

April 10 (?),
1884
→ LT lost

My Benjamin,

Send me the little book as soon as possible, for I'm eager to complete it.[1] Marie will write down a few days on some paper so

that your preparation won't be stopped, and I will hurry with it so that I'll keep it the shortest time possible.

Your little letter, my baby, gave me very deep joy. I was able to see and to feel that your little heart was really being adorned and purified for the entrance of Jesus, the little King. Ah! my darling, how good this sweet Child is to desire to come down from heaven where He is honored, where He has such a beautiful home, in order to descend into your poor little heart which, though well-prepared, will not be able to offer Him a single ray of heaven's beauty. But this is how He loves His Thérèsita. He loves her more than the heavens, and the garden in bloom that she's preparing for Him will be more delightful than all heaven's gardens!...

Oh, my little child, isn't this thought ravishing and very fitting for filling us with love!

Adieu. The great day is approaching for you as well as for me! I am praying for you; pray for me!

Your Agnes

Your Mother[2] kisses you as her true little daughter.
Bonjour to all.

* Autograph.
1. See LC 26, note 1, March 13, 1884.
2. Mother Marie de Gonzague.

LC 30 *From Sister Agnes of Jesus to Thérèse.*
April 24 (?), 1884

J. M. J. T.

My dear baby, here is something for you alone.[1] ... Oh! how quickly time is passing![2] Prepare your little heart well. The Child Jesus is already preparing to leave the Tabernacle. Don't you hear

His *knock knock* from within so that we come and open the door for Him? My little darling, would your desires be less great than His? Oh, no, it's impossible. You, too, are going to *knock, knock* a thousand times a day at the door of little Jesus' amiable prison. Tell Him to come, and tell Him to look through the keyhole at His dear little girl and to help her prepare her heart for the great day when the gold door will finally swing open!. . .

Be brave in the planting of the flowers!

Adieu, my darling. I love you more and more.

A of J
†

* Autograph.

1. Perhaps a holy picture? Sister Agnes of Jesus' letter seems to be a commentary on a lace picture entitled: "A model for our Faith" (the same subject as the holy picture of July 5, 1891, in the Appendix); it is a picture of a child seated on the altar and knocking on the Tabernacle door.
2. We suggest April 24 as the date for this letter with the idea that the visits of Easter Week (April 13) could have freed Sister Agnes from her weekly letter; she went on retreat for her Profession on April 28.

LC 31 *From Sister Agnes of Jesus to Thérèse.*

May 6, 1884

Two days before Thérèse's First Communion and Pauline's religious Profession. On Sunday evening, May 4, Thérèse remained at the Abbey as a boarder in order to make the retreat with more recollection. The Autobiograhy speaks of "the sweet memory," "the unspeakable happiness of those few days spent awaiting Jesus" (Ms. A, p. 75).

J. M. J. T.

Come Jesus!

My dear Benjamin,

I am not forgetting what I promised you. I'm sending you my whole heart with this little note. Well, now, only a few hours sepa-

rate us both from the Great Day! There is still the whole day tomorrow, and then Jesus will come to dwell in Thérèsita's garden in bloom. At the same time, He will come to dwell in Agnes' poor garden!. . . Which of the two gardens will carry Him off in its beauty and riches? Ah! I know, but I also know that Thérèsita's little Jesus is not difficult or rather that He is merciful and indulgent. In spite of everything, then, He will become Agnes' Jesus, and when He caresses Thérèsita with one hand, He will caress His Agnes with the other. That is what I hope for and what I expect.

And is your retreat going well, my darling?[1] Are you a little upset by the emotional experience of Sunday? When learning about the good superior's death,[2] I couldn't help thinking of you and praying that your retreat would not be affected by it. A First Communion retreat is somewhat like a Profession retreat. . . both come only once in a lifetime, and so it is good to put all one's heart and mind into the retreat.

I'm thinking very much about my Benjamin. The thought of her joy moves me to tears. I can picture Jesus finally opening the little golden door of His prison of love. I picture the Ciborium entirely filled with white Hosts on the blessed morning of the great Day, and I say to myself: Among these little Hosts, there is one for Thérèsita! And in this little Host, when I look at it with the eyes of faith, I see a beautiful Child with an inexpressible smile, with the sweetest look, and with hands filled with graces. When I ask this beautiful Child who He is and why He is present in this white Host, I hear a voice, more melodious than all heaven's concerts, answering me: "I am Thérèsita's Jesus; I have just left heaven to visit the little flower garden she has been preparing for Me for three months. I have a great desire to walk in it and to take my rest in it. Thérèsita's heart is about to become my heaven; I prefer her heart to the throne of gold and precious stones destined for me up above. I will never leave the pretty lily cradle[3] where I'm going to sleep. . . . I'll remain there forever. . . as long as the lilies don't fade. . . for sin alone can make me leave it, and sin alone can fade the lilies of her heart!"

This is what Jesus answers when I question Him for May 8,

1884, this is what He says to me, but what He will say to Thérèse, oh! this will be even more beautiful still! My darling, listen well to Him when He is in your little garden; listen to Him, and then speak in your turn.[4] Marie will have to tell you all you should ask for, and don't forget me. Tell little Jesus that all my intentions are yours, that He must answer all my requests on that Day of Days, the most beautiful of days for me also!. . .

Adieu, my darling. Let us think of nothing but Jesus![5]

Your Agnes

* Autograph.

1. The instructions were given by Abbé Domin, chaplain of the Abbey. Thérèse wrote a résumé of these instructions in a notebook (see integral text in Mss. II, p. 22). From these conferences there comes an atmosphere of fear in contrast with the tone of Sister Agnes' letters to little Thérèse.
2. This was Mother Saint-Exupère, prioress at the Abbey. Thérèse wrote "During our retreat, we missed many instructions because the Prioress died and Monsieur l'abbé Domin was not able to spend time with us."
3. The "lily cradle" is the theme of the prayers beginning the month of May in the "little copybook" of preparation; and the lily is the only flower kept from May 1 to 7. For these seven days, the child totaled 245 sacrifices and 320 short aspirations.
4. In fact, few were the words spoken between Jesus and Thérèse on May 8 (see Ms. A, p. 76).
5. This letter must have been given to Thérèse on May 7, when the "*whole family*" came to visit her (Ms. A, p. 76). Pauline (Sister Agnes) sent her a "*beautiful picture*" through Marie: "I never grew tired of admiring it and having it admired by everybody!. . ." (Ms. A, p. 76). This picture has not been identified.

LC 32

May 6, 1884

→ LT lost

From P. Pichon to Thérèse.

Thérèse met P. Pichon in August 1883 (see p. 174). At the time of her First Communion, she shared her joy with him: "I had written to good Père Pichon, recommending myself to his prayers, telling him that soon I would be a Carmelite and then he would be my director. . . . Marie gave me a *letter from him*; truly, I was too blessed! . . ." (Ms. A, p. 76.) Five years later, P. Pichon recalled these confidences: 'You give me great joy, recalling my letter for your First Communion. Doesn't my adoption of you date from then?'" (To Thérèse, LC 116, August 16, 1889.)

† Paris, May 6

My good and blessed Child,

I am placing my good angel in charge of accompanying you to the Holy Table on Thursday and presenting you to Jesus, adorning you to please Him, and, above all, giving you to Him forever.[1] But I don't cede my place to him in the midst of all those who are praying for you, nor my right to share in your joy, still less the share you promise me in your prayers. Your dear little letter pleased me very much.[2] I was very happy to find in it the promise of a very childlike remembrance on this beautiful day when He, who will be the God of your heart, will be unable to refuse you anything. Ask for yourself, along with me, the grace of loving Him as much as He wills to be loved by your heart, and for myself a great number of souls to save.

I will offer the Adorable Victim[3] at the altar for you and your Pauline.

I bless you just as a father blesses his youngest child on the day of her First Communion.

A. P.[4]

* Autograph.

1. See her First Communion prayer: "I love you and give myself to You forever!" (Ms. A, p. 77).
2. Père Almire Pichon did not keep any of Thérèse's letters.
3. See Ms. A, p. 76: "What gave me the greatest joy in his letter was the sentence: 'Tomorrow, I will offer Mass for you and your Pauline.'" Thérèse was quoting freely.
4. The initials of Almire Pichon. This letter was accompanied by a holy picture which has not been identified.

A sky without clouds
(May 1884 - May 1885)
Age eleven and twelve

Although this year (May 1884 - May 1885) was outstanding for the spiritual heights attained by Thérèse as a child, we have only a few words written by her on the back of holy pictures and hardly any letters. Later on, we shall point out that what was expressed in words by her cannot be compared with what she actually lived. Ten years later, her Autobiography explained the compactness of the mystical experience connected with the following dates:

May 8, 1884: her First Communion: "It was no longer a look, it was a fusion" between Jesus and Thérèse (Ms. A, p. 77).

May 22, Ascension Day: her second Communion (not to be confused with the solemn renewal, May 21, 1885): "It is no longer I who live, it is Jesus who lives in me!. . . " (Ms. A, p. 79; Mss. II, p. 24).

June 14: reception of the "sacrament of Love" (Ms. A, p. 80), her Confirmation: Céline never forgot the "fervor," the "holy inebriation" of her little sister during those days (NPPO, 1908, p. 4).

In the course of the year 1884, there was another Holy Communion, which gave rise in her heart to "a great desire for suffering" (Ms. A, p. 79): "Oh! Jesus! unspeakable Sweetness! change all consolations of this earth into bitterness for me!. . . " (Ms. A, p. 79).

This desire was answered later. For the moment, however, Thérèse enjoyed peace: "The period of my First Communion has remained engraved in my heart as a memory without any clouds. . . my spiritual trials left me for almost a whole year" (Ms. A, p. 73).

At the Abbey, Thérèse spent the school year of 1884–1885 in the second class (orange class), in the first division. She had as her main teacher, Mother Saint-Léon (d. 1938). "I succeeded very well in my studies, was almost always first, and my greatest success was in history and composition. All my teachers looked upon me as a very intelligent pupil" (Ms. A, p. 82).

Complementing these memories, her correspondents' letters draw attention to Thérèse on vacation in the country at Saint-Ouen-le-Pin, at the seashore, and at Trouville-Deauville.

Thérèse is described as "radiant with joy" (LD, August 7, 1884), "very happy here" (LD, May 4, 1885).

→Read Ms. A, pp. 76–84.

LT 12 **From Thérèse to her sister Marie.**

May 8, 1884

On the back of a lace picture, "The Shepherdess," Thérèse wrote in pencil:

To my dear little Marie, souvenir of the First Communion of

Your little daughter, Thérèse

* Autograph.

LT 13 **From Thérèse to Céline.**

May 8, 1884

On the back of a holy picture painted by Sister Agnes of Jesus, she wrote in pencil:

Souvenir of my First Communion for dear little Céline from her little sister,

Thérèse

* Autograph.

LC 33 *From Mother Marie de Gonzague to Thérèse.*

May 8, 1884

Mother Marie de Gonzague to her dear child, her Thérésita!... Souvenir of a day twice dear to the mother's heart of her beloved children!!!

Her Thérèse received her Jesus for the first time.

Her Agnes was united to the Spouse of virgins, to the King of kings!! blessed day for her heart!

May 8, 1884[1]

* Autograph.

1. These words are written on an envelope; the enclosed holy picture has disappeared and has not been identified.

LT 14 **From Thérèse to Marie Guérin.**

1883-1885

These words were written in pencil on the back of a holy picture. Date is unknown.

To little Marie from her little sister[1] Thérèse.

* Autograph.

1. The title "sister" is frequently used between the Martin and Guérin children.

LT 15 **From Thérèse to Céline.**

1883-1885

These words were written in ink on the back of a holy picture. Date is unknown.

To my darling little Céline. Souvenir from her little sister, who loves her with all her heart.[1]

Thérèse

* Autograph.
1. Transcribing this text on a sheet of paper Sister Geneviève wrote: "We were at the Abbey." Céline left the boarding school the first days of August 1885.

LC 34 *From Mother Marie de Gonzague to Thérèse.*
After June 21, 1884-1885

Thérésita, my angel, you don't have a relic. Poor Mother Marie de Gonzague, who loves her Benjamin, has been blessed by her venerated Mother Prioress,[1] who gave her two reliquaries as a feast-day gift.[2] I am placing one in my dear little one's hands and my heart in her heart.

Sister Marie de Gonzague
r.c.ind.

* Autograph.
1. Mother Geneviève of St. Teresa, prioress from January 31, 1883 to February 3, 1886.
2. June 21, feast of St. Aloysius Gonzaga. We don't know the content of the reliquaries.

LC 35 *From Marie to Thérèse.*
Summer 1884 (?)
Conjectured date; see note 2.

My Benjamin, are you always behaving well with Marie?[1] Enjoy yourself and don't give too much trouble to Aunt.

This is my will.

Your godmother, who loves you dearly.[2]

* Autograph.
1. Marie Guérin.

2. The year 1883 seems to be out of the question, according to this note. Marie was not with Thérèse from March 23-28. For the year 1884, there are two assumptions: 1) from June 23-29, Marie was away on a retreat with P. Pichon at Vitré (Ile-et-Vilaine); 2) in August 1884, Céline and Thérèse were on vacation at *Saint-Ouen-le-Pin*. See following LD.

Saint-Ouen-le-Pin

"This was over five miles from the town,"[1] *Céline tells us. "We used to go there and spend a whole day in September, gathering hazelnuts on the property of Mme. Fournet, Aunt Guérin's mother. . . . We went in a large wagon, and we left with the Guérin family. . . . It was a modest little house on a farm which was rented to some farmers, but we enjoyed ourselves there very much. . . . At Saint-Ouen everything was rustic, even to the dishes, and this pleased us"* (*see* G/NPHF, p. 553).

"Thérèse stayed there for several days with our aunt and our cousins Jeanne and Marie Guérin. She was there in order to get a change of air during a spell of whooping cough. Thérèse was very much interested in the ponds and the little brook on the farm, and, beyond the meadows, a tiny little woods, perhaps a section of a former park, called 'le Theil.' This woods was often the goal of our walks. We also went, but not very frequently, into the village by way of a pretty little road which was well shaded" (Sister Geneviève, Notes on Thérèse's trips, p. 1).

Were she to return today to Saint-Ouen-le-Pin, Thérèse would have to make very few alterations on a sketch she signed on August 8, 1884. Seated in the meadow beyond the brook, with her back to the "le Theil" woods,

she drew very carefully the minutest details of the main building on the farm. During this time, too, Céline sketched all the buildings along the entrance road to the left, and, in the background, the "owner's house." On the following page, a portrait of Jeanne Guérin doing some sketching. Marie Guérin has even left us a sketch of the dog Biribi, a very feeble dog, indeed!

The site is typical of the Auge countryside with its gently sloping foothills and those "distances" mentioned at times in Thérèse's writings; apple orchards, rich meadows, wooded crests, in a word, Normandy at its best.

Describing the property, Céline wrote: "It spread out into the surrounding countryside which was studded with castles that we could see in the distance" (G/NPHF, p. 553). *In one of these castles, no doubt the most ostentatious,*[2] *less than half a mile from the Fournet home, François Guizot had died about ten years previously (September 12, 1874). It was there that Louis-Phillipe's former minister had written several of his works on French history. He rests in the parish cemetery.*

Thérèse was at Saint-Ouen-le-Pin during the last days of July 1885. These vacations in the country are undoubtedly to be counted among the most pleasant of her childhood because of her love of nature.

1. *Saint-Ouen-le-Pin* was about six miles from Lisieux; there were 196 inhabitants there in 1968.
2. Ancient Cistercian Abbey of the XIIth century. In ruins from the XIVth to XVIth centuries, it was rebuilt in the XVIIth, and transformed into a castle by Guizot.

LD *From Mme. Guérin to her husband.* (Extracts).

August 7, 1884

Saint-Ouen-le-Pin, August 7, 1884

My dear little Husband,

We are all very happy here. Thérèse's face is always radiant with joy. She is enjoying herself very much at sketching; she and Marie have undertaken to do the house on the farm. I am *Mademoiselle* Godard,[1] and I supervise my pupils closely. Like her, I am very severe but also very much inclined to compliments,[2] so I see two future *artists*[3] in my two pupils. Céline and Jeanne are doing another landscape. They are sketching the buildings on the farm, taken from different angles. We're very fortunate for having discovered this delightful distraction, for the heat is such that we can't dream of going very far. Yesterday morning, we went to Mass at seven. It was charming. We were witnesses, it seemed, of nature's awakening. In the afternoon, we went with Ernest[4] to Mourerie, and we were present, in the evening, at the milking of the cows. We go there every evening and each has a glass of very warm milk. I think this is a good remedy for the whooping cough, although I still can't see any great change in our patients. However, I think Thérèse is coughing less frequently.[5] She is throwing up *very, very little*, and last night she did so only twice, one spell being very, very bad; she slept very well. Her appetite is always good. Jeanne seems to be much better also. Léonie's coughing seems to me the most persistent, although her night was good. We received, yesterday, M. Martin's short note, as well as the fishhooks and the lines. I beg you to thank him for us for his kindness. Céline caught a small trout. . . . This morning, Mme. Grip gave us a whole dissertation on her honeybees. She even gave our children some wax cells where the bees place the honey. This piece had fallen to the ground and she picked it up. The children were in admiration over the work of the bees.

Try to convince Marie Martin to come and see us on Saturday evening. We can easily put her up, as well as yourself.

See you soon, dear little husband. All our girls and I kiss you tenderly with all our heart.

Your devoted wife,
C. Guérin

* Autograph.

1. Céline was taking instructions in art from her since 1882. It was difficult for Thérèse not to share these lessons with her sister at this time. "I was thirteen," Sister Geneviève (Céline) tells us, "when my father told me he was going to have me take drawing lessons. We were together, Thérèse and I, and I saw her eyes light up with envy, expecting to receive the same favor. In fact, my father said: 'And you, my little Queen, would you like to learn how to draw?' She was about to answer when Marie spoke up, saying that the house was already cluttered with 'smearings' that had to be framed, and she won the case. Thérèse didn't answer, and we did not think about what she was experiencing. Later on, some weeks before her death, she recalled this incident, and she told me that she experienced such a strong desire to complain that she wondered still, after so many years, how she had the strength to resist it" (Sister Geneviève, NPPO, 1908, p. 77). A similar testimony was given by Sister Marie of the Sacred Heart (Marie). (See PO, 1653; PA, 819.)
2. She had written: "Very, very good, C. Guérin," on Thérèse's sketch, August 8, 1884. Similar sketches are in copybooks of Céline Martin and Marie Guérin, same date.
3. She mistakenly writes: "*satistes*" for "*artistes.*"
4. No doubt, Ernest Maudelonde, Mme. Guérin's nephew, age twenty-two.
5. Thérèse had been coughing very much ever since the month of May (Ms. A, p. 76). On July 12, 1884, Mother Geneviève, prioress at the Lisieux Carmel, wrote M. Martin: "We are praying with all our heart for your charming little Thérèse's cure so that we may have the consolation of seeing her take up the offering (at the ceremony for Sister Agnes of Jesus' reception of the Veil, July 16). Around the same date, Sister Agnes wrote to Marie: "I would really like to get

some news about my dear little collector. I can hear her coughing from here and this causes me grief."

LC 36 *From Sister Agnes of Jesus to Thérèse.*

December, 1884 (?) Uncertain date; see note 1.

→ LT lost

J. M. J. T.

Long live Jesus!

Dear little Thérèse,

Your pretty blue letter pleased me very much, and even more so because it was written *perfectly.* I'm coming to scribble (for I haven't the time to write so well) a little letter for you, not *blue* but *black*, and I am making it a reward for your letter!...

Always be good, my darling. It's not enough to make pretty little cribs in your garden.[1] This is very good, no doubt, but the prettiest crib must be in your heart. Little Jesus loves to come and rest there, and this not only for a certain time but forever. A little heart, very innocent, very gentle, filled with good will and the desire to please Him, oh! what a delightful home, what a pleasant crib for Him!...

Little darling, from now on place all your joy in goodness, in love for Jesus! Later on, you will see from the experience of all things that on earth we cannot be truly happy except with this only joy.

Adieu, my dear little girl. I give you all the kisses of my heart.

Your Agnes

* Autograph.

1. One of these miniature cribs was rebuilt in the garden at Les Buissonnets. The mention of cribs shows this letter was written around Christmas time. The year remains uncertain.

LC 37 *From Mother Marie de Gonzague to Thérèse.*
1884-1885 Date unknown.

Mother Marie de Gonzague sends the tenderest kisses from her heart to her little Thérésita.

* Autograph.

LC 38 *From Sister Agnes of Jesus to Thérèse.*
End of January
1885 (?)

(with a thousand congratulations and a million kisses, five hundred thousand of which, that is, one half, are for my little Benoni).[1]

I thank you both for your little letters and holy pictures[2] of January 21. . . . I asked St. Agnes to bless and protect my beloved little daughters all through their life.

* Autograph.
1. Ben-Oni, the name originally given to Benjamin, Jacob's twelfth son (Genesis 35:18). Though it meant "son of my sorrow," the Martin-Guérin family used it for Thérèse in the sense of the "favored" one. See LT 95, note 3, July - August 1889.
2. These letters and holy pictures have been lost. Though this paragraph is written to Céline and Thérèse, this letter without a heading is preserved in the collection of letters to Thérèse; this is why we place it in the category "LC."

Trouville

It was on August 8, 1878, we may recall (see LD, August 9, 1878), when Thérèse first saw the sea at Trouville. She was then only five and a half. She returned there frequently with her father and sisters for one-day outings.

In 1885, 1886, and 1887, M. Guérin wanted to provide his daughters, especially Marie, who was experiencing difficulties in adolescent development, with fresh air at the seashore. He used to rent a villa for a whole month at the seashore, avoiding the busy season (July -August). Thérèse and her sisters were invited to share these vacations with their cousins. It is easy to reconstruct the framework and the chronology of these stays at the country, thanks especially to the Guérin Chronicle,[1] Thérèse's Autobiography, and the Correspondence of both families. We are able, then, to determine Thérèse's four stays on the Côte Fleurie:

1) *from May 3 to 10, 1885, at the Chalet des Roses, 17, quai de la Touques at Deauville;[2]*
2) *the last ten days of September 1885, at the Villa Rose, rue Charlemagne (today, 25, rue Victor-Hugo), at Trouville;*
3) *the first days of July 1886, at the Chalet des Lilas (today "La Pluie de Roses"), 29, rue de la Cavée, at Trouville;*
4) *from June 20 to 26, 1887, at the same villa, Trouville.*

Seven letters (May 1 to 10, 1885)[3] offer much information, such as is usually found in a diary. It is enough here to recall the occupations and the outings of the "ladies" at Maison Colombe.

Mme. Guérin was in charge of four girls, whose average

age was fifteen and a half: Jeanne (seventeen), her older daughter; Marie (fifteen), her younger daughter; Thérèse (twelve and a half), her niece; and Marcelline, the maid (almost nineteen). Mme. Guérin wrote to Marie, Thérèse's oldest sister: "We are doing some needlework; we cook; and today we are doing the washing." (See LD, May 4, 1885, letter to Marie Martin.) She could also have added: ". . . and we are doing some sketching." We can easily picture this little "blonde girl" (LC 41), seated in the garden,[4] concentrated on reproducing in her sketchbook the complicated architecture of the Chalet des Roses, flanked by its "tour de Mme. Malboroug" (LC 39).

The first goal of their outings was evidently the seashore; at times, Deauville; and most frequently, Trouville. They had to take the ferryboat at the end of the Quai de la Touques. They passed by the Casino, still closed at this season, and then went along the bank as far as Roches Noires. The children's attention was drawn to the excessive activity in the port: the disembarking of the passengers from Le Havre (over a hundred and thirty-two thousand for the year 1885),[5] the departure of the fishing boats (Trouville had as many as 420 boats, with 650 workmen). What an attraction it was for them to buy live fish at the market!

At times, these young girls explored the locality, with its labyrinthine little streets ascending the hill dotted with little green patches of vegetation. Trouville's stable population, usually about six thousand inhabitants, welcomed as many as fifteen thousand visitors during the months of July and August. The first in the Calvados department to set up spas, it had become famous in the past sixty years through the paintings of Ch. Mozin.

Regarding monumental structures, Trouville has nothing to offer but two churches: Notre-Dame-des-

Victoires in pseudo-Byzantine style, with a flight of steep steps from which one can look out upon the quays and the sea; and Notre-Dame-de-Bon-Secours, the main door of which is a replica of that at Trinity church in Paris. Thérèse frequently attended services in both these churches.

And, now, an interesting question: What was Thérèse's preference: the countryside or the sea? Perhaps her answer is in her words: "I choose all!" (see Ms. A, p. 27). This is how she described the house of her dreams at age fourteen: "If my dreams come true, one day I'll go to live in the country. When I think of my plans, I am transported in spirit to a charming little house or chalet, well-lighted by the sun; all its rooms face the sea, for my little house is in a village at the seashore.... My garden is rather large... behind my garden is a field with a stable.... My greenhouse is always filled with the most beautiful flowers. I have a little boat so that I can sail, from time to time, on the sea." (Composition exercise, without any date; beginning of 1887?)

1. It contains some errors in dates and names, corrected in the Appendix, volume II.
2. And not Trouville as the greater part of the letters in May 1885 indicate, with the exception of those from Mme. Guérin.
3. Five are quoted in whole or in part; the others have no interesting material for the present *Correspondence.*
4. Unlike the farm at *Saint-Ouen-le-Pin,* the *Chalet des Roses* underwent many changes over the years! It became the *Chalet Bellevue,* and in 1972 it was in ruins. The former *jardin Colombe* is now a *café-bar* called: "*Au petit Navire.*"
5. According to the Guide de Normandy (Hachette), 1887, p. 306.

LC 39 *From Marie Guérin to Thérèse.*

May 1, 1885

Trouville, May 1, 1885, Friday

My dear Thérèse,

I'm writing you at this moment from our little garden, in the shade of a parasol which M. Colombe[1] lent us. All through these past days, the good weather permitted us to go out, but today the bad weather is inviting us to stay at home. We are enjoying ourselves very much; the day before yesterday,[2] we went to the *Roches Noires* (black boulders) with Mme. Maudelonde[3] to get some sea water. I assure you it's no good, for I took half a glass of it yesterday and felt sick to my stomach all morning long. We returned from our outing, walking along the seashore, and it was a delightful spectacle. Yesterday morning, we settled down on the balcony, and we sketched a ship; in the afternoon, we went to see the beach at Deauville, and when seeing the shellfish, we thought of you; I returned very much fatigued by my walk. We were at Notre-Dame-des-Victoires[4] this morning for Mass; the flight of steps is very steep, so steep that I fell. Everybody is falling this week. The day before yesterday, Mamma fell when sitting on her chair; I must say the chairs are very light. Today, Jeanne took a tumble when reaching over for her work, and I just fell, slipping on the pavement in the garden. We returned from Mass by way of the fish-shop, and we bought some little fish. We saw a steamboat arriving when we were getting off the ferry; and, on the quay, we had a lot of trouble holding on our hats, and I was even afraid I'd be carried off into the Touques river. Mamma bought us some straw sunbonnets; mine is trimmed in white, Jeanne's, in red. We weren't able to buy two the same. Our lodgings are very good here; our little garden is larger than we thought it would be; the

house is poorly arranged. I won't describe it to you because I believe you will be coming with little Father[5] on Sunday. Like Mme. Malboroug, we climb up into the tower each day to watch the steamboat leaving, and I don't even get dizzy. Tell Céline I'm not forgetting her and that I'll write her the next time; it's only that my hand is tired out because I have written to Céline and Hélène.[6] Tell me in your next letter how Louise Renier is,[7] for it appears she is very sick; tell me, too, when the First Communion will be.

Adieu, dear little Thérèse. Kiss Uncle, Marie, Léonie, and Céline for me and be assured of the sincere affection I have for you.

Your little sister,
Marie
enf. de Marie

Till Sunday

* Autograph.

1. M. Alphonse Colombe (d. 1889), who had graciously placed his chalet at the disposition of the Guérin family.
2. April 29. ChrIG p. 34, seems to suggest this as the date of arrival; however, this date should be set at several days before April 29.
3. Sister of Mme. Guérin.
4. Trouville parish; taking the ferryboat cut the distance down to about half a mile.
5. Busy at his pharmacy during the week, M. Guérin joined his family on Sundays, usually taking along one of his nieces, who never traveled alone, including Marie at age twenty-five.
6. Céline and Hélène Maudelonde, aged twelve and nine respectively, first cousins of the Guérin children.
7. Born October 5, 1881, her mother, *née* Amandine Fosse, was first cousin of Mme. Guérin (on the Fournet side).

LD *From Mme. Guérin to her husband.* (Extracts.)

May 2, 1885

Deauville, May 2, 1885

My dear friend,

. . .

Little Thérèse will be welcome here if you judge it good and if her father allows it. So we expect you on Sunday, the children are counting on it. Now with regard to sleeping, I think I should keep her with me. I would not want to have her stay on the second floor. In any case, you know there is room enough and that we'll be very happy to have one more little girl. However, follow whatever your heart tells you.

. . .

We are expecting you, then, tomorrow with Thérèse at 9:15 in the morning. You know, too, if one of the older ones wants to come with her, being acquainted with our accommodations, you know this is possible. Whatever you do will be all right.

. . .

Au revoir, dear Friend. You can't imagine my joy when writing you this note. Until tomorrow, then. You will come to the High Mass with us; what a joy! We're a little lonely, you know, without our family! We are so accustomed to all being together.

Your devoted wife
C. Guérin

* Autograph.

LC 40 *From Marie to Thérèse.*

May 3, 1885

As agreed upon by M. and Mme. Guérin, Thérèse arrived at Deauville on Sunday, accompanied by her uncle.

Sunday, May 3

Well, Thérèse, I wasn't intending to write you, but here I am.

I gave you all my messages in Aunt's letter[1] so perfectly that there is nothing more to say. What to do? Ah! I'm really a fairy godmother who can refuse her big baby[2] nothing. Here I am, then, freed from my baby! This morning, some lovable people were pleased to show an interest in my little nuisance[3] whom they no longer saw at my side. I told them to go to Trouville to see what she had become under her beautiful straw hat.

While awaiting the return of the straw hat and its owner, I must work away and mend her dresses.... What a poor slave Marie is!... Gather some shells for her to fill up the holes when you make some more in your splendid dress with a thousand little pleats.... I am doing my best to take care of your little rabbit. He is well and he sends you all his little jumps as a sign of his love. Today, somebody came to see my beautiful May altar. Guess who? Félicité's sister.[4] She saw mine in the garden, and to please her I had her visit all the May altars in the house. It's too bad there wasn't one in your little garden.

Au revoir, darling big baby. I have to go and pour the soup on the bread. That is altogether different from going out on the beach. It is seven o'clock and Félicité hasn't yet brought back the *Abbey's lover.*[5] Léonie has been there since one o'clock this afternoon. Abbey, my loves!!! If I knew how to compose verses like Pauline, I would compose a pretty romance about it.

Meanwhile, the soup and bonsoir, Thérésion.[6]

* Autograph.

1. This letter reached Deauville on May 4 (not preserved): "nice letter and so comical at the same time," Mme. Guérin said (to M. Guérin, May 5, 1885).
2. See Ms. A, p. 89: "I was still very much of a child in spite of my twelve and a half years."
3. Thérèse.
4. "Félicité" (Marie Hubert) was a maid in the Martin family since 1884. She left them in the winter of 1886-1887 to get married. We don't know her sister's name.

5. Céline? or more likely Léonie. Léonie had finished her schooling there in 1881. She was now twenty-two years old and it seems she was interested in entering the novitiate of the Benedictine nuns. See P. Pichon's letter to Marie, July 4, 1885: "Your beloved Léonie a Benedictine nun! Oh! what good news!" She never went through with this plan.
6. This is the only time this name is used in the correspondence.

LD *From Mme. Guérin to Marie.* (Extracts.)

May 4,
1885

Deauville, May 4, 1885

Dear Marie,

It's only ten o'clock, and I've already read your letter three times.[1] Ah! this is really a letter and above all a very interesting letter. It's an event at the Chalet. My poor worn-out niece really knows how to write a letter, and from her heart, too! Her little aunt thanks her for all her affection, returning it to her a hundredfold. . . .

. . .Don't get the idea we are staying here without any work to do. We're doing some needlework, cooking, and today we are doing the wash. What work for ladies! Our little Thérèse slept perfectly in the beautiful big bedroom, and this morning she looks very good. I told her she had to eat with all her might and that from today I'll not relent in this matter. She seems to be very happy here and she isn't lonesome. The weather is not very good this morning, but yesterday we were able to go to the beach. All our little girls were at the water's edge, waiting for the waves to come in. Thérèse was armed with a spade,[2] and all of them were very happy. We were at High Mass this morning at Trouville, and in the afternoon we attended Vespers at *Bon Secours*. I listened there to a meditation on the rosary such as I had never heard

before. The Curé[3] speaks well, and I admired this way of reciting the rosary very much. You can see, dear Marie, that we really made our Sunday holy, and so God permitted us to have good weather for taking a walk. He rewarded us because during Vespers the rain came down in torrents. But we didn't fall asleep when *singing our psalms* like a certain little inhabitant at Les Buissonnets, who will go down with a crash one of these fine days, perhaps at the very moment when the Curé comes to incense our chapel.[4] I'm always the tease, am I not, dear Marie, but, you see, I do have to tease a little those whom I love very much. . . . Come next week. Keep in mind that we have to return to Lisieux for Thérèse's second Communion, on May 21. Afterwards, we shall not have even a full week here since we shall be returning on the following Thursday or Friday. . . .

Au revoir, very dear Marie. I believe I'll not come to an end with you. I left my letter to take some breakfast. Then we went to the pier to see the little boats leaving, and the sun was smiling at us all the time. . . . Thérèse, Jeanne, and Marie kiss you tenderly and their sisters also. Thérèse isn't forgetting her father and kisses him with all her heart. . . .

Your very devoted aunt,
C. Guérin

Thérèse would very much like to write to her dear Marie, but since she has a slight headache, I have forbidden her to do so. So you will have to be vexed with me. She would have to be racking her brains thinking what to say; that's why I think I did well not to let her.

* Autograph.
1. This letter is lost; see preceding LC, note 1.
2. This was a long and narrow iron spade.
3. Undoubtedly Abbé Le Fournier, pastor of *Bon Secours* since 1882.
4. Her teasing is directed to Marie Martin. The Martin and Guérin families used to attend Vespers at the cathedral of *Saint-Pierre* at Lisieux in one of the little chapels.

5. Thérèse's headaches are mentioned several times during her stay; see Mme. Guérin's letter to her husband, May 5: "Thérèse seems to be very happy. Today, especially, her headache seems to have vanished. I'm always seeing her good and cheerful face." See, too, Jeanne's letter to her father: "Yesterday, we followed your advice, and we were at the Deauville pier. We saw several ships leaving, but Mamma and Thérèse got a little dizzy from the noise and motion of the sea" (May 5, 1885). See below, LT 16. We have, then, good reason to believe that the episode of the "donkey and the little dog," recalled as happening during the vacation of September 1885 (Ms. A, p. 89), should be placed in May. Besides, Céline is absent, and this makes it all the more incomprehensible if it took place in September.

LC 41 *From Sister Agnes of Jesus to Thérèse.*

May 3-10 (?),
1885

Thérèse,

Good day, little Benjamin of my heart. Enjoy yourself very much and kiss Aunt and my little cousins for me.

If you see again the *luminous trail* on the waves of the sea, think of times past, of your old teacher,[1] of Grandmother's[2] *Tirelire*.... All this is far behind, isn't it? But what is always very close to my heart is your little heart.

Adieu, little blonde. Be a pearly little shell yourself,[3] filled with beautiful pearls for your heavenly crown.

Your *petit Paulin* of times past.

Agnes of Jesus
r.c.ind.

* Autograph.

1. Pauline.

2. *La Tirelire aux histoires* by S. W. Belloc. One of the stories, entitled "The Golden Trail," was filled with memories for Pauline and Thérèse; see Ms. A, pp. 48-49. This story describes the scene of a lit-

tle girl sailing on the sea in the golden trail left by the setting sun. Concerning the difficulty of dating this "meditation," see LD, August 9, 1878, note 3.

3. We have already taken note of the reference to shells in LC 39 and 40. When a child, Thérèse loved playing with shells; see LD, October 13, 1877. Some little baskets made from shells are in the collection of her knickknacks as a little girl (Ms. A, p. 90).

LT 16 — From Thérèse to Mme. Guérin. (Fragments.)

May 10-17, 1885

Probably Thérèse returned to Les Buissonnets on Sunday, May 10, accompanying her uncle, M. Guérin.

My dear Aunt,

You told me to write and give you some news about my health. I am better than I was on Sunday; however, I have a constant headache.[1] I hope you are well, Jeanne, too, and that Marie is completely cured.[2]

I am thinking of you often and I remember how good you've been to me. I am not forgetting my little cousins either, and I beg you to tell Marie that I'm not writing her today, but that I will write her the next time so that I will have more things to tell her.

I go on retreat on Sunday evening,[3] the First Communion being set for the 21st; it is now certain that it will not be changed.

Au revoir, dear Aunt. Kiss Jeanne and Marie for me, and keep the biggest kiss for yourself.

Thérèse
enf. des. Sts. Anges[4]

* Three fragments of the autograph.
1. See LD, May 4, 1885, note 5.
2. Marie Guérin had a boil on her neck.
3. The 17th; preparatory retreat for Thérèse's "second Communion."

4. "Child of the Holy Angels," a confraternity which Thérèse joined on May 31, 1882; she was named one of its counselors, December 14, 1884 (*La Petite Thérèse à l' Abbaye,* p.51).

LT 17 — **From Thérèse to her sister Marie.**

May 21, 1885

Words written in pencil on the back of a holy picture painted by Thérèse:

To my dear little Marie,

Souvenir of the second Communion of her little girl, May 21, 1885.

Thérèse

* Autograph.

LC 42 — *From Marie to Thérèse.*

May 26, 1885
→ LT lost

After Thérèse's second Communion, Marie spent a few days on vacation with the Guérins at Deauville. Thérèse could have hoped for a longer visit at Carmel with Pauline, but..."I see, Céline, that you have become a thief in my absence. Thérèse complains that you took up all her visiting time. You just wait! I'll teach you a lesson! Ah! yes, *adieu* to the *misery, adieu* to the torment caused by little Céline, who pinches my cheeks affectionately but is gritting her teeth at me, who never lets me rest, who makes me age two years in one hour by the way she worries me!" (Letter of Marie to Céline, May 26, 1885.)

Poor little Martyr,

You have nothing, then, except disappointments. It's sad. Well, I shall return soon to protect you and to share my visit with

you since I promised you this. We were talking about you this morning when we were taking our chocolate. We're well treated at Aunt's house. That's true! I have remained for the bouquet, and, as a reward for allowing me to leave, I'll bring back a bouquet from your cousins and Aunt on Friday. Aunt is so good to all of us.

The sun is hardly as cheerful at Trouville as it is at Lisieux, dear Thérèse, but, to make up for it, we are laughing in its stead. Yesterday, it was raining from time to time. They wanted to stop me from opening my umbrella, and they were teasing me as much as they could. Poor farmer unaccustomed to wearing her beautiful Sunday clothes every day; she even has to protect herself from the fog. Well, it just can't be done. Oh! I am unhappy here in this chalet, which is so highly praised! Fortunately, under my window, I have silent little boats that say nothing to me. . . . How good it is to see them. They open their sails, and, then, very softly, very softly, they go very far away, perhaps to catch some beautiful fish which God has made for us. God has done many things for us. So, little Thérèse, we must do very many good things for Him also. Let us go with our little boat to fish for pearls. There are many beautiful ones at the bottom of the sea which we are crossing. When Céline is a thief and when she tells her secrets at the Carmel, cast your net, dear little fisherman. A beautiful big pearl!

Adieu, Thérèse. Your letter isn't as long as Céline's, but I must think of Léonie. You will not be jealous now, you little rascal, or never again Marie's bed.

Jeanne and Marie kiss you. I gave them your pictures. You see that I didn't forget your messages; they thank you for them and find them very pretty.[1]

Marie

Aunt is asking if you've finished the one for her which you began at Trouville.

* Autograph.

1. These were pictures probably painted by Thérèse.

"In the swaddling clothes of childhood" (*Ms. A, p. 97*)
(May 1885-November 1886)
Age twelve and thirteen

From May 17 to 21, 1885, Thérèse made the preparatory retreat for her "second Communion" at the Abbey. "What M. l'Abbé [Domin] told us was frightening. He spoke about mortal sin, and he described a soul in the state of sin and how much God hated it." (Thérèse's retreat notes.) Coming at a time when she was in a weakened physical state (see LT 16, note 1), this teaching on salvation, mortal sin, death, judgment, and a good confession, etc., gave rise in Thérèse to "the terrible malady of scruples. . . . A person would have to pass through this martyrdom in order to understand it well; it is impossible for me to say what I suffered for a year and a half. . . ." (Ms. A, p. 84).

Her oldest sister Marie became her "sole adviser": "It was Marie who guided me, consoled me, and aided me in the practice of virtue" (Ms. A, p. 88). Her godmother had to have very much patience to listen each evening to the tearful confession of her little sister's scruples (Ms. A, p. 84). Thérèse seemed to be sinking more and more into childishness. She became "really unbearable because of her extreme touchiness" (Ms. A, p. 97).

All happiness, however, was not banished from her life. In July 1885, we see her "really happy" at Saint-Ouen-le-Pin (LD, July 29, 1885). In September, during her father's trip to Central Europe, Thérèse was "happy at Trouville" in Céline's company (Ms. A, p. 89).

But in October 1885, she could not become accustomed to making the trip to the boarding school without her "inseparable Céline" (Ms. A, p. 85). She soon became sick through sadness. Before the end of the second quarter, M. Martin had to take his daughter out of

the boarding school. She was only thirteen. She had to complete her studies by taking special lessons from Mme. Papinau (LT 19, note 1, June 26, 1886).

Even at Trouville, in July 1886, she felt that she was out of her element at her aunt Guérin's house because she could not do without her godmother. She had to be taken back to Les Buissonnets after two or three days (LC 45, July 13, 1886).

We can easily imagine her amazement when she learned, shortly afterward, of Marie's coming departure for the Carmel. She was about to lose "the only support that attached her to life!. . ." (Ms. A, p. 90). The last feast day of her older sister, August 15, was very sad at Les Buissonnets (see the two LD for this date).

Doubly sad was the farewell trip to Alençon. On October 7, 1886, Léonie, who was blindly searching for her own vocation, unexpectedly entered the Poor Clares of that city. "She was at port!" she thought (LD, October 15, 1886).

On October 15, Marie crossed the threshold of the cloister without any real enthusiasm: "I have found God's mercy too bitter at times, but we must nevertheless respond to it no matter how hard it may be." (Letter of Marie to Mme. Guérin, 1886.)

And so, "from the joyous and large family at Les Buissonnets there remained only the two last children. . . ." (Ms. A, p. 92). Humanly speaking, there was no escape for Thérèse.

But, just as in 1883, grace came to the aid of nature. After an insistent prayer to her four little brothers and sisters in heaven, Thérèse was freed from her scruples: "Very soon peace flooded my soul with its delightful waves" (Ms. A, p. 93).

However, this was still not her "complete conversion"

(Ms. A, p. 98). She was still to cry "like a Magdalene" (Ms A, p. 97). And it is in tears that this part of the Correspondence comes to an end (LC 46, November 1886).

→*Read Ms. A, pp. 84–97.*

LD *From Mme Guérin to her husband.* (Extracts.)

July 29, 1885

St. Ouen, July 29, 1885

My dear Friend,

Yesterday, we received some charming letters from Marie and Pauline.[1] Marie is always the same. She has a way of telling things which is proper to herself alone. I think I will not be able to answer her before the mailman arrives. Kiss her for all of us and Céline as well.[2] Jeanne would like to know who won the ball of wool. Léonie is a very good girl. Had you seen her yesterday taking care of grandpapa and grandmamma,[3] you would have been charmed with your niece. She shows me very much affection, and she shares little confidences with me. I have just allowed all four of them to make a tour of the property by way of the field, the meadow, and the Theil woods; they left filled with delight. Mme. Papinau's[4] lessons are falling a little behind; however, we should take advantage of the country. They've neglected their homework and lessons for only a few days. Besides, Marie and Thérèse are enjoying themselves very much. Thérèse is delightfully happy. Mamma was telling me yesterday that she had never seen Thérèse so gay, with her face so frankly happy. Yesterday, she and Marie came home all decked out in little bouquets. Marie had cornflowers, Thérèse had forget-me-nots. All was perfectly arranged. They were wearing their Breton aprons, with well-made bouquets at each of the cor-

ners, on their heads, at the end of their pigtails, and even on their shoes. One was Rosette, the other Bluette. . . .

Your devoted wife,
C. Guérin

* Autograph.
1. These letters were not preserved.
2. Only Léonie and Thérèse were on vacation at *Saint-Ouen-le-Pin* at this time, with Jeanne and Marie Guérin.
3. M. and Mme. Fournet, parents of Mme. Guérin.
4. Regarding this teacher, see LT 19, note 1, June 26, 1886. These lessons must have included Marie Guérin: ". . . almost always ailing" (Ms. A, p. 89), she hardly ever went to the Abbey, which she left definitively in August 1885. It is possible that Thérèse was sharing her homework with her cousin; judging from the sudden interruption in her school copybooks, from April 29 to October 8, 1885, Thérèse does not seem to have returned to the Abbey after she made her second Communion, during the third quarter.

LT 18 **From Thérèse to M. Martin.**

August 25, 1885

This was written for the feast of St. Louis. M. Martin had gone on a tourist trip to the Balkans through Central Europe (August 22? to October). He received this letter in Vienna, Austria. Thérèse decorated it by sewing a flower on it, with these words surrounding the flower: "A reseda plucked from my garden," a patch of ground she cultivated at Les Buissonnets.

My dear little Papa,

If you were at Lisieux, today is when we should wish you a happy feast; but since you are not here, I want just the same and all the more to wish you for your feast very much happiness and, especially, very much joy on your trip. I trust, dear little Father,

that you are enjoying yourself very much and that you are happy on your travels. I'm thinking of you continually, and I'm praying to God to give you much pleasure and that you return soon in good health. Dear Papa, Pauline composed some pretty stanzas for your feast, so that I would recite them on your feast day,[1] but since I can't do this, I'm going to write them for you:[2]

Les Souhaits d'une petite Reine pour
la fête de son Papa-Roi.

Si j'étais petite Colombe
Papa sais-tu bien où j'irais?
Ton coeur serait mon nid, ma tombe
Là je resterais à jamais.

Si je m'appelais hirondelle
Bien souvent pendant les beaux jours
Je viendrais reposer mon aile
Père à l'abri de ton amour.

Si j'étais petit rouge-gorge
Je resterais dans ton jardin
De ta main le moindre grain d'orge
Me deviendrait un vrai festin.

Si j'étais rossignol sauvage
Je quitterais vite mon bois
Pour venir en ce frais bocage
Chanter tous mes airs à la fois.

Et si j'étais petite étoile
Je voudrais toujours être au soir
A cette heure où le jour se voile
Pour t'offrir un rayon d'espoir.

Longtemps à travers ta fenêtre
Je brillerais de mille feux
Et ne voudrais point disparaître
Sans te parler un peu des Cieux.

Et si j'étais un bel archange
Aux ailes toutes garnies d'or
Papa si j'étais petit ange
Vers toi je prendrais mon essor.

Je te montrerais ma Patrie
Dans un songe mystérieux
Je te dirais après la vie
Pour toi ce trône lumineux.

Si tu voulais de blanches ailes
Je t'en apporterais des Cieux
Et vers les rives éternelles
Nous nous envolerions tous deux.

Mais je n'ai point d'aile qui brille
Je ne suis point un Séraphin
Je suis une petite fille
Qu'on tient encore par la main.

Je suis une timide aurore
Un modeste bouton de fleur
Le rayon qui me fait éclore
Cher petit Papa c'est ton coeur!

En grandissant je vois ton âme
Toute pleine du Dieu d'amour
Cet exemple béni m'enflamme
Et je veux te suivre à mon tour.

Je veux devenir sur la terre
Ta joie, ta consolation
Je veux t'imiter Petit Père
Toi si tendre si doux, si bon.

J'aurais bien autre chose à dire
Mais il faut enfin s'arrêter
Papa donne moi ton sourire
Sur mon front dépose un baiser.

Au revoir, beloved Papa. Your Queen, who loves you with her whole heart.

Thérèse

* Autograph.

1. We have about ten of these poems (1881–1888) composed by Pauline (then Sister Agnes of Jesus) to be recited by Thérèse to M. Martin on January 1 or August 25. Whatever their literary value may be, these pieces merit attention insofar as they influenced the attitude of Thérèse as a child and adolescent towards her father. We still see traces of them in her letters to her father when she was a postulant (1888–1889); for example, LT 58, July 31, 1888. When in the infirmary in Carmel, Thérèse recited some stanzas of these poems (see DE/G, p. 631, number 8).
2. We see some differences when comparing the poem with the LT 1948 edition (see pp. 50–51). These differences appeared in the copy of the poem in CMG III, pp. 99-101. In the notebook there are some corrections made by Mother Agnes of Jesus, which are still evident. Sister Geneviève transcribed the poem in ink. The first edition omitted the tenth stanza, here lines 54–57, because at age twelve and a half, Thérèse should no longer be considered as a "little girl, whom you are still holding by the hand."

[The following is a literal translation of the above poem.]

The Wishes of a little Queen for
the feast of her Papa-King

If I were a little Dove
Papa, do you know where I'd go?
Your heart would be my nest, my tomb
There I'd stay forever.

If I were called a Swallow
Very often during beautiful days
I'd come to rest my wings
Father, in the shelter of your love.

If I were a little Robin
I'd remain in your garden
From your hand the smallest grain of corn
Would be for me a real feast.

If I were a wild Nightingale
I'd quickly leave my woods
To come into this fresh grove
To sing all my tunes at once.

And if I were a little star
I'd always want to be out at night
At the hour when the day grows dark
To offer you a ray of hope.

A long time through your window
I'd shine with a thousand fires
And I'd not want to disappear
Without speaking a little about heaven.

If I were a beautiful Archangel
With wings all garnished in gold
Papa, if I were a little angel
Towards you I'd take my flight.

I'd show you my Homeland
In a mysterious dream
I would tell you that after life
For you, this luminous throne.

If you wanted white wings
I'd bring you some from heaven
And toward the eternal shores
Both of us would fly.

But I haven't any wings that shine
I am not a Seraph
I am only a little girl
Whom you still hold by the hand.

I am only a timid dawn
A modest flower-bud
The ray that makes me open
Dear little Papa, is your heart!

While growing up I see your soul
All filled with the love of God
This blessed example inflames me
And I want to follow you in my turn.

I want to become on earth
Your joy, your consolation
I want to imitate you, little Father
You, so tender, so gentle, so good.

I'd have much more to say
But I must finally end
Papa, give me your smile
On my forehead place your kiss.

LD *From Jeanne Guérin to M. Guérin* (Extracts.)

September 29, 1885

September 29

Two more days, dear little Father, and you will no longer be alone without your family in your big house[1] . . . . At the moment, Trouville isn't cheerful; all the visitors have left and the beach is deserted. We spent two hours there yesterday in the shelter of a cabin, where we weren't too badly off. Céline, Marie and Thérèse[2] took there shoes off to play a little at the seashore. It wasn't cold, and today I think the weather will be good . . . . You can come on Thursday if the weather is good, and this would please us, and it would give you two days to spend at Trouville since you have to come to get us on Friday . . . .

Your little daughter,
Jeanne
Enf. de Marie

* Autograph.

1. According to the ChrIG, p. 34, they returned to Lisieux on Wednesday, September 30; according to this statement, it should have been recorded as Friday, October 2.

2. Regarding the stay of Céline and Thérèse at Trouville (*rue Charlemagne*), see Ms. A, p.88. Céline's sketchbook has a seaside scene dated "Trouville, September 23, 1885," with a correction: September 20.

LC 43 *From Sister Agnes of Jesus to Thérèse.*

1885 (?)
→ LT lost

J. M. J. T.

Little Thérèse,

I was very much pleased with your little bottle;[1] when receiving it, I'd have liked to show you my delight. You, who love so much to see me act the baby, would have had a real party. I was fiddling around with my little bottle so much that I ended up breaking half the seal, and then I gathered up the contents to put it away until next week when I'll use it.

Thanks, little Benjamin! You were asking me on Friday if you were still my little girl! Yes, my darling, always, and even more and more. Good Jesus wills it so, and He will never will it otherwise. Pray to Him for me, and let's both of us be very good.

Adieu, my little blonde. I am kissing you with all my heart, and Mother Marie de Gonzague, before me, kisses you tenderly, too.

Tell Léonie I'd be delighted to see her; she must have many things to tell me.[2] Kiss her for me, and Papa, too, and the most unfortunate of all, the one whom I never see, Marie![3] . . .

Good night, Thérésita. Thanks again for your bottle and your good little letter.

Sister Agnes of Jesus,
r.c.ind.

* Autograph.
1. Material, no doubt, for Sister Agnes' painting.

2. With regard to her vocation to the religious life? See LC 40, note 5, May 3, 1885.
3. "This was said playfully; she was the one who took up all the visits" (Sister Geneviève's note). See Ms. A, p. 88: "The visits were only for Marie; Céline and I had permission to come in only at the *end*, to have just enough time to crush our heart . . . ."

LTS 18a **From Thérèse to her father.**

October 15, 1885 Composition homework

My dear little Father,

It's almost three weeks since you've left us.[1] Three weeks is a long time for your little daughter when she is separated from you. If you only knew how I long to have you return. Often I picture your arrival: Everybody is happy; they all hurry to reach the station; they are afraid not to arrive there on time, and so they end up getting there a quarter of an hour early. Finally the train arrives, and we kiss you. You are well and we are all delighted. But more frequently, the picture is black. I imagine that you are delayed, and, instead of the two weeks that we have to wait, it will be a month or even more. Or else you are sick because you don't take enough care of yourself. Dear little Father, you are going to tell me that I am not reasonable, that I am creating idle fancies for myself. This is perhaps somewhat true, but what do you expect since that's the way I'm made. And I believe I'm not totally wrong, for couldn't you be delayed,[2] and, then, admit it, little Father, you never take enough precaution against sickness. You are always saying that there is no danger, but there is a proverb which says: Help yourself, and heaven will help you. But now I see that I'm on the road to giving you a lecture; pardon me, dear Father. It is the fear your little daughter has that you'll get sick that makes her talk this way.

Everyone at home wants you to return; you're being riddled with prayers.[3] We are invoking I don't know how many saints, and, among them, St. Raphael so that he guide your trip as he did that of Tobias and that he bring you back to us in good health.

All of us want you to return as soon as possible. I'm sure that Tom[4] has the same opinion as I, for he is lonesome because of your absence, and I am sure that, for your arrival, he is preparing to wag his tail in the same way that Tobias' dog did[5] and to welcome you with his joyful bounds.

Au revoir, beloved Papa.

I kiss you with all my heart.

Your daughter,
who loves you as much as one can love a Papa like you.

Thérèse
enf. des Ss. Anges[6]

* School copybook.

1. Thérèse speaks below about a wait of two weeks to a month; this brings the duration of the trip to five or seven weeks. This is the approximate length of M. Martin's absence; he had left Lisieux on August 22. Regarding the date of his return, see note 2. It is difficult to separate fact from fiction in Thérèse's composition exercise.
2. See M. Martin: "You ask me when I shall arrive? I hope it will be on Saturday night, at 9:30. But remember that I will be returning from Alençon, for I have to go there next Tuesday." (M. Martin's letter to Marie, from Milan, October 6, 1885.) October 6 was a Tuesday, so "next Tuesday" would be October 13; the Saturday of his return would be the 17th. In this case, Thérèse's composition was written before her father's return. There is another assumption: The date of October 6 is wrong (copyist's error?) and the return would have taken place on October 10; in this case, Thérèse would be simply reliving her former sentiments. We cannot solve the problem because we do not have the autograph copy of M. Martin's letter. ChrIG, p. 99, has "August 22, 1885, M. Martin leaves for Constantinople; October, his return during the first days."

3. See M. Martin: "You tell me that good Mother Marie de Gonzague and the whole Carmel are riddling me with prayers; I want you, in return, to bombard them for me with big boxes of tuna fish." (Letter to Marie, Constantinople, September 11, 1885.)
4. A spaniel that M. Martin had given to Thérèse the preceding year; she had asked for "an animal with hair." He answered: "But, my little Queen, you have animals with hair; you have rabbits." She replied: "That's true, but I'd like an animal with hair that follows me everywhere and jumps around me!" (Sister Geneviève CMG III, p. 102; this is erroneously dated 1885.) Thérèse wrote in her diary: "Tom arrived at our house on June 26, 1884." See LT 91, note 4, May 1889; also AL, May 1969, pp. 14-16.
5. "Your friend Tom is certainly ready to play his role of wagging his tail like Tobias' dog for your return." (Sister Agnes of Jesus to her father, August 24, 1885.) See Tobias 11:9.
6. See LT 16, note 4, May 10-17, 1885.

LTS 18b From Thérèse to a friend.

February 11, 1886

Composition exercise. The friend is as fictitious as is the letter written to her. However, the content appears to be a faithful account of one of Thérèse's "free Thursdays."

Dear little Friend,

Last Thursday,[1] I spent my day very peacefully but also very pleasantly. I didn't go out in the morning. I paid a visit to my little birds[2] and my flowers which I don't pay much attention to because of a lack of time. I learned my composition on French history. In a word, I did a lot of things which would take too long to recount and which, besides, would not interest you very much. We went out around two o'clock in the afternoon. We went with Aunt to see Pauline and we had a pleasant visit. And I assure you it is this that gave me the most joy in my whole day. We made a

little trip afterward by carriage,[3] and then we returned to spend the rest of the afternoon at Aunt's house. We worked and played; we spent our evening very pleasantly. Aunt, Uncle, my cousins, and the young Maudelonde girls[4] came to dine at our house. We enjoyed ourselves very much by playing all sorts of games. Finally, since all things come to an end, we had to separate. This wasn't without regret, but this is the way it is for all things here on earth; troubles and pleasures come to an end. You can see, my dear friend, that I was not bored. However, there is no pleasure without its sorrow. I, too, was sorry, and it was because you were not there for my free Thursday. But I hope you had much joy in spite of our separation and that you will write to tell me about it, for it will interest me very much to know how you spent your free Thursday.

Adieu, dear little friend. I kiss you. How I love you.

Your sister at heart,
Thérèse, aspirant for
the Children of Mary[5]

* School copybook.

1. February 4. On the first page of her homework, Thérèse wrote by mistake: "February 13, Thursday," but on the next page she corrected it to "February 11, Thursday," the correct date.
2. In a diary, Thérèse had written: "I got my linnet in the month of July 1885." She was going to arrange an attic on the second floor into a "garden and aviary"; see Ms. A, p. 90.
3. The carriage was horse-drawn.
4. Marguerite, Céline, and Hélène Maudelonde; see LC 39, note 6, May 1, 1885.
5. Thérèse had just been received into the "Children of Mary" on February 2.

LC 44 *From Marie Guérin to Thérèse.*

June 23, 1886

The Guérin family rented the "*Chalet des Lilas,*" *rue de la Cavée,* Trouville, from June 15 to July 31.

My dear Thérèse,

I understand very well that you haven't been able to write me, and, to prove you are excused, I am coming to talk a little with you. I returned from the market where I met the *demoiselles* Colombe. Up until now, we've been at the beach every afternoon, but today I believe the weather will not permit this; it is very windy and a few drops of rain are falling. If my Thérèse were here, she'd enjoy herself watching the children[1], for we are surrounded on the beach only by babies and they amuse us very much. We have cheerful lodgings, and our large room looks out upon a little garden where Jeanne and I have good games of shuttlecock. My bedroom is charming, and I like it very much. The view from it is delightful; I can see the ocean, especially from the Deauville side, shrimp boats with blue and red sails, boats fishing for eels, and a steamboat arriving. So you see I am cheerful in my little room and our artist[2] would find charming subjects to sketch. I'm not alone in looking at the sea; I have a companion, little Pauline is on my fireplace.[3] You can tell her that, without suspecting it, she is with us at Trouville. How is Madame Papinau?[4] Is she as monotonous as ever? And are your lessons always going well? Tell me all this in your next letter, or tell me this *viva voce*, which would please us much more, for I hope to see you soon.[5]

Adieu, dear little Thérèse. Kiss Godfather[6] for me and my good little Father when you see him. Don't forget your sisters and receive, for yourself, a great part of my kisses.

Your little sister,
Marie

Don't forget my *petit Paulin.*

Trouville on the sea, June 23, 1886

* Autograph.

1. When she was at the Abbey, "Thérèse had a very special affection for the very little pupils in the baby class. . . . Often she would leave the games of the big children and return to watch the babies playing." (*La Petite Thérèse à l'Abbaye,* p. 22.)
2. Céline Martin.
3. Pauline's photograph, no doubt, when she was twenty.
4. See LD, July 29, 1885, note 4.
5. Very likely, Thérèse arrived at Trouville during the early part of July; perhaps even on June 29 or 30, accompanied by her sister Marie. "Uncle will go to see you on Tuesday or Wednesday with Marie, who is making much of it; I will go the next time. How happy I will be to spend a day with you." (Letter from Léonie to Mme. Guérin, June 26, 1886.)
6. M. Martin.

LT 19 From Thérèse to Marie Guérin.

(Fragments.)

June 26,
1886
→LC 44

Aux Buissonnets, Saturday, June 26, 1886

My dear little Marie,

I thank you for being so kind as not to expect me to have written you, and so I'm hastening to answer your nice letter very quickly. You can't imagine how much joy it gave me. I'm very happy that you're well and enjoying yourself very much. I haven't any news from Lisieux that I can give you; I know only that we are all well.

You asked me in your letter to give you some news about Madame Papinot;[1] she is very well and often inquires about your health. Regarding my lessons, all goes well; for some time now,[2] their number has been increased, and this is why I wasn't able to

write you on Sunday. I am very happy, for tomorrow I will be in white for the Procession.[3] Marie made me try on my things and they fit me very well.

Dear little Marie, I ask you to kiss good Aunt and dear little Jeanne for me.

Au revoir, dear little cousin; pardon me if my letter is poorly done and badly written. It is because I am in such a hurry, and I didn't have time to make an outline. Céline asks me to kiss you, Jeanne, and Aunt. I have not yet carried out your message to Pauline, but I'll do it this afternoon. Your little cousin, who loves you with her whole heart.

Thérèse

* Seventeen fragments; see CMG + LT 1948.

1. Incorrect spelling of Mme. Papinau, the "... very good person, very well educated but a little old-maidish in her ways" (Ms. A, p. 85). Thérèse was taking special lessons at her home ever since March 1886. She was fifty years old.
2. Her lessons were increased in number. For the school year (1886-1887) an invoice shows that her lessons went from four to eight a month, each one hour in length; see Mss. II, p. 27.
3. For the feast of *Corpus Christi* (June 24), solemnized on Sunday, June 27.

LC 45 — *From Marie Guérin to Thérèse.*

July 31, 1886

Between this letter and the preceding (LT 19), Thérèse had joined her cousins at Trouville, "but she was homesick for Les Buissonnets and was forced as a consequence to cut her vacation short" (Ms. A, p. 90).

My dear Thérèse,

Pardon me for having been so long a time without writing you; you're going to believe I have forgotten you. Not in the least; I

think of you a lot, but many obstacles have come to upset my correspondence. These are the excuses for my delay, and I trust you will accept them.

On Sunday,[1] we went on an outing to La Grâce[2] with Uncle Petit.[3] We had a carriage with two horses, a coachman in uniform, and off we went, then, for the whole afternoon. The route was charming. When going, we traveled along the edge of the Saint Gatien forest, where we stopped to go and see the home of our ancestors; each of us brought back a souvenir from this farm. Uncle Petit was delighted to see the house again in which he had spent so many happy days. Afterward, we continued on our way to La Grâce. During the trip, we saw a balloon that came from the Honfleur carnival. When we reached La Grâce, we went into the chapel, and there I prayed for my Thérèse and her whole family. You cannot imagine the pretty panorama that unfolded before our very eyes. It was enchanting; the Seine flowing into the sea and, facing us, the coast of Le Havre, Barfleur, etc. On our return, we went along the side of the sea. We came back by way of Villerville. The weather was in our favor and the sea was as calm as a lake. You can imagine the joy that reigned all during this outing. I have nothing else worthy of note to tell you. Our life is always the same; our outings always have as their goals the seashore or the park.

If you are too pressed for time to answer me, don't write, and I won't be the least bit annoyed. I'll write you as though you had answered me, and that will be my revenge. See you soon, darling. I kiss you with all my heart. Don't forget my Godfather and your charming sisters. Be assured of Marie's affection for you.

Trouville-on-the-sea, July 13, 1886

* Autograph.

1. July 11, 1886.
2. Normandy shrine called *Notre-Dame-de-Grâce,* near Honfleur.
3. M. Gustave Petit (1820-1895), brother of Mme. Fournet, who was Mme. Guérin's mother; he was Marie Guérin's great-uncle.

LT 20 **From Thérèse to Marie Guérin.**
(Fragments.)

July 15,
1886
→ LC 45

Aux Buissonnets, Thursday, July 15, 1886

My dear Marie,

You're very good for having written to me, and your letter pleased me very much. I am very happy that you're having beautiful trips like the ones you told me about. I was very much interested in them.

I was using the swing just now. Marie is afraid that I'm becoming hunchbacked,[1] and she asked Papa to put up the rings and the swing; the rings don't please me as much as the swing;[2] my hands are all red from using them.

We went yesterday to spend the afternoon at Madame Maudelonde's home, and I had a lot of fun with Céline and Hélène. Madame Papinot[3] gave me a holiday for tomorrow in honor of the feast of Our Lady of Mt. Carmel so that I can go to listen to the sermon.[4]

You can see, Marie, that I don't have interesting things to tell you, and I haven't, like you, made a delightful trip that I can share with you. But I trust that in spite of this my poor little letter is going to give you a little bit of pleasure.

Au revoir, dear little Marie. Kiss Aunt and Jeanne for me.

Your little sister, who loves you very much.

Thérèse

* Twelve fragments of the autograph; see CMG.
1. Thérèse was already showing signs of an inclination to stoop; see Ms. A, p. 159. This was the reason for the physical exercise prescribed by Marie.

2. The swing was one of Thérèse's favorite playthings even in her early childhood days at Alençon; see Ms. A, p. 17, where she is quoting CF, July 25, 1874. It was the same at Les Buissonnets. M. Martin installed a swing there. And he used to set the swing in motion for her, and it had to go high enough for her to see over the wall an old woman in a cotton bonnet, who was always out in her garden; a poor soul, who did not believe in God or the devil. As soon as Thérèse cried out: "I can see mother Godet," it was a signal that the swing had reached its highest point and was to be slowed down. (G/NPHF, pp. 545-546.)
3. See LT 19, note 1.
4. In Carmel.

LD *From Mother Marie de Gonzague to Céline and Thérèse.*

August 15, 1886
→ LT lost

Marie had just received P. Pichon's decisive call: "After having prayed very much, I believe I am the interpreter of Our Lord, giving you the signal of departure, of going out of Egypt. Go quickly with a joyful heart to hide in His Heart." (*Sainte-Anne de Beaupré*, August 1, 1886.) From Carmel, they were trying to lessen the sorrow experienced at Les Buissonnets.

†J. M. J. T.

Carmel of Lisieux
August 15, 1886

My dear Children,

I want to thank you![1] *May my Thérèsita receive all the gratitude of my heart for her great generosity.* I am sending Céline and Thérèsita a little gift to offer your dear Marie.[2] I hope this will please you.

I kiss you. How I love you both and your dear Léonie. Love your older sister for me.

Your best friend and Mother,[3]
Sister Marie de Gonzague
r.c.ind.

* Autograph.

1. Their feast-day wishes. However, Mother Marie de Gonzague's "real feast" was on June 21; see LD, August 14, 1887.
2. This has not been identified, unless it is the "beautiful holy picture" Céline thanks her for the same day; see LD that follows.
3. She was elected prioress on February 3, 1886 and remained in charge until February 20, 1893.

LD *From Céline to Mother Marie de Gonzague.* (Extracts.)

August 15, 1886

At least as much affected as was Thérèse by Marie's approaching departure for Carmel and on the verge of being promoted to mistress of the house at the age of seventeen, Céline poured out her soul at great length to the prioress. (The following extracts represent about one-third of her letter.)

Dear Mother,

I can wait no longer nor silence my heart any more. How I thank you for your charming gift! If you only knew how much it pleased me.... How well you understood, dear Mother, my great sorrow at seeing dear Marie's feast coming and having nothing to offer her. This was going to be the last one and she was going to be doubly sad! I wasn't able to resign myself to this thought...and, thanks to you, dear Mother, our last feast was somewhat happy. Happy, however, is saying too much, for the

sorrow we are experiencing is too great for us to be consoled in this way!

Dear Mother! Once again we are about to lose our mother. God should have been content with the one He now has at His side. How often I think of her! It is unbelievable how much I love praying to her. Often, too, she has been able to see how much I'd love to have her near me. The other day, I was thinking of her, and it seemed to me I was able to see her, to hear her. But, no, I was unable to experience these joys.[1] . . . God willed to compensate for these by giving to Marie a mother's heart, and, now that I was beginning to understand her, that my soul loved to confide in her, that I was enjoying her spiritual conversations, now she is about to be taken from me! Oh, Mother, it is too difficult. . . . I am all alone in life,[2] I am deprived of my dear Marie, whom I love so much! I cannot resign myself to this thought; it seems to me it is something unreal, and, yet, it is only too true. . . .

Oh! Mother, God must help me very much during these terrible days. . . .

Thanks a thousand times, dear Mother, and thanks for the beautiful holy picture also.[3] How beautiful it was and what joy it gave me!

Your very sad little daughter,
Céline

* Autograph.

1. Céline was eight when Mme. Martin died; the following day she chose Marie as her second mother.
2. Léonie, at twenty-three, was also thinking of the religious life; and Thérèse, at this time, was still much of a child: "A distance separated us still!. . ." (Ms. A, p. 103). We don't know what Céline's rapport with her father, now sixty-three, was.
3. A picture painted by Sister Agnes; she had written that same day to Céline: "Dear little Céline, here is Marie's picture; it seems to me you will be happy with it and Marie also."

LT 21 **From Thérèse to Marie.**

October 2, 1886

In Canada since October 1884, P. Pichon was preparing to return to France. Marie wanted to see him for the last time before she entered Carmel. She persuaded her father to take her to Calais and Dover. It was a useless trip, filled with misunderstandings. From Les Buissonnets, Céline and Thérèse tried their best to support their sister's plans.

Saturday, October 2, six in the evening,
Feast of the Holy Angels

My dear little Marie,

We just received your telegram; I'm very happy, for I believe this means that you've seen Father at Dover.[1] He sent you a letter on Wednesday[2] which was telling you to go there before him today. You can't imagine how worried we were. Céline has sent some letters to Dover and Calais "hold till called for."

The Blessed Virgin has had a candle each day, and I have prayed and begged her so much that I can't believe Father will not return today. Monsieur Pichon[3] also sent a letter to Papa; we were not daring to open it, but Pauline told us it would be better because it may have something important inside. However, it was only that Monsieur Pichon did not know as yet the day when Father would return and that he was going to write the superior to find out.

Oh, little Marie, if you only knew how I find that what you told us is true; God is spoiling us, but you don't know what it is to be separated from a person who is loved as I love you.[4] If you could only see all I'm thinking, but I cannot say it. It is too late, and I've written my letter in all directions because I can't see it. Dear little Godmother, I asked Pauline if the little gold-bronze bottles were used for painting in water colors. She told me "no," that these were used for painting the saints and statues. I'm telling you this

so that you won't buy me any as souvenirs. I beg you not to bring me anything; this will really distress me. Léonie kisses you and also Papa.

Au revoir, beloved Marie. Kiss my dear little Papa for me.

Your true little daughter,
who loves you as much as one can love,
Thérèsita

Don't forget especially our messages and the stool for Aunt. Félicité[5] sends her regards; she's in a delightful mood ever since you left. Aunt, Uncle, Jeanne, and Marie send their best regards. We haven't brought the telegram to Carmel as yet.

* Autograph.
1. M. Martin and Marie met P. Pichon at Paris, on the return trip. See DCL, *Le Père Pichon et la famille Martin,* article cited in VT, October 1967, pp. 197-198.
2. Letter sent from Dublin, September 26, and received at Les Buissonnets on the 29th; it was quoted fully in VT, p. 198 (see note 1).
3. M. Alphonse Pichon (1846-1927), P. Pichon's brother.
4. See Ms. A, p. 91: "I didn't want to leave, for one single moment, the dear sister who was soon to fly away. . . . *Each time* I passed the door of her bedroom, I knocked until she opened it, and I kissed her with my whole heart. I wanted to provide myself with kisses for the time when I was to be deprived of them."
5. Servant of the Martin family; see LC 40, note 4, May 3, 1885.

LD *From M. Guérin to Sister Marie of the Sacred Heart.* (Extracts.)

October 15, 1886 — This was written on the same day as Marie's entrance into Carmel.

Lisieux, October 15, 1886

My very dear Daughter,

I'm interrupting my letter to Mother Prioress of the Poor Clares[1]

in order to speak to you for a few moments. I will not go to see you so as not to tire your courage and to steal from your dear sisters the precious time you owe them and to which I have no right whatsoever. The sacrifice, then, is complete, and what a sacrifice: your youth, your beauty, family, tastes, well-being, freedom, and the world! . . . How incomprehensible are God's ways and how poor human reason must bow before His unfathomable designs! For Pauline, He casts roses beneath her feet; she is pierced by the thorns, but the scent of the roses inebriates her, and the Beloved's melodious voice lessens the suffering. She hears His loving call distinctly: "Come, my Dove, rest on my Heart. Fly quickly away from the despicable and misleading world which can only soil your white plumage in the black and fetid mud in which it wallows." From you, my dear, He hides the roses; the thorns alone strike your view, and He is spreading them abundantly beneath your feet. The path you must follow becomes invisible because of them, and your poor feet are made bloody by them. However, you advance without turning your head, being guided by a feeble voice whose few sighs you can distinguish amid the outbursts of the storm raging within your heart. "This way, my beloved daughter; here you will discover the peace and perfect joy after which you hunger. I will shelter you within my Heart burning with an inextinguishable love for you; we will share our sufferings, and you will forget your pains in the immense profundity of mine. Come quickly, then, my fiancée, so that I may place on your forehead the seal of our covenant which will unite you to Me and my Mother, taking henceforth the name of Marie of the Sacred Heart."

To Léonie, He is showing an immense desert in which sandy paths crisscross in all directions. She hears His voice only indistinctly at a distance, and the poor child walks timidly in His direction, but the further she advances the further away His voice seems to be. She gets lost, always returning to her point of departure. Suddenly, the lightning will tear through the clouds, a whirlwind will carry her off, her eyes will be opened, and she will be at port![2]

God's hand is upon us, my dear child, and we would have to be blind not to see it. What have we done for this Merciful God that He guides our steps in this way and showers the treasures of His blessings upon us? Alas, we have no other virtue except that of listening to His voice and being the children of relatives whose accumulated merits, through successive generations, are being poured out on our souls in a fruitful dew.

Oh, my admirable and heroic daughter, how blessed are you now for having so courageously carried out your sacrifice, and how God's voice will be heard distinctly in your heart now that it rests in His! I am not worthy to have such adopted daughters, always expecting them to listen to the counsels of human prudence[3] whereas their ears are so close to the lips of infinite Wisdom.

One day, God showed me an old tree[4] laden with five beautiful fruits awaiting maturity; he ordered me to transplant that tree into my own garden. I obeyed Him. The fruits matured successively, and the Child Jesus—just as He had done on the flight into Egypt—passed by three times and made a sign.[5] The old tree bent down lovingly, each time without any complaint,[6] and it allowed one of the ripe fruits to fall into the Child-God's hand. What an admirable spectacle, the spectacle of this new Abraham! What simplicity! What faith! What greatness! We are but dwarfs at this man's side!

Adieu, dear daughter. Pray to God for me and mine.

Your second father,
I. Guérin

* Autograph.

1. At Alençon, where Léonie had just entered the Poor Clares very suddenly on October 7; see Ms. A, p. 91.
2. Léonie left the Poor Clares the following December 1. It was only in 1899, after her fourth attempt at the religious life, that she was finally "at port."
3. M. and Mme. Guérin had at first doubted Marie's vocation: "They did not want to believe me; they were absolutely stunned. I, the independent one! I, who never seemed to be able to stand convents,

and I was about to become a religious! They could not get over their surprise." (Sister Marie of the Sacred Heart, *Souvenirs autobiographiques,* p. 76.)

4. M. Martin.
5. This is a reference to the apocryphal writings on the childhood of Jesus.
6. Marie's departure was a great shock for M. Martin. When his daughter spoke to him about her vocation (in April-May 1886?), "...he sighed when hearing such a revelation! He was far from expecting it, for nothing in me could have made him suspect that I wanted to be a religious. He stifled a sob and said: 'Ah!...ah! but...without you!...' He could not finish. And to prevent him from being too much affected, I answered reassuringly: 'Céline is big enough to replace me; you will see, Papa, that everything will be all right.' Then dear little Father said: 'God could not ask a greater sacrifice from me! I believed you would never leave me!' He kissed me in order to hide his emotions. I am crying while writing these memories." (Sister Marie of the Sacred Heart, ibid., p. 76.)

LD *From Sister Marie of the Sacred Heart (Marie) to Céline and Thérèse .*

October 22-24 (?), 1886

For housework-washing, sweeping, etc.-in which all the Carmelite nuns shared, the postulant needed a suitable bonnet, but Céline and Thérèse were able to find only a very stylish one in the town. (See LD, which follows, written on the same day.)

My darlings, I thank you with all my heart for your kindness, but I don't need this stylish bonnet for sweeping the floors. Our Mother does not want it, and I'll tell you in confidence that I'd be ashamed of myself if I were to have such little spirit as not to wear a nightcap.[1] What does it matter? Provided God is content and finds you beautiful, you don't have to worry about pleasing anyone but Him. See you soon, little sisters, whom I love so much. Kiss Papa for me, and buy something else at Mme. Caval's shop.[2]

* Autograph.

1. To appear in the Community wearing a nightcap was somewhat humiliating for postulants. Marie was willing to face this humiliation boldly.
2. Mme. Caval had a shop in which she sold women's hats and bonnets.

LD *From Sister Agnes of Jesus to Céline and Thérèse.*

October 22-24 (?), 1886

Little Immortelle and little Lily,

Sister Marie of the Sacred Heart prefers her nightcap to this piece of vanity. I'm sorry for having given you this trouble uselessly. You should return this bonnet and get something else. When Thérèse comes, Our Mother said this evening, *she herself* will make her little bonnets.[1] . . . I'm sure that nothing less will be done for the Immortelle than for the Lily.

I kiss my two dear flowers. I see that their perfume is not being wasted on earth, that they are flying straight to heaven, and this gives me joy because these are my flowers and I love them only for the sake of Jesus.

We are doing the washing on Monday and Thursday of next week.[2] Come on Tuesday[3] if you can.

Sister Agnes of Jesus
r.c.ind.

Your little nightcap-sister kisses you and loves you.

To the Governess,[4] who watches over you, the best tokens of affection and prayers from her two little Carmelites, who love her very much.

Tell Aunt we are doing the wash on Thursday.[5]

* Autograph.

1. "Not an *old lady's* bonnet," Sister Agnes told Thérèse at the end of March 1888. However, Céline was the one who made Thérèse's bonnet which was made with "a plain little ruffle of fine silk netting"; see LC 77.
2. Probably October 25 and 28? On Monday, October 18, the feast of St. Luke and the anniversary of establishment in France of the Carmelite Order (1604), the Blessed Sacrament was exposed all day long; there could be no question, then, of doing the washing that day or on Monday, feast of All Saints.
3. Tuesday, October 26?
4. Undoubtedly this was Mme. Guérin, who was watching over her two young nieces more than ever.
5. Sister Agnes wrote, then, after Thursday, October 21, so that there can be no possible confusion about the date of the following Thursday, the 28th. Céline and Thérèse did not fail to come for a visit on October 21, feast of St. Céline.

LC 46 *From Sister Marie of the Sacred Heart to Thérèse.*

November, 1886 Date obtained through cross-references; see note 1.

(To Thérèse)[1]

I don't want my darling to cry like this, but I want her to be good and reasonable. After all, we shouldn't say that today was the last time in her life that she was seeing me! And when we think that on Thursday morning this baby will return for a visit and again on Friday! Will we not have time to say many things to each other? Come, then, tell me quickly that you're no longer sad, and kiss one another, Céline and Thérèse.[2] Nevertheless, you are my jewels. Dear little jewels, adorn yourselves for heaven with tears and little sacrifices here on earth. These are what become *diamonds* when you know how to profit from them.

See you soon, my love.... But I don't want my darling to despair when God has spoiled her *so much*...*so much*. Let her reflect a little on God's treats. That is something which will dry all her tears.

Your little godmother, who loves you.

Marie of the Sacred Heart

* Autograph.

1. We have a letter with the same format, the same arrangement, and even the same folds as this present note, with the heading: (For Céline). Its content indicates that it was written in November 1886.
2. We don't know what misunderstanding had arisen between the two sisters. Here are a few lines from the note to Céline: "Doesn't my hope want to be called *hope* any longer?... However, it is this dear little sister who is my hope! From her I expect everything, everything that is good and devoted. Dear little Céline, always be a little star in the heaven of my life. Let me see you shining, GENTLE and joyful, embellishing two lives: our good little Father's and your little sister's, who is now entrusted to you. Yes, you will do this and it is already done; you will give them joy and dry their tears; you will be their smile and the peace of the home." (Sister Marie of the Sacred Heart to Céline, November 1886.)

SECOND PERIOD

ADOLESCENCE

(Christmas 1886 - April 1888)

THE CHRISTMAS GRACE

The night of Christmas 1886 was the beginning of a very definite change in Thérèse's life. In her Autobiography, she writes that it began ". . . the third period of my life, the most beautiful of all, the most filled with graces from heaven" (Ms. A, p. 98). When describing it, she refers to this grace as a "miracle," "her conversion": "God would have to work a little miracle, and this miracle He performed on that unforgettable Christmas day" (p. 97). "It was December 25, 1886, that I received the grace of leaving my childhood, in a word, the grace of my complete conversion" (p. 98). In fact, she became very poetic when recalling this incident in her life: "On that luminous night which sheds light upon the delights of the Holy Trinity, Jesus, the gentle little Child of an hour, changed the night of my soul into torrents of light. . . . On that night, when He became weak and vulnerable out of love for me, He made me strong and courageous, He clothed me with His weapons, and ever since that blessed night I have not been defeated in a single combat, but, on the contrary, I have walked from victory to victory. I began, so to speak, to run 'a giant's race!. . .' (p. 98). See also LT 201, November 1, 1896, in which she again refers to this grace as "the night of my conversion."

The transformation was such that, within fifteen months, this child, always on the verge of tears and extremely sensitive, was able to take her place in the ranks of the daughters of St. Teresa of Avila. And St. Teresa wanted her nuns to be very strong. (See LT 201.)

This "giant's race" can be divided into several stages:

Christmas 1886–October 1887, months of human and spiritual fullness;

October 1887, the month of combat for her vocation (p. 286);

November–December 1887, the trip to Rome (p. 303) and its effects upon Thérèse (p. 379);

January–April 1888, quiet waiting for her entrance into Carmel (p. 389).

"The perfumed breezes of the dawn" (*LT 142*)
(Christmas 1886–October 1887)
Age thirteen and fourteen

Is this expression, sounding so much like some of St. John of the Cross's expressions in his poems, in agreement with Thérèse's "correspondence" during these nine months, an "April fish" for Céline (LT 22) and the four playful letters to her Guérin cousins (LT 23 to 26)? Thérèse has answered this question in her Autobiography. In spite of appearances, this period was for her a "dawn," the awakening of her entire being.

Her physical development: she was now fourteen years old, and, within a few months, she became "tall in stature" (Ms. A, p. 103; see also LC 49 and LD, June 24–25, 1887).

Her intellectual development: "Freed from its scruples, its excessive sensitiveness, my spirit developed. I had always loved the great, the beautiful, but at this time I was seized with a great desire for learning. . . . I applied myself alone to special studies in history and science" (Ms. A, p. 101). Mme. Papinau's quiet pupil began to study on her own.

She also took lessons in art: "I was taking lessons with Céline, and my clever teacher found that I had an aptitude for her art" (Ms. A, p. 112). As evidence of this, there are about a dozen studies of heads, most of them dated, done between January 1887 and May 8; there is also a sketch of the church in Ouilly-le-Vicomte (April 12). She also did some clay modeling with Céline.

Her spiritual development: "Jesus was instructing me in secret on things pertaining to His love" (Ms. A, p. 105). We must be satisfied here with an account of the most outstanding graces:

May 1887: "The reading of the conferences of l'abbé Arminjon on the end of the world and the mysteries of the future life was one of the greatest graces of my life" (Ms. A, p. 102);

spring and summer: the spiritual conferences with Céline in the belvédère at Les Buissonnets (Ms. A, p. 103);

July: an awakening to an apostolic dimension, caused by a picture of Christ Crucified, when she was in the cathedral of Saint-Pierre (Ms. A, p. 99);

July-August: total preoccupation with the salvation of the assassin Pranzini, "my first child," as she was to call him later on (Ms. A, p. 99);

"transports of love" for God (Ms. A, p. 112).

Henceforth, the hope of entering Carmel at the age of fifteen is no longer a "sweet thought" which she entertains (Ms. A, p. 97). It is the necessary response to "the divine call which was so urgent that, if I had to walk through flames, I would have done it in order to be faithful to Jesus" (Ms. A, p. 106).

M. Martin was under no illusions. On March 19, the day on which Sister Marie of the Sacred Heart received the Habit, he confided to some priests: "I am very happy; the salvation of two of my daughters is already assured. I still have one more who is only fourteen and who is already burning with the desire to follow them." (Testimony of P. Godefroy Madelaine, PO, 131.) And Thérèse received his permission to enter without any difficulty, on Pentecost Sunday, May 29: "In deep faith, he cried out that God was giving him a great honor in thus asking him for his children" (Ms. A, p. 108).

Very early, too, Thérèse found an ally in Céline, or better still, a friend, a "spiritual sister" (Ms. A, p. 103). Ever since Marie's departure for Carmel, they enjoyed

"the sweetest life that two young girls could ever dream of" (Ms. A, p. 106), they experienced "ideal happiness." Henceforth, it was "together"[1] that they were going to live out their spiritual adventure for years.

→ *Read Ms. A, pp. 97–112.*

1. Thérèse used this adverb "together" sixteen times in Ms. A: nine times for Céline; six times for this period alone. It appeared some forty times in her *Letters*: twenty-six times with reference to Céline and Thérèse, twenty-three of which have reference to Céline before her entrance into Carmel, September 14, 1894.

LD *From Sister Marie of the Sacred Heart to Céline and Thérèse.*

December 31, 1886

Happy New Year! to my beloved little sisters. Who of us five will wake up the first in 1887? . . . No doubt Agnes of Jesus and Marie of the Sacred Heart since they will be keeping watch before God right up until midnight[1] in order to wish you a Happy New Year before everyone else! . . .

* Autograph.

1. "In Carmel, on the eve of the first day of the year we keep watch until midnight; at the foot of the Tabernacle, we spend the last moments of the year that is about to fall into eternity and the first moments of the year that is about to begin." (Letter of Sister Agnes of Jesus to Mme. Guérin, December 31, 1883.) Marie was undoubtedly writing before the eve, between ten and eleven o'clock.

LC 47 *From Sister Marie of the Sacred Heart to Thérèse.*

January 1,
1887

My dear Thérèse,

Tomorrow you will be fourteen! *Your godmother* is not forgetting it, and so she is coming to wish you a Happy Birthday. If only I had something to give you! But I have nothing except this little picture[1] which I like very much and which I'm sending you for your feast.

With it, I'm sending some Spanish licorice and a beautiful blue ribbon to make you laugh. Adieu, my darling. Always love good little Jesus, who is smiling at you from His crib[2] and who extends His little arms to you in order to hug you tightly.

Your Marie, who loves you with her whole heart.

January 1, '87

You're the one who has my first letter of this year.
Kiss little Céline and Léonie and our dear little Father.

* Autograph.
1. This picture has not been identified.
2. Let us take note here of a passage in one of Thérèse's composition homeworks on the theme: *Christmas.* It was written between December 19, 1886 and January 6, 1887. Her presentation is unusual. The illumination in the heading and the garland which runs along the whole margin are expressive of a great happiness. Here are a few lines of the text: "In order to save men Jesus willed to be born the poorest of the poor. While it would have been sufficient for Him to shed one drop of His Blood to save the human race, He willed to become a little child and to be born in a stable, having only borrowed swaddling clothes to cover Him and an ox and an ass to warm His delicate little members. Who could ever understand this mystery of love! A God descends from heaven where He is adored

and praised to save a creature who is ungrateful and culpable. How will we ever be able to praise and thank this little Child enough, who comes to us and asks from us as a return for all He has done that we give ourselves to Him without reserve? Oh, Jesus, who will dare refuse You this heart which you have so well won?"

LC 48 *From Sister Agnes of Jesus to Thérèse.*

January 1, 1887

My beloved little girl,

Happy Birthday! See how big you are. Courage! Jesus will soon pluck His little flower,[1] but you must be patient and courageous and wait gently for the passage of the divine Lamb.

How I love you, my darling! Pray for your *petit Paulin* of former days. She must become a saint first since the choice fell on her first.

I'm sending you a little chaplet that comes from Jerusalem.

Your Agnes of Jesus
r.c.ind.

* Autograph.

1. To transplant her in Carmel.

LT 22 From Thérèse to Céline.

March 31, 1887

"At Les Buissonnets, Thérèse gave me a comb to put in my hair. On the eve of April 1, I received a folded piece of paper inside of which she had sketched a fish in red, green, and purple ink. This fish had a comb as its diadem!" (CMG IV, p. 378.) The fish was carrying a little broom (or tassel?) on its tail and in its mouth a little net. It was swimming among weeds and shells.

(Above the fish, in large letters) *Poisson d'Avril!...*

(beneath) *Je garde mon Diadème j'usqu'à Demain matin*
Mais après sur ta tete passera mon Destin

(from one side to the other, beneath two strips of paper glued at the ends) *Demain tu auras un peigne que le poisson d'avril te donnera.*

April fish!...

I'm keeping my Diadem until tomorrow morning

But afterward my Destiny will pass to your head

Tomorrow you will have a comb which the April fish will give you.[1]

* Autograph.

1. The handwriting and the inks used are proof that this was done in 1887.
[Among French people, to give a "*poisson d'avril*" is the same as playing an April-fool prank on someone.]

LTS 22 **From Thérèse to Léonie.**

April 15, 1887

Incomplete inscription.

To my very dear little Léonie

Souvenir of April 15, 1887 Your lit

* Autograph. This is in pencil. After these two lines there are some school notes which are hardly legible.

LD *From Sister Agnes of Jesus to M. Martin.*

May 3-4, 1887

On the morning of May 1, M. Martin suffered a slight paralytic stroke. Thanks to the care of M. Guérin, he quickly recovered.

J. M. J. T.

Jesus!

Beloved little Father,

Uncle tells us that you have been ailing since Sunday.[1] In case you cannot come on Friday, I am sending you a short note from my heart. Surely, the Blessed Virgin will cure you entirely, for the Carmel is praying so much for you! Dear little Father, don't be thinking yet about heaven; the repose of the homeland will not be yours until the moment when your mission to the three jewels who remain with you is completed. I say three jewels, for Léonie[2] is also a pearl. Our Mother was very much edified by her last visit. She has so much kindness and humility in her heart! It is impossible that God will not finally set this timid violet in the garden of the religious life.[3] And, then, Céline! and Thérèse! You would have to listen to their Friday spiritual talks in order to know what is within these two beautiful little souls. As our Mother has said, they are truly the *privileged* of the *privileged*.

Dear little Father, may all your desires be accomplished!Your crown in heaven will be all-virginal! Oh, what a glory for you to have given here on earth spouses only to the King of heaven! the loved ones of the Lamb without spot, who are destined to sing to Him and follow Him eternally. . . . I am very much moved when writing these lines, I, the poor little pearl that was set first in the jewel box of the Heart of Jesus! However, I am not ungrateful, and, in spite of my lack of all virtues, my love and my thankfulness speak loudly of my happiness.

Adieu, beloved little Father. The hymn of the *Nunc Dimittis* is still not yours; before becoming Simeon,[4] you will still be Abraham for a long time, and the Lord's angel will not hold back your obedient arm[5] until it is on the last little dove to be led by you to the mount of sacrifice.

In the meanwhile, kiss and bless the one whom you offered first to Jesus.

Sister Agnes of Jesus
r.c.ind.

Our beloved Mother sends you her heart and her prayers! We are learning every day to appreciate this treasure that God has given to us.

* Autograph.
1. "May 1, the first paralytic stroke on the entire left side." (CMG IV, p. 177.)
2. Léonie had returned to Les Buissonnets on December 1, 1886, after a short trial with the Poor Clares at Alençon. (See LD, October 15, 1886.)
3. She was soon to make another attempt at entering the religious life at the Visitation convent at Caen; see LT 25, note 2, July 14, 1887.
4. See Luke 2:28-32.
5. See Genesis 22:12.

LC 49 *From Sister Marie of the Sacred Heart to Thérèse.*

May 31 (?), 1887 Probable date; see note 3.

My dear Thérèse,

Sister Agnes of Jesus would like to have the parchment that Céline gave you as a New-Year's gift. Hers is too beautiful for the pictures they are asking her to make.[1] One just like yours should come here next week, and she will send it to you.

I just placed a candle before the Blessed Virgin for my darlings (a little candle as long as my finger); however, the Blessed Virgin is not demanding. When we burn only a piece of straw for her, if we possess nothing else, what does it matter, provided we love her and pray to her?

I imagine I'm at Les Buissonnets; I hear a thrush singing, and it is making an endless warbling for us from morning till night. Just this moment it thundered, and it sang on just the same. Little birds have more spirit than we have; they always praise God, no matter what the weather is, even when the sky is dark.

Darling of my heart, my very tall baby! yet always a baby in my eyes, how much reason we have for singing to our good Jesus. Oh! yes, even when our heart is sad. It has so many reasons for being happy, so many! so many! especially *a little heart that I know*[2] and two others also, not to count the *paternal heart* that delights in the joys of all our hearts.

But my little candle is burning away, and I must go and say my rosary before the Blessed Virgin to celebrate the end of Mary's month.[3] I hear the beautiful bells of Saint-Pierre, speaking to me about heaven. Ah! when God calls us that will be the feast of feasts. . . .

See you soon, sweet darling, whom I would eat with kisses. Tell Céline I can't write her but that I am praying *very much* for her and that God is *very well pleased* with His *little flower*. . . .

My Léonie, whom I never forget and my little Father, whom I

love above all! Don't forget to thank Uncle and Aunt for their good Grenache wine.

Sister Agnes kisses all of you. She scolded me because I had not carried out her messages for her. It is for *this afternoon* that she needs the parchment.[4]

* Autograph.

1. Sister Agnes was painting miniatures on parchment, especially pictures for First Communion; this was to help the Community financially.
2. Thérèse's heart; this was probably a reference to the permission she had just received from her father on May 29 to enter Carmel for Christmas 1887.
3. This is, then, May 31? That same day, Thérèse was received as a "Child of Mary" at the Benedictine Abbey.
4. This statement was written at the bottom of the page in a different ink; it could have been written on June 1.

LD *From Sister Agnes of Jesus to Céline and Thérèse.*

June 16, 1887

Sister Agnes was on retreat, for she was about to leave the novitiate on June 21, after three years of Profession. She was not able to visit with her sisters on Friday, the 17th; hence the written message.

On this same day of June 16, M. Martin and his three daughters spent the day in the country at Touques. L'abbé Lepelletier, pastor of *Saint-Pierre* at Lisieux, accompanied them in order to get a lesson in fishing. The priest, on this occasion, gave Céline a lesson in sketching, and so we have a sketch of Thérèse, her hair flowing freely, while she picks wild flowers. (See AL, June 1967, pp. 5-7.)

J. M. J. T.

Darlings,

If our Mother permits it, the little white dove[1] will show you a little cherry which was the object this evening of a sweet meditation during collation.[2]

Notice how beautiful the fruit is, but where did it come from? You will tell me that it is from a flower. Yes, from a flower; the fruit came and replaced the flower. But this is precisely what delighted me. Do you see the poor little flower at the end of the stem? Its discolored remains are all you can recognize now. Well, this is an image of youth and good desires; this is an image of you and me, too. We love, we desire, and that represents the flower; this love and these desires will become the little red fruit in the gentle sun of the Heart of Jesus.

Oh, my darlings, pray that my flower will soon dry out and the cherry will be good to pick.

* Autograph.

1. Sister Marie of the Sacred Heart, who was wearing the white veil of a novice ever since March 19.
2. The collation was a light lunch replacing the evening meal during the days of fast. Thursday, the vigil of the feast of the Sacred Heart, was a day of fast in the Carmel.

LD
June 24-25, 1887

From Jeanne Guérin to Céline. (Extracts.)

Around June 20, Mme. Guérin and her two daughters were at the *Chalet des Lilas, rue de la Cavée*, Trouville. Thérèse was with them for the first week. Beneath the red "J" at the top of the page, Jeanne sketched with her pen the steamboat serving Trouville and Le Havre. Within a few days, a letter from Thérèse in reply had a sailboat.

My dear Céline,

This time, I'm the one who is late with you; you are so kind for having written me so quickly. The postman is always awaited with impatience at Trouville. Yesterday morning, however, I wasn't waiting for him; he came about seven o'clock to our house. I must

confess I was still sleeping, but what a sweet awakening when casting a glance at my night table, two letters. I read them while rubbing my eyes, and your letter made me laugh. How many incidents have taken place in your quarters since my departure! Thérèse was not the least bit disturbed by the death of her silkworm.[1] The tall Thérèse is very well and is enjoying herself, too, I believe. Yesterday, we gathered aspens in the park. Just picture to yourself a field with tall daisies and aspens; never had we seen anything like it, and we gathered two large bouquets of them. We went to the rocks to get some sea water, and Thérèse removed her shoes for a moment. We go to the seashore every day, twice a day. . . .

For the past few days it has been much colder. Marie is really suffering from toothaches. I don't know if she'll be able to bear the filling of her tooth.[2] The poor girl hasn't been able to profit from her trip; she hasn't really had a chance. Fortunately, we have Thérèse to cheer her up a bit; she really needed that. I haven't done any painting this week. All our outings have been to the seashore, so I haven't done much in either painting or sewing.

Will you come to see us, little Céline? You could come on a Sunday with Papa. Uncle could spend a day at Trouville next Thursday, for example, and bring you back.

Write me when the spirit moves you and when you have the time. Your letters always give us much joy. . . .

Adieu, dear Céline. I kiss you with all my heart, and a good kiss for Léonie.

All yours,
Jeanne

Bonjour to Uncle for me.

* Autograph.
1. See LT 24.
2. See LT 23.

LT 23 **From Thérèse to Marie Guérin.**

June 27, 1887

After a sojourn at Trouville, Thérèse returned to Les Buissonnets on Sunday, June 26, accompanied by her uncle, M. Guérin.

Aux Buissonnets, Monday, June 27, '87

My dear little Patient,

How are you this morning? Did you sleep well last night? Is your tooth causing you less suffering?[1] . . . Dear little Marie, look at all the questions I'm asking you this morning, but, alas! nobody can answer me, and I am forced to answer them myself, so I'll do it to my own advantage, and I can see you are much better.

I'm obliged to turn the page, for I just noticed that I was writing in all directions. It's been such a long time since I held a pen[2] that it seems strange to me. I have returned from the Carmel. I told Marie and Pauline how much you are suffering, and they're going to pray to God that He cure you and that you can enjoy your time at Trouville. . . . I'd have many things to tell you, dear little Louploup,[3] but I haven't the time, for I intend to write a note to Jeanne,[4] and, besides, I would be afraid of hurting your eyes. My letter is a real muddle, and I don't know how I can dare send it to you this way.

I leave you, kissing you not on your two cheeks, for I fear hurting your teeth, but on your pretty little forehead.

Thérèse
e.M.[5]

I recommend especially that my dear little *Louploup* not put herself out by writing me. This will not prevent me from sending her letters often. My little *Louploup* must merit her name and eat like a real *Louploup.*

* Fifteen fragments of the autograph. CMG.
1. See preceding LD.
2. There were no lessons with Mme. Papinau between June 17 and 28, judging by the 1887 bill.
3. One of Marie Guérin's nicknames, whose second name was Louise.
4. See LT 24. Thérèse was going to use the second sheet of the same paper and the same purple ink; this gives us a hint about the dating of LT 24.
5. Abbreviations for "*enfant de Marie.*" Thérèse was just received into the "Children of Mary" on May 31; see LC 49, note 3.

LT 24 — From Thérèse to Jeanne Guérin.

June 27, 1887

Concerning the date of this letter, see LT 23, note 4.

(here, a sailboat sketched by pen)

My dear little Jeanne,

Not having the artist Darel[1] to sketch a boat for me and desiring, however, to place one at the top of my letter, I was obliged to apply myself to daubing one. I am coming, dear Jeanne, to annoy you for a few moments. I hope your migraine headache has entirely passed away. Now that the tall English lady[2] has left, you will be less tormented and certainly everybody will be much better.

I suppose you are very happy not to be listening any longer to my sermons on death, to no longer see my eyes which fascinate you so, and to be no longer pushed when going to see the Pigeon ladies.[3] . . .

I have to announce to you the death of *eight* of my silkworms; I have only *four* left. Céline lavished so much care on them[4] that she made almost all of them die from sadness or a fatal seizure of apoplexy. I very much fear that the four that are left have caught

the germ of their brothers' sickness and that they will follow them in death.

It seems strange to me to be again at Les Buissonnets. This morning, I was surprised to see myself at Céline's side. We spoke to Papa about the amiable offer that good Aunt made to us,[5] but it is absolutely impossible because Papa leaves on Wednesday and he will remain a very short time at Alençon on this occasion.

Au revoir, dear Jeanne. I always love you with my whole heart.

Thérèse
e.m.

* Autograph.

1. Not identified, but it was undoubtedly Jeanne herself, who was doing a lot of sketching, and Thérèse could have seen her, just three days before, decorating her letter to Céline with a sketch of the steamboat; see LD, June 24-25, 1887.
2. This was no doubt Thérèse herself. In 1887, Thérèse was tall and phlegmatic.
3. See LD, June 4, 1879, note 2.
4. When Thérèse was away at Trouville, Céline, having no mulberry leaves, fed the silkworms with leaves from the other trees at Les Buissonnets.
5. Offer of another visit to Trouville during M. Martin's absence.

LT 25 From Thérèse to Marie Guérin.

July 14,
1887
→ LC lost

Aux Buissonnets, July 14, 1887

My good little Marie,

I received your dear little letter just this minute, and I'm still laughing when thinking of all you're telling me. Well, then, you

naughty little thing, I must first begin by scolding you. Why did you take your face again to the sculptor?[1] He has really done a fine job on it!. . . I was really sorry when I learned your naughty little cheeks had once again taken on the form of a balloon. However, experience should have taught you. It seemed to me that you had enough the first time.

I'm happy that Aunt is doing better. I was dismayed when I learned that she was ailing; truly, God is sending you many trials this year.

This week we're no longer cheerful at Les Buissonnets; it's the last week that Léonie is spending with us. The days are passing by rapidly, and she has only two more days with us.[2]

However, what do you expect, my poor darling? A certain joy is mixed with my sorrow, and I am happy to see dear Léonie finally in her element; yes, I believe that there only will she be happy. In the Visitation, she will find what she is missing in the world.

Céline is mourning her two little finches;[3] the male rejoined his companion the next morning, and now its mortal remains are at the taxidermist's. I trust, my darling, that the end of your visit to Trouville will be happier than its beginning. I hope that God, who has so tried you, is now going to give you very much joy.

Céline is sorry she is unable to write to Jeanne, but she is so busy with all Léonie's preparations that it is impossible. Tell Jeanne that she could not imagine how touched Léonie was by her letter and yours, too. She kisses you with her whole heart as well as dear little Aunt. Kiss Jeanne for me. Tell Aunt how much I love her, and keep for yourself a great part of my kisses. (I heard about the letter from Carmel;[4] it seems it was very amusing.) Papa sends you all his love, and especially to his dear goddaughter.[5]

Thérèse[6]

* Nine fragments of the autograph. CMG.

1. The dentist; see LT 23.

2. Léonie entered the Visitation at Caen on July 16.

3. Birds from the islands that Thérèse had just bought for Céline at the International Exhibition at Le Havre in June or July.
4. This letter was not preserved.
5. Marie Guérin.
6. We should recall that during this same month of July, undoubtedly on a Sunday, when seeing a picture of Jesus on the Cross, Thérèse was "...struck by the Blood flowing from the divine hands," and she made the resolution to "...remain in spirit at the foot of the Cross to receive the divine dew pouring from His hands, understanding that she was then to pour this out upon souls" (Ms. A, p. 99). At this time, too, Thérèse and Céline received "...graces of an order as elevated as those granted to the great saints," during their spiritual conversations in the belvédère (Ms. A, p. 103). Thérèse wrote: "Already faith and hope were no longer necessary, and love helped us find on earth Him whom we were seeking." (Ibid.)

LC 50
July 20, 1887
→ LT lost

From Léonie to Thérèse.

Having entered the Visitation, Léonie was preparing for her admission to the postulancy by a retreat of ten days. She left the monastery after six months.

From our Caen monastery
July 20, 1887

My beloved little Sister,

I don't want dear Céline's letter to leave without adding a short note for you. Thanks for your charming little letter; you have understood my intentions well, and this is how I want you to write me.

It is already a month since I have had the joy of knowing our honored Mother and our good Mistress of Novices for the first time.[1] I am very happy, dear little sister, in my new family; here, I am surrounded by affection. How different from the Poor Clares,[2] and how good it seems to me! God has given me great

graces, for He is the One who led me here as though by the hand; I believe He wants me to be here. Pray for me, my beloved little Thérèse so that I make no mistake. As for myself, I think much about you, and I am not forgetting the grace that you want so much to obtain.[3] Be at peace, then, my darling, nothing is impossible with God.

Our cell looks out upon the garden where I see a beautiful Calvary scene placed there this year on Passion Sunday. Oh! how it gives me courage to suffer all that is most bitter, when I consider a God, who has suffered so much for us. I see, too, the two steeples of St. Stephen's,[4] and I think that God is very close to me since He is really present in our churches. And so you can see I am very happy; envy my happiness because this is permitted, for it is the only thing worthy of envy on earth, all the rest is but nothing.

I beg you, beloved little sister, to give my best regards to all whom I love, especially to my good little Father, whom I love so much.

Your sister, who has more affection for you than ever.

* MSC copybook.

1. These were respectively: Mother Marie-Stéphanie Lejeune, who was born September 1, 1841, and died February 25, 1888, and Mother Marie de Sales Lefrançois, who was born on March 25, 1858, and died on September 17, 1907.
2. In LC 56, October 14-16, 1887, Léonie will emphasize again this "difference." Having entered the Poor Clares without sufficient reflection, she seems to have been very much adversely affected by this first experience in the religious life.
3. Probably the grace for Thérèse to enter Carmel at age fifteen.
4. Steeples from the *Abbaye aux Hommes* (over 260 feet high); this church was built in the XIth century by Lanfranc, thanks to the kindness of William the Conqueror.

LD *From Sister Marie of the Sacred Heart to M. Martin.*

August 14, 1887

Dear little Father, would you tell Céline and Thérèse that I'd be very happy if they were to write a short note to Mother for tomorrow.[1] Her name is Marie, and it is her feast day; not her real feast day,[2] but it doesn't matter. In Carmel, we don't think twice before celebrating; in Carmel it's always a feast day. You remember how we used to say this: "They are always celebrating in Carmel!" Well, it's true. This is a proof that we are not inclined towards sadness. "The soul of the just man is a perpetual feast."[3]

I believe, beloved Father, that you are not the least of the guests at this blessed table. May God grant you as much as you deserve.

Sister Agnes of Jesus, who is our painter in miniatures and house-painter on occasion, has written this beautiful passage from the psalms in our Mother's cell: "The Lord led them by a marvelous road; He Himself was their shelter by day and their starlight through the night."[4] All of which I see as beautiful; I find this applies to you . . . .

Your diamond,[5]
Marie of the Sacred Heart

* Autograph.

1. These letters have not been found. However, we do have a visiting card of M. Martin when he offered his best wishes to the prioress on that August 15, 1887.
2. Her feast day was on June 21; feast of St. Aloysius de Gonzague.
3. Proverbs 15:15.
4. Wisdom 10:17.
5. M. Martin, jeweler, nicknamed Marie his diamond and Pauline his pearl.

LD *From Sister Agnes of Jesus to M. Martin.*

August (?), 1887 Approximate date; see notes 2 and 4.

J. M. J. T.

My dear little Father,

Would you tell your little *gypsies*[1] not to come until Saturday because of the washing we have to do on Friday.

Thanks, dear little Father, for your kindness this week. When eating some of the angelfish brought by you, we will think of the angel from heaven who is recording your kindness.

I am writing some beautiful sentences on the walls of our dormitory.[2] We cannot raise our eyes in Carmel without thinking of God and the homeland awaiting us. This is very sweet to my heart, and I love my task very much. I love writing this verse from a psalm: "The Lord has taken me by the hand and drew me out of the deep waters,"[3] for this is what He has done for us. Oh! how gentle a support is this hand of the Lord!

I wish for the two little doves remaining at Les Buissonnets[4] the same grace as the one their older sisters are enjoying. I know that they desire it ardently. May this desire, which is also that of an incomparable Father, be accomplished one day!

Adieu, dear little Father. What a joy to be your daughter!

Sister Agnes of Jesus
r.c.ind.

The diamond kisses you.

* Autograph.

1. Céline and Thérèse. It was usually to Marie that this nickname was given because of her nonconformist character.
2. This was the corridor outside the individual cells of the Carmelites. With reference to these sentences, see the preceding LD; this is why we think this letter was also written in August.

3. See Psalm 17:17.
4. This letter was written after Léonie's entrance into the Visitation (July 16, 1887).

LT 26 **From Thérèse to Marie Guérin.**

August 18, 1887

Mme. Guérin and her daughters were spending a few days of vacation with their cousin M. David, at the *chateau de la Musse*, near Evreux.

Aux Buissonnets, August 18, '87

Dear little Marie,

Uncle just told me that you were sick. You naughty little thing, as soon as you can have a little bit of pleasure, you hurry to get sick. You're fortunate that I'm far from you, otherwise you would have to deal with me. . . .

And how is good Aunt? Always better, I hope. Alas, how things turn out just the opposite of what we imagine. I was picturing you running happily in the park, looking at the fish,[1] enjoying yourself very much with Jeanne; in a word, I thought you were living the life of a lady. But instead of this, you're living the life of a patient there. Oh! my darling, I pity you with all my heart, but you must not be discouraged, for you still have time for outings and to enjoy yourself. You have only to leave your bedroom quickly which, though beautiful and gilded, is † nothing but a beautiful Cage for the little bird that would like to hop in the beautiful Sun it sees through the bars †.

(I notice that I just put the cart before the horse; I beg you to understand the little crosses which I placed in the preceding sentence.)

Yes, my DARLING little sister, you need the fresh air of the park just like the little birds. When you return to us, you must be fresh like a pretty rose which has just bloomed. Oh! my darling, I

want, when speaking of roses, to kiss your cheeks. They are not perhaps roses, but I love a beautiful white rose as much as a red rose. Take care to make your little cheeks less white and ask Jeanne to kiss them for me. Tell her that I'm thinking very much about her, too, and I am sending her a kiss with all my heart. Dear Marie, I've let my pen run like a little fool, and it has written things which are hardly easy to read[2] or understand. I beg you to blame the pen only for these ugly things, but what I don't want you to attribute to the pen is the affection your little sister has for you.

Kiss dear Aunt for me, whom I love with my whole heart.

Adieu, dear little sister. I am sending you a kiss with the recommendation to cure yourself quickly in order to have a little bit of pleasure.[3]

Your sister, who loves you,
Thérèse
c.M.

* Autograph.

1. *La Musse* was a property owned by M. David, cousin to the Guérins.
2. Written in pale blue ink, this letter is difficult to decipher because Thérèse wrote her lines not only in the usual manner but also perpendicularly, writing across her lines.
3. We should remember that during this same month of August, Thérèse was using "all the means possible" to prevent the criminal Pranzini "from falling into hell." Condemned to death on July 13, he was guillotined at *La Roquette* on August 31; see Ms. A, p. 99.

LC 51 *From Marie Guérin to Thérèse.*

August 22, 1887
→ LT 26

My dear little Thérèse,

A very important person is writing you these words; this morning I awakened to the sounds of my seventeen years. It is some-

what shameful to wake up at eight o'clock, but this is poor Jeanne's fault, who had a very bad migraine headache last night. I believe I remember it is also August 22, my Godfather's birthday.[1] I beg you, then, dear little Thérèse, to wish him a happy birthday, kissing him with all your heart for his goddaughter.

I'm going to show you just a little how my life as a lady is spent. First, in the morning, after my breakfast, I take a stroll in the park; then we go to a delightful little spot which we've called the hermitage, and we make our meditation.[2] After lunch, we go for an outing of two or three hours in the woods or the meadow, and in the woods we have already seen two little squirrels.

I saw my little "Miss" again; this is a little dog very tiny and very obedient, answering at the first call. However, to make her decide to follow us we have to draw her by her predominant fault, which is gluttony, or by carrying a rifle under our arm. Then we hear her endless barks; Diane joins the party, running through the thickets to scare out the game for us. But we're like the monkey showing the magic lantern; we have the instrument, but the powder is missing, which means we kill nothing. Since we have been here, we've had really beautiful weather, not too hot, and only a few storms.

Dear little Thérèse, I have followed your advice, and my cheeks are red as apples; the country air is doing me much good, and it has been decided that we remain until Friday.

Yesterday, we heard Mass at Evreux, and in the afternoon I answered Léonie, who had written me on Monday to wish me a happy feast.[3] In the evening, we always have a little music, and the game of billiards is always our favorite game, so much so that with all these amusements, my piano gets hardly a few minutes.[4] I assure you that my armchair covering[5] is hardly making any progress because I'm always on the move.

Adieu, dear little sister. I kiss you. How I love you.

Best regards from me to your whole family.

Your sister,
Marie
La Musse, August 22, '87

* Autograph.
1. M. Martin was born on August 22, 1823.
2. Marie and Jeanne; Jeanne wrote to Céline: "Marie and I often speak about you. We are so happy at this moment in peace and solitude that our thoughts are constantly about you, the faithful admirers of nature and God's marvels." (Letter from Jeanne Guérin, August 21, 1887.)
3. These letters were not preserved.
4. "Marie is always somewhat delicate; to restore her strength her father gave her a pretty piano as a New Year's gift." (Letter of Sister Marie of the Sacred Heart to Sophie Bohard, January 16, 1887.)
5. This was an embroidered chairback, with a pale blue lining, Marie was making for her mother's feast; see LC 65, note 2, November 20, 1887.

LC 52 *From Sister Agnes of Jesus to Thérèse.*
September (?), 1887 Approximate date; see notes 2 and 4

J. M. J. T.

My Cherub,

I am afraid I caused your little heart some pain, and I love you so much that this makes me suffer. Be very brave, dear little Benjamin. Don't torment yourself with anything and for no reason. This does not please God, who loves to see the little hearts of His children always joyful.

When you have a headache, you must eat just the same or no *Carmel*. Our Mother is going to write this to you, too,[1] and so I won't say anymore.

Don't be distressed about the visit to Carmel. It is *understood* that every Tuesday and Friday the two little Carmelites of Les Buissonnets[2] will see the two real Carmelites on *Rue de Livarot*.[3]

You will have three long quarters of an hour, and then Papa

will come to have his little visit, which will make up an hour or close to it, for we will not worry over a few minutes more in cases of *big secrets* or *big sorrows*.

This was what was decided during recreation this afternoon.

And so, little Benjamin, courage. Carmel will reward[4] you for all the sacrifices you are making at this moment and, then, heaven will come after Carmel!... How incredible we are for causing ourselves so much sorrow for such a short time. It is true that we are allowed to suffer on this poor earth, but we should not *suffer just for the sake of suffering*, for this spoils the whole thing. Understand? *Adieu*, beloved little girls. All my heart is yours.

Sister Agnes of Jesus

Thank Papa for the fish. There were 180 of them; the Sisters will never end frying them. What providence! what a Father!

* Autograph.
1. See LC 53.
2. Léonie was no longer at Les Buissonnets; the letter was written between July 16, 1887 and January 6, 1888.
3. Former name, until 1933, of the actual *rue du Carmel.*
4. Her approaching entrance to Carmel does not seem to be in question. This letter had to be written before October 8, the date when Thérèse asked her uncle's permission and was refused.

LC 53 *From Mother Marie de Gonzague to Thérèse.*
September (?), 1887

† J. M. J. T.

My dear Thérèsita,

I have learned through the voice of an older and dear sister[1] that my child is not being obedient!... Where, then, is the prom-

ise made by my little child to eat *much, much*? We must act as if we were in Carmel. Well! when we are in the refectory, we must take all that obedience gives us. If you have a headache, this is weakness, and you must eat *more. Understood*?

Doesn't my angel want to come and be with her older sisters, who are so happy in God's service? If you do not take the necessary nourishment, you won't be able to succeed! Courage, child of my heart, patience and hope. The years are passing, months are short, and days are but hours, and soon the much desired hour will sound. But I WANT my child to eat *much, much*. . . .

Understood, promised, and our Marie of the Trinity[2] will give me news about the obedient child of my heart (*my Thérèsita*).

Sister Marie de Gonzague

* Autograph.

1. Sister Agnes of Jesus? See LC 52.
2. Future name for Céline when she entered Carmel, chosen by Thérèse (see CSG, p. 81); actually, she never received this name.

"At the point of the sword" (LT 201)
(October 1887)
Age fourteen

On October 8, 1887, less than three months before Christmas, the date chosen for her entrance into Carmel, Thérèse spoke to her uncle about her plans. This step (see LT 27) forced him to take a stand for or against her plans. It was the hour of human prudence.

The Correspondence introduces us to the tortuous course of a very subtle diplomacy. It would be good here to present the persons involved in this struggle regarding Thérèse's vocation.

First, there was her uncle Guérin. He was almost forty-seven years old. When she begged for his permission to enter Carmel at age fifteen, his first reaction was negative. She was to wait another three or four years (LT 27). Two weeks later, October 22, he changed his mind completely, under Sister Agnes of Jesus' influence (LD, October 21, 1887).

Then, there was Canon Delatroëtte, ecclesiastical superior of the Lisieux Carmel since 1870, pastor of Saint-Jacques for almost twenty years. He was already in his seventies. Canon Delatroëtte was totally opposed to Thérèse's idea. "No one had thought of this opposition, the most invincible of all" (Ms. A, p. 111). His main motive: the youth of the aspirant (LD, October 29, 1887). But there were other very serious reasons for his action (LD, November 25, 1887). The Carmel's willingness to appeal to a higher authority displeased him very much. During the following weeks, his refusal becomes more adamant. On November 24 (see LD of Sister Agnes of Jesus to M. Guérin, November 28), in a visit to the Carmel he gave a very harsh explanation for his stubborn "no," and he was not to retract it for the next four years.

Such stubbornness surprised the chaplain of the Carmel, l'abbé Youf. "Such a charming child! Ah! I want her to enter!" (LD, October 25). He approved the Carmel's having recourse to the bishop of Bayeux.

A meeting was arranged, and Thérèse went to see Bishop Hugonin, accompanied by her father, October 31. She had tied her hair up in a knot to look older, and she tells us she used all the eloquence at her command (Ms. A, p. 111). The bishop was very paternal, showed her many signs of affection, but he did not say "yes" or "no." He would take up the matter with M. Delatroëtte. "I could not have heard anything which gave me more

distress. . . . It seemed to me my future was forever ruined" (Ms. A, p. 111).

Ultimately, the decision rested with M. Révérony, the vicar general. In his fifties, this priest was a good listener, but he did not give in easily. He was a wise man, filled with a great esteem for the religious life, and he soon had the opportunity of observing Thérèse at close range.

When she later on recalled these matters, in 1896, Thérèse gave much credit to the superior, Canon Delatroëtte, referring to him as "our good Father" (LT 201, November 1, 1896). "His conduct was prudent, and I have no doubt that in putting me to this trial he was carrying out the will of God, who willed that I conquer Carmel at the point of the sword."

→*Read Ms. A, pp. 109 to 118.*

LT 27 **From Thérèse to Sister Agnes of Jesus.**

October 8, 1887

Saturday, October 8, '87

My dear little Sister,

Ever since Wednesday,[1] I was looking for a chance to speak to Uncle; this morning, I had the chance. Uncle was very kind. I was afraid that, since it was a Saturday, he would not be pleased, for on that day he is very busy.[2] On the contrary, as soon as I asked him to come, he very eagerly put down the book he was reading.

He told me that for some time he had suspected that I had something to tell him; then he went on to give me a *very* AFFECTIONATE little sermon which I had expected.[3] He told me he was

very sure of my vocation, that it was not this which prevented him from allowing me to leave. It is only the world, I believe, which is the obstacle. It would be a real *public scandal* to see a child entering Carmel; I would be the only one in all of France, etc. . . . However, if God wills it, He will be able to prove it. In the meanwhile, Uncle told me that according to the rules of human prudence, I must not dream of entering before the age of seventeen or eighteen, and this will still be too soon.

Uncle told me a lot of other things along this line, but it would take too long to recount them. As you can well imagine, I did not speak to him about a date.[4] Dear little Pauline, I am very happy that Uncle found no other obstacle but that of the world. I think that God will not be at a loss to show Uncle, when He wills to do so, that it is not the world that is going to stop Him from taking me into Carmel. You realize, dear little sister, Uncle told me very many other nice things, but I am telling you only the obstacles that he has found. Fortunately, as far as God is concerned, these obstacles don't exist.

Oh! dear Pauline, I can't tell you today all the things that fill my heart. I can't get my thoughts together. In spite of everything, I feel that I am filled with courage; I am sure that God is not going to abandon me. Now, as Uncle told me, my time of trial is about to begin. Oh! pray for me; pray for your Thérèsita. You know how much she loves you; you are her confidante. I would really have to see you, but this is still a sacrifice to offer Jesus.[5] Oh, I want to refuse Him *nothing*, and even though I feel sad and alone on this earth, He still remains with me. And has not St. Teresa said: "God alone suffices."[6] . . .

Pardon me, dear Pauline, for sending you this letter or this scribbling in which the thoughts don't even follow each other. I don't even know if you will be able to read it so poorly is it written, but my heart had so many things that my pen was unable to follow them. Tell dear Godmother that I am thinking very much about her during her retreat.[7] Ask her not to forget her goddaughter.

See you soon, dear sister. Once again, I really don't want to send you this letter, but I don't have the courage to begin it all over again.

Your little Thérésita

I am sending you your little penholder.
Tell dear Mother[8] that her Thérésita loves her with all her heart.

* Autograph.
1. October 5. The evening before, evidently was the last visit Thérèse was able to make to her sisters before the retreat began on the evening of October 6; see note 7. Sister Agnes must have told Thérèse then that she should speak to her uncle.
2. This was shopping day at Lisieux, and the Guérin pharmacy was very busy on Saturdays.
3. Thérèse tells us that she spoke to her uncle "not without trembling" (Ms. A, p. 109). She gives the details of this interview on this page of Ms. A.
4. Thérèse had made the resolution to enter Carmel on Christmas night 1887. See LC 55.
5. Because of the retreat; the next visit would take place on Monday, October 17; see LC 55.
6. The last sentence of St. Teresa of Avila's bookmark.
7. This retreat was preached by P. Pichon, bringing a special joy to Sister Marie of the Sacred Heart, for he was her spiritual director.
8. Mother Marie de Gonzague.

LC 54 — *From Sister Marie of the Sacred Heart to Thérèse.*

October 14, 1887

Happy feast to Thérésita of the Child Jesus! May the gentle Jesus give her all His caresses and all His tokens of affection.

Darling, I have only a Christmas picture to offer you,[1] but I find it says something to the soul and it can do good even though

it is not Christmas. Does Jesus come to you only on Christmas day? Would Thérèse's Jesus be able to stand it if He were not to stop often to kiss and bless His little Benjamin?

Our Mother is not going to be able to write her Thérèse, but how she kisses her and how tenderly she loves her!

While waiting for the angels to throw some flowers from heaven, I am sending her two little flowers from Carmel which have a little perfume, I believe, flowers from heaven.

Kiss dear little Father. Tell him that all through the week the fish were crying for mercy. . . . Yes, at the bottom of my heart, these mute little fish are speaking to me all the time and they tell me to bless him always for all his kindness to us.

I kiss little Céline, who is spoiled by God.[2]

Marie of the Sacred Heart

* Autograph.

1. This picture has not been identified.
2. A probable reference to the fact that on October 12, Céline had just chosen P. Pichon as her spiritual director (CMG I, p. 125). She was soon to become P. Pichon's favorite child among her sisters.

LC 55 *From Sister Agnes of Jesus to Thérèse.*

October 14, 1887
→ LT 27

J. M. J. T.

Little jewel of my heart, I wish you a happy feast. Oh! how I'm going to pray to St. Teresa for you![1] You have every right to her motherly caresses and her special favors.

I received your letter, and I will have many things to tell you on Monday.[2]

Adieu, little Benjamin. *Adieu*, ripe little fruit which Jesus is getting ready to pick. Always be faithful to Him and fear nothing. . . . Oh! what a blessing for you to be only fifteen and to love

Him alone, alone, without any sharing!... You are the little St. John of Jesus always leaning on His Heart;[3] you listen only to Him, you want only Him. If you only knew what a privilege this is!

I am always thinking of you. Pray for your poor little Confidante.

Sister Agnes of Jesus
r.c.ind.

Kiss little Father for me. I have received his good and beautiful fish. I am waiting for Monday in order to thank him better.

Will Céline have nothing to say at the next visit?[4]...

She forgot me in her short note, but I don't want to take revenge, and if I do, I will revenge myself by more tenderness than ever.

And Léonie?[5]...

Our Mother wishes her dear little daughter a happy feast.

* Autograph.

1. See, in the Appendix, the picture which may have been sent with this letter.
2. October 17, first free day after the retreat, which ended on the evening of the 15th (feast of St. Teresa of Avila).
3. See John 13:23, 25.
4. See LC 54, note 2.
5. What is understood here is: "How was she on your last visit?" Thérèse had made a visit to Léonie at the Visitation convent a few days before (see LC 56, note 2). They were beginning to be concerned in the family over Léonie's perseverance as a postulant.

LC 56 *From Léonie to Thérèse.* (Fragment.)

October 14-16, 1887

October 15, 1887

My beloved little Thérèse,

I come to wish you a happy feast. I know what I want the most for you; I don't have to name this grace,[1] for you know it well, privileged little child of Jesus.

It is now already one year since our dear Marie is in Carmel.

You were there at her departure, but I wasn't there. I had entered the Poor Clares a week before. When I think of that, I thank God for having made me leave there in order to lead me into my dear Visitation where I am so happy, in spite of the thorns which pierce my heart at times. But what is that in comparison with the Poor Clares! These are roses which I trample under my feet at times through my cowardliness, for it will take a lot to make me a saint. But little by little we approach this just the same with the grace of God. Since the day I saw you,[2] I've exerted many efforts; however, I could still do better for Our Lord. I feel it. Ah! how I'd like to throw myself courageously into every sacrifice.

You see, dear little sister, it does me good to talk with you. I know that you understand me in spite of your young age; so I want to confide to you one of the greatest desires of my soul, which is intimate union with Jesus. For the one who possesses Jesus possesses all; He is the treasure of treasures. In Him alone we find our joy and not in the creature. There we find only sorrow and sadness of every kind. Because our heart is made solely for God, He alone can fill it entirely. It is too big for the world; so what folly to have too much attachment for creatures, isn't that true? You know this. I can judge it by my own experience, for until now I have not known how to control my poor heart. You, dear little sister, God has so enraptured your very pure heart that you have not known all the agonies to which foolish affections give rise. So Jesus will have your heart in all its freshness. May your heart be a thousand times blessed. I take delight in this for your sake.

Pardon me, darling, for not having sent you this letter for your feast; it was begun on Friday,[3] but until now I've been so busy that it was impossible to finish it, and you know that I need more time than others for writing, and I explain myself so badly that you are going to have trouble understanding me. I have prayed very much for you all day, and this morning especially in my Holy Communion. This is all I can offer you; you know that now I have nothing but my poor prayers.

Tomorrow is the 17th, the feast of our Blessed Sister Margaret Mary. You know that she cured me miraculously.[4] You also know

my devotion to her. She is no stranger to the joy I have in being at the Visitation, this blessed Order whose glory she is. Pray for me in order that, if necessary, she will obtain a second miracle so that I become a holy Visitandine.[5]

* MSC copybook.

1. Thérèse's entrance into Carmel for Christmas.
2. We don't know the exact date of Thérèse's visit to Caen, where Léonie was in the convent. It must have been between the 6th and 10th of October. See LD, October 25, 1887, note 4.
3. October 14.
4. This was a cure obtained after a novena made by Sister Marie-Dosithée Guérin, the child's aunt, to Blessed Margaret Mary, March 1865. At the age of twenty-one months, Léonie was in a pitiable condition, but "immediately after the novena she was running around like a little rabbit," according to Mme. Martin's statement; see CF, March 5, 1865 and June 27, 1865.
5. Thérèse answered her on the 23rd; see LT 29.

LD *From Sister Agnes of Jesus to M. Guérin.*

October 21, 1887

Thérèse did not dare speak again to her uncle about her vocation ever since October 8 when he refused his permission. What was the alarming news she was given at the Carmel on October 17 (see LC 55, note 2)? She passed through a painful crisis for three days: "It was *the night*, the profound night of the soul. . . . Like Jesus in the garden of agony, I felt *alone*, finding consolation neither on earth nor in heaven. God seemed to have abandoned me! . . ." (Ms. A, p. 109). Overcome by sadness, Thérèse came to the Carmel on Friday morning, October 21, accompanied by her sister Céline, whose feast it was. In the evening (see note 1 below), at Thérèse's request, Sister Agnes of Jesus wrote M. Guérin, ". . . not to plead but to explain the case" of her young sister.

Dear Uncle,

I have asked the Blessed Virgin to inspire me in what I have to say, for I don't know myself what I am about to confide to you. . . .

Poor little Benjamin of a Thérèse was so pale, so sad, so unhappy this morning[1] that it was very necessary for her to admit the cause of all this. A whole week of agony, and why? I was about to give her a scolding, but in her little eyes filled with sweetness and tears I believed I saw something other than the pain of a child. Céline herself was very much moved.... Well, what is the matter? Are you sick? No, Pauline, but I have never suffered so much; if this continues, I will die from sadness. I can see that Uncle is waiting for a miracle; God, however, will not work a miracle for me.... He says it is extraordinary for me to enter at age fifteen. It's unfortunate that this is extraordinary, but I don't understand why God is asking, then, something impossible. It seems to me that God always asks only for possible things, and He is asking this from me.... Oh, Pauline, I have only one hope, and it is prayer. I am praying, I am praying, if you only knew with what fervor! Every day I say to God: My God, You are all-powerful and Uncle always listens to You; when You are in his heart, tell him very loudly that You want me without any delay.... I was really tried this week; I suffered very much, be content with that and give me some consolation now.... The trip to Rome is but a burden to me as long as You don't tell me it is *my honeymoon trip*.... Oh, Jesus, take me for Christmas!...

I admit, dear Uncle, that this confidence moved me more than gave me pleasure. This evening, during prayer,[2] there in the intimacy of a heart-to-heart talk with Jesus, I was unable to restrain myself from making some gentle reproaches to Him. A thousand thoughts, more *human* than divine, came into my mind, especially this bitter reflection which would condemn both Sister Marie of the Sacred Heart and myself: It is her sisters who have attracted her!... And this other reflection: What a Father! He does not love His children, He wants to get rid of them, that's evident.

But Jesus, in his turn, scolded His lamb. He reproached her for her small spirit of faith.... "Am I not the Master of hearts? Which is better, to listen to My voice or that of the blind and senseless world?... I will be stronger than all of you. I want this child. She is a lily-bud opened before the dawn. She is a fruit

ripened before the autumn. From on high, I have desired this lily, the beauty of this fruit. . . . My divine hand is ready to pluck My treasure[3]. . . . Who will dare say to Me: Lord, it is too soon, if I find that it is time?. . .

Beloved Uncle, I don't know how I can trace these lines, for my heart and my eyes are filled with tears. I come to you as to a Father, a real Father, not to plead but to explain the cause of this dear child. . . . I think nothing, I want nothing, I understand nothing. . . . Let God do what He will do! At the present moment, I fear more than ever to hold back this hand lowered with love on our lily in flower! After all, this incomparable privilege of belonging to Jesus almost from the cradle, isn't this privilege worth what it will cost, namely, the blame of a most bitter world?

I beg you, dear Uncle, to pardon my heart this filial outpouring. It is not to give you any advice. You know better than I how you must act. . . . I just wanted to instruct you in the whole matter, and, besides, the Benjamin asked me to do it. Send me your paternal kiss and believe me to be always,

Your *older* little daughter,[4]
Sister Agnes of Jesus
r.c.ind.

* Autograph.

1. Friday, October 21. Sister Agnes did not put a date on her letter. We can still see, although almost totally erased, the heading: J.M.J.T. M. Guérin wrote in pencil the date of its *reception* (as he did in other circumstances): "October 22, '87." Between 1905 and 1910 (?), Sister Geneviève (Céline) recopied an extract from this text in CMG III, p. 147, dating it from October 22, '87. In 1943, she revised the originals and the copies for P. Piat's documentation; at this time, he was writing *Histoire d'une Famille.* She noted on a sheet of paper: "After reflecting well on this, I state that my uncle made an error when dating this letter in the month of October. He must have dated it after the event, misguided by this sentence: 'The trip to Rome is but a burden to me as long as You don't tell me it is my honeymoon trip.' I erased this wrong date, in pencil, and I replaced it with 'August,' putting in nothing else, for we should leave some leeway. But

it isn't possible that it was before August: Léonie had entered the Visitation on July 16, and there was no talk of a trip to Rome at that time. We had knowledge of the pilgrimage and we decided to go there only after Léonie's entrance. I feel that everything comes together in this way." (G/NPHF, p. 679, July 30, 1943.) However, this was all corrected later on in 1947 when the first edition of the "*Letters*" was in preparation, and the date of "October 22" was restored.

2. About 5:00 or 6:00 in the evening. Sister Agnes was writing during the "silence," the free time between Compline and Matins. The letter was delivered the next day to the Guérin pharmacy.
3. M. Guérin changed his decision the next day, using the same image as Sister Agnes: "He told me that *I was a little flower that God wanted to pluck*, and he himself would no longer oppose it!. . ." (Ms. A, p. 110).
4. She meant older in the religious life. Sister Agnes of Jesus was always highly esteemed by M. Guérin, and his favorite among the Martin children. Sister Marie of the Sacred Heart always claimed that it was Sister Agnes' letter that changed his attitude.

LT 28 From Thérèse to P. Pichon.

October 23 (?), 1887

In a fragment of a letter to Sister Marie of the Sacred Heart (November-December 1887), P. Pichon mentions his much-enjoyed visit to Les Buissonnets during his sojourn at Lisieux (October 6 to 15, 1887). We get the impression from her letter that Thérèse, still a little timid, is sparing in her words. She was not experiencing the need for a spiritual director: "The way I was walking was so direct, so luminous, that I needed no other guide except Jesus. . . ." (Ms. A, p. 105). Besides, her "confidante," Sister Agnes of Jesus, was sufficient. However, when about to enter Carmel, she remembered her promise of 1884: in Carmel, she had stated, P. Pichon would be her director (see LC 32, May 6, 1884).

Reverend Father,

I thought that since you were attending to my sisters,[1] you would be willing to take the last one also. I would like to be able to

make myself known to you, but I am not like my sisters. I don't know how to express in a letter all I am feeling.[2] I believe, Father, that, in spite of everything, you will understand me. When you come to Lisieux, I hope I will be able to see you at Carmel in order to open my heart to you.

Father, God has just granted me a great grace. For a long time I have wanted to enter Carmel, and I believe the moment has arrived. Papa is willing that I enter at Christmas.

Oh, Father, how good Jesus is to take me so young. I don't know how to thank Him.

Uncle thinks me very young, but yesterday[3] he told me he wanted to do God's will. Father, I come to beg you to pray for your last child. I just returned from the Carmel. My sisters told me[4] that I could write you to tell you simply what was taking place in my heart. You see, Father, that I did this, hoping you would not refuse to accept me as your little daughter.

Bless your second Lamb.[5]

Thérèse

* Autograph (rough draft).

1. P. Pichon was Marie's (Sister Marie of the Sacred Heart) spiritual director ever since April 17, 1882, and had become Céline's on October 12, 1887 (see LC 54, note 2). After the 1887 retreat at the Carmel, Sister Agnes of Jesus began a regular correspondence with him for several years. Léonie did the same around 1889 and 1891.
2. See LT 36: "I cannot write these things; I would have to express them." However, even *viva voce* Thérèse was rather sober in matters of conscience, a characteristic which P. Pichon stressed in his testimony ("timid and reserved," PO, 318; "recollected and rather silent," PA, 134; "she did not express herself in a flow of words. She asked her questions very clearly but with great sobriety," PA, 361). On October 5, 1971, a person who had been acquainted with P. Pichon said: "He told me that Thérèse was extremely uncommunicative; I can still picture the gesture he made which meant that he had to make the first moves in order to *delve* into her mind." (DCL.) Concerning the relationship between Thérèse and P. Pichon in 1887 and 1888, see VT, January 1968, pp. 53–55.

3. October 22. It is this exact information that suggests this letter was written on October 23. The rough draft reads: "but for some time he has changed his mind."
4. First draft of the letter: "Marie told me." This first version seems to be the better one from the psychological standpoint. From the correction we may deduce Thérèse saw both her sisters. They told her about M. Delatroëtte's opposition to her entrance, but she was confident she would change his mind. (See Ms. A, p. 111, and LD, October 25, 1887.)
5. The first "lamb" was Sister Agnes of Jesus. We may question whether this letter was ever sent to P. Pichon. If we answer affirmatively, then why did he not answer? If he did, why did not Thérèse preserve his letter as she did for all the others he wrote her, including that of 1884?

LT 29 From Thérèse to Léonie.

October 23-30
(?), 1887
→ LC 56

Dear little Sister,

I can't tell you how much joy your letter gave me. Thanks for wishing me a happy feast in such a nice way. I would have liked to write you immediately, but we are so busy now[1] that it was impossible. Céline cannot write you, for she has too much to do, but this doesn't prevent her from thinking of her little sister, whom she loves so much. She told me to kiss you. You told me to pray to Blessed Margaret Mary so that she may obtain the grace for you to become a holy Visitandine. I will never fail[2] to do this for one single day.

I thank you for warning me to look at the pretty little Jesus;[3] He is not damaged. He is as fresh as when He left you. I kissed His little foot for you, and His little hand seemed to bless you from a distance.

Dear Sister, I would have many things to tell you, but. . .[4]

* Autograph (rough draft)
1. They were preparing for the trip to Rome.
2. Thérèse omitted the word "fail" which we supplied.
3. This warning is not in the letter; perhaps Léonie had told Thérèse when the latter was visiting her at Caen. See LC 56, note 2.
4. An incomplete draft. The remainder of the page is taken up with an exercise in arithmetic (changing Arabic numerals to Roman numerals) and the sketch of a fisherman on the bank of a river.

LD

October 25 (?), 1887

From Sister Agnes of Jesus to M. Martin.

On Sunday, October 23, Thérèse was informed of Canon Delatroëtte's opposition to her entrance into Carmel; see LT 28, note 4. On Monday, the 24th, it seems, she went to see the superior, accompanied by her father and Céline to plead her cause. All for nothing. "He received us coldly; my *incomparable* father joined his own insistence to mine but in vain. Nothing could change his attitude" (Ms. A, p. 111). Tuesday, Thérèse shared her disappointment at Carmel. In the afternoon of the same day, Sister Agnes informed Abbé Youf, chaplain of the Carmel. In the evening, she reported this interview to M. Martin.

J. M. J. T.

Dear little Father,

I saw M. Youf just this moment, and I told him our angel's whole affair. He could not get over Our Father's refusal.[1] "She is such a charming child," he said. "Ah! I want her to enter!" I told him you intended speaking to Monseigneur during the trip. . . . "Monseigneur!" he replied, "But IT IS NOT PROBABLE that he will go to Rome, and what a disappointment for the child at the moment of departure to learn this news! All the joy of her trip would vanish. No more hope! She would have to wait the return to know her fate. Since her incomparable father has the *heroism* to be

willing to take her to Monseigneur, let him go straight to Bayeux; this will be more certain. Monday, Tuesday, and Wednesday, the bishop will not be away *because of the feasts of All Saints and All Souls.* It is a favorable occasion and I trust there will be a good decision made."

This, little Father, is quite close to what good M. Youf told me; I admit that the interest which he seems to be taking in this matter really touched me. I saw a priest who understands perfectly that God is free to call souls at any age He pleases. If the fruit is ripe before its time, isn't it right that His Divine Hand stretch forth to gather it?

The whole Carmel is praying for our lily's Father, that fruitful tree that produces only virgins. . . . We are praying, too, for the little lily whose petals today were so filled with *diamonds.*[2] Let her not lose courage, let her hope, nothing is lost. . . . Oh! how angry the demon is to see the lily already in bloom! The wicked one, he cannot stand her precocious desires for a life all for God! But he is wasting his time by placing obstacles in her path, for trial is such an incontestable sign of God's action! He it is who is permitting everything and that for our greater good. "After the night comes the day, and after the tempest comes a great calm,"[3] says the Imitation.

Dear little Father, come to Carmel as soon as possible; I would like to talk to you, for by letter I don't say one quarter. . . . I fear it is daring too much *to ask again* for a trip to Bayeux;[4] however, it is necessary if you want the Benjamin's great trip not be be covered with a cloud of sadness. . . .

As for myself, I am convinced that Monseigneur will say "*yes,*" and what a joy for the little lily *with the diamonds*!

I kiss you, little Father. . . . Oh! how good you are, how I love you! how much the whole family of Carmel cherishes you! . . . If you only knew how touched my heart is when thinking of all you want to do for your Queen, and of all you have done for us! . . .

Your poor little pearl,

Agnes of Jesus
r.c.ind.

If you could come today,[5] I would be pleased.

* Autograph.

1. The superior of the Carmel, Canon Delatroëtte, who was given the title "Our Father" until his death, October 8, 1895.
2. Thérèse had cried in the Carmel's speakroom, just as she had the evening before when leaving the rectory (see Ms. A, p. 111).
3. Imitation of Christ, II, 8:5.
4. Sister Agnes wrote first "to ask you," and, then, "to ask you again." This would suggest that there had recently been a trip to Bayeux, undoubtedly to settle questions regarding the pilgrimage to Rome.
5. "Today": perhaps with reference to the receiver? Sister Agnes was writing in the evening. There was no time, then, for another visit on that Tuesday, the 25th. M. Martin would come to the Carmel on Wednesday, the 26th. We must gauge, between this meeting and the following note (LD, October 29, 1897), the time to make an appointment with the bishop through the intermediary of M. Révérony (see Ms. A, p. 114), to obtain an answer from the latter, to communicate its content to M. Delatroëtte, thus receiving the written answer from the superior on Saturday, the 29th.

LD *From Sister Agnes of Jesus to M. Martin.*

October 29, 1887 — Last communication before the trip to Bayeux, set for Monday, October 31.

J. M. J. T.

Saturday, 4:00 o'clock

My beloved little Father,

I just received this note from our good Father Superior. I believe that I should send this short statement which has pleased me and which you may, if need be, repeat to Monseigneur: "Let Monsieur Martin tell Monseigneur that the age is the only reason[1] for which I hesitate to say 'yes.' But if His Excellency judges in favor of not delaying the entrance, *I will bless Providence.*"

Adieu, dear Father. I have only time to send you my heart.

May God protect and bless you as you deserve! Your courage and your faith make up the object of my meditations today.

Hope for the little lily,
Sister Agnes of Jesus
r.c.ind.

* Autograph.
1. The given reason. There was another; see LD, November 25, 1887, paragraph 4.

The trip to Rome
(November 4-December 2, 1887)
Age fourteen

A trip to Rome was an event at this time. On the human level, it was the event in Thérèse's life: "It taught me more than long years of study" (Ms. A, p. 121)

Thérèse would have written more during the trip were it not for Céline, who was the guardian of her rest. We have, nevertheless, eight letters from her hand (LT 30 to 37; two others are lost).

Their content gives us some information about her conduct. Aside from her persistent difficulty in expressing herself in writing (LT 28, note 2), Thérèse appeared to be preoccupied by one objective: "to have one word from the pope" (LT 35). Did she spend her trip unconscious of the world around her? Her letters to her father, within a few months (LT 46, 51, 58, 72), will prove that this little Norman did not lose contact with reality, appreciating "the sumptuous Italian cuisine," nor did she lose her sense of humor, registering in her memory the picturesque jargon of Rome's guides.

The Autobiography brought out two great lessons she learned from the trip: the fragile nature of human greatness (Ms. A, p. 121), and the necessity of prayer for priests (ibid.). Of the 197 pilgrims, among whom the nobility was largely represented, the train was carrying close to seventy-five priests. Among them, "there were many holy priests," but Thérèse is greatly surprised to discover in them "weak and fragile men. . . ." (Ibid.).

The family correspondence was very pronounced during those four weeks. Its value for a future biography of the Saint would suggest its publication without any restraint. There are, then, thirty-six letters (or extracts) supplying information about the trip to Rome:[1]

fourteen are addressed to Thérèse (LC 57 to 70);

six have reference to her as well as to Céline and her father;

six are from Céline;

ten others are exchanged among the various correspondents.

The letters from the Guérin family (eight) reflect the peaceful life of the city of Lisieux, now immersed in the winter fogs. They are a faithful witness of the affectionate atmosphere of a much unified family.

From the Carmel comes spiritual guidance. . . and, at times, a little bit of diplomacy. Sister Agnes of Jesus excels in each of these areas (twelve letters), and she is firmly supported by Mother Marie de Gonzague. The prioress has no hesitation in committing herself totally to "the child of our heart" (LT 62). And Sister Marie of the Sacred Heart's ordinary good sense comes through all the time (nine letters).

In the background, there are two priests. Concerning M. Delatroëtte, we already know that "nothing will ever

be able to make him change his mind" (LD, Sister Agnes, November 26) once he has taken his position. M. Révérony comes through as a little more flexible. At first, a friendly observer (see Ms. A, p. 124), Céline and Thérèse begin to feel he is a possible ally. His conduct, however, at the audience with the pope on November 20 convinces them that he is the one responsible for their failure (LD, Céline, November 20, note 2). The vicar general's kindness towards Thérèse (LD, Céline, November 23 and 29) restores them to a state of equanimity. And after a few weeks, his intervention was the determining factor in favor of Thérèse's entrance (see LT 39, note 2).

→Read Ms. A, pp. 122 to 143.

1. The Carmel archives has forty-four letters; eight of these have nothing to do with Thérèse and so they are omitted.

LD *From Céline to Sister Agnes of Jesus and Sister Marie of the Sacred Heart.*

November 5-6, 1887 Schedule of the visits at Paris on the second and third days of the trip.

My dear little Sisters,

Paris is very beautiful, yes, very beautiful, but I find that my *Lisieux is still more beautiful.* It possesses riches that Paris knows nothing about. For me, it is heaven on earth; it contains my treasures. . . .

Today, we went to the *Champs Elysées*, the *Tuileries*; we saw the panorama and the diorama. This time, they were presenting the Bosphorus and Constantinople, and I believed I was actually there. We passed under the *arc de triomphe de l'Etoile*, climbed

up to the tower of the Bastille (250 steps); we saw the statues of the République, Joan of Arc, and Louis XVIII. We saw the royal palace, the Bourse, the Louvre Museum. There was in the Museum a head of a ravishing woman. What I do [when I paint], do you know what it is good for? To be thrown into the fire without taking the trouble to look at them. The tints are subdued and pretty, and the half-tints instead of being reddish, the way I make them, are of a bluish-pink transparency. I would believe it was the real thing. We went to the Louvre to find some raincoats,[1] and it was only last spring that I got my bargain. Papa was helping me buy them, asking everybody where the counters were for women's raincoats; if you only knew how good he really is! We were in the elevators,[2] and it was very amusing. Although we went often either by carriage or tramway, we are tired. Everybody is now in bed, and I'm going to do the same thing. Good night until tomorrow.

We saw, too, the grand opera and several theatres and circuses, etc.

Sunday, November 6

Today and especially towards noon, we made *no headway*, our feet refused any further service.

We enjoyed ourselves just the same. It was the steps at Sacred Heart that caused us so much fatigue. We made the tour of the underground church with Monseigneur de Coutances in a procession; it was very pretty. The Chancel is almost finished being covered. We received Holy Communion.[3]

This afternoon, we saw Guignol at Champs Elysées, the little wagons drawn by goats, the wooden horses, the Invalides, the Vendôme tower, a beautiful exhibition of machines for making beer, etc.

I'm going to say *au revoir*, because I intend writing poor Léonie.[4]

The ink at the *Grand hôtel de Mulhouse* seems to me less

beautiful than that of the *hôtel du Bouloi,*[5] but I don't see the color.

Céline

Papa tells me to kiss you. I kiss Mother Marie de Gonzague and all my dear ones.

* Autograph.
1. "*caoutchoucs,*" same meaning as "*imperméables.*".
2. Thérèse spoke of these "ascenseurs" in her recreations at Carmel and again in June 1897 when giving the account of her discovery of the "little way" (see Ms. C, p. 207).
3. This ceremony is described in the *Bulletin mensuel de l'Oeuvre du Voeu National du Sacré-Coeur de Jésus,* but it is mistakenly dated for Monday, the 7th. There is an excerpt from Monseigneur Germain's discourse; he was the bishop of Coutance and was leading the pilgrimage.
4. Letter is lost. See LT 30, note 3.
5. November 4 and 5, M. Martin had chosen the *hôtel du Bouloi* because of its proximity to *Notre-Dames-des-Victoires.* At the request of the organizers, the pilgrims gathered at the *Grand Hôtel de Mulhouse et de Champagne* on the 6th. This hotel was close to the East Station, and it was difficult to obtain carriages at six in the morning.

LT 30 From Thérèse to Sister Agnes of Jesus and Sister Marie of the Sacred Heart.

November 6, 1887

Paris. *Hôtel de Mulhouse.*

My dear little Sisters,

Céline did not want me to write yesterday; however, I don't want you to receive a letter from her without a word from your little

Thérésita. I see that I'm writing like a real little cat, but I trust you will not be vexed with me, for I am *extremely* fatigued. Everything is turning around me. Tomorrow, we shall no longer be in France. I cannot get over all I am seeing. We have seen some beautiful things at Paris, but all this is not happiness. Céline is going to tell you if she wants the marvels of Paris; as for myself, I'll tell you only that I am thinking *very often* of you. The beautiful things of Paris don't captivate my heart in the least.

I am somewhat like my dear Godmother. I'm always afraid of being crushed;[1] at each moment, I am hemmed in by carriages. Oh, dear little sisters, all the beautiful things I see don't give me any joy; I will not have this until I will be where you are already....

I was very happy at *Notre-Dame-des-Victoires.*[2] I prayed very much for you and for *dear Mother*.

I would like to write my little cousins, but this will be at another time, for I am going to write Léonie.[3] Poor Léonie, what will become of her?... I beg you to tell them[4] that I think of them very much. I asked *the grace* for Jeanne at *Sacré-Coeur de Montmartre.*[5] I think she'll understand. Don't forget *good Uncle* and dear Aunt. *Adieu*, DEAR Godmother and my DEAR little Confidante.[6] Pray for your little Thérésita.

I hope that you will remember that I wrote my letter in the evening and when very fatigued. If it were not for this, I would not dare send it to you.

Kiss dear Mother for me.

* Autograph.

1. Marie spent several days at Paris on three occasions: June-July 1878 (see LD, June 26, 1878); March 1883; and October 1886, after having missed P. Pichon at Calais (see LT 21).
2. Having reached Paris on the 4th, around eight in the morning (Lisieux-Paris is about five hours), "...we began to visit it immediately," wrote Thérèse in her Autobiography. One of the first visits was to *Notre-Dame-des-Victoires,* dear to the family (see *Correspondance familiale*). "Ah! what I felt at her feet; I could not

express it. . . . The Blessed Virgin made me feel it was *truly she who had smiled at me and had cured me*" (Ms. A, p. 123).

3. This letter was not preserved. Léonie was again uncertain about her vocation.
4. Her cousins, Jeanne and Marie Guérin.
5. We don't know the object of this request; see LD, November 10-11, '87.
6. Sister Agnes of Jesus; see LT 27 and 43 B.

LD *From Sister Agnes of Jesus to Céline and Thérèse.*

November 8, 1887

J. M. J. T.

Jesus! November 8, '87

My dear little girls,

Are you enjoying yourselves?[1] Are you happy? We are happy to think that you are happy. What a beautiful trip!

Darlings, God is spoiling you very much. Love Him very much, and spoil Him in your turn by refusing Him nothing of the sacrifices He is asking from your heart. When seeing the beautiful things of this world, think that heaven and the beautiful things on high are still preferable.

When visiting the holy sanctuaries, pray for our Léonie[2] with fervor and *confidence*; prayer obtains all. Let little Céline ask for herself the grace of carrying out *well* her *present vocation* and her future vocation.

Let the Benjamin pour out her little heart in front of all the Tabernacles in order to obtain the desired grace, but, before all else, that she really remain the Divine Child's toy.[3] Who could prevent her, then, from belonging to Jesus? *Nobody, nobody* in this world. Yes, the bonds are already formed between Jesus and His

little Thérèse; Jesus is already Thérèse's Fiancé and Thérèse the fiancée of Jesus. To suffer a little before the nuptials is not asking too much!... In order to enter the House of the heavenly Spouse you must have some trials, you must knock several times, you must weep, knock and weep again. Then there will come a moment when the door will finally open, and what has opened the door if not desire, suffering, and love?

In order to merit the suffering of the cloister,[4] you must bear the suffering of waiting. Oh, darling little dove, courage, the flood will pass away, soon the window will open and you will escape[5] into the desert, into the oasis of Carmel.

Adieu, little girls, my *true little ones*. You will know only in heaven the affection I've had for you.

Little Céline, kiss Thérèse. Thérèse, kiss little Céline for

the Lamb of Jesus,

the very happy traveler in Carmel's field.

Our beloved Mother kisses her two travelers very tenderly.

When arriving at Loreto, check at the post office to see if there is a letter, for we do not have the name of the hotel and perhaps we would have to write.[6]

* Autograph.
1. She had not yet received the letters from Paris (LD, November 5-6, '87 and LT 30).
2. See LT 30, note 3.
3. On the important theme of this Theresian imagery, see LT 34, note 2.
4. A study of Sister Agnes of Jesus' correspondence manifests a stress on suffering ever since the October retreat of 1887, preached by P. Pichon. She maintained this characteristic for several years, but it was softened later on.
5. See Genesis 8:10-11.
6. The present letter is addressed to Venice, *Hôtel Beau Rivage*, previously chosen as the lodging place for the Bayeux pilgrims (who will, in fact, remain at *Hôtel de la Luna*). It reached there on November 10.

LD *From Sister Marie of the Sacred Heart to Céline.*

November 8, 1887
→ LD lost
LD, November 5-6, 1887 and LT 30

Letter addressed to Venice with the preceding letter from Sister Agnes of Jesus.

I understood little Céline; when she will return to the dear Carmel, I will take charge of unraveling all her affairs, and this will not be long. It is useless that she be worried about her confessor.[1] This is the least of her worries. At this time, my darling, be taken up with profiting from all the joys God is giving you, for there are still more on this earth. When you see such a good father who does not know what next to devise in order to please you, isn't there something to celebrate every day?

Observe well the marvels of this world in order to give us poor little hermits some news about them. Don't you know that this raises the heart to God? It is true that all is vanity under the sun,[2] but still you yourselves are not attracted to vanity but to the holy realities of the earth, to the martyrs, to the Sovereign Pontiff. This is very beautiful.

We received your dear little letters this morning. I see that you are expert Parisians. How good this dear Father is to tire himself out so much for his imps.

Tell Thérèse that I'd rather she go *to bed* than that she write us at night; my dear little girls must not waste your nights in this way, for they are not long enough to give you the rest you need.

You will find in this envelope a little *treat from God.*[3] How thankful you must be to Him!

I kiss my little Céline. How I love her and Our dear Mother loves her also.

Marie of the Sacred Heart

* Autograph.
1. Céline was wondering at this time how to reconcile P. Pichon's direction with the advice of her usual confessor ("M. l'abbé Baillon, I believe," Céline wrote in an undated note). From LC 73 and 75, we know that when she came back from Rome, she went to confession to M. Delatroëtte.
2. See Ecclesiastes 1:2 and LT 58, note 3.
3. Undoubtedly a letter from P. Pichon to Céline.

LC 57 *From Sister Agnes of Jesus to Thérèse.*

November 9, 1887
→ LT 30

Mail addressed to Loreto, at the same time as two letters to M. Martin and Céline (omitted) and the note from Sister Marie of the Sacred Heart (LC 58).

My dear Thérésita,

Monseigneur is awaiting the end of the trip in order to make his decision.[1] Today, really *confide your entire affair* to the Blessed Virgin. There, in that blessed house where she worked, prayed, suffered, what delightful things she is about to make your heart understand. One does not go to *the Blessed Virgin's home* without coming back with hands filled with graces. Oh, little home of Nazareth, you are worth a thousand times more than all the palaces of this world! There, truly, is heaven's vestibule!... Little Friend and fiancée of little Jesus, don't forget that He grew up under this roof of mystery.... Don't forget that He wept there often, very often; He wept there with love and with the desire to see all souls take flight towards Him, and He wept with sorrow when seeing so few would love Him in the future!

When the Blessed Virgin noticed that her Darling was weeping, it was then that she quickly placed the mysterious ball in His hand,[2] and He smiled immediately... on the dear ball was written this name: *Thérésita of the Child Jesus.*

Adieu, adieu, little pilgrim, little toy of Jesus. Fear nothing, for

Jesus says to you as He said formerly to St. Teresa: *"Nobody will be able to snatch you from My Hands!"*[3]

Your confidante,
Agnes of Jesus
r.c.ind.

You should also pray to *good St. Joseph*, for he, too, worked for Him and suffered in this little house, thrice blessed.[4]

Your little letter pleased me *very much*; don't worry about your handwriting. When we are traveling this is insignificant.[5]

* Autograph.
1. With reference to Thérèse's entrance at Christmas.
2. See LT 34, note 2.
3. *Histoire de Sainte Thérèse, op. cit.* (LT 27, note 6).
4. See Ms. A, pp. 126ff., concerning the visit to the Holy House of Loreto.
5. Thérèse answered on November 14, in the evening (LT 34).

LC 58 *From Sister Marie of the Sacred Heart to Thérèse.*

November 9, 1887

My dear little Thérèse,

I made a rash judgment, for I imagined that before reading my note you had already read through another.[1] Is it true? And yet your poor godmother was a good prophetess. Monseigneur said what I was thinking: "It seems to me that we can wait to decide everything after the trip to Rome." I think he intends speaking about it to M. Révérony.[2] In the meanwhile, my darling, rest in the Heart of Jesus; abandon yourself to Him, and He will not abandon His little Thérésita. *At the hour, at the minute* that He

wills it, she will enter His own house, and He will not be hampered in the least opening the doors. I am praying for my little goddaughter, who is so much loved. Let her eat much especially in order to have strength to make her beautiful and holy pilgrimage. Do you realize that you are going to visit the true home of the Blessed Virgin and the little Jesus!... That is delightful. Pray for us all so that one day we will no longer see only the house but Jesus Himself and His beautiful heaven. I kiss my darling Thérésita, and I tell her to hope *always*, for the last word has not been spoken. God reserves it to Himself. And He does well, He who loves His little Thérèse so much. He will not be able to cause her any distress.

"I am sleeping, but my Heart is watching."[3]

Marie of the Sacred Heart

* Autograph.
1. She was referring to Sister Agnes' letter (LC 57); Thérèse's answer regarding this (LT 33).
2. M. Révérony, vicar general of Bayeux.
3. Canticle of Canticles 5:2.

LC 59 *From Sister Agnes of Jesus to Thérèse.*

November 10, 1887

Letter written the evening of the 10th (see LC 60, note 5), and sent the next day to Rome, *Hôtel de Milan*, which was the first place the Bayeux pilgrims were supposed to stay (see LT 32, note 4).

J. M. J. T.

(Confidential letter)

Jesus' little Toy,

I had told you to ask nothing from the Holy Father;[1] today, Our Mother and Mother Geneviève[2] advise you to speak, in case

you really want to do so. I can't explain why; it would take too long.

If the Holy Father blesses each pilgrim in particular, what will be easier? I would fear that in preventing you from speaking, little Jesus will be vexed with me. The opportunity is so beautiful, since He has made His little ball roll all the way to Rome! It is not right to demand anything further from poor dear little Father, he has done enough for you, more than any other father would want to do. Pray to the Child Jesus, your dear Fiancé, and He will aid you.

Don't let your little heart be troubled; pay no attention to the crowd which will be around you. What does it matter if they hear you? *Not the least bit*. . . .

Ask Jesus how you should go about it. It's up to Him to instruct you since it's for His love that you will speak. I believe it would be good to say *first: Most Holy Father, I have a great favor to ask you*. . . . If he doesn't hear you and passes on to another pilgrim without paying any attention, repeat, don't get tired: Most Holy Father, I have a great favor to ask you. Finally, the good Holy Father will end up by understanding. When he seems to be listening to you or if he asks you a question, you will explain then in a few words the object of your request: Most Holy Father, in honor of your jubilee, permit me to enter Carmel at age fifteen. They find me very young, but since I have the vocation and since Papa is really willing!

. . . .

You will then see what he answers. . . think that it is to Jesus Himself that you are speaking, and this will help you. Formerly, in His mortal life, the Jews had no shame revealing their needs to Him in the midst of crowds; don't you blush either. Speak and fear nothing.

Above all, let M. Révérony know nothing about this letter. If you only knew the trouble this would cause. . . . I have written you my thought only after reflection. Mother Geneviève was saying to me yesterday: Above all, don't hinder her from speaking to the Holy Father; and Our Mother is of the same opinion. This is,

therefore, an obligation[3] for me *to lift the prohibition*. However, *it is up to you*; do only what Jesus will inspire you to do. . . . It's true that *the opportunity is beautiful!*

Our beloved Mother, Mother Geneviève, the whole Carmel is in prayer for Thérésita. Courage!. . .

Above all, don't allow yourself to be rebuffed by a first refusal; think of the perseverance of the Canaanite woman.[4] If the Holy Father seems to say "no," then you answer: Oh, most Holy Father, you can't refuse me; you know that Jesus said: Let the little children come to me.

Our Father[5] has said: If the Holy Father were to say "yes," we would open the doors to you without any difficulty.

You may show your letter to Céline before tearing it up.[6]

* Autograph.

1. Advice given in the last visit at Carmel before their departure. Thérèse was the first one to get the idea of speaking to Leo XIII (see LD, November 11, 1887, note 8).
2. Mother Geneviève of St. Teresa, prioress from 1883 to 1886.
3. She felt this was an obligation because her prioress and Mother Geneviève were of this opinion. From this word on, the text takes up all the margins of the four pages in both directions. It is difficult to build up the logical sequence with any certainty.
4. See Matthew 15:21ff.
5. The superior; (see LD, Oct. 25, 1887, note 1).
6. This communication justified Céline's intervention, who witnessed her sister's fear at the last moment. "Speak!" she told her.

LT 31 A **From Thérèse to Marie Guérin.**

November 10, 1887
→ LC lost

This letter was begun at Venice where the pilgrims were staying from Wednesday night to Friday morning, the 9th to the 11th. Céline kept it until their arrival at Rome. It was completed by Thérèse the evening of the 14th (LT 31 B), and reached Lisieux on the 17th.

Venice,[1] Thursday, the 10th (evening)

My dear little Marie,

Finally, the moment has come when I can write you. We will not go out this evening. I preferred to come and relax a little with you.

I beg you, tell *dear* little Aunt that she could never imagine *how much* her letter TOUCHED me. I'd like to write her to thank her, but I trust she is going to excuse her little daughter and that she will guess at what my heart would say to her. Besides, I have very little time, for Céline does not want me to stay up too long.

Dear little sister, you can have no idea of all the things we see. It's really marvelous. I would never have imagined that we would see such beautiful things. There are so many that I must refrain from recounting them to you. I will do this much better when I shall be in my dear little Lisieux, which all the beauties of Italy cannot make me forget.

Dear little sister, how are you? How are all of you? You are well, I trust. You are as happy as when we left?

Oh! Marie, if you only knew how often I think of all of you in the beautiful churches to which we go. I don't forget you. I thought of you, too, in the presence of nature's marvels on the slopes of the Swiss mountains which we crossed.[2] One prays so well; one feels that God is here!

How little I seemed in the presence of these gigantic mountains.

The country of Italy is very beautiful. We are now enjoying its beautiful blue skies.[3] This afternoon, we visited the monuments of Venice in a gondola; it is delightful.[4]

It appears strange to me to hear the language of Italy spoken around us. It is very beautiful, very musical. The people at the hotel[5] call me *Signorella,* but I don't understand anything else but this word which means *"petite demoiselle."*

I would like to write often, but it is incredible how our days are filled. We can write only very late at night. I am very much ashamed of my letter; I wrote it very fast and the thoughts don't follow. I see that I haven't begun to tell you what I wanted to tell you. I have so many things to tell you and so many things to ask you that if I were to listen to myself I would continue a very long time, but Céline would not let me finish. She has even made me hurry up.

Thank Uncle for the nice little note he sent us. He gave us all much joy. Hug him *very* TIGHTLY for me. Don't forget my little Jeanne. I think of her very often.

Adieu, dear little sister. Think of your little Thérèse sometimes, who thinks so often of you. (You know I haven't forgotten what you did for me one Sunday.)

Your little Thérèse

Papa is well; he sends his regards to all of you.
P.C.T.[6] *Bonjour* to Maria[7] and Marcelline.[8]

* Autograph.

1. Thérèse wrote from the *Hôtel de la Luna.* "In this hotel, everything bears the moon coat of arms: the glasses, the dishes, even the pats of butter which they serve at our meals." (Abbé Hamel, correspondent for the *Indicateur de Bayeux,* quoted from Sister Geneviève's manuscript copy, in her copybook "*Souvenirs du voyage de Rome,* November 1887.")
2. On the evening of November 8, Céline and Thérèse shared with Mother Marie de Gonzague their astonishment over the beauties of Switzerland; these letters were not preserved (see Mme. Guérin, LD,

November 11, 1887). We still get an echo of this astonishment in the Autobiography, Ms. A, p. 124.

3. "Today, for the first time, we are enjoying the beautiful skies of Italy. The weather, cloudy until today, has completely cleared up, and the sun is bright." (Abbé Huet, *Journal du Pèlerinage de Bayeux à Rome*, p. 6, November 10.)
4. Céline lists them in her *"Carnet de voyage"* (her diary). This unpublished document is an excellent source for the itinerary of the trip. Written from memory, it is not always exact on the chronological order of the visits. Here is a summary of the two pages on Venice: *Place Saint-Marc et église, Palais des Doges, Palais des Chambord,* Glassworks, lace factory employing five thousand workers, *église Sainte-Marie des Frères,* with mausoleums of Canova and Titien, *église des Dominicains, des Carmes,* near the station, etc. With the passing of time Thérèse seems to have retained an impression of sadness when she visited Venice; see Ms. A, p. 126.
5. Thérèse had written *"autel"* instead of *"hôtel."*
6. This undoubtedly meant "P.S."
7. One of the servants at Les Buissonnets; very young, she stayed only a few months and was sent away because of a drinking problem, January 1, 1888.
8. Marcelline Husé, servant of the Guérins.

LD *From Sister Marie of the Sacred Heart to Céline and Thérèse.*

November 11, 1887

Dear little girls, I saw that the little lamb had scribbled some things[1] and I nothing at all. . . . You know, however, whether I love you, but I haven't the time this morning to write you. If I were Céline, every night I would make a resumé (only four lines) of all that I saw, for example: Seen, today, St. Peter's, the Colosseum, the Catacombs, etc. This is a way of recalling everything.[2] And you will not be making this trip every year. . . .

I think of my little Thérèse. I believe that little Jesus is not so asleep in His little cradle as He appears to be, and I imagine His very much loved *little toy* really touches His Heart.

Adieu, my darlings. Meditate on these last lines that we used to love to repeat together: "Time is your boat and not your home. . . ."[3] See how you have covered ground . . . . And we are running just as quickly and even more quickly towards heaven, our true home.

Marie of the Sacred Heart

* Autograph.

1. See LC 59. On the evening of the 9th, Sister Marie of the Sacred Heart also wrote her father (letter omitted). These three letters were sent off together on November 11 to Rome. The Martin family found them at the *Hôtel de Milan*, Monday, in the morning (see LD, November 14, 1887).
2. Was it this advice that made Céline decide on beginning her "*carnet de voyage*" (her diary)? See LT 31 A, note 4. The notes concerning Rome begin on page 12. In that case, those relative to Milan (pp. 1-5), Venice (pp. 6-7), Padua (pp. 8-9), Bologna (pp. 9-10), Loreto (pp. 10-11) would have been written from memory. However, it is possible that Céline had anticipated her sister's advice, beginning the "*carnet de voyage*" on November 9 or 10.
3. Lamartine, *Réflexion (Recueillement poétiques, Epîtres et poésies diverses*, Hachette, 1884). They used to recite this text in the family. Thérèse quotes it in Ms. A, p. 87. Lamartine's poems appear in the copybooks of both Marie and Pauline when they were at the Le Mans boarding school (1874-1877).

LD

November 10-11, 1887

From Jeanne Guérin to Céline. (Extracts.)

A comparison of this letter with the two following would suggest that Jeanne Guérin wrote it over a period of two days. It seems we should line up the dates as follows: Wednesday, the 9th, the visit of the Guérins to Les Buissonnets, gathering the pears; Thursday, the 10th, visit of "more than an hour" to the Carmel; Friday, the 11th, M. Guérin's trip to the Carmel, from which he brings back the letters from Céline and Thérèse received by Mother Marie de Gonzague (lost; see LC 62).

Dear Céline,

I just got back from the sermon; the novena for All Souls ended this evening. It is at this hour that we used to get together usually.[1] For a week now everything is very much changed for us; instead of speaking with you, we are dreaming of you. If you only knew how our thoughts often take flight in your direction; they have quickly left Lisieux to follow you in your visits to Milan, Venice, Bologna, where else? All I can tell you is that I fear that poor Tom[2] doesn't have the same consolation as I, dreaming of you. We feel sorry for him with his poor sad eyes and the yelps he makes when he sees us. Everything seems to be very sad at your house when you are not there, even to the Saint Joseph statue in the small room, which appeared saddened by your departure. I have just learned at this instant that you were awe-struck over Switzerland; Papa returned from Carmel where he saw Mother Prioress and he brought us back some news about you. Yesterday, we had a nice visit with her and our dear cousins; we remained more than an hour talking about you. We very often think of our little Thérèse, and we hope that God will draw a great good from her trip to Rome, and that He will allow Himself to be touched by all the prayers that are being directed to Him. I want to thank this dear little angel for having thought of me in the church of the Sacred Heart.[3] I was very much touched by it.

Adieu, little Céline. I kiss you and I beg you to give Thérèse a good kiss for me.

All yours,
Jeanne

P.S. Remember me to Uncle.

* Autograph.
1. Thursday evening.
2. Thérèse's spaniel (see LTS 18a, note 4); his sadness is spoken of several times during the absence of the Martin family. See Mme. Guérin, LD, November 17, 1887; and LC 63.
3. See LT 30.

LC 60 *From Marie Guérin to Thérèse.*

November 10-11, 1887

At this time (1886-1887), Marie was placing the date at the end of her letters; she must have, like her sister, begun her letter on the 10th and finished on the 11th.

Dear little Sister,

It's a week ago today that we left each other, and what a long journey you've made since that time and what marvels have passed before your eyes! We follow you everywhere, and we think that you must be very tired. As for myself, time seems very long, and on Sunday I didn't sing at Mass, not having my singing teacher behind me.[1] Yesterday, I went to your house, and I used the swing, but this swing, which usually pleases me so much,[2] bored me, and I left it very quickly. As for the pears, you may tell Céline that there were some much too ripe, and Mamma gave some to the poor of the district (I can't remember their names).[3] There was a little pear tree and its fruit was yellow and nobody knew the name. I called them Normandy pears, but everybody laughed at me and said that pears of this kind don't exist; finally I insisted

that they were cooking pears, having heard Céline say it. I was not mistaken, they were English pears, and Marie[4] gave us the explanation of this famous pear tree; I knew they were pears that had a kingdom as their name, but I had forgotten only to cross the English Channel!

I notice that I have filled my pages and that I am always saying trite things; I am always the same, no more serious than I was formerly, falling always into the same faults.

We just returned from the Carmel where we spent a nice visit, and Pauline told me to tell you that she really wanted you to speak to the Sovereign Pontiff on the matter of your entrance to Carmel. If he does not pass near you, she would like that you go up to him to ask the favor you desire with so much fervor.[5] On my part, I assure you, dear little Thérèse, that I won't forget you; I'm praying for you enough to break the prie-dieu. This evening I was at my half-hour of daily Adoration, and I recited a whole rosary for my dear little sister. I don't know if the Blessed Virgin is going to answer me; let it suffice that I wanted to pray with fervor. I had a lot of thoughts that came to disturb my meditation on the Sorrowful Mysteries. Each time I was aware of this, I roused myself again to fervor. Finally, I had only one "Hail Mary" to say for my little Thérèse, and this one had to be good or bad. I prayed so much to the Blessed Virgin to listen to this prayer made with so much confidence that I believe these few words were worth all possible prayers.

If you only knew how I love you, dear little Thérèse; I love you so much that I can't express it. We were speaking yesterday to Pauline[6] about this, and we were saying that we love you not like cousins but like *sisters*, and *real sisters*.

Adieu, dear little Thérèse. There are very many leagues to travel to kiss you, but for my heart distances are not an obstacle, and fatigue knows no distances to tell you that I love you; I love you a million times over.

Your sister, who loves you,
Marie

It isn't necessary to sign Marie Guérin. I believe you recognized the heart that dictated these pages so poorly written although I am not on a train bound for Rome.

Kiss Céline and my *dear Godfather* for me. *Bon voyage* and good night.

November 11, '87
Lisieux

Mme. Mansonnet[7] asked me for some news about you, and I told her you were at Bologna. I believe she understood the woods of Boulogne, for I told her you had passed through Venice, and she made an "ah!" which showed me she was beginning to understand that it was in Italy. The other day, she asked Jeanne if Rome was farther away than Lourdes!

* Autograph.

1. This singing teacher was M. Martin. "He had a very beautiful voice; it was remarkable, full and sonorous, exact and pleasing" (G/NPHF, p. 465. See also Ms. A, p. 43).
2. With reference to this swing, see LT 20, note 2, July 15, 1886.
3. See Mme. Guérin's letter (LD following).
4. Sister Marie of the Sacred Heart; she explained it during the visit to Carmel, Thursday, November 10.
5. This passage was written on the 10th. Not satisfied, however, telling Marie Guérin to give Thérèse this message, Sister Agnes developed her thoughts at length in a letter to her young sister (LC 59), written very likely that same evening, during her free time (between eight and nine). This letter (LC 59) was mailed on November 11 before the Carmel received the letter from Milan (which Céline and Thérèse wrote to Mother Marie de Gonzague), indicating the new addresses of the hotels (see Sister Agnes of Jesus, LD, November 11, 1887).
6. This "yesterday" was Thursday, November 10.
7. This person is mentioned nowhere else and so nothing is known about her relationship to the Martin family.

LD *From Mme. Guérin to Céline and Thérèse.*

November 11, 1887

This letter takes up the fourth page of Jeanne's letter (LD) written on November 10 and 11. Posted on November 12, these three letters from Mme. Guérin and her two daughters arrived at Rome (*Hôtel du Sud*) on Monday morning, the 14th.

My dear little nieces,

I am very happy with the good news you gave this evening to Mother Marie de Gonzague.[1] I still haven't seen your letters, but my husband told me that the sight of Switzerland enraptured you and that *our artist*[2] is totally amazed. I have no trouble believing this. This is a little trip which will leave its mark *on your artistic life, Céline.* In the meantime, I must render an account to the mistress of the house[3] of what is happening at her place. I went on Wednesday to pay my visit to all the pears, and I found that many of them were overripe, others were rotten. The overripe ones were given to the Dauphin and Déliot children, who were very happy and very grateful. I chose some ripe pears, *a good ripeness,* about thirty of them, for Mademoiselle Carré.[4] Then I made some preserves with a basket of big pears which were just about ripe. I made the compote at the house; Maria[5] stayed at our place to make it. I made a little more than your large pot holds, so I'm going to send a pot to the Carmel and keep the other for ourselves. I had the English pears picked up which were in the grass. You will find them on your return. Marie[6] told me that these were cooking pears. You can do what you want with them; they will keep well. I believed it was better to use for the compote the pears that would be spoiled before your return. Was that good?. . . Maria was suffering very much on Monday from her boils, so she took a purgative. She was not able to do the wash this week because she still has a very sore wrist, but I trust she will get to work on Monday. She did some sewing. You can see, dear Céline, that I'm talking to you about serious matters, I, who would like so much to talk about your trip. I am busy about the house all the time. And little Thérèse, what does she say in the midst of all these things? We are

thinking about her a lot here at Lisieux. An important matter: Pauline wrote a letter for you addressed to Rome, *Hôtel de Milan*. Don't fail to go and pick it up when you arrive.[7] *Adieu*, dear children. I kiss you. How I love you with my whole heart. Your Uncle shares with me in this. Both of us ask you to give our best regards to your good father.

Céline Guérin

Pauline had also written to Venice, *Hôtel Beau Rivage*.[8]

* Autograph.
1. Letters (lost) from Céline and Thérèse, sent from Milan, the 9th.
2. This was Céline, who was in drawing and art for a period of five years already.
3. Céline.
4. See LC 63. We find the name of "Mlle. Carrey" at the end of Céline's red notebook (notes on the trip), in a list of persons to whom she brought a souvenir from Rome. She was undoubtedly a close neighbor at Les Buissonnets.
5. See LT 31 A, note 7.
6. Sister Marie of the Sacred Heart.
7. The "confidential letter" of November 10; LC 59.
8. Letter of November 8; LD, Sister Agnes of Jesus.

LD *From Sister Agnes of Jesus to M. Martin, Céline, and Thérèse.*

November 11, 1887

This letter and the two following (LC 61 and 62) reached Rome at the *Hôtel du Sud, via Crispi* (today, *via Capo le Case*, 56), on the 14th, in the evening.

J. M. J. T.

Happy Feast

For the Travelers

Friday evening, November 11
Feast of *St. Martin*

Dear Travelers,

One more word this evening, but only one word; I have only

half an hour to give you. Our beloved Mother received the letter from Milan.[1]

We did not know early enough the change of hotels for Venice and Rome. This will make two letters or rather three letters to claim. One sent to *Hôtel Beau Rivage, Venice,*[2] one to Loreto, to be picked up, addressed *to Céline,*[3] and the third to Rome, *Hôtel de Milan.*[4] Don't forget to look into this.

I hope you are happy, spoiled little children of God and of the best of Fathers!. . . Write us as often as possible, this gives us *so much joy.*

Tell us about Papa; tell us whether he is tired,[5] and whether he, too, is happy.

Dear little Father, your two little Carmelites, their Mother, and the whole Carmel never cease thinking of you. May you be thanked a thousand times for giving your two jewels this great joy of such a beautiful trip.

Sister Marie of the Sacred Heart will write you another day. It is impossible for her to write this evening[6] . . .

You are very fortunate to be at Rome! It is the goal of the trip, as heaven is the goal of our pilgrimage in this world. Oh! heaven, what a beautiful Rome!

I kiss all three of you with my whole heart, beginning, it is understood, with the beloved Patriarch. May Thérésita not allow her little soul, so dear to Jesus, to be troubled! May she be confident and fear nothing! The Child Jesus loves it very much when we come to lay at His feet the homage of *our desires.*

Let her abandon her desires to the Heart of the Child Jesus! Oh! how sure and sweet this is at one and the same time!

Adieu, adieu, much joy! and see you soon!

The Lamb

P.S. Above all, dear little Father, don't tell Monseigneur or M. Révérony that I have lifted the prohibition and allowed Thérèse to speak to the Holy Father, just as she had always wished.[7] They would believe the inspiration came from the Carmel while it came only from the little Queen of France and Navarre,[8] Fiancée of Jesus and Carmelite in desire. Happy Father!

* Autograph.
1. See preceding LD, note 1.
2. Mail of November 8 (two LD).
3. See LC 57 and 58; the same mail delivery containing the letters of Sister Agnes to M. Martin and Céline (omitted here).
4. See LD, November 11, 1887 (Sister Marie of the Sacred Heart), note 1.
5. Ever since his paralytic stroke on May 1 (see LD, May 3-4, '87), M. Martin remained somewhat weak. This trip was very tiring for him. "I remember that one day in the train at Rome, our father, tired out from sight-seeing, closed his eyes; he was deathly pale and his lips were purple. I was frightened and, filled with anxiety, I said to him: 'Papa, are you sick?'" (G/NPHF, p. 683).
6. She added a short note for Thérèse (LC 61).
7. See LC 59.
8. Nickname given to Thérèse in her early childhood. The statement in this last sentence is confirmed in the Autobiography (Ms. A, p. 117), and even in the following letter: "Before Pauline wrote me, I was thinking of this" (LT 32).

LC 61 *From Sister Marie of the Sacred Heart to Thérèse.*

November 11, 1887

Thérésita of my heart,

Godmother is not forgetting her darling; she sees the dear little girl of her heart, far away, far away...and yet still close to her.... She believes that Jesus does not leave His dear Thérésita for the space of a step; she believes that in His eyes these marvels[1] are not worth one of Thérésita's sighs.... How sweet to be so much protected and so much loved....

This is all that Marie will say tonight to her Benjamin. Let her little heart understand all the rest and let it lean on Jesus *always.*

Marie of the Sacred Heart

* Autograph.

1. The marvels of Switzerland, the enthusiastic descriptions of which had just reached Lisieux the same day.

LC 62 *From Mother Marie de Gonzague to Thérèse.*

November 11, 1887

It is possible that Mother Marie de Gonzague had written these lines before receiving letters from Céline and Thérèse; she makes a reference to this only in the postscript.

†J. M. J. T.

My Thérèsita of Jesus,

Thérèsita's Jesus is very happy with His fiancée's joy! Yes, confidence, dear child of my heart; everything that Jesus wills is marked with the seal of the Cross, and we must not drag this Cross but carry it! The longer you live, my treasure, the more you will understand all the sacrifices for His love that the grace of the vocation Jesus has given you merits. . . . Monseigneur[1] will be at the reunion at the Vatican; don't allow yourself to be intimidated and do what you will be able to do to go to Confession to M. Révérony. And then place the whole matter under the protection of the holy Apostles with hope, confidence, and all will work out for the greatest glory of God and your own greatest good, child of our love. We are eager to know if you received the three letters sent to Venice, Loreto, and Rome?[2] It seems to us that we are with you in the Eternal City; we don't leave you, incomparable Father, and children so dear to our hearts, and the distance makes us think more than ever of our reunion in the heavenly city!!!

In the meanwhile, my heart knows nothing about space and it is with you, there where you are! I bless you; I love you; and the trinity from the Carmel[3] is united with and kisses the trinity at *Rome.*

Your Mother,
Marie de Gonzague

I am very happy with the two little pages from my dear children!. . . A great thank-you from my motherly heart.

* Autograph.

1. Monseigneur Germain, bishop of Coutances. In fact, he was absent after the pilgrims from Bayeux were presented to Leo XIII; see LT 36, note 1, November 20, 1887.
2. See LD, November 11, 1887 (Sister Agnes of Jesus).
3. Mother Marie de Gonzague, Sister Agnes of Jesus, Sister Marie of the Sacred Heart; "the trinity at Rome": M. Martin and his two daughters.

LD *From Céline to Mme. Guérin.* (Extracts.)

November 14, 1887
→ LD

Letter written from the *Hôtel du Sud,* in the evening of the first day of the visits. "The first day was spent outside the walls. . . . This trip into the Roman countryside left a sweet impression on me" (Ms. A, p. 129).

Dear Aunt,

You're the first to whom I'm writing from Rome, the Eternal City, the unique City, the homeland of martyrs and saints. And in union with these heavenly inhabitants, I come to wish you a happy feast[1] . . . . Your two letters[2] gave me much joy. I think you are so good! If you only knew how I pitied you; I can see you looking for the pears, making preserves, such annoying things! while your lazy goddaughter spends the rainy season happily in a delightful country where the sun smiles every day, where the fields are bedecked with daisies, and where the gardens are all in bloom.

If it were only this! . . . It is very beautiful but passing. These delightful pearls that God casts under our feet are nothing; they pale in the presence of the marvels which we are witnessing. Rome! Oh, dear Aunt, how can I speak to you about it? My heart is so moved. Today, we visited ancient Rome, that is, outside the walls; we went through the Roman countryside, passed along the Appian Way,[3] so famous because of historic and holy memories.

St. Paul walked it to go to his martyrdom.... I drank some water from the fountain produced by the bounds made by the head of this great Saint.[4] I saw the little prison where he spent three days; it is walled in, but through a little window I was able to thrust in my hand quite far, perhaps farther than many people. When treading this holy ground in this way, my heart leaps and my tears are hidden with difficulty. Dear Aunt, I could not begin to tell you all the things we see; each step uncovers something new; my heart is overflowing and I'm going to stop. Oh! at the sight of these sacred relics, what heart would remain silent? They cry out: be saints! life is short, very short, so work while it is still day. The dead in their tombs tell you that all is passing away....

We saw in the catacombs[5] a skeleton lying within its tight enclosure, but I'm staying up too late, I could continue in this way until midnight.

Au revoir, dear Aunt. I kiss you. How I love you, and I wish you an exceptional feast celebrated by the angels.... I kiss dear Uncle, *dear* little Jeanne, Marie, Marie and Pauline. We received *all* their letters;[6] we were on the lookout, and there was no danger of allowing one of them to escape.

I kiss Marcelline and Maria and all those dear to us, our friends, everybody....

Céline

If the Carmel were to see this letter because of some information I have given, I believe they would be happy.

Papa told me to give all best regards and to wish you a happy feast.

* Autograph.

1. See LT 32, note 1.
2. Letter of the 8th (?) received at Venice (lost); and letter of the llth (LD) received the morning of the 14th at Rome.
3. Excursions noted down by Céline in her red notebook, pp. 12-14.
4. Red notebook, p. 15; "The three fountains; we drank some water springing from them."

5. "The catacombs of St. Calixtus. Inscriptions, paintings, an altar where Mass was celebrated, tomb of St. Cornelius, St. Cecilia, skeleton of a woman, skull of a child, an anchor, Jonas, the Chananean woman, a bird, a knife, etc." (ibid. p. 15). On the visit to the catacombs, see Ms. A, p. 131.
6. Answer to Sister Agnes' anxious inquiry; see LD, November 11, '87.

LT 32 From Thérèse to Mme. Guérin.

November 14,
1887
→ LC 60 and LD

Monday, the 14, evening

My dear little Aunt,

If you only knew how happy your little daughter would be if she could be near you to wish you a happy feast,[1] but since this happiness is refused her, she wants at least that a short note from her heart depart from beyond these mountains[2] to take her place. Poor little note, how insufficient it will be to tell dear Aunt all the love I have for you.

How happy we were this morning when we received your dear letters.[3] Oh! Aunt, if you only knew how good I find you....

We received all the letters from Carmel; none of them went astray. I'll do what Pauline tells me in the letter (*Hôtel de Milan*).[4] I don't know how I'll go about speaking to the pope. Really, if God were not to take charge of all, I don't know how I would do it. But I have such a great confidence in Him that He will not be able to abandon me; I'm placing all in His hands.

We still don't know the day of the audience.[5] It appears that to speak to everybody the Holy Father passes in front of the faithful, but I don't believe he stops; in spite of all, I am very determined to speak to him, for even before Pauline had written me I was thinking about it, but I was saying to myself that if God willed me to speak to the pope, He would make it known to me....

Dear Aunt, I'd like to be able to have you read into my heart. You would see in it much better than in a letter all I wish for your feast. I am far, very far, from you, dear little Aunt, but it is incredible how this evening I seem to be close to you. I'd like to tell you how much I love you and how much I think of you. However, there are things that cannot be said in words, they can only be divined....

Dear Aunt, I beg you to thank dear little Marie for her charming and very AFFECTIONATE little letter.[6] It gave me very much joy. Thank, too, my DEAR little Jeanne for thinking of her little sister.

Au revoir, dear little Aunt. I beg you to kiss dear Uncle for me. I'm sending you, dear Aunt, the best wishes I have ever addressed to you, for it's when we're separated from those we love that we feel all the affection we have for them.

Your little daughter,
Thérèse
e.m.

* Autograph.

1. Saint Elizabeth of Hungary, November 19. Mme. Guérin had as her names: Céline, Elisa, Emilie. The family had adopted the custom of celebrating her feast along with that of Mme. Guérin's mother: Elisa Fournet-Petit.
2. Thérèse used the word "mers" (seas), but she meant "mountains."
3. See LD, November 11, 1887 (Mme. Guérin).
4. LC 59. *Hôtel de Milan* was unable to welcome all the Normandy pilgrims; twenty-three of them were directed to *Hôtel du Sud*. Céline and Thérèse (in room no. 1) were the only young ones of this group that comprised fifteen priests, three gentlemen (besides M. Martin) and three old ladies. Their stay there came to an end on November 24, in the morning.
5. Final information was given the pilgrims on Tuesday evening, the 15th: "At dinner in the evening, we learned to our joy that the Holy Father would allow us to attend his Mass on Sunday and that the au-

dience would follow immediately afterward." (Abbé Huet, *Journal du Pèlerinage de Bayeux à Rome, op. cit.*, p. 13.)

6. LC 60. When she discovered that her letter of November 10 to her cousin (LT 31 A) had not been mailed, Thérèse added a postscript (see below, LT 31 B).

LT 31 B **From Thérèse to Marie Guérin.**

November 14, 1887
→ LC 60

Thérèse completed the letter to her cousin, begun at Venice on November 10; see LT 31 A.

Monday, the 14th. You see the date of my letter, dear little sister. I thought Céline had sent it a long time ago.[1] I believed you had received it!... Really, you will be thinking I have forgotten you.

Oh! little sister, how pleased your letter made me. I found once again my little Marie in it....

THANKS!... *Adieu*.... I'm sending you this *old* letter. Just remember it should have been sent four days ago....

* Autograph.

1. Céline had begun writing to Jeanne on November 12 when on the train, undoubtedly between Bologna and Loreto; see LT 37, note 4, at the end, November 25, 1887.

LT 33 **From Thérèse to Sister Marie of the Sacred Heart.**

November 14, 1887
→ LC 58 and 61

Dear Godmother,

You made a real rash judgment when thinking I was going to read Pauline's letter before yours; it's just the opposite that happened....

Oh! yes, Marie, you said enough to me in the short note this evening,[1] and my heart understood all.... How this note pleased me.

When I read the letters you send me, I feel—I don't know what it is—something very sweet flowing into my heart.

Papa is well, and he is happy with your letters.

I asked at the monks' monastery if I could have some relics of St. Agnes; this is *impossible.*[2]

Your Thérèsita loves you with her whole heart.

* Autograph.

1. LC 61 was received at *Hôtel du Sud,* Rome, and LC 58 was held back at *Hôtel de Milan.* Thérèse went to get it in the morning.
2. See Ms. A, p. 132. Thérèse brought back to Sister Agnes: "... a little red stone which came from a rich mosaic, the origin of which goes back to the time of St. Agnes."

LT 34 From Thérèse to Sister Agnes of Jesus.

November 14,
1887
→ LC 57 and 59

Dear Pauline, I cannot really refrain from thanking you for all you are doing for me. Oh! really pray to God for me. Since *Monseigneur* isn't willing, the last step that remains for me is to speak to the pope,[1] but this has to be possible. It has to be Little Jesus, who is preparing all in order that His little ball[2] has only to roll where He wills. If you only knew how what you said in your letter to me at Loreto pleased and consoled me. Oh! Pauline, continue protecting me. I am so far from you.... I can't tell you all I'm thinking! It's just impossible.... Jesus' little toy,

Thérèsita

* Autograph.

1. In the "Loreto letter" (LC 57), Sister Agnes told Thérèse about Bishop Hugonin's decision to postpone his answer until after the trip to Rome was over. Thérèse took this as a negative answer: "I had

learned he was no longer very well disposed towards me, so my only plank of salvation was in the Holy Father's permission. . . but to obtain it, I had to ask; I had *to dare to speak up* in front of everybody '*to the pope*,' and this thought made me tremble" (Ms. A, p. 132).

2. The image of the "little ball" or the "little toy" appears for the first time under Sister Agnes of Jesus' pen on November 8, 1887. It tends to supplant the image of the "lily" which was used until October 29. The leaflet which is the source of this image must have been given to Thérèse at the Carmel between the trip to Bayeux (October 31) and the departure for Rome (November 4). This image is recalled by Thérèse in her letters or in those of her correspondents whenever she meets with trials which demand abandonment to God's will; thus for her entrance into Carmel or her reception of the Habit (January 1889). Here is the list of those letters:

from Thérèse: LT 34, 36, 74, 76, 78, and 79;

from Sister Agnes of Jesus: LD, November 8, 1887; LC 57, 59, 66, 69, 75, 76; LD, February 12-15, 1888, LC 100, 102;

from Sister Marie of the Sacred Heart: LD, November 11, 1887, and November 20, 1887; LC 67, 70, and 101;

from Sister Marie of the Angels: LC 92;

from P. Pichon: LC 97, (151), and 158.

Thérèse explained the spiritual meaning of this image in a letter to Léonie (LT 176, April 28, 1895), and then in her Autobiography, Ms. A, p. 136.

LD

November 17, 1887

→ LT 31 A and B and 32

LD November 14, 1887

From Mme. Guérin to Céline and Thérèse.

The Guérin family had not received any letters from the pilgrims since their departure for Rome. At the Carmel, the last letter had been received on November 11, and they were beginning to be a little bit disturbed.

Lisieux, November 17, 1887

My dear and good little Nieces,

What a joy to receive letters from Italy! How long we have been hoping for them! At the Carmel, they were beginning to get a lit-

tle disturbed; fortunately, M. Gosset received a letter yesterday from his father,[1] who was telling him that all the pilgrims were in good health. So we were a little bit reassured. Nevertheless, when your letters arrived, it was a question as to who would read them first. Thanks, dear children, for your good wishes to me; thanks, too, for your kind affection which distance cannot diminish. I am very grateful for this, and, if you could only see my heart, you would see that my heart loves *very much, yes, very much* those whom it is pleased to call its dear little daughters. I gladly accept this beautiful feast day bouquet which will never fade since it is God Himself who has formed this affection uniting us and making up our joy here on earth. Thank, I beg you, your good father for me, and tell him that we advise him not to tire himself out too much during his trip. I will pray to my holy patroness for you, little Thérèse, so that you will really love God's good pleasure in all He wills. If He permits you to be able to speak to the Holy Father, we will bless Him, and if He does not permit it, we will still bless Him, isn't that true, Thérèse? His good pleasure always comes before ours; we shall always be happy, and my little Thérèse will not make herself sad, above all. She is so far away that we will not be able to go and console her. I sent your letters to the Carmel[2] immediately after we received them. Pauline and Marie will be happy to receive this news. Yesterday, we went to see them, and they could not explain how they had not received any letters. But I can explain this now, thinking that you are overworked and that you haven't a moment's respite. Take care not to tire yourselves too much. You're blessed to have such a beautiful blue sky; we had snow on Monday, and now it is freezing. You are even more blessed than M. Lepelletier,[3] who was telling my husband that when he was at Naples it was cloudy and he was prevented from seeing many things. He brought us a little photograph of the Holy Father. I sent it to the Carmel today so that your sisters can see it.

I went to your house this afternoon with my daughters and your uncle. We paid another visit to the pears, but they are well thinned out now. I had forgotten to take the key of the cellar, but I shall return next week. Poor Maria is beginning to long for your

return. She did the washing yesterday and the day before. Today, she began to repair your father's last two shirts. Your uncle removed the snow from the *arbor vitae* on the lawn. The unfortunate tree was bending over from the weight of the snow. We always feel very sorry for Tom. He is crying all the time over your departure; however, Maria takes him out every day, she tells me. But see how faithful this beast is and how he loves you. And so *beasts and people* long for you. You are missed everywhere and we can't get accustomed to your absence. Hurry up, then, to return, little pilgrims. If you had been at home yesterday, you would have received a visit from Mademoiselle de la Croix, who came to ask you for some information about the former Maria Detettre.[4] So not finding you, she came to our home, and I gave her the information, the good as well as the bad. I believe she is going to accept her. So, then, poor Maria has once again changed her place. I hope the black dresses will still be in good condition for your being presented to the Sovereign Pontiff[5] and that up to now they haven't suffered much damage. I thought the reception had taken place on Tuesday, but I see I was mistaken. You will write to the Carmel, won't you, immediately afterward?

Adieu, my darlings. We kiss you, your uncle and I, with our whole heart.

All the families Fournet, Maudelonde, Pigeon are following you in spirit on your trip, and they entrust me with their best regards to you and your good father. Both good Marcelline, who is complaining, and Maria wish to say "*bonjour*." Best regards to good M. Martin.

Your very devoted Aunt,
C. Guérin

Above all, Céline, take note of all you see; you know you will have much to do upon your return, telling us about all the beautiful things. Profit well from your trip, it will be a memory for your whole life. I believe you're going to return to us very holy after visiting that blessed soil. How blessed I think you are when seeing

all you are seeing and seeing it with the eyes of faith, which permits you to appreciate so many beauties. Once again, *au revoir, à bientôt*.

* Autograph.

1. M. A. Gosset of Lisieux traveled in the same compartment as M. Martin and his daughters; he, too, lodged at *Hôtel du Sud*.
2. Undoubtedly Thérèse's note to her sisters (LT 33 and 34) and Céline's letter to Mme. Guérin (see the P.S. of LD, November 14, 1887).
3. Pastor of *Saint-Pierre*, Lisieux, confessor of M. Martin (G/NPHF, p. 557); he was also Thérèse's confessor after she left the Abbey boarding school. See Marie's and Jeanne's letters of the same day.
4. This was another Maria (see LT 31 A, note 7), who served the Martin family for four or five months in 1887. She was at Les Buissonnets during the Lent of 1887 (according to Sister Geneviève's notes).
5. "The style of dress for the pontifical audience is as follows: for men, a black suit, tie and white or black vest, no gloves. . . . Women should be in black silk or woolen dresses, a black veil covering the head, no gloves." (Feuillet *Pèlerinage de Rome*, printed at Coutances.)

LC 63 *From Marie Guérin to Thérèse.*

November 17, 1887
→ LT 31

This letter repeats in part some details given by Mme. Guérin in the preceding letter.

Thursday, November 17, 1887

Dear little Thérèse,

I am coming to spend the evening at Rome in order to take refuge from the winter cold that is sweeping through Normandy and freezing the poor inhabitants of Lisieux on the spot. How fortunate you are over there; at least, you are avoiding a good month of chilblains. You are nice and warm there, just as in summer,

while your cousins are in the depths of winter. The snow falls, it is freezing, and it's a case of who will shiver the most.

In spite of the winter cold, we paid a visit to your cellar. There were a few pears lost, but what most attracted our attention and our compassion was your dog. Tom does nothing but whimper day and night; he arouses deep pity in us. If, at least, I had a place to put him at our house, I would take him and this would distract him.

Continuing the news about your house, I will tell you that the large tree at the entrance was bent over under the weight of the snow and also the two rosebushes on the side. Now I'm going to inform you of the decease of one of your hens that succumbed after several days of sickness. Maria, not seeing it eat, brought it to Mademoiselle Carré,[1] who told her that the poor beast had distemper; I wonder what she will do with it, and I don't know if she will think about its burial.

We had a visit from M. l'abbé Lepelletier, who told us about his trip to Rome and gave us a photograph of the Holy Father.

I was at the Abbey this week where I was well received and was invited to the feast of Mother St. Placide[2] next Tuesday; I shall have to play my piece[3] at the end of the meeting, which I don't relish at all. Everybody came up to me, asking for news about the travelers, and I didn't know which way to turn my head. You can flatter yourself for giving me the beastly task of always repeating the same thing. I was more fatigued than if I myself had made the trip. Nothing new at our Lisieux, but as for Rome it is another matter. It has a treasure which it does not suspect and which it would do well to return to me soon; my dear little Thérèse's absence is beginning to appear too long. However, to pass the time I pray every day for this dear little sister, not for her to return but for her special intentions, and I ask God to bless her trip.

Adieu, dear little Thérèse. I thank you for your good little letter. I am not kissing you, but I am sending you my heart which will know better than I know how to say: I love you.

Your sister,
Marie, the rascal

Kiss Uncle and Céline for me. Pray for me. Mamma Papineau[4] has put on her warmest clothes and her woolen veil.

* Autograph.

1. See LD, November 11, 1887 (Mme. Guérin), note 4.
2. Directress of the Abbey boarding school. See LT 70, December 1888.
3. A piece she played on the piano.
4. Concerning Mme. Papinau, see LT 19, note 1, June 26, 1886. At the end of her notebook in which she wrote down the lessons to be learned and the division of material for the week, Thérèse wrote: "Lessons: three lessons, one hour before the trip." These lessons were not resumed until January 18, 1888. There was nothing in December. Hoping to enter Carmel for Christmas, Thérèse was not much worried about pursuing her studies.

LD *From Jeanne Guérin to Céline.* (Extracts.)

November 17, 1887

This letter was written on the fourth page of Marie's letter (LC 63). All mail was read by all four cousins whenever they received any.

Dear little Céline,

I pity poor Thérèse for being subjected to reading Marie's long scribbling instead of resting from her travels or going out to admire the splendors of the city. So I'm not going to speak very long. . . . On Sunday, M. Lepeltier gave us a magnificent sermon on Loreto and other places in Italy he had visited. A. Godard[1] was weeping; it had to be touching, isn't that so? We thought that it was exactly that morning that you were visiting the Holy House, and we assisted at Mass in union with you. How fortunate you are to visit so many beautiful things.

Adieu, dear little Céline. I kiss you both with my whole heart. . . .

Your Jeanne

* Autograph.

1. Undoubtedly Jeanne's and Céline's art teacher.

LT 35 **From Thérèse to Marie Guérin.**

November 19, 1887 Eve of the papal audience.

→ LC 60

Saturday, November 19, '87

Dear little Marie,

Tomorrow, Sunday, I will speak to the pope. When you receive my letter, the audience will be over. I find that the post office doesn't send letters fast enough,[1] for when you will have my letter, you will know nothing about what has happened. I'm not going to write to the Carmel this evening, but tomorrow I'll tell them what the pope said to me.

Oh! my dear little sister, if you only knew how fast my heart is beating when I think about tomorrow.

If you only knew all the thoughts I have this evening; I'd like to be able to tell you them, but, no, this is impossible for me. I see Céline's pen running over her paper;[2] mine stops, it has too much to say.

Oh! little Marie, I don't know what you're going to think of your poor Thérèse, but tonight she can't really tell you about her trip. She is going to leave this care to Céline.

I hope you are well, that you are always playing some beautiful music. In Italy, we hear very much music. You realize it is the country of artists;[3] you would be able to judge much better than I what is beautiful, for I'm not an artist. Jeanne would see some very beautiful paintings. You see, little sister, that there is nothing for me at Rome; it's all for the artists! If I could only have one word from the pope, I'd ask for nothing more. . . .

Today is dear Aunt's feast. I'm thinking a lot about her, and I hope she has received our letters.[4]

Dear little sister, hug all those whom I love very tightly for me. I think often of dear little Jeanne. Thanks for your letter;[5] you don't know the pleasure it gave me. It was like a ray of joy.

Au revoir, little sister, and pray for me.

Your little Thérèse

* Autograph.

1. The average delivery was only forty-eight hours. Thérèse had not received as yet the three letters from the Guérin family, written on the 17th and mailed on the 18th; see below, note 4.
2. Céline was writing to the Guérin family and to Maria (the maid); letters lost; see LC 68.
3. November 18 was "the day of the artists in music, painting, and sculpture" (Abbé Huet, *op. cit.*). There were solemn services at the St. Peter's Basilica (solemnity of the Dedication) and, in the afternoon, a visit to the Vatican museums. The Martin family often followed an independent schedule, but we can be somewhat sure they participated in this one.
4. LT 32 and LD, November 14, 1887, for which Mme. Guérin offered her thanks on November 17.
5. Letter of November 11.

LD — *From Sister Marie of the Sacred Heart to Céline and Thérèse.*

November 20, 1887
→ LT 33

Postscript of a letter addressed to M. Martin; it reached Rome on November 23, along with the three following letters from Sister Agnes of Jesus.

My little darlings, I don't have time to write you. Your letters pleased us very much. Let little Thérèse never grow weary of being the ball of the Child Jesus. It will be so good one day to roll into heaven, we shall be so well-off there! But, in the meanwhile, we must, in order to merit it, stumble a little on the stones[1] in the stony paths on earth. Let the little ball not be deflated. This would make little Jesus, who loves it so much, cry.

Marie of the Sacred Heart

* Autograph.

1. Sister Marie used the word "*pierrotter*," which apparently she coined.

LD *From Sister Agnes of Jesus to M. Martin.*

November 20, 1887

J. M. J. T.

Sunday, November 20, '87

Jesus!

My beloved little Father,

There you are, then, all three of you, on the eve of departure![1] See how all passes in this life! We are rejoicing very much at seeing you again, but we are happy, nevertheless, to know you are happy. I believe the two jewels are delighted, or rather I am sure of it, for their letters express it. The Signorella,[2] in spite of her apparent calm, wrote us some little pages filled with enthusiasm. She is only fifteen, but I believe the impressions of this trip will last through her whole life, for *her soul is already old*. Céline has almost replaced "*la semaine religieuse*" in her description of Switzerland. But since then she has become a little lazy, and details have come to us only from Aunt,[3] but this is really pardonable since her time is so precious.

Léonie is doing better; however, we must pray for her always, for it takes such a little matter to make her fall. Yes, let us pray always, so that God does not abandon the little children of dear Papa Martin, so that He bless them more and more and treasure them in order that they may one day form the crown of the Holy Patriarch, their Father!

See you soon! There you are on the return journey! May God keep you and lead you back in good health and *happy*!

I kiss you, little Father. Send also your good kiss to your poor little pearl,

Agnes of Jesus

Aren't you very tired?[4]

* Autograph.
1. This letter reached Rome on November 23, eve of their departure.
2. Thérèse; see LT 31 A.
3. See LD, Mme. Guérin, November 17, note 2.
4. Question already asked on November 11; see on this date Sister Agnes of Jesus, LD, note 5.

LD *From Sister Agnes of Jesus to Céline.* (Extracts.)

November 20, 1887
→ LD

J. M. J. T.

Jesus Sunday, November 20

Dear Céline,

Your little letters really pleased us; they are somewhat *rare*. We long so much for a sign of life! But now it's almost over. See how all passes!...

We have received some better news about Léonie! But we must not cease praying, for she is so *inconstant*! We must obtain for her the energy and courage which she absolutely lacks. This is not her fault in God's eyes, but it is certain that we could not have her take on obligations without seeing her very firm in generosity. It is almost a miracle to ask for, but confidence obtains all! Let us pray! Let us pray!

And our darling Benjamin! Surely, she was not able to speak to the Holy Father.[1] But let her not be sad; events are conducted by the Hand of the Beloved, the Hand of God! It would not be difficult for Him to direct all for our satisfaction; if He directs everything for trial, it is because trial is better for us.

Adieu, little Older One, and darling of my heart. Our beloved Mother is on retreat;[2] she is praying for you and I kiss you for her and myself.

Sister Agnes of Jesus
r.c.ind.

* Autograph.

1. Yes, Thérèse did speak to the Holy Father. At the moment when Sister Agnes was writing, Céline and Thérèse were in the act of recounting the audience with Leo XIII (see LD of this date and LT 36).
2. "Mother has been on retreat since yesterday. This will be for ten days. She is not making a big trip like you, and yet we are deprived of her just as much. She does not come any longer to recreation; we don't see her anymore." (Sister Marie of the Sacred Heart, November 20, 1887.)

LC 64 *From Sister Agnes of Jesus to Thérèse.*

November 20, 1887

J. M. J. T.

Carmel

Jesus *Sunday*, November 20, '87

Dear little toy of Jesus,

Oh! how I'm praying for you! Do you feel it? Listen, my darling, no matter what happens, be very certain that you are the little privileged one of the Holy Child Jesus. Do you know why I say this to you? Well, it's because little Jesus never sends anything but Crosses to His loved ones. . . . To those who don't love Him entirely, He sends roses; those who don't love Him entirely wouldn't love Him at all unless He did this. . . . Do you understand? Oh! how blessed the little ball is whom no one wants to use except Jesus alone! The little ball that does not wish to find its pleasure except in the pleasure of its Little adorable Master! Yes, this little ball is very blessed!. . .

Darling, I don't know why I just wrote these lines, for I haven't received any news and I don't even know the day of the audience.[1] . .

. . . .

As soon as I learn when it is, I will write you again (check at the post offices of Florence, Pisa, and Genoa).[2]

You are seeing many beautiful things at Rome, aren't you? Doesn't all this make you dream more about virtue and heaven? Think that sanctity is synonymous with suffering;[3] think that the little heart torn by thorns is a thousand times closer to the Heart of the Child Jesus than the heart filled with joy, even holy joy. It is not our satisfaction that pleases our Jesus but our readiness to deprive ourselves of all satisfaction to please Him. . . .

"Oh, my dear little ball," says the Holy Child Jesus, "fear nothing, you are safely in my little hands. While waiting for Carmel, make a retreat in my Heart. Don't go far from Me, for you are the toy I prefer to all others. Do you want to allow me to play always with you?" And I hear the little ball answering, while bouncing: "Jesus, Jesus, YES, YES, always!"

Adieu, my own little soul.[4] In joy and in sadness, you will find my heart rejoicing or weeping with you.

I hope to receive a letter from Rome soon. What will it teach me?. . . But I wait for nothing and I want nothing but the Will of my little ball's Master.

See you soon! All passes, *all, all,* except the love of Jesus for Thérèse and the love of Thérèse for Jesus!. . .

Agnes of Jesus

Our beloved Mother is on retreat; she is praying for the child of her heart.

* Autograph.

1. The pilgrims were informed in the evening, Tuesday, the 15th (see LT 32, note 5). Thérèse wrote this to Marie Guérin on the 19th (LT 35), but her letter did not reach Lisieux until November 22.
2. The next letters from Lisieux will be addressed to Pisa and Nice.
3. See LD, Sister Agnes of Jesus, November 8, 1887, note 4.
4. "How happy God is when He encounters a little soul totally abandoned to His pleasure!. . ." (P. Pichon, October Retreat 1887, during his second conference on the second day.)

LC 65 *From Marie Guérin to Thérèse.*

November 20, 1887

Thérèse received this letter at Rome on November 23; she answered it in Florence on the 25th (LT 37).

My dear little Thérèse,

I am going to ask you to excuse the handwriting. M. Puchot[1] is in the large room with Papa, and we are obliged to write on the counter of the Pharmacy, with a very poor pen.

This evening, there is a meeting at the Catholic Club, and we are going to it with the Maudelonde girls. It is a music evening party and would not amuse you very much.

Yesterday, we celebrated Mamma's feast. We gave her our chairback,[2] and you can't imagine how pretty it is and how rich the pale blue lining makes it. Afterward, I played a piece on the piano and sang a sentimental song. The feast was not complete like last year's, for you were missing from our little reunion. Mamma gave us a little present, and I give you a hundred, a thousand chances to guess what it is. You would never guess, and that's why I'm going to tell you. A little watch chain in gold but very tiny; it's the style. Are you amazed, dear Thérèse? I assure you I wasn't expecting this surprise.

Marcelline and Maria are going to go to the Club; Mamma has given them this little distraction in honor of her feast, and they are very happy.

Well! dear little sister, the audience must be over! How eager I am to know the result. Oh! I beg you, write us at the earliest moment. Your letters are awaited with great mp ience, and when they are late like the last time, this begins to cause worry. I beg you, too, to tell us in your next letter what are the hotels you must stay at in the cities you will be visiting.

Were you always in good health during your trip, are you always seeing beautiful things? I'm burning with the desire to see

you once again so that you can tell us all the marvels that passed before your eyes. I see the same thing all the time, a muddy street, a fog that doesn't permit you to see ten feet ahead of you, a coating of ice that just misses making you tumble,[3] this is not as cheerful as the fields of Rome covered with daisies and Italy's beautiful blue sky doesn't appear in Lisieux.

Adieu, my dear little Thérèse, kiss uncle and Céline for me.

Your sister,

Marie

* Autograph.

1. M. Charles Puchot, director of the Catholic Club of the city. The Martins and the Guérins attended the meetings of this Club regularly.
2. A covering for an armchair that Marie Guérin was working on the summer before (see LC 51).
3. In her letter dated November 20 (omitted), giving the same news as her sister's letter contained, Jeanne wrote to Céline: "At present, we are in a fog, a real London fog; at the beginning of the week, we had snow and severe cold." She described Lisieux as "a real Siberia where our poor fingers can't hold our paint brushes."

LD *From Céline to Sister Marie of the Sacred Heart.*

November 20, 1887

On November 20, Leo XIII received in audience the pilgrims from Coutances, Bayeux, and Nantes. Thérèse was able to speak to the pope, but matters developed altogether differently from what she and Céline had expected. This is how Céline described the incident twenty years later: "I was struck with dismay; it would be quite impossible to have a more definite setback. We hid it from our father in order not to sadden him, and we hardly ever spoke about it afterward. It was like a memory you wanted to cast far from you. I regarded it so much as a shameful humiliation that I used to think interiorly: If later on they write Thérèse's life, this fiasco will mar its beauty, and, when in Carmel Mother Agnes of Jesus gave her the command to write her memories, I said to myself: Poor little thing, she'll have to recount the audience with the pope which succeeded so poorly." (NPPO 1910.) The following letter was written from this point of view.

Dear little Marie,

Today I am crushed; in my head there is an immense void. Oh! how I would like to be at my dear Carmel to tell all my thoughts. Thérèse is going to recount this morning's audience to you. Each time it comes into my mind, it's like a very sharp sword which is being plunged into my heart.

I'm exhausted, dear little Marie; it's as if this were aimed at me, it's even worse, I believe. We assisted at the Holy Father's Mass; we were supposed to receive Communion from his hand, but they feared to tire him too much, so this did not take place.[1] When our turn came to be at the Holy Father's feet, Thérèse knelt down, but, unfortunately, M. Révérony was with the Bayeux pilgrims, and it was he who was presenting them to the Sovereign Pontiff. When Thérèse made her request, tears in her eyes, the Holy Father bent over and said: "I don't understand very well."

You know, he is so old that it brings tears to your eyes just looking at him; he is as pale as death; he could hardly support himself or speak. He appears to be broken by age but what a kind face! He is truly a Holy Father.

But to return to Thérèse's request, M. Révérony answered immediately with a sarcastic tone:[2] "She is a child who is asking to enter Carmel at fifteen, but the matter is being examined by the superiors." Then, after Thérèse's *repeated entreaties*, the Holy Father answered: "My dear child, if God wills it, you will enter; leave it up to your superiors." This lasted hardly two minutes, and I came afterward. I had tears in my eyes, but would you believe that I had the audacity to say: "Most Holy Father, a blessing for the *Carmel*."[3] He blessed me, saying: "Oh, it is already blessed!"

After this request made by me, M. Révérony was careful not to say that I was Thérèse's sister, but he replied, laughing a little: "It is already blessed." The Holy Pontiff, who is so kind, seemed to understand it in another way, and it was then he said to me: "Oh, yes, it is already blessed! . . ." Then he extended his hand for me to kiss. Papa came afterward with the gentlemen.[4] M. Révérony introduced him to the Holy Father, saying: "This is the father of two Carmelites and a Visitandine," but he did not say that he was Thérèse's father . . . .

The Sovereign Pontiff looked intently at Papa, and he extended his hand to Papa, who kissed it and *pressed* it lovingly. Papa, when returning, was weeping a little.

Here are the details, but I believe they can be of interest to you. I assure you that I've spent quite a week![5] It was nothing but nightmares and swords every time I thought of this . . . .

If we want to lose out a little on the trips, it[6]

* Autograph.

1. "The crowd was quite large, so the Sovereign Pontiff found it impossible to give Holy Communion. The pilgrims, warned the day before, in the evening, had received at the morning Masses" (Abbé Hamel, *op. cit.*, p. 21).

2. From the reading of this letter and that of Ms. A, p. 134, we get the impression that M. Révérony deliberately obstructed Thérèse's plan. At least, it was she whom he had in mind especially when he gave his directive for silence during the reception. This is not true. The pope's Mass was followed by a Mass "in thanksgiving," and this was attended by Leo XIII on his knees. The audience began immediately afterward by the presentation of some 125 pilgrims from Coutances. M. Révérony then offered the wishes of the Bayeux diocese and its jubilee gift, a lace rochet, which had required six thousand days of work. The Holy Father examined it closely. Then the pilgrims were presented to him in single file: ladies (about twenty-five, Thérèse and Céline were last); the clergy (some thirty priests); gentlemen (about twenty). At first, Leo XIII had a kind word for each one. But "after the long preliminaries which had caused some fear of fatiguing the Holy Father, M. Révérony did not hesitate to forbid any speaking to him, and the audience was hurried up." (Note of Sister Geneviève, p. 22 from the account of Abbé Hamel.) The Nantes pilgrims came afterward.
3. Before meeting the pilgrims individually, the Holy Father, at M. Révérony's request, had extended his blessing to the whole Bayeux diocese, especially the religious communities and the Christian schools (Abbé Huet).
4. By mistake Ms. A, p. 135, mentioned that the procession of the gentlemen preceded that of the ladies.
5. "What I suffered before the audience only God knows, *and dear Céline*. Never will I forget the part she played in all my trials. It seemed that my vocation was hers." (Ms. A, p. 132.) This apprehension did not entirely "destroy" the trip to Rome for Céline and Thérèse. See LC 68, note 6.
6. The next page has disappeared. In 1897, Sister Geneviève was to recall this audience in more positive terms.

LT 36 **From Thérèse to Sister Agnes of Jesus.**

November 20, 1887 Her account of the papal audience.

My dear little Pauline,

God is making me pass through real trials before having me enter Carmel. I am going to tell you how my visit with the pope went. Oh! Pauline, if you could only have read my heart, you would have seen there a great confidence. I believe I did what God wanted me to do, and now there remains nothing for me to do but to pray.

Monseigneur was not there.[1] M. Révérony was taking his place. For you to get an idea of the audience it would be necessary for you to be there. The pope was seated on a large chair, very high.[2] M. Révérony was very close to him; he was looking at the pilgrims who were passing in front of the pope after kissing his foot, and he was saying a word about some of them. You can imagine how my heart was beating when seeing my turn come, but I did not want to return to my place without having spoken to the pope. I said what you were telling me in your letter[3] but not all, for M. Révérony did not give me time. He said immediately: "Most Holy Father, this is a child who wants to enter Carmel at fifteen, but the superiors are considering the matter at this moment." (The good pope is so old that one would say he is dead; I would never have pictured him like this. He can hardly say anything. It is M. Révérony who talks.)[4] I would have liked to be able to explain my business, but there was no way. The Holy Father said simply: "If God wills it, you will enter." Then they made me pass into another room.[5] Oh! Pauline, I cannot tell you what I felt. I was crushed. I felt I was abandoned, and, then, I am so far, so far. . . . I was crying a lot when writing this letter; my heart is heavy. However, God cannot give me trials that are above my strength. He has given me the courage to bear this trial. Oh! it is very great. . . . But, Pauline, I am the Child Jesus' little ball; if He wishes to break His toy, He is free. Yes, I will all that He wills.

I have not written what I wanted to write. I can't write these things; I'd have to speak them.[6] And, then, you are not going to read my letter for another three days. Oh! Pauline, I have only God, Him alone, Him alone. . . .

Adieu, dear Pauline. I can't speak to you any longer. I am afraid Papa may come and ask me to read my letter, and this is impossible.[7]

Pray for your little girl.

Thérèsita

I would really like to write to dear Mother, but I can't this evening. Ask her to pray for her poor[8] Thérèsita.

Kiss dear Marie for me. I have written this letter also for her, but I prefer to speak to only one person. I hope she will understand her little Thérèsita. I haven't the time to read my letter over. It is certainly filled with mistakes. Pardon me.

* Autograph.

1. This was Bishop Germain from Coutances; he presented the members of his own diocese but not those from Bayeux.
2. The accounts are in agreement: the Holy Father was seated not on a throne but on a chair set on a platform in such a way that the pilgrims could easily kneel and kiss his slipper.
3. The "letter from Loreto," see LC 57.
4. The parentheses are erased in the original but are still legible. The pope's pallor, he was then seventy-seven, is emphasized in all the accounts. It was to save his strength that M. Révérony tried to prevent the pope from speaking; see preceding LD, note 2. Leo XIII did not die until 1903, six years after the death of Thérèse, September 30, 1897.
5. Two noble guards had to take the kneeling girl "by force"; see Ms. A, p. 135. That same evening, one of these guards, still much moved by the scene, told his family: "Oh! it would be impossible ever to see a more charming girl asking for something so difficult." (Testimony of his daughter, who was only a child in 1887; she became a religious of the Sacred Heart. She wrote this letter to the Lisieux Carmel from her convent at Heliopolis, Egypt, August 26, 1936.)

6. See LT 28, note 2, October 23, 1887.
7. Thérèse was afraid to cause her father any anguish because he was taking her vocation very much to heart.
8. Word enlarged.

LD *From Céline to Sister Agnes of Jesus and Sister Marie of the Sacred Heart.*

November 23, 1887

"On November 21, we leave for Pompei and Naples. The number of pilgrims staying at Rome during these few days is small. Nobody stayed there because of any sickness; everybody's health was excellent." (Abbé Huet's Journal, *op. cit.*, p. 19.) Céline and Thérèse took part in this excursion, while M. Martin and M. Révérony remained at Rome.

Wednesday

My dear little Sisters,

Rejoice! it is when all seemed lost that all is gained.... We went to Naples and Pompei yesterday and the day before with Mme. Bénard.[1] During this time, Papa went to see the superior of the Brothers,[2] to shake his hand and to thank him for the reception he had given him two years ago with M. l'abbé Marie.[3] The Brother was charmed. Papa spoke to him frankly; he recounted the audience we had on Sunday, Thérèse's desires, her request, all the ups and downs, the sadness she experienced. The superior knew that Marie, Papa's oldest daughter, had entered Carmel. He had never seen such a thing and he was very much enthused about our family. He understood this very well, and he himself—if he had not entered the Brothers when young—believes that he would not have gone, and he thanked God every day for having called him when young (he is fifty years a Brother). He was noting down what Papa was saying about Thérèse, and he offered to speak about her to M. Révérony. But listen to the very end:

Papa stood up to leave and whom did he see enter but M. Révérony!... You may judge his surprise and that of the brother. M. Révérony was very much charmed by Papa; he seemed to be repentant. He reminded Papa that the Sovereign Pontiff had spoken to him particularly because he [M. Révérony] had introduced him by telling the pope that two of his daughters were Carmelites. Papa asked him if he had heard anything regarding the bishop's decision, and he added: "You know very well that you had promised to help me." What a good Father! Then he recounted Thérèse's grief at the audience and especially when he had replied that the matter was being examined by the superiors, etc. M. Révérony was touched, I believe, and he is beginning to believe that Thérèse's vocation is extraordinary. He even said: "Well! I will assist at the ceremony; I'm inviting myself." Papa told him he would be happy to have him and all sorts of amiable things were exchanged between them. That is what Papa told us this morning.[4] I could not keep this in and I am writing you immediately. To show you the promptitude with which I am writing this, I hardly waited for Papa to finish and in the office of the hotel I seized a piece of paper[5] and a pen and here I am!...

Are you happy, dear little sisters? Perhaps even before this letter you have some rays of hope, perhaps you even know more good news than we do. I believe we have won M. Révérony's sympathy. Thérèse was so pretty at the feet of the Holy Father. She was kneeling at his feet, her hands joined on the pope's knees, and her eyes were so pleading! It was beautiful to see her this way, and then I followed, in tears, asking for a blessing for the Carmel. This scene was touching, I assure you.

It could have influenced M. Révérony. So all goes well, what joy! I believe the trials are quite close to being over.[6]...

Au revoir my darlings. We must go to dinner.

Your little Céline

Pisa, *Hôtel de la Minerve*
Nice, *Beau Rivage*
Marseille, *Grand Hôtel de Marseille*,
you know the dates.

* Autograph copy.

1. M. and Mme. Victor Besnard of Lisieux. They had traveled in the same compartment with the Martin family. "Mme. Besnard loved to tell how on the night of the first day, little 'Thérèse,' only fourteen, was so tired that she stretched out on the floor, leaned her head on her knees where she slept for part of the night." (Obituary notice of Sister Pauline de Sales Besnard, †September 7, 1937, daughter of M. Besnard.) M. and Mme. Besnard lodged at the *Hôtel du Sud*, Rome; see LT 32, note 4.
2. Brother Siméon (1814-1899) of the Christian Schools. Thérèse wrote him in 1890, at the time of her Profession; see LC 134.
3. On his return from Constantinople, in September-October 1885.
4. The group from Naples returned to their hotel at midnight (night of November 22).
5. The paper had the stamp of: HOTEL DU SUD ROME G. PAOLUCCI.
6. This letter reached Lisieux on the 25th; in her answer on the same day (see LD of this date), Sister Agnes of Jesus tempered Céline's optimism.

LC 66
November 23, 1887
→ LT 36

From Sister Agnes of Jesus to Thérèse.

The account of the audience reached Lisieux Wednesday morning. From the Carmel, they tried to console Thérèse and Céline (letter to Céline is omitted). Sister Agnes does not say a word to her father (letter to him is omitted) because he was thought to be unaware of the affair (LT 36, note 7). This letter was sent to Pisa; see note 2.

J. M. J. T.

Thérèse,

Wednesday night, Nov. 23

Oh! how Jesus loves His little toy! Yes, He loves it more than the entire universe. He could play with wild flowers, make Himself a ball out of the beautiful mountains of Switzerland, have toys of gold and precious stones; He could with a glance call the stars and

the stars would come around His cradle; He could create millions of creatures more perfect than those which have existed and will ever exist; He could do much else besides. But He wants nothing, He desires nothing, He asks for nothing but His little toy: Thérésita of the Child Jesus. . . . With His dear little ball He dries His tears! When He falls asleep, it is there near Him; always His little hand presses it to His Heart; always He looks at it, always. . . .

"But, little Jesus, what have You done, then, today to Your little ball? How, You who love it so much, have You pierced it so? Look, it no longer bounces. You will not be able to play with it anymore, but it's Your fault."

"What did I do with My little ball, ah!" replies the Divine Child, "it is very simple. I wanted to know what was inside it! . . ."

"And what did you see, Jesus?"

"I saw, I heard a sigh, and this sigh said to me: 'Jesus, I love You.' No, never had My little ball given me so much pleasure, never; I have already pierced it several times and each time a gentle breeze caressed My blond curls; today, I made a bigger hole, and I learned that My little ball was filled only with My love. I learned that it really wants to suffer for Me. I learned that it wants only Me. In a word, I learned everything! . . . Presently, I am going to repair it, and this is how I'm going to do it! I am going to take it into My two little hands and blow very hard into it. Then in order to close it, I am going to do nothing else but place a kiss on the hole I have made. This kiss will be the seal of My Heart; no one will be able to break it, no one. . . . Oh! how happy I am! How I love My little ball! I can pierce it; I can do all I want with it and always it repeats: 'Jesus, I love You! Jesus, I love You! To rejoice, to suffer, to suffer again! All that You will, my dear little Jesus.'"

Oh, dear Thérèse, aren't you proud, aren't you blessed by the *distinct preference* Jesus is showing you? So young, at fifteen, He finds you already worthy to carry His Cross; He finds you worthy to suffer! What an honor for you! If you only knew what these trials do to advance your soul in the way of sanctity! You want to

be a saint, a great saint. Be at peace, Jesus wills this also. He is giving proof of it today.

Adieu, darling of my heart. This trip is marked with the Child Jesus' kiss, marked with His blessings! This trip has made you travel more leagues toward heaven than you have travelled on earth; this trip is a pearl in your crown. . . . Yes, you will enter Carmel when God wills it! Oh! what a beautiful word, what a grace to have heard it from the mouth of *Jesus Himself*. It is an act of abandonment that you must make, that is God's will for you! How beautiful it is! Jesus seems to be sleeping in your little boat, but fear nothing, *His Heart is watching.*[1]

She who loves you more than herself.[2]

* Autograph.

1. See Canticle of Canticles 5:2; see LC 69, note 1.
2. Letter is unsigned. They still have the envelope addressed to: "Mademoiselle Thérèse Martin *Poste restante à Pise Italie*," and bearing the stamps: Lixieux 24 NOV 87, Paris 25 NOV 87, Pisa 26 11 87.

LC 67 *From Sister Marie of the Sacred Heart to Thérèse.*

November 23, 1887

J. M. J. T.

My dear Thérèse,

You can say in all truth as the virgin Agnes said: "He has set His seal on my forehead!"[1] Yes, dear little child of Jesus, He has marked you as His little spouse with the sign of the Cross. But you would not be His if it were not this way. You would not be one of His privileged ones if you never brought your lips to His bitter chalice. But, dear child, what sweet things He is hiding from you. . . . Yes, under this cross, there are only roses. . . . It's not just to console you that I am telling you this: *it is my conviction.*

Did you notice the word of the Holy Father addressed to you: "You will enter if God wills it!" It is very profound, little Thérèse. Ah! if you only knew what mysteries it contains!. . . "You will enter if God wills it." A word from the Holy Father is a word from Our Lord Himself; it is as though Jesus were saying to you: "My child, if I will it, you will enter; if I will it, in spite of all contradictions, in spite of all no's, you will enter; if I will it, tomorrow hearts will be changed, for I hold them all in my hands!" Yes, dear child, the Holy Father has spoken truly; he could not have spoken a more consoling word to you. "You will enter if God wills it!" For me this is a balm, and I would say this always without getting tired. He did not say to you: "Wait, child; listen to the voice of the superiors." He said: "You will enter, if God wills it!" To give joy to your heart I know that it had to hear a 'yes.' But Jesus wills to try to the limit the confidence and abandonment of His Thérésita. He wills to adorn His little ball and *not break it at all*. . . . Ah! He loves it too much for that. Let her heart not be troubled. Jesus is saying to her as He said formerly to His Apostles: "It is I! Fear not."[2] No, Thérèse, no, there is nothing to fear, you have only to bless Jesus! This Jesus, who loves her so much, gave me a thought this evening, which I will not tell her today. I shall wait until the next letter.[3] Let the dear little ball rest gently in the hands of the Child Jesus. If she only knew how dear she is to Him, how much He desires her for Himself alone and how He will have her at Christmas, if He willed it!!!. . .

Yes, Thérèse, yes, the Holy Father bent over to hear you. And Jesus also. . . . Ah! how He bends over with love towards His dear little toy. You know better than I that I have hardly paid any attention up until now to your desires. I was wondering if God's hour had not been advanced by us. But at present I know it hasn't! He has given us proofs of this. And I am sure that His will will be done. It is only that very often, my poor darling, His will is not done. . . . Very often men place obstacles in its way.[4] But for you they will not be able to place any. Has not the Holy Father told you: "You will enter if God wills it!"

Adieu, dear little child. Let your heart rest on the Heart of Jesus.

Your Marie, who loves you

* Autograph.

1. The Response in the Office of St. Agnes at that time; it is used in the ceremonial for the reception of the Veil at Carmel.
2. John 6:20
3. Perhaps the thought Marie shared with Céline on November 26? See LD this date, before the last paragraph.
4. See Ms. A, p. 135, where Thérèse comments in this manner on Leo XIII's answer (spontaneously or under the inspiration of this letter?). See also her prayer of September 8, 1890 (Profession note, Ms. A, p. 275) and her wish at the end of 1895, (Ms. A, p. 181).

LC 68 — *From Mme. Guérin to Thérèse.*

November 23, 1887

Mme. Guérin had just heard at the Carmel about Thérèse's "tribulations." She sets about consoling her, or better, reasoning with her niece. This letter reached Florence on November 25 or 26; *see below*, LT 37, note 4.

Lisieux, November 23, 1887

My dear little Thérèse,

My letter today is for you because I know you are somewhat unhappy and my heart tells me that you are suffering. I would like to be near you, my darling, to console you and to tell you all that I think regarding the trials which have come to you. If you only knew how I see in all this the hand of God. His Providence is guiding you, be sure of it, and be very trusting. You are doing all that you can, and you're doing it to please God, and this God is pleased to try His little child. Don't be surprised at what has happened to you; your good uncle finds this very natural, and he finds it even extraordinary that you were so disturbed by this.

Why, then, cause yourself any grief? Cannot God change hearts in one instant? And, then, if His will is different from ours, or, at least, if He wills to try us for a time, even a long time, in patience, must we complain about it? Have you not done all that you had to do? Really believe, then, I beg you, my darling, that everything that took place comes from God's hand. It is He who permits all this, and, in tormenting yourself, you give Him grief because it is too human a feeling, and God wills that His little daughter allow herself to be directed entirely by Him.[1] Your uncle is so convinced of this that he wants me to repeat it with insistence.

Little Thérésita, Jeanne and Marie wanted to write you, but I prevented them because the hour is late and tomorrow is Mama Papineau's[2] lesson. Poor Marie has still very much to learn. Jeanne is making a cincture for a woolen skirt, and this shows you that the sun is hardly smiling at us. I received your letters yesterday.[3] I delivered Maria's. But the poor girl is hardly in any condition to make a palace out of your home, for those ugly boils don't leave her. She wanted just the same to begin the cleaning yesterday, but she had a large, large boil which caused her much suffering in the whole arm. I advised her to wait for two days, and it will no doubt burst. I see with pleasure the time advancing, and soon you will be in France. What a joy for all of us! We saw Marie and Pauline this afternoon for the last time until Christmas.[4] They shared with us all your tribulations, Thérèse. Tomorrow, they must celebrate the feast of St. John of the Cross, and we would not have been able to see them.[5] The whole family is always very much interested in the travelers. They are following you in spirit and find you very fortunate to see such beautiful things. You must not prove them wrong; you must chase away sadness far from you and lose nothing of this beautiful trip. Come, then, Céline, you who are always cheerful, could you not console and cheer up your little Thérèse?[6] I have firm confidence in you, and I am sure that today you are going to make her laugh a little for my sake.

Adieu, little Thérèse. We all think of you and we are following you both in spirit. We all kiss you will all our heart and also your Céline, and we beg you to give our regards to your good father.

Your devoted aunt,

C. Guérin

The families Fournet, Maudelonde, and Pigeon want to be remembered to you.

Maria and Marcelline say "*bonjour.*"

* Autograph.
1. These sentiments of abandonment to Providence appear often in Mme. Guérin's letters.
2. See LD, July 29, 1885, note 4.
3. Two of Céline's letters (not preserved); and LT 35.
4. Visits to the Carmel were not permitted in Advent, beginning that year on November 27.
5. Because of the exposition of the Blessed Sacrament throughout the day.
6. As a matter of fact, even during this anxious week, Céline and Thérèse had their hours of gaiety; these hours were quite late in the estimation of their neighbor in the next room, a certain Father Vauquelin, who occupied room 2, *Hôtel du Sud*: "At night, overcome by fatigue from the comings and goings of the day and also somewhat intoxicated by the novelty of their encounters, the two sisters did not decide to go to bed immediately; they stretched out on the carpet in their bedroom, trying to relax, and they exchanged their impressions with each other so animatedly and joyfully that the sounds at times passed through the wall, preventing the good priest from falling asleep." (Céline's memories, reported by A. Noché, S.J., *La Petite Sainte Thérèse de Maxence Van der Meersch devant la critique et devant les textes*, Ed. Saint-Paul, Paris 1950; p. 296.)

LD *From Sister Marie of the Sacred Heart to Céline.*

November 24, 1887 — This letter was sent with four others (LC 66 and 67 and two letters from Sister Agnes, omitted) to Pisa.

My dear Céline,

You won't be annoyed by this half-page. I would like our letters to go out this morning, and I haven't the time to write very much. You should, Céline, see everything from heaven's viewpoint. . . . What do you expect? That's life. . . . This very beautiful trip is life, a true image of life that is never without clouds. God loves you too much to strew only roses in your path. But you must not, my darling, give yourself too much distress over Thérèse's answer. I myself find it so beautiful! The good Holy Father could not express an affirmative "yes." Don't think it was M. Révérony who stopped everything. No, no. If Thérèse had spoken at greater length, the pope would not have answered her any more than he did. Our Mother says this. But I admit that I believe God has His plans in all this, ravishing plans of mercy. Live, *be joyful* right to the end, *God wills it*; live, be JOYFUL in spite of all that can happen. You will see that I am right in inviting you to joy.

Adieu, dear little sister. Be grateful to God and to our good Father, who has made you a gift of a trip like this. BE BIG, *generous*, bold. It just does not suit you to be otherwise. Be *happy, happy, happy* about the Holy Father's audience. And don't paint clouds in the sky. You would then be an unskillful artist. But if you want to see clouds at any cost, look, at the same time, at the sun hidden behind this little cloud. When it hides itself, it is only so as to become more resplendent. . . .

I leave you as a last thought, this word *from Father* during the retreat: "Unfortunate are souls who are not protected by their Cross!"[1] Oh! yes, the Cross protects, it defends, it is victory's arm. . . . Your sister, who loves you,

Marie of the Sacred Heart

* Autograph.
1. P. Pichon. Retreat at Carmel of Lisieux, October 1887, first day, first instruction.

LT 37 **From Thérèse to Marie Guérin.**

November 25, 1887
→ LC 65

The pilgrims left Rome on the morning of the 24th. They visited Florence on the 25th, in torrential rain (Céline's letter to Jeanne Guérin, the same day, omitted), and then in better weather, on the morning of the 26th. Ms. A, p. 139, seems to ignore the city's treasures, recalling only the tomb of St. Mary Magdalene de Pazzi.

Friday, November 25, '87
Florence

My dear little Marie,

Time is passing quickly; a few more days and we will be reunited. I hope that a week from today we shall be with you.[1]

I assure you I will leave all Italy's marvels behind with pleasure. All this is very beautiful, but I can't forget those whom I have left at Lisieux. There is a kind of magnet which is attracting me to Lisieux, so I shall return there with *very much* pleasure.

You just don't know the joy your nice letter gave me. I was very happy that you spoke to me about dear Aunt's feast. I was near you in spirit at that moment; there was no longer any distance between Rome and Lisieux. You did well to tell me about the present Aunt gave you, for I would never have been able to guess it. What a beautiful surprise!

I will not speak to you about my visit to the Sovereign Pontiff. I think that you have the news about it from the Carmel. I was very miserable, but since it is God's will. . . .

I hope, dear little sister, that you are going to continue to pray for me. I have very much confidence in your prayers. It seems to me that God can refuse you nothing.

You were complaining that your letter was poorly written; really, if you are that fussy, I shall no longer dare to send you mine which are veritable scribblings. I think very often of you, of you all, so often that I dream of you at night. I would like to be already with you.

It is a long time since we have had any news from the Carmel. I am afraid their letters went astray.[2]

Yesterday, we were at Assisi. When returning from one church, I found myself all alone and without any carriage; there was no longer any left but that of M. Révérony. He made me climb up into it with him; he was very friendly, and he did not want me to pay my way.[3] He did not speak to me at all about my business, and I don't know what he is thinking about the audience.

I see that I am putting in "he's" without any end. My letter has taken a strange turn.

Thank Aunt for her letter.[4] It touched me in such a way that I would not be able to express it. Kiss all whom I love for me.

Adieu, dear little sister,
see you soon, *au revoir*,
Thérèse

* Nine fragments from the autograph. CMG.

1. The return to Lisieux took place on Friday at two in the afternoon.
2. Thérèse received a letter at Pisa on the 26th.
3. See Ms. A, p. 138, where this incident is reported in detail, taking place in the afternoon of the 24th. See, too, Céline's account to her sisters, on the 28th (LD of this date).
4. Letter of the 23rd (LC 68), undoubtedly received at Florence on the 26th, for it seems difficult (not impossible) that a letter mailed at Lisieux on the 24th would reach Florence on the 25th. Thérèse would have terminated her letter, then, on Saturday morning, the 26th. In her letter of the 25th, mentioned above, Céline enumerates some of their noble company; she ends this way: "How stupid I am! I picked up an old piece of paper on which there was the beginning of a very old letter written on the train." On the text, we read, in fact,

in pencil: "My dear little Jeanne. I am late. It is two days since Thérèse's letter was finished." (See LT 31 A, November 10. Céline was writing, then, on the 12th.)

LD *From Sister Agnes of Jesus to M. Martin.* (Extracts.)

November 25, 1887

At the moment when the difficulties between M. Révérony and Thérèse are leveling off (see Céline, LD, November 23 and November 28, 1887), the situation is becoming worse between M. Delatroëtte and the Carmel (see Sister Agnes of Jesus, LD, November 26 and November 28, 1887). They did not speak to Thérèse about it (see LC 69 and 70), but Sister Agnes of Jesus transmitted some information about it to her father. This letter, the last from the Carmel, reached Nice on November 28th.

J. M. J. T.

Beloved Father,

How good you are! Céline's letter told us about your visit to the good superior of the Brothers at Rome, M. Révérony's providential arrival, the whole thing which was so delightful! Dear little angel, Thérèse, how fortunate she is to have you! It is through you that her grief is assuaged; you are the real Holy Father, whose single word she was hoping for so much....

I was far from expecting a letter of this kind after the letters of desolation received yesterday.[1] Thérèse's short note was heartbreaking. Her whole heart was in it, palpitating with sorrow and yet resigned. What virtue in this child! Oh! how God loves her. She is a privileged soul among all privileged souls, but we must take care not to tell her so.

I saw Our Father Superior yesterday. He is more and more opposed, and nothing can convince him. There is a mystery here for us! But God is there in this mystery. It is only a matter of

repeating with P. Ponlevoy: "There must always be something in God's way that we do not understand and should not want to understand so that there may be room for faith and the Cross."

If Thérèse enters at Christmas, this can be only because of Monseigneur; if Monseigneur decides, he[2] will consent to open the door, that is understood; but for him to take upon himself the responsibility of this act, never will this happen. I believe that he has very grave reasons to act in this way and these reasons are easy to guess at. This poor Father has been so calumniated by Monsieur Fl.[3] at the time of his daughter's[4] plan. It was frightful.... And what would Monsieur Fl. say today when seeing him giving us a child of fifteen? It is necessary, then, that Our Father be able to tell everybody that it is Monseigneur who had our angel enter. In that case, nobody would say anything.

Adieu, beloved Father....

Your poor little pearl,
Sister Agnes of Jesus

* Autograph.

1. LT 36 and Céline's LD, November 20, 1887. We must admit either that Sister Agnes wrote over a period of two days, the 24th and 25th, or that she meant: "before yesterday," the 23rd, for she speaks in the following paragraph of a "yesterday," which means the 24th, the date of M. Delatroëtte's visit.
2. The superior of the Carmel, M. Delatroëtte.
3. M. Fleuriot (d. 1913).
4. "...to enter the Carmel. She was his oldest daughter, Jeanne. He did so much and this so successfully that she remained in the world. Thérèse inherited the furniture of the cell they had prepared for Jeanne, and this furniture displeased her very much because it was nicely finished." (Sister Geneviève's note.)

LC 69 *From Sister Agnes of Jesus to Thérèse.*

November 25, 1887

In answer to Céline's joyful letter (LD of November 23), received at Lisieux that Friday, the 25th.

J. M. J. T.

Jesus' little Toy,

You see that I was right when thinking Jesus was going to repair His little ball! I would never have expected Him to do it so well and so promptly. Remember, my darling, that the desperate hours are always God's hours.[1] It is when there is no longer any hope, when everything seems lost that the sleeping Jesus awakens and commands as Master the winds and the tempest.[2] Yes, intimate little friend of the Divine Child, yes, you are really His little ball; abandon yourself forever into His hands. You will really suffer during your life, your heart is especially made to suffer,[3] but when Jesus is there, when it is He who is sending His little ball into the midst of thorns, the thorns will change into flowers.

Let us pray; let us pray. . . . The Child Jesus is taken up at this moment with His little ball repaired by His divine kiss. He truly seems to be aiming at Carmel in order to send it there with one throw and make it bounce into His crib to remain there forever. Let us say to Him at each moment: May your will be done! Let us say: Jesus, arrange all things so that Your little ball be sent where You will, at the hour You will, and the way You will; don't let it escape Your little hands.

Darling of my heart, I really know that you are thinking all this. Oh! how Jesus loves you, and do you know why I believe more than ever in His divine call? It is because *you have suffered*. . . . Without the Cross, one is sure of nothing; without the Cross, there is only the human element, the mundane; without the Cross, Jesus is not there. But, take consolation, your vocation is marked with this sacred sign. The Child Jesus in His poor crib

sighed only for the Cross, dreamt only of the Cross, and He has told His dream to His dear Thérésita.[4]

Your little Confidante, who has suffered
still more for you than you for yourself

If you only knew how much Our Mother loves you.

* Autograph.

1. See P. Pichon: "The desperate hours are God's hours! . . . Sometimes Jesus seems to sleep in the midst of tempests, trials, waves agitated in our soul! He is only pretending! . . . His Heart is watching!" (October retreat of 1887, fifth day, second instruction.) Sentence cited also at the closing sermon, October 15, 1887. P. Pichon attributed this at times to Mother Madeleine-Sophie Barat (died 1865; canonized 1925).
2. See Matthew 8:24-27.
3. Same "prediction" under the pen of Mother Marie de Gonzague (LC 118, autumn 1889); this judgment was ratified by Thérèse at the end of her life (Ms. C. p. 217; CJ 29.7.14 and 26.8.8).
4. Concerning this "dream of the Child Jesus," dear to the piety of Sister Agnes of Jesus, see LC 125, note 1, January 2, 1890.

LC 70 — *From Sister Marie of the Sacred Heart to Thérèse.*

November 25 (?), 1887 — That same evening or in the morning of the 26th, a letter from her to M. Martin (omitted).

My dear Thérèse,

Have you understood now the word of the pope? And do you realize, today, that a word from the Holy Father is a word from God Himself? I knew nothing about all this[1] when I wrote you my letter.[2] Well, then, did not your poor Marie speak the truth? Yes, privileged child of Jesus, yes "you will enter if God wills it." And for me, this is at Christmas that He wants you and it is at

Christmas that He will have you.[3] See, then, how He has turned hearts in one instant. Ah! never forget this remarkable grace. Never forget that one day at the feet of the Holy Father, leaning on him as upon Jesus Himself, you opened your heart to him and that he blessed you!... Never forget these words from heaven which you did not understand at first because they were enveloped in mystery.... A mystery filled with light, filled with the *special* love of Jesus. Ah! how good is the Jesus of Thérèse! Do you see how He loves His little toy? Do you see how good it is to be the little toy of Jesus? Would you say that He has broken His toy? I myself am beginning to say that He has adorned His little ball. And that now that it is well-adorned, nobody will dare dispute it with Him. Oh! good little Jesus. Dear little ball, believe me, don't roll one single instant far from His cradle. It is so good to approach it and remain there always.

See you soon, blessed child! And you must never forget what our Father, unique among all, has done for you. And thank Jesus for so many good things He gives you through him!...

Marie of the Sacred Heart

* Autograph.
1. What Céline reported in her letter of the 23rd.
2. LC 67, also written on the 23rd.
3. Thérèse will not enter until April 1888.

LD *From Sister Agnes of Jesus to Céline.*

November 26 (?), 1887

J. M. J. T.

My dear Céline,

How good you are! How grateful we are to you for your desire for Thérèse's happiness. God is blessing you and He will bless you.

We are very much touched by your conduct, and this trip will make us love you more, if that is possible.

Yes, yes, you did well in asking for a blessing for the Carmel! Our beloved Mother was delighted by it. Oh! how I would like you to be here in order to hear all this in detail.

Darling, don't believe that all is won! If you only knew how much Our Father is opposed to the entrance! . . . Never had I seen him before as he was on Thursday.[1] He said that the more he goes on, the more he is rooted in his *no* and what a no! If you had only heard him! We can see so well that nothing could change him. However, God is permitting this. Must there not always be a bitter drop in the chalice of our consolations? The only way of having Thérèse enter at Christmas would be to ask M. Révérony to ask Monseigneur to write Our Father his sentiments about her. Without this, there is no way, *it's too delicate a matter for us*. . . . How can you expect us to tell Our Father that M. Révérony is attending to Thérèse's vocation?[2] This would offend him. Everything must come from Monseigneur and you, and nothing must give rise to the suspicion that the Carmel is acting in an underhanded way. . . . However, all is in God's hands, that is evident, and I believe that all will go well in spite of Our Father's opposition; and furthermore he is always saying that if Monseigneur decides, the door is opened for Thérèse. But as far as he is concerned, if he is to decide, *the door is far from being opened.*

I'd like everything to be decided before your return, that is, that M. Révérony promise Papa that he will have Monseigneur write; in this way, we shall be entirely protected! . . .

Adieu, darling of my heart.

Our beloved Mother kisses you and I join my kisses to hers.

Write what happens.[3]

* Autograph.

1. The 24th; see LD of Sister Agnes of Jesus, November 25, 1887. The fact that she does not say "yesterday" as she did in the letter to M. Martin indicates that she is writing to Céline on the 26th.

2. Vocation. (This was abbreviated in the French.)
3. Céline answers this request on the 28th (LD of this date).

LD *From Sister Marie of the Sacred Heart to Céline.* (Extracts.)

November 25-26, 1887

Not having seen the Father Superior on the 24th, Marie is not as upset as Pauline about M. Delatroëtte's opposition. In the letter to Céline, as in her letter to her father (omitted), Marie is very optimistic.

Céline, just a short note to you who, however, wrote three large pages of joy to us![1] Is not God's conduct beautiful, is it not good to abandon oneself to Him!. . .

Darling Céline, you will be rewarded without any doubt for the generosity you are showing to God in giving Him your little Thérèse so lovingly. . . . I have always believed (especially since the opposition of the superiors) that God wanted Thérèse. This is a proof without parallel.

I intended to tell Uncle to speak to M. le curé at St. Jacques.[2] Now all is useless, Jesus has said everything Himself. He has allowed the Holy Father to say: You will enter if I will it, and He does will it, that is evident. Ah! what words; they delighted me as soon as I read them . . . . I am not surprised that these words are being carried out. Be happy, darling Céline, this is a blessed, an unforgettable trip . . . .

Marie of the Sacred Heart

* Autograph.
1. LD, November 23, 1887.
2. M. Delatroëtte. Would this plan be the "idea" mentioned by Marie in her letter to Thérèse on the night of November 23? See LC 67, note 3.

LD *From Céline to Sister Agnes of Jesus and Sister Marie of the Sacred Heart.* (Extracts.)

November 28, 1887

This Monday, the 28th, the pilgrims enjoyed a magnificent sight as they traveled along the Mediterranean ocean from Genoa (see Ms. A, p. 140). They crossed into France in the late afternoon, reaching Nice in the evening. A large package of letters (six in all) was awaiting M. Martin and his daughters at *Hôtel Beau Rivage.*

Monday, November 28, 1887

Dear little Sisters,

I really need to rest this evening, but I cannot resist the pleasure of sending you a short note. It's the first in France. France! Oh! I am so happy to see it again. . . .

Dear little sisters, it is not to talk about this that I come this evening, but rather to thank you for your nice letters.[1] Papa is delighted and they were our consolation. Since I wrote you,[2] M. Révérony has not spoken to us about all that happened. All seems to be asleep. All is at rest. Jesus is sleeping for a long time! He is allowing the boat to rock softly at the mercy of the waves, but we don't see the port coming into view. I would like to wake Him up a little bit[3] to remind Him that the hour is getting late and we are cold. . . .

Thérèse and I have thought that M. Révérony, intelligent as he is, had perhaps said all this just to oblige, just to please, and we have noticed that he is always in agreement with everybody; he says one thing with some and another thing with others. What can he be held to? The other day, Thérèse by accident found herself in the same carriage as himself[4] with several handsome gentlemen who never leave him; at the end of the trip, they all gave twenty-five cents to the coachman. Thérèse took out her purse, but M. Révérony gave a fifty-cent piece, saying to Thérèse: "We

have an account to settle together." That is what we know. It seems to us that it would be a mistake for Thérèse to go and speak to him;[5] moreover, there is never an opportunity, numerous friends are around him all the time. And for a matter so serious, this would be begging, seeking favor, and this would do more evil in our opinion. There is only one thing to do and this is to let little Jesus wake up by Himself; "even in sleep, He is never sleeping."[6]

Adieu, dear little sisters. *Au revoir*, and see you soon. Thérèse would have liked to write you at all costs, but I forbade her. Her sentiments are mine, and what good is it to fatigue ourselves writing them twice? She would have liked to send a short note also to dear Aunt. She was very happy with her nice letter.[7]

Kiss our dear Mother for us.

We arrive on Thursday at midnight at Paris. Being *very eager* to see all of you again, we shall probably not stay at Paris, and we are counting on taking the 11:45 train which will bring us into Lisieux around 4:30 on FRIDAY. If you don't receive any other letters or telegrams, it is because nothing has changed. It is understood that we shall stop at the Carmel immediately.[8]

We kiss everybody.

Céline

* Autograph.

1. Letters from Sister Agnes of Jesus to her father (LD, November 25), to Thérèse (LC 69), to Céline (LD, November 26); letters from Sister Marie of the Sacred Heart to M. Martin (omitted), to Thérèse (LC 70), and to Céline (LD, November 26).
2. The 23rd, (LD).
3. See Matthew 8:24-27; see LC 69, notes 1 and 2.
4. At Assisi, the 24th; see LT 37, note 3.
5. See suggestions of Sister Agnes to Céline (LD, November 26).
6. See Canticle of Canticles, 5:2.
7. LC 68, November 23, 1887, received at Florence.
8. There is no reason to think this visit did not take place, thus obliging them to postpone it until Saturday, December 3.

LD *From Sister Agnes of Jesus to M. Guérin.*

November 28-29, 1887

In its November 24 issue, *L'Univers* related the audience given the pilgrims from France on November 20 by Leo XIII. In one passage it pointed out: "Among the pilgrims was a young girl of fifteen, who begged the Holy Father for permission to enter a convent immediately to become a religious. His Holiness encouraged her to be patient, to pray very much, and to seek counsel from God and her conscience. This caused the young girl to break down into sobs." (*Univers* article was not signed.) This account caused some commotion in Lisieux.

J. M. J. T.

Dear Uncle,

M. Lepelletier[1] knows all. He came to see Sister Marie of the Sacred Heart on Saturday.[2] He is in admiration, and he said this child is privileged and destined for great things. . . .

Thank you, dear little Uncle, for your two short notes.[3] You speak to us as a father and you love us as your children.

I know a will that is not so easily bent as you imagine.[4] . . . But God can do all things!

I saw Our Father on Thursday evening.[5] He told me among other things: "If your little sister should get sick because of grief, I shall say that she did not have the strength to be a Carmelite. That's it. But this would not make me give in."

To tell you, dear Uncle, what I experienced when hearing these words is impossible. *I was crushed.* Immediately coming out of there, I found the only Confidant, who can place balm on all wounds. He is the One who consoled me, and I don't know what inner voice said to me: Fear nothing, this child will not die in the world. . . .

What followed[6] proved that this voice was really God's voice.

Adieu, dear little Uncle. I kiss you and I love you, as well as Aunt and my two little sisters.

Your *daughter* and GODDAUGHTER,
Sister Agnes of Jesus

These beautiful words of the Canticle of Canticles keep coming back to my mind: "Come from Lebanon, my Spouse; come to be crowned, for you have wounded my heart."[7]

* Autograph.
1. Thérèse's Confessor for the last eighteen months; see LD, November 17, 1887 (Mme. Guérin), note 3. Not aware of his penitent's decision to enter Carmel at Christmas, he came seeking an explanation at the Carmel.
2. The 26th. This information would suggest that the letter was not written before Monday, otherwise Sister Agnes would have written "yesterday"; and not before Thursday, November 1, otherwise there would have been confusion regarding "Thursday evening" of paragraph 4.
3. These letters were not preserved.
4. That of "Our Father," the superior.
5. The 24th; see letters from Sister Agnes on the 25th and 26th to M. Martin and Céline.
6. M. Révérony's sudden change, pointed out by Céline (LD, November 23, 1887). Sister Agnes does not seem to have received the following letter (LD, November 28) in which Céline's optimism is on the decline.
7. Canticle of Canticles 4:8-9.

LD *From Céline to Sister Agnes of Jesus and Sister Marie of the Sacred Heart.*

November 29, 1887 — Last letter before the return to Lisieux. Céline wrote in the train on the way to Marseille.

Tuesday, November 29, '87
Cannes

My dear little Sisters,

Jesus seemed to have awakened a little.[1]
! ! ! ....

This morning, when being taken to the station, we were in the

omnibus[2] with M. Révérony. Papa was next to him, and he said in a whisper: "Would you say something to Thérèse." M. Révérony answered with a smile, and Papa said: "You know that she is always thinking of her little Christmas Jesus. . . ." The same smile, the same response. Then without being aware of anything, we got up into the omnibus, Thérèse and I, and we were behind Papa. By God's permission, Thérèse was next to M. Révérony. She was very close to him, for we were sixteen in the carriage, eight on each side, crushed in like sardines. M. Révérony leaned over to Thérèse and said to her: "Well! where will we go when we are at Lisieux?" Thérèse, searching for an answer, responded with a smile. M. Révérony repeated his question. Thérèse then said: "I will go to see my sisters at Carmel." He answered: "We will do what we can, won't we?" "Oh! yes," Thérèse said. "I *promise* to do all I *can*." Thérèse then answered with this word which came from her heart: "Oh! Thank you! . . ."

This was the whole little scene; I wrote it immediately such as it took place.

Au revoir, my darlings. Pardon me for this very poorly written note, but it is on the train that I am tracing these lines and it is very difficult to write.

Céline

* Autograph.

1. See her letter of the preceding day (LD, paragraph 2), in which Céline finds His "sleeping" very long.
2. This was a horse-drawn vehicle. The episode took place at Nice and not at Cannes. In fact, not one of the schedules issued to the pilgrims before the trip from Rome, and not one of the Chroniclers (Abbés Hamel, Huet, and M. de la Thuillerie) mentions any visit or stay at Cannes. The crowding of the passengers in the vehicle is explained by the arrival of almost two hundred persons from the *Hôtel Beau Rivage* (Nice) at the station at seven o'clock in the morning. Céline was reporting the incident within an hour after it took place, and her note in pencil shows the effects of the jerking of the train.

"Why call me so strongly. . . ." (*LT 39*)
(December 1887)
Age fourteen

The three pilgrims arrived at Lisieux on December 2 in the afternoon. Without delay, they resumed negotiations in order to bring the "matter" to a close, namely, Thérèse's entrance into Carmel for Christmas.

Sister Agnes of Jesus was on the point of capitulating to the aggravated intransigence of the superior (LD, December 10, 1887). Mother Marie de Gonzague and M. Guérin then took hold of the situation (LD, December 10 and 15). It was a question of playing the last card cleverly: recourse to the bishop of Bayeux. The prioress doubted a "miracle." But Thérèse's confidence never weakened: ". . . since God is calling me" (LT 38 A).

Each morning, from December 18 to 24, the young girl went to the post office with her father (Ms. A, p. 141), hoping for an answer to her letters of December 16 (LT 38 C and 39) to Monseigneur Hugonin and Abbé Révérony.

LT 38 A From Thérèse to Monseigneur Hugonin.

December 3-8 (?), 1887

No doubt on December 3 (see note 1), Thérèse had a talk with Sister Agnes of Jesus. "I had done everything that depended on me, even to speaking to the Holy Father, so I didn't know what I still had to do. You told me to write to Monseigneur and to remind him of his promise; I did this immediately, the best way possible for me, but in words Uncle found a little too simple. He wrote my letter over again. At the moment I was about to send it off, I received a letter from you, telling me not to write, to wait for a few days. I immediately obeyed, for I was sure that it was the best way not to make a mistake. Finally, ten days before Christmas, my letter left!" (Ms. A, p. 141.) We have this letter in three different drafts from Thérèse's hand (LT 38 A, unedited, and 38 B) and a copy of the text written by M. Guérin (see below, LT 38 C). The passages in parentheses were erased by Thérèse.

Monseigneur,

I am coming today[1] to ask Your Excellency to give me the answer I have desired for a long time. Oh! Monseigneur, I hope for everything from your paternal kindness; yes, I believe it is through you that Jesus is really going to carry out His promise. Oh! Monseigneur, they say that trials are a sign of a vocation, and you know that God has not spared me from them, but I felt (in the center of my heart a great calm through Jesus, little Jesus) that I was suffering for Jesus, and I have not ceased hoping for a single instant, (oh! yes, since He judged me worthy).

(He was in my heart) Little Jesus made me feel so well that He wanted me for Christmas that I was not able to resist the grace He was giving me, (it is true) that I am very young, but Monseigneur (God is pleased) since God is calling me and Papa is willing.

Monseigneur (I hope that) I think that M. Révérony really

wanted to speak to Your Excellency about me; he promised me this during the trip from Rome.[2] Oh! I will never forget his kindness to me.

(Monseigneur, Christmas is approaching, and I am waiting the answer that Your Excellency will be willing to give me with a great confidence.)

Oh! Monseigneur, Christmas is approaching, but I am awaiting your answer with a great confidence in the promise that little Jesus made me at the bottom of my heart. I will never forget that it is to Your Excellency that I will owe the accomplishment of God's will.

Pardon me, Monseigneur, the liberty I took in writing to you. My heart told me to do so, and I have written simply to Your Excellency, thinking that in your kindness you would not refuse me.

* Autograph.

1. Probably on Saturday, December 3. In the evening, the day of their return, the three travelers made a quick visit to the Carmel; see Céline, LD, November 28, 1887, note 2. A more intimate visit could have been postponed until the next day.
2. See Céline, LD, November 29, 1887.

LT 38 B From Thérèse to Monseigneur Hugonin.

December 3-8 (?), 1887

The second draft contains more erasures than the first. This is how it was transcribed for the "Process of the Writings."

1887

Monseigneur,

I am coming to ask Your Excellency to give me the answer I have desired for a long time.

Monseigneur, I place all my hope in your paternal kindness;

yes, I believe it is through you that Jesus is going to carry out His promise.

Oh, Monseigneur! they say that trials are a sign of a vocation; yes, truly, you know that God has not spared me from them. But I felt that I was suffering for Jesus, and I never ceased hoping for a single instant. Little Jesus made me feel so much that He wanted me for Christmas that I am unable to resist the grace He has given me. It is true that I am very young, but, Monseigneur, since God is calling me and Papa is willing.

I hope that Monsieur l'Abbé Révérony has spoken about me to Your Excellency; he had promised me this during the trip from Rome. Never will I forget his kindness to me.

Oh, Monseigneur! Christmas is approaching, but I am awaiting your answer with a great confidence. I will never forget that it is to Your Excellency that I will owe the accomplishment of God's will.

Please bless your child, Monseigneur.

I am Your Excellency's littlest and most grateful daughter,

Thérèse Martin

* CE.

LD *From Mother Marie de Gonzague to M. Guérin.*

December 10, 1887

This Saturday, Thérèse went to the Carmel (paragraph 2) with the letter destined for Bishop Hugonin; this was the letter held back at Sister Agnes of Jesus' orders (see LT 38 A). Now the idea of writing to the bishop is being called into question.

†J. M. J. T. December 10, 1887

Monsieur,

I sincerely believe that our dear Thérèse's letter[1] is going to produce a bad effect. Monseigneur is going to send it to our Su-

perior, and I am convinced the latter will make a *formal* decision.[2] It might have been better, I think, that the request addressed to His Excellency to learn about his decision might have been done in another way: either a *viva voce* request or through a note from you, Monsieur, pressured by the dear child's anxiousness regarding the hope or the disappointment she has to have.

Pardon this scribbling, Monsieur; I am expressing my thoughts while the angel is in the speakroom.

I fear the *obstinate* Superior much; this note is for you alone. He does not really know the child's reasons.

My deepest respect in Jesus,

Sister Marie de Gonzague
r.c.ind.

* Autograph.

1. The letter already corrected by M. Guérin no doubt (LT 38 C).
2. It seems that Mother Marie de Gonzague wrote *before* the superior's visit, about which Sister Agnes gave an account (see LD following, note 3). However, she was already aware of M. Delatroëtte's opinion. See this incident recorded at the Apostolic Process: "On a big feast day, Father Superior came into the cloister to visit Mother Geneviève, our Foundress, sick in the infirmary. Asked beforehand by Mother Marie de Gonzague, Mother Geneviève begged for the favor of Thérèse's entrance at Christmas, doing so before the whole Community. The superior answered emotionally: 'You are speaking to me again about that entrance. With all these requests is one to believe that the Community's salvation depends on this child's entrance? There is no danger in this home; let her stay with her father until she is twenty-one. Besides, do you think I offer a refusal such as this without seeking God's counsel? I beg that you don't speak again about this matter.'" (Mother Agnes of Jesus, AP, 368.) This was most likely on December 8, feast of the Immaculate Conception.

LD *From Sister Agnes of Jesus to M. Guérin.*

December 10, 1887 Date written in by M. Guérin, see note 1.

J. M. J. T.

Dear Uncle,

Let Thérèse make the sacrifice. Our Father came this afternoon[1] and asked for Our Mother. He told her *the most painful things*: that she had acted underhandedly, that it was a fine thing to do knowing what she knew about the Fleuriot family,[2] etc., etc. This beloved Mother listened with her customary kindness and serenity, but her very tender heart was moved, and I saw her come out of the speakroom in tears![3] I must admit to you, Uncle, that I cannot see this incomparable Mother suffer without suffering with her. My heart is broken.... I don't know what I am writing.

Come to the Carmel as soon as you can and ask for her.

Don't write to Monseigneur.[4] We must abandon the matter completely. May God be blessed and glorified in this trial!

I kiss you and I love you.

Your child,
Sister Agnes of Jesus
r.c.ind.

* Autograph.

1. According to the Carmelite schedule at this time, this visit took place either between one and two or three and five o'clock. Having seen the serious side of the situation, Sister Agnes must have written without delay so that the letter be brought to the Guérin pharmacy in the evening. The date of the writing and the reception of the letter are the same.
2. See LD, November 25, 1887. Let us point out that M. Fleuriot's attitude did not destroy the good relationship of his family with that of the Martins and especially the Guérins (Mme. Fleuriot, *née* Adèle Méry Samson, was related to Mme. Guérin by a common ascending line: Fournet-David-Monsaint).

3. At first, she wrote: "in sobs." It is very unlikely that Sister Agnes of Jesus was present at this interview between M. Delatroëtte and the prioress.
4. This nullifies the preceding suggestion of Mother Marie de Gonzague; this would suggest that the prioress had written (preceding LD) before the superior's visit. Thérèse would have, then, come to the Carmel on Saturday morning?

LC 71 *From Sister Agnes of Jesus to Thérèse.* (Fragments.)

Winter 1887-1888 Approximate date; see note 1.

Let Thérèse console her little heart. Trial is always precious; we have only this life to suffer and *Eternity* to rejoice.

Kiss[1] . . . .

* Autograph.

1. The verb "kiss" in the plural suggests that the letter was addressed to both Celine and Thérèse. The handwriting, the paper, the very pale ink, all permits us to place the date of this letter in December 1887 or early 1888. Would this fragment be part of the letter (lost) about which Thérèse spoke in Ms. A, p. 141 (see LT 38 A, short introduction)? In this case, it could be dated, then, around December 8.

LD *From Mother Marie de Gonzague to M. Guérin.*

December 15, 1887 Date written in by M. Guérin. Since Sister Agnes' counter-order (LD December 10), the affair of Thérèse's vocation remained pending.

J. M. J. T.

Monsieur,

I am a bother, but I understand your heart and I'm coming to you as a child to tell you what I'm thinking.

I was making this reflection, what is Monseigneur going to say of everybody's silence, he who had said that he would decide the matter after the return from Rome?[1] . . . and especially after the step taken by the venerable Father,[2] don't you think this abstention is hurting him? . . . I myself can do nothing for the present; the child must remain in silence. How can you help us now?

It seems to me, Monsieur, that it is only your perspicacity that can effect something; the Superior still has the same sentiments. I am anxious to know if at the time of your visit the Superior asked any questions?[3] I believe a miracle is necessary for the dear child to be answered in her desire for Christmas.

Accept, Monsieur, our most religious respect and sincere gratitude.

Would you please, Monsieur, send us our bill next week?[4]

Your humble servant
Sister Marie de Gonzague
r.c.ind.

* Autograph.

1. See LC 57.
2. Undoubtedly the visit to Bayeux, October 31.
3. The documents are silent concerning this step which must have been decided upon between himself and the prioress in the Carmel speakroom on Sunday, the 11th; a step which must be placed between December 12 and 15. This present letter must have led to another meeting with M. Guérin in the speakroom and the decision taken to have Thérèse write to Monseigneur Hugonin and M. Révérony (LT 38 C and 39).
4. Bill from the pharmacy.

LT 38 C **From Thérèse to Monseigneur Hugonin.**

December 16, 1887

"Finally, ten days before Christmas, my letter went off!" (Ms. A, p. 141.) The text was "reviewed and corrected" by M. Guérin; see LT 38 A.

Monseigneur,

I am coming humbly to remind Your Excellency of the request for authorization to enter Carmel which I had the honor of directing to you.

I am awaiting with confidence, Monseigneur, this remarkable favor from your paternal kindness. I believe it is through you that Jesus is going to carry out His promise.

They say that trials are a sign of a vocation. You know, Monseigneur, that God has not spared me from them, but I felt I was suffering for Jesus and I never ceased hoping for a single instant.

Little Jesus had made me know so well that He wanted me for Christmas that I cannot resist the impulse of His gentle violence.

It is true that I am very young, but, Monseigneur, since God is calling me and Papa is willing!

All the distractions of my trip to Rome, the beautiful things that I admired, all these could not chase from my mind for a single moment the ardent desire that I have to unite myself to Jesus. May I hope that the frequent meetings I had during my trip with Monsieur Révérony and which permitted me to appreciate his kindness were for him the opportunity of judging the truth of my vocation and a motive for pleading my cause with Your Excellency?

Christmas is approaching, Monseigneur, and I await it with great confidence, for I am thinking of the promise that Jesus made me at the bottom of my heart. I will never forget that it is to Your Excellency that I will owe the accomplishment of God's designs on His little servant. However, I do not fear to state that

no matter what the pain a refusal would cause me I will accept it with the fullest submission as coming from God Himself.

I dare to call myself, Monseigneur,
the littlest daughter and obedient
servant of Your Excellency,
Thérèse Martin

* Copy of Mother Agnes according to M. Guérin's outline.

LT 39 **From Thérèse to l'abbé Révérony.**

December 16, 1887

Lisieux, December 16, 1887

Monsieur le Vicaire Général,

I just wrote to Monseigneur. Papa and Uncle permitted me to do so. I am always awaiting with confidence the "yes" of the Child Jesus. Monsieur l'Abbé, it is only a week from now until Christmas! But the more time advances the more I hope; this is perhaps temerity, but, nonetheless, it seems to me that it is Jesus who is speaking within me.

All the distractions of the trip to Rome were not able to chase from my mind for one instant the ardent desire of uniting myself to Jesus. Ah! why call me so strongly if it is only to make me languish far from Him?

Monsieur l'Abbé, I hope you have pleaded my cause with Monseigneur as you had promised me.[1] If Jesus has consoled me in my trials it is through your intervention, and if I enter Carmel at Christmas, I know that I shall owe it to you. But I am not ungrateful, and all my life I shall remember this.

I humbly ask you, Monsieur le Vicaire Général, to bless me.
Your most respectful and grateful

little servant,
Thérèse Martin

* Autograph (outline).
1. In the omnibus at Nice, November 29; see LD of this date, note 2.

"The value of time" (*Ms. A, p. 143*)
(Christmas 1887-April 9, 1888)
Age fifteen on January 2, 1888

At Christmas, Thérèse was still at Les Buissonnets. The answer from Bayeux had not come. . . . "This trial was very great for my faith." (Ms. A, p. 142.) The pleasure of wearing "a beautiful blue hat, decorated with a dove" (CSG, p. 24) or Céline's kindness (Ms. A, p. 142; LC 96, December 24, 1888) could not compensate for this disappointment. The Carmelites reserved "a very sweet consolation" for her by singing a hymn to her composed by Sister Agnes of Jesus on the theme of the little ball (Ms. A, p. 142).

On December 28, Mother Marie de Gonzague received from Moneigneur Hugonin the authorization to receive the aspirant without delay. She informed Thérèse of this on January 1. But "this time it was the holy ark that was refusing its entrance to the poor little dove. . . ." (Ms. A, p. 142). By a disconcerting about-face, "Sister Agnes of Jesus suddenly no longer wanted her to enter before Easter because of Lent. . . . Monsieur Martin was very much upset by this decision of his Pauline; in the speakroom, he pointed his finger, saying: 'She is always the same; she says something, then

she takes it back.' Oh! he was angry. . . he had gone to so much trouble so that she could enter at Christmas."[1]

Thérèse reacted generously. She resumed her weekly lessons with Mme. Papinau (LC 63, note 4). Above all, she understood "the value of time" and got the most out of it through fidelity in little things (Ms. A, p. 142). Concerning the month of March 1888 she said at the end of her life: "It was one of the most beautiful months of my life." (DE/MEu, p. 779). And it was no doubt one of the times filled with spiritual exchanges, through writing, with her "confidante," Sister Agnes of Jesus (LT 43 B). The latter was "ambitious" for her little girl: with Jesus, she wanted her to be "a saint, a great saint and, at the same time, a little saint" (LC 77).
→ Read Ms. A, pp. 143–144.

1. Sister Marie of the Sacred Heart, according to the notebook of Sister Marie of the Incarnation, p. 114.

LT 40 From Thérèse to Monseigneur Hugonin.

Beginning of
January 1888

Monseigneur,

I am very late in thanking Your Excellency for the beautiful New Year's gift you sent me.[1] All the beauties of this world would never have given me so much pleasure. The Child Jesus, then, has not misguided me! He said "yes" to me in His cradle.

Monseigneur, I don't believe that[2] . . . .

* Autograph.

1. This was the authorization to enter Carmel; Thérèse was notified on January 1

2. Incomplete text without any erasings. It seems to be less a draft than a first copy. Perhaps Thérèse thought the handwriting was not good enough. The outline could have been supplied by Sister Agnes of Jesus just as it was for LT 41 and LT 44. The back of the paper has "*Personal* For His Excellency Monseigneur Bishop of Bayeux Calvados."

LC 72 *From l'abbé Révérony to Thérèse.*

January 12, 1888

→ LT lost

Bayeux, January 12, 1888

My Child,

I gladly share in your joy[1] and with you I thank with my whole heart God, who is treating you as a very tenderly loved child. I am counting on your prayers; I have a pressing need of them. I, too, will pray for you and also for your excellent father. Please remember me to him and also to your sister.[2]

A Dieu, my child. Be His with all your heart and with all your strength. I bless you.

M. Révérony
v.g.

* Autograph.
1. At the same time as she wrote Monseigneur Hugonin (LT 40), Thérèse had to write the vicar general to thank him for the authorization obtained through his intervention.
2. Céline, whom M. Révérony got to know as well as M. Martin during the recent pilgrimage to Rome.

LC 73 *From Sister Agnes of Jesus to Thérèse.*

January 13-30, 1888

J. M. J. T.

Darling,

You must write this short note[1] to *Monsieur le Curé de St. Jacques.*[2] Céline will give[3] it to him when giving him M. Révérony's letter.[4]

Let Céline tell him *that he must return it.* This is a letter to preserve.

* Autograph.
1. See LT 41.
2. M. Delatroëtte.
3. When she went to Confession; see LD, November 8, 1887 (Sister Marie of the Sacred Heart), note 1.
4. LC 72.

LT 41 **From Thérèse to Canon Delatroëtte.**

January 13-30, 1888

Draft from the hand of Sister Agnes which Thérèse was satisfied to recopy.

Monsieur le Curé,

I want to thank you for the beautiful picture[1] you had Sister Agnes send me. I will treasure it as a souvenir which will always be dear to me.

Please, Monsieur le Curé, bless the littlest of your children from a distance; at this moment, she is working to prepare her soul for the life of Carmel. I realize it is a great grace to be called

so young, but I shall not be ungrateful, and God will give me, I trust, the means of being faithful to Him just as I desire with all my heart.

I humbly beg you, Monsieur le Curé, not to forget me in your prayers.

Your very little child,
T

(P.S.) Here is a short note from Monsieur Révérony that I asked Céline to give you.[2]

* Autograph (Sister Agnes of Jesus).
1. This picture is not identified.
2. See the answer from the superior: LC 74.

LC 74 *From Canon Delatroëtte to Thérèse.*

January 30,
1888
→ LT 41

To Sister Thérèse of
the Child Jesus Lisieux, January 30, 1888

My good Child,

One of your sisters[1] told me that you want to have M. Révérony's letter which you sent me, and that she will take it back the next time. For fear of its going astray, I am going to return it to Sister Agnes of Jesus with the request that she return it to you herself.[2] I am happy that you are asking God for the grace of being a holy Carmelite. With you, I will pray to Him with my whole heart to make you worthy of being numbered among the true daughters of St. Teresa, but I cannot refrain from regretting that you pressed for your entrance with so much insistence. I fear that later on you and your own sisters will have to regret it.

Please pray for me and accept my most devoted sentiments in Our Lord Jesus Christ.

Delatroëtte
Curé de St. Jacques

* Autograph.
1. Céline (see LC 73, note 3) or Léonie (LC 75, note 3).
2. This was a shrewd step to emphasize the fact that he had identified the inspirer of this request!

LD *From Sister Agnes of Jesus to Céline* . (Extracts.)

February 12-15 (?), 1888

J. M. J. T.

My dear little Céline,

Our beloved Mother and Mother Geneviève find that it would be better not to talk again about Thérèse's matter immediately.[1] You will see that all will go well at the suitable moment.

I kiss all three of you[2] with my whole heart. Spend a good Lent[3] and be very fervent. . . .

Pray for Monsieur de Virville, whom you saw at Caen.[4] He is very *sick.* It is a great trial for our dear Mother.

Your little sister,
Agnes of Jesus

I would like to have Thérèse read the life of several Carmelites[5] who entered Carmel after so many trials that it would make you shudder. There is one who was to enter at the age of fourteen and a half, but she was obliged to wait until she was *thirty-one.* But this is not the case with Jesus' little toy; it will come bouncing into Carmel when spring shows up, soon, soon! Oh! what a grace! It is not too much to have suffered very much to obtain this.

* Autograph.
1. Read: don't speak again to the Superior about Thérèse's coming entrance into Carmel; see LC 75.
2. Léonie had returned from the Visitation at Caen on January 6, after a postulancy of six months.
3. Lent began on February 15 (Ash Wednesday).
4. See LT 42, note 3.
5. Perhaps in the *Chroniques de l'Ordre des Carmélites de la Réforme de sainte Thérèse depuis leur introduction en France*, by the Poitiers Carmel (four volumes; about 630 pages; Oudin, Poitiers, 1887-1889). The first two volumes came out in 1887. In volume I, pp. 239-249, we find, for example, the account of a Mother Marie-Rose, who entered Carmel only at the age of thirty, after waiting for fifteen years. But we cannot say that this Carmelite was the one Sister Agnes of Jesus was speaking about.

LT 42 From Thérèse to Sister Marie of the Sacred Heart.

February 21, 1888

Tuesday, February 21, '88

My dear Godmother,

I am not forgetting that tomorrow is your birthday. I've already been thinking of it for a long time. I would be very happy if I could see you to celebrate your twenty-eight years, but since we are in Lent, we must make sacrifices.[1]

Dear little Marie, on Ash Wednesday, Papa gave me a gift. In vain would I give you one hundred guesses, even a thousand; I believe you would not guess. Just imagine, dear Marie, at the bottom of Papa's big bag was a little ravishing lamb, all in curls. Good little Father told me, when giving it to me, that he wanted me to have the pleasure of having a little lamb before I entered

Carmel. Everybody was happy. Céline was delighted that we had a little lamb, one day old. What touched me above all was Papa's kindness in giving it to me; and then a lamb is so symbolic. It reminded me of Pauline....

Up until now, everything was going well, everything was delightful, but you must wait for the end. Already we were building castles in the air with the little lamb. We were expecting to see it leaping around us at the end of two or three days. But, alas! the pretty little beast died in the afternoon. It had been too cold in the wagon where it was born; poor little thing, it was hardly born when it suffered and then died.

The little lamb was so nice. It had such an innocent look that Céline made its portrait on a little piece of linen, and then Papa dug a hole into which we placed the little lamb which seemed to be sleeping. I did not want the earth to cover it, and we threw some snow on it and then all was over.......................

You don't realize, dear Godmother, how much the death of this little animal made me reflect. Oh, yes! on this earth we must attach ourselves to nothing, not even the most innocent things, for they fail you at the moment when you are least expecting it. It is only what is eternal that can content us. Dear Marie, I see that I have spoken to you the whole time only about the lamb, and now Léonie wants me to leave her a little space at the end of my letter.[2] *Adieu,* then, dear Godmother. Your little daughter loves you much more than you can ever imagine.

Thérèsita

Tomorrow, I will offer my Communion for my dear Godmother.... Kiss dear Mother for me and Pauline as well. Tell her I am well.

I prayed very much for Monsieur de Virville.[3]

* Autograph.

1. Visits to Carmel were not permitted during Lent.

2. Léonie added some twelve lines after Thérèse's signature.

3. This was according to Sister Agnes of Jesus' suggestion in the preceding LD. M. Alexander Davy de Virville (March 12, 1832 to August 21, 1889) was commissioner of administrative supervision at the train station at Caen. Céline and Thérèse had seen him the preceding months when visiting their sister Léonie at the Visitation convent.

LC 75 *From Sister Agnes of Jesus to Thérèse.*
Around March 10, 1888 Approximate date; see note 1.

J. M. J. T.

Jesus' little Toy,

We don't know the precise time that Mother Geneviève asked Our Father for your entrance on the 9th;[1] I will tell you the details on Easter Monday.[2]

Let Céline not say a word about it until the last moment. The last time she will go to Confession before the 9th, she can say only: Father, Thérèse's entrance is on Monday. We will expect you at Carmel at the hour you designate. . . .

He is certainly offended because we had recourse to Monseigneur. He told us, "Never will I change my opinion. Don't you realize that I have been considering this matter for a long time!. . ." I was heartbroken. But must not all earth's joys be mingled with some trials? The drop of gall makes all chalices bitter.

Little Céline, dear little toy of Jesus, love the Cross, it is the blessed mast to which the sails of love are attached. A breeze from heaven then pushes the boat of our heart, and we are separated from earth. This is what is necessary. *Don't be too distressed.* But let Thérèse prepare herself to give herself TOTALLY from the beginning of her religious life. Let her have no fear of her Jesus; the strikes He will give His little ball will never be able to do anything else but make it bounce more promptly toward Him, toward heaven. . . .

Adieu, darlings. Sanctity is the only beautiful thing on earth. Let us ask for it, let us work to acquire it, our eyes fixed upon the model: Jesus!

I send my whole heart to my dear little girls.

Sister Agnes of Jesus

Tell Léonie that I love her and suggest that she say not a word about Thérèse at Confession.[3] This would cause trouble and all is useless. We can see that he imagines we are trying to make him change his mind.

* Autograph.

1. April 9, the desired date of Thérèse's entrance. The mention of the 9th, without a precise mention of the month suggests that Sister Agnes was writing after March 9; there was no possible confusion in the mind of the recipient.
2. April 2, the first day of a possible visit after Lent.
3. Since her return from the Visitation, Léonie was going to Confession to M. Delatroëtte.

LT 43 A **From Thérèse to Sister Agnes of Jesus.**

March 10-12(?), 1888
→ LC 75

Draft in pencil, except for the last paragraph, written on the back of an arithmetic exercise of February 2, 1888. The words in parentheses were erased by Thérèse.

St. F.X.P.P.M.[1]

My little boat is having a lot of trouble reaching port! For a long time, I have seen the shore and always I find myself far off, but it is Jesus who is guiding (it) (over the rocks) my little boat. And I am sure that the day when He wills it it will be able to approach the port safely; (I believe that God is sending me these trials so that I desire nothing, not even what I believe the best[2]. . . .)

Oh, yes! Pauline, when Jesus will have set me on the blessed shore of Carmel, I want to give myself totally to Him. I want to live only for Him. Oh! no, I shall not fear His strikes, for even in the most bitter sufferings, I always feel that it is His hand that strikes (He has really shown me this). I have felt it at Rome at the moment when I would have believed that the earth would give away beneath my steps. I desire only one thing when I am in Carmel, it is always (to preserve my place) to suffer for Jesus. Life passes so quickly that truly it must be better to have a very beautiful crown and a little trouble than (not) to have an ordinary one without[3] any trouble and then for a suffering borne without joy, when I think that for all eternity I shall love God better. Then in suffering, one can save souls. Ah! Pauline, if during my life I could have suffered to offer one soul to God, one soul that would be snatched from the fire of hell, oh! how happy I would be. Really, how could one complain about sufferings when one sees the fruit[4] of suffering.

Dear little sister, I see that I have not yet spoken about your letter which, however, really pleased me. Oh! Pauline, I am very fortunate that God has given me a sister like you. I hope that you will pray for your poor little girl in order that she correspond with the graces that Jesus wants to give her. She has great need of your help, for she is very little what she would like to be.

* Autograph.
1. This means: *St. Francis Xavier, pray for me.* This is a chronological indication that this was written during the "Novena of grace" (March 4-12). However, the definitive writing was postponed until the following Sunday (LT 43 B).
2. This characteristic sentence was not retained in the final draft.
3. She spelled "*sans*" as "*sas.*"
4. She spelled "*fruits*" as "*fuits.*"

LT 43 B **From Thérèse to Sister Agnes of Jesus.**

March 18 (?), 1888
→LC 75

Definitive rendition of the preceding draft.
Date deduced from content; see note 3.

My dear little Pauline,

I would have liked to write you immediately to thank you for your letter, but this was impossible for me. I had to wait until today.

Oh! Pauline, it is very true that the drop of gall must be mingled in all chalices; I find that trials help very much in detaching us from this earth. They make us look higher than this world. Here below, nothing can satisfy us. We cannot enjoy a little rest except in being ready to do God's will.

My little boat is having a lot of trouble reaching port. For a long time, I have seen the shore and I always find myself far off; but it is Jesus who is guiding my little boat, and I am sure that on the day when He wills it, it will be able to approach the port safely. Oh, Pauline, when Jesus will have placed me on the blessed shore of Carmel, I want to give myself totally to Him, I want to live no longer but for Him. Oh, no, I shall not fear His strikes, for, even in the most bitter sufferings, I always feel that it is His gentle hand that is striking. I really felt this at Rome at the very moment when I would have believed the earth could have given way beneath my steps.

I desire only one thing when I shall be in Carmel, and it is to suffer always for Jesus. Life passes so quickly that really it must be better to have a very beautiful crown and a little trouble than to have an ordinary one without any trouble. And then for a suffering borne with joy, when I think that during the whole of eternity I will love God better. Then in suffering we can save souls. Ah! Pauline, if at the moment of my death I could have a soul to offer to Jesus, how happy I would be; it would be a soul that would have

been snatched from the fire of hell and would bless God for all eternity.

My dear little sister, I see that I have still not spoken to you about your letter which, however, pleased me very much. Oh! Pauline, I am very fortunate that God has given me a sister like you. I hope that you will pray for your poor little girl so that she will correspond with the graces that Jesus wants to give her; she has a great need of your help, for she is FAR FROM what she *would like* to be.

Tell my dear Godmother[1] that I am thinking often of her. We would like to know when she will make her Profession inside[2]. . . .

Céline kisses you. This poor little sister has a sore foot. I think she will not be able to go to Vespers.[3] Almost everybody is sick at Uncle's house. Truly, life isn't cheerful. It is very difficult to be attached to it.

Au revoir, dear Pauline, my *Confidante.* Until Easter Monday[4] but especially April 9[5]. . . . Kiss DEAR Mother[6] for me.

* Autograph.

1. Sister Marie of the Sacred Heart.
2. Having received the Habit on March 19, 1887, Sister Marie of the Sacred Heart would make her vows on March 20, 1888, on the "inside," that is, in the Community chapter room. This ceremony took place on May 22, 1888, and was completed on May 24 by the public ceremony of the reception of the black Veil.
3. Thérèse was writing, then, on a Sunday? No doubt on March 18, Passion Sunday. See the following LD from Sister Agnes of Jesus to M. Martin. The autograph copy has "March 1888" in pencil, in Thérèse's hand, but in a handwriting that suggests it was done in 1895-1897. This suggests this letter was given her by Mother Agnes of Jesus when she was writing her Ms. A, 1895 or at the end of her life.
4. For the visit to Carmel; see LC 75, note 2.
5. Date of Thérèse's entrance into Carmel.
6. Mother Marie de Gonzague. "*Dear*" is underlined five times.

LD *From Sister Agnes of Jesus to M. Martin.*

March 18-19, 1888

Dear little Father, I am sending you a delightful letter from Thérèse, received today[1] . . . .

I beg you not to let her know I showed it to you.

When you have read it, will you please return it; I would be pleased to read it over again.

I am answering with a short note to Thérèse;[2] I would be happy if you gave it to her without Léonie's noticing it, for poor Léonie could think we are forgetting her!

The diamond and the fine pearl[3] kiss their very good little Father! Happy feast to the Saint Joseph of Carmel![4]

* Autograph.
1. LT 43 B.
2. LC 76.
3. Sister Marie of the Sacred Heart and Sister Agnes of Jesus.
4. We are, then, at March 19 (or the eve)? M. Martin was then called "foster father of the Carmel."

LC 76 *From Sister Agnes of Jesus to Thérèse.*

March 18-19, 1888

→ LT 43 B

J. M. J. T.

Thérèse

Darling,

Your little letter pleased me a lot. I see that Jesus is teaching you Himself. Is it not said in the Imitation: "It is I who give

understanding to little children, and he whom I instruct Myself makes rapid progress in virtue. . . ."[1]

You must thank God for this grace, for it is a great one.

My darling, prepare your heart, for behold the port! Don't you see at last the mountain of Carmel. It is there, for in intimacy with Jesus you will live hidden in His Heart. . . . Oh! yes, HIDDEN! I desire that Jesus' little Toy be not admired by anyone in this world. If Jesus wills to play with a grain of sand,[2] He is free, the whole earth is His.[3] Why does He not always take the most beautiful souls for His spouses? Why, instead of a grain of sand, does He not play with a diamond? But Jesus loves humility. Jesus loves what does not appear before the eyes of men, what they trample underfoot, what they despise. Oh! humility, how beautiful it is! Jesus loves it so much that He seeks for it everywhere on the earth in order to make His heaven out of it. But it is rare. All the beautiful, the truly beautiful is almost not to be found here below.

I am sure that the little grain of sand understands me and that it will not ever wish to become a mountain, but, on the contrary, always littler, lighter, in order to be lifted more easily by the breeze of love.[4]

Until April 9!. . .

For the cover of the littlest book all that is needed is one centimeter at least at the top and on the side.[5]

* Autograph.

1. A free citation of the Imitation of Christ III, 43:2.
2. On this theme, see LT 45, note 4.
3. See Psalm 23:1.
4. See LT 103, par. 1.
5. The fourth page is addressed to Céline. We read: "Darling, Jesus will reward you for your generosity in giving Him Thérèse. He does not love you less, and He is waiting for you also!. . "

LC 77 *From Sister Agnes of Jesus to Thérèse.*

March 25-26, 1888 — Date obtained through cross-references. See note 4, and Thérèse s answer (LT 44).

Darling,

I am sending you the little draft of the letter for Monseigneur.[1] Write it very nicely, and then wrap the picture[2] in a piece of silk paper and place it in the second paper as it is. Don't fold your letter in four, that would crumple it.

It is, then, for April 9!. . Often, very often, I think of my little girl. I am ambitious for her. And Jesus! It is He who wants her to be a Saint! Oh, yes, a saint, a big saint and, at the same time, a *little* saint, so little and so humble that He can read always on her face and in her heart the words of the Blessed Virgin which she will have to say when entering: "I am the Handmaid of the Lord."[3]

Adieu, darling. Don't think of rejoicing here below since Jesus has suffered so much for us,[4] but think of loving Him since He has loved us so much! Forget all in order to think of Him.

Our beloved Mother does not want a fancy bonnet,[5] just a plain little ruffle made of fine silk netting, like a First Communion[6] headdress but in black for every day. Céline could make it since it cannot be found ready-made in the shops.

Adieu, my darlings. I kiss you and I love you tenderly. This note is for you both.

Kiss Léonie for me; I think of her very much.

Regarding the little bonnets, I think a white one for Sundays would be nice, with pretty chin ties. For this, you can just buy a First Communion cap. Not *an old lady's bonnet!* Let's agree on that!

* Autograph.

1. See LT 44.

2. A picture on parchment, painted by Sister Agnes of Jesus.

3. Luke 1:38. Interior attitude suggested by the date of entrance: feast of the Annunciation, postponed to the Monday of *Quasimodo*, its celebration having been hindered by the liturgy of Holy Week on March 25.
4. Letter written on Palm Sunday or Monday of Holy Week.
5. Postulant's bonnet; see the two letters of October 22-24, 1886 (LD).
6. On May 8, 1884, Thérèse wore the little bonnet of the school uniform, a white ruffle, the one reproduced in the portrait painted by Mother Saint-Léon at the Abbey of Lisieux. See LT 53.

LT 44 — From Thérèse to Monseigneur Hugonin.

March 27, 1888

Incomplete copy of the draft supplied by Sister Agnes of Jesus (see LC 77). Date deduced from that of the following (LT 45).

Monseigneur,

I am taking the liberty of coming to ask a blessing on the eve of my entrance to Carmel. I am not forgetting that I am Your Excellency's[1] little daughter, and I know what I owe to your paternal kindness. Now your little[2] . . .

* Autograph.
1. See Ms. A, p. 156, and, in the same sense, this episode written into the chronicles of the monastery: "On February 21, Bishop Hugonin entered the cloister with P. Basile, a Carmelite and the Lenten preacher in the diocese that year. Before the assembled Community, the bishop asked: 'Where is my little novice?' Mother Marie de Gonzague, then prioress, told him that because of the winter and Lent she had postponed her entrance until after Easter. Monseigneur approved the delay." (*Fondation du Carmel de Lisieux*, III, p. 154, which places the incident at the beginning of March; date rectified according to the *Semaine Religieuse de Bayeux*, February 19, 1888, p. 124.)
2. We do not know the rest of the text. The Bishop's archives have not preserved any of Thérèse's letters. Bishop Hugonin answered on March 31 (LC 79).

LT 45 **From Thérèse to Sister Agnes of Jesus.**

March 27,
1888
→LC 76 and 77

Tuesday, March 27, '88

My dear little Sister,

I just wrote Monseigneur the letter[1] you composed for me; I thank you very much. Oh! how beautiful your picture is; it is a marvel.

I am sending you this note quickly to learn if you want me to say at Uncle's house that you painted a picture and that I wrote. If later on they know this, they will not be happy,[2] but I prefer to ask you. I will tell them, too, that it is for the 9th. Since it is on Thursday that we go to Uncle's place, I would like you to put a note in the turn[3], which Papa will pick up tomorrow morning.

Oh! yes, Pauline, I always want to be the LITTLE grain of sand.[4] . . . How much good your letter did me; if you only knew how much it has been at the bottom of my heart.

I would like to say many things regarding the little grain of sand, but I haven't any time. . . . (I want to be a saint. . . .)

The other day, I saw some words that pleased me very much; I no longer remember the Saint who said them. It was (I am not perfect, but I *want* to become perfect.)[5]

What disconnected words! Pardon me, dear little sister, I am hurrying very much.

Until April 9![6]

Thérésita

* Autograph.
1. LT 44.
2. "not be happy," that is, because they were not informed.

3. The "turn" was a barrel-shaped object which rotated, making it possible for the Carmelites to place notes, articles, etc., for persons on the outside.
4. This image—symbol of hiddenness—was henceforth going to be used alternately with that of the little "toy" (see LT 34, note 2) in the letters of the two sisters. Thérèse used it up to her Profession (September 8, 1890). We meet it in LT 45, 49, 54, 74, 82, 85, 86, 95, 103, 114. Sister Agnes was the first to use it (see LC 76), and she uses it again in LC 78, 127, 137. Sister Marie of the Sacred Heart avoids it. It does not please Céline (LD, March 1, 1889; LC 110). Mother Marie de Gonzague used it (LC 94 and 95), also Sister Marie of the Angels (LC 119). This image is absent from P. Pichon's letters, but he had quoted, in his closing sermon during the October retreat of 1887, the prayer of General de Sonis, which was really the origin of this image.
5. Saint Augustine, according to *Petites Fleurs ou Extraits de la Doctrine et de la Vie des Saints et des auteurs approuvés*, by Abbé Bourbonne; the word "*veux*" is underlined and written in large letters.
6. Address on the back of the note: "Agnes of Jesus Carmel E.V." Sister Agnes of Jesus answered the same evening (LC 78).

LC 78 *From Sister Agnes of Jesus to Thérèse.*

March 27, 1888
→ LT 45

Last letter from Sister Agnes addressed to Thérèse at Les Buissonnets.

J. M. J. T.

Darling, you could have shown the picture to Uncle; it's no secret. Tell him whatever you want.

Pray much to God so that He arrange all things for the best on the day of your entrance. *I don't believe* that Our Father wishes to be here at the great moment.[1] Let Céline ask him as was agreed upon,[2] but I doubt it. . . . It is sad for our beloved Mother and for us all; it places us in such a false position. We seem to be doing *something forbidden, almost a sin!!!*

Poor little grain of sand! It is really very difficult to raise it up to the blessed soil of Carmel. . . . This demands much trouble, gives rise to many miseries and contradictions. But if the little soul hidden in the little grain of sand becomes a home of love and virtue, everybody will be well repaid and the devil will be trapped. This is what I hope for my darling, for my so much loved little girl. . . . Let her entrust to the suffering Jesus the great matter of her entrance. He will refuse nothing to her childlike prayer.

What does Céline say about the little bonnets?[3] Does she understand? She would have to tell this to Mademoiselle Léonie[4] and explain to her what we want; she would arrange it.

I kiss you, my darlings. Let us not be frightened by the sorrows of this earth, for it is they that merit for us the joys of heaven! Let us welcome, then, suffering as a future joy. Life! It is so short; it's a point in space. "A thousand years are in the Lord's eyes just like yesterday which has passed!" we sing in one of the psalms.[5] Let us raise our hearts and fight the good fight in order to carry off the victory and merit the crown.[6]

Adieu! Let us love Jesus, who has loved us so much! Let the little fiancée have no fear of following her Beloved on the road to Calvary. She must learn that He is "a Spouse of blood"[7] and that, to resemble Him and bear the name of Spouse worthily, she must always prove her love through suffering.

* Autograph.

1. M. Delatroëtte did finally assist at this entrance ceremony, but he spoke these harsh words: "Well! Reverend Mothers, you can sing a *Te Deum!* As the delegate of Monseigneur, the Bishop, I present this child of fifteen whose entrance you so desired. I trust she will not disappoint your hopes, but I remind you that if she does, you alone will have to bear the responsibility." (Reported by Mother Agnes of Jesus, AP, 370-371.)
2. See LC 75, par. 2.
3. The postulant's bonnets; see LC 77.
4. This was the seamstress for the Martin family.
5. Psalm 89:4.

6. See 2 Timothy 4: 7-8.
7. Rather than from Exodus 4:25, this expression seems to be borrowed from P. Pichon; see LT 82, note 1, February 28, 1889. The last paragraph is inspired by the liturgical readings for Holy Week.

LC 79 *From Monseigneur Hugonin to Thérèse.*

March 31, 1888

→LT 44

Bayeux Diocese

Bayeux, March 31, 1888

Dear Child,

I bless you with all my heart. Your wishes have been answered. Our Lord is receiving you among His faithful spouses, whom He has chosen one by one through a privileged grace. Unite yourself more and more to Our Lord in order to be more and more detached from yourself. Such will be your program.

I recommend myself and the whole diocese to the prayers of your Community.

All yours in Our Lord,
† Flavien[1]

* Autograph.
1. It is addressed:

Mademoiselle Thérésita
at the Lisieux Carmel (Calvados)

THIRD PERIOD

THE POSTULANCY

(April 9, 1888 - January 10, 1889)

IN CARMEL

"I am here forever, forever! . . ." (*Ms. A, p. 148*)

On the morning of April 9, 1888, after a "last look at Les Buissonnets, that delightful nest of my childhood" (Ms. A, p. 147), Thérèse assisted with her family at the seven o'clock Mass at the Carmel. Then there came the heartbreaking separation, the last kiss to her family, to her aged father especially, who blessed her, sobbing. "Ah! what a moment that was! One must pass through it to know what it is . . . ." (ibid.). M. Delatroëtte's harsh admonition (see LC 78, note 1) did not break her enthusiasm. With firm step, she crossed the threshold of the cloister.

Situated at the bottom of an unhealthy ravine, close to the Orbiquet River, the monastery was hardly fifty years in existence. This postulant was acquainted only with its exterior: its outside courtyard, upon which faced the lodgings of the Extern Sisters and that of the chaplain, Abbé Youf; the chapel and the speakroom with its somber grilles. Now she was about to discover "the other side." It was a pleasant surprise: "Everything

seemed delightful to me." (*Ms. A, p. 148.*) *In fact, there was nothing grim about this quadrangular structure in red brick;*[1] *rather, there was something human and balanced about it. The arcades of its cloister in perfect symmetry opened out on a courtyard in the center of which was a Calvary* (*built in 1877*). *Around the choir* (*west wing*), *the center of the monastic life, were grouped some twenty cells and the principal conventual areas, for example, the chapter room, the library* (*north wing*), *the refectory, the kitchen, and the recreation room* (*south wing*). *Beyond the fourth wing* (*east*), *which had no second floor in order not to cut off the air and the sun, there was a triangular garden. A chestnut walk skirted a little hayfield, "the meadow," in which were planted some pear trees.*

They led Thérèse to her cell. There were just the essentials in this little room[2] *with its plaster walls: a bed, a simple bookshelf, no water, no electricity, and no heating. The view from the window was obstructed by the slate roof of an adjoining building. However, through its spacious window the sun could shine all through the afternoon when it showed itself in that foggy country. A person experienced here a physical sense of solitude and peace: "I believed that I was transported into a desert; our little cell especially delighted me"* (*Ms. A, p. 148*). *Thérèse was to live in this same cell for the next five years.*[3] *It was here that she wrote her letters, seated on a little bench, a writing desk* (*portable*) *on her knees, with an oil lamp for light in the evenings.*

The postulant did not receive a special Habit; she wore a black cape over her long blue dress, and the traditional little bonnet. From the very first day, she made a deep impression on the Community, even upon her own sisters. ". . . in her bearing she was marked by a kind of majesty that one was far from expecting in a child of fifteen." (*Sister Marie of the Angels, AP, 405.*)

The twenty-six Carmelites, who lived in the monastery,[4] were already known to her for the most part for the past six years. There was first "her dear Mother," henceforth to be called "our Mother." At the age of fifty-four, Mother Marie de Gonzague had not lost anything of her tall stature, her distinguished bearing, and those qualities of understanding and affection which so attracted others from the very beginning, helping them to forget her rather leonine features. During those first months, Thérèse had to exercise a firm control over herself lest she yield to a misguided affection for the prioress (see LC 80, note 5). Having succeeded in this, she carried out faithfully that chapter of the "Imitation of Christ" which she recited from memory for the prioress on the same day of her entrance, April 9: "That we must love Jesus Christ above all things" (Imitation II, 7). "The love of created things is deceitful and inconstant; the love of Jesus is faithful and lasting. . . . The nature of thy Beloved is such that He will not admit of a rival, but He will have thy heart for Himself alone."

Thérèse glimpsed that morning the kind look of Mother Geneviève (see Ms. A, p. 148), the foundress of the Lisieux Carmel, who was filled with infirmities, a saint, gentle and humble of heart.

In the novitiate quarters, she was welcomed by a religious of forty-three, Sister Marie of the Angels, ". . . a real saint, the finished type of the first Carmelites" (ibid. p. 151). The novice mistress already had three novices under her care: Sister Marie-Philomène, forty-eight, and professed since March 25, 1886; Sister Marie of the Sacred Heart, Thérèse's own sister and godmother, who was twenty-eight; and Sister Martha of Jesus, twenty-three, a lay-sister, already a postulant for three months, an orphan, with mediocre intelligence and a poor upbringing, who was frequently to test Thérèse's patience.

Sister Thérèse of the Child Jesus approached her demanding vocation with no illusions: "I found the religious life to be such as I had imagined it; no sacrifice astounded me" (Ms. A, p. 149).

Apart from some slight alteration to fit the different seasons, the Carmelite nun followed the same horarium (schedule) from January 1 to December 31: in the summer, six hours of sleep, to which was added one hour of optional siesta, and in the winter, seven hours of sleep; meals at ten o'clock in the morning and six in the evening, with no meat allowed; six hours and a half of prayer in the choir (Mass, three and a half hours of Divine Office, and two hours of silent prayer); an hour of recreation in common after each of the meals; one hour of free time in the evening; five hours of manual work.[5]

In Thérèse's case, this manual work was reduced to three very hidden tasks: mending the linen, under the affectionate guidance of Sister Marie of the Angels, who interspersed spiritual exhortations with her sewing lessons; the sweeping of the dormitory and a staircase (see Her Last Conversations, July 13, no. 18); and, from time to time, a little weeding in the garden for physical exercise. Every day, the novice mistress gathered her charges together to explain the Rule, the Constitutions, and the customs proper to the Order. The novice mistress testified later with regard to Sister Thérèse of the Child Jesus: "She had such an understanding of religious virtues and perfection that I had only to instruct her in these matters and she carried them out immediately to perfection." (Sister Marie of the Angels, AP, 406; see, too, Mother Marie de Gonzague, LT 50, note 4.)

1. Each side of the cloister was thirty meters in length.
2. Roughly, ten feet by seven feet; the furniture is the same as described in DE, p. 821.
3. We do not know at what date Thérèse occupied, in the same dormitory, a second cell looking out upon the courtyard, before going, in August 1894, into the cell of the "Saint Elias' dormitory" (see DE, pp. 577 and 820).
4. The average age of the nuns on April 9, 1888, was close to forty-seven.
5. For a detailed schedule, see DE, pp. 825-826.

First steps: "more thorns than roses" (*Ms. A, p. 149*)
(April 9, 1888 - January 5, 1889)
Age fifteen and sixteen

On the letter-writing level, Thérèse's postulancy period represents a collection of fifty-four documents.[1] *The chronology of this correspondence is generally well substantiated.*

Of the twenty-eight letters written by Thérèse (LT 46 to 73), twenty-four were written for persons outside the cloister. The recipients were: M. Martin (eleven letters) and Céline (four); M. and Mme. Guérin (five); her cousin Marie Guérin (three); and finally, a letter to Mother Saint-Placide, her former directress at the boarding school.

The other four notes were exchanged with her two Carmelite sisters during their respective retreats: Marie of the Sacred Heart (one), and Agnes of Jesus (three).

Totally missing are the letters she wrote to P. Pichon when he was in France and in Canada; and the notes to her prioress, Mother Marie de Gonzague, and to Sister Marie of the Angels, her novice mistress.

Twenty letters to Thérèse (LC 80 to 99) and six LD complete this collection.

In spite of the infrequency of external events, these documents contain nothing of a monotonous repetition. We can perceive two tones in Thérèse's "song," which are closely connected with the mishaps occurring in her "dear King's" life: June 23–27, M. Martin's sudden and unexplained trip to Le Havre; October 31, a serious attack, again at Le Havre. Thérèse's postulancy, then, may be divided into the three following periods:

1. April 9 – June 23 (LT 46 to LC 82): All goes well at Carmel. The postulant's conduct surprises even the pri-

oress: "We don't have to say a word to her; all is perfect. . . ." (LT 50, note 4). The delightful celebrations of the month of May—Sister Marie of the Sacred Heart made her Profession and received the Veil—are crowned for Thérèse by a liberating interview with P. Pichon. After she had made a general confession to him, she received the assurance that she had never committed a mortal sin (Ms. A, p. 149), and she felt that she was freed, too, from an interior trial she had borne for five years (LC 82, note 3). She never again saw P. Pichon, whom she had chosen as her spiritual director, but from now on she wrote him frequently, at least once a month (see Ms. A, p. 151).

At Les Buissonnets, her father compensated for his recent sacrifice of Thérèse by multiplying his gifts to the monastery. Hardly a day went by that he did not place some gift at the turn. The Benjamin received the assignment of thanking him for these gifts. She resumes once again her talk of the "little Queen" (see LT 18, note 1). She enjoys, too, recalling her memories of their trip to Rome (LT 46, 51).

2. June 23 - October 31 (LD, June 26 to LC 92): Shaken by Céline's statements relative to her own religious vocation (see LT 53, note 3), M. Martin, one week later, leaves his home without a moment's warning. It is only a brief alarm, but it traumatizes his daughters, and Thérèse's handwriting bears traces of its effect upon her. She finds, however, the strength to control her anxiety in order to bolster Céline's courage (LT 57 and 67).

Added to this, the adaptation to her new form of life, especially to life in the Community, was accompanied by some suffering. The "little reed" experiences its weakness (LT 55); it quivers under pinpricks (ibid.). However, her generosity does not fail. And the Commu-

nity decides to admit Thérèse to investiture (LC 89 and 90). All is ready when another paralytic attack suffered by M. Martin necessitates the postponement of the ceremony.

3. October 31 – January 3, 1889 (LC 92 to LC 99): the deterioration of the mental powers of the "venerable old man, who has become like a child" (LC 97, note 2) causes his daughters to live the month of November 1888 in great anxiety. Then an unexpected "recovery" is an invitation to set a date for the reception of the Habit by Thérèse. Mother Marie de Gonzague had to calm the desolation of her "little lamb" because of delays on the part of the bishop of Bayeux (LC 93 and 95). However, it is with joy that Thérèse welcomes the dawn of her sixteenth birthday (LT 73).

A statement from P. Pichon could be taken as a balance sheet for Thérèse for the year 1888: "God is molding your heart in its most delicate fibers" (LC 97). "Yes," Thérèse answers, "suffering stretched out its arms to me, and I threw myself into them with love. . . . " (Ms. A, p. 149.)

→ Read Ms. A, pp. 143 – 158.

1. It is completed by the seventeen letters and notes exchanged from January 6 to 10, 1889 (retreat for the reception of the Habit).

LT 46 **From Thérèse to M. Martin.**

April 29, 1888

This is Thérèse's first letter since her entrance into Carmel on April 9. Céline's nineteenth birthday was celebrated on April 28 in the speakroom of the Carmel (according to a letter of Sister Agnes of Jesus, April 27 or 28, 1888). It seems that M. Martin was not there, and this is the reason for thanking him by letter.

Sunday, April 29, '88

J. M. J. T.[1]

Dear little Father,

How good you are, then, to your little Queen;[2] almost no day passes that she does not receive some present from her King.

Thanks for everything, good little Father. If you only knew how much the little *Orpheline de la Bérésina*[3] loves you! But, no, you will know this only in heaven. It is there that we shall see beautiful *Estatues* on beautiful *Cornichons,*[4] and we shall then really be able to enter into *Extasaison*, and then what a guide we will have for visiting heaven's marvels!. . . I think that very many of the saints will have a *Bysantine* Cross in their *halo*. There will no longer be any *sarcophaguses* for us to see, for in heaven there will no longer be any tombs.

Dear little Father, I see the hour is going by, and I must leave you, but beforehand I kiss you from a distance with my whole heart.

The bright little pearl[5] kisses you. Oh! Papa, if you only knew how *precious* is your bright little pearl. . . .

The brilliant Diamond,[6] the gypsy,[7] kisses you, too, with her whole heart.

Adieu, and thanks, little Father.

Your little Queen, who is at last pulled from under the cart.[8]

Thérèse of the Child Jesus

* Autograph in eighteen fragments; CMG.

1. This means: Jesus, Mary, Joseph, Teresa (Saint Teresa of Avila), a heading then in use in the Order of Carmel.
2. This was one of the nicknames given to Thérèse by her father in her childhood days (see LD, November 11, 1887, note 8). It appears fifty times in the twelve letters from Thérèse to M. Martin; three times only in the following (LT 142, 169, 261, to other correspondents).
3. Another affectionate nickname given by M. Martin to Thérèse as a child, inspired by a novel read at Les Buissonnets: *L'Orpheline de Moscou ou la Jeune Institutrice*, by Mme. Woilliez. We find it again in LT 63, 66, 72, to M. Martin; and LT 116, to Sister Marie of the Sacred Heart.
4. That is: *"des statues sur de belles corniches"* (statues on beautiful cornices); see Ms. A, p. 131: *"les petits* CORNICHONS *et les* CUPIDES *posés dessus"* (the little CORNICES carrying figures of CUPIDS). Also, farther on: *"en extase"* is rendered *"en Extasaison."* To amuse her father, Thérèse mimicked the guide she was listening to at Rome in November 1887. She mimicked him more than once during the recreations in the Carmel. According to Léonie, Thérèse had "a special knack of imitating the tone of voice and the mannerisms of others, but never, to my knowledge, did this little amusement ever degenerate into mockery. . . . Thérèse knew when to stop at a certain point, with perfect tact." (PO, 285.) This talent, inherited from M. Martin, appeared very early in her life (see CF, March 12, 1876). It was revived in many "games" in the infirmary of the Carmel during her last illness in 1897 (see DE, *passim*).
5. This nickname given to Pauline by M. Martin appears again in LT 48, 52, 58, 61, 63, all letters from Thérèse to M. Martin.
6. Nickname of Sister Marie of the Sacred Heart (Marie), given her by her father; see, too, LT 48, 51, 52, 58, 61, 63, to M. Martin.
7. Another nickname given Marie by her father.
8. A note on the autograph, written in pencil by Sister Agnes of Jesus: "Papa said to each of us when seeing us enter Carmel: 'So you're pulled from under the cart.' This was an expression in Normandy which meant in our case: 'There you are sheltered from the dangers of the world!'"

LT 47 **From Thérèse to Céline.**

May 8,
1888

May 8, 1888

I am sending you, little Céline, two little tablecloths to be stitched on the sewing machine. I know that you are very busy, but you are not going to refuse this service to your little Thérèse.[1] I think that two rows would be good. There is one on which the hem is too little, and you could widen the second row of stitches. I would really like to have them for tomorrow after dinner at the latest, for it is Ascension Thursday.[2]

It is four years ago today that I made my First Communion,[3] do you remember?... What graces God has given me since that time.

Dear Céline, there are moments when I wonder if it is true that I am in Carmel; at times, I can't believe it. Alas, what have I done for God that He gives me His graces in this way.

Tomorrow, it will be a month that I am far from you, but it seems to me that we are not separated. What does the place matter where we are? Even if the ocean were to separate us, we would remain united, for our desires are the same and our hearts beat together.... I am sure that you understand me. (What does it matter after all whether life is cheerful or sad, we would nonetheless reach the end of our journey here below.) A day of a Carmelite spent without suffering is a day lost.[4] For you it is the same thing, for you are a Carmelite at heart.

Kiss Léonie for me.

Your little Thérèse of the Child Jesus

* Autograph.

1. Ever since her entrance, Thérèse was assigned to the linen room, working under the direction of Sister Marie of the Angels. Without

having had any previous experience in manual work, she was more than once corrected for her slowness and even judged "little devoted to her tasks" (see CJ 13.7.18).

2. May 10, so Thérèse was writing on Tuesday.
3. May 8, 1884; see Ms. A, p. 77.
4. This is a probable reference to one of the sayings of St. Mary Magdalene de Pazzi: "A day spent without some mortification is a day lost." (*Direction spirituelle pour les novices, maxime 44*, page 278.) The same thought appears in a "*Testament de Ste. Magd. de Pazzi*," no. 15 of the little sayings which the Sisters drew by lot, no doubt on May 25, the feast of the Saint. We read there: "It is in suffering and not in rejoicing that true love is proven; a day without the Cross is lost for heaven."

LT 48 From Thérèse to M. Martin.

May 8,
1888

May 8, 1888

My dear little Father,

Your beautiful little candles pleased me so much that I cannot refrain from writing you a little note to thank you.

Jesus' postman[1] is very good to furnish his little Queen in this way with the means of making *beautiful* lightings.[2]

The Queen is thinking continually of her King; besides, the postman of good Jesus comes so often carrying His messages that I could not forget him.

Dear little Father, really, I almost believe you are going to bring yourself to ruin, but I am going to surprise you by telling you that I am not very much worried about it. It is because you have so many plans that you'll not be caught short . . . even famine would not frighten you. Do you remember when you used to tell me: "We shall eat this or that in the famine." Or: "We shall do

this when we are ruined." With such dispositions, you will not be frightened by any misfortune.

Thanks for the fish, dear little Father. Thanks, thanks, you give us so many things that I see myself forced to thank you for all in general, but each thing, nevertheless, brings its particular pleasure.

Adieu, dear King. Your Diamond and your Pearl thank you as well as your Queen.

Thérèse of the Child Jesus

* Autograph in twenty-one fragments; CMG.

1. This was M. Martin himself, who came often to leave letters and gifts at the turn of the Carmel. The same name in LT 52.
2. In honor of the Child Jesus whose statue under the cloister was decorated by Thérèse.

LC 80 *From Sister Marie of the Sacred Heart to Thérèse.*

May 12-20, 1888 Date deduced from content; see note 3.

The Child Jesus is happy! . . . Tonight, the loved little Thérèse of His Heart has offered Him such beautiful flowers. . . . The flowers of sacrifice . . . she well understands . . . . Ah! these flowers are more scented for Him than all flowers here below. How he goes *knock knock*[1] on the window to get some more, for the wicked don't want to give Him any. So it is from His future little spouse that He seeks them. He knows well enough that she will refuse Him nothing. Knock knock . . . you who did not see your Mother this evening, or who has seen her very little, come, see how I smile at you. In heaven, I will flood you with joys for all the little joys here below which escaped you.[2] In heaven, I'll have you

enjoy in My turn the perfume of My flowers. Knock knock. . . . Come back again to console Me for those who don't love Me. Ah! I am in such a hurry to see you again. Have you any other flowers to give Me? If you wish, I'll make them grow under your steps. But only if you so wish, I never force hearts. Oh! let Me always go knock knock in your heart.

A little hermit[3] to whom Jesus said all this *in a whisper.*[4]

* Autograph.

1. It seems, according to the context, that Thérèse went to see her Mother Prioress. The "knock knock" repeated throughout this note could be a reference to the disturbances that shortened her interview.
2. "I recall that as a postulant I had at times such violent temptations to go to you for my own satisfaction, to find a few crumbs of joy, that I was obliged to pass quickly before your office and to cling to the bannister of the stairway. There came to my mind a multitude of permissions to ask, in a word, beloved Mother, I discovered a thousand reasons just to please myself. . . . How happy I am now for having deprived myself at the beginning of my religious life!" (Ms. C, p. 237.) This was a very meritorious asceticism since, in this matter, Thérèse was different from her older sisters. Sister Agnes of Jesus wrote this undated note (perhaps May 12-22, 1888) to Sister Marie of the Sacred Heart: "I will not see Our Mother until tomorrow, I think. Just recently I suffered a little because I gave in to the desire of seeing her today. This will be three days; that is long. But how blind we are; who will deliver us from our darkness? To be always wanting to satisfy ourselves, always enjoying something!" Sister Marie of the Sacred Heart talks in the same way: "One day, we were passing our Mother's cell together, and I made a sign to her [Thérèse] to come in with me. But instead of following me, she quickly descended the stairs to distract herself from the temptation of seeking herself in anything. Seeing her heroism, I admit that I was embarrassed when I compared myself to her" (NPPO 1908, p. 7). See, too, LT 75, note 3.
3. Sister Marie of the Sacred Heart was preparing for her Profession (May 22) by a retreat of ten days.
4. Thérèse answered the same evening; see LT 49.

LT 49 **From Thérèse to Sister Marie of the Sacred Heart.**

May 12-20,
1888
→ LC 80

The Hermit of the Heart of Jesus gave her little daughter a sweet joy; she read into her heart! . . . Jesus speaks, then, when we are on retreat? . . . I am so *thrilled* by your note and the very charming way that it was presented[1] to me that I cannot refrain from answering it this evening; soon the bell will ring. It is ring[2]

I interrupted my note just at the moment when I wanted to speak at length. . . .

Life is filled with sacrifices, that is true! But what a joy. Must it not be better that our life which is a night spent in a bad inn[3] be spent in a hotel that is *entirely bad* than in one only half-bad? . . .

If you *only knew* how much I LOVE you. When I meet you, it seems to me you are an angel. . . . You, who are an EAGLE called to soar in the heights and to fix your gaze on the sun, pray for the very feeble little reed[4] that is at the bottom of the valley, the least breeze makes it bend. Oh, pray for it on the day of your Profession.

Ask that your little daughter always remain a little grain of sand,[5] truly unknown, truly hidden from all eyes, that Jesus alone may be able to see it, and that it may become smaller and smaller, that it may be reduced to *nothing*. . . .

Pardon me for all the sorrows that I have caused you; if you only knew how sorry I am for having told you that you were calling me too often.[6] . . .

Oh! after your Profession never will I cause you any pain. . . . *Adieu*! . . . Pardon me. . . .

Pray for your OWN little daughter.

I have dried out your little violet with great care.

* Autograph.

1. The note was accompanied by a violet.
2. Thérèse had written: "*elle son,*" not completing the whole verb: "*elle sonne*" (it is ringing). Through fidelity to obedience, Thérèse ceased to write at the first sound of the bell for a community exercise. She forgot to complete the word, and she marked the interruption with a dash. When she was in the infirmary, Thérèse recommended this same promptitude in obedience to her sisters; see DE/MSC 13.7.1.
3. Saint Teresa of Avila, *Way of Perfection*, ch. 42. Thérèse could have read this sentence even before her entrance into Carmel, in *L'Histoire de Sainte Thérèse* by the Carmelites at Caen, volume I, pp. 353-354 (see LT 27, note 6).
4. On this symbolism, see LT 54, note 7, July 4, 1888.
5. See LT 45, note 4.
6. Sister Marie of the Sacred Heart was Thérèse's "angel," that is, she had to initiate her into the customs of the Carmel. She was to write later on: "From the very first days of her novitiate, I saw the degree to which she would be faithful to the Rule. It was hardly three weeks that she was in Carmel, and, thinking that she did not know how to find the Office alone, I wanted to keep her with me to teach her how to find the commemorations. But instead of taking advantage of this opportunity, she answered sweetly: 'I thank you, I found them today. I would be happy to stay with you, but it is better that I deprive myself, for we are not at home!'" (NPPO 1908, pp. 6-7.)

LT 50 From Thérèse to Marie Guérin..

May 13,
1888
→ LC lost

Sunday, May '88

My dear little Sister,

If you have "Pott's disease"[1] at the end of your tongue, you certainly don't have it in your *mind* or at the tips of your fingers. What a charming letter!...

If you wanted to make me laugh, you did not lose your time, you little rascal. Naughty little thing, now you have a sore foot; it's extraordinary, for your feet are so little that there really is no room for it.

Fortunately,[2] Pentecost will be soon, and the Holy Spirit will certainly repair a grave oversight He made on the day of your Confirmation. He gave you all His gifts, but unfortunately He forgot one which would be very useful for you. Can you guess which?. . .

I am going to pray during my retreat[3] that on the day of Pentecost you will be as *strong* as a little Samson. If you still have a sore foot, watch out for your *Loulou.*[4]

Last night, I dreamt very much ABOUT Jeanne.[5] Since I have been in Carmel, it is incredible how often I dream of her. Hug her tightly for your little Thérèse.

What beautiful weather! The sun is radiant; it is really more brilliant than the one that was on your letter, for that one hardly brightened the earth, and if the sun were the same today, I would be forced to use your lamp.[6]

I was fortunate to have had the word lamp to place on this page; otherwise, I would have been obliged to behave discourteously to you, turning the page to bid you *Adieu.*

See you soon, dear Sister. Kiss good Uncle for me, and tell him we shall not forget his recommendation. A thousand kisses for dear Aunt.

(Your strength will have to be not in your hair[7] but in your foot.)

Dear little imp, I kiss you with my whole heart.

Your little sister,
Thérèse of the Child Jesus
p.c.In.[8]

Our big sister[9] is on her Profession retreat. She has her big white veil lowered. I would say she's an angel.[10] She is going to pray for her little Marie.

* Autograph in thirteen fragments.

1. Thérèse writes: "*Si tu as la Pott,*" which is a pleasant way of saying: "le mal de Pott."
2. She spelled "*heureusement*" incorrectly as "*heureusent.*"
3. Community retreat between Ascension and Pentecost, in memory of the Apostles in the Cenacle (see Acts 1:14).
4. Nickname given to Thérèse by Marie Guérin; it was used a few days later on by Mother Marie de Gonzague: "We will not cease praying for your angel Marie; how lovable and nice this child is. Her *Loulou* is praying very hard for her and her cure! This *Loulou* is perfect; never would I have believed in a judgment so advanced in a fifteen-year-old!... Not a word has to be said to her; everything is perfect...." (Letter to Mme. Guérin, May 17, 1888.)
5. Thérèse used the expression: "...*j'ai beaucoup rêvé* DANS *Jeanne*...." This was only to amuse her cousins.
6. This was an ordinary little oil lamp which Marie Guérin got for Thérèse. Later on, the mechanical device for raising the wick wore out. At the end of her life, Thérèse had to force the wick up with the aid of a pin (see CSG, p. 126).
7. Reference to Samson; see Judges 16:17.
8. Abbreviation for "*postulante carmélite indigne,*" a formula then in use.
9. Sister Marie of the Sacred Heart.
10. See LT 49.

LT 51 From Thérèse to M. Martin.

May 17 (?),
1888

J. M. J. T.

My dear King,

I know that the diamond wrote you a note,[1] and that is why I am not going to speak to you very long, for your poor Queen would be eclipsed by the splendor of the Diamond.... I only

have to repeat to you that I love you as though you did not know it as yet; and, then, how could a Queen not love her King and a King like you, so holy, so good. Yes, you are as holy as St. Louis himself. . . .

Thanks, dear little Father, for all you have given to me, the beautiful shovel,[2] etc., etc., . . . and all that follows.[3] . . .

Do you recall, Papa, when at Genoa we were shadowing from a distance M. Benoit[4] and the others?[5] Ah! what fun we had. The memory of this beautiful trip made with my dear little Father will always remain with me.

I kiss you, dear King.

Your Queen of France and Navarre.

Thérèse of the Child Jesus
p.c.ind.

* Autograph in eight fragments.

1. Probably a letter written on "Thursday" (May 17) in which Sister Marie of the Sacred Heart was announcing that her Profession was advanced from May 23 to 22, and she was asking for M. Martin's blessing for the occasion.
2. They had prescribed a little gardening for the postulant in order to have her get some fresh air. She used to go to pull out the weeds at half-past four, just before the hour of prayer in the evening.
3. "Thanks to dear little Father for his good mackerel, etc., etc., for his kindness to us is like an endless chain!" (Letter of Sister Marie of the Sacred Heart to M. Martin, May 17, 1888.)
4. M. Félix Benoit, magistrate at Caen; he is not to be mistaken for M. Auguste Benoit.
5. This happened on the morning of November 28, 1887, during the trip from Rome. "At times, when we had free time, we used to take walks without knowing too much where we were going. It was then that, seeing someone from the pilgrimage, Papa used to say to us playfully: 'Let's shadow him!' This amused us very much. But it was not done out of curiosity, nor for a long time!" (G/NPHF, p. 652.)

LC 81 *From Sister Marie of the Sacred Heart to Thérèse.*

May 20, 1888

To Thérèse of the Child Jesus
My dear little daughter,
Souvenir of my dear
Retreat![1] . . .

Pentecost Sunday
May 20, '88

* Autograph.

1. Lines written on the reverse side of a page from a calendar, which carried this printed text (the "souvenir" that Marie was giving to Thérèse): "Oh, Cherubim, lead me into the Bridegroom's garden! There He is. . . . He is coming. . . . Will He stop at me! . . . Will I be the little plant upon whom He is going to look with pleasure and whose flower He will pick in order to breathe in its scent! . . . Open your petals and bend the flower of your heart towards Him, and He will look at you with love! . . ."

LD *From Sister Agnes of Jesus to Sister Marie of the Sacred Heart.*

June 7, 1888

I, the poor little rose of Jesus and the dear bud, Thérèse of the Child Jesus, offer the blessed Rose of the Heart of Jesus all their good wishes for the Holy Feast![1]

The Lamb and the little lamb kiss the dove.

* Autograph.

1. Feast of the Sacred Heart, June 8. The note was no doubt accompanied by some roses; see the letter following, LD, June 10, 1888.

LD *From Sister Marie of the Sacred Heart to M. Martin.* (Extract.)

June 10 (?), 1888

Sunday

Thanks to good Jesus' little Monitor, who is giving us good things and joys. The fine pearl, the Queen, and the Diamond[1] make up only one heart to love him. The Queen placed the three roses and the bud[2] at her little Jesus' statue, and I said a prayer for the little Monitor so dear to God's Heart.

Dear little Father, your Queen is really worthy of this title; she is a little Queen, a perfection worthy of her King. . . .

* Autograph.

1. Sister Agnes of Jesus, Thérèse, and Sister Marie of the Sacred Heart.
2. Perhaps the roses offered to Sister Marie of the Sacred Heart by Sister Agnes of Jesus (see LD, June 7, 1888)?

LT 52 **From Thérèse to M. Martin.**

May-June (?), 1888

Uncertain date; see notes 1 and 3.

J. M. J. T.

Little Jesus' postman[1] is very kind, and I am sending him all my love and kisses. I shall gladly take the wine he is giving me,[2] imagining it is coming from the cellar of the Child Jesus.

Dear little Father, it's you who are Jesus' postman; I know it. Oh! thank you. . . how kind you are to me!

Yes, I will always remain your little Queen, and I will try to be your glory by becoming a great saint.

Thérèse of the Child Jesus, the brilliant Diamond, and your *very* bright pearl kiss you.

They just showed me this instant the birds.[3] Oh! dear little Father, how good you are. There are three birds, one for Papa's diamond, one for the bright pearl, and one for the little Queen. She will take care to do her best to resemble her King a little.

* Autograph in eleven fragments, CMG.

1. See LT 48, note 1, May 8, 1888. At the same time, Sister Marie of the Sacred Heart spoke of "good Jesus' Monitor." The handwriting and the tone of this letter suggest it was written between May 8 (LT 48) and June 24 (see LD, June 26, 1888). The CMG III copy, p. 172, transcribed it immediately after the April 29 letter (LT 46). However, see note 3.
2. No doubt a medicinal wine.
3. These were waterfowl which, according to the interpretation of the time, were part of the fish family (the Rule of Carmel prohibited the eating of meat). If these were sea ducks—usually caught during the foggy season—mentioned at various times in the correspondence of the Martin and Guérin families, we would perhaps have to place this letter at the beginning of winter: November - December 1888 as was done in the first edition of the *Letters* (ed. 1948, p. 88). However, in 1892, it happened that Sister Marie of the Sacred Heart thanked Céline for a gift of sea ducks between April 10 and 17.

LT 53 From Thérèse to Céline.

June 17,
1888

Sunday, June 1888

J. M. J. T.

My dear Céline,

You would be very nice to send me AS SOON AS POSSIBLE the material you bought for making yourself an apron. I would need, too, the Scotch cincture you had in which you dressed up. Send

me, too, all the white ribbons you have; there is one I had around my head on the day of my First Communion. You can also take the one off the bonnet.[1] . . . All this is for representing St. Agnes.[2] . . .

Dear little sister, how good God is to you! If you could only see what a grace you received on Friday.[3] I believe really that this is the grace you were awaiting. You know, you used to say to me: but I have not received any definite grace.[4] I am convinced that you have this grace. Now you must be all for Jesus; more than ever He is all yours. He has already placed on your finger the mysterious ring of the espousals. He wants to be the sole master of your soul.

Dear sister, we are truly SISTERS in the full *strength* of the term. *Adieu*; from a distance, my heart is reading your heart.

Thérèse of the Child Jesus
p.c.ind.

Kiss my incomparable King[5] for me.

* Autograph.

1. The First Communion bonnet; see LC 77, note 6.
2. For the feast of Mother Marie de Gonzague, June 21; a little play composed by Sister Agnes of Jesus. A copy has been preserved from the hand of Thérèse, dating from 1894-1895.
3. "June 15. I announced to Papa my vocation for Carmel, and these were the circumstances. I was showing my dear father a painting I had just completed; he was in the belvedere, seated at his little work table, and he seemed to be meditating. He turned to me, and he studied my canvas with joy and suggested that he take me to Paris to have me pursue a course in painting. I immediately answered that I would prefer to give up this art completely rather than expose my soul to any danger, that, having given my heart to Jesus a long time ago, I wanted to keep it pure. . . ." (Sister Geneviève, CMG IV, pp. 183-184.)
4. An offer of marriage, received the evening of April 9, the same day as Thérèse's entrance into Carmel, had left Céline undecided as to what way she should follow.

5. On the reverse side of the sheet folded in two, Thérèse wrote: "*Very busy* Céline."

LC 82
June 18, 1888
→ LT lost

From P. Pichon to Thérèse.

First letter in spiritual direction since he had taken official charge of Thérèse at the end of May.

† S. Brieuc, June 18, '88

Happy Benjamin of the Heart of Jesus,

May I not add: and of my heart? Yes, God wills it and you, too, isn't that true?

The first little sample of your soul[2] gave me great joy. I read, I understood what your pen wrote and better still what it could not say. Your lines are dear windows through which I saw your soul. I love these windows very much which permit me to see the soul of my child and open out even on her heart.

There is nothing more precious than your great peace. Don't allow the enemy to break into it. Listen to Jesus saying to you as to His intimate friends: Peace be with you![3]

You will always carry out those ardent desires for sanctity, for the apostolate, by aiming at nothingness out of love for God. In your little nothingness, you will find the great ALL! And with Him what can you not do?

Love for love! That is your motto.[4] Try to rival. You will always be conquered. Oh! the blessed defeat.

In union of prayers, merits, and sacrifices! I depend on them always. I bless you paternally in union with the Sacred Heart of Jesus.

A. P.

Pray for my retreat from July 3 to 12.

* Autograph.

1. P. Pichon very frequently indicates the month when he is writing by the first letter of that month. The announcement in the postscript of

his personal retreat from the 3rd to the 12th of July suggests he was writing in June.

2. A reference to the first letter sent by Thérèse (it is understood that P. Pichon is now her spiritual director). P. Pichon did not save one of Thérèse's letters. Concerning the relationship of the director to the directee, between the Jesuit and the Carmelite nun, the reader is referred to the study cited, DCL, *Le Père Pichon et la famille Martin*, 1882-1897, pp. 24-28, for these months of May-June 1888.
3. See Luke 24:36. See Ms. A, p. 62 and p. 149, where Thérèse recalls her confession of May 1888, the source of such a peace for her, relative to her illness—simulated, she feared—of May 1883. It is perhaps this peace to which P. Pichon is referring and which he is confirming in this paragraph.
4. This was repeated in LC 87. It was current in the pious literature of the time. Mother Marie de Gonazgue, as many other Carmelite nuns, had it engraved on her Profession Crucifix. Compare it with the motto inscribed by Thérèse on her coat of arms: "Love is repaid only by love."

LD *From Mme. Guérin to Sister Marie of the Sacred Heart, Sister Agnes of Jesus, and Thérèse.*

June 26, 1888

On June 23, M. Martin left Les Buissonnets without any warning to his family. From Le Havre, he wrote Céline asking her to send him some money. Upon receiving this letter, June 25, Céline and M. Guérin and Ernest Maudelonde went in search of him. Their search was fruitless at the time Mme. Guerin traced these lines to the Carmel.

June '88

My Darlings,

I am sending you a letter from your father which we have just received.[1] You can see he is still at Le Havre since the letter was delivered yesterday evening. I sent a message immediately to my

husband. He is going to watch the entrance to the post office. I would be surprised if he did not succeed in finding him. Calm, then, your great sorrow, I beg you. I am sorry you saw this morning's telegram[2] since it has caused you so much trouble. I thought it over for a moment, but then I told myself that you were going to pray even more if you could and then I sent it to you. But, I beg you, don't push matters to the extreme; look at the handwriting of this recent letter. It is good, it seems to me. Now how he needed money I don't know at all. But I cannot believe that God will allow things to get worse. Look at this morning's fire and how your sister was protected.[3] The fire could have taken place at night, and I don't know what would have happened. It is always possible that your house could have been seriously damaged, and Léonie perhaps not have awakened; then what would have happened? I tremble to think of it. But God watches over us all. He did not permit the fire to touch your house. I assure you that I who was a witness to all this cannot refrain from believing that God will never allow a very great misfortune to take place. I believe He is holding you in His hands. He will perhaps allow things to go very far to test your confidence, but He will stop all in time.[4] I will tell you soon about a little detail[5] which will help you see that God will not permit anyone to touch a hair of your head.

See you soon, my darlings. We kiss you all from the depths of our heart. Remember me to your good Mother Marie de Gonzague.

Céline Guérin

Please return your father's letter sealed to the bearer. It could be useful to me sometime.

* Autograph.

1. This letter was not preserved; it was probably addressed to the Guérins.
2. This was no doubt from M. Guérin stating that they had not yet found M. Martin.

3. "This morning (Tuesday), shortly before five o'clock, a fire broke out in Lisieux, *chemin des Bissonnets* [sic], in a little house rented by a M. Prévost. . . . The property was destroyed as well as the greater part of the furniture. . . . Under the direction of Captain Lepage, two pumps were put in action and extinguished the fire; the first from the hydrant at the City Hall, brought in by Corporal Leminoux, was able to preserve the house occupied by M. Martin and his family; a piece of wood in the roof was beginning to burn." (Journal *Le Normand*, Tuesday, June 26, 1888.) It is this incident concerning the fire that makes it possible to date the present letter. In July M. Martin bought the burnt property in order to enlarge Les Buissonnets. Its site today is occupied by the stairs and the embankment.
4. M. Martin was found at Le Havre on June 27 (ChrIG, p. 36).
5. We don't know the nature of this "little detail."

LC 83 *From Sister Agnes of Jesus to Thérèse.*

July 3 (?), 1888

Approximate date. Sister Agnes of Jesus began her private retreat of ten days on the night of July 1 (according to her letter to M. Martin, July 1, 1888). This first note to Thérèse was found in one of Thérèse's books: *Direction spirituelle à l'usage des novices* (see LT 47, note 4, May 8, 1888).

A moment!... An eternity![1] We sow in tears in order to reap with laughter.[2] In the lessons on the Martyrs, we read these beautiful words:[3] "The Lord Himself will wipe the tears from their eyes.[4] They have entered into the sojourn of light. . . . There the sun will no longer burn them, and the night will not envelop them in darkness. . . ."

The martyrs of the religious life are included here, and it is to them also that God is making this promise.

Ah! blessed Eternity, it is worth suffering a little and even very much in order to attain it.

* Autograph.
1. On the same day, it seems, Sister Agnes of Jesus wrote to Sister Marie of the Sacred Heart: "I am absorbed today with the thought of Eter-

nity. What an unfathomable abyss!" Judging by this note and several others, she read this in *Conférences théologiques et spirituelles sur les grandeurs de Dieu*, by P. d'Argentan. Céline transcribed a long passage from the same author into a former school copybook of poetic fragments and notes from her reading. We read there: "O moment! O eternity! how closely you are allied!" (*Op. Cit.*, vol. II, XIth conference. "The eternity of God," art. I, p. 13.) See LT 96, note 2, October 15, 1889.

2. Psalm 125:5.
3. Office of Several Martyrs, first response from the first nocturn at Matins. According to the Carmelite *Ordo* of 1888, this response, in June-July, was recited on the night of June 25 (feast of Sts. John and Paul) and on the night of July 27 (Sts. Nazaire and Celse).
4. See Apocalypse 21:4.

LT 54 From Thérèse to Sister Agnes of Jesus.

July 4 (?), 1888
→LC 83

Concerning the date of this note, see LC 85, note 2.

J. M. J. T.

The bleating of Jesus' dear lamb[1] has resounded like sweet music in the ears of the little lamb![2]... Where, then, has the lamb learned Cecilia's melody?[3]

Eternity, oh! the little lamb is plunged into it; following the lamb, it tries to advance by leaps, but the road must be opened up for it by the sweet lamb's music.

The grain of sand,[4] in spite of its littleness, *wishes* to form beautiful Eternities; it wishes to form some for the souls of sinners, but, alas, it is still not little enough or light enough.

The palm of Agnes[5] is needed for the lamb and the little lamb, and if this is not through blood, then it has to be through love.... That is the dream of the grain of sand!...

Jesus alone! Nothing but Him. The grain of sand is so little that, if it wanted to place someone other[6] than Him in its heart, there would be no room for Jesus....

May the white Lamb pray for the unknown grain of sand in order that in eternity it may become brilliant and bright.

The little Reed of Jesus[7]

* Autograph.

1. On July 11, 1888, Sister Agnes wrote to Sister Marie of the Sacred Heart: "Since the dear lion loves so much the poor lamb's bleatings. . . ." We do not know who was the first to make use of this expression, Thérèse or Sister Agnes of Jesus.
2. This nickname for Thérèse, coupled with that of Sister Agnes of Jesus, "the lamb," appears in LT 54, 55, 56, 75, 78, 91, 95, 106 (all letters addressed to Sister Agnes of Jesus with the exception of LT 91, which is an answer to LC 112 from Sister Marie of the Sacred Heart). We find it, too, in the following correspondents: Sister Agnes of Jesus (LC 115); Sister Marie of the Sacred Heart (LC 98, 101, 106, 112); Mother Marie de Gonzague (LC 118, 143, 144); but above all P. Pichon who utilized it until 1897 (LC 87, 94 where Mother Marie de Gonzague cites these words of Père Pichon, 97, 116, 126, 146, 151, 157, 161, and LD, July 26, 1897).
3. See LT 55, note 3.
4. See LT 45, note 4.
5. On June 21, Thérèse had just played the role of St. Agnes; see LT 53. And the note from Sister Agnes of Jesus speaks of martyrdom.
6. This is a probable reference to her very deep affection for Mother Marie de Gonzague; see LC 80, note 2.
7. This image, presented already in LT 49, appeared again in LT 55. In her answer, Sister Agnes of Jesus used it in LC 84 and 85. See, too, LC 120, from Sister Marie of the Angels; the latter could have influenced her novice at times in this regard. Sister Marie of the Angels loved to call herself "the little reed." (See the sermon given by P. H. de Chaumontel, her relative, for her golden jubilee on April 9, 1918.) No doubt this image was used in imitation of Sister Marie de Saint-Pierre of the Tours Carmel (d. 1848), whose writings the novice mistress loved to read. When Thérèse received the Habit, she was given the "reed" as the emblem for her clothing. This was customary in the Lisieux Carmel, emblems being used in preference to numbers. Thérèse used the "reed" on her coat of arms.

LT 55 **From Thérèse to Sister Agnes of Jesus.**

July 5-9, 1888 Approximate date.

→ LC lost

Thanks to the dear lamb for having made the little lamb hear once again the music from heaven. The gentle breeze made the little reed sway softly. . . .

It was after nine o'clock when the reed noticed the dear little paper;[1] there was no earthly light,[2] but its heart more than its eyes knew how to decipher St. Cecilia's[3] music. It did not miss one single word! . . .

Yes, I desire them, these agonies of the heart, these pinpricks about which the lamb speaks. What does it matter to the little reed if it bends? It is not afraid of breaking, for it has been planted at the edge of the waters, and, instead of touching the ground when it bends, it encounters only a beneficent wave which strengthens it and makes it want another storm to come and pass over its frail head. Its weakness gives rise to all its confidence. It cannot break since, no matter what happens to it, it wants only to see the gentle hand of its Jesus. . . . Sometimes the little gusts of wind are more unbearable for the reed than the great tempests, for in these latter it will be refreshed in its dear brook, but the little gusts of wind don't make it bend low enough; these are the pinpricks. . . .

But nothing is too much to suffer to gain the palm.[4] . . .

* Autograph.

1. A note slipped under the door of her cell by Sister Agnes of Jesus before the Office of Matins at nine o'clock. Thérèse was dispensed, then, from this Office that night.
2. The Carmelites were following sun time; on July 24, 1888, Sister Marie of the Sacred Heart wrote Jeanne Guérin: "I can say that I'm writing you by the light of the moon, for I'm no longer able to see in my little cell, it is 8:30" (which would be 9:30 today). Thérèse, no doubt already retired, did not want to light her lamp just out of curiosity; see Ms. C, p. 210.

3. See LT 54. Perhaps Thérèse is taking up here an expression of Sister Agnes? See the latter's letter to Céline on October 20, '88: "To the fiancée who is awaiting the day of the divine nuptials, this is no longer the silence of the exile, that crushing silence that darkens the soul; it is already the melody of the great day, the melody of Cecilia. . . ." Concerning the origin of this comparison, see LT 87, note 9.
4. See LT 54, note 5.

LC 84 *From Sister Agnes of Jesus to Thérèse.*

July 7-9 (?),
1888
→ LT 55

If the little reed is always so faithful to the lightest breeze of grace, its sweet face will often be caressed by the Lily from heaven, Jesus, who remains always at its side!. . . While sinners rise up like lofty oaks to mock His power, the little reed will offer Him all her possessions, that is, the swayings of its stem which are the sighs of love. . . .

* Autograph.

LD *From Sister Agnes of Jesus to Sister Marie of the Sacred Heart.* (Extract.)

July 8,
1888

Poor much loved lion![1] . . . Do you want me to tell you something? This little adventure[2] proves that really we must not be concerned in anything regarding Thérèse of the Child Jesus. As for myself, I shall leave her to do entirely what she asks and

what she wants; let them give her all she asks. We shall not have to answer for it. Let us keep our peace; let us keep our soul. . . . It is really enough to be occupied with ourselves. God will bless us if we act in this way!. . . Let us go straight along our path. . . . Unless we act this way, we shall find so many occasions of worry that we will not be able to stand it.[3] . . .

* Autograph.
1. See LT 75, note 1.
2. We don't know what this was about.
3. The solicitude of Marie and Pauline for their young sister made the observance of this resolution difficult; see, for example, LC 122, 123, 124, in the winter of 1889-1890; LC 102, note 1.

LC 85 *From Sister Agnes of Jesus to Thérèse.*

July 10, 1888 Date obtained through cross-references; see note 2.

We cannot live without a heart, and our heart cannot live without love, but to give it life, let our heart love Jesus alone, for every other love will cause it to die.

Père Nouet[1]

See you soon! In two days,[2] I shall return to the field of battle to fight and to suffer. Little reed, pray that the timid lamb may give Jesus the proofs of a true love.

* Autograph.
1. This citation appears on p. 24 of a notebook of notes from readings of Sister Agnes, begun on January 16, 1886, ended around 1891. In this notebook, the citation begins thus: "You cannot live without a heart and your heart, without love, but if you want to give it life, let. . ." We were not able to identify the source. Apparently it is from a book of the same author: *La grandeur du chrétien dans ses rapports avec la Très-Sainte Trinité,* based on the teachings of Père Nouet of the Company of Jesus, a work collected and put in order by a priest of the same Company of Jesus (Haton éditeur, Paris).

2. Begun the evening of July 1, Sister Agnes' retreat ended on the morning of July 12. The note following suggests the year 1888. In fact, on July 10 or 11, 1888, Sister Agnes of Jesus transcribed the same thought for Sister Marie of the Sacred Heart; the notes are identical in format and presentation; their tearings fit together perfectly. Now, on the reverse side of the note destined for Sister Marie of the Sacred Heart, we read: "Let Céline make arrangements with the house at Paris. It is certain that they cannot sleep on the ground." These lines make a reference to a short visit of Céline to Auteuil with her father and Léonie in July 1888 (mentioned in CMG IV, p. 187). The notes LT 54, 55, 56, being contemporaneous with this same retreat, it is not possible to uphold the date of May 1889, proposed by the first edition of the *Letters*. The study of the handwriting and the type of paper confirm the dating of July 1888.

LT 56 From Thérèse to Sister Agnes of Jesus.

July 11,
1888
→ LC 85

What a joy to see once again the sweet face of the lamb,[1] but the little lamb begs the lamb not to leap towards heaven as yet.[2] If its place is already prepared, let it think of the poor little lamb; let it wait a little until the little lamb can leap too. Then both of them will go into their homeland. Their heart which is never satisfied on earth will go to quench its thirst at the real spring of love.[3] Oh! the sweet banquet. What a joy to see God; to be judged by Him whom we shall have loved above all things.[4] I dreamed that the lamb was going to fly away into its homeland, but I hope that it will remain a little while more in this exile in order to guide the poor little lamb.

* Autograph.

1. On the morning of July 12, Sister Agnes would lift her veil. It was customary for the nuns, when on their private retreat, to keep their veils lowered as an aid to recollection.

2. Nothing in Sister Agnes' note justified this fear. But the anxiety which her dreams bring out (see end of the note) and which comes through again in LT 78: "Don't die right now," reveals how vital for her, in these two first years of her religious life, was the presence of her "Mamma" (see LT 76, note 7).
3. Probable reference to the sentence from P. Nouet, quoted by Sister Agnes.
4. Saint Teresa of Avila, *Way of Perfection*, ch. 42; or *Histoire de Sainte Thérèse*, vol. I, p. 354. This thought appears also on the leaf of a calendar preserved by Thérèse in one of her books. (We have found some twenty of these leaves; the choice of the sentences is significant, but we don't know at what date Thérèse collected them.)

LC 86 *From Céline to Thérèse.*

July 22, 1888

M. Martin's health improved in July. He went to Auteuil for a few weeks with his two daughters (see LC 85, note 2). They were uncomfortable there, and they broke the lease and returned to Les Buissonnets.

Sunday, July 22, 1888

My dear Thérèse,

How express my whole soul to you! You know, Sunday is sometimes sad; I feel emptiness everywhere. Oh! you understand what I want to say.... I found your copybook which speaks of heaven;[1] I read it, but my sole consolation is to come and speak to you a little.

Do you remember the evenings in the belvedere,[2] our long chats, our dreams of sanctity, our resolutions? We had as witnesses only the stars and the silvery moon. In this profound silence, there were only two souls, and what a sweet language was theirs!

Everything in the house is filled with memories of you. In the little study, the two drawers of your desk have remained intact; if you only knew what heart aches I get when I open them. Every-

thing is arranged as you placed it, your copybooks, your books.... In my bedroom, your linen drawer has not been touched. Beloved little sister, I'm crying while writing these lines.

Yesterday evening, I believed my heart was about to break; this is with regard to poor little Father. I put a plaster poultice[3] on him, and he told me that he wanted to take a purgative because of the dizzy spells he was experiencing. He appears so old to me now, so worn out. If you were to see him kneeling every morning at the Communion Table; he leans over, he helps himself as well as he can, and it's enough to make you weep. My heart is torn; I imagine that he will die soon. Oh! I believe I would die myself of sadness. This thought pursues me; I am always seeing him in his hour of agony, and my soul is so heavy that I can no longer breathe.

He is so good. Ah! darling, if it is only up to me to refuse him anything, this will never be true. I am going to wear myself out for him; if you only knew how much I pity him! The other day, at Paris, he would have loved to find a little bantam hen for Léonie, who had expressed the desire to have one.

However, he is affected by his condition, so I try to make him happy; I am doing *the best* I can.

Dear little sister, it's true that all passes, but all is so long! And now P. Pichon is preparing to go to Canada[4] and for a long time. What a blessed moment when God will say to us: "Now it is my turn!"[5]

It is our turn at the present moment. Ah! how necessary it is to make good use of it! Yes, there is nothing but suffering on this earth, and we must expect nothing else.

Thérèse, this letter is for you *alone*.[6]

Your little sister who loves you,
Céline

* Typed copy, G.

1. A former school copybook from the Benedictine Abbey boarding school. On the four pages in the middle, Thérèse had copied, June 4

and 5, 1887, extracts from the conference: "On eternal beatitude and the supernatural vision of God," the seventh conference of Abbé ARMINJON, in *Fin du monde présent et mystères de la vie future* (2nd. ed., Saint-Paul, 1882). The new edition of this book in 1970, *l'Office Central de Lisieux*, gives a concordance of the pages 1882/1970 at the end of the volume. In these notes of the *General Correspondence*, we are giving only the 1882 pagination. We know that this reading exerted a considerable influence upon Thérèse as an adolescent (see Ms. A, pp. 102-103). Céline recopied this extract in her copybook of "Poetic Fragments," a few pages before P. Argentan's extracts (see LC 83, note 1).

2. See Ms. A, p. 103.
3. This was placed on a wound he had behind his left ear; this was a skin condition he got from an insect bite years before. See LD, May 9, 1877, note 8.
4. P. Pichon left for Canada on November 3, 1888.
5. This is from Abbé ARMINJON, *op. cit.*, in note 1 above.
6. She meant that it was better to hide it from Sister Agnes of Jesus and Sister Marie of the Sacred Heart; hence the step taken by Mother Marie de Gonzague, who came very early in the morning to give Thérèse this letter personally (LT 57, note 10). The two older sisters believed, at this time, that M. Martin's decline in health came from a lack of *savoir-faire* on the part of Céline, mistress of the house since Marie's departure for Carmel (October 1886); see LD, Sister Agnes of Jesus to Léonie and Céline, end of January 1889.

LT 57 From Thérèse to Céline.

July 23,
1888
→ LC 86

J. M. J. T.

Monday, July 23, '88

Jesus alone †

Darling Sister,

Your Thérèse understood your whole soul; she read still more deeply into it than you wrote about it. I understood the sadness of

Sunday; I experienced it all. . . . It seemed to me when I was reading it that the same soul animates us. There is something so sensitive between our souls that makes them so much alike. We have always been together, our joys, our pains, everything has been in common. Ah! I feel that this is continuing in Carmel; never, no, never shall we be separated. You know that it is only the yellow lily[1] that could separate us a little. I tell you this because I am sure that the white lily will always be your lot since you have chosen Him and He has chosen you first. . . . Do you understand the lilies. . . .

I was sometimes wondering why Jesus had taken me first; now I have understood. . . . You know that your soul is a lily *immortelle*.[2] Jesus can do all He wills with it. It matters little whether it be in one place or another; it will always be immortelle. The tempest cannot make the yellow of its stamen fall on its white scented calyx; it is Jesus who made it that way. He is free, and no one is to ask Him why He gives His graces to one soul rather than another.[3] At the side of this Lily, Jesus has placed another, its faithful companion.[4] They grew up together but one was *immortelle*, and the other was not. It was necessary that Jesus take His lily before its flower opened so that the two lilies be for Him. . . . One was weak, the other was strong; Jesus took the weak one, and He left the other so as to embellish it with a new splendor. . . . Jesus asks ALL from His two lilies; He wills to leave them nothing but their white dress. ALL! Has *immortelle* understood her little sister? . . .

Life is burdensome. What bitterness. . . but what sweetness. Yes, life is painful for us. It is hard to begin a day of work. The feeble bud has seen it just as the beautiful lily has. If we feel Jesus present, oh! then we would really do all for Him, but no, He seems a thousand leagues away. We are all alone with ourselves. Oh! what annoying company when Jesus is not there. But what is this sweet Friend doing then? Doesn't He see our anguish, the weight that is oppressing us? Where is He? Why doesn't He come to console us since we have Him alone for a friend? Alas, He is not

far; He is there, very close. He is looking at us, and He *is begging* this sorrow, this agony from us. He needs it for souls and for our soul. He wants to give us such a beautiful recompense, and His ambitions for us are very great. But how can He say: "My turn,"[5] if ours hasn't come, if we have given Him nothing? Alas, it does pain Him to give us sorrows to drink, but He knows this is the only means of preparing us to "know Him as *He knows Himself* and to become *Gods ourselves*."[6] Oh! what a destiny. How great is our soul. . . .

Let us raise ourselves above what is passing away. Let us keep ourselves a distance from the earth. Higher up the air is pure. Jesus is hiding Himself, but we can see Him. When shedding tears, we are drying His, and the Blessed Virgin smiles. Poor Mother, she had so many sorrows because of us, and it is only right that we console her a little when we weep and suffer with her. . . .

I read this morning a passage of the Gospel where it says: "I have not come to bring peace but the sword."[7] There remains nothing else for us to do but to fight, and when we don't have the strength, it is then that Jesus fights for us. . . . Together let us lay the axe to the root of the tree.[8] . . .

Poor muddle-headed Thérèse. What a letter, what turmoil. . . . Oh! if I could only have said what I am thinking, Céline would have very much to read. . . .

Jesus is good to have allowed us to meet a mother like the one we have.[9] What a treasure. Little sister, if you had seen her this morning at six o'clock,[10] bringing me your letter. I was really moved. . . .

Jesus is asking ALL, ALL, ALL.[11] As much as He can ask from the greatest Saints.

Your poor little sister,
Thérèse of the Child Jesus
p.c.ind.

* Autograph.

1. "The 'yellow lily' in our common language signified marriage." (Sister Geneviève, PO, 1857.)
2. *Immortelle*: this was a symbol given to Céline by Sister Agnes of Jesus; see LD, October 22-24, 1886.

3. Compare this with the first chapter of Ms. A.
4. Thérèse herself.
5. Arminjon, *op. cit.*, p. 290; see LC 86, note 5. The "now, my turn!" appears again in LT 94, 107, 157, 169; all these letters were written to Céline.
6. *Ibid.*, p. 290. However, Arminjon, quoting St. Paul, 1 Cor. 13:12, wrote: "in order that knowing me, as I know them, they may become Gods themselves."
7. Matthew 10:34.
8. Imitation of Christ I, 11:4.
9. Mother Marie de Gonzague.
10. At the end of morning prayer, which was made between five and six in the summer; see LC 86, note 6.
11. Written three times in capital letters, this word is underlined respectively two, three, and five times.

LT 58 From Thérèse to M. Martin.

July 31, 1888

July 31, '88. Carmel

J. M. J. T.

My dear King,

If you only knew the pleasure your carp, your *monster*, gave us. The dinner was held back for half an hour. Marie of the Sacred Heart made the sauce, and it was delicious. It tasted like "*la cuisine du monde.*" It was even better than the sumptuous "*cuisine d'Italie,*" and that is not saying little, for what banquets[1]...and what company! Do you remember, little Father?... But it isn't always that that gives appetite, at least to me, for I haven't eaten so much since I've been in Carmel. I feel that I am entirely in my element; if Mademoiselle Pauline[2] were here, she would say that: "I have found my way."

Your Diamond can't write you, for she is doing the washing,

but this doesn't stop her from thinking of you, dear little Father. She kisses you with her whole heart, and you know the heart of your biggest daughter is not little.

I think of all you used to say to us frequently: "Vanity of vanities, all is vanity,[3] vanity of life which passes, etc. . . ." The more I live the more I find this is true, that all is vanity on this earth.

When I think of you, dear little Father, I naturally think of God, for it seems to me that it is impossible to see anyone more holy than you on the earth.

When I think that in a week it will be four months since I am in Carmel, I can't get over it. It seems to me that I have always been here, and, on the other hand, it seems that my entrance was yesterday. How everything passes. . . .

The more I live, dear little Father, the more I love you. I don't know how this can be, but it is the truth, and I wonder what this will be at the end of my life. . . .

I am very proud of my title of Queen of France and Navarre; I hope to merit it always. Jesus, the King of heaven, when taking me for Himself, has not taken me away from my holy King on earth. Oh! no, always if my dear little Father wills it and does not find me too unworthy, I shall remain Papa's Queen.

The bright pearl hugs you *very tightly*.

Adieu, and see you soon, dear King.

Your little Queen,
Thérèse of the Child Jesus
p.c.ind.

* Autograph in ten fragments, CMG.

1. They still have the menu of the *Hôtel du Sud*, Rome (see LT 32, note 4). It was made up of: "*Potage. Pâte d'Italie au Consommé. Entrées. Matelotte de poisson. Noix de veau glacées Nivernaise. Rôti.*" The second half is missing.
2. Mademoiselle Pauline Romet, friend of the family; see LT 6, note 2. Céline had just written her on July 27 to ask for lodgings on the occa-

sion of a trip to Alençon, August 6, with M. Martin and Léonie (ACL).

3. Imitation I, 1:3, quoting Ecclesiastes 1:2. It was, in fact, to the *Imitation* that M. Martin must have been referring when writing to his daughter Marie: "Be more reasonable than your aged father, who has enough of the beauties which surround him and who is dreaming of heaven and infinity. Vanity of vanities, and all is vanity, except to love God and to serve Him!" (Letter to his daughter Marie, August 30, 1885.)

LT 59 — From Thérèse to M. Guérin.

August 22, 1888

M. David, first cousin of Mme. Fournet, Mme. Guérin's mother, is very sick. The Christian influence of M. Guérin, who had hastened to his bedside at La Musse on August 10, had just brought the dying man back to God.

Carmel, August 22, '88

J. M. J. T.

† Jesus

Dear Uncle,

We just received a letter from Aunt[1] in which she was telling us about all your sorrows. Although far away from you, your little niece is sharing in your pain. She would like to be near her good Uncle to console him, but, alas! what would she be able to do?... No, it is better for her to be in Carmel; there, at least, she can pray as much as she wants to Him who alone can give consolation and pour it abundantly into her dear Uncle's heart.

Good Monsieur David's condition saddens us very much. I understand, dear Uncle, how much you must be suffering, for there is nothing so painful as seeing those whom we love suffering.

However, I thank God with my whole heart for the great grace He willed to grant this beautiful soul. What a disposition he has for appearing before Him; it is really admirable. Everything dear Aunt told us about him has touched me very deeply.

It was impossible, Uncle, that God not grant you this consolation after all you've done for His glory. Ah! how beautiful the crown reserved for you appears to me. It can't be otherwise since your whole life was a perpetual cross and since God acts in this way only with the great saints.

What a joy to think that in heaven we shall be reunited, never again to leave each other; without this hope, life would be really unbearable. . . .

Dear Uncle, I don't know what you're going to think of your poor little niece; she has let her pen run on without thinking of what it's saying. Her heart, if it could write, WOULD SAY something entirely different, but it is obliged to trust in this cold pen which doesn't really know how to express what it feels. I place myself in my good angel's hands; I think that a messenger from heaven will carry out my message well. I'm sending him to dear Uncle to pour some consolation into his heart insofar as our soul can contain it in this valley of exile. . . .

Adieu, good Uncle.

I beg you to remember me to Madame Fournet; I share her pain. For you, Uncle, I'm sending all the love my heart contains, and I will continue to pray unceasingly for good Monsieur David.

Your little niece, who would like to be able to lessen your sorrow a little.

Thérèse of the Child Jesus
p.c.ind.

* Autograph.

1. Letter not preserved.

LT 60 **From Thérèse to Mme. Guérin.**

August 23, 1888

News of M. David's death reached the Carmel the night before. Thérèse wrote this letter after her morning prayer, around six o'clock.

Carmel, August 23, '88, six o'clock.

J. M. J. T.

Jesus †

Dear Aunt,

Yesterday evening, we heard of the death of good Monsieur David. Although we were expecting to receive this sad news at any moment, when learning the reality I was very much touched. I am praying that God may take this very holy soul into His paradise; perhaps his soul is already there, for with dispositions as perfect as this one can go straight to heaven.

I am begging God to pour consolation into your soul, dear Aunt. He has already been good for having answered all the prayers you offered in order to give Him your dear relative's soul. If from the depths of her solitude your little daughter could hope that she had a feeble share in this, she would be very happy.

I find, dear Aunt, that in these moments of great sadness, we must look to heaven; instead of weeping, all are rejoicing, for Our Lord possesses one more of the elect, a new sun[1] lights up the angels of heaven with its splendor, all are in the rapture of divine ecstasy. They are astonished that we call death the beginning of life. In their eyes, we are in a narrow tomb, and their souls can be transported to the extremity of the heavenly shores, infinite horizons.[2] . . . Dear Aunt, when we consider the death of the just man, we cannot refrain from envying his lot. The time of exile no longer exists for him; there is no longer anything but God, nothing but God.

Oh! Aunt, your little daughter would have many things to say to you; her heart is thinking deeply on this. This morning she is

totally lost in sorrow at the death of the saints, but time is lacking for completing my little draft. I must stop, for the bell has just warned me that it is time[3] to finish. I offer this little sacrifice to Jesus in order that He console you with His gentle little hand.

Your little daughter who is at heart near you as well as near her dear little sisters.[4]

Thérèse of the Child Jesus
p.c.ind.

* Autograph.

1. On the comparison of the Elect to a new sun, see ARMINJON, *op. cit.*, p. 312. This whole paragraph brings out "the reception which God must give to His Elect at the moment when *He Himself* will become the great and eternal reward," a passage from this author that particularly struck Thérèse; see Ms. A, p. 102.
2. Extract from *Une Voix de Prison by* LAMENNAIS. Mme. Martin used to love quoting this passage which she knew from a collection of selected texts.
3. Thérèse meant to write "*temps*" and wrote instead "*tant.*"
4. These were her cousins Jeanne and Marie Guérin. On the fourth empty page of her letter, Mother Marie de Gonzague wrote a few words of sympathy.

LT 61 From Thérèse to M. Martin.

August 25,
1888

J. M. J. T.

Carmel, August 25, '88

Jesus †

Dear little Father,

It has finally arrived, then, the day when your Queen can wish you a happy feast with all her honors, for she is in Carmel in the company of your jewels: the Diamond and the fine pearl. . . . Poor little Queen, she would have to withdraw to give place to the

two splendid gems of her King, but she really cannot resign herself to this, for she has her title, too. She can show it to whomever wants to see it; it is signed by her King's own hand: Queen of France and Navarre. She has nothing else, but it seems to me that this suffices for her to be admitted next to her King. Besides, no one tries to contest her right, it is recognized even by the stranger. In Italy, at Rome, they knew that the Queen was there. . . .

Dear King, your little Queen would like to have some magnificent gifts to offer you, but she has nothing, and, besides, it would be too difficult. For her King, all the palaces of the Vatican, loaded down with gifts, would not be beautiful enough; she is dreaming of something else more kingly. She needs the immense treasures of the infinite horizons;[1] what she would like to give her King is not found on earth. It is Jesus alone who possesses this, so she is going to pray to Him to give her King heavenly consolations. For a Father who is not of this earth all that is earthly cannot satisfy him.

You see, dear little Father, that, while appearing to offer you nothing, I am giving you a magnificent gift; if it doesn't delight your eyes, at least your heart will feel it, for I hope that God will answer my prayer.

However, dear little Father, while telling you that I desire to charm only your heart, I am giving you a little picture[2] made by your Queen. I hope that in spite of my little talent it will please you. The fine pearl helped me with her artistic advice and formed the charming design for me, but she wanted me to paint it *all alone.* It doesn't merit much, but my powerlessness is so great and my King is so indulgent that I hope to give him a little pleasure in giving him this little picture.

See you soon, dear little Father. If your Queen is not near you today, she is really there in mind and heart. She wishes you the best of feasts you have ever had in your whole life,[3] and she kisses you with her whole heart.

Your little Queen,
Thérèse of the Child Jesus
p.c.ind.

* Autograph in twenty-one fragments; CMG.

1. See LT 60, note 2.
2. This picture has not been identified; they have preserved the paper in which it was wrapped and on which Sister Agnes wrote in red ink: "Papa's Queen did this picture by herself." These two last words were underlined fifteen times. Across these lines, we can still read: "Stated at Carmel, August 24, '88 under our sign and the seal of our arms. . . . Sister Agnes, the little pearl."
3. The tone of this letter gives us a hint about the worry of M. Martin's daughters; he had just suffered a new relapse on August 12 (CMG IV, p. 187, which gives no details). The circulatory troubles of 1887, localized in the members, were followed in 1888 by cerebral troubles.

LT 62 From Thérèse to Marie Guérin.

September 1888 Date deduced from the content; see note 4
↔ LC lost

J. M. J. T.

Carmel, Thursday

Jesus †

My dear little Sister,

I had already begun to write you on Tuesday evening, and just now I wanted to continue my letter, but the things I was telling you are not what I want to tell you today so I have instead begun it over again.

Thanks for your delightful letter; if Madame de Sévigné had written me, this would not have given me as much pleasure. . . .

Though my little cousin thinks about me often, I, too, am often close to her in spirit. Like you, I have to hear my little Marie spoken about frequently, and above all to speak about her myself. So to satisfy myself, when conversing with God about my dear little sister, I have never any fear that He will find that I'm speaking too long about her, for I am sure that my little Marie is deeply within His Heart.

Dear little imp, how many things I have to tell you, but how quickly the time is passing; I see it escaping me with a frightful rapidity. It's late, and I am writing you in the light of your dear little lamp.[1] You can see that my handwriting reflects my eagerness. What consoles me for having such an ugly handwriting is the thought that in heaven we will no longer need this means of communicating our thoughts; and this is really fortunate for me. . . .

Yesterday, I received a visit, and I give you a hundred guesses. . . . A beautiful woman of the WORLD, her dear husband, a tall *Mademoiselle* of sixteen, a *Monsieur* of fourteen. Did you guess?. . . It is the godmother, who used to plant the verbena.[2] . . . She was accompanied by her niece Th. Gilbert and her nephew Pierre. High society! If you had only seen her in the speakroom. She was almost singing: "*Que mon coeur, que mon coeur a de peine,*"[3] when seeing us behind the grille.

It's time that my chattering come to an end. I haven't, however, said anything interesting to my dear little cousin. But what can you expect from a person like me, who writes without paying any attention to the fact that the paper is being filled with banalities when she has so many serious things to say?. . . Pardon me!. . .

I am coming to an end, dear little Marie, asking you a favor; you would be very kind if you could, when taking a walk in your beautiful park,[4] find some little pieces of dried moss, some bark from a tree, etc. . . . This is for making little things, such as cribs, for example. If this is any trouble to you, don't bring me any; it's only if you find some when taking a walk.

I was very sorry that dear Aunt was sick; I think very much of her, and I am praying for her prompt cure. Hug her very TIGHTLY[5] for her little daughter, however, not in a way to hurt her!. . .

Hug, too, for me DEAR little Jeanne and Céline and Hélène.[6] For those who are not sick I have no pity, so I beg you to hug them as tightly as you can.

I can see, dear little Marie, that all my kisses are not coming to an end. However, I am not at the end, for I haven't given you any, who are charged with distributing everything. So I beg all the

dear persons to whom you are going to give these kisses to return them to you as much as they can. I doubt that my request will be carried out, so I hug you from my heart, but very strongly, so strongly that if you had a boil, it would burst just like the time before the trip to Rome.

Your little sister,
Thérèse of the Child Jesus
p.c.ind.

* Autograph in twenty-four fragments.

1. See LT 50, note 6.
2. Madame Tifenne, friend from Alençon and godmother of Léonie.
3. This was a song they used to sing at Les Buissonnets.
4. See LT 26. When M. David died (LT 60), the Guérin family inherited the *chateau de la Musse.* Up to 1899, the family used to spend their summer vacations there. This summer of 1888, Mme. Guérin and her two daughters stayed there from August 25 to September 29 (ChrIG, p. 36).
5. This word is underlined four times.
6. Céline and Hélène Maudelonde, first cousins to Jeanne and Marie Guérin.

LT 63 From Thérèse to M. Martin.

September 30, 1888

The postulancy was usually of six months duration. M. Martin had already sent, in preparation for Thérèse's reception of the Habit, some *point d'Alençon* as an ornament for her wedding dress. In fact, the postulancy was prolonged for another three months (LC 89 and 90).

J. M. J. T.

Carmel, September 30

My dear King,

Your little Queen is crushed under the weight and the magnificence of your gifts; one really can see that it is a King who is offer-

ing them to His Queen. First it was the *point d'Alençon* that I saw arriving; it was truly regal. I don't know how to thank you for these beautiful gifts. Where, then, is the time when your little Queen would have leaped with joy before something like ONE SOU which her King gave her?[1] Even now her heart would be joyful, but the King's heart has to give more; that is why he is giving his Queen lace *worthy* of: THE QUEEN OF FRANCE AND NAVARRE.

It is true, dear little Father, that if the Queen is unworthy of so much riches, they are not too beautiful for the divine Bridegroom to whom you have given her, and that is why I shall be happy to wear them. Otherwise I would not really dare to, for I am still only the *Orpheline de la Bérésina.*[2] It is only on the day of my reception of the Habit that I will deserve to carry my title of Queen.

I still have a sweet mission to carry out, and it is that of thanking you, in my name as Queen and in the name of the Diamond and the fine pearl, for an avalanche of pears, onions, prunes, and apples, which came from the turn as from a horn of plenty. Where did all this come from? An old gentleman said it was from a Monsieur who lived at the side of the *"jardin de l'Etoile."*[3] This could be no one else but you, so, dear little Father, the provisions were well received; we gave these provisions a good reception without having to be coaxed. The strange thing is they had less trouble entering than your Queen, who was obliged to go to Rome to have the door opened for her. . . .

The enormous onions delighted my heart; they made me think of those of Egypt. We shall not have to sigh for them[4] as the Israelites did. I thought again of those from Lyons[5] that cost fifty *centimes* and are so big. Well, my King, I believe your Queen is going to bore you with her babbling, but she is so happy that she was unable to refrain from telling you so. She thanks you for everything and kisses you with her whole heart.

Thérèse of the Child Jesus
p.c.ind.

* Autograph in twenty fragments, CMG.
1. See Ms. A, p. 36.
2. See LT 46, note 3.
3. See LD, September 10, 1877, note 6; and LD, June 4, 1879.
4. See Numbers 11:5.
5. On the return from Rome, the Martin family spent the whole day of December 1, 1887, visiting Lyons.

LT 64 From Thérèse to M. Martin.

October 8-15(?), 1888

No precise information on the date or the circumstances of this letter.

My dear King,

I would like to write you a long letter, but I am on retreat[1] and this is impossible. You don't know how much your little Queen loves you!... Having to send a letter[2] to the daughter of the King, Princess Léonie, I thought I could not have my message reach her but through the King himself, so it is for this reason that I am addressing myself to His Majesty, the King of France and Navarre. If his dignity does not appear in the eyes of men, I know myself that in heaven it will be shown to the eyes of God. Then the least of the Elect will be like the head of a numerous people,[3] and my King, oh! what a place!...

Your little Queen,
Thérèse of the Child Jesus

* Autograph in eight fragments.
1. Probably the Community retreat preached in October 1888; see LC 87, note 2. The chronicles of the monastery mention erroneously the name of P. Pichon as preacher in 1886 (he gave the October 1887 retreat), and the chronicles don't mention the preachers for 1887

and 1888; it was no doubt P. Blino who preached in 1888. See LT 107, note 2.

2. This letter is lost; we don't know where Léonie was at this time.
3. Isaias 60:22; quoted in the Imitation of Christ III, 58:9.

LC 87 *From P. Pichon to Thérèse.*

October 14, 1888
→ LT lost

† Poitiers, October 14

Sister Thérèse
of the Child Jesus

My very dear Child
in the Sacred Heart,[1]

You are the Benjamin of St. Teresa, and under this title (under a thousand others) I claim for you her most loving blessings.

This week, I followed you in the holy Exercises,[2] and I shared in all your joys, the joys of Thabor or Calvary. But how much I would like to see you in the livery of Jesus.[3] Will your Seraphic Mother tell me "no" tomorrow?[4]

Mass, Office, rosary, prayers, all for you. A good and holy feast!

Thanks for your wishes on September 9[5] and for all your beloved little sheets.[6] Thanks for your pretty little picture. It really spoke to my soul.

Oh! yes, paint Jesus in your soul. Tell the Blessed Virgin to take up the brush[7] herself. Ah! that your heart may reflect only Jesus, Jesus alone! Confidence! The divine Child will continue His work in you. Haven't you felt this during these blessed days of retreat?

You feel the need of God; alleluia. May you be consumed with the desire of possessing Him, of loving Him to distraction.

Love for love![8] I pity you if you attempt to rival Our Lord. You will never love Him as much as He has loved you.

I am charmed with my little Lamb, for it explains its soul to me well. If you only heard all the echoes answering you in my own heart.

Canada is always threatening on the horizon, but a little less. It is more probable that God will keep your Pastor near you. The end of the week will bring me, I hope, the last word from God.[9] Let us love the word in advance whatever it may be.

I bless you lovingly with the hands and the Heart of St. Teresa.

Almire Pichon

* Autograph.
1. Address placed in the corner; this is a peculiarity of his appearing several times. P. Pichon used to group the letters of his correspondents in the same envelope.
2. The Community retreat. See LT 64, note 1.
3. The Habit of Carmel; Thérèse's clothing in the Habit was still not set. See LT 63.
4. The 15th of October was the feast of the "Seraphic Mother" of the reformed Carmel, St. Teresa of Avila.
5. On the feast of St. Almire, September 11th.
6. That is all the letters received from Thérèse since his last answer of June 18, 1888 (LC 82); this would be at least four letters, if we follow what Thérèse said herself: a letter each month. See Ms. A, p. 151.
7. Ms. C, p. 235. Thérèse began painting without any help; see LT 61, note 2 and 67, note 2.
8. See LC 82, note 4.
9. As a matter of fact, P. Pichon will leave for Canada on the following November 3, embarking from Le Havre.

LC 88 *From Céline to Thérèse.*

October 14,
1888

October 14, 1888

My dear little Sister,

Happy feast!... What sadness for your poor Céline not to be able to wish it as in other years. I cannot get used to being separated from you; yesterday, I shed bitter tears at the feet of Jesus.

Do you remember when, last year the both of us used to go into the side aisles[1] in order to see the Tabernacle better? Well, I was there again; no one saw me, only Jesus.

Yes, I cry over you often, I who formerly never used to shed tears; they are always ready to flow now, and I believe that the more this goes on, the more I feel our separation. I find myself without any support, without any counsel. What conformity of ideas, of affections, what sweet outpourings we used to have together, and all this is past! At Aunt's house, there is no longer that happy family life as it was before; there are always sick people; you hear them always moaning. Here I have no support; Léonie is thinking incessantly about the Visitation, and my little affairs don't interest her.

Thérèse! is this the way to wish a happy feast! Don't be disturbed by my complaints. Jesus is here! He must take the place of all. When He is absent, it is then that we must say with St. Francis Xavier: "The absence of the Cross is the absence of life."[2] Or again: "Don't cease to suffer for a moment and you will not cease to love."

Happy feast, darling, happy feast!... And here is another disappointment for me. I had a little present to give you; I went to a lot of trouble, and I don't have it.[3] But you know, there is no feast without its octave, so, during the octave of your feast, you will

find my little souvenir at the feet of your little pink Jesus.[4] Don't forget to look there. In the meantime, I am giving you four pink candles; they are transparent like my heart and my love for you, no cloud, no veil.

Good little Father is sending his Queen some clowns. He alone had the idea; if you only knew how much this touched me! Furthermore, he is giving you fify *centimes* worth of pink cashmere which, alas! has not arrived either. It was impossible to find any in any of the stores, and he had to write to Paris.

Because of your feast, he bought you some fish, all the most beautiful fish there were at the fish-market; never yet has he bought any so expensive, and he did not want to tell me the price. Everybody is feasting you, my darling; I have the least of gifts, but I have my heart!. . .

And the Holy Face,[5] I found it beautiful. I think we should have brought it to you today.

Kiss dear Mother.[6] I love Marie and Pauline, and they know how much!

Your little Céline

* Typewritten copy, G.

1. At the cathedral of Saint-Pierre, Lisieux.
2. We find this quote (the source has not been identified) in Céline's copybook, immediately after the excerpt from Père Arminjon about which she speaks on July 22 (see LC 86, note 1). Céline quotes this same sentence to Jeanne Guérin on January 27-28, 1889.
3. Céline had a little bird stuffed; this bird had been purchased for her by Thérèse at Le Havre (see LT 24, note 3).
4. Statue of the Infant Jesus in the cloister, entrusted to Thérèse's care (see LT 48).
5. A painting of the "veil of Veronica," based on the model at Tours. Céline had framed it. It was placed in the choir; in 1895-1897, it was above the prioress' place in the choir (see CJ 5.8.7). Today, it is in the infirmary where Thérèse died.
6. Mother Marie de Gonzague.

LT 65 **From Thérèse to Céline.**

October 20, 1888

J. M. J. T.

Carmel, October 20, '88

Jesus †

My dear Céline,

Tomorrow, then, is your feast day.[1] Oh! how I would like to be the first to wish you a happy feast; if this is not possible, at least I can do it in my heart. What do you want me to offer you for your feast? If I were to listen to myself, I would ask Jesus to send me all the sorrows, all the sadness, all the annoyances in the life of my dear Céline, but, you see, I am not listening to myself, for I would fear that Jesus may say to me that I am an egoist. I would be wanting Him to give me all there is of the best without leaving a little for His little fiancée whom He loves so much. It is to prove her love for Him that He is making her feel the separation,[2] so I can't ask this from Jesus. And, then, He is so rich, so rich, that He has much with which to enrich both of us. . . .

When I think that if God were to give us the entire universe with all its treasures that this would not be comparable to the *lightest* suffering! What a grace when, in the morning, we feel no courage, no strength to practice virtue; that is the moment to put the axe to the root of the tree.[3] Instead of wasting our time gathering a few baubles, we can dip into diamonds, and what a profit at the end of the day. . . . It is true that sometimes, for a few moments, we look with scorn at gathering our treasures, and this is the difficult moment. We are tempted to leave all behind, but in one act of love, even *unfelt* love, all is repaired, and Jesus smiles. He is helping us without seeming to do so, and the tears that the wicked make Him shed are dried by our poor and feeble

love. Love can do all things, and the most difficult things don't appear difficult[4] to it. Jesus does not look so much at the grandeur of actions or even their difficulty as at the love which goes to make up these actions.[5] . . .

Some time ago, I found a saying which I find very beautiful, and here it is, it will please you, I believe: "Resignation is still distinct from God's will; there is in it the same difference as exists between union and unity. In union, we are still two; in unity, we are only one."[6] Oh! yes, let us be only one with Jesus; let us despise all that passes away. Our thoughts must be drawn to heaven since the home of Jesus is there. I was thinking the other day that we should not attach ourselves to what is around us since we could be in another place other than where we are;[7] our affections and our desires would not be the same. I can't explain my thought to you; I am too stupid for that, but when I see you, I will tell you about it.

Why have I told you all these things which you know *much* BETTER than I? Pardon me. I had to have a little talk with you just like our talks of former times. But that time is not past; we are always the SAME SOUL, and our thoughts are always the *same* as they were at the windows of the belvedere[8] . . . .

I take delight in the day when we shall celebrate[9] in the heavenly city. Your little sister,

Thérèse of the Child Jesus

Oh! yes, it is very sad to think that Père Pichon[10] is going to Canada, but Jesus remains for us! . . .

* Autograph.

1. Saint Céline, virgin, patroness of Meaux, and companion of Saint Geneviève. At the approach of her feast and her birthday, Céline used to abstain from going to the Carmel in order to get a letter from her sisters.
2. The separation from Thérèse; see LC 88.
3. Imitation of Christ I, 11:4.
4. Ibid., III, 5:4.

5. St. Teresa of Avila, *Interior Castle*, VIIth Mansions, ch. 4.
6. Madame Swetchine. Thérèse, when in the infirmary, told her sisters how much this thought helped her during the trial of M. Martin's illness (CJ 23.7.5).
7. Thérèse drew this same conclusion when she saw the chestnut trees pruned at the wrong time; see CJ 24.9.2.
8. See Ms. A, p. 103.
9. Perhaps she meant: "we will celebrate your feast"; however, we find in the correspondence of the Martin-Guérin families other examples of the use of this verb (fêter) without any object.
10. P. Pichon. See *Le Père Pichon et la familee Martin.*

LC 89 *From Monseigneur Hugonin to Thérèse.*

October 25, 1888
→ LT lost

The time for the reception of the Habit having arrived, Thérèse, at the invitation of her prioress, applied for permission from the bishop of the diocese and then from the superior of the Carmel to present her request to the conventual Chapter.

Bishop's Residence
Bayeux

Bayeux, October 25, 1888

Dear Child,

I can only yield to your desires and pray to Our Lord that He may preserve the holy dispositions which He has given to you.

All in Our Lord,
† Flavien

* Autograph.

LC 90 *From M. Delatroëtte to Thérèse.*

October 26,
1888
→ LT lost

My good Child,

After receiving Monseigneur's permission,[1] Reverend Mother Prioress has no need of mine to present you to the Community. I can only give my approval and I join with you in thanking Him whom you have chosen for your Bridegroom for blessing you more and more and for granting you all your heart desires.

I recommend very specially to you an unfortunate young man, who is dying[2] and who is anything but prepared to appear before God. . . .

I send you my paternal blessing with the assurance of my devoted sentiments in Our Lord Jesus Christ.

Delatroëtte
sup. of the Carmel

October 26, '88

* Autograph.
1. See LC 89.
2. See following letter (LD).

LD *From M. Delatroëtte to Mother Marie de Gonzague.*

October 27,
1888

Lisieux, October 27, '88

Reverend Mother and dear daughter
in Our Lord Jesus Christ,

Since Monseigneur granted the little Benjamin of the Carmel[1] the permission she requested from him,[2] mine is, as you know, of

no utility. In any case, I have only to offer my prayers that all the desires of those who know your deservedly loved child may be totally fulfilled.

I recommend very specially to your prayers and to those of your Community Mme. Nasse's son, who is dying and far from being prepared to appear before Him who judges justly.[3]

Receive my paternal blessing with the renewed assurance of my most devoted sentiments in Our Lord Jesus Christ.

Delatroëtte
sup. of the Carmel

* Autograph.
1. This was Thérèse; see LT 71, note 5.
2. See LC 89.
3. See psalm 9:5.

LC 91 *From Sister Marie of the Angels to Thérèse.*
End of October(?), 1888 Approximate date; see note 3.
→ LT lost

†J. M. J. T.! Jesus!

It is my turn to surprise my little Benjamin, so much loved![1] Jesus has told me something for her; first, before all else, He is very content with her, always!... What I have to tell her is my own little adventure, for my Nightingale from Paradise must know that it is not the only one that is dry, very dry with God! Behold, only yesterday, an imbecile or the poor mistress might have been the same thing at the feet of Jesus-Victim; and this morning I could not better express my stupidity than by looking upon myself as a log, nothing but a log! When contemplating myself in this way in my prayer, I set myself to reflecting on what a log was and what purpose it served. I saw that a log was nothing but a piece of wood, bigger than other pieces, and that to be very good it had to be very, very dry! There, already, is a light; after-

ward, I saw that, well-dried out, this poor log was destined for nothing less than making a very warm and beneficent fire. Why, then, I asked myself, not accept very humbly and even joyfully the position of being the little log or even the *heavy* log of good Jesus? Did He not come on earth to kindle in souls the sacred fire of holy love?[2] Well, then: My Jesus, take me as such and make use of Your poor little creature to kindle a blaze of love in all souls!... Burn me, consume me so well that I may no longer be anything but the same fire with You and that even my ashes may be destroyed. I thought of sharing my prayer with my little Benjamin to make her smile and to amuse her just a little! Even though this thought may not be poetical, at least, it is practical, and when we are poor, we refuse nothing.

Little Sister Thérèse of the Child Jesus! yes, I thought very much of you today. Here I am already more than half way through my retreat.[3] With what joy will I see you once again! Each day, Jesus increases my attachment to my little chicks[4] and especially to the littlest and much loved of the nest.

Sister Marie of the Angels

* Autograph.

1. This suggests that Thérèse had "surprised" her novice mistress with first note (lost). Sister Marie of the Angels was on retreat; see note 3.
2. See Luke 12:49.
3. The retreat for the year 1888; see also LC 92, note 7, which is an indication justifying the choice of October for this note. No definite document gives the precise date of the private retreats of Sister Marie of the Angels. She had entered Carmel on October 26, 1866.
4. The little chicks are the two novices (or newly professed): Sister Marie-Philomène, forty-eight, Sister Marie of the Sacred Heart, twenty-eight, and the two postulants, Sister Martha of Jesus, twenty-three, and Thérèse, fifteen.

LD — October 30, 1888

From Sister Agnes of Jesus to M. Martin.

A note written and signed in the name of her two sisters. M. Martin, Céline, and Léonie were getting ready to meet P. Pichon at Le Havre, whence he would embark for Canada.

My dear little Father,

Above all, don't forget what you promised me; confide to the good Father[1] all your little affairs and think that God's will is to do only what he will advise you to do.[2] The diamond and the Queen kiss you tenderly and long already for your return as does, too, your poor little fine pearl.

We love you so much! Don't travel any more, little Father, I beg you; remain with us.[3] This is what God wills. We are praying very much for you so that Our Lord continue always to shower His blessings on our little family which is so dear to Him.

The Queen is going to receive the Habit soon.[4] What a beautiful celebration! What an honor for her to be led to the altar by a Father like you.

Adieu, dear little Father. See you soon.

Sister Marie of the Sacred Heart
Sister Agnes of Jesus
Sister Thérèse of the Child Jesus

* Autograph.

1. This is P. Pichon.
2. Ever since June 15, the day when Céline told him about her vocation, M. Martin was grappling with "a sort of fixed idea. . . to retire into some sort of solitude and live there as a hermit." (*Le Père de Saint Thérèse de l'Enfant-Jésus*, p. 76.) After his flight of June 23 27 (see LD, June 26, '88), this plan disturbed his daughters.
3. On November 29, Sister Agnes confided to a friend: "What is unfortunate is that there always remains with him the desire to travel. . . . Very often he talks about Alençon and makes some plans! . . . But it is very imprudent for him to go at this time. Could you not, dear

Godmother, advise him against it with all your power, and M. Vital, too? Here we can do nothing, not one of us. It is distressing." (Letter to Pauline Romet, November 29, 1888.)

4. See LC 89 and 90.

LC 92

From Sister Marie of the Angels to Thérèse.

November 2-4 (?), 1888
→ LT lost

This note could have been written after a grave relapse suffered by M. Martin. This took place at Honfleur, October 31. "Honfleur. . . Le Havre. . . most painful stages! Papa is very sick. . . ." (Notes of Sister Geneviève, CMG IV, p. 187.) Céline wrote on the same day to her sisters: "No, there are no words, no expressions, which can express our agony, our anguish. . . . It is not one sword but a thousand that come with their poisoned dart to be plunged into the gaping wound of my heart. . . . Oh! how I pity Papa! I can see that he is suffering VERY MUCH. Today, his poor face had a deathly pallor on it." (Honfleur, October 31, 1888.)

J. M. J. T! Jesus

My beloved little Benjamin, I found your good little note[1] which Jesus made me notice and pick up immediately. Thanks, my dear little child, for having told me about your pain. Yesterday, at the entrance to the choir, judging by what our beloved Mother told us, I felt immediately that a sword of sorrow had transpierced your poor heart! Its sharp point entered even into my own heart, for I cannot sense a pain in my dear child but that pain becomes deeply my own!. . .

You must hope against hope and pray to heaven which can do all things. Our Jesus is so kind even when He is trying us! Oh! how much He loves His dear little fiancée at this very moment; and even though He is hidden, He is watching her all the better, and His divine eyes and His Sacred Heart are not losing a single one of her agonies which make her merit so much. The wedding dress

was still not beautiful enough, and so He wants to embellish it, to adorn it with precious stones and brilliant jewels so that, on the day of the alliance, the eyes of heaven much more than those of earth may be fixed on it in admiration![2] Jesus is a Spouse of blood,[3] and He is drenching your nuptial dress in the blood of the Lamb;[4] let Him, you will not regret it! Little Thérèse of the Child Jesus, let the Child play games with His very dear ball;[5] smile at Him still, smile at Him always,[6] and the more He makes you suffer the more you are to love Him! Let everything in your soul sing the intoxicating songs of Calvary, and, in this, be more than a cicada on the ground but be rather a little Nightingale from Paradise![7]

How I would like to remain and talk with my little daughter, whom I love a thousand times over; oh! how I am going to pray to Jesus for her so that He may take my place by her side! He will be able to console her much better than I, and He will speak to her words that dry all tears and heal all wounds.

Needless to say, I will continue to pray for your venerable patient. I still don't look upon myself as beaten down, and I still want to hope in a kind Providence.[8]

Courage and confidence. Knowing that my little Thérèse is a prey to sadness is a cloud in the heaven of my retreat; may Jesus scatter the cloud and bless the dear little Benjamin of my heart a thousand times.

Sister Marie of the Angels SC[9]
r.c.ind.

* Autograph.
1. This was not preserved.
2. This is a reference to the bridal adornment in view of the reception of the Habit (see LT 63); there is no question here only of a mystical adornment since the eyes *of earth* will be able to admire it. In Ms. A, p. 160 and LT 178, Thérèse retains only the spiritual meaning of the comparison.
3. See LC 78, note 7.

4. See Apocalypse 7:14; there is a similar thought ir LC 105.
5. See LT 34, note 2.
6. See P. Pichon: "Be obstinate in smiling at Jesus just the same" (LC 111); "As strongly as you cry, I want you to be able to smile at Jesus always" (LC 116).
7. See LC 91; a slight indication of the proximity of the two notes?
8. No doubt, hope for the recovery of M. Martin for the coming taking of the Habit. See Ms. A, p. 154: "However, the time for my reception of the Habit had arrived; I was received by the Chapter, but how dream of having any ceremony? Already they were talking of giving me the holy Habit without my going out of the cloister, when they decided to wait."
9. Abbreviation for "Sacred Heart," which completed the name of Sister Marie of the Angels.

LT 66 From Thérèse to M. Martin.

November 15, 1888

Thanks to the energetic care of Dr. Notta and M. Guérin, "against all hope, our dear Father recovered from his second stroke" (Ms. A, p. 154).

J. M. J. T.

November 15, '88

My dear King,

How good God is, then, for having cured you! I assure you that your little Queen was really worried, and really there was good reason, for you were very sick. The whole Carmel was in prayer,[1] so God finally listened to its sighs and restored my King to me, but you know, dear little Father, now that God has done what we desired, it's your turn to make us totally happy. The *Orpheline de la Bérésina* comes, then, to ask you to take GOOD care of yourself, as much as will be necessary; you know that the *Intrépide* No. 2[2] knows what to do, so, I beg you, to have *respect* for her *title* (given by the King himself) of taking care of you insofar as it is necessary.

Your little Queen is always near you at heart; how could she forget her very good King?... And, then, it seems to me that affection is still greater, were this possible, when one has suffered so much!...

Au revoir, dear King. Above all, take good care of yourself to please your Queen.

Thérèse of the Child Jesus
p.c.ind.

* Autograph in fourteen fragments, CMG.

1. "To tell you how much Our Mother and the whole Community shared in our pain and in our worries is quite impossible.... The little Benjamin was very courageous in suffering.... She is an elite soul, a heart filled with extreme tenderness but which nothing gets down. It is admirable!..." (A letter already quoted from Sister Agnes of Jesus to Pauline Romet, November 29, 1888.)
2. A nickname given by M. Martin to Céline; see the latter's letter to her sisters, October 31, 1888: "Once (when we were in a carriage) he kissed me in a very kind way, calling me 'son intrépide.'" Marie was "intrépide No. 1."

LT 67 From Thérèse to Mme. Guérin.

November 18, 1888

Her feast day (see LT 32, note 1, November 14, 1887).

J. M. J. T.

My dear Aunt,

Permit your little daughter to come, too, to offer you her feeble wishes; they will appear to you as a small matter compared to those which you have already received. But this does not make any difference; her heart cannot refrain from telling her dear Aunt how much she loves her.

This morning, during my Holy Communion, I prayed very much to Jesus to give you His joys; alas! this is not what He is sending us for some time. It is the Cross, the Cross alone, which He is giving us in order to test us.... Oh! Aunt, if it had been only myself who was suffering, this would have been nothing, but I know the large share you took in our trial.[1] For your feast, I would like to take away all sorrow and to take for myself all your pains. This is what I was asking for just now from Him whose Heart beats in unison with my own. I then felt that all He could give us of the best was suffering, and He was giving this only to His *chosen* friends; this answer proved to me that I was not answered, for I saw that Jesus loved dear Aunt too much to take away the Cross!...

I was really touched, Aunt, by the beautiful cake you sent us; instead of our wishing you a happy feast, it is you who are wishing it to us. This is really too much! I have only a poor little picture[2] to offer to dear Aunt, but I hope she will look at her little daughter's intention.

Au revoir, dear Aunt. It seems to me that during the trial you are still closer to your

little daughter,
Thérèse of the Child Jesus
post.carm.ind.

Sister Marie of the Sacred Heart's letter was finished when we received the cake; she told me to thank you.

* Autograph.

1. M. Martin's illness.
2. The picture has this sentence: "Oh! how sweet it is to suffer with Jesus and for Jesus!..." It is illuminated according to the taste of the time. On a solitary rock, a dove receives drops of Blood from the transpierced Sacred Heart. At the top of the first page of the letter from Thérèse, Mother Marie de Gonzague wrote: "Sister Agnes of Jesus did not touch this picture; the child did it alone."

LT 68 **From Thérèse to M. Martin.**

November 25, 1888

J. M. J. T.

Carmel, November 25, '88

Dear little Father,

Your Queen is thinking of you continually, and she is praying all day long for her King. I am very happy in the nest of Carmel, and I no longer desire anything on earth, except to see my dear King entirely cured, but I know why God is sending us this trial; it is so that we win His beautiful heaven. He knows that our dear Father is all that we love most on this earth, but He knows, too, that it is necessary to suffer to gain eternal life, and it is for this that He is trying us in all that we hold most dear.

I feel, too, that God wills to give my King a magnificent throne in His Kingdom; it is so beautiful and so elevated above all human thoughts that we can say with St. Paul: "The eye of man has not seen; his ear has not heard, and his heart cannot understand what God reserves for those whom He loves."[1] Is there anyone whom God loves more on this earth than my dear little Father?... Really, I cannot believe it!... Today, at least, He is giving us the proof that I am not wrong since God always tries those whom He loves. I really believe that God makes us suffer in this way on earth so that heaven may appear better to His Elect; He says that on the last day He will dry all the tears from their eyes,[2] and, no doubt, the more tears there will be to dry the greater the consolation will be!...

Adieu, dear King. Your Queen rejoices when thinking of the day when she will reign with YOU in the beautiful and only true *kingdom* of heaven.

Thérèse of the Child Jesus
post.carm.ind.

* Autograph.

1. I Corinthians 2:9. The Apostle had written: "...those who love him." In LT 94, Thérèse wrote at first: "...those who love him," and corrected it to: "...those whom he loves." The correct text ("...those who love him") in LT 173, January (?), 1895 and Ms. A, p. 126, 1895; but in LT 182, February 23, 1896, Thérèse returns to her own version: "...those whom he loves." This is a characteristic *lapsus* under her pen.
2. Apocalypse 21:4.

LT 69 **From Thérèse to Marie Guérin.**

November (?), 1888
→ LC lost

Approximate date; see note 3

Jesus M. J. T.

My beautiful Doll,

I cannot resist the desire to thank you for your letter; it pleased me very much. You cannot imagine how much I think about you. My little Marie is always coming into my mind. Besides, if I wanted to forget my dear little cousins, I would not be able to, for my pretty little lamp lights me up so well![1]...

Thérèse is coming to ask for another favor. Sister Agnes just told me that I need a pair of boots lined with fur,[2] just like the ones I saw you with many times in the winter; they are a kind of little ankle-boot that are bordered with Astrakhan fur. If Aunt wanted to buy them for me, I would be very happy. Jeanne could try them on, for she has exactly the same foot as I.

I have many things to tell my Doll, but they are waiting for my little note, so I must leave you. On Thursday,[3] I shall have many things to say to my dear little sister; in the meanwhile, I kiss DEAR Aunt, GOOD Uncle, and dear little Jeanne.

As for my *Louploup,*[4] I can't tell her how much I love her; my heart is too full of affection for her.

If I could have the boots this afternoon, I would be very happy. You cannot imagine how well they take care of you in Carmel; I always have to be eating and keeping my feet warm.[5]

Until Thursday, little darling, my beautiful living doll. I am *very, very* happy, at the height of my desires.

Thérèse of the Child Jesus

I often think of my dear Marcelline.[6]

* Autograph in twenty fragments,CMG.
1. See LT 50, note 6.
2. The reception of the Habit was postponed, and so the postulant had to be properly equipped for the winter, especially severe that year.
3. Visits were suspended during Advent; that Thursday was, then, on November 29.
4. Marie Guérin; see LT 23, note 3.
5. Thérèse was dispensed from the fast until she was twenty-one. She was given thick soups, generous portions of starchy foods, glasses of milk; the menu did not please her, but she was not allowed to leave things on her plate (see LC 53). As for heating in the monastery, this consisted of one wood fire kept continually burning during the severe cold in the fireplace of the recreation room; perhaps, during that first winter, Thérèse was given a charcoal foot-warmer.
6. Marcelline Husé, servant of the Guérin family; see LT 121, September 28, 1890.

LT 70 **From Thérèse to Mother Saint-Placide.**

Beginning of December, 1888

As a former pupil of the Benedictine boarding school and a Child of Mary, Thérèse received an invitation to the celebration on December 13, the twenty-fifth anniversary of the establishment of the Children of Mary Sodality. According to an oral tradition, Sister Agnes of Jesus wrote the letter and Thérèse copied it.

J. M. J. T.

Jesus † Carmel, December, '88

Dear Mistress,

I was very much touched by your kind attention. I received the dear circular letter of the Children of Mary with pleasure. Certainly, I won't fail to be present in spirit at this beautiful celebration, for was it not in this beautiful chapel that the Blessed Virgin adopted me on the beautiful day of my First Communion and on the day of my reception into the Children of Mary. I could not forget, dear Mistress, how kind you were to me at the time of these great events in my life, and I cannot doubt that the remarkable grace of my religious vocation germinated on that blessed day[1] when, surrounded by my good teachers, I made the consecration of myself to Mary at the foot of the altar, taking her for my Mother in a special way, when in the morning I had received Jesus for the first time. I like to believe that she did not look then on my unworthiness and that, in her great kindness, she considered the virtue of the dear teachers who had, with so much care, prepared my heart to receive her divine Son. I like to think that it was for this reason she wanted to make me become more perfectly her child by giving me the great grace of leading me into Carmel.

I think, dear Mistress, that you are aware of my beloved Father's illness. I feared for several days that God was going to steal him from my love, but Jesus has seen fit to give me the grace

of restoring him for the time of my reception of the Habit. I was intending every day to write you to let you know of my acceptance by the Chapter,[2] but, not knowing the time the bishop would decide upon, I was waiting. I hope, dear Mistress, that you have not taken my tardiness as indifference; oh! no, my heart is always the same. I believe that, since my entrance into Carmel, it has become more tender and more loving. So I am thinking frequently of all my good teachers, and I love to name each in particular to Jesus during the blessed hours I spend at His feet. I dare to beg you, dear Mistress, to speak for me to them and to remember me to them, especially to *Madame la Prieure*, for whom I retain a most filial and grateful affection. Please, too, remember me to my happy companions,[3] whose little sister in Mary I remain always.

Adieu, dear Mistress. I hope you will not forget in your holy prayers her who is and always will be your grateful child.

Sister Thérèse of the Child Jesus
post. carm. ind.

* Facsimile of the draft, reduced in form.

1. A gratuitous interpretation on the part of Sister Agnes to please the recipient.
2. See LC 89, 90.
3. According to the statement of one of them, received as a Child of Mary, December 13, 1888, this letter was read to all those present on the day of the celebration (testimony, dated September 14, 1938, of Valentine Loutrel, who became Sister Saint Stanislaus at the Hôtel-Dieu, Rouen).

LC 93 *From Mother Marie de Gonzague to Thérèse.*

December 6-10, 1888 Date deduced from the content; see notes 1 and 2.

→ LT lost

I don't want the child of my tenderness to allow herself to go into such a great sorrow. I don't know anything about the reception

of the Habit. Monseigneur appears to say that he cannot come here in January, but let us wait. I will write to the lamb[1] that she may tell you what I have known. Before causing ourselves any distress, let us wait. On Thursday, we shall see if His Excellency would have given Monsieur Révérony any messages for us.[2] A dream is only a dream,[3] and our Holy Mother does not want us to pay any attention to it.[4]. . . No, Jesus isn't weeping, He is smiling at His fiancée. But my dear child must not cause herself any sorrows about things here below; let her soul prepare itself, without any preoccupation, for the great grace granted to it by the Divine Child in the crib!!! God's good pleasure, that is my will, my desire!. . . Write to our holy exile.[5]. . .

I am carrying you in my heart, which blesses you, very darling child!!!

* Autograph.

1. Sister Agnes. This written message seems to suggest that the prioress was on retreat. Different documents show that she made her annual retreat in November 1887 (see LC 64), December 1892, and October 1893. A custom permitted the nuns to write their prioress twice during her private retreat.
2. Thursday, December 13, M. Révérony presided at the Benedictine Abbey on the occasion of the 25th anniversary of the establishment of the Children of Mary Sodality (judging by a letter from Sister Saint Stanislaus, September 14, 1938).
3. This is a difficult sentence because a word was written over another word: "the dream is only a dream," and so perhaps Thérèse had dreamed Jesus was weeping? Or: "Life is only a dream," which would explain the reference to St. Teresa of Avila immediately afterward.
4. See St. Teresa of Avila: "the dream this miserable life is" *(Exclamations* 13). See LT 82 and 108; LC 135, last paragraph.
5. P. Pichon, in Canada. He answered Thérèse on December 27 (LC 97).

LC 94 *From Mother Marie de Gonzague to Thérèse.*

December 10 (?), 1888
→ LT lost

This note seems to have been written shortly after the preceding LC 93, but the absence of any reference to the date for the reception of the Habit seems to indicate that M. Révérony had not come to the Carmel (a visit expected on December 13).

†

Let my Benjamin, my little grain of sand, say all to her Mother; she understands. The Father[1] is perfect, but I had a thorn in my heart when I opened the folded sheet and when I saw that the sheets were for me alone.[2]. . . When speaking[3] of my child: "It will be said, then, that the dear little lamb will undergo contradiction at each step. Blessed privileged one of the Cross!"

Yes, child of Jesus, the Cross is our lot! Let us rejoice in this blessing! It is from heaven and not from earth! What a joy, *a humiliation*![4] This is worth all the treasures of Panama!!![5] Let us repeat this to ourselves when we make a blunder: *happy fault that merited for me this humiliation*!!! As for our miseries, we have only one thing to do, form a little package out of them and place it in the Heart of Jesus so that He change them into so many merits for the homeland. I pass on to you the holy blessing of the exiled Father, who thinks so much of his little lamb. . . . As for my own blessing, it is for every minute and each hour of the day.

* Autograph.
1. P. Pichon. This mail must have crossed with that from the Carmel.
2. Mother Marie de Gonzague would have preferred if the letter were for Thérèse.
3. A difficult reading here, a word being written over by another word: "he told me," then, "When speaking."
4. The following note, LC 95, speaks again of the "*little* humiliation." We don't know the precise object of this.
5. The building of the Panama canal was very much in the news those days. In May-June, M. Martin increased his visits to Paris, regarding

the loan which was financing this undertaking (according to CMG IV, p. 183). On July 1, 1888, Sister Agnes wrote her father: "Men of genius may very well occupy themselves with cutting through Panama. We, too, shall cut through whatever could hold us to this earth, and it is then that the ocean of love will surround us on every side." According to Sister Geneviève (Céline), the Martin family "lost fifty thousand francs on the Panama enterprise and different sales of property," at the time of (and because of?) her father's illness (G/NPHF, p. 583). This would be worth 100,000 francs in 1972.

LC 95 *From Mother Marie de Gonzague to Thérèse.*

Around December 13, 1888 Approximate date; see note 2.

→ LT lost

†

My darling grain of sand laughed at my Panama jackpot[1] as compared to her *little* humiliation.... My darling angel must know that Jesus is not so much concerned about the value, the grandeur, or the size of the gift which we offer to Him as to the way of offering Him this gift. A *very little* humiliation well-received, accepted with joy, is worth more to the Heart of Jesus than all the greatest Crosses of the world if there nests in their acceptance a little bit of self-seeking, a little grain of vanity, a tiny drop of self-love, an iota of anything unworthy of the Heart of Jesus!... Let my little nothing prepare herself well, taking advantage of all the thorns of each hour that she finds under her steps, for the great grace that is granted to her by the Divine Child during the month of January,[2] the month consecrated to the Divine Child.... Let all be offered to obtain from Jesus the grace of understanding this favor insofar as the mind of man can grasp it, for in heaven alone will we understand the remarkable honor that the Divine Spouse gives our souls in uniting them to Himself.

Our hearts are united *in the Heart of Jesus.*

* Autograph.
1. See LC 94, note 3.
2. The choice of January was confirmed, perhaps by M. Révérony (see LC 93 and 94), but the precise date was not yet determined.

LC 96 *From Céline to Thérèse.*

December 24, 1888

Christmas Eve, December 24, 1888

My dear Thérèse,

While awaiting Jesus, I cannot refrain from talking a little with you. Little sister of my heart, "Christmas night," what memories! Do you recall last year when we were hoping up to the last minute for a letter from Monseigneur permitting you to enter Carmel?[1] Then, the little surprise I prepared for you?[2]. . . I am experiencing still all that I experienced at that moment; ah! how I feel my soul is united with yours. It seems to me they make up only one soul. . . .

If you only knew how your thoughtfulness this evening touched me even to the depths of my soul! I have my dear picture[3] right before my eyes while writing you. What joy you gave me! I have tears in my eyes. Thérèse, in your absence everything here is exile; I am suffering more and more from our separation, and often I have to hold myself back from crying.[4]

But the Divine Child is about to come. I must receive Him with joy; is it not He who is taking the place of all for me!

This evening, you touched me so much; you showed me that you loved me. If you only knew how grateful I am. Your slipper was badly stocked; if there is anything you want, tell me, I beg you.

Your little Céline

* Typewritten copy, G.

1. An answer to the letter Thérèse wrote the bishop, begging permission to enter Carmel at Christmas 1887 (see LT 38).
2. Upon her return from midnight Mass 1887 Thérèse found in her bedroom "in the middle of a charming basin, a *little* boat carrying little Jesus, who was sleeping with His *little* ball at His side; on the white sail, Céline had written these words: 'I sleep but my heart watches,' and on the boat, the word: 'Abandon!'" (Ms. A, p. 142).
3. This picture has been lost. Céline had placed a picture in her own letter with these words on the reverse side: "Souvenir of Christmas Eve 1888. Your little Céline."
4. "Our father's illness was becoming worse from day to day; I was passing through many interior emotions and sufferings." (Note of Sister Geneviève, p. 7, from her typed copy.) As a matter of fact, December 1888 showed a marked improvement in M. Martin's health: "Our dear Father is getting better and better; he is as well as he possibly can be. I am happy that you will see him; he will be going to Alençon toward the middle of this week." (Letter of Céline to Pauline Romet, December 30, 1888.)

LC 97 *From P. Pichon to Thérèse.*

December 27, 1888
→ LT lost

† Montreal, December 27

Sister Thérèse of
the Child Jesus

My dear Benjamin in Our Lord,[1]

Entirely surrounded by thorns, your vocation appears to me more beautiful and more radiant. Oh! I envy your privileged lot: suffering for Jesus and what sufferings! This is the engagement gift. God is molding your heart, even its most delicate fibers. Let

Him do with you and with your holy patriarch[2] all He wills to do. There is nothing in divine Providence that is not inspired by the love of a Father.

Little toy of Jesus, broken by the adorable hand, dear orphan crucified in your two fathers, poor little lamb whom Jesus wills to see totally immolated to His glory and His divine whims, I love the lines along which your whole interior life is painted. My sorrow is not being able to answer you immediately. Have pity on me and don't stop your pen. Souls, here, don't leave me any leisure. How can I hide myself from their eager pursuit. Ah! the chances for saving them superabound. Pray, pray!

I am waiting for that much-desired letter which will announce the date of your reception of the Habit in January.[3] That blessed day, that heavenly day on earth, I will celebrate it with you in the Heart of Jesus. My Mass belongs to you by right, and along with my Mass you will have all I can give you, namely, my rosary, my breviary, etc.

My dear child, how right you are to think yourself more joyful on Calvary than on Thabor. On Thabor, would you find the Blessed Virgin?

There is no ocean between your soul and mine, there isn't even the point of a needle, a thread of silk. In the Heart of Jesus, there is union, there is fusion.

Reverence all the secrets of Jesus. In spite of appearances, they are so lovable!

Yes, yes, the dress of sorrow[4] is a thousand times better than the homespun dress, even if it be the dress of St. Teresa.

When giving thanks to God during these last days of this year, I cry out my thanks very loudly for all the favors it has brought you.

The dear little lamb will find in the crib in the Heart of the divine Lamb my prayers and my best blessings at the dawn of the New Year.[5]

Almire Pichon

* Autograph.

1. A photographic vignette (picture of the Sacred Heart), stuck at the top of the letter, partly covers the title and the first line of the text.
2. This is M. Martin; on that same day, P. Pichon wrote to Sister Marie of the Sacred Heart: "The venerable old man, now become a child, will not be long, no doubt, in taking his flight to heaven." (December 27, 1888.) We should remember that P. Pichon had seen M. Martin at Paris on November 1 or 2 in a very painful condition (LC 92).
3. When Thérèse wrote him at the beginning of December (see LC 93, note 3), she was able to give him no specific date for the reception of the Habit.
4. When writing P. Pichon, perhaps Thérèse had taken something from the comparison suggested by Sister Marie of the Angels (see LC 92).
5. It was no doubt on January 7, 1889 that Thérèse received this letter; see LT 76, note 6.

LT 71 From Thérèse to Mme. Guérin.

December 28, 1888

J. M. J. T.

December 28, '88

Jesus †

My dear little Aunt,

I am very sorry, for, yesterday evening, not knowing my sisters were going to write you, I slept like a lazy thing![1] . . . This morning, I have only a bit of time, and I even have to take it from the Office.[2]

Dear Aunt, I would like to be the first to wish you a Happy New Year for 1889! . . .

When I think, dear Aunt, that it will soon be nine months since your little daughter is in Carmel, I can't get over it. It seems to me it was only yesterday that I was still with you!... How quickly life passes; it is already sixteen years since I have been on earth. Oh! soon we shall all be reunited in heaven. I love these words of the psalms very much: "A thousand years in the eyes of the Lord are like yesterday that has passed already."[3] What rapidity! Oh! I want to work during the day while it is still light, for afterwards will come the night when I shall be able to do nothing.[4] Pray for your little daughter, dear Aunt, so that she does not abuse the grace which God is showering on her in the fertile valley of Carmel.

I cannot refrain from laughing when seeing my letter; it is not really a New Year's letter, but, dear little Aunt, with you I am like a child who lets its heart go without searching in any way for what it is going to say!...

If you only knew, dear Aunt, all I will ask for you and *dear Uncle* on New Year's day!... No, you don't know, and I am not going to undertake telling you, for it would bore you because it would take too long.

And my little cousins (my *dear* little *sisters*), how I will pray for them!...

Au revoir, dear Aunt. I beg you to tell Uncle how much I love him. I should have written him at the same time as I wrote you, dear Aunt, but I am too stupid to talk to two persons together.... I beg him to pardon me, and I send to both of you the best kiss from your littlest Benjamin.[5]

Thérèse of the Child Jesus
post.carm.ind.

I just remembered that I haven't thanked dear Aunt for the crown that she wants to give me for my reception of the Habit.[6] Oh! if she only knew how grateful I am and also how dear this souvenir will be to her little daughter's heart!...

* Autograph.

1. It was permitted to rest during the free hour which preceded Matins, between eight and nine o'clock.
2. The canonical obligation of reciting the Divine Office began only after Profession; a postulant could be very easily dispensed from the "Little Hours" (Prime, Terce, Sext, None) recited at seven in the morning during the winter. Furthermore, on this December 28, feast of the Holy Innocents, the novices enjoyed a little more freedom from the schedule.
3. Psalm 89:4.
4. See John 9:4. See also the *Reflections* which follow the first chapter of the *Imitation of Christ*: "Work while the day is light; hasten to amass a treasure that does not perish. The night is coming when no one can do anything."
5. It is only in the correspondence with the Guérin family that Thérèse, up to the time of Marie Guérin's entrance into Carmel (August 15, 1895), gives herself the nickname of "Benjamin." See LT 100, 125, 139, 152, and 180. Before her entrance into Carmel, the nickname was often applied to her by her sisters (see LC or LD, *passim*). In Carmel, the nickname is used frequently, especially in the sense of "Benjamin of the Community," in letters and notes from her "superiors": Mother Marie de Gonzague (LC 94 and 103); Sister Marie of the Angels (LC 91, 92, 104, 119, 120, 141, 145); P. Pichon (LC 87, 97, 108, 111, 116, 117, 157, 158); and even M. Delatroëtte (LD, October 27, 1888). Sister Marie of the Sacred Heart uses it only once (LC 169).
6. This was a crown of artificial lilies which held the bridal veil in place. The gift was still only a promise, and it became an actuality in a few days (see LT 73).

LT 72 **From Thérèse to M. Martin.**

December 30, 1888

J. M. J. T.

December 30, '88

Jesus!...

My dear King,

What a joy to be able to send you this year from the *Kingdom* of Carmel my wishes for a Happy New Year. Never has your little Queen been able to offer her affection with more joy; she feels *so close* to her King, so close that nothing could separate her from him!...

Earthly Kings are very happy when they can form noble alliances for their daughters, and what gratitude these children have towards their parents!... For your little Queen it is a totally different matter. You *as a Father*, and really *as a King*, you wanted to entrust her only to the *King of heaven*, to Jesus Himself, and from *Orpheline de la Bérésina* I passed to the very noble title of Carmelite.

How I must love a Father who wanted to obtain such a great happiness for me, and how I do love him!... If the guide at Rome were here, he would be able to say: "*Messieurs les Abbés*, I am going to have you look upon a father, the like of whom you've never seen; there is something here that will make you fall over in *admiration*."[1] Is it not true, dear little Father, that you could not do more for your little Queen.[2] If she is not a Saint, it will really be her own fault, for with a father like you she really has the means for this!...

Dear Father, the day is ending, and it is time that I leave you, but only in finding you again at the side of Jesus, your true place.

Soon the day without shadows will light up for us, and then never will we end our conversation!...

Happy New Year, dear King, and thanks for all the treats you gave us this week!...and throughout the WHOLE *year*!...

May Jesus grant you His blessings, and may He give you, as He has promised, the hundredfold in this life and His BEAUTIFUL heaven in the next.[2] That is the wish of your little Queen, who loves you more than ever any Queen loved her King.

Sister Thérèse of the Child Jesus
post.carm.ind.

* Autograph in twenty-eight fragments, CMG.

1. See LT 46, note 4. Mimicking the guide at Rome, Thérèse spelt the French word "*merveille*" as "*emerveillaison.*"
2. See Matthew 19:29.

LC 98 *From Sister Marie of the Sacred Heart to Thérèse.*

January 2, 1889 — This was for Thérèse's sixteenth birthday

Jesus!

I have nothing to give my dear little girl; it's up to Jesus, then, to put Himself out for me, who am so poor. He is rich! May He adorn His little fiancée for the great day which is approaching in giant strides.[1] Ah! already His wedding presents are prepared, already diamonds of an inestimable value are hidden in them. Her Jesus was really able to give her the most beautiful dress;[2] He was eager to run as soon as there was a question of a celebration! May the little fiancée of sixteen not regret the years that are flying by. Her fifteenth year was rich in sacrifices. In heaven she will

know their value! May little Jesus caress His little lamb with His dear little hand on this day of her sixteen years! May Mary bless her and hide her under her virginal mantle, and may St. Joseph present her to Jesus and Mary, and may our little Mother in heaven[3] rejoice with them when seeing her forever in the sheepfold of Carmel.[4]

* Autograph.
1. The reception of the Habit.
2. Suffering. See LC 92.
3. Madame Martin.
4. See, too, for this same date, the picture offered by Mother Marie de Gonzague to her "daughter of sixteen" (Appendix, Pictures).

LT 73 **From Thérèse to Mme. Guérin.**

January 2, 1889

J. M. J. T.

January 2, 1889

Jesus!...

My dear Aunt,

Your little daughter is at the height of her joy!... How kind you are to her, it's really too much...and how to thank you?... But isn't a Mother able to read into her little daughter's heart, so I am not going to worry, being sure that you are going to understand my gratitude.

The lilies are RAVISHING;[1] I would say they have just been picked! How good of my little *sisters* to offer them to me. It will be a great joy for me, on the day of my reception of the Habit, to

think that they were the ones who adorned me to go to my divine Fiancé. These flowers will speak to Jesus for them, who, I am sure, will give them His graces and you, too, dear Aunt.

If you only knew how happy I was to have the *enormous* stick of sugar-candy to offer our Mother.[2] I recognized dear Aunt here, who is always looking out for what will give her little daughter the most pleasure. My joy was not less great when seeing the beautiful package of gingerbread. I was very proud in the refectory when our Mother told the Community that you were giving us this treat in honor of my sixteen years.

Thanks, dear Aunt. If you only knew how good I find you are! On the day of my reception of the Habit, I will pray for you and for dear Uncle, too, whom I thank with my whole heart, for I know that it is he also who has given me all these beautiful gifts I received this evening.

Our dear Mother finds the crown very beautiful and so does the whole community. Never have I seen flowers that pleased me so much; lilies are so pure. I would really like my soul to be adorned with them to go to Jesus, for it is not enough to have them in my hair; it is the heart that the eyes of Jesus are always looking at!. . .

Au revoir and thanks, dear Aunt. Pray that your little daughter may be adorned interiorly as well as exteriorly!. . .

Sister Thérèse of the Child Jesus
post.carm.ind.

* Autograph.

1. This word was underlined four times; this was a crown of artificial lilies for Thérèse's reception of the Habit; see LT 71, note 6.
2. Mother Marie de Gonazgue was subject to attacks of bronchitis.

LC 99 *From M. Révérony to Thérèse.*

January 3, 1889
→ LT lost

To excuse himself for not being able to attend her reception of the Habit ceremony.

Bayeux, January 3, 1889

My dear Child,

I will be with you in spirit! But this is very probably all I will be able to do.

God is kind to you! Be very generous with Him!

I beg Him with my whole heart His choicest blessings for you and for your dear father.

M. Révérony
v.g.[1]

* Autograph.

1. Vicar general of the Bayeux diocese.

"All will be for Him, all" (*LT 76*)
(January 5-10, 1889)
Age sixteen

The reception of the Habit was finally set for January 9. This was a "delightful" date (LT 76) for Thérèse of the Child Jesus, for it was exactly nine months to the day when she entered Carmel (it took place on the feast of the Incarnation of Our Lord, LC 77, note 3). However, at the last moment, an unexpected event frustrated this "shadow of joy" (LT 76, note 3). The ceremony of the investiture took place on January 10.

Having entered upon her retreat on the evening of January 5 (a retreat of three full days according to the custom at this time), Thérèse's solitude was prolonged

for another day, just as it had been for her Confirmation (see Ms. A, p. 80).

During these four days, Thérèse exchanged fourteen notes with those around her.

Written in haste, without any preoccupation as to style, on shabby pieces of paper that had already been written on, on the reverse side, Thérèse's messages often had a pathetic note. She admits this: "all is sadness" (LT 78):

"deprived of all consolation" (LT 76) during the three or four hours of daily prayer: "Nothing near Jesus. Aridity!. . . Sleep!. . . " (LT 74);

riddled with "pinpricks" in the Community life: "creatures; oh! creatures!. . . " (LT 74);

undoubtedly no less anxious than her sisters about M. Martin who was always threatened by another attack (LC 105, note 2).

The unanimous encouragement of her two sisters, her prioress, her mistress of novices, even the "heavenly" letter from P. Pichon (see LT 76) had hardly any influence upon the feelings of the "chéri tristotin" (LC 103). At least, all this brought out Thérèse's faith: "it is divine silence that works wonders" (LC 105); "very great strength and peace" (LT 78); desires "infinitely great" (LC 104) to love Jesus "more than He has ever been loved!. . . " (LT 74); a total detachment "from all that is not Jesus. . . . " (LT 78).

Then, after the trial, joy: "what a beautiful celebration!" was this January 10; "nothing was missing, nothing, not even the snow" (Ms. A, p. 154). M. Martin "was admired by everybody, this day was his triumph, his last celebration here below" (ibid.).

LC 100 *From Sister Agnes of Jesus to Thérèse.*

January 6, 1889

Date deduced from that of the response; see **LT 74**, note 3.

All the days in Carmel are days of *retreat.* When we are really united to God and when we think only of pleasing Him in all things, then the soul begins here below the great Retreat of Eternity.

Thus ever since the dear little ball of Jesus made its entrance into Carmel, the retreat has begun for it and will be continued on earth in suffering and in the labors of this exile to terminate in the rest *without end* of the homeland.[1]

* Autograph.

1. Thérèse answered the same evening in this note (LT 74).

LT 74 **From Thérèse to Sister Agnes of Jesus.**

January 6, 1889
→LC 100

Date deduced from the content; see note 3.

J. M. J. T.

Dear little lamb of Jesus, thanks!... If you only knew how much your note pleased me!...

Ask Jesus to make me generous during my retreat. He is riddling me with *pinpricks;* the poor little ball is exhausted. All over it has very little holes which make it suffer more than if it had only one large one!... Nothing near Jesus. Aridity!... Sleep!... But at least there is silence!... Silence does good to the soul.... But creatures! oh! creatures!... The little ball shudders from them!... Understand Jesus' little toy!... When it is the sweet Friend who punctures His ball Himself, suffering is only sweetness, His hand is *so gentle*!... But creatures!... Those who sur-

round me are very good, but there is something, I don't know what, that repels me!... I cannot give you any explanation. Understand your little soul. I am, however, VERY *happy*, happy to suffer what Jesus wants me to suffer. If He doesn't directly puncture His little ball, it is really He who directs the hand that punctures it![1]... Since Jesus wants to sleep[2] why will I hinder Him? I am only too happy that He doesn't bother with me, for He is showing me that I am not a stranger when treating me this way, for, I assure you, He is going to no trouble about carrying on a conversation with me![3]...

If you only knew how much I want to be indifferent to the things of this earth. What do all created beauties mean to me, I would be unhappy possessing them, my heart would be so empty!... It is incredible how big my heart appears to me when I consider all earth's treasures. But when I consider Jesus, how little it appears to me!... I would so much like to love Him!... Love Him more than He has ever been loved!... My only desire is to do the will of Jesus always! to dry away the little tears that sinners make Him shed.... Oh! I do not WANT Jesus to have any sorrow. On the day of my espousals, I would like to convert *all* the sinners of this earth and to save all the souls in purgatory![4]...

The Lamb[5] of Jesus is going to laugh when it sees this desire of the little *grain* of sand!... I know that it is folly, but, nevertheless, I would like it to be this way so that Jesus have not one single tear to shed.

Pray that the grain of sand become an ATOM seen only by the eyes of Jesus!...

Thérèse of the Child Jesus
post.carm.ind.

* Autograph.

1. This hand, for the moment, is often that of Sister Saint Vincent de Paul; see LT 76, note 1.
2. "dormir," was spelt incorrectly; this letter has many mistakes and alterations.

3. This reflection suggests that Thérèse has already spent at least a few hours in retreat; she was writing, then, on January 6 (Sunday during free time) or in the evening. In LT 76, Thérèse spoke of an even greater spiritual aridity: "Today more than yesterday. . . ."
4. There is a similar wish expressed in her prayer of September 8, 1890 (Ms. A, p. 275).
5. Thérèse makes a mistake here in the spelling of the French word "*agneau*," writing "*angnau*"; it, of course, means "lamb."

LT 75 From Thérèse to Sister Marie of the Sacred Heart.

January 6 or 7, 1889

J. M. J. T.

Jesus †

Dear Lion[1] of Jesus, the little lamb really must borrow from you a little strength and courage, that courage which makes the Lion surmount all things!. . . The poor little lamb can say nothing to Jesus, and, above all, Jesus says absolutely nothing to it; pray for it so that its retreat be pleasing just the same to the Heart of Him who ALONE reads into the depths of the soul!. . .

Why seek joy on earth; I admit to you that my heart has a burning thirst for it, but this heart sees that[2] no creature is capable of quenching its thirst. On the contrary, the more it drinks at this delightful spring the more burning does its thirst become![3] . . . I know another spring; it is the one at which, after one has drunk, one is still thirsty, but with a thirst that is not panting.[4] It is very sweet, on the contrary, because it has something satisfying in it, and this spring is the suffering that is known to Jesus alone!. . .

Dear Lion, I have many things to say to you, but I haven't the

time; *read* into the heart of YOUR[5] *little daughter*, as you so well know how to do!. . .

Thérèse of the Child Jesus
post.carm.ind.

* Autograph.

1. A nickname given to Sister Marie of the Sacred Heart by P. Pichon; see LD, July 8, 1888; LC 111; Thérèse used it in LT 79 and 91.
2. Thérèse uses the word "*et*" instead of "*que.*"
3. An allusion to her too great affection for Mother Marie de Gonzague which she had to control; see LC 80, note 2. The symbol of the spring or the fountain – same meaning – is used several times in the notes of Sister Agnes of Jesus to Sister Marie of the Sacred Heart, in 1887-1888; let us cite, for example: "Little dove. . . never go to drink unnecessarily at the fountains of creatures; we return with a more burning thirst" (May 12-22, 1888).
4. Thérèse spelled the French word "*haletante*" (panting) as "*alle-tante.*"
5. This is underlined five times.

LC 101 *From Sister Marie of the Sacred Heart to Thérèse.*

January 7 (?),
1889
→ LT 75

I am not surprised that the little lamb so dear to Jesus finds nothing here below to satisfy its hunger. There is *nothing* either for the lion or the little lamb. The dreamed of spring is the Heart of Jesus; the bubbling fountain where we'll be able to drink long draughts in an endless ecstasy is the homeland! It is heaven! Here below, the Cross; here below, the exile, the arid desert. Doesn't the Child Jesus on His straw say this to His darling little fiancée? What did He come looking for in this world where He was so little loved after having loved so much!. . . A Cross to die on!!. . . Dear

child, never shall we suffer as much as Jesus did; never shall we know as He did the garden of the agony. He does give us a few drops of His chalice, but He reserves for Himself all the gall. He is not speaking to the heart of His little fiancée. Ah! the language of Jesus is not in any way the language of earthly bridegrooms. Sometimes it is silence ON THE MOST BEAUTIFUL DAYS; one would say that He wants to hide. Why? It is He alone who knows the ravishing mysteries of the other life and what treasures of graces, what precious diamonds He is amassing for His spouses when He will call them to the eternal banquet. It is for this reason that He often says nothing to us here below; it is for this reason that He keeps silent! This short moment of life will pass so quickly and the real day of the nuptials will be so beautiful that Jesus does not think twice with us before sending us suffering. He hungers and thirsts for this so as to crown us better. Let the little lamb fall asleep in the heart of its little Jesus. And let her, until heaven comes, remain His dear little toy among all others.[1]

* Autograph.
1. Thérèse answered this note on January 8, no doubt (LT 79).

LT 76 **From Thérèse to Sister Agnes of Jesus.**

January 7, 1889

J. M. J. T.

Jesus †

This morning, I had trouble with Sister St. Vincent de Paul;[1] I went away with a heavy heart. . . .

What do you have that is so attractive for my soul? You cannot imagine how much I am deprived by not being able to talk with you.[2]. . .

Do you understand something regarding Jesus' conduct?. . .I used to tell you that children don't know what they want. Jesus is acting that way with His little ball. He has undoubtedly found that the date of the 9th was too ravishing;[3] He wants nothing ravishing for it!. . . I really know why. It is because He alone is ravishing in the full STRENGTH of the term, and He wants to show His little ball that it would be mistaken in looking elsewhere for a shadow of beauty which it would be taking for beauty itself!. . .

How good He is to me, He who will soon be my Fiancé; how divinely[4] lovable He is when not wanting to allow me to attach myself to ANY created thing. He knows well that if He were to give me a *shadow* of HAPPINESS, I would attach myself to it with all my energy, all the strength of my heart, and this shadow He is refusing me; He prefers leaving me in darkness to giving me a false light which would not be *Himself!*. . . Since I can't find *any* creature that contents me, I want to give all to Jesus, and I don't want to give to the creature even one *atom* of my love. My Jesus always makes me understand that He alone is perfect joy, when He appears to be absent!. . .

Today more than yesterday,[5] if that were possible, I was deprived of all consolation. I thank Jesus, who finds this good for my soul, and that, perhaps if He were to console me, I would stop at this sweetness; but He wants that *all* be for *Himself!*. . . Well, then, *all* will be for Him, all, even when I feel I am able to offer nothing; so, just like this evening, I will give Him this nothing!

Although Jesus is giving me no consolation, He is giving me a peace so great that it is doing me more good!. . .

And Father's letter?[6] . . . I find it heavenly, and my heart finds many beautiful things in it, but joy? . . . Oh, no! no joy . . . joy is to be found only in suffering and in suffering without any consolation!. . .

Little sister, my own *Mamma*,[7] what are you going to think of your little daughter? Oh! if it were not you, I would not dare send these thoughts, the most intimate of *my soul!*. . . *I* BEG YOU, tear up these sheets after you have read them!. . .

Pray for your little daughter that she may refuse Jesus not one *atom* of her heart.

Thérèse of the Child Jesus

* Autograph.

1. This was undoubtedly on the occasion of fitting out Thérèse with the *alpargata* (sandals made of a heavy linen and corded soles); Sister St. Vincent de Paul made them. This Sister, who was very intelligent but somewhat eccentric, hid a kind heart under a very rough exterior. She never had any sympathy for Thérèse, who was always slow and clumsy in doing anything of a practical nature. Sister St. Vincent de Paul directed many biting remarks at Thérèse, speaking loud enough for Thérèse to hear these remarks. However, Thérèse always answered with a smile. After some years of acting in this way, this Sister did not hesitate to pay respect to Thérèse's extraordinary virtue.
2. During her retreat, the postulant was permitted to speak only to the prioress and the mistress of novices.
3. This sudden disappointment, shared in by Sister Agnes of Jesus (see LC 102, par. 2), was very probably motivated by the change in plans received that same day. On Saturday evening, January 5, Abbé Voisin, honorary vicar general (1827-1889), died at Bayeux. "Very early on Sunday, this sad news was announced by telegram to the communities of Caen, Lisieux, Vire, Pont-l'Evêque, and Honfleur, all Carmelite communities of which M. l'abbé Voisin was superior." (*Semaine religieuse de Bayeux*, January 13, 1889, p. 23.) The funeral at the Bayeux Cathedral, presided over by the bishop, was set for Wednesday, January 9, the date already set for the reception of the Habit by Thérèse. Bishop Hugonin advised the Lisieux Carmel, Monday the 7th, that the ceremony was to be postponed until the 10th. See in LC 108, note 1, the problem posed by the letter from P. Pichon.
4. Thérèse wrote "*divienent*" instead of "*divinement*."
5. See LT 74, note 3.
6. Letter from Père Pichon (LC 97).
7. Thérèse had chosen Pauline for her "mother," after the death of Mme. Martin; this name "Mamma" appears in LT 106, 110; then in LT 252, July 13, 1897; see, too, CJ 30.7.2, note 1, DE p. 502.

LC 102 *From Sister Agnes of Jesus to Thérèse.*

January 7,
1889
→ LT 76

Dear little ball of the heavenly and divine Child, I am thinking only of you, I am offering up all for you. . . . This morning, *bitter tears*. This evening, I don't understand the feeling of exile that placed my heart in suffering. I was very wrong to criticize the advice of your mistress, and I am sorry; Our Mother did well to scold me, for I deserved it. This did me some good.[1] . . . We need to be humbled from time to time; yes, this is necessary.

Dear little sister, your date of the 9th! ah! I understood all before reading your note.[2]

But don't say that you are in darkness; it seems this way to you, but eternal light is shining on you. . . . Without it, would you have these sentiments? No. . . . You fill my heart with joy; I would really cry with joy when seeing that my little daughter, the *dearest*, holds nothing back in her holocaust. . . . She is saying just like the Spouse in the Canticles: "Come, my Beloved, let us go down into our garden; it is time to taste my fruits. I have reserved the best and the most beautiful for you.[3] . . ." And the Beloved runs over the hills; He is coming; He is here; only two days more![4] . . .

"Dear garden of my little fiancée," He says from a distance, "always be *the garden enclosed*,[5] open only to me; I am the sun of your flowers. My divine eyes will cast such a ray of flame upon your budding fruits that they will ripen in one instant; my mouth will open to sing melodious words to you . . . all of nature's concerts will not be even a faint echo of my song. Come, my friend, my sister, my dove, open to me, for my head is covered with dew,[6] the moisture of the night, that is, the sins of men, has flooded my beautiful face. Come, open to me. You will henceforth be the little Veronica of my choice.[7] I am cold, I weep, but when I look at you, oh, my garden *enclosed*, there are no more tears for me, for I see in your hands the white veil of virginity. . . . Bring it close to my divine Face, and I will imprint my Face on it forever."

* Autograph.

1. We don't know the incident to which this paragraph is referring (perhaps with regard to the change of date for the reception of the Habit). From time to time in Thérèse's religious life, Sister Agnes' solicitude for her little sister was the occasion of conflict with the superiors (see LD, July 8, 1888, note 3). It took Thérèse's prudence to safeguard the freedom of her religious life with regard to the members of her family in the cloister.
2. See LT 76, note 3.
3. This is a free citation from the Canticle of Canticles 7:12, 14.
4. That is, two more days of retreat, the 8th and the 9th.
5. See Canticle of Canticles 4:12.
6. Ibid. 5:2. Sister Agnes of Jesus was attracted to the Canticle of Canticles at this time; she used these same images in a prayer she composed in honor of the Holy Face, which Thérèse loved to quote; see LT 103.
7. On January 10, Thérèse added to her name the title of the "Holy Face"; see LT 80. The ending of this note shows us the understanding Sister Agnes of Jesus had of this devotion, based on the teachings of Sister Marie de Saint-Pierre of the Tours Carmel (see LT 98).

LC 103

January 7 (?), 1889

From Mother Marie de Gonzague to Thérèse.

According to the custom of the time, the retreatant had a spiritual conference with the prioress each day. Mother Marie de Gonzague was trying to make up, in this note, for the many interruptions mentioned by Thérèse (see LT 78).

†J. M. J. T.

My dear *tristotin*[1] is really hidden in the heart of the Child Jesus,[2] and I would prefer that the Christmas divine Child put joy into the soul of His Benjamin. However, if His holy and divine will is to leave my dear little soul in this mysterious sadness, I will bless His will just the same; and this, especially if the Divine Child of Bethlehem grants my child spiritual consolations on the day of

her espousals. You will have to rejoice in the alliance contracted with a privileged love and not be thinking of the day that is past, which was the day desired.[3] . . . Alas! darling child, Jesus will not ask His privileged Spouse: "Were you clothed in the livery of my Mother on November 25 or January 10?" But He will ask her soul, *united to His love*: "Did you understand my Heart, which chose you to form only one heart with Me? . . ." The month is a matter of indifference, but the sacrifice, but the immolation of our most cherished desires, but the giving of our entire self. . . ah! that is what will give joy to the Heart of the Beloved. . . . Spoiled child, think only of the great honor that Jesus is giving us, and let us give Him all the blood of our heart. I bless you from the bottom of this heart which is all yours! . . .

* Autograph.

1. Thérèse used this word "*tristotin*" in two ways: "*tristotin remplissant*" and "*tristotin minotant.*" "When it was a question of a 'sorrow' in which one was filled with joy, or a 'sorrow' which brought on sadness." (Note of Sister Geneviève, p. 173, in a copybook typed by her, from her letters to Mother Agnes of Jesus.)
2. This is a probable reference to the fact that Thérèse was on retreat, hidden in solitary prayer more than hidden from the current activity of the Community.
3. January 9, the date the postulant would have preferred to January 10 (see LT 76 and LC 102).

LC 104 *From Sister Marie of the Angels to Thérèse.*

January 6-9, 1889 (?) → LT lost?

Approximate date; see note 1.

† J. M. J. T! Jesus

My dear little Benjamin,

I think much about you, and your note comes again[1] to console both my heart and my soul! Rejoice in your lot; it is well prepared by the Beloved Himself of your heart! Bless him for the ardent desires He is giving you to love Him and gain souls for Him. What

does it matter if your heart is little, provided your desires are very great! Desire, desire again and always to love Him whom you will never love enough. Your aridities, your sufferings, these are something to offer Jesus both for Himself and for souls! You know very well, there are little flowers which don't always have to be touched by the rays of the sun; for them to develop to their plenitude, they need more shade than sun. Well, then, if Jesus wills that you be one of these flowers, what does it matter, as long as in the eyes of heaven you were blooming with all the splendor that the divine Gardener had given your soul in treating it in the way that He knows is suitable for it! See you soon,[2] darling little child. I am extending to you in advance both my heart and my arms.

Sister Marie of the Angels

* Autograph.

1. She used the word "again." Either there was a first note (lost) or this written communication followed an oral interview between Thérèse and the novice mistress. There is no certitude regarding the date of this note; we present it here because it is in agreement with the sentiments expressed by Thérèse at this time in other notes: ardent desires (see LT 74), spiritual darkness (LT 78).
2. The retreat was about to end.

LT 77 — From Thérèse to M. Martin.

January 8, 1889

This is the last letter Thérèse wrote to her father at Les Buissonnets. All the others that she wrote afterwards were destroyed.

J. M. J. T.

Jesus † January 8, 1889

My incomparable King,

If you only knew how much I was touched by your kindness!. . . a melon![1] . . . champagne, oh! it would make me want to

cry if I were not to control myself. But I am controlling myself, and I am very much delighted by Thursday's beautiful celebration.

Usually, the wedding of a Queen is celebrated with great rejoicing, and it is no doubt because of this that the Queen of France and Navarre will have some fireworks. . . . The king is paying all the expenses for the Queen, and he is an expert at providing surprises; the little *blond rascal*[2] has only to thank him! . . .

If on Thursday there will be a beautiful celebration on earth, I think it will be more magnificent in heaven; the angels will be in admiration when seeing a Father so pleasing to God, and Jesus will prepare a crown to be added to all those that my King has already gathered together.

No, never are earth's celebrations as ravishing as those of heaven; however, it seems to me that it is impossible to find a celebration more heavenly than the one in preparation. I have, nevertheless, done nothing to be worthy of such a great grace, but God has been pleased to look upon the merits of my dear Father, and it is because of this that He is granting me this remarkable favor.

I am now on retreat, and on retreat we are not permitted to write, but Our Mother has allowed me to send you this note to thank you, for you are so kind to your Queen. And, then, no doubt, if it is forbidden to write, it is so as not to trouble the silence of the retreat, but can I trouble my peace by writing to a Saint? . . .

Until Thursday, dear King. Your little Queen kisses you from her heart while waiting until she can do it in reality.[3]

The Queen of France
and Navarre
Thérèse of the Child Jesus
post.carm.ind.

* Autograph in six fragments, CMG.

1. A surprise fruit which made an explosion by a wick which, when lighted, threw out a shower of candies.

2. One of the affectionate nicknames given to Thérèse by her father because of her beautiful blond hair.
3. At this time, the postulants went out of the cloister for part of the ceremony; she could then kiss her father and the members of her family.

LT 78 **From Thérèse to Sister Agnes of Jesus.**

January 8, 1889
→ LC 102

J. M. J. T.

Jesus†

I haven't seen the lamb *of the day*, but I know that it has a bad headache,[1] and this causes pain to the little lamb which fears that Jesus is sprouting wings on the lamb. . . . What delightful lines! . . They are heavenly; they give a sense of the homeland! . . . The lamb is mistaken in believing that Jesus' toy is not in darkness; it is immersed in darkness. Perhaps, and the little lamb agrees with this, this darkness is light, but in spite of everything it is darkness . . . . Its *only* consolation is a strength and a very great peace, and, then, it wants to be as Jesus wills it to be; that is its joy, otherwise, all is sadness . . . . When I go to Our Mother, I am continually interrupted,[2] and then when I do have a moment, I can't tell her what is taking place in my soul, and I go away without joy after having entered without joy![3] . . .

I believe that the work of Jesus during this retreat has been to detach me from all that is not Himself . . .

If you only knew how great my joy is not to have anything with which to please Jesus! . . . It is a refined joy (but in no way felt).

Dear lamb, only one more day to be the fiancée of Jesus! . . .

Don't die immediately; wait until the little lamb has wings in order to follow you .[4] . . .

Thérèse of the Child Jesus, the little toy of Jesus!

post.carm.ind.

Will you, if you please, give me first, your indian ink and some gold; secondly, tell me if the Responses of St. Agnes are suitable for my little pictures for the reception of the Habit; and thirdly, open our door ajar at six o'clock if you are here, otherwise I will wake up by myself. If all these things put you to any trouble, give me nothing; I can do without.[5]

* Autograph.
1. Sister Agnes frequently had migraine headaches.
2. These interruptions were because of Sisters coming to see the prioress when Thérèse was speaking with her; see LC 103.
3. She had the same difficulty when speaking with her novice mistress; see Ms. A, p. 151.
4. See LT 56, note 2.
5. Sister Agnes answered all these requests that evening; LC 105.

LC 105 *From Sister Agnes of Jesus to Thérèse.*
January 8, 1889 (Fragments.)
→ LT 78

Dear child, the hour is approaching! Although Jesus is saying nothing to you, He is acting at the bottom of your heart, and this is worth more than all consolations. See how this suffering is bringing you close to Him; see how you feel freed from all attachment. It is the divine silence that works these marvels.

Really pray for Papa. He was really good today[1] but tired out. This is the time. . .Jesus will refuse you nothing on the day of your espousals; ah! ask Him to have pity on us.[2] Papa is so good; it's enough to make you cry . . . .

I am very eager to see my dear little hermit again. I will help her on Thursday to put on her white dress. . . the martyr's dress, for it will have to be dyed in the blood of sacrifice, *blood from your heart*.

Ah! my darling, really, on Thursday morning, you will be able to sing like St. Agnes:[3] "It is Jesus, whom I love; I have sucked from His mouth milk and honey, and *His Blood stains my cheeks*. . . ."

Meditate on this mystery. . . . Formerly, you were sucking from the mouth of Jesus the milk and honey of His love, but today *His Blood stains your cheeks*. . . .

Adieu,[4] second little Lamb; rejoice in your lot!. . . In heaven, the honey and the milk will be restored to you. . . also your white dress and your crown of lilies, an immortal dress, an imperishable crown!. . .

I will give you tomorrow what you are asking me.[5]. . . Some of the Responses of St. Agnes are suitable but not all. I will wake you up. . . pray that Jesus make me a saint, I am far from it.

* Autograph.

1. M. Martin came to the Carmel's speakroom, bringing the gifts for which Thérèse thanked him (LT 77).
2. Much later, Mother Agnes of Jesus revealed the depth of her anxiety concerning her father. She wrote to Mme. La Néele (Jeanne Guérin), recalling the day of Thérèse's reception of the Habit: "It is already twenty-five years ago! How time flies! Oh! how I suffered that day! Poor little Father was in danger of an attack at any moment. I was afraid of an accident during the ceremony. I still tremble just thinking about it, and I recall on the day before, in the evening, I begged God to have pity on us and that Father would not weep in the chapel. I thought: tomorrow, at this time, all will be ended, what joy. How I would like now to be at tomorrow evening!" (Letter of Mother Agnes of Jesus to Mme. La Néele [Jeanne Guérin], January 1914). It was undoubtedly when she was recalling these fears that Thérèse underlined these words in her Autobiography: ". . . never had he looked so handsome, so dignified. Everybody admired him" (Ms. A, p. 155).
3. The texts that follow in Sister Agnes' note to Thérèse are free cita-

tions from the Responses of Matins for the Office of St. Agnes (January 21). The choice of Thérèse for her reception of the Habit (see LT 78) was probably inspired by a little play put on in 1888 (see LT 53). Later on, she put these "Responses of St. Agnes" in verses for the feast on January 21, 1896 (P 22).

4. Before this word, three lines are missing, cut out at the top of the page, and the same goes for the back of the same page.
5. See LT 78, postscript.

LT 79 From Thérèse to Sister Marie of the Sacred Heart.

January 8, 1889
→ LC 101

J. M. J. T.

Jesus †

Dear Lion, your note gave GREAT PLEASURE[1] to your little daughter's heart!... Thanks.... How good you are!... Oh! how I would like to resemble you. But the toy of Jesus[2] is weakness itself; if Jesus does not carry it, or if He does not Himself throw His little ball, it will remain inert in the same place!

Only one more day, and I will be the Fiancée of Jesus, what a grace!... What to do in order to thank Him, to make me less unworthy of such a favor?...

Oh! the homeland...the homeland![3] How I thirst for heaven, there where I shall love Jesus without reserve!...

But we must suffer and cry in order to arrive there...well, then, I want to suffer all that will please Jesus; let Him do whatever He wills with His little ball.

Thérèse of the Child Jesus
post.carm.ind.

* Autograph.

1. The words "great pleasure" are underlined respectively four and five times.
2. See LT 34, note 2. Thérèse never used this image again in her correspondence; however, she did recall it again in LT 176, April 28, 1895.
3. These words were filled with memories for the Martin family: "You recall this sigh from her heart, so frequent and so much felt by our Mother: 'Oh! the homeland! the homeland!' I believe, little Father, that all this world's beauties will only make you repeat with fervor this cry of an exiled soul: 'Oh! the Homeland! the Homeland! Heaven! . . .'" (Letter of Sister Agnes of Jesus to M. Martin, then on a trip in Central Europe, August 24, 1885.) Again: "The words of our dear Father repeated to us are true: 'For this exile, there is nothing but tears and sad thoughts. . . . Oh, the Homeland! the Homeland! It is beautiful, the Homeland!' I can still hear the sound of his very lovable voice, telling us the profound sentences upon which his heart was meditating for whole days." (Letter of Céline to Sister Marie of the Sacred Heart, June 27, 1889.)

LC 106

From Sister Marie of the Sacred Heart to Thérèse.

January 8, 1889

This note seems to have crossed that of Thérèse (LT 79).

Dear little daughter, my heart is filled with sweet things that I don't have time to tell the little lamb. After having really tried us, we could say that Jesus is pleased to give us joy. Everybody is joyful; they are talking of nothing but the nuptials of this little Queen. A real Queen! who has received the most magnificent jewels that any queen has ever received. Oh! yes, the King of heaven has treated His little fiancée royally. Ah! on the day of her espousals, let her ask for very special graces for the dear patriarch who is so much loved by Jesus! Let her beg Him that he may not have a relapse as he did before; let her beseech[1] Him, let her em-

brace Him, let her hold Him so tightly against her heart until He has said: "Yes, I have answered you!"

With regard to *my little daughter's* blond hair which will fall under the scissors on that day,[2] do you know what I thought which was sweet? In the Canticle of Canticles, it is said: "You have ravished my heart, my sister, my spouse, by one of your eyes, and by ONE *of your hairs.*"[3] I thought that my little lamb's hair would delight still better the Heart of Jesus! For she will give it without counting the cost.

And countless treasures up above also!!!. . . will be given to her in exchange!

* Autograph.

1. Just as Sister Agnes of Jesus was very much worried about her father, so also was Marie (see LC 105, note 2).
2. At the ceremony of the reception of the Habit, a strand of hair was cut symbolically from the postulant's head. Thérèse had long hair, and it fell in long strands over her shoulders on January 10. According to the custom of this time, the novice was to have her hair cut off a few months later. Because this operation was being put off, Thérèse asked for it herself. Mother Agnes testified: "We had not cut her hair after the reception of the Habit because she was too young. But a short time afterwards, she insisted in such a way with Our Mother to obtain this permission that it was finally given to her. She then came looking for me to perform the operation, but I was not happy. 'You are too young,' I told her, 'wait; we don't know what will happen.' Finally, I gave in to her insistence, thinking I would please her. I was wrong. She looked silently on the magnificent head of hair that had fallen into my hands, and, when I asked her what she was thinking, she said: 'I think I am happy for having made this sacrifice for Jesus. I was eager to give Him my hair.'" (NPPA, Temperance, p. 1.) When making this answer, Thérèse had tears in her eyes (DCL).
3. Canticle of Canticles 4:9. See LT 163, May 20, 1894. Some of the versions read: ". . . you have ravished my heart with one glance of your eyes, with one bead of your necklace."

LC 107 *From Sister Marie of the Sacred Heart to Thérèse.*

January 9, 1889

Jesus †

My dear little daughter, I don't want the eve of such a beautiful day to pass by without speaking a little word to her from her Jesus. Her Jesus! He has made her a bed of lilies![1] "My beloved browses among the lilies!"[2] says the spouse in the Canticle. I want to give my little daughter the only picture that is dear to me among all others. . . . Aunt at Le Mans gave it to me, and I am attached to it,[3] for it says much to my heart. But all for the little fiancée of Jesus! What is too beautiful for her? Oh! yes, ". . . happy the lily that remained without spot until the hour of reaping."[4]

One day, we shall reap, rejoicing![5] And this hour will come! And it will be a day without clouds, and the more we shall have suffered the more radiant that day will be. Then! then! Ah! I keep silent. . . . This day will be so beautiful, it will be so sweet, this day which will have no setting!! My whole heart to my dear angel, whom I adorned for Jesus on the day of her First Communion and whom I will adorn on the day of her espousals.

Marie of the Sacred Heart

* Autograph.

1. This is a probable reference to the rough carpet ornamented with artificial lilies and spread out in the choir of the religious; the novice prostrated upon it at the end of the ceremony, during the singing of the *Veni Creator* (in fact, the *Te Deum*, on that January 10, because of an error on the part of the celebrant). See Ms. A, p. 155.
2. Canticle of Canticles 6:3.
3. On the back of this picture given to her by her Aunt, Sister Marie-Dosithée Guérin, a Visitation nun, Marie Martin had written as a child: "Souvenir *from Aunt at Le Mans; I shall keep it forever.*"

4. This was the sentence on the front of this picture, under a painting of Jesus as a boy, cutting lilies. Thérèse chose a similar picture as a souvenir of her own "*adieu*" to her sisters (LT 245, June 1897).
5. Psalm 126:5.

LC 108 *From P. Pichon to Thérèse.*
January 10, 1889

† Les Cèdres
January 10, '89

My very happy Child
in Jesus Christ,

It is today, then.[1] My whole heart is at Lisieux, in the blessed sanctuary where Jesus is clothing you in the livery of His spouses. Your espousals fill me with joy. You have been prepared for them by the Cross, and I find you very much privileged. Meditate on these words of St. Mary Magdalene de Pazzi: "God takes greater pleasure here below in the soul transformed by sorrow than in the soul transformed by love."[2]

Presently, I am going to ascend the holy altar and offer the adorable Victim for you. Better still, I am going to unite you to the divine Holocaust in order to consecrate you to God.

Do not complain about my absence. No one is more present than I at the Carmel of my much-loved children.

Enjoy your happiness. I envy your "tête-à-tête" with Jesus. I myself am in the mêlée, battling against all the demons of hell. These past days, in the course of a mission, I did not leave the confessional until between eleven and midnight. Long live Jesus! How good it is to vow oneself to Him, to sacrifice oneself for His love.[3] I want this joy to be all yours and all mine.

May the Sacred Heart of the Master tell you and repeat to you all that my heart says to you. In eternity, we shall make up for this ugly Canada.

My most tender and holy blessings to my happy Benjamin on this day of eternal memory.

Almire Pichon
S.J.

* Autograph.

1. Depending on the places of residence of P. Pichon in Canada, we observe that the letters from Lisieux reached him within eight to fourteen days. If he had been informed by letter about the date of the reception of the Habit, it would have been necessary for Thérèse to write him on January 2 at the latest; this would constitute a serious objection to the assumption of a change in date taking place during the course of her retreat (see LT 76, note 3). However, it is not unreasonable to think that Céline transmitted the news by cablegram; she used this means on other occasions, for example, to announce to him the death of M. Martin in 1894.
2. This sentence appears textually on an illuminated picture given by P. Pichon on January 11, 1890, to one of the nuns under his direction (we don't know her name). Under the sentence, Sister Geneviève commented in pencil "error!"
3. Thérèse cites this sentence in her letter to Céline, March 12, 1889 (LT 85).

LT 80 From Thérèse to Sister Martha of Jesus.

January 10, 1889

Lines in pencil on the reverse side of a lace picture.

Souvenir of my reception of the Habit, offered to my dear little Sister.

Soon the divine Fiancé of Thérèse of the Child Jesus will also be the Fiancé of Sister Martha of Jesus![1]

Ask Jesus that I become a great saint; I will ask the same grace for my dear little companion!

Sister Thérèse of the Child Jesus of the Holy Face.[2]
nov.carm.ind.[3]

* Autograph.

1. Sister Martha of Jesus, who had entered the Carmel on December 23, 1887, had to make one year of postulancy as a lay sister; her reception of the Habit was put off until May 2, 1889.
2. This was the first time that the title ". . . of the Holy Face" appeared in Thérèse's signature. Introduced to this devotion by Sister Agnes of Jesus (see Ms. A, p. 152), who was influenced by the writings of Sister Marie de Saint-Pierre of the Tours Carmel, Thérèse entered very deeply into this devotion in a very personal way because of the events in her life and also her own reading, but especially when she made her discovery of chapter 53 of Isaias (LT 108). See also DE, pp. 516-518. However, the novice continued to be called in the daily life of the Carmel: Thérèse of the Child Jesus.
3. Abbreviations for "*novice carmélite indigne*" (unworthy Carmelite novice).

LC 109 *From Sister Marie of the Angels to Thérèse.*

January 10, 1889

J. M. J. T! Jesus!

My dear little Child,

Souvenir of the day, the object of all her desires and her most ardent aspirations! . . .

May the Divine Child recall to her mind that when, on January 10, 1889, she entered the cloister and the Cross was presented to her to be kissed, it was He Himself, this gentle little Brother Jesus,

who was presenting it to her, carried in the arms of His Immaculate Mother.[1]

May good little Jesus be forever the Jesus of little Thérèse, and may little Sister Thérèse be truly Thérèse of the Child Jesus.

During this octave of the Kings, He espoused her to Himself in order to make her soon the *Queen* of His most tender love. Be happy, then, very happy for long years in Carmel, dear little child. Share in the kingship of Jesus. His kingdom will become yours, His crown awaits you, refuse Him nothing. The kingdom of Jesus is not of this world,[2] and yours will not be either. Aid Jesus in extending His divine kingdom in souls; save them by your sacrifices, by your generosity. Work for heaven. Jesus will count all you do for Him, and nothing will escape His loving and constant gaze!

On the night of this beautiful day, I bless you and give you before you fall asleep, His sweetest and most tender kiss.

Your little Sister, who loves you most tenderly.[3]

Sister Marie of the Angels of S.C.
r.c.ind.

* Autograph.

1. A probable reference to a picture preserved in the Theresian collection which corresponds in every way with the commentary that Sister Marie of the Angels was making on it.
2. See John 18:36; on the day of her Profession, Thérèse took up this same theme of the hidden kingship of Christ (see LT 117).
3. See in the Appendix the picture offered by Mother Marie de Gonzague, January 10, 1889.

FOURTH PERIOD

THE NOVITIATE

(January 1889 - September 1890)

THE NOVITIATE
(1889–1890)

The reception of the Habit (January 10, 1889) began the canonical year of novitiate for Thérèse. In one year, the young religious would be able to pronounce her perpetual vows, for temporary vows were not made in those days. But, in January 1890, she would be seventeen, the age required by the Constitutions for making a definitive promise. The superiors judged it to be more prudent to delay, and her vows were postponed for eight months (Ms. A, p. 158).

The religious setting remained the same as the preceding year. Mother Marie de Gonzague was elected again for three years (February 13, 1889), and Sister Marie of the Angels was retained in her office as mistress of novices. In March, three years after her Profession (March 25, 1886), Sister Marie-Philomène left the novitiate and joined the rest of the Community. Sister Marie of the Sacred Heart was now the oldest member in the novitiate. Thérèse took her place before Sister Martha of Jesus, the latter's reception of the Habit having been postponed (May 2, 1889).

Exteriorly, the novice was formed more and more by her milieu. At the choral Office, "my joy and my martyr-

dom" she described it one day (CJ 6.8.6.), she intoned the antiphons, recited the versicles, and read the lessons at Matins (LC 122). All was in Latin, recto tono.

Thérèse took her turn at carrying out the house assignments for each week, for example, the ringing of the bells, serving at table, and reading during the meals. Appointed as "second in charge" of the refectory, under the supervision of Sister Agnes of Jesus, she prepared the water and beer, at noon and in the evening, swept the refectory, and kept clean a little alcove called "Saint Alexis," a refuge of spiders for which she had a horror (CJ 13.7.18).

Two photographs taken a few days after her reception of the Habit bring Thérèse's face alive at this time. Bundled up in the rough habit and heavy veil, the adolescent exudes joy. Her plump features, it is true, justify the humiliating compliment paid to her by Sister St. Vincent de Paul: "Oh! how well she looks! Is this big girl strong! Is she plump!" (CJ 25.7.15.) Her mischievous look and happy face were so perfectly misleading that Thérèse had to correct this mistaken view of herself: "Ah! what a surprise we shall have at the end of the world when we shall read the story of souls! There will be those who will be surprised when they see the way through which my soul was guided!" (Ms. A, p. 149). However, when referring to the year 1889, she wrote: ". . . exteriorly, nothing revealed my suffering which was all the more painful since I alone was aware of it" (ibid.). Her autobiography is sparing in revelations: ten pages are sufficient to describe the twenty months in the novitiate. There was a deliberate reserve here: "All that I have just written in a few words would require many pages of detail, but these pages will never be read on this earth" (Ms. A, p. 160).

→ *Read Ms. A, pp. 154–166.*

"Our great riches" (*Ms. A, p. 156*)
(January-May 1889)
Age sixteen

The ceremony of January 10, 1889, was for M. Martin "... his triumph, his last celebration here below... never was he more handsome, more dignified.... Everybody admired him" (Ms. A, p. 156). However, "... his glory of a day was followed by a painful passion" (ibid.). This passion is already suffused with light when Thérèse briefly recalls it, in 1895, in cloaked words, in her manuscript. M. Martin was already dead for a whole year. But in the letters of 1889, his illness is described in all its realism. The drama opened on February 12 when his hallucinations had taken on a disquieting form for those around him (LD, February 18, 1889). M. Martin had to be transferred to a mental hospital, Bon Sauveur at Caen. The trial entered deeply into the "little Queen's" heart: "Ah! that day, I did not say that I was able to suffer even more!!!" (Ms A, p. 157). And Thérèse was not unaware of the fact that, in Lisieux, certain persons were making her responsible for her father's misfortune, shaken as he was by the successive departures of his daughters for the convent (LT 81, note 4). Her suffering had such a sharpness about it that, during a whole year, the names of "father" or "papa" appear only rarely in her correspondence (see LT 82, 83, 88, 91, 100).

In this combination of circumstances, her courage was admired by the Community. A Sister Aimée of Jesus, little inclined to emotionalism, was very emphatic about this: "Her fortitude was heroic during her venerable father's illness through her admirable submission and through her punctuality at being present at the Community exercises, even at a time when her sisters were absent; and she used to speak to us with perfect se-

renity, while large tears, which escaped from her eyes, showed that she was not indifferent to these sufferings." (*PO, 2223.*)

The twelve letters from Thérèse written during this period (end of January to end of May 1889, the most acute stage; LT 81 to 92) confirm Sister Aimée's statement. Their content manifests the triumph of her faith, and the handwriting reveals her broken heart. The alterations, the irregular and painful motion would cause one to believe in the imminence of an emotional breakdown. Then Thérèse regained control of herself.

The greater part of the letters are addressed to Céline, who, with Léonie, went to live at Caen, close to M. Martin. An untiring correspondence was carried on between "the exiles at Caen" (Ms. A, 157) and the Carmel; the first letters transmitted the news which was frequently heart-rending, and the three Carmelites supported their sisters confronted with a "novitiate of sorrow" (LT 82).

The shadow of this trial hovers like a funeral veil over the whole period of Thérèse's novitiate year. But for the kind of faith lived by the Martin family the veil of sorrow was transformed gently into a Veronica's veil. Through her tears, Thérèse learns to "recognize,"[1] *behind the face of her humbled father, the features of the Suffering Servant.*

1. See LT 116, note 3.

LT 81 **From Thérèse to Céline.**

January 23-25(?), 1889 Approximate date; see note 1.

J. M. J. T.

Jesus and His Cross!...

Dear Sister,

Yes, *darling* of my heart, Jesus is there with His Cross![1] Privileged one of His love, He wills to make you like Him! Why be frightened at not being able to carry this Cross without weakening? Jesus on the road to Calvary fell three times, and, you, poor little child, you would not be like your *Spouse*, you would not be willing to fall a hundred times if necessary to prove your love for Him, rising with greater strength than before your fall!...

Céline...Jesus must love you with a special love to be trying you in this way. Do you know that I am almost jealous of you? To those who love more He gives *more*, and to those who love less He gives less!...

But you don't feel your love for YOUR SPOUSE. You would like your heart to be a flame that rises up to Him without the lightest smoke.[2] Don't forget that the smoke that surrounds you is only for yourself in order to remove from you the sight of your love for Jesus, while the flame is only for Him. At least, then He has this love entirely, for if He were to show it to us just a little bit, swiftly self-love would come like a fatal wind which extinguishes everything!...

You give me the impression, at this moment, of a person who is surrounded with immense riches...the sight of them is lost over the horizon.... This person wants to turn her back because, she says, too many riches embarrass her, she does not know what to do with them; it is better to lose them, or that *another* take them!... That other will not come, for these riches are prepared

for the fiancée of Jesus. . . and for her alone! . . . God would turn the world upside down to find suffering in order to give it to a soul upon whom His DIVINE *glance* has rested with an indescribable love![3] . . .

The things of this earth . . . what do they mean to us? . . . Should this be our homeland, this *slime*, so unworthy of an immortal soul . . . and what does it matter to us that cowardly men *harvest* the mustiness that grows on this slime? The more our heart is in heaven the less we feel these *pinpricks*.[4] . . .

But believe that this is a *grace* and a *great grace* to feel these pinpricks, for, then, our life is a *martyrdom*, and one day Jesus will give us the palm. To suffer and to be *despised*![5] . . . what *bitterness* but what glory. That is the Lily Immortelle's[6] motto! . . . No other could suit her. My heart is following you in the *noble task* that Jesus has entrusted to you. You are not a soldier but a General. . . . Suffer both again and always. . . . But all passes.[7]

* Autograph.

1. M. Martin's condition manifested around January 22, it seems, alarming symptoms: overstimulation and drowsiness (according to Céline's letter to Jeanne Guérin, January 22-23, 1889). Sister Geneviève (Céline) later dated Thérèse's autograph as "January 1889."
2. A possible reference to the Imitation of Christ III, 49:2.
3. A thought expressed by P. Pichon, according to Sister Geneviève's note, in CMG IV, p. 13. The first edition of the *Letters* (LT LVII, p. 108) puts it in quotation marks; there is no trace of this quotation in P. Pichon's retreat notes (1887-1888), or in his letters to Thérèse and her sisters. However, between the publication of the first edition of the *Letters* (1948) and her death (1959), Sister Geneviève destroyed in part P. Pichon's letters to Sister Marie of the Sacred Heart and herself.
4. These were humiliating reflections on their father's illness. "Outside the monastery, many persons made us responsible for this misfortune, caused, they said, by his extreme sorrow, especially when Thérèse entered the Carmel" (Sister Agnes of Jesus, *Souvenirs intimes*, 1905, p. 84).

5. This was one of St. John of the Cross' desires, and it was taken up by both Thérèse and Céline in their conversations in the belvedere at Les Buissonnets during the summer of 1887; see Ms. A, p. 157.
6. Nickname of Céline; see LT 57, note 2.
7. Thérèse was thinking of St. Teresa of Avila's bookmark (see LT 27, note 6)? "Let nothing trouble thee. . . . Nothing affright thee. . . . All things are passing. . . . God never changes."

LD *From Sister Agnes of Jesus to Léonie and Céline.* (Extracts.)

End of January, 1889

J. M. J. T.

My dear little Sisters,

Dear little Céline, always be devoted!. . . Your letter heartened me,[1] also Sister Marie of the Sacred Heart and the little lamb.[2]

Yes, *we have confidence in you.*[3] And what blessings are reserved for you! Your task is difficult but so beautiful!. . .

Above all, tell dear little Father to show the photographs only to Uncle and not to tell anyone that M. Gombault photographed the angel.[4] People would believe that he entered the cloister precisely for this, which is not true, since Monseigneur had given him the permission to come with the contractor to see the old house.[5] You can say, in case you are asked, that someone had lent me the apparatus[6] for two or three days. This secret is very IMPORTANT.

* Autograph.
1. News about M. Martin was better: "Papa said to us this morning: 'Poor children, I'm still not fully recovered, but I am improved; it is strange, all that has happened for several days. It is like a dream.' He spoke joyfully about you, his face was radiant." (Letter from Céline to her sisters, end of January 1889.)

2. This was Thérèse.
3. "At Carmel, they did not believe Papa was as sick as he was, and they thought I was not taking good care of him. P. Pichon had to come to my defense. . . ." (Sister Geneviève's note.)
4. "Photograph of Thérèse as a novice, taken by M. l'abbé Gombault, professor at the minor seminary at Lisieux; he frequently did architectural work" (Sister Geneviève's note).
5. "The house of the Extern Sisters was tumbling down, and the Carmelite nuns decided to have it repaired. It was a heavy burden for the Community. . . . They began the work in May. Because the nuns had neither turn or speakroom, messages from the outside were transmitted through the sacristy turn, and they used the confessional as a speakroom." (*Foundations* III, p. 156.)
6. This was Céline's own photographic apparatus.

LD
February 18, 1889
→ LD lost

From Céline to Pauline Romet.

After a grave attack of paralysis, M. Martin was hospitalized at Caen, Tuesday, February 12.

Lisieux, February 18, '89

Dear Aunt,[1]

I was very much touched by your very loving and consoling letter. Oh! yes, we are sad, very sad, and without any comfort. It is the greatest trial that could come to us; we love our dear little Father so much! He was our glory, our whole love. We loved him all the more because he had loved us so much; he had left his dear Alençon and his friends for our sake, and he acted as a Mother to us. He always watched over us with a fatherly love; I could say it had no equal. He was the best of fathers, the most excellent of men; everybody loved him, and in the town they call him: "the holy patriarch." And now he is gone! . . . Oh! dear Aunt Pauline, our heart is torn; we find no consolation whatever in the bitter-

ness of our sorrow. As for myself, never will I be able to accustom myself to this separation; hours follow hours, days follow days and the sorrow is the same, or rather it becomes more intense, the wound deepens.

Dear Aunt, I am not going to try to describe my sorrow to you, for deep emotions cannot be described, but I know you understand; in fact, our language, as rich as it is, is still too poor for the language of the heart.

On Saturday, [2] we were at Caen to see our dear little Father; he was sleeping, and he was feeling no pain. For me, this was the beginning of an attack. The last one was signaled in exactly the same way. At first, he had been going along for some ten days, then he ended up by sleeping; I don't know how he is today. We intend to return there in one or two days. I want only one thing and that is to be a servant girl in some Community[3] in order to be *near him* and to run at the slightest sign; I can no longer live here. Lisieux seems to me like a desert; I feel that I am too far from the one I love. I want to dedicate myself to him; my life is now useless so I am going to try to carry out my plan. Dear Aunt, I am sure that you are going to approve; you understand dedication so well!

We went to see M. and Mme. Benoît;[4] they told us they had left for Alençon. We wanted to thank them. Knowing that they will be near you, I think they will give you some details that would take too long in a letter. The doctor at the establishment told us that it was a general paralysis, the whole nervous system was attacked; he believes that the time will come when all his strength will be so weakened that we shall be able to take him home and take care of him until his last breath; this hope gives me courage. It is very sad that the paralysis settled in his brain,[5] otherwise we would still have our very much-loved Father at home. He is incredibly good; he was far from wanting to do us any harm with his revolver; on the contrary, he wanted to defend us. In his imagination, he was seeing frightful things, slaughter, battles; he was hearing the sounds of cannon and the drum. I tried in vain to correct his mistake. An attempt at robbery in the town served only to

confirm him in his ideas, so he took his revolver and wanted to carry it on him in case of danger, for, he said, "I would not want to harm even a cat." In fact, I don't believe that he would have made use of it; it was just an idea that was passing and it would have vanished. Perhaps they should have waited before acting, and should have tried ways of taking it away from him,[6] for he was so good, so gentle; he used to kiss us with such tenderness!

Dear Aunt Pauline, God has permitted this trial; that is what we have to say. The consolations of religion can alone strengthen us in such circumstances.

The consolations of friends are very sweet, too, especially when they are dictated by a heart like that of our good Aunt.

My regards to M. Vital.

Céline Martin

* Autograph.

1. This was a title given only through affection; there was no blood relationship but very close ties of friendship between the Martin and Romet families.
2. February 16, 1889.
3. On Monday, the 19th, Céline and Léonie took a room at the Sisters of St. Vincent de Paul, *rue de Bayeux,* close to the *Bon Sauveur,* on *rue Caponière.*
4. M. Auguste Benoît (1826-1903) had married in 1857 Hortense Romet (1825-1898), sister of Vital and Pauline Romet. They lived at Caen. M. Romet took M. Martin to the *Bon Sauveur;* see note 6.
5. And not in the limbs as happened in May 1887.
6. This was not the opinion of M. Guérin, who feared for his nieces' lives and that of the maid, Maria Cosseron. Without any hesitation, he called in their mutual friend, a tall, vigorous man, to disarm M. Martin and take him to Caen under the pretext of a trip. The precise circumstances of this departure are not too well known. The actual witnesses have all died. We may well imagine that, during their lifetime, Thérèse's sisters avoided recalling these painful memories. We find only this fragment of a letter from Céline to her sisters: "Léonie and I were mute, we kept silent the whole time; we were crushed, broken. It seemed to me that my heart was bleeding and that it had

a large wound. . . ." (February 12, 1889, CMG IV, p. 163). And we have these few details written down by the infirmarian of the Carmel, following a conversation with Sister Marie of the Sacred Heart: "February 12, 1939. This morning. . . Sister Marie of the Sacred Heart spoke to me at length about M. Martin. It was the 50th anniversary of his entrance at *Bon Sauveur,* and our Mother (Agnes of Jesus) had just come in to tell us that during her breakfast with Sister Geneviève (Céline), they had been speaking about their Papa and they began to cry. Then Sister Marie of the Sacred Heart continued: 'The other day, our Mother was telling me that she recalled, as though it were yesterday, M. Martin's short visit to the Carmel when he was about to take the train for Caen. Our Mother was portress; she knew it was that morning that a friend had to take Father to Caen. Suddenly, our Extern Sisters told her: 'M. Martin is asking for you.' She went to the speakroom, and he said to her: 'It is I, Pauline, and I've brought you some fish.' Actually, he had put two or three little fish in his handkerchief! Then he turned to the dog Tom and said to him: 'Go away, you.' M. Martin believed he was going to Caen on a trip, but our Mother, who knew he was to stay there, felt her limbs giving way under her. That day, it was snowing, and when she left the speakroom, she went out to wash the handkerchief in the snow in the Lourdes courtyard, in the exact place where the shrine is (since 1923). When Papa was taken to Caen, they told him that it was to take care of him and he said nothing.'" (Sister Marie of the Incarnation's notebook, p. 229.) It is not known whether Thérèse had any knowledge of all these circumstances at the time; see LT 83, note 2.

LD *From Céline to her sisters Agnes of Jesus, Marie of the Sacred Heart, and Thérèse.* (Extracts.)

February 27, 1889

Uncle must have given you an account of yesterday's visit,[1] so I am not going to give you a lot of details.[2] I need only have you hear the song of the exile sighing for his homeland.

The more I travel, the more I see things, the more I am detached

from the earth, because at each moment, I notice the nothingness of what is passing away.

The Sister said to him [M. Martin] that he was rendering them a great service by bringing back the fallen-away patients to God. "You are an apostle," she told him. "That's true," answered dear little Father, "but I would prefer to be an apostle elsewhere; however, since it is God's will! I believe it is to break down my pride." If you only knew, dear little sisters, how these words struck me to the heart. I think Papa is so holy! . . . But it was when I saw him go back inside, the moment when the door was shut on him again that my heart was torn. He is so good! He follows the infirmarian with such meekness!

I showed Papa's portrait to the Mother Superior of St. Vincent de Paul, and she thought it was very beautiful. . . . I am here in a real cell; nothing pleases me more than this poverty, and I would not exchange it for the brightest *salon*.

(Caen, February 27, 1889, from the Orphanage of St. Vincent de Paul.)

* CMG.
1. Céline's visit to M. Martin at *Bon Sauveur*; she was accompanied by Léonie and M. Guérin.
2. Sister Geneviève's notebook does not contain any other details on the patient's illness but those cited here.

LT 82 From Thérèse to Céline.

February 28, 1889
→ LD February 27

J. M. J. T.

Carmel, February 28, 1889

Jesus †

Dear Céline,

Is it possible that I am writing you at Caen? . . . I wonder if I am dreaming or if I am awake. . . . But, no, it is a reality! . . . I

am going to surprise you, dear little sister, by telling you that I am far from pitying you, but, you see, I think your lot is worthy of envy. Jesus has designs of an indescribable love for you; He wants His little lily-immortelle all for Himself, but He is Himself taking charge of having her make her first novitiate. It is His divine hand that is adorning His spouse for the day of her wedding, but His dear hand makes no mistake about the adornment . . . . Jesus is a Spouse of *blood.* [1] . . . He wants for Himself *all* the blood of her heart . . . .

Oh! how it costs to give Jesus what He asks! . . . What *joy* that it costs . . . . What an unspeakable joy to carry our Crosses FEEBLY. Has the Lily-Immortelle understood the poor grain of sand? . . . Your novitiate is one of sorrow; what an inexplicable privilege . . . .

Ah! dear little sister, far from complaining to Jesus about the Cross He is sending us, I cannot understand the *infinite* love that has drawn Him to treat us in this way . . . . Our dear Father must be much loved by Jesus to have to suffer this way, but don't you find that the misfortune that is striking him is really the complement of his beautiful life? . . . I feel, little Lily-Immortelle, that I am speaking real follies to you, but it does not matter. I still think very many others things about the love of Jesus which are perhaps much stronger than what I am saying to you . . . . What a joy to be humbled; it is the only thing that makes saints! . . . Can we doubt now the will of Jesus concerning our souls? . . . Life is only a *dream,* [2] and soon we shall wake up, and what joy . . . the greater our sufferings are the more infinite will be our glory . . . . Oh, let us not lose the trial that Jesus is sending us, it is a gold mine to be exploited. Are we going to miss the chance? . . . The grain of sand wants to get to work, without *joy,* without *courage,* without *strength,* and it is all these titles which will facilitate the enterprise for it; it wants to work through love.

The *Martyrdom* is beginning. Let us enter the arena together, if the Lily-Immortelle is willing not to look down upon

the poor *grain of Sand*

* Autograph.

1. This expression was made popular in Carmel by P. Pichon; see LC 78, note 7. Thérèse takes it up again in LT 112, and Sister Marie of the Angels does so in LC 92. We find it, too, in the correspondence of Sister Agnes of Jesus with her other sisters.
2. A possible reference to St. Teresa of Avila? See LC 93, note 4. The same thought is expressed in LT 108, July 18, 1890.

LD *From Céline to her sisters Agnes of Jesus, Marie of the Sacred Heart, and Thérèse.* (Fragments.)

March 1, 1889

When Papa sees me, he asks for news about all of you; he is thinking about all of you. I believe they are going to allow us to come no more than once a week; we come every day inquiring about him.

Sister Costard,[1] after having talked about other patients, told me, when speaking about Papa: "This is not M. Martin's case, *he is paralyzed.*" She claims that he is rapidly approaching a general paralysis; she finds his tongue a little impaired, his movements are slow, and he walks with difficulty.

My heart is filled with melancholy; there is nothing around me that does not speak of exile .... Life! Life appears to me as something whirling around that is passing by very quickly. Yes, all passes! Soon we shall rejoice over our sorrows. Oh! what good this thought from St. Ignatius does me: "You have told me, Lord, that . . . if anyone wishes to follow me, he must be content to live under my tent, to eat at my table, and to drink the same cup; he must work like me and with me. He will share with me the fruits of victory after he has shared with me the fatigue of the combat."[2]

Little sisters, I want to be very happy about tribulations, and to do more: thank God for the bitterness of our humiliations. I don't

know why, but instead of receiving these trials with bitterness and complaint, I see something mysterious and divine in the conduct of Our Lord in our regard. Besides, did He not Himself pass through all humiliations! . . . I admit that the opinion of the world amounts to nothing in my mind.

Oh! if you only knew how I see God in all our trials. Yes, everything in them is visibly marked with His divine finger.

Thanks, little Marie, thanks, little Pauline, for your very dear letters.[3] Thanks, dear Thérèse . . . but I don't want you to call yourself the little grain of sand because this is not true. If you persist in calling yourself this, then give me the name of imperceptible atom, and then things will be right. I always come *after* you; I am another you, but you are the reality while I am only your shadow.[4] . . .

Your little sister,

Céline
Caen, March 1, 1889

* CMG.

1. This religious of the Bon Sauveur (1846-1897) was directing the section of the establishment that had five hundred male patients. (CMG IV, p. 191.)
2. This is a free citation of the *Spiritual Exercises* of St. Ignatius Loyola, second week, meditation on the Kingdom of Jesus Christ.
3. Letters sent with that of Thérèse, February 28 (LT 82). Only Sister Agnes of Jesus' letter was preserved.
4. Thérèse took up this thought on March 15 (LT 86).

LD *From Céline to her sisters Agnes of Jesus, Marie of the Sacred Heart, and Thérèse.* (Fragments.)

March 4, 1889

Sister Costard takes care of Papa simply as though he were her father; yesterday she was crying when she was giving me information about him: "You see, it's heartbreaking to see this handsome patriarch in such a condition; we are sad, deeply pained, and our staff is dismayed. In the short time that he has been here, he has made himself loved, and, then, there is something so venerable about him! He bears no ordinary stamp . . . . We can see that it is a trial; it doesn't suit him to have this illness, and this makes it all the more distressing!"

This good religious kept repeating: "There is something so venerable about him!" Oh! how true this is. He seems to be so incredibly good. The doctor wouldn't be surprised if paralysis were to follow this attack.

Dear sisters, Papa will certainly have no purgatory in the other world, but these sorrows are so sharp for us that they can, I think, bring about changes in our souls that will make us saints. I don't believe the saints had harder trials . . . .

Just think of it, Uncle sent me two urgent and forceful notes[1] in which he was advising me and almost commanding me to obey; he wanted to see us at Lisieux today. As you can see, I held my ground, and I remained at my post.

And, nevertheless, I am struggling against my heart which calls me to be near you, and I want, on the other hand, to remain on duty, even to die because of it.[2]

I would not have believed that so weak a creature could bear such an amount of suffering. Oh! dear sisters, I feel that without a special grace I would be unable to remain here, this exile is too deep.[3]

Let us trust in Jesus, all that He permits can be only good.

Céline
Caen, March 4, 1889

* CMG.

1. These notes were not preserved; a month later, we find a comparable demand from M. Guérin's hand in the postscript of a letter from Mme. Guérin to Céline: "I find that it is absolutely useful for your health, your rest, and to regain new strength, that you come *every two weeks at least.* You must rely on our experience and obey. There is *no reason* whatsoever, *any valid motive* to excuse yourself from this obligation. I expect you, then, on Thursday. I. Guérin." (April 2, 1889.)
2. Thérèse makes a reference to this decision in her answer to this letter (LT 83, par. 4).
3. This letter was addressed to the Carmelites through Mme. Guérin, who wrote to Céline on March 5: "I went to the Carmel immediately, bringing your little letter and telling them about the one you had written to us .... Your sisters and I talked for a long time."

LT 83 From Thérèse to Céline.

March 5,
1889
→ LD, March 4

J. M. J. T.

Jesus †

My dear Céline,

I cannot tell you how much good your dear little letter did me!... Now you are truly the *Lily-immortelle* of Jesus. Oh! how pleased He is with His lily, how lovingly He looks on His dear flower, who wants *Him alone*, who has no other desire except that of consoling Him ....

Each new suffering, each new agony of her heart is like a light breeze which will carry to Jesus the perfume of His lily; then He will smile lovingly, and He will immediately prepare a new sorrow. He is filling the chalice to the brim, thinking that the more His lily grows in love the more, too, must it grow in suffering!...

What a privilege Jesus grants us in sending such a great *sorrow.*

Ah! ETERNITY will not be too long to thank Him. He is giving us His favors just as He gave them to the greatest saints. Why this great predilection?. . . It is a secret which Jesus will reveal in our homeland on the day when "He will dry all the tears from our eyes."[1] . . . It is necessary that it be to *my soul* that I am speaking in this way, for otherwise I would not be understood, but it is to her that I am addressing myself, and all my thoughts were anticipated by her. However, what she does not know perhaps is the love that Jesus has for her, a love that demands ALL. There is nothing that is impossible for Him. He does not want to set any limit to His Lily's SANCTITY; His limit is that there is no limit! . . . Why should there be any? We are greater than the whole universe, and one day we *ourselves* shall have a divine existence . . . .

Oh! I thank Jesus for having placed a lily near our dear Father, a lily that fears nothing, a lily that wishes rather *to die* than to abandon the *glorious* field in which the love of Jesus has placed it! . . .

Now we have no longer anything to hope for on earth, no longer anything but suffering and again suffering. When we have finished, suffering will still be there, extending its arms to us. Oh! what a lot worthy of envy . . . . The Cherubim in heaven envy our joy.

It was not for this that I was writing to my Céline, but it was to tell her to write to Mademoiselle Pauline[2] about the misfortune that has struck us in Papa's illness. Laugh in your turn at your poor Thérèse, who approaches her subject at the end of her letter. Poor Léonie, I love her also; she is more unfortunate than we are, for Jesus has given her less. But *much* will be demanded from those to whom much has been given.[3]

Your little sister,

Thérèse of the Child Jesus
post.carm.ind.[4]

* CMG.

1. Apocalypse 21:4.

2. Mademoiselle Pauline Romet; actually, she was one of the first to be informed by her brother-in-law and her sister, M. and Mme. Auguste Benoît; see LD, February 18, 1889.
3. See Luke 12:48.
4. Thérèse signs "postulant" instead of "novice"; the same mistake in LT 127, April 26, 1891.

LD *From Céline to her sisters Agnes of Jesus, Marie of the Sacred Heart, and Thérèse.* (Fragments.)

March 9, 1889

The other day, Papa said to the doctor: "I had always been accustomed to commanding, and I see myself reduced to obeying; I never had any humiliations in my life, and I needed one." The doctor answered: "Well, then, this one can count!"...

I feel more and more that my duty is to remain here;[1] yes, it is better to suffer and not abandon dear little Father. At least, here, if we can do nothing for him, we can run at the least call; even for yourselves, this must be a kind of assurance to know that we are here.

Dear little sisters (I'm talking also to my little Thérèse even though I am writing her specially),[2] oh! how bitter life is! What I cannot understand is that I'm not able to accustom myself to realizing where Papa is; it seems like a dream, a nightmare to me....

Well, certainly, we can tell ourselves that God can turn everything to good; He never gives us anything above our strength, and the moment Papa seemed to be carrying too heavy a load, God lightened it for him, removing from him the bitterness of his sorrow.

Yes, God willed it so; it is He who has arranged this matter, all by Himself. We would have acted in vain and only disturbed ourselves, poor little atoms. All would have taken place just the same.

Certainly, this trial was needed for Papa in order to crown his sanctity . . . .

(March 9, 1889)

* CMG.
1. At Caen, in spite of her uncle's objections; see LD, March 4, 1889, note 1.
2. This letter was not preserved.

LT 84 **From Thérèse to Mme. Guérin.**

March 12, 1889
→ LC lost?

J. M. J. T.

Carmel, March 12, 1889

Jesus †

Dear little Aunt,

I find it impossible for me to obey you, for it would be too difficult not to say *merci*! . . . How little a thing these five letters[1] are to express my gratitude to you, but dear Aunt, I beg you, understand all that your little daughter cannot say to you. Oh, Aunt, how kind you are! . . . And how I will pray for you. Alas, it is true that I am incapable of doing anything good, and instead of earning money, I know only how to lose it, and so dear little Aunt's loving attention has really touched me.[2] I couldn't get over seeing myself so rich all of a sudden without having done anything to earn so much money . . . . I can't help smiling when thinking that, thanks to *my* kind relatives, I am going to be able to supply the whole Community with fish . . . .

I trust, dear Aunt, that you will thank dear Uncle for me and express my gratitude to him.

God must love you, dear Aunt, very specially when making you

suffer in this way; however, if He were to answer me, you would never be sick again, for I would be happy if He were to send me all the pains that He reserves for you.

Alas! dear Aunt, may my letter go a little way in expressing the sentiments of my heart . . . . I should like to be able to show you all my gratitude!. . .

How kind Jesus is in allowing us, in the cruel trial He is sending, the consolation of seeing our sorrow shared and understood by our kind relatives!. . .

I kiss little Jeanne and also my little *mistress* of the house[3] with my whole heart.

Adieu, dear little Aunt. I thank you once again and dear Uncle, too, and I kiss you very tenderly.

Your very grateful little daughter,

Sister Thérèse of the Child Jesus
nov.carm.ind.

* Autograph in four fragments; CE and CMG.

1. The letters of the word "*merci.*"
2. "Aunt had paid for a work done by Thérèse." (Note of Sister Geneviève in CMG III, p. 207.)
3. This was Marie Guérin; see her letter to Léonie, March 14, 1889: "My role as mistress of the house is very serious." Marie Guérin was paying regular visits to Les Buissonnets in the absence of Céline and Léonie. This letter of March 14th gave a detailed account: meeting the laundry women who came to pick up the wash, recommendations to "père Guéret," the gardener, inspection of the rabbits, hens, and pigeons, and also the dog: "Poor Tom was so happy to see me that he broke his collar."

LT 85 **From Thérèse to Céline.**

March 12,
1889

J. M. J. T.

Carmel, March 12, 1889

(Long live Jesus!... How good it is to vow oneself to Him, and to sacrifice oneself for His love).[1]...

Céline!... This dear name echoes sweetly at the bottom of my heart!... Don't our hearts answer each other perfectly?...

I have a need this evening to come with my Céline in order to plunge myself into infinity.... I have to forget this earth.... Here below, everything tires me, everything is a burden to me.... I find only one joy, that of suffering for Jesus, but this *unfelt* joy is above every other joy!...

Life is passing away.... Eternity is advancing in great strides.... Soon we shall live the very life of Jesus.... After having drunk at the fountain of all sorrows, we shall be deified at the very fountain of all joys, all delights.... Soon, little sister, with one look, we shall be able to understand what is taking place within the inner depths of our being!...

The image of this world IS PASSING AWAY.[2]... Soon we shall see new heavens, and a more radiant Sun will light up with its splendors ethereal oceans and infinite horizons![3]... Immensity will be our domain.... We shall no longer be prisoners on this earth of exile.... All will have PASSED AWAY!... With our heavenly Spouse, we shall sail on lakes without any shores.... Infinity has no limits, no bottom, no shore![4]... (Courage, Jesus can hear the very last echo of our sorrow.)[5] Our harps, at this moment, are hung on the willows which border the river of Babylon.[6]... But on the day of our deliverance, what songs will be heard... with what joy shall we make the strings of our instruments vibrate!...

Jesus' love for Céline can be understood only by Jesus!... Jesus has done foolish things for Céline.... Let Céline do *foolish things* for Jesus.... Love is repaid by love alone, and the *wounds* of love are healed only by love.[7]

Let us really offer our sufferings to Jesus to save souls, poor souls!... They have less grace than we have, and still all the Blood of a God was shed to save them .... And yet Jesus wills to make their salvation depend on one sigh from our heart .... What a mystery! If one sigh can save *a soul,* what can sufferings like ours not do?... Let us refuse Jesus nothing!...

The bell is ringing and I haven't yet written to poor Léonie. Give her my suggestions, kiss her, and tell her that I love her!... Let her be *very faithful* to grace, and Jesus will bless her. Let her ask Jesus what I want to say to her. I entrust Him with my messages!...

See you soon!... Oh , heaven, heaven. When shall we be there?

Jesus' little *grain of Sand*

* Autograph.

1. See letter of P. Pichon to Thérèse, LC 108, January 10, 1889.
2. 1 Corinthians 7: 31.
3. Lamennais, *Une voix de prison*; see LT 60, note 2, August 23, 1888.
4. Arminjon, *op. cit.*, p. 300; without quoting them textually, this letter has also other quotes from this author, especially from the seventh Conference: "Concerning Eternal Happiness and the Supernatural Vision of God."
5. See P. Pichon to Sister Marie of the Sacred Heart: "Confidence! Jesus hears the very last echo of our sorrow." (Letter of December 27, 1888.)
6. See Psalm 136: 1-2.
7. St. John of the Cross, *Explanation of the Spiritual Canticle*, stanza 9 and 11. See LT 109, note 3, July 27-29, 1890.

LD *From Céline to her sisters Agnes of Jesus, Marie of the Sacred Heart, and Thérèse.* (Fragments.)

March 13, 1889

Knowing that we are at Caen, near him, Papa does not feel deserted; each day the Sister reminds him that we are here and

that we come every day looking for news about him. This seems to please him.

He thinks very often of us and has only good things to say about us; sometimes he cries when speaking about his children. Dear Sisters, don't be sad; alas! I know I am saying this in vain, for the heart cannot refrain from suffering and being very sad. If it were possible, I would like to gather all Papa's tears in a golden vase, and, to save a single one of these very dear tears, I would joyfully do my utmost.

Papa was very, very pleased with your letters.[1] They did him much good; he improved all day and he seemed to take on new courage. They made him look upon the situation as a trial of a great friend of God, and these thoughts gave him strength. Write him, then, often, as often as you want, for the least thing does him some good. You know how a single thought is sometimes enough for Papa.

March 13

* CMG.

1. See letter of Sister Marie of the Sacred Heart to Céline and Léonie: "Let me know if it would please Papa to receive a note from us. Perhaps it is better not to awaken memories of us; you will let me know, little Céline" (March 10-12, 1889). Around the 11th of March, Sister Agnes wrote: "You will place Papa's letters in an envelope with the picture, won't you?" (Letter to Céline, March (?), 1889.) None of the letters from the Carmel were preserved.

LC 110 *From Céline to Thérèse.* (Fragments.)

March 13, 1889
→LT 85

My dear little Thérèse,

I cannot refrain from putting in a little note for you.[1] If you only knew the good your letter did to me. . . . Oh! I have too much

in my heart to tell you everything.... My heart is filled with love for my dear little sister. Jesus' little atom loves Jesus' little grain of sand so much!... Your letter and those from Marie and Pauline are nourishment for my soul, they are my treasures; I feel enriched by them, my broken-down courage is renewed, and I take on strength again.... Oh, dear little sister, thank you....

If you only knew what I dreamt the other night! You had just died a martyr; a man had taken you into a woods to kill you. With envy, I saw you leave for martyrdom.... I was awaiting what was going to happen when suddenly we saw a light smoke arising to heaven, and then a bird sang. We said to ourselves: the sacrifice is accomplished! Thérèse is a martyr..... My heart leapt at this news: And what about me! Am I going to be separated from my Thérèse? Oh! no, this could not be; there was something which gave me hope for the same blessing. As I was wandering in the countryside, a little boy, a shoemaker's apprentice, jumped on me and plunged his awl several times into my throat. I was so happy that I had no thought of running away, but, the child being undoubtedly too weak, I did not die. However, his rage increased more and more, and he ended up by tearing out my eyes.[2] This time I collapsed but saying always: more, more!... I wanted more, but I didn't end up dying; I was envying your lot when, after having undergone all these horrors, I awakened, and I greatly regretted that this dream was not a reality. No doubt, it was a time of persecution, but, you see, these were unknown martyrdoms, you killed in a woods and I by the hand of a child. All the same, you won't fail to say to yourself: I can see that she wasn't suffering when she was always wanting more! It's true that in my dream I was trying to suffer and I couldn't, so it's not surprising then that I wanted more sufferings.

Dear little sister, in spite of what is very unlikely in this dream, I assure you that it said something to my heart.... You know what it is, you can guess what it is.... No, we two cannot be separated.[3]...

....

. . . like you: let us suffer, suffer, and not cease suffering. . . . Let us give our whole life, all our blood, all the strength of our soul and our heart for Jesus. . . . The Cross that we are carrying is very bitter!

Tell Marie and Pauline how much good their letters did me.

I have not yet received a letter from Father,[4] and you? Oh! you would have told me if you had received any?

I understood your whole letter. . . .

Another time I won't be so long without writing;[5] what held me back one day was M. Guérin's[6] visit. I thought she was going to give you the news. When you are surprised at not receiving a letter, think that there is nothing new and that the news is insignificant. At times, I have trouble getting any news; I have to keep questioning.

The little Atom is united to the Grain of sand in the Heart of Jesus.

A kiss for dear Mother.[7]

My heart is filled with "*mercis*" to little Marie and very dear Pauline. . . . I could be saying them until tomorrow morning and I would still not have begun to say what is in my heart. . . .

* Incomplete autograph.

1. Besides the collective letter of the same day (see preceding LD), perhaps written before the reception of the letters from Marie and Pauline, and for which Thérèse is asked to thank them?
2. See Thérèse's answer: "Let Jesus *tear* from us all that is most dear to us" (LT 86, March 15, 1889).
3. There is a line of dots ending the first side of the page of Céline's autograph copy. The top of the next page is cut off; judging by the format and the folds of the paper, we would say only one line of the manuscript is missing; the date on the first side, of course, was cut off, but it was replaced by Sister Geneviève (Céline). The typewritten copy made by Sister Geneviève, containing a few alterations when compared with the original, gives the following to fill in the missing line: ". . . and we are the only ones who understand the thirst

that Jesus has placed in our heart, the fire that consumes our heart *night and day*. . . . We two, all *alone*, knelt in the Colosseum, in the very place. . . . Oh! Thérèse, who knows if Our Lord has not destined us for martyrdom? Oh! yes, I say like you. . . ." It is evident this development exceeds a line of manuscript; hence, it is a later interpolation of Sister Geneviève, who is interpreting in 1950 her sentiments of 1889.

4. This is P. Pichon.
5. A relative delay; see note 6. Céline wrote on March 10: "For several days now Papa no longer asks to leave; he is resigned to stay as long as they like" (CMG IV, p. 193).
6. Marie Guérin, who mentioned this recent visit in her letter to Léonie, March 14, 1889. She is thanking them for a letter from Céline received that same March 14 and says she is "furious because of the long wait" which has been only since March 12. They all seemed to want a letter every day from Céline.
7. This is Mother Marie de Gonzague.

LT 86 From Thérèse to Céline.

March 15,
1889
→LC 110

J. M. J. T.

March 15, 1889

Jesus †

Thanks for your dear letter; it *pleased* the little grain of sand!. . .

In one of your letters, you were telling me recently that you were my shadow.[1] Alas! this would be very sad if it were true, for what is the shadow of a little grain of Sand?. . .

I thought of something better for my dear Céline; this idea of shadow pleased me; I said to myself that, in fact, my Céline had to be the shadow of something but what?. . . I was able to find

nothing in creation which could satisfy the idea I have of this reality of which my dear Céline should be the faithful shadow . . . . And it is Jesus Himself, who must be this *divine reality*! . . .

Yes, Céline must be herself the little shadow of Jesus . . . . What a humble and, nevertheless, glorious title, for what is a shadow? . . . But the shadow of Jesus, what a glory! . . .

What things I'd have to say regarding this little shadow of Jesus, but I have too little time, and so it is impossible! . . .

Céline's dream is very pretty, and perhaps one day it will be carried out . . . but, in the meanwhile, let us begin our martyrdom, let Jesus *tear* from us all that is most dear to us, and let us refuse Him nothing. Before dying by the sword, let us die by pinpricks . . . . Does Céline understand? . . .

The little grain of Sand is united in suffering to the little *shadow* of Jesus.

Sister Thérèse of the Child Jesus of the Holy Face
nov.carm.ind.

* Autograph.
1. See LD, March 1, 1889.

LT 87 **From Thérèse to Céline.**

April 4,
1889

J. M. J. T.

Carmel, April 4, '89

Jesus! . . .

Dear little Céline,

Your letter[1] gave great sadness to my soul! Poor little Papa[2]! . . . No, the thoughts of Jesus are not our thoughts, and His ways are not our ways[3] . . . .

He is offering us a chalice as bitter as our feeble nature can bear! . . . Let us not withdraw our lips from this chalice prepared by the hand of Jesus . . . .

Let us see life as it really is . . . . It is a moment between two *eternities*[4] . . . . Let us suffer in *peace*! . . .

I admit that this word peace seemed a little strong[5] to me, but the other day, when reflecting on it, I found the secret of suffering in peace . . . . The one who says *peace* is not saying joy, or at least, *felt* joy . . . . To suffer in peace it is enough to will all that Jesus wills . . . . To be the spouse of Jesus we *must* resemble Jesus, and Jesus is all bloody,[6] He is crowned with thorns! . . .

"A thousand years in your eyes, Lord, are as yesterday, which has PASSED"[7]! . . .

"On the banks of the river of Babylon, we sat and wept when we remembered Sion . . . . We hung our harps on the willows in the fields . . . . Those who led us into captivity said to us: 'Sing for us one of the pleasant songs from Sion.' How could we sing the song of the Lord in a foreign land!" . . . Psalm of David[8] . . . .

No, let us not sing the canticles of heaven to creatures . . . . But, like Cecilia, let us sing a melodious canticle in our heart to our Beloved![9] . . .

The canticle of suffering united to His sufferings is what delights His Heart the most! . . .

Jesus is on fire with love for us . . . look at His adorable Face! . . . Look at His eyes lifeless and lowered! Look at His wounds . . . . Look at Jesus in His Face . . . . There you will see how He loves us.[10]

Sister Thérèse of the Child Jesus of the Holy Face
nov.carm.ind.

* Autograph.

1. This is either a letter to all her sisters in general, March 26 or 28, only a few fragments of which remain, or it is a personal letter to Thérèse, which is lost. At the end of her life, Sister Geneviève destroyed all the letters she (Céline) had addressed to Thérèse between March 13 and December 24, 1889.

2. Because of a calming sirup that was being administered to him, M. Martin's health improved from March 15 to 23; however, his health broke down when this treatment was suspended. The end of the month was rather bad for the patient (judging by a letter from Céline to Jeanne Guérin, March 29, 1889).
3. See Isaias 55:8.
4. A possible reference from the chapter of P. d'Argentan on Eternity? See LC 83, note 1.
5. This remark suggests that the "... let us suffer in peace" is not from Thérèse but from her meditation on it. It is perhaps a reference to the *Reflections* of P. Lamennais on the Imitation of Christ III, 47: "Let us wait; let us suffer in peace; the hour of rest is approaching." In these same *Reflections* we find the sentence: "Console yourself, my soul; listen, don't you hear in the distance the first murmur announcing the arrival of the Bridegroom?" (Quoted in part in Ms. C, p. 211.) This chapter is entitled: "We must be ready to suffer everything that is most painful for Eternal Life."
6. This is from the Vespers of the Divine Office on Thursday; they had begun the celebration of the feast of the *Precious Blood of Our Lord Jesus Christ*.
7. See psalm 89: 4.
8. See psalm 136: 1-4.
9. See the Divine Office for the feast of St. Cecilia, first response at Matins: "While the instruments were sounding, the virgin Cecilia was singing in her heart to the only Lord." See, too, LT 55, note 3. Sister Marie of the Angels, her mistress of novices, confirms Thérèse's spiritual outlook: "During this great sorrow (her father's illness), she enjoyed a profound peace, which explains her imperturbable calm when they brought her the worst news. It was during this great trial that she said to Mother Agnes of Jesus: 'Everything is singing in my heart just as it was in the heart of Saint Cecilia.'" (PA, 1145.)
10. The handwriting in this letter, almost upright, is usual for this period in her life.

LT 88 **From Thérèse to Marie Guérin.**

April 24, 1889

J. M. J. T.

Wednesday, April '89

Jesus †

My dear little Sister,

I'm coming to ask you for a favor, and it's to you I am addressing myself, for I know that Les Buissonnets, now, alas! deserted, was formerly your domain.

Do you recall a book which Mme. Tiffenne[1] had given me at the time of my First Communion? . . . It was entitled: "The Young Girl's Bouquet." This book must be in one of the drawers of the bureau belonging to poor little Father. I'd be very happy if I could have it as soon as possible, as well as another *smaller* book that the *Mesdemoiselles* Primois[2] had given me. It's a brown book surrounded with a gold border; I think these are meditations on the Eucharist.[3] This book is on one of the shelves of the cupboard in Céline's bedroom (the cupboard next to the door). Dear little sister, pardon me for asking you this favor! . . . If it were possible, you could perhaps explain to the maid what you want without going to Les Buissonnets yourself! . . .

It is incredible how now, it seems to me, our bonds have been tightened; it seems to me that after our terrible trial we are *Sisters* even more than before! . . .

If you only knew how *I love* you! . . . and how I think of all of you . . . . Oh! when we are suffering, it does so much good to have friendly hearts whose echo responds to our own sorrow! . . . How I thank Jesus for having given us such kind relatives . . . such good little sisters. Our poor little sisters *over there* were tireless the other day[4] when telling us all the good things you have done for them. I saw that my little Marie's *heart* had touched my Céline's *heart*, and this gave great joy to my poor *heart*, for I love my Marie so much! . . . All the compliments they give her would have trouble in measuring up to what I *think of her* myself.

I am hurrying like a little foolish thing without realizing that my pen cannot keep up with my heart and that, no doubt, I am going to have the embarrassment of not being able to be read.

Very dear little sister, kiss *all* those whom I love so much; thank them for having spoiled us at Easter with the good chocolate and the good fish . . . . Ah! I can't even think of the *fish*.[5] . . . Uncle had something so PATERNAL about him that day, something out of the ordinary! . . . Never will I forget that visit.

Your little sister, who loves you,

Sister Thérèse of the Child Jesus

* Autograph in seventeen fragments; CMG.

1. Mme. Tifenne, Léonie's godmother.
2. Marie and Jeanne Primois, friends of the Martin family.
3. *Perhaps* the book: *Le Mois Eucharistique* by Mme. Bourdon (Putois-Cretté, Paris, 1866)? We cannot state this with any certitude because the two books mentioned in this letter were given to Mother Marie de Gonzague's family.
4. Easter Monday, April 22. Céline had written on April 17: "We shall arrive on Saturday on the ten o'clock train . . . . We shall be able to see you only on Monday, but if our Mother so desires, I will arrive early for my little visit with Thérèse." (CMG IV, pp. 172-173.)
5. This gift of fish touched Thérèse, reminding her of her father, who used to be so happy when offering his catch of fish to the Carmelites.

LT 89 From Thérèse to Céline.

April 26, 1889

J. M. J. T.

Jesus†! . . . Carmel, April 26, '89

Jesus Himself is taking charge of saying HAPPY BIRTHDAY for His fiancée's twenty years![1] . . .

What a twentieth year fruitful in *sufferings*, in choice graces! Twenty years! an age filled with *illusion* . . . tell me what illusion are you leaving in the heart of my Céline?. . .

What memories between us!. . . It's a world of memories . . . . Yes, Jesus has His preferences; there are, in His garden, fruits which the Sun of His love ripens almost in the twinkling of an eye . . . . Why are we of this number?. . . A question filled with mystery . . . . What reason can Jesus give us? Alas! His reason is that He has no reason!. . . Céline! Let us make use of Jesus' preference which has taught us so many things in so few years, and let us neglect nothing that can please Him!. . . Ah! let us be adorned by the Sun of His *love*!. . . this sun is burning . . . let us be consumed by *love*!. . . St. Francis de Sales says: "When the fire of love is in a heart, all the furniture flies out the windows."[2] Oh! let us allow nothing . . . nothing in our heart except Jesus!. . .

Let us not believe we can love without suffering, without suffering much . . . . Our *poor* nature is there! and it isn't there for nothing!. . . Our nature is our riches, our means of earning our bread!. . . It is so precious that Jesus came on earth purposely to take possession of it.

Let us suffer the bitter pain, without courage!. . . (Jesus suffered in *sadness*! Without sadness would the soul suffer![3] . . .) And still we would like to suffer generously, grandly!. . . Céline! what an illusion!. . . We'd never want to fall?. . . What does it matter, my Jesus, if I fall at each moment; *I see* my weakness through this and this is a great gain for me . . . . *You can see* through this what I can do and now You will be more tempted to carry me in Your arms . . . . If You do not do it, it is because this pleases You to see me *on the ground* . . . . Then I am not going to be disturbed, but I shall always stretch out my arms suppliant and filled with love!. . . I cannot believe that You would abandon me!. . .

(It was *when* the saints were at the feet of Our Lord that they encountered their Crosses!. . .)[4]

Dear Céline, sweet echo of my soul!. . . If you only knew my misery!. . . Oh! if you only knew . . . . Sanctity does not consist in

saying beautiful things, it does not even consist in thinking them, in feeling them!... It consists in *suffering* and suffering *everything*. (Sanctity! We must conquer it at the point of the sword; we must *suffer* ... we *must agonize*!)[5] ...

A day will come when the shadows will disappear, and then there will remain only joy, inebriation....

Let us profit from our one moment of suffering!... Let us see only each moment!... A moment is a treasure ... one act of love will make us know Jesus better ... it will bring us closer to Him during the whole of *eternity*!...

Sister Thérèse of the Child Jesus of the Holy Face
nov.carm.ind.

* Autograph.
1. Céline was twenty years old on April 28.
2. See Camus, *Esprit de saint François de Sales*, III, 27; a sentence cited by P. Pichon in his second instruction of the seventh day, October 13, 1887; see VT, January 1968, page 68. This quotation from P. Pichon and the three following appear on a page of excerpts which Thérèse recopied at the beginning of 1889; see VT, April 1968, p. 140.
3. P. Pichon, retreat of 1887, conference for the seventh day.
4. P. Pichon, retreat of May 1888, Saturday evening, May 26, according to the notes of Sister Marie of Saint Joseph.
5. P. Pichon, same source as in note 4.

LC 111 *From P. Pichon to Thérèse.*

April 27, 1889
→ LT lost

† Lachine, April 27

My most dear Child
in Jesus Christ,

I challenge you ever to suffer as much from my silence[1] as I suffer from it myself. God preserve you from this! It is the most tor-

menting of my martyrdoms. I desire so much to shed all your tears, to drink long draughts with you from your whole bitter chalice!

If you only knew what my life is! I don't understand myself any longer in the whirlwind in which my dear apostolate engulfs me.

There is not one of your little sheets[2] that hasn't failed to touch me sweetly and console me interiorly. How kind Jesus is for having given me my very dear Benjamin. On your pages I read even what your pen is not writing, although your heart is saying it aloud. Do the same thing for me and understand my silence.

Love all that comes to you from Jesus, everything, even the most bitter gall, the sharpest thorns, your most filial agonies, the divine absences. Be obstinate in smiling at Our Lord just the same.[3]

Yes, you are right, it is better to love Jesus on His terms; there is more love on Calvary than on Thabor.

Yes, yes, take joy in being nothing since Jesus is all. Bless God that you feel nothing, possess nothing, find nothing in yourself.

How I approved your blessed vow of chastity.[4] What a joyous "alleluia" for my heart!

May Jesus acquire more and more a taste for our sacrifices, our incense, our myrrh! Is He not admirably kind in asking us for our tears?

All, even to the snow of your espousals,[5] appeared to me as a token of love from Jesus' Heart. Among all the letters, your loving letter of January 10 was dear and sweet to me.

Your new name[6] is rich in expectations. Alas! these expectations have been quickly carried out. Is not the martyrdom of the holy patriarch your wedding gift?

The great peace which you are enjoying is a treasure *par excellence* which Our Lord has bequeathed to us in His divine testament.[7] Be very grateful and guard this gift from God. May Jesus be ever free to sever us from our consolations and from all the most seductive Thabors. Your Calvary is worth more, dark as it is. . . . Open your eyes, and you will see me at your side. I shed every one of your tears. And every one of your prayers for the holy patriarch has an echo in my own heart.

No, no, don't doubt the Heart of Jesus; believe in His divine tenderness; proclaim His love!

I bless you just as a most loving father blesses his Benjamin.

Almire Pichon

I enclose you, along with the Lamb[8] and the Lion,[9] within the Heart of Jesus.

* Autograph.

1. P. Pichon's previous letter was written on January 10, 1889 (see LC 108).
2. If Thérèse was really faithful to her monthly letters (see Ms. A, p. 151), then P. Pichon had at hand at least four letters from her, counting the one of January 10.
3. See LC 92, note 6.
4. We know nothing about the date and circumstances of this private vow of chastity; the testimonies at the process of beatification and canonization are silent on this point.
5. See Ms. A, p. 152.
6. Her title "of the Holy Face."
7. See John 14:27.
8. Sister Agnes of Jesus.
9. See LT 75, note 1.

LT 90 From Thérèse to Céline.

April 27 (?), 1889

For April 28

J. M. J. T.

Once again, I want to wish my dear Céline a Happy Birthday,[1] and I am sending her a little bouquet from little Jesus. He thanks her for all the beautiful flowers that she has given to Him.[2] Alas! these flowers are not bright, for Carmel's little Jesus is poor;

however, in heaven, He will show us His riches, and I know well the one to whom He will give these riches . . . .

Tomorrow, I shall receive my Jesus![3] Oh! how I'll speak to Him about my Céline, about that other *myself.* I'll have many things to tell Him, but it will not be difficult for me because a single sigh will tell Him all.

What scribbling this is! But I went so fast that you will have to excuse me. I'd like my heart and all that it holds for you to be known to you; however, there are things that cannot be written and that the heart alone understands.

(The bouquet from Jesus spent a few hours before Him in a vase even poorer than He is! . . .)

Dear Céline, one day we shall go to heaven forever, and then there will no longer be day or night as there is on earth . . . . . Oh! what a joy. Let us walk in peace, looking at heaven, the ONLY goal of our works. The hour of rest is approaching. Kiss Léonie for me whom I love so much. I am not forgetting the day of her twenty-five years.[4] Since I've been in Carmel I have a good memory for dates.

See you soon, Céline,[5] immortelle of Jesus . . . . I love you more than I can say.

Your little sister,
Thérèse of the Child Jesus

* Autograph.

1. Thérèse had already wished this on April 26; see LT 89.
2. Flowers to decorate the statue of the Child Jesus in the Cloister.
3. Her Communion on Sunday; daily Communion was not in vogue even in the Carmel.
4. Thérèse makes a mistake, for Léonie will be twenty-six years old on June 3. The number "26" is written over this by a strange hand.
5. April 28, Céline announced her visit for Saturday, May 4. Marie Guérin wrote to Céline on May 1: "You will come, then, to celebrate with us the centenary anniversary of the convocation of the *Etats Généraux*, on May 5. There will be a big celebration at Lisieux,

torchlight procession with drums, fireworks, etc., etc." Céline wrote for the last time from Caen, May 8: "I thought of little Thérèse and little Pauline today. . . . ." (Reference to May 8, 1884.) Léonie and Céline returned definitively to Lisieux on May 14.

LC 112 *From Sister Marie of the Sacred Heart to Thérèse.*

End of May (?), 1889 Uncertain date; see note 1.

My dear little lamb, I don't want my retreat[1] to pass without saying a little word to you.

Pray much for me so that I become a saint, for it is only this that remains to us at the end of our life . . . . Then we shall regret not having suffered the *martyrdom of our heart*! Then we shall bless the Cross that makes us weep so much today. Then our dear Father, clothed in *glory* measured by his humiliations and his sorrows, will come to us and will be able to call us better than ever before: "my Diamond," "my fine Pearl," and "my Queen." The diamond will have been purified in trial, the fine pearl will shine among all the pearls, and the little Queen, dressed in the white robe of Virgins, will be truly Queen forever!

Dear little lamb, all passes, all passes! The night of life will come just as the night of this day and the morning of eternity will be without a night and a tomorrow! A note to your poor big sister; Sister Marie of the Angels has permitted me this.[2] Console me a little, my heart is sad in spite of everything when I think of our dear little Father. Above all, don't write me this evening; you have to sleep.

* Autograph.

1. It is difficult to be precise about the date of this retreat in 1889; the normal time would be around May 22, the anniversary of Sister Marie of the Sacred Heart's Profession. But this note has as back-

ground the disposal of the furniture at Les Buissonnets (see LT 91, note 4), and this took place in October 1889. Because of the work on the house for the Externs (see LD, end of January 1889, note 5), there was no preached retreat in October 1889. Would Sister Marie of the Sacred Heart have said anything here about her annual retreat? We have preferred to leave this note and Thérèse's answer in the month of May.

2. The newly professed used to live in the novitiate quarters for three years after making their vows; the mistress of novices' permission was necessary for spiritual exchanges.

LT 91 **From Thérèse to Sister Marie of the Sacred Heart.**

End of May (?), 1889
→LC 112

Uncertain date; see LC 112, note 1.

J. M. J. T.

Jesus †

Dear Lion, thank you, thank you!... What do you want the little lamb to tell you?... Wasn't it instructed by you?... Do you remember the time when, seated in the *big chair*, holding me on your knees, you were speaking to me about heaven?[1] ... I can still hear you saying to me: "Look at the merchants, how much trouble they go to in order to earn money, and we can gather treasures for heaven at each moment without giving ourselves any trouble; we have only to gather diamonds with a RAKE."

And I went off, my heart filled with joy, filled with good resolutions!... Without you, perhaps I'd not be in Carmel!...

Time has passed since those blessed moments that slipped away in our sweet nest.... Jesus has come to visit us.... He has found us worthy to pass through the crucible of suffering....

Before my entrance into Carmel, our *incomparable* Father

said when giving me to God: "I would like to have something better to offer to God." Jesus has listened to his prayer. . . that other better thing was *himself*![2] . . . What a joy for a *moment* of suffering. . . . It *is the Lord* who has done this.[3] . . . And the Lord loves Papa incomparably better than we love Papa; he is God's little child. And God, in order to spare him *great* sufferings, wills that we suffer for him! . . .

It is up to us to thank Him! . . .

Dear Lion, life will pass very quickly. In heaven, it will make no difference to us when we see that all the *relics* of Les Buissonnets have been carried off here and there![4] . . . What does earth matter? . . .

Your little daughter, whom you reared! . . .

Sister Thérèse of the Child Jesus of the Holy Face
nov.carm.ind.

* Autograph.

1. See Ms. A, p. 74.
2. This sentence was recalled on the death card of M. Martin in 1894: "God has honored me by asking for all my children; I am giving them to Him joyfully. If I possessed anything better, I would be eager to offer it to Him."
3. See Psalm 117: 23.
4. Some articles of the furniture at Les Buissonnets were given to the Carmel. During this same retreat of Sister Marie of the Sacred Heart, Sister Agnes of Jesus wrote her: "Are you going to be always crying about what you will smile at for all eternity? Let Les Buissonnets be stripped of its furniture, let everything crumble, let what is perishable, perish." (Note without a date; May [?] 1889.) We should note that the Guérin family was living temporarily at *la maison Sauvage*, 16, *rue Condorcet* (from March 25, 1889, according to ChrIG, p. 37). The Guérins left there on June 7 and came to live at Les Buissonnets (same source, p. 38), while they were waiting to move to the house at 19, *rue de la Chaussée* (today, *rue Paul-Banaston*). This house was bought by M. Guérin the preceding April 20.

No doubt, then, it was necessary to make room at Les Buissonnets for the new arrivals. There was another disposal of furniture a short time before October 21, 1889: "I was unable to refrain from crying when I saw them moving out these old remains from Les Buissonnets that recalled a thousand memories, and poor Tom following the wagons." (Letter of Sister Marie of the Sacred Heart, October 1889.) With reference to this breaking up of the home in October, Sister Geneviève (Céline) wrote: "Once inside the cloister, the faithful Tom raised his ears, then, looking in all directions as if to get his bearings, he sprang on his little mistress [Thérèse was in the cloister yard], leaping up at her face and making a thousand bounds in all directions. She was obliged to lift her large veil and hide Tom under it, for he could not control his joy. . . . She was forced to tear herself away from all this, so great was her emotion." (CMG III, p. 103.)

LC 113 *From Marie Guérin to Thérèse.*

May 29, 1889

The Guérin family, accompanied by Céline and Léonie, visited the Paris Exhibition from May 23 to 31 (ChrIG, p. 38). This letter seems to be a continuation of some written or spoken confidences of Marie to her cousin Thérèse; we have no trace, however, of these confidences.

May 29, '89

My dear Thérèse,

I am coming again to bother you, and I know in advance that you are not going to be pleased with me, but what do you expect, I am suffering so much that it does me good to pour all my pains into your heart. Paris was not made for healing the scrupulous;[1] I no longer know where to turn my eyes. If I flee from one nudity, I meet another, and so it goes on all day long. It's enough to make you die of sorrow; it seems to me I do this out of curiosity, I have to be looking everywhere. It seems to me that it is to see evil. I don't know if you will understand me; I have so much in my poor

head that I don't know how to sort it out. Neither does the demon fail to bring to my mind all these evil things that I saw during the day, and this is another subject of torment. How do you expect me to receive Holy Communion tomorrow and Friday? I am obliged to abstain from it; this is the great trial, for never have I felt so much love for Holy Communion. I feel that I would be flooded with consolations; I would feel fortified if I could have God in my heart. Otherwise, my poor heart is so empty; it is filled with sadness, and nothing can distract me. Oh! what a city Paris is; one is much happier in the little house on the *rue Condorcet*.[2] Do you know where I feel the most joy? It is when I am in Church; at least, there, I can rest my eyes on the Tabernacle. I feel at home, and all the rest is not made for me; I don't know how one can live here. As far as I am concerned, this is a veritable hell.

I am sorry, dear Thérèse, for not having written you earlier. At least, you would have been able to answer me, and this would have done me so much good to be consoled a little. However, I would really like to receive a little note of consolation when I return to Lisieux, if this is not asking too much, and if you can't answer me at Paris; to do this you would have to write me tomorrow, Thursday,[3] in order for me to receive the letter on Friday morning. On Friday night, I shall be in the city of my birth, and it is the best of all. I look upon Paris with horror.

Pray for your little sister Marie, who loves you with her whole heart.

Pay my respects, I beg you, to Mother Marie de Gonzague and Mother Geneviève, and recommend me to their good prayers. Kiss Marie and Pauline for me.

* Autograph.

1. Marie Guérin retained this scrupulosity for a long time; see LC 130, May 23-25, 1890; and LC 183, June 2, 1897.
2. This was the temporary home of the Guérin family at Lisieux; see LT 91, note 4.
3. This is what Thérèse will do; see LT 92.

LT 92 **From Thérèse to Marie Guérin.**

May 30,
1889
→LC 113

J. M. J. T.

Thursday, May 30, 1889

Jesus †

My dear little Sister,

You did well to write me, and I understand *everything* . . . *everything, everything, everything*! . . .

You haven't committed the *shadow of any evil*; I know what these kinds of temptations are so well that I can assure you of this without any fear, and, besides, Jesus tells me this in the depths of my heart. . . . We must despise all these temptations and pay no attention whatsoever to them.

Should I tell you something that has given me *much* sorrow? . . .

It is that my little Marie has given up her Communions . . . on the feast of the Ascension[1] and on the last day of Mary's month! . . . Oh! what sorrow this has caused Jesus! . . .

The devil has to be very clever to mislead a soul in this way! . . . But don't you know, my dear, that this is the only goal of his desires? The evil one knows well that he can't make a soul that wants to belong totally to Jesus commit a sin, so he tries to make the soul believe it has. It is already much for him to put disturbance in this soul, but to satisfy his rage something else is needed; he wants to deprive Jesus of a loved tabernacle, and, not being able to enter this sanctuary, he wants, at least, that it remain *empty* and without any Master! . . . Alas, what will become of this poor heart? . . . When the devil has succeeded in drawing the soul away from Holy Communion, he *has won everything* . . . . And Jesus weeps! . . .

Oh, my darling, think, then, that Jesus is there in the Tabernacle expressly for *you*, for *you alone*; He is burning with the desire to enter your heart . . . so don't listen to the devil, mock him, and go without any fear to receive Jesus in peace and love! . . .

However, I hear you saying to me: "Thérèse is saying this because she doesn't know . . . she doesn't know I really do it on purpose . . . it pleases me . . . and so I cannot receive Communion since I believe I would commit a sacrilege, etc., etc., ..." Yes, your poor little Thérèse does know; I tell you that she understands it *all*, and she assures you that you can go without any fear to receive your only true Friend . . . . She, too, has passed through the *martyrdom* of scruples,[2] but Jesus has given her the grace to receive Communion just the same, even when she believed that she had committed *great sins* . . . . And so I assure you that she knew this was the sole means of ridding herself of the devil, for when he sees that he is losing his time, he leaves you in peace! . . .

No, it is IMPOSSIBLE that a heart "which rests only at the sight of the Tabernacle" offend Jesus to the point of not being able to receive Him; what offends Him and what wounds His Heart is the lack of confidence! . . .

Little sister, before I received your letter, I had a presentiment of your anxiety; my heart was united to your heart. Last night, in my dreams, I tried to console you, but, alas! I was unable to succeed! . . . I am not going to be any more fortunate today unless Jesus and the Blessed Virgin come to my help; I hope my desire will be fulfilled and that on the last day of her month, the Blessed Virgin will heal my dear little sister. But for this you must pray, *pray very much*. If you could only place a candle at *Notre-Dame-des-Victoires*[3] . . . I have so much confidence in her? . . .

Your heart is made to love Jesus, to love Him passionately; pray so that the *beautiful years of your life* may not pass by in chimerical fears.

We have only the short moments of our life to love Jesus, and

the devil knows this well, and so he tries to consume our life in useless works . . . .

Dear little sister, *receive Communion often*, very often.[4] . . . That is the *only remedy* if you want to be healed, and Jesus hasn't placed this attraction in your soul for nothing. (I believe that He would be pleased if you could receive the two Communions you missed, for, then, the devil's victory would be less great since he would not have succeeded in separating Jesus from your heart.) Have no fear of loving the Blessed Virgin *too much*, you will *never* love her enough, and Jesus will be pleased since the Blessed Virgin is His Mother.

Adieu, little sister; pardon my scribbling which I can't even read over since I don't have the time. Kiss all my dear ones for me.[5]

Thérèse of the Child Jesus
nov.carm.ind.

* Autograph.

1. That same day, May 30.
2. From May 1885 to the autumn of 1886; see Ms. A, p. 84 and p. 93. See Conrad de Meester's analysis in *Dynamique de la confiance, Genèse et structure de la voie d'enfance spirituelle chez sainte Thérèse de Lisieux* (Ed. du Cerf, 1969), pp. 407-411.
3. See LT 30, note 2.
4. On October 29, 1910, Monseigneur de Teil, vice postulator for the cause of beatification and canonization of Sister Thérèse of the Child Jesus, in a special audience with Pius X, asked him to read this letter, cited in Articles, p. 55: "Most Holy Father, this little saint has made a commentary in advance on your Holiness' decree on frequent Communion." In the course of his reading of the letter, Pius X said: "*Est opportunissimum! Est magnum gaudium pro me.*" (This is most opportune! It's a great joy for me.") And he ended his talk with the vice postulator by saying: "*Bisogna far presto questo Processo.*" ("We must hurry this cause.") See DCL.
5. We still have a fragment of the envelope addressed by Thérèse to "Mademoiselle Marie Guérin 17 Hôtel d'Orléans rue Richelieu Paris."

"The blood-stained Face of Jesus" (LT 95)
(July–October 1889)
Age sixteen

The months passed by, and the hope for M. Martin's cure gradually dimmed. His daughters had to learn to live with the poignant pain in their heart. Thérèse, who had cast aside "resignation" (LT 65), was not content with passive acceptance; she was at all times totally aware of the event, and, hence, her immense capacity for suffering.

From her suffering, there came cries of distress: "Oh! how hard it is to live" (LT 94); "I am suffering" (LT 95). But she recovers immediately, sustained by the hope of heaven, the eternal face to face vision of God (LT 94 and 95). The expression, encountered in her reading of Abbé Arminjon, took on a special significance for Thérèse, and she longs to take flight to the Face of Jesus (LT 96, note 3).

The influence of the Carmelite of Tours, Sister Marie de Saint-Pierre, is perceptible in the correspondence of the time (LT 95, note 5). A picture received from Mother Marie de Gonzague (see LT 98) stimulated Thérèse's piety in this same direction. This was a picture of the blood-stained Face of Jesus. We can still read these lines from the printed text: "Speak, my Jesus! speak . . . what must I do to console You?" And Jesus answers: "What I want from you, faithful Soul, is LOVE*. . . . Humble love that reduces self to nothing . . . generous love that forgets self." To reduce herself to nothing, to forget herself in order to console Jesus, this was Thérèse's ambition. When in January 1889 she admitted she had an ardent thirst for joy and love (LT 75), from now on the perspective was reversed:*

it was up to her to quench the thirst of her Beloved (*LT 96, 98, etc.*).

To this time in her life belong, par excellence, those confidences in her Manuscript that state: "The little flower transplanted to Mount Carmel was to expand under the shadow of the Cross. The tears and blood of Jesus were to be its dew, and its Sun was His adorable Face veiled in tears . . . . I thirsted for suffering and to be forgotten . . . . " (*Ms. A, p. 151–152*).

In a letter written during a private retreat in the month of July or August, Sister Agnes of Jesus confirmed her sister in these aspirations (*LC 115*).

One evening of this same summer of 1889, Thérèse was the recipient of a mystical grace that she experienced in the grotto of Saint Mary Magdalene in the monastery cemetery. She explained that this grace was followed by several days of "quietude": "It was as though a veil had been cast over all the things of this earth for me . . . . I was entirely hidden under the Blessed Virgin's veil. At this time, I was put in charge of the refectory, and I recall doing things as though not doing them; it was as if someone had lent me a body. I remained this way for one whole week" (*CJ 11.7.2*).

In September or October, during the absence of the sacristan and the Sisters in charge of the turn, the sweeping of the outside chapel was entrusted to two novices, Sister Martha of Jesus and Sister Thérèse. One day, the latter, "seized by an impulse of love, went and knelt at the altar, knocked at the door of the Tabernacle, and said: 'Are You there, Jesus; answer me, I beg You'" (*Sister Martha of Jesus, PA, 1273*).

LC 114 *From Marie Guérin to Thérèse.*

July 10 1889

Marie was on vacation at *La Musse*, from July 6 to 20 (ChrIG, p. 38), at the château inherited from M. David the year before (see LT 62, note 4, September 1888).

Your little Marie has obtained permission to write you, and her letter will not be read.[1] I really see God's will here, for He wills me to seek consolation in the heart of my little Thérèse. If you only knew how I thank you for having wanted me to confide in Céline.[2] I obeyed you that same evening, and I opened my whole soul to her, and there isn't even a shadow hidden from her. I cast everything into her heart, and now my soul is an open book for her. What balm for my poor heart; I felt that I was understood, loved, and consoled!!! I don't know how I was able to live thus far always withdrawn into myself, not having anyone to whom I could confide my pains. I used to have to wait two weeks for consolations from the Carmel, and then in a half-hour[3] I could only speak of what was most urgent. There are always some little sufferings in my heart, mere nothings, and I compare these to thorns which, though they are little, wound one more deeply than big thorns; however, these troubles I don't have time to talk about, and I have to keep them to myself.

Dear little sister, I am going to tell you something that will really please you, I am much less scrupulous. There is, however, a point on which I have been very much tormented. It was on the eve of one of my Communions, and I feared or rather I was sure that I committed my sin (you understand, don't you).[4] I found that I was not worthy to go to receive God, and I was not able to find Mamma in order to have her share in my troubles, and so I told Céline everything. Did I do well, I don't really know? I always made sufficient reflections on this matter; I feared that this may give some thoughts to Céline. I was thinking that perhaps I should not tell my sins to everybody, and, then, since M. l'abbé Domin[5] had forbidden me to speak to Jeanne about my scruples,

this prohibition was perhaps for Céline also. Well, Thérèse, if you want to give me some advice on this matter, this will be one less great weight on my conscience. I don't want to leave you with the belief that I am gravely concerned; oh! no, I am very calm, and I am not over-worried, but it's just that I'll be very happy to have your approval. Beloved little sister, you may write me without any fear, for your letter will be for me alone. Oh! how I love you!!! Allow me to tell you this, it gives such consolation to my heart. Oh, yes! I have a heart that I feel only too much, it has too much ardor; when it loves, its love has no limits. At times, I feel that my body is too narrow to contain it. There is between us an affection that isn't of this earth; we are united through the bonds of the soul. How sweet this affection is; nothing can describe it, and the word "sister," which is, nevertheless, one of the sweetest names, is not the expression we must use.

Well, yes, Thérèse, God is pleased to break my heart; when He wills to make me suffer, it is always to my heart that He turns. My lot is interior sufferings. At times, I feel as though I am abandoned; I am experiencing a deadly *ennui*. You should not believe I love life, no, I'm meeting only with disappointments. There are some persons who would be in their glory if they had a château and if they had all they desired; let them come, then, to my place, I'll grant it to them gladly. As for myself, there is no place where I'd be happier than at Les Buissonnets.[6]

I'd like you to recommend my vocation to God; pray especially for this. I can see that I'm not at the end of my sufferings. If God wills to catch me in His nets as you have already told me, I would throw myself into them with love. I have only one fear, to be mistaken.[7] Trials are beginning, and they haven't ended; I don't see the future with a happy outlook. I am passing through a moment of great loathing, and I haven't the courage for anything. I used to desire so much to receive Holy Communion more than twice a week, and, this week, when this was granted to me, I am finding no taste whatsoever for Communion; I shall even say that my thanksgivings could not be more arid.

Dear litle sister, I recommend myself to your prayers, and I tell you that I love you with all my heart.

Kiss your sisters for me.

Offer my respects to Mother Marie de Gonzague and Mother Geneviève.

Marie

July 10, '89

* Autograph.

1. She meant here that the letter would not be read by her mother, who usually read her daughters' mail, according to the custom of those times.
2. Judging by LT LXXII, p. 131, no. 2 (ed. 1948), ". . . it was upon the advice of P. Pichon, S.J., that Marie Guérin was entrusted to Céline." We have no written trace of this advice. Marie Guérin never had P. Pichon as a spiritual director, but he was aware of the friendship between the two cousins, approved it, and regretted the restrictions imposed on it: "I deeply regret that they are hindering her from confiding everything to you, even her scruples. There is nothing better than the theological counsels and solutions which Jesus was dictating to you for her. I really like your theology, your excellent simplicity which preserves you from all scruples. Continue to travel your road uprightly and with simplicity." (Fragment of the autograph of P. Pichon to Céline, October 1, 1889.)
3. This was the customary length of a visit.
4. Probably these were troubles pertaining to purity; see LC 113, May 29, 1889 and LT 92, the answer.
5. This was the chaplain at the Benedictine Abbey; Marie had kept him as her confessor after she had left the boarding school (1885).
6. The temporary residence of the Guérin family; see LT 91, note 4, end of May 1889.
7. The final doubts of Marie Guérin regarding her vocation to Carmel ended on September 24, 1890, the day Thérèse received the Veil.

LT 93 **From Thérèse to Marie Guérin.**

July 14,
1889
→LC 114

J. M. J. T.

Sunday, July 14, '89

Jesus †

My dear little Sister,

Since you have the humility to ask advice from your little Thérèse, she cannot refuse you, but the poor little novice without any experience would fear making a mistake, and you yourself could have some doubts about what she tells you. But, today, have no fear, this is the answer of Jesus Himself that I am bringing you . . . . Oh! how happy I am to transmit it to you . . . .

This morning, I asked our good Mother what I should answer you regarding what you said to Céline. In doing what this dear Mother told me for you, you will have no fear of making a mistake, for God has placed in her heart a deep knowledge of souls and all their miseries. She knows *all*; *nothing* is hidden from her, your little soul is perfectly known by her. This is what she told me to tell you *from Jesus*: "*You did very well* to tell Céline everything; however, it is better not to converse about these things, it is better to pay no attention whatsoever to them, for our Mother is sure that you are doing no wrong." So, are you reassured?. . . It seems to me that, in your place, if she had said as much to me, I would have been cured, and I would have allowed myself to be led blindly, for this is the only way to have any peace and, especially, to please Jesus.

Even if you were certain of doing something wrong, there is still no danger, for *our Mother,* who has (I think) more experience than *you,* is telling you that you haven't done any wrong. . . .

Oh! Marie, how fortunate you are to have a heart that can *love*

in this way . . . . Thank Jesus for having given you such a precious gift, and give Him your heart *totally*. Creatures are too little to fill the *immense void* that Jesus has dug out in your heart, don't give them any place in your soul . . . .

God will not catch you in His nets, for you are already imprisoned within them . . . .

Yes, it is really true that our affection is not of this *earth*, it is too strong for that; even death would not be capable of breaking it . . . .

Don't be troubled about feeling no consolation in your Communions; this is a trial that you must bear with love. Don't lose any of the *thorns* you are meeting every day; with one of them you can *save a soul*! . . .

Ah, if you only knew how much God is offended! Your soul is so well made for consoling Him . . . love Him to *folly* for all those who don't love Him! . . . Little sister, after its foolish race, my pen must stop. I have five letters to write today,[1] but I began with my little Marie . . . I love her so much and so *unselfishly*! . . . Kiss Uncle, Aunt, and my dear Jeanne, and tell them that I love them. And you, little privileged one of Jesus, pray that your unworthy little sister may love as much as you do, if that is possible! . . .

Sister Thérèse of the Child Jesus of the Holy Face
nov.carm.ind.

* Autograph.

1. One of these letters was addressed to Céline (LT 94). Another could have been for M. Martin; see Sister Costard to Mother Marie de Gonzague: "Our venerable patriarch is a little calmer these days. I gave him the little package from his dear Carmelites, and he seemed very happy . . . . He is really admirable; not only does he not complain, but he finds that everything we give him is perfect" (July 17, 1889; CMG IV, pp. 202-203).

LT 94 **From Thérèse to Céline.**

July 14,
1889

J. M. J. T.

Jesus † Carmel, July 14, '89

My dear Céline,

My soul doesn't leave you[1] . . . it suffers exile with you! . . . Oh! how hard it is to live, to remain on this earth of bitterness and anguish . . . . But, tomorrow . . . in an hour, we shall be at port, what joy! Ah, what a good it will be to contemplate Jesus *face to face* all through the *whole* of eternity! Always, always more love, always more intoxicating joys . . . a happiness without clouds.[2] . . .

What has Jesus done, then, to detach our souls from all that is created? Ah, He has struck a big blow . . . but it is a blow of love. God is admirable, but He is especially lovable; let us love Him, then . . . let us love Him enough to suffer for Him all that He wills, even spiritual pains, aridities, anxieties, apparent coldness . . . . Ah, here is great love, to love Jesus without feeling the sweetness of this love . . . this is martyrdom . . . . Well, then, *let us die as martyrs*. Oh! Céline . . . sweet echo of my soul, do you understand? . . . Unknown martyrdom, known to God alone, which the eye of the creature cannot discover, a martyrdom without honor, without triumph . . . . That is love pushed to the point of heroism . . . . But, one day, a grateful God will cry out: "Now, my turn."[3] Oh, what will we see then? . . . What is this life which will no more have an end? . . . God will be the soul of our soul . . . unfathomable mystery . . . . The eye of man has not seen the *uncreated* light, his ear has not heard the incomparable harmonies, and his heart cannot have any idea of what God reserves for those whom He loves.[4] And all this will come *soon*, yes, soon. Let us hurry to fashion our crown; let us stretch forth our hand to seize the palm. And if we love much, if we love Jesus with a passion, He will not be so cruel as to leave us for a long time on this earth of

exile . . . . Céline, during the SHORT MOMENTS that *remain to us,* let us not lose our time . . . let us save souls . . . souls are being lost like flakes of snow,[5] and Jesus weeps,[6] and we . . . we are thinking of our sorrow without consoling our Fiancé . . . . Oh, Céline, let us live for souls . . . let us be apostles . . . let us save especially the souls of priests;[7] these souls should be more transparent than crystal . . . . Alas, how many bad priests, priests who are not holy enough . . . . Let us pray, let us suffer for them, and, on the last day, Jesus will be grateful. We shall give Him souls! . . .

Céline, do you understand the cry of my soul? . . . Together . . . . Together, always, Céline and Thérèse of the Child Jesus
of the Holy Face
nov.carm.ind.

Sister Marie of the Sacred Heart cannot write you because the letter would weigh too much.

* Autograph.

1. Céline and Léonie are on vacation at *La Musse* with the Guérin family (see LC 114). After their return, they will live definitively with their aunt and uncle until May 1892.
2. See LT 95, the next to the last paragraph.
3. Abbé Arminjon, *op. cit.*, p. 290; see LT 57, note 3, July 23, 1888.
4. See 1 Corinthians 2:9. See LT 68, note 1, November 25, 1888.
5. P. d'Argentan, *op. cit.*, vol. II, pp. 83-84. The preceding year, Sister Agnes of Jesus had been impressed by the same sentence: "Père d'Argentan is very frightening in his description of hell and I feel myself shuddering and my hair standing on end. He says that souls fall into this place of eternal horror like flakes of snow on a winter's day! . . . It is frightening!" (Undated note; July 1888.) We can imagine that Thérèse was reading certain chapters from *Conférences théologiques et spirituelles sur les grandeurs de Dieu*, a work in the novices' library. See LT 96, note 2.
6. The tears of Jesus, frequently mentioned at this time (LT 95, LC 117, LT 98), are very evident on the picture of "Veronica's Veil," venerated at Tours and very much loved by Thérèse (CJ 5.8.7 and 5.8.9, note 3).

7. This is the first time concern for priests is shown in Thérèse's writings. In 1895, she wrote that it was during her trip to Italy that she understood the "principal end of the Carmelite Reform" (Ms. A, p. 122). In her canonical examination on September 2, 1890 (LC 136), she explained: "I came to save souls and especially to pray for priests" (Ms. A, p. 149). In her correspondence of 1889-1890 with Céline, this theme is repeated: "Let us pray for priests" (LT 94, 96, 101, 108, 122; see also LT 201, November 1, 1896, concerning September 8, 1890). The experience of the trip to Rome, which the two sisters underwent together, made them aware of the main apostolate of the Reformed Carmel; see Saint Teresa of Avila: "Let the Carmelite nuns all be devoted to praying for preachers and theologians" (Way of Perfection, ch. 1). We don't know how much the Carmel of Lisieux was influenced at this time by the appeals of Thérèse Durnerin in favor of priests. In 1889-1890, 200,000 copies of her brochure *L'Hostie et le Prêtre* and her eight pamphlets (Thérèse was acquainted with at least the third one, see LT 101, note 4) were distributed and principally to the Carmels of France. Concerning this apostolate, see Msgr. Laveille, *Thérèse Durnerin, Fondatrice de la Societé des Amis des Pauvres*, 1848-1905 (Ed. Téqui, Paris 1922, pp. 54, 68, 72-74).

LT 95 **From Thérèse to Sister Agnes of Jesus.**

July-August (?), 1889

During the latter's private retreat; approximate date; see note 2.

J. M. J. T.

Jesus †

Dear little lamb, allow your poor little lamb to bleat a little.[1] . . . The lamb did me some good on Sunday![2] . . .

There is especially one sentence that was very enlightening for me, and it was "Let us hold on to a word that can elevate us." It's true that we must keep all for Jesus with a *jealous* care . . . . Dear lamb, how good it is to work for Jesus *alone*, for Him ALONE! . . .

Oh, then, how full the heart is, how light one feels . . . . Little Belloni[3] of Jesus, pray for the poor little grain of sand, that the grain of sand be always in its place, that is to say, under the feet of all, that no one may think of it, that its existence be, so to speak, *unknown*. The grain of sand does not desire to be *humbled*; this is still too glorious since one would be obliged to be occupied with it. It desires only one thing, to be FORGOTTEN, counted for *nothing*![4] . . . But it desires to be *seen* by *Jesus*. If the eyes of creatures cannot be lowered to look at it, may, at least, the blood-stained Face of Jesus[5] be turned towards it . . . . It desires only one look, one look! . . .

If it were possible for a grain of sand to console Jesus, to wipe away His tears,[6] there really is such a grain that would like to do it . . . .

May Jesus take the poor grain of sand and hide it in His adorable Face . . . . There, the poor atom will no longer have anything to fear, it will be sure of *no longer sinning*![7]

The grain of sand wants at all costs to save souls . . . . Jesus must grant it this grace. Little Veronica,[8] ask this grace from the *luminous* Face of Jesus! . . . Yes, the Face of Jesus is *luminous*, but if in the midst of wounds and tears it is already so beautiful, what will it be, then, when we shall see it in heaven? Oh, heaven . . . heaven. Yes, to see one day the Face of Jesus, to contemplate eternally the marvelous beauty of Jesus, the poor grain of sand desires to be despised on earth! . . .

Dear lamb, beg Jesus that His grain of sand hurry to save many souls in a short time in order to take its flight promptly towards *His dear Face*![9] . . .

I am suffering! . . . But the hope of the homeland gives me courage, soon we shall be in heaven! . . . In heaven, there will no longer be day or night, but the Face of Jesus will make an incomparable light shine! . . .

Dear lamb, understand the grain of sand; it does not know what it is saying this evening, but certainly it had no intention of writing one single word of all it has scribbled.[10] . . .

* Autograph.

1. This introduction would suggest that Thérèse was the first to write.
2. No doubt in a conversation. The sentence cited does not appear in any of Sister Agnes of Jesus' notes to Thérèse.
3. This is a deformation of the name "Bennoni"; see LC 38, note 1. The autograph has an erasing and the word "lamb" written over.
4. Imitation of Christ I, 2:3. See Ms. A, p. 152, citing this passage from the *Imitation of Christ.*
5. See the picture Thérèse will give to Céline for her feast (LT 98). Among the letters from Thérèse, mentioning the Face of Jesus (in 1889: LT 87, 95, 98; in 1890: LT 102, 105, 108, 114, 117), this one is no doubt the most closely associated with the devotion to the Holy Face as it was propagated by the *"l'Oratoire de Tours."* In 1889, the *Neuvaine en l'honneur de la Sainte Face* was just published again, followed by some prayers in which we can easily find some expressions which could have inspired Thérèse's own words.
6. See LT 94, note 6.
7. Thérèse seems to have been attacked by a new set of scruples. P. Pichon soon had to encourage her (LC 117); Sister Marie of the Angels had to do the same (LC 120). In this context, her letters to Marie Guérin (LT 92 and 93) are all the more amazing.
8. Thérèse here recalled the words of Our Lord to Sister Marie de Saint-Pierre, the Carmelite of Tours: "Find Veronicas for me." These words appear in the prayer-book of the Arch-Confraternity of the Holy Face of Tours, to which the Martin family belonged since 1885.
9. See LT 96, note 3.
10. Sister Agnes of Jesus' answer has not been preserved, nor have Thérèse's other notes written during this retreat.

LC 115 *From Sister Agnes of Jesus to Thérèse.*

July-August (?), 1889 Approximate date; see note 3.

Little lamb of Jesus,

This is my last note.[1] I read the day before yesterday in the Life of the Holy Mother, Teresa of Jesus (Poor Clare)[2] that at the

death of her sister she was sad at not having seen her soul when, two days later, she saw it rise to heaven under the form of a light cloud from which came a voice saying: "I am going to God; oh! I am not sorry for having humbled and annihilated myself for Jesus on earth. If you only knew what glory I am going to have, but God has not permitted me to reveal it to you because you would experience too great a joy and your way is the way of suffering."[3]

I cannot tell you, dear little lamb, the good that this passage did me. Ah! let us work, then, for Jesus, annihilating ourselves and hiding from the eyes of all, and our souls will soon rise like light clouds and go to the homeland of glory.

See you soon.

* Autograph.

1. This would suggest that there were other notes from Sister Agnes to Thérèse during this retreat, but they have not been preserved.
2. Mother Saint Teresa of Jesus (1828-1884), abbess of the Poor Clares at Lavaur (Tarn). Her Life was published in 1884. The third edition (Privat, Toulouse, 1886) is entitled: *"Aimer et souffrir ou la Vie de la Révérende Mère Sainte Thérèse de Jésus Abbesse du Monastère Sainte Claire (de Lavaur), écrite par elle-même, mise en ordre et annotée par M. l'Abbé Roques, archiprêtre de Lavaur."*
3. Free citation from Mother Saint Teresa's notes, September 15-16, 1871 (ed. 1886, p. 243). Her sister had died on September 12, 1871, after seven years of religious life. Sister Agnes quotes this same text, with some changes, in a letter to Céline, undated, but written between the death (August 27, 1889) and burial of Victor Bonaventure, the gardener and sacristan of the Carmel. She began the letter in this way: "I was reading *recently* that a holy religious, having her sister in the same monastery," etc. We have underlined the adverb. It is because of this letter and the words "the day before yesterday" in LC 115 that we are placing the retreat of Sister Agnes in July, perhaps even in August 1889.

LC 116 *From P. Pichon to Thérèse.*

August 16, 1889
→ LT lost

Sister Thérèse of the Child Jesus

† Clermont, August 16[1]

My Dear Child
in Jesus Christ,

How good to find you once more in the Heart of Jesus, or rather to feel that our souls don't leave each other in His Heart. Your loving little letters[2] open doors and windows for me, and Jesus is giving me the joy of reading your soul.

I was pleased with you during your great trial.[3] You considered everything from God's viewpoint, and this is really the only way of remaining in the truth and keeping one's peace.

Give God a free hand . . . regarding yourself and all your dear ones, especially in whatever concerns the beloved patriarch.

Yes, the school of Calvary is good. It is there that the adorable Master fashions His disciples, molds His friends according to His Heart, and unites His little spouses to Himself. As much as you may cry, I want you to smile always at Jesus. How good it is to be Jesus' little toy.

Meditate on the words of Venerable Father de la Colombière: "Lord, I shall not believe You love me unless you have made me suffer much and for a long time."[4]

You pleased me very much when you reminded me of my letter for your First Communion.[5] Doesn't my adoption of you date from that time? You are, then, in the name of Our Lord, my child in a twofold way. Consequently, I have a double right to give you to Jesus on my paten. God knows if I fail in this.

Let the little lamb remain in its poverty, and let its misery be its hope . . . oh! what an excellent program.

I bless you just as a father blesses his dearest Benjamin.

Almire Pichon

* Autograph.
1. Date written in pencil on the autograph by Sister Geneviève.
2. These were the letters received by P. Pichon since April 27 (LC 111), at least four.
3. Hospitalization of M. Martin.
4. This quotation from *Notes Spirituelles* of P. de la Colombière appears already in P. Pichon's first instruction of the sixth day of the October 1887 retreat preached at Lisieux.
5. LC 32.

LC 117 *From P. Pichon to Thérèse.*

October 4, 1889

† Joliette, October 4, '89

My very dear Child
in Our Lord,

I was counting so much on writing you a long letter for your feast! And Jesus did not will it! Here I am at the last minute.[1] Crushing work, without either respite or thanks. In seventeen days, I just preached eighty-one sermons. There are five retreats for the month of October alone! See how I need to be sustained by your prayers!

There is not a single line in your blessed pages, in all the dear little letters from your soul, which does not fail to touch me, console me, attach me more and more to the adorable Jesus, who has given me my Benjamin in Carmel.

I'm really going to pray to your Holy Mother for you! Do you know what a Canadian religious said to me after I had preached a retreat to her Community? "I believe that if Saint Teresa were not in heaven, P. Pichon would not be so keen on entering there!" On the 15th, my whole heart will emigrate to your dear Carmel. That day I'll be all yours, and my soul will not even respect the cloister, I'll keep faithful company with you, especially in the choir. My Mass will be for my children in Carmel, but you will head the list.

The Cross! Always the Cross planted at Caen[2] and so heavy on your hearts. Let Jesus hear from us only our cries of filial gratitude. The divine Beloved does well in all that He does!

How annoyed I was at your telling me that your letters must bore me! It's hardly possible to lie better. It is, then, the father of lies who inspires you when you speak this way.

Oh! yes, let your ambition be to wipe the tears of Jesus.[3] Offer to cry and to suffer in His stead.

You're calumniating your soul; it is able to make itself understood much better than you think!

Be hungry for love; be insatiable . . . . To suffer is to love, and to love here below is to suffer.

I forbid you in the name of God to call into question your being in the state of grace.[4] The devil is laughing heartily at you. I protest against this ugly mistrust. Believe obstinately that Jesus loves you.

Thank you for the charming little pictures.[5] I'm making good use of them for the glory of Our Lord.

It is not only a part that you have in my apostolate: the whole thing is yours! Is it surprising that Jesus is generous with His Cross with you when I have so many souls to save?

I am awaiting with impatience for your next letter which will explain, I hope, the mysterious grace[6] about which your last letter spoke. As a gift for your feast, I will ask the privilege of daily Communion for you.[7]

My whole heart pours out its tenderest blessing on you.

Almire Pichon

* Autograph.

1. We know that, depending on his place of residence, P. Pichon's letters took between ten and fourteen days between Canada and Lisieux for delivery. This letter ran the risk of not arriving exactly for the feast of St. Teresa of Avila (October 15), which, of course, was Thérèse's feast day.
2. M. Martin's state of health remained the same.

3. See LT 94, note 6.
4. Concerning Thérèse's fears, see LT 95, note 7.
5. These were pictures painted by Thérèse.
6. Perhaps he is referring to the week of "quietude" which followed the grace Thérèse received in the grotto of St. Mary Magdalene. See CJ, 11.7.2.
7. Thérèse never received this privilege during her life, except at the beginning of 1892, during the influenza epidemic; see Ms. A, p. 171.

LC 118

From Mother Marie de Gonzague to Thérèse.

Autumn (?), 1889
→ LT lost

Uncertain date; see notes 2 and 4.

†

J.M.J. to my little lamb,[1] whom I understand to the very depths of her soul. Oh, child, yes, the exile is long,[2] but we must fill it up. Mine is coming to an end and yours is beginning; I'm not going to make you laugh, but we must tell the truth in all things! Jesus has formed my violet for suffering, and I don't want to be a prophet today, but I can, nevertheless, say to my little daughter, that it is suffering and more sacrifice still that will make you[3] a great saint. We shall be spared nothing, and we shall have a beautiful bundle at the end of our exile, and, like another St. Teresa,[4] if we are faithful, we shall see the Jesus of Teresa.

Pray for my poor soul, for Jesus loves it also in spite of its poverty. Its place will be at the door of heaven, but obtain for it, privileged child, the favor of seeing God. I bless you.

* Autograph.
1. This beginning would suggest that the note was accompanied by a picture; it has not been identified.

2. Echo of a note from Thérèse, which has been destroyed. This exchange by writing suggests that Mother Marie de Gonzague was on retreat. The tone of this note reminds us of the "climate" of 1889. We don't know the date of the prioress' retreat that year.
3. A word written over: *vous? nous?*
4. See LT 107, note 8. It is difficult to know whether these reflections were inspired in Mother Marie de Gonzague by the proximity of St. Teresa of Avila's feast on October 15. (We should recall that there was no preached retreat in October 1889; see LC 112, note 1.) Or perhaps her remarks were inspired by the picture she had given Thérèse.

LT 96 **From Thérèse to Céline.**

October 15,
1889
→ LC lost

J. M. J. T.

Jesus† October 15, '89

My dear Céline,

If you only knew how you touched the heart of your Thérèse! . . . Your little flowerpots[1] are DELIGHTFUL, and you DON'T KNOW the pleasure they gave me! . . . Céline . . . . Your letter pleased me very much; I felt how much our souls were made to understand each other, and to walk by the same way! . . . Life . . . ah, it's true, for us it has no more attraction . . . but I am mistaken. It's true that the attractions of this world have vanished for us, but this is only a smoke . . . and the *reality* remains for us. Yes, life is a treasure . . . each moment is an *eternity*, an eternity of joy in heaven,[2] an eternity of seeing God *face to face*[3], of being one with Him! . . . There is only Jesus who *is*; all the rest *is not* . . . . Let us love Him, then, unto folly; let us save souls for Him. Ah! Céline, I feel that Jesus is asking *both of us* to quench *His thirst* by

giving Him souls, the souls of *priests* especially. I feel that Jesus wills that I say this to you, for our mission is *to forget* ourselves and to reduce ourselves to nothing .... We are so insignificant ... and yet Jesus wills that the salvation of *souls* depends on the sacrifices of our love. He is begging souls from us .... Ah, let us understand His *look*! There are so few who understand it. Jesus is giving us the remarkable grace of instructing us Himself and of showing us a *hidden light*! ... Céline ... life will be short, eternity is without end .... Let us make our life a continual sacrifice, a martyrdom of love, in order to console Jesus. He wants only a *look*, a *sigh*, but a look and a sigh that are for *Him alone*! .... Let all the moments of our life be for *Him alone*; let creatures touch us only in passing. There is only one thing to do during the night, the one night of life which will come only once, and this is to love, to love Jesus with all the strength of our heart and to save souls for Him so that He may be *loved* .... Oh, make Jesus loved! Céline! how easily I talk with you ... it's as if I were speaking to my soul .... Céline, it seems to me that I can say everything to you ....

(Thank you again for your pretty jars; little Jesus is *radiant* when He is so well adorned.)

Sister Thérèse of the Child Jesus of the Holy Face
nov.carm.ind.

* Autograph.

1. These were for flowers for the statue of the Child Jesus; see her parenthetical remark at the end of her letter.
2. This is possibly a new statement from the chapter of P. d'Argentan on eternity; see LT 94, note 3. Céline transcribed some excerpts from it, about this same time, judging by the handwriting. We read: "If I fill up this moment of my life with some good work, I am certain that it will procure for me a blessed eternity; and the more moments I shall use in this way, the more eternities will necessarily come from them." (*Op. cit.*, vol. II, p. 13.)

3. Thérèse had first written: "an eternity to see Him face to face"; she corrects it: "an eternity to see Jes": she corrects it again and replaced "Jesus" by "God." These corrections are revealing. We have noticed in her letters 94, 95, 96, the various changes in Thérèse's thought: *here below,* a generous apostolic effort ("to save many souls in a short time, " LT 95); *in heaven*, the enjoyment of the face to face vision of God. It was only in the last months of her life that Thérèse glimpsed the possibility of imitating the angels, "continually interested in us without ever ceasing to see the divine Face" (LT 254, July 14, 1897).

LT 97 From Thérèse to Mme. Guérin.

October 15, 1889

J. M. J. T.

Jesus † October 15, 1889

My dear Aunt,

I could not tell you how much I was touched by all your treats! . . . I am asking my saintly patroness to thank you by granting you her graces, as well as dear Uncle. I ask you to thank my dear little sisters Jeanne and Marie for me for their pretty bouquets and their delicious grapes.

My letter was interrupted by the arrival of a new gift, two magnificent plants for little Jesus . . . . Really, I am just overwhelmed, and I'd be embarrassed if this were not to decorate the Child Jesus' altar. He is the one, no doubt, who will take charge of paying my debt to my dear relatives. I don't know the name of the person who made this delightful gift to Thérèse's Jesus . . . if you know the person, I beg you to let him know how grateful I am.

Oh, Aunt, how I am praying today for St. Teresa to return to you a hundredfold all you have done for us. In her little letter for

my feast,[1] Céline was speaking to me about all your kindness to her, and I was very much touched by this; however, I was not surprised, for I know all the maternal *tenderness* you have for us.

Dear Aunt, my heart is filled with sweet things that I'd like to be able to say, but I am obliged to leave you in order to go to Vespers.[2]

I am sending you my best kisses, as also to Uncle and my four little sisters.[3]

Your very grateful little daughter,

Sister Thérèse of the Child Jesus
nov.carm.ind.

* Autograph.
1. This letter was not preserved.
2. Vespers was said at two o'clock in the afternoon.
3. Her two sisters Léonie and Céline and her two cousins Jeanne and Marie.

LT 98 **From Thérèse to Céline.**

October 22, 1889

J. M. J. T.

Jesus † Carmel, October 22, '89

My dear Céline,

If you only knew the sorrow I have when I think that I allowed the 21st to pass by without wishing a happy feast to my Céline![1] ... Will Céline have doubted the heart of her Thérèse? ...

She had been thinking, nevertheless, of this dear feast for a long time, but the life of Carmel is so eremitical that the poor little hermit never knows what the date is .... Céline this forget-

fulness was in my heart, but, you see, I think that this year Jesus wanted our feast to be on the same day; and isn't today the octave of St. Teresa. Yes, Céline, St. Teresa is also your patroness since you are already her dear daughter . . . .

If you only knew how I look upon this sorrow that I have today as willed by Jesus, for He is pleased to sow our life with little sorrows . . . .

I am sending you a beautiful picture of the Holy Face[2] that our dear Mother gave me some time ago. I think it suits Marie of the Holy Face[3] so well that I can't keep it for myself, and, for a long time already, I was thinking of giving it to my Céline . . . my own Céline . . . . May Marie of the Holy Face be another Veronica,[4] who wipes away the blood and tears of Jesus, her *only* Beloved; may she win souls for Him, and especially the souls whom she *loves*;[5] may she be tireless in braving the soldiers, that is, the world, in order to reach Him . . . . Ah, how happy she'll be when one day she will be able to contemplate in glory the *mysterious* drink with which she had quenched her heavenly Fiancé's thirst, and when she sees His lips, once desiccated, open to speak that *unique* and *eternal* word of *love*! . . . The *Merci* which will have no end . . . .

See you soon, dear little Veronica. Tomorrow, no doubt, the Beloved will ask a new sacrifice, a new alleviation of His thirst, but this does not matter, let us die with Him.[6] . . .

Happy feast, dear Céline . . . .

Your poor little sister,

Thérèse of the Child Jesus of the Holy Face
nov.carm.ind.

Don't forget to pick a little Céline[7] flower; my heart will offer it to you . . . .

* Autograph.
1. Sister Agnes of Jesus wrote in the same way: "Dear little Céline, how could we forget your feast when we are thinking of you all day long? It's incomprehensible . . . ."
2. A double image, in lace (Ch. Letaille's collection). First side in colors has the blood-stained Holy Face, with these words: "Insults and Reparation. Offended every day!" The second side, in black, has hearts on fire, surrounding a Ciborium and various symbols, with the words: "Consoled every day."
3. A name given spontaneously by Thérèse to Céline; see LT 149, October 20, 1893. Mother Marie de Gonzague used to write to Céline, using this name from March 1889 on. In Carmel, Céline had this name during her postulancy (see LT 174, January (?), 1895).
4. See LT 95, note 7.
5. The souls of priests; see LT 94, note 7.
6. See John 11:16.
7. The aster; it bloomed in October, and each year at Les Buissonnets Thérèse used to give one to Céline on her feast.

"Totally abandoned to God's good pleasure"
(*P. Pichon, LC 126*)
(November 1889-March 1890)
Age sixteen and seventeen

There are few events in this winter of 1889–1890.

Among the twelve documents gathered together here, only three are from Thérèse's hand, and two of these are quite dull (LT 99 and 100, to her uncle and aunt Guérin).

The other nine letters or notes from correspondents throw only an indirect light upon the existence of the novice, who was now applying herself "especially to the practice of the little virtues" (Ms. A, p. 159) and "deprived of all consolation in her life of prayer" (Ms. A, p. 157).

It is almost impossible to date five of these notes. Two are from Sister Agnes of Jesus, who is on retreat (LC 119 and 120); she is intent on sustaining the generosity of her "little reed."

In the three notes from "godmother" (LC 122, 123, 124), which her "naughty little daughter" did not tear up, Thérèse is able to discern, in spite of her "angel's" abuse of power, the rough tenderness of her who was her second Mamma at Les Buissonnets.

Two new detachments are demanded from Thérèse around Christmas time:

1) *that of Les Buissonnets, the now deserted nest. The lease was terminated on December 25, and, in a final visit, Céline picked for Thérèse a last leaf of ivy, "souvenir of so many souvenirs!" (LC 121);*

2) *that of the postponement of her Profession, which she hoped to make on January 11, 1890. "At first, it was very difficult for me to accept this great sacrifice" (Ms. A, p. 158), "I was really sorry" (LT 176, April 28, 1895). Meditation on the* Fondements de la vie Spirituelle *by P. Surin helped her in accepting these sacrifices.*

The texts received from Céline for her seventeenth birthday (LC 125) repeated Sister Agnes of Jesus' composition: "The first dream of the Child Jesus," enacted on Christmas night 1889. Thérèse played the role of the Blessed Virgin. She did so "with so much piety and simplicity that the whole Community was deeply moved" (note of Mother Agnes). The Child Jesus was dreaming about His future Passion: "nails, thorns, bitter gall and chalice" (see LC 126), and Thérèse took up this theme in 1894 (LT 156). As a counterpart to the sufferings an angel presents Him with the "immense army" of those who will respond to His love. The poem ends with this prophetic stanza:

Parmi ces coeurs, il est une famille
Que je présente au petit Roi des Cieux;
Dans l'avenir, voyez comme elle brille,
Rêvez, Enfant, le Carmel de Lisieux.*

This family, for the moment, was witnessing the continued decline of its head (LD, March 27, 1890). "Yes," whispers Thérèse, "but humiliation, too, will pass away . . . in heaven, one of his white hairs will illuminate us!" (Letter of Sister Agnes of Jesus to Céline, February 16–19, 1890.)

* Among these hearts there is a family
I present to the little King of heaven;
In the future, see how it will shine,
Dream, Child, of the Carmel of Lisieux.

LC 119
November
1889 (?)
→ LT lost

From Sister Marie of the Angels to Thérèse.
Approximate date.

J. M. J. T! Jesus! My dear little daughter, your good little note gave me great joy when seeing in your sentiments and dispositions the blessed work of Jesus on His Sacred Heart's little grain of dust[1] and on His Immaculate Mother's young dove[2] so well protected under her virginal mantle. What can you desire more? You are right, dear Benjamin, to be pleased with your lot, for it is the best! Attach yourself to the Cross like the ivy in order to die there if Jesus so wills. May divine suffering be the center of your life; plunge into this bottomless ocean, and may it engulf you as it did Jesus, for there alone are life and happiness.

Always love to be little, so little that the eyes of Jesus only may find you! Little grain of dust, be unseen by all in order to be seen by God alone.[3]

Be filled with confidence that good Jesus will do everything; rejoice at being poor, at feeling yourself so poor in order that, little beggar, you may have everything from the infinite charity and love of Jesus!

Take flight to the All of your heart with wings of humility, simplicity, and love. Jesus loves you with a tender predilection, so pay Him in return, and be happy to love Jesus in suffering for Jesus! I am not forgetting my dear little Benjamin, and, soon, we shall see one another; in the meanwhile, profit well from all the good talks our beloved Mother will give you.[4] Much more than I, she is Jesus for you, and, better than I, will know how to speak about Him and make Him loved by you.

Your very devoted,
Sister Marie of the Angels

* Autograph.
1. This is a change from the "grain of sand" image; see LT 45, note 4.
2. This is perhaps a reference to the white veil the novice was wearing since January 10, 1889 (and would wear until September 24, 1890).

3. See LT 95, July-August 1889.
4. This reflection suggests that Sister Marie of the Angels was on retreat, because the prioress was supplying for her in daily interviews with the novices, in the afternoon.

LT 99 From Thérèse to Mme. Guérin.

November 18, 1889

J. M. J. T.

Jesus! Carmel, November 18, '89

My dear little Aunt,

How time flies . . . . It is already two years ago since I sent you greetings for your feast,[1] and still it seems like it was only yesterday.

Many things have happened during these two years, and God has granted me some great graces . . . . He has also visited us with His Cross, and, at the same time, He has revealed to us all the tenderness He has placed in our dear Aunt's heart . . . .

What memories there are for me in that date of November 19, and what a joy when I saw the moment arrive! . . . And it is always with the same joy that I come to repeat to my dear Aunt all the wishes I'm arranging for her; but I am mistaken, I'm not going to waste my time enumerating them, for I believe a whole volume would not be enough for me . . . .

If you only knew, dear little Aunt, how your little daughter is going to pray for you on the day of your feast. Alas! I am so imperfect that my poor prayers have, no doubt, no great value, but one of the privileges of beggars is that they can obtain what they desire on the strength of their importunity; I shall do as they do, and God will not be able to send me away with empty hands.[2] . . .

Four o'clock is ringing, and I must leave you, dear little Aunt, but I assure you that my heart remains near you.

I beg you, dear little Aunt, to remember me to Madame Four-

net,[3] for I'm not forgetting that it is her feast. It goes without saying that I am kissing Uncle and my dear little sisters with my whole heart.

And for you, dear Aunt, I am sending the best kiss from the heart of the *littlest* of your seven little daughters.

Sister Thérèse of the Child Jesus
nov.carm.ind.

* Autograph.
1. LT 32, November 14, 1887.
2. Luke 11:5-8.
3. This was Madame Guérin's mother, whose name was Elisa.

LC 120 *From Sister Marie of the Angels to Thérèse.*

November 21,
1889 (?)
→ LT lost

J. M. J. T! Jesus!

Little reed,[1] infinitely loved by Jesus and profoundly dear to my heart!. . . Jesus does not will any joys for you!. . . Why are you surprised by this?. . . Isn't this what He chose for Himself and the lot He gave to His Immaculate Mother? Isn't it the lot of His loved ones, His predestined?. . . You are right, then, in thanking Him for this, blessing Him a thousand times for this, and, above all, for having given you the grace *par excellence* of understanding that it is a favor with which He wills to honor you!. . . He finds so few souls capable of understanding this secret of His love that, when He meets one on His road, He makes up for it and goes to no trouble whatsoever when He is sure that He will be more loved, more supported!. . .

You tell me, dear little child, that you have felt all your misery! Oh! again, what a grace from Jesus! To be nothing, to feel noth-

ing, and, especially, to love nothing in oneself, in order to find everything only in Jesus, and, consequently, to have Him alone as one's support, what security, what joy for the soul that truly loves. We are nothing, but Jesus is all, we have nothing, but He has all! We can do nothing, but He can do all and for all if we are really convinced that we can do nothing!... Yes, my beloved little daughter, Jesus is very, very much pleased with you,[2] be also pleased with Him; ah! if you could be as pleased with Him as He is with you, what waves of joy would inundate your soul! Tomorrow, the feast of St. Cecilia,[3] I will offer my Holy Communion for my beloved little reed, and I will ask Jesus that she may love Him just as the virgin martyr did! Time seems long for me without my Benjamin; if she were not suffering, I would feel it less, but courage, little reed of Jesus! The storm will not break the reed; it will make it bend, but afterward it will quickly stand up straight and its head will again look up to heaven. Remember that Jesus carried it in His hand on the day of His Passion! Be, then, the privileged reed of your heavenly Fiancé.[4]

Pray, too, for your little mistress, who loves and cherishes her Benjamin.

Sister Marie of the Angels

* Autograph.
1. See LT 54, note 7.
2. Perhaps Thérèse had revealed some disturbances in her conscience; see LT 95, note 7.
3. Therefore, it was November 22.
4. This expression would indicate that Thérèse was still a novice; it was only her Profession, September 8, 1890, that gave her the title "spouse."

LC 121 *From Céline to Thérèse.* (Fragments.)

December 24, 1889

My dear little Thérèse,

Your Céline is sending you a little souvenir for your little Christmas crib; she did not want this feast to bring nothing to "her heart . . ." My own Thérèse, Th.[1] . . .

Tomorrow, Les Buissonnets will no longer be ours.[2] I was there, yesterday, to visit it for the last time. I took some moss and some branches for my crib . . . . As a souvenir, not finding the smallest flower, I took several ivy leaves.[3] This is *the* souvenir of so many souvenirs!!! . . .

The little ivy leaf was detached from Les Buissonnets, but it will wrap itself around Jesus! . . .

Thérèse! your little Céline loves you! . . .

I kiss Marie and Pauline . . . .

* Incomplete autograph.

1. The end of the first fragment of the autograph; the lower part is cut and repeated.
2. The lease was broken on December 25, 1889. For several months already (LT 94, note 1), Léonie and Céline were living with their uncle and aunt. Part of the furniture was taken there; part was brought to the Carmel. See LT 91, note 4. On December 31, Sister Agnes of Jesus wrote to Céline: "Ah, who could have told us on December 31, '88, that Papa's clock would ring 'midnight' in the Carmel's choir on December 31, '89? . . . What upheavals there are in life!"
3. One of these ivy leaves is still attached to the autograph by a pin.

LT 100 **From Thérèse to M. and Mme. Guérin.**

December 30,
1889

J. M. J. T.

Jesus † December 30, '89

Dear Uncle and Aunt,

Your Benjamin comes in her turn to wish you a Happy New Year!... Just as each day has its last hour, so each year sees its last night coming also, and it is on the night of this year that I feel drawn to cast a look over the past and on the future. When I consider the time that has just run out, I feel drawn to thank God for, although His hand has offered us a bitter chalice, His divine Heart has been able to sustain us in the trial, and He has given us the strength necessary for drinking His chalice[1] even to the last dregs .... What is He reserving for us for the year that is about to begin?... I have not been given the power to penetrate this mystery, but I'm begging God to reward my dear relatives a hundredfold for all the touching kindness they have for us!...

The first day of the year has a world of memories for me .... I still see Papa giving us his caresses .... He was so good!... But why recall these memories? Dear Father has received the reward of his virtues;[2] God has sent him a trial worthy of himself.

Nine o'clock is ringing,[3] and I am obliged to terminate my letter without having said anything of what I should have spoken about, but I trust that my dear relatives will excuse their little Thérèse, and, above all, *pardon the writing*[4] which isn't readable ....

Happy New Year to my dear little sisters!... Above all, may Marie be cured very quickly; I shall be vexed with her if the INFLUENZA[5] prevents her from coming to see us!...

Au revoir, dear Uncle and dear Aunt. Your little daughter wishes you a *Happy New Year* and kisses you with her whole heart.

Sister Thérèse of the Child Jesus
nov.carm.ind.

* Autograph.
1. See Matthew 20:22.
2. For Thérèse's faith, trial is already a reward; M. Martin's illness was to last another four and a half years.
3. This was the hour for Matins.
4. Thérèse wrote "*l'écrire*" for "*l'écriture*," and this was corrected on the autograph by a strange hand.
5. The captitalizing of all the letters and the underlining suggests a point of humor on Thérèse's part. However, there was an epidemic of influenza that invaded that section of France. It became a real calamity, and Bishop Hugonin ordered special prayers to be said to *Notre-Dame de la Délivrande* (Semaine Religieuse de Bayeux, January 19, 1890, pp. 35-36). There were seventy thousand victims that year. And in 1891-1892, the Carmel of Lisieux was severely hit.

LT 101 From Thérèse to Céline.

December 31, 1889

J. M. J. T.

Jesus † December 31, '89

My dear Céline,

You are the one getting my last "*adieu*" for this year! . . . In a few hours, it will have passed forever . . . it will be in eternity! . . .

Since my Céline is in her bed,[1] it is up to me to go and wish her a *Happy New Year* . . . .

Do you remember times past? . . . The year which is just running out was good; yes, it was precious for heaven, and may the one that will follow resemble it! . . .

Céline, I'm not surprised at seeing you in bed after such a year; at the end of a *day* like that, there is reason to rest! . . Do you understand? . . . Perhaps the year about to begin will be the last!!!!!! . . . Ah! let us profit, let us profit from the shortest moments; let us act like misers, and let us be jealous of the littlest

things for the Beloved! Our New Year's day is very sad this year . . . and it's with a heart filled with memories that I'm going to watch, waiting for midnight . . . . I remember everything . . . now we are orphans,[2] but we can say with love: "Our Father, who art in heaven."[3] Yes, there still remains to us the only *All* of our souls! . . .

Another year has passed! . . . Céline! it is gone, gone, and it will never return, and just as this year has passed so also will our life pass and soon we shall say: "It is gone." Let us not waste our time, soon eternity will shine for us! . . . Céline, if you wish, let us convert souls; this year, we must form many *priests* who love Jesus! and who *handle* Him with the same *tenderness* with which Mary *handled* Him in His cradle![4] . . .

Your little Sister Thérèse of the Child
Jesus of the Holy Face
nov.carm.ind.

I wish a Happy New Year to *Lolo*[5] also, but I believe I'll see her! . . . Thank Uncle and Aunt very much, and tell them that I was really touched by their gifts; thank, too, Jeanne and Marie very much. They are truly kind.

* Autograph.
1. Thérèse was writing this letter after Matins and before the hour of prayer between eleven and midnight to usher in the New Year; see LD, December 31, 1886, note 1.
2. There was almost no communication between M. Martin and his daughters because of his mental illness; see LT 169, August 19, 1894, where Thérèse speaks of "a *death* of five years."
3. Mt. 6, 9.
4. See *Prière a Jésus Prêtre et Hostie*, composed by Thérèse Durnerin: "Oh! give us priests! priests filled with the fire of true children of Mary, who will give Jesus to souls with the same tenderness and care with which you carried the little Child of Bethlehem in your arms! In the Host, oh, Mother, your Jesus is even poorer than in the crib! He no longer has hands as tender as yours to touch Him . . . . Give

Him a generation of priests formed in your school, in the tenderness of your virginal love." (*Le Coeur Eucharistique de Jésus*, Feuillet, a leaflet without the name of the author, *Imprimatur* given at Verdun, July 21, 1888.) We find a repetition of this prayer at the end of the "pious recreation" entitled: *Les Anges à la crèche de Jésus*, December 25, 1894; in the prayer, also, that was composed by Thérèse in October 1895 for Abbé Bellière; in 1896-1897, Thérèse, who knew the prayer by heart, had the novices recite it daily (CSG, p. 108). Concerning Thérèse Durnerin, see LT 94, note 7.

5. Nickname for Léonie.

LC 122 *From Sister Marie of the Sacred Heart to Thérèse.*

Winter 1889/1890? Uncertain date.

I have already told you that it causes me distress to see you go up at 8:30; you had promised me 8:15.[1] When I see you doing the same thing almost every evening, it makes me very sad, and it is because of this that I'm crying, for you never listen to me anymore. You can read your lesson at the beginning or end of prayer, but, no, you don't want to do that. Then your poor little godmother is sad at heart, very sad over her poor little daughter, who seems to be fading away.[2]

Is it not enough that she is no longer able to give her nice things as she did at Les Buissonnets? No, her dear little daughter must break her heart *deliberately*.

* Autograph.

1. After Compline, ending at eight in the evening, Thérèse used her free time of "silence" to prepare the Latin text of the lessons at Matins; these lessons were from the first nocturn, and she had to read them when she was a novice. However, her sister Marie would have preferred that Thérèse go up to her cell and rest during this hour of free time; see LC 123.
2. On the contradictory opinion concerning Thérèse's good or bad appearance, see CJ 25.7.15.

LC 123 *From Sister Marie of the Sacred Heart to Thérèse.*

Winter 1889/1890?
→ LT lost?

Perhaps this note followed the preceding (LC 122).

All I can say is that you're causing me much sorrow. Ah! when I think that you refuse to take this hour of rest which is given us by obedience.[1] I can no longer give you anything as I did at home. When I feel that you're tired, I have[2] no other hope than that of having you take the helps permitted us by the Rule. Since you don't want to do anything I tell you, I, who love you so much, well, then, do what you want in everything. I really see now that I can no longer do anything for you, and I am very sad at heart. . . .

In the evening, when I bring a glass of milk to the others who have colds,[3] I'd be so happy to enter the cell of my poor little daughter. But, no, nothing, not one single consolation of this kind. And to refuse me what you can give me without anyone's taking exception to it!

Tear this up immediately.

* Autograph.
1. A reference to a response (destroyed) from Thérèse to the first note from her sister (LC 122)?
2. She wrote first: *"je n'ai"* and changed it to *"je n'avais."*
3. Sister Marie of the Sacred Heart was at this time aide to the infirmarian.

LC 124 *From Sister Marie of the Sacred Heart to Thérèse.*

Winter 1889/1890?

Little godmother begs her little daughter to put on her woolen stockings tomorrow.[1] She will wash her feet at the same time; little godmother will give her a footbath.

The naughty little girl will, no doubt, find some pretexts for not pleasing her poor little godmother.

TEAR THIS UP.

* Autograph.

1. Normally, it was after their Profession that the nuns received woolen stockings (homespun stockings, white); this would suggest that the note was written during the winter of 1890-1891. That Thérèse should have to wait for her older sister to give her a footbath (zinc basin) is proof, however, that she was still a novice; Marie was able to supply her with stockings because Thérèse's novitiate had been extended.

LC 125 *From Céline to Thérèse.*

January 2, 1890 For Thérèse's seventeenth birthday.

My dear little Thérèse,

Did you think I was going to allow your birthday to pass by without a greeting? Oh! no, you don't have any doubts like this about your Céline. I'm sending you, in order to please you, two beautiful extracts from the Liturgy[1] that you used to love so much. In this thought, you will see all my love. . . . I'm poor and have nothing to give you, but, in my opinion, gifts from the heart are what enter more deeply and afford the greatest joy.[2]

I kiss you, my dear little sister, I love you, and I prayed for you during my Holy Communion.

Ah! in another thirty years, will we still be greeting each other on our birthdays? No, undoubtedly. But while we are awaiting to be crowned, we still have a "good game to play."[3] I'll tell you all my thoughts on this matter when I see you.

Your little sister,
Céline

* Autograph, G copy.

1. Two texts cited by Dom Guéranger in his *l'Année Liturgique*, "*Temps de Noël*," vol. I, 4th ed., 1875:
   i) pp. 325-328: "*Cher petit enfant, que tu es doux!...*" This was a translation in prose from the English poem of Father Faber: "Dear Little One! how sweet Thou art" (thirteen stanzas, four verses).
   ii) p. 489: "*Lui pleurant, dit Saint Bonaventure*" (*Méditations sur la Vie de Notre-Seigneur* by Saint Bonaventure, vol. I, p. 51; reference indicated by Dom Guéranger.

   The text from Father Faber seems to be one of the sources for Sister Agnes of Jesus' composition: "The first dream of Jesus," enacted on Christmas night 1889, in which Thérèse played the part of the Blessed Virgin. It was the inspiration, too, for the picture painted by Thérèse for Mother Agnes of Jesus, January 21, 1894 (see LT 156), and for her play on Christmas 1894: "The Angels at Jesus' Crib" (RP 2). We should take note of Céline's statement: "...two beautiful extracts from the Liturgy that you used to *love* so much." Thérèse enjoyed reading these, then, before her entrance into Carmel; the Martin family used to read *l'Année Liturgique* at Les Buissonnets.
2. End of the autograph; the end of the first page was cut off. The completed text was made by Sister Geneviève. The authenticity, therefore, of the second part is not certain.
3. This is a reference to the game of billiards that M. Martin used to love very much: "He was very good at this game. There was a billiard table at the '*Cercle Vital.*' We remember how our father used to say: '...on earth, we have a good shot to make.' (He meant this with reference to eternity, to the goods of heaven to be won.)" See Sister Geneviève, NPHF.

LD *From Sister Costard to Sister Agnes of Jesus, Sister Marie of the Sacred Heart, and Thérèse.* (Fragment.)

March 27, 1890

I gave your letters[1] to your good Father, and he was so happy to receive them; he asked me when they were going to come and get

him to bring him back to Lisieux. "When I am going to my home, I'll say *adieu* to my Carmelites, for, undoubtedly, I will not see them again. . . ."

* CMG.

1. These letters were not preserved. See the letter from Sister Costard to Céline: "Your excellent father is about the same as when you saw him, but his limbs cannot support him. Monsieur Martin does not leave his bed. If you are living in an isolated spot, I would advise you to take him, for he is not difficult to handle. . . . Your good father doesn't even try to wash himself. His limbs must have been really affected by the paralysis for him to be acting this way. . . . He received the letters from his Carmelites, and, when reading them, he cried very much." (CMG IV, pp. 204-205.)

LC 126 *From P. Pichon to Thérèse.*

March 27, 1890
→ LT lost

† Montreal
March 27, '90

My dear Child
in Jesus Christ,

Oh! you are my child, and you feel this in spite of my silence, just as I feel that I am your father! Five months without writing you![1] I would not excuse myself if the fault were not God's. I suffer too much from my silence for it to be deliberate.

Each day, I find the dear little lamb in the Sacred Heart, without ever leaving it. How good, sweet, and heavenly is this union of souls at the Tabernacle!

Jesus has a weakness for nothingness, for our poor little nothings; let us rejoice, then, to be of such little consequence.[2]

Let it not be enough for you to love Jesus. You must make Him loved.[3] Without that, would you be a daughter of St. Teresa?

Now, to make Jesus loved we must suffer, suffer very much. Be happy, then, since everything is suffering and exile for you.

Your wedding[4] will carry the seal of the Cross just as your espousals did. How pleased I am to see you totally abandoned to God's good pleasure! Come to the defense of Providence, even if human wisdom tears its hair out in despair. All that Jesus does is done well. His gifts are the best: nails, thorns, bitter gall, and chalice![5]

Let us bless all Crosses, even the Cross of Caen. We are really crucified in the person of our venerable patriarch. Do you think that Jesus is not interested in our martyrdom?

My little lamb will be led to the altar adorned in thorns from head to foot; there are not more beautiful flowers in the eyes of Jesus.

Keep your ardent desires, and be God's little match.

Les Buissonnets and Carmel, Caen and Canada, all God's desires must be dear and precious to us. Heaven will make up for everything.

Will my letter arrive in time to bring you my prayers for April 9, your very sweet anniversary?[6] Tell my dear older one that I did not forget March 19[7] and that I won't be forgetting the very dear April 17, the ninth anniversary.[8] I am going to celebrate April 6th[9] with the lamb.

You are right, your thanks must be multiplied on the nights of days of aridity and bitterness.

I can read all the unwritten things in your soul. I see it. It is totally clear to my eyes and to bless it is so great a joy for me!

Almire Pichon

* Autograph.

1. His last letter was on October 4, 1889 (LC 117).
2. Compare this to LC 120, when he is approving the same dispositions in Thérèse.
3. See LT 96.

4. He is referring here to her Profession which was postponed.
5. Perhaps this is a reference to the play put on at Christmas about which Thérèse would have spoken.
6. The second anniversary of Thérèse's entrance to Carmel.
7. The third anniversary of Sister Marie of the Sacred Heart's reception of the Habit.
8. In fact, the eighth anniversary of P. Pichon's first meeting with Marie Martin at Lisieux, April 17, 1882.
9. Seventh anniversary of Sister Agnes of Jesus' reception of the Habit. In 1890, April 6 was Easter Sunday.

"The most beautiful of Lilies" (*see LT 105*)

(April-July 1890)

Age seventeen

No decision was made regarding Thérèse's Profession before the end of July. Fourteen documents bring these four months to life.

The reason for the eight letters or notes from Thérèse's hand was: Sister Agnes of Jesus' retreat in May (LT 103, 104, and 106); Céline's birthday (LT 102), her trip to Lourdes (LT 105 and 107), and her vacation at La Musse in July (LT 108). One letter was written to Marie Guérin (LT 109). These letters have a great spiritual richness in them.

At this time, the "Holy Face" remained the privileged object of Thérèse's contemplation. She nourished herself more and more on biblical texts (obtained probably from the Liturgy of the preceding Lent; see LT 108, note 13 and 17). The "fourth song of the servant of Yahweh" (Isaias 53) made an indelible impression on her. She stated on her deathbed: "These words of Isaias: 'Who has believed our report?... There is no beauty in

him, no comeliness, etc.,' have made up the whole foundation of my devotion to the Holy Face, or, to express it better, the foundation of all my piety. I, too, desired to be without beauty, alone in treading the winepress, unknown to everyone" (CJ 5.8.9).

Once again, a picture made a "deep impression" (see Ms. A, p. 71) upon Thérèse, setting before her eyes the suffering "Face." This was a miniature on parchment, painted by Sister Agnes of Jesus for Céline, and it was a Veronica Veil supported by a branch of nine lilies (LT 102, note 1). Thérèse was struck by one detail in particular: "The divine Blood moistens our petals" (ibid.). The lilies become indistinct in her eyes, giving place only to "the Face of the most beautiful and the whitest of Lilies" (LT 105). A prayer to the Holy Face, composed by Sister Agnes, helped Thérèse (LT 102 and 103) to discover "the hidden beauties of Jesus" (LT 108). Her desire to offer the Beloved "a new wine that would quench His thirst" and "which would return love for love" (ibid.) became more intense. It was at this time that she met a spiritual teacher in the person of Saint John of the Cross (LT 108, note 18), "the Saint of Love par excellence," she was one day to call him (Sister Marie of the Trinity's notes).

LT 102 **From Thérèse to Céline.**

April 27, 1890

J. M. J. T.

Jesus †

Dear Céline,

I was taking delight in the thought of writing you a long letter for your *twenty-first birthday*, and now I have hardly a few

moments!... Céline, could you believe that your Thérèse would forget April 28?... Céline, my heart is just filled with memories ... it seems I've loved you for centuries, and still it is only for twenty-one years .... But now I have an eternity before me ....

Céline, the lyre of my heart will sing for you on the 28th, and your name will frequently ring in the dear ears of my Jesus!... Ah! since our heart is the SAME, let us give the whole of it to Jesus; we must travel *together*, for Jesus cannot dwell in *half a heart*!... Ask that your Thérèse not remain behind ....

When I was looking at the image of the Holy Face,[1] tears came into my eyes; isn't it an image of our family? Yes, our family is a *branch of lilies*, and the *Lily without a name*[2] dwells in our midst. He dwells there as King, and He is giving us a share in His kingship. His divine Blood moistens our petals, and His thorns, while tearing us, allow the perfume of our love to spread.

Adieu, Céline, they are coming to break off my conversation; understand *all*.

Thérèse[3]

* Autograph.

1. This was a miniature painting, depicting the Holy Face, bleeding, surrounded by nine lilies, which were on a green stem that was intertwined by a branch of thorns. On the same day, Sister Agnes explained the symbolism to Céline: "You are the beautiful white lily, and its petals are supporting the Holy Face; you have this honor since this is your name! The stem is our little Mother in heaven and Papa [the branch of thorns] is the victim whom Jesus has chosen in our family. The four little buds are the four angels who took flight." [These four angels, of course, were the four Martin children who died in infancy, two boys and two girls.] On the painting, we can still read the words: "Blessed the hearts crushed by the jealous love of Our Lord .... P.P." (Père Pichon). We find the quotation, attributed to P. de la Colombière, in the prelude to the conference on the seventh day of the October 1887 retreat preached by P. Pichon at the Carmel of Lisieux (notes written down by Sister Marie of Saint Joseph). Besides the references made to this painting in LT 104 and 105, there is also a reference to it at the beginning of the Autobiog-

raphy (Ms. A, p. 16). It was a source of inspiration, too, for Thérèse when she did a painting for a chasuble (around 1894).

2. Jesus, whose divine Name is ineffable in human language. In her prayer to the Holy Face, composed at this same time, Sister Agnes of Jesus wrote: "*la Fleur sans nom, la Fleur des fleurs aux charmes incréées . . . .*"
3. Thérèse's signature ends in a flourish, which seems to indicate that she was interrupted; this is the only time in her correspondence when there is such a flourish.

LT 103 — From Thérèse to Sister Agnes of Jesus.

May 4 (?), 1890 — Approximate date; see note 1.

J. M. J. T.

Jesus †

Dear little lamb, my heart follows you into solitude.[1] You know, light *lark*, that you have a thread on your foot, and, as high as you may soar, you will have to drag your burden . . . but a grain of sand isn't heavy, and it will be lighter if only you ask Jesus . . . . Oh! how it longs to be reduced to nothing, to be unknown by all creatures. Poor little thing, it desires nothing any longer, nothing but to be FORGOTTEN[2] . . . not contempt, insults, this would be too glorious for a grain of sand. Were one to despise it, one would have to see it. But to be FORGOTTEN! . . . Yes, I want to be forgotten, and this, not only by creatures but by *myself*. I'd like to be reduced to nothing to such an extent as to have no desire whatsoever . . . . The glory of Jesus, that is all; as for my own glory, I abandon it to Him, and, if He seems to forget me, He is free since I am no longer my own but His . . . . And He will more quickly grow tired of making me wait than I shall grow tired of waiting for Him![3] . . .

Dear lamb, do you understand?. . . Understand, just the same, what my heart cannot express. You, who are a luminous light that Jesus gave me to light up my steps in the dark paths of this exile, take pity on my weakness, hide me under your veil[4] in order that I may share in your light . . . . Tell Jesus to *look at me* so that the *belles-de-nuit* may penetrate with their bright rays the heart of the grain of sand, and, if this be not too much, ask Him, too, that the Flower of flowers may open its petals and that the melodious sound coming from it may make its hidden teachings vibrate within my heart.[5] . . . Dear lamb, don't forget the grain of sand! . . .

* Autograph.

1. Sister Agnes of Jesus began her private retreat of ten days on May 1: "I'm coming to say a little '*adieu*' because I am leaving for my big retreat . . . . I must offer Jesus the sacrifice of our visit tomorrow" (Sister Agnes' letter to Céline, May 1, 1890). It was perhaps during her free time on Sunday, May 4, that Thérèse began her dialogue with the retreatant.
2. See LT 95; also the note of her Profession day, September 8, 1890 (Story of a Soul, p. 275).
3. A probable reference to the postponement of her Profession.
4. It was customary for the nuns when on retreat to keep their veils lowered.
5. Thérèse had written "*mes mystérieux enseignements,*" instead of "*ses mystérieux enseignements.*" The concluding lines of this letter were inspired by the symbolism in Sister Agnes of Jesus' prayer to the Holy Face in which she compared each of the Lord's features (eyes, mouth, etc.) to a flower, the whole forming "*Mon bouquet de Fête.*" The "*belles-de-nuit*" (four o'clocks) represent His eyes, and the "Flower of flowers," of course, was the Lord Himself.

LC 127 *From Sister Agnes of Jesus to Thérèse.*

May 3, 1890 Date deduced from the content; see note 3.

→ LT 103

Dear little grain of sand, don't say that I am your light! Ah! if you only knew what darkness! Pray for me; I'm not troubled, but there's not a single ray! It's like a sky with no thunder, no lightning, but all covered with clouds . . . . Not a single star! And you know what a sky is without stars!

In "The Foot of the Cross" by Father Faber, I read that Our Lord, on the night of His Passion, was so mistreated by His enemies that the blows He received were so violent He had trouble opening His eyes, so painful was the light of day to Him.[1] . . . Little grain of sand, in this bitter detail I find one consolation: since nothing bright can strike the wounded eyes of Jesus without making Him suffer, He can walk, then, in my darkness without suffering too much . . . . Dear little grain of sand, you are very close to me. Ah! Let us both remember that on earth there can be only suffering for those who love and seek with ardor the gentle, suffering Face of Jesus . . . . Let us not be so cowardly as to desire consolations with such a love in our heart! . . .

But, oh, my God! how sweet the homeland will be after this exile of struggles and tears! what a blessedness to hope for! and what a thing to wait for! To see this great Eternal Vision lighted up not by the lamps of this world but by the divine Lamb![2]

Give me some news about Céline;[3] our Mother tells me she is suffering very much! And the itinerary for the trip,[4] what day does she arrive at Lourdes?[5] And the Holy Face,[6] won't she arrive there tomorrow?

* Autograph.

1. F. W. Faber, *The Foot of the Cross, or The Sorrows of Mary* (Bray et Retaux, Paris 1877, 10th ed.), ch. 1, p. 15, "Mary's Martyrdom."
2. See Apocalypse 21:23.

3. Thérèse had received, around 1:30 that Monday afternoon, a visit from Céline and Léonie, who were leaving on a trip with the Guérin family and would be away from May 6 to 17 or 18.
4. Céline had written down the itinerary in a notebook that she had used for her trip to Rome (see LT 31 A, note 4). On pages 26-38, there are descriptions of the following cities: *Le Mans, Tours, Lourdes,* trip to *Gavarnie,* then *Pau, Bayonne, Saint-Sebastien, Biarritz, Bordeaux,* with no mention of dates; she stated that for the trip to *Gavarnie* the tourists boarded a carriage at six in the morning and that the trip from *Lourdes* required twelve hours. M. Guérin completed the return trip, in his chronicles, citing, after *Bordeaux*: *La Rochelle, Nantes, Angers* (ChrIG, pp. 38-39).
5. See LT 104, note 8.
6. This was the *Oratoire de la Sainte Face* at Tours. Céline wrote: "The chapel of the Holy Face in M. Dupont's house was on the ground floor; this chapel was made up of three little oratories; upstairs was his bedroom in which there was a plaster bust of M. Dupont" (Carnet, p. 27).

LT 104 From Thérèse to Sister Agnes of Jesus.

(Fragments.)

May 5-6, 1890
→ LC 127

J. M. J. T.

Thank you for your letter, ah! thank you!...

It doesn't surprise me that you are having no consolation, for Jesus is so little consoled that He is happy when He finds a soul in whom He may take His rest without a lot of ceremony....

How proud I am to be your sister! And your little daughter, too, for it's you who taught me to love Jesus, to seek Him only[1] ...and to despise all creatures....

As for Céline, I don't know anymore than you, and even less,

for I didn't know she was suffering,[2] if this is not . . . troublesome. At first, Céline spoke to us about our poor Father; she remarked that it . . . .

she . . . . of Jeanne. She told us also to pray very much for Léonie, for she is suffering from her illness,[3] and I believe that Uncle thinks this is dangerous; it's swollen all around[4] . . . .

Céline spoke to us about poor little Father; she remarked that it was on Saturday, the day of the Finding of the Cross, that we, too, found our Cross![5] Léonie was here. She hopes to be cured at the Holy Face[6] or at Lourdes. She will go down into the bath. Poor Léonie, she was so kind and she wanted to deprive herself of her visits just to please Céline . . . . They rang for Vespers,[7] and I left. I don't know when they will be at Tours, but I believe next week they will be at Lourdes. We must write them on Monday or Tuesday before noon in order that the letter arrive on Saturday.[8]

Oh! how earth is an exile!. . . There is no other support to seek outside of Jesus, for He alone is *immutable*. What a joy to think that He cannot change . . . . What a joy for our heart to think that our family loves Jesus so tenderly; this is always my consolation; is not our family a virginal family, a family of lilies?[9] . . . Ask from Jesus that the littlest, that the *last* may not be the *last* in loving Him with all her power to love!. . .

* Autograph in four fragments; CE, LT 1948 (LXXXII).

1. End of the first passage which was restored according to the copy of the Process (CE II, p. 49), with the exception of the line: "It doesn't surprise me that you're having no consolation," still remaining from the autograph. What follows, right down to " . . . it's swollen all around," is cited from pieces of the autograph.
2. Moral suffering and, at this time, physical suffering. During the year 1890, Céline was having some heart trouble and this disturbed her sisters; these troubles were of a nervous origin, the result of sorrows and worries because of M. Martin's condition. See LT 124.
3. Perhaps eczema? From childhood, Léonie was afflicted with this sickness, and it lasted for a very long time, even throughout her religious life.
4. End of the autograph. The following paragraph is cited according

to the first edition, LT LXXXII, p. 148, all other sources having disappeared since then.

5. This Saturday, May 3, Céline and Léonie went to visit their father at *Bon Sauveur* at Caen. His condition was very distressing for them, and perhaps Thérèse was giving some details about M. Martin's illness, hence, the destruction of the original and the copies by the sisters of the Saint.
6. This was a reference to the Holy Face at Tours; see LC 127, note 6.
7. Vespers was recited at two o'clock in the afternoon. We see several times, in the Martin-Guérin correspondence, meetings in the speak-room of the Carmel set for one o'clock.
8. Thérèse makes a mistake here (see LT 105). Céline had no doubt said to write on Saturday (May 10), at the latest, so that the letter would arrive on Monday or Tuesday, May 12 or 13, before the departure for Lourdes (Tuesday noon?). Here the paragraph cited from LT 1948 ends. The following paragraph is from the Process (CE II, p. 49).
9. See in LT 102, note 1, the description of the picture painted by Sister Agnes of Jesus.

LT 105 From Thérèse to Céline.

May 10, 1890

This letter was sent along with a letter from Sister Marie of the Sacred Heart, dated "Saturday," and Sister Marie's letter began this way: "If this little note doesn't reach you in time, complain to Thérèse of the Child Jesus. She assured me that I was mistaken and that you were not to be in Lourdes until next week. I'm sorry about taking this chance; I'd have been happy if you received a note from us at Lourdes. Well, at any rate, pray for us!. . ."

J. M. J. T.

Jesus †

My dear Céline,

Are you happy with your trip?. . . I hope the Blessed Virgin grants you her graces, if these are not graces of consolation, they

will no doubt be graces of light! . . . And the Holy Face![1] . . . Céline, do you know it is a great grace to visit all these holy places? . . . My heart would like to follow you everywhere, but, alas, I don't know the itinerary of the trip; I even thought that you would not be at Lourdes until next week.

Céline, you should be happy to be contemplating the beauties of nature, the mountains, the silvery rivers; all this is so magnificent, so well made for lifting up our souls . . . . Ah! little sister, let us detach ourselves from this earth, let us fly to the mountain of love where the beautiful Lily of our souls is to be found . . . . Let us detach ourselves from the *consolations* of Jesus in order to attach ourselves to *Him*! . . .

And the Blessed Virgin! Ah, Céline, hide yourself well in the shadow of her virginal mantle in order that she may virginize you![2] . . . Purity is so beautiful, so white! . . . Blessed are the pure of heart, for they shall see God![3] . . . Yes, they will see Him even on this earth, where nothing is pure, but where all creatures become crystal clear when seen through the Face of the most beautiful and whitest of Lilies![4] . . .

Céline, *pure hearts* are sometimes surrounded by thorns . . . . They are often in darkness, and then these lilies believe they've lost their whiteness, they think these thorns surrounding them have succeeded in tearing their petals! . . . Céline, do you understand? . . . The lilies in the midst of thorns are the loved ones of Jesus, and it is in their midst that He takes His delight! . . .

Blessed is he who has been found *worthy* to suffer temptation![5]

Thérèse of the Child Jesus of the Holy Face
nov.carm.ind.

I'd have liked to write to my dear Léonie, but this is impossible for me because of a lack of time. Tell her how much I am praying for her, and how much I am thinking of my dear godmother.[6] I wanted, too, to write to little Marie, but I can't. I am praying very much so that the Blessed Virgin may make her a *little lily* that thinks very much of Jesus and *forgets itself* as well as all its

miseries within the hands of obedience![7] I'm not forgetting my Jeanne . . . .

We have received nothing from Canada.[8] Sister Agnes of Jesus can't write because of her retreat.

If you have not bought anything for N.M.,[9] you could bring back a statue of Our Lady of Lourdes, *unpainted,*[10] around four or five francs.

* Autograph.
1. She meant the Holy Face at Tours in the "*Oratoire de la Sainte Face.*"
2. Thérèse writes "*virgine*" instead of "*virginise.*" In the prayer to the Holy Face already mentioned (LT 103, note 5), Sister Agnes wrote, making Jesus speak the words: "[This bouquet] is for you, and the more you look at it, the more the mysterious petals of these divine flowers will be turned toward you in order to cover your soul and virginize your heart."
3. Matthew 5:8.
4. Reference to the picture of April 28; see LT 102.
5. James 1:12. Thérèse is referring here, in a very delicate way, to the temptations regarding chastity that tortured Céline for some months past (see Piat, *Céline,* pp. 46-48) and that would persist for a long time (see LC 157). Citing the preceding paragraph in her testimony, Sister Geneviève introduced it in this way: "In spite of her angelic purity, here is what the Servant of God thinks of temptations contrary to this virtue" (PA, 1013).
6. Léonie was Thérèse's godmother at her Confirmation (June 14, 1884).
7. Reference to the scruples from which Marie Guérin was suffering (see LT 92 and 93).
8. Reference to P. Pichon, who was in Canada.
9. Abbreviation for "*Notre Mère,*" that is, Mother Marie de Gonzague.
10. At the end of her notebook (see LC 127, note 4), Céline noted down, with their prices, the objects of piety she had purchased at Tours and Lourdes. There is no mention of a statue.

LT 106 **From Thérèse to Sister Agnes of Jesus.**

May 10, 1890

Date deduced from the content; see note 1.

J. M. J. T.

Jesus†

Dear lamb, still one more day[1] and you will come back to fight on the plain![2] . . . The little lamb[3] will again find its Mamma.[4] . . . How happy I am to be *always a prisoner* in Carmel; I have no desire to go to Lourdes to have ecstasies.[5] I prefer (the monotony of sacrifice)! What a joy to be so hidden that nobody thinks of you! . . . To be *unknown* even to persons with whom you live . . . .

Dear lamb, how I thank Jesus for *having given me to you,* for making you understand my soul so well![6] . . . I cannot tell you all I am thinking about . . . . Ah! HEAVEN!!!!!! Then a single glance and all will be understood! . . .

Silence, this is the language that alone can tell you what is happening in my soul! . . .

* Autograph.

1. Sister Agnes came out of retreat on Monday, May 12; we could say, then, that Thérèse wrote on Saturday evening. Had she written on Sunday, she would no doubt have said: "tomorrow you will come back," etc.
2. See Exodus 17:8-13; see LT 201.
3. This is the last time in her correspondence that Thérèse calls herself by this nickname; see LT 54, note 2.
4. See LT 76, note 7.
5. A possible reference to the "consolations" received by Céline at Lourdes. See the letter from Marie Guérin to Céline, October 15, 1890: "Thérèse told me yesterday that certainly you would receive consolations from the Sacred Heart just as the Blessed Virgin gave you at the grotto. You had not told me that you had received any consolations at Lourdes."

6. Was Thérèse making a reference to a second note from Sister Agnes of Jesus, now lost? Or was she speaking about her sister's customary attitude towards her? In any case, we should compare this text to the later testimony of the two sisters, which would hint at a certain misunderstanding between them in 1889-1890, the years when both were assigned to taking care of the refectory; see Ms. A, p. 160, and especially CJ 13.7.18: "You had come to the point where you no longer knew me."

LT 107 — From Thérèse to Céline.

May 19-20, 1890

Approximate date; see note 2.

J. M. J. T.

May '90

Jesus†

My dear little Céline,

I have been told to write you to tell you not to come and give us any news about Papa[1] during the retreat for Pentecost.[2] If you were to write us a short note, you would be very kind, and then you could come on Monday[3] to see us. Dear Céline, I am happy for having been given this charge, for I have to tell you how much I think that God loves you and is treating you as one of His privileged souls . . . . Ah! you can well say that the *reward* is *great* in *heaven* since it is said: "Blessed are you when they *persecute* you and say *falsely* all kinds of evil against you."[4] So rejoice and leap for joy![5] . . .

Céline, what a privilege to be unknown on this earth! . . . Ah, God's thoughts are not our thoughts.[6] If they were, our life would be only a hymn of thanksgiving! . . .

Céline, do you think St. Teresa received more grace than you? . . . As for myself, I shall tell you not to aim for her *seraphic*

sanctity, but rather to be perfect as your heavenly Father is perfect![7] . . . Ah! Céline, our *infinite desires* are not, then, either dreams or fancies, since Jesus Himself has given us this commandment![8] . . .

Céline, don't you find that on this earth there is *nothing* left for us! Jesus wills to have us drink His chalice to the dregs by leaving our dear Father *over there*. Ah! let us refuse Him nothing; He has so much *need of love* and He is so *thirsty* that he expects from us the drop of water that must refresh Him! . . . Ah! let us give without counting the cost. One day, He will say: "now, my turn."[9]

Thank my dear little Marie very much for her delightful bouquet; tell her that I offered it to Jesus as coming from her, and I asked Him in return to adorn her soul with as many virtues as there are rose buds! . . .

Your little Sister Thérèse of the Child Jesus of the Holy Face
nov.carm.ind.

* Autograph.

1. Céline and Léonie went to visit M. Martin at *Bon Sauveur* at Caen, Monday or Tuesday, May 19 or 20; see LD, May 20.
2. Pentecost Sunday was May 25. Céline returned from the trip with the Guérin family on May 17 or 18. On May 15, Ascension Thursday, Sister Agnes of Jesus wrote her: "You know that today we are entering the retreat for Pentecost. If our beloved Mother allows you to see the little lamb on Saturday, it is because she pities her little lamb Céline so much. She is really a little lamb exiled from the sheepfold! . . . (When you have asked our Mother in the little confessional, she will do what she wants.)" We do not know if this visit took place on Saturday, May 17; or if Céline had to content herself with a written communication; perhaps it was to this letter (lost) that Thérèse was responding here.
3. Monday, May 26.
4. Matthew 5:11. We do not know the source and the nature of the "persecutions" Céline was suffering, but no doubt these had something to do with her father's illness.

5. Matthew 5:12.
6. Isaias 55:8.
7. Matthew 5:48, cited, among others, in the Imitation of Christ I, 17, *Reflection.*
8. See in this same matter Thérèse's conversation with P. Blino, S.J.: "'Father, I want to become a saint; I want to love God as much as St. Teresa,' she said to a retreat master. 'What pride and what presumption!' he replied. 'Confine yourself to correcting your faults, to offending God no longer, to making a little progress in virtue each day, and temper your rash desires.' She answered: 'But, Father, I don't think that these are rash desires; I can aspire to sanctity, even to a more elevated sanctity, if I wish, than that of St. Teresa, since Our Lord said: 'Be perfect as your heavenly Father is perfect.' See, Father, how vast the field is, and it seems to me I have the right to run in it!' The religious was not convinced, and the *Servant of God* was seeking, without being able to find it, the answer to her thoughts, her inner longings, someone in authority who would tell her: 'Launch out into the sea and cast your nets, you are in the truth.'" (Mother Agnes of Jesus, NPPA, *Hope,* p. 2.)

   It is difficult to date this conversation (and even to guarantee its literalness). If we are to believe Sister Marie of the Trinity in this matter, it should have taken place a short time before the month of August 1890, the time when she herself, at the age of sixteen, made a retreat at the Paris Carmel, *l'avenue de Messine,* and met the same Jesuit priest: "During this retreat, I saw Père Blino, S.J., extraordinary confessor at the Paris Carmel. He spoke to me with praise of Sister Thérèse of the Child Jesus at the Lisieux Carmel where he had just preached the 'Ignatian Exercises,' and he told me how she had even gone to the Holy Father to obtain entrance to the Carmel at fifteen. I told him that I felt I had the courage to go to Rome on foot, if it were necessary, to obtain the same favor." (*Circulaire de soeur Marie de la Trinité,* pp. 4–5.) Research, up to this day, has not shed any light on this point of chronology. As for Thérèse's aspirations to sanctity, these were answered in the Carmel; apart from Sister Agnes of Jesus, see Mother Marie de Gonzague (LC 118, 144, 162, and the Christmas picture, 1890); Sister Marie of the Angels (LC 141 and 145).
9. Arminjon, see LT 57, note 5.

LD *From Céline to Sister Agnes of Jesus, Sister Marie of the Sacred Heart, and Thérèse.*

May 20, 1890 (Fragments.)

When going for the visit,[1] I met M. Vital[2] and Mme. Benoit,[3] who were going there; they stopped their carriage and we climbed up with them. Poor little Father was really touched; it gives him such evident joy when he sees his old friends.

He was charming. M. Vital, wishing to leave, said to him: "Now, I am going to leave you with your children." With a very kind look in his face, he replied: "Oh! stay a while, you are not in the way!" Finally, they left.

God had arranged a consoling day for us. When we saw him, he was just returning from the May devotions at which a reading had been made on the respect due to old people, on the veneration for white hair; Papa was very much moved.

His limbs are numbed at present, and it was with difficulty that he made a tour of the garden with us. At first, he let go Léonie's arm and was satisfied with mine, but it was as if his head were heavier than his whole body, and it wouldn't have been long before he fell over. He noticed this, for he supported himself by the wall, saying that he wasn't tired but that everything was spinning around him; Léonie then gave him the support of her arm.

Poor little Father spoke about you, our Mother, and Mother Geneviève; he was delighted with your letters.[4] "I was not able to read them entirely," he told me, "because it was too beautiful, and I was weeping . . . ." He did not ask to leave, and when I said: "Nothing is long which comes to an end!" "That's true, and I believe all this is approaching its end, it won't be long now . . . ." (He wanted to talk of his return.)[5] He made this answer with such a resigned and kind look! . . . I really think that the more time goes on, the more the expression on his face is peaceful and saintly.

* CMG.

1. Judging by this letter, we are unable to determine whether Céline wrote it on that same day or the day after her visit to M. Martin at *Bon Sauveur*. At this time, families did not enter the hospital quarters but saw their sick in a visiting room.
2. M. Vital Romet, Céline's godfather, and one of M. Martin's best friends in their younger days.
3. *Née* Hortense Romet, sister of Vital Romet; see LD, February 18, 1889, note 4.
4. These letters were not preserved.
5. M. Martin did not return to Lisieux until two years later.

LC 128 *From Céline to Thérèse.*

June 17, 1890

My dear little Thérèse,

You're going to be surprised to receive a letter from your Céline[1] in poetry, but, you see, I wasn't able to write otherwise. Pauline told me yesterday what you thought about flowers, what you said to Jesus on their behalf.[2] I understood everything . . . and you know how!

Once I returned to my little room, alas! what was I to do if not to meditate? Yesterday, it was easier for me to do this in poetry . . . . My own little Thérèse . . . oh! you understand me, you know my whole soul. I thought about this so long, and I would have liked so much to say it in my poor clumsy verses! Understand your Céline! . . .

We leave for Caen tomorrow on the 7:00 o'clock train, and it is possible that we shall return by 4:30; in this case, I shall be bold enough to pass by to give you some news . . . . Oh! ask our dear Mother to be willing [3] to allow me. I shall be deprived of so many visits during our tiresome sojourn at the much-overrated La Musse.[4]

Kiss my beloved Mother for me and my dear little sisters.

For you, my whole heart,
Your Céline

I did my shopping this morning;[5] did you receive your asparagus?[6]

P.S. In case I should return only at 7:00 o'clock, I would not be able to go and see you; so would you answer this question which Jeanne asked me: In what material should she buy her white dress?[7] In other words, what kind of silk, precisely? (I believe she intends to give it to you,[8] but she hasn't told Aunt about this as yet.)

* Autograph.

1. A poem entitled: "*Le Divin Charme.*" The original has disappeared, but we have found a complete copy in one of Sister Geneviève's notebooks (*Notes intimes*, I, pp. 36-37), dated June 26, 1890. This poem was inspired by the picture of April 28 (see LT 102, note 1) and by Jeanne Guérin's recent wedding engagement (see note 7). The poem is mentioned in LT 108, 120, and LC 149.
2. Thérèse never ceased to develop, ever more deeply, this symbolic language of flowers. In 1910, Sister Marie of the Angels emphasized this fact as one of Sister Thérèse's characteristics: "In the Servant of God's piety, there is a matter which strikes me very much because I never saw it in our Carmel, and I never heard it spoken about in the lives of the saints, and this is the role she gives to flowers. All had a special language for her, revealing to her God's infinite love and perfections. She made use of them, too, in order to express her own love and her heart's sentiments to God." (PO, 2016.)
3. Céline could have expected a refusal because of the proximity of her last visit with Sister Agnes of Jesus, Thursday, June 26.
4. Céline and Léonie accompanied the Guérin family to the château at La Musse, and they remained there from July 10 to 31 (ChrIG, p. 39).
5. Instead of Saturday, the customary day for shopping at Lisieux.
6. Perhaps to celebrate the feast of Saints Peter and Paul, Pauline's feast.

7. This was for her wedding; Jeanne Guérin was engaged since June 8 to Dr. Francis La Néele. The Guérin chronicles mention a trip to Paris, July 2-5: "Purchases for the wedding" (ChrIG, p. 39).
8. After her wedding, Jeanne Guérin made a gift of her dress (satin) to the sacristy of the Carmel, and the nuns used it to make curtains for the little Communion grille. Thérèse painted eucharistic symbols on it.

LC 129 *From Céline to Thérèse.*

July 17, 1890

Céline was on vacation at La Musse with the Guérin family since July 10.

La Musse, July 17, 1890

My dear little Thérèse,

Here I am, then, for a moment with you, my dear confidante. I am leading a life of the exiled here. It's true that I have Marie, who is very loving and devoted to me, but I feel that her soul has not been matured through suffering. At times, I find her a little too childish and not sufficiently submissive to sacrifice; this is what makes her less looked up to than Jeanne, less respected, less listened to by Uncle and Aunt. However, I believe that she is called to a high perfection. A director would really be necessary for her, but her parents would be opposed to this, fearing he would influence her to choose the religious life.

Thérèse, it would be impossible for me to tell you what I am suffering when I think of our dear little Father, I miss him so much! Oh! if you only knew what my heart feels when seeing itself deprived of Father, Mother, even home . . . . Yes, deprived of all this, for I have nothing of all this. And when I see others at my side who are enjoying the paternal home, lavishing their filial affection, and I who cannot serve close by the father whom I love so much! by the father who challenges any comparison with other earthly fathers, so incomparable is he. Nobody approaches him, he was so good! . . . Papa!

Oh, Thérèse, let us be saints. I feel that Our Lord has placed everything at our disposal so that we may attain this unique goal. I have noticed that, in our soul, He knew how to touch the most sensitive chords; He presses all of them under His divine fingers, and there is not one of them that remains without producing some sounds. And what sounds! Our soul is the harp of Jesus, and this harp alone knows for what concerts it is employed . . . .

Have you noticed how Jesus does not will that there remain anything human in our heart? He explores it and He explores it again, right down to its very depths. He is looking to see if, there where one would suspect nothing, He will not discover a gold mine. Oh, Thérèse, I want to make my heart all gold, even in its most intimate hiding-places; Jesus will be so pleased. He alone delights me. Each evening, when contemplating immensity, I repeat my little poem to Him: "*Le Divin Charme*,"[1] and I never grow tired of it. Everyday, when walking through the woods, gathering flowers, I catch myself meditating on "the tears of Jesus," a divine charm that fascinates me.

The other day, we went by chance into a poor little church. I believed that my tears were going to betray my heart, I had all the trouble in the world holding them back. Just think: a Tabernacle without a veil, a real black hole, perhaps the refuge of spiders, a Ciborium so poor that I think it was copper, and what did it have for a cover?. . . A dirty rag, no longer retaining the form of a Ciborium veil .[2] . . . In the Ciborium, a single Host. Alas! there is no need of others in this parish, for there is not a single Communion throughout the year, outside of Easter. Then, in these country places, there are unrefined priests who close their churches all day long. Besides, they are old and without financial support.

Oh, Thérèse! I remained deep in thought before this spectacle, my soul was torn into shreds. Now I hate La Musse, for I am in a château with gilded panellings,[3] while Jesus dwells in the most frightful poverty in the valley opposite us. Now I detest stylish clothes, for I have silk dresses and wear diamonds and gold, while Jesus has nothing for Himself but rags. Now I desire only one thing: since Jesus is poor, I want to be poor with Him; I long for

the moment when I shall no longer have a single *sou*! I must possess nothing. Oh! were I free with my fortune, I would rid myself of it in order to give all to Jesus.

Kiss our Mother for me in order to make amends for my mistake in having written her such a scribbled little letter[4] and on such poor paper. I think of Marie and Pauline, whom I love *so much*. For you, your Céline's heart.[5]

P.S. Did you receive the tarts?[6] I think Aunt would be flattered to receive a "thank-you" for the ones she gave.

* Typewritten copy G.
1. See LC 128, note 1.
2. "We made plans to buy a suitable Ciborium, and the Carmel made an embroidered Veil." (Sister Geneviève's note.)
3. "Even the keys were gilded," said little Jean Lahaye, son of the pharmacist at Lisieux, who was welcomed at La Musse in 1893, along with his mother and his sister Charlotte (DCL).
4. This letter from Céline to Mother Marie de Gonzague has not been preserved.
5. Thérèse answered this letter the following day (LT 108).
6. Undoubtedly on the occasion of July 16, the feast of Our Lady of Mount Carmel.

LT 108 From Thérèse to Céline.

July 18,
1890
→LC 129

J. M. J. T.

Jesus †!... Carmel, July 18, '90

Dear Céline,

If you only knew what your letter said to my soul! ... Ah! joy inundated my heart like a vast ocean!... Céline, you know all that I have to say to you since you are myself .... I'm sending you

a page[1] which says much to my soul, and it seems to me your soul, too, will be immersed in it . . . .

Céline, it's *such a long time ago* . . . and already the soul of the prophet Isaias was immersed, just as our own soul is, in the HIDDEN BEAUTIES of Jesus . . . . Ah, Céline, when I read these things, I wonder what time really is? . . . Time is only a mirage, a dream . . . already God *sees us in glory*, He TAKES DELIGHT in *our eternal beatitude*![2] Ah! what good this thought does my soul, and I understand now why He is not bargaining with us . . . . He feels that we *understand* Him, and He is treating us as His friends, as His dearest spouses . . . .

Céline, since Jesus was (alone in treading the wine)[3] which He is giving us to drink, let us not refuse in our turn to wear clothing stained in blood . . . let us tread for Jesus a new wine which may quench His thirst, which will return Him love for love. Ah, let us not keep back one drop of wine that we can offer Him . . . and, then, looking about,[4] He will see that we are coming to help Him! . . . His face was as though hidden![5] . . . Céline, it is still hidden today, for who understands the tears of Jesus? . . .

Dear Céline, let us make a little tabernacle in our heart where Jesus may take refuge, and then He will be consoled, and He will forget what we cannot forget: (the ingratitude of souls that abandon Him in a deserted tabernacle! . . .)[6]

(Open to me, my sister, my beloved, for my face is covered with dew, my locks with the drops of night) (cant. of cant.).[7] That is what Jesus says to our soul when He is abandoned and forgotten! . . . Céline, *forgetfulness*, it seems to me that it's this which causes Him the greatest sorrow! . . .

Papa! . . . Ah, Céline, I cannot tell you all I am thinking, it would take too long, and how say things that the mind itself can hardly express, deep things that are in the innermost recesses of the soul! . . .

Jesus has sent us the best chosen Cross that He was able to find in His immense love . . . how can we complain when He Himself was looked upon as a man struck by God and humbled![8] . . . The

divine charm[9] delights my soul and consoles it in a marvelous way, at each moment of the day! . . . Ah, *the tears of Jesus, what smiles!* . . .

Kiss everybody for me, and tell them *all I would like to say!* . . . I think very much about my dear Léonie, my dear little Visitandine.[10] Tell Marie of the Blessed Sacrament[11] that Jesus asks much love from her, He wants from her reparation for the coldness He receives, and her heart must be a furnace in which Jesus may warm Himself! . . . She must forget herself entirely in order to think only of Him . . . .

Céline, let us pray for priests, ah, pray for them. May our life be consecrated for them; Jesus makes me feel every day that He wills this from the both of us.

C.T.[12]

J. M. J. T.

From the Prophet Isaias (ch. 53).[13]

"Who would believe what we have heard? To whom has the arm of the Lord been revealed? The Christ will grow up like a sapling before the Lord and like a shoot that comes from a parched soil. He is without beauty and without stately bearing; we have seen him; he had nothing that would attract our eyes and we despised him. He appeared to us as an object of scorn, the least of men, a man of sorrows, acquainted with suffering! . . . His face is as though hidden! . . . He seemed to be despicable, and we did not recognize him . . . . He truly took our infirmities upon himself, and he was burdened with our offenses. We looked upon him as a leper, as a man struck by God and humbled! . . . And yet he was pierced for our iniquities, he was broken for our crimes. The chastisement which was to procure our peace fell upon him, and we were healed by his wounds."

Continuation of ch. 53[14]

"Who is this that comes from Edom, in crimsoned garments, from Bosra, this one arrayed in majesty, marching in the greatness of his strength? . . . 'It is I, I who announce vindication, I who am mighty to save.' Why is your apparel red, and your garments like those of the one who tramples wine in the winepress? 'The winepress I have trodden alone, and of my people there was no one with me. I looked around me, and there was nobody to help me; I searched and I found no help! . . .'"

"These who are clothed in white robes, who are they? and where do they come from? . . . 'These are they who have come out of the *great tribulation* and have washed their robes in the blood of the Lamb. Therefore, they are before the throne of God and serve him day and night . . . .'"[15]

"My beloved is a bundle of myrrh, he will rest on my heart! . . . My beloved shines with the whiteness and beauty of his face, the hair on his head is like royal purple.[16] My beloved is lovable, his face inspires love, and his bowed *face* urges me on to return love for love."[17]

"I abandoned and forgot myself,
Laying my face on my Beloved;
All things ceased; I went out from myself,
Leaving my cares
Forgotten among the lilies." (Fragment of a poem
of Our Father, St. John of the Cross.)[18]

* Autograph.

1. This is a page of excerpts from Sacred Scripture, that Thérèse will comment on in the letter. This page could have been transcribed before she wrote the letter. Her handwriting, straight up, differs from that of the letter itself.

2. On October 20, 1888, Sister Agnes of Jesus (who was reading P. d'Argentan that year, see LC 83, note 1), wrote to Céline: "Père d'Argentan tells us that all is *present* to God. It is an immense consolation to search the depths of this mystery! He has always, then, looked upon me as His spouse since I must be this one day. I am always in His Heart just as I will be throughout eternity." However, we can not really determine if, and to what extent, P. d'Argentan influenced Thérèse's statement on the mystery of "time," with its relationship to "eternity."
3. Isaias 63:3.
4. *Ibid.* 63:5.
5. *Ibid.* 53:3.
6. In spite of the parentheses, which Thérèse used instead of quotation marks, it is possible that this is not a textual quotation but is simply recalling Céline's letter regarding this matter.
7. Canticle of Canticles 5:2. This was a quotation, dear to Sister Agnes of Jesus, who had painted it on a wall in the dormitory in 1887, between the linen room and the chapter room (writing, however, "my head" instead of "my face").
8. Isaias 53:4.
9. Céline's poem; see LC 128, note 1.
10. Léonie persevered in her desire to enter the Visitation, which she had left in January 1888.
11. Marie Guérin; see LC 130.
12. Initials of Céline and Thérèse, which the latter wrote below the words "*the both of us*," putting them in a circle. Sister Agnes added a postscript to this letter; see LC 130, note 1.
13. Isaias 53:1-5. These verses form the first reading of the first nocturn of the Office for the "Five Wounds of Our Lord Jesus Christ," recited on Friday of the third week of Lent (March 14, 1890) and the first reading of the first nocturn of the Office for the "Sorrows of the Blessed Virgin Mary," recited on the fifth Friday of Lent (March 28, 1890). Thérèse transcribed this quotation almost textually in her second "pious recreation": "The Angels at the Crib of Jesus" (December 25, 1894). See, too, CJ 5.8.9.
14. This was really Isaias 63:1-5, in which Thérèse omits verses 3 and 4 in part, concerning God's anger and the day of vengeance. The whole excerpt, including verses 3 and 4, makes up the third lesson

for the Divine Office of the "Five Wounds" (March 14, 1890); divided into verses, it appears as antiphons for the Divine Office of the "Precious Blood of Our Lord Jesus Christ," for the fourth Friday of Lent (March 21, 1890) and the first Sunday of July (July 6, 1890).

15. Apocalypse 7:14-15. These verses form the first three antiphons of Lauds, in the Divine Office of the "Precious Blood."
16. Canticle of Canticles 1:12, 11, 16; these are the fourth and second antiphons of Vespers for the "Sorrows of the Blessed Virgin Mary" (note 13).
17. First response of the first nocturn of the same Divine Office; Thérèse keeps only what has reference to the Face, omitting "the extended hands and the opened heart." This response was according to the text from Isaias (note 13).
18. *Ascent of Mount Carmel,* Canticle of the Soul, stanza 8. The same stanzas are repeated at the beginning of the *Dark Night of the Soul.* This is the first time that Thérèse quotes St. John of the Cross explicitly. It seems we are approaching the period about which Ms. A speaks: "Ah! what lights I have drawn from the Works of Our Father, St. John of the Cross! . . . At the age of seventeen and eighteen, I had no other spiritual nourishment" (Ms. A, p. 179). Thérèse was undoubtedly acquainted with the Doctor of Carmel at Les Buissonnets, through her two Carmelite sisters and through quotations in the *Petites Fleurs* (see LT 45, note 5). On the occasion of the Saint's first feast day celebrated by her in the Carmel, she drew out by lot a saying of St. John of the Cross (November 24, 1888). However, the decisive discovery of his writings came in 1890. The Carmelites were preparing for the celebration of the third centenary of St. John of the Cross' death (December 14, 1591). For this occasion, the Carmelite nuns at Paris published a second edition of his Works (volumes I and II in 1890; III and IV in 1891). In the Lisieux Carmel, the knowledge and influence of St. Teresa of Avila exceeded that of St. John of the Cross (judging by the correspondence of Mother Marie de Gonzague, Sister Agnes of Jesus, etc.). Thérèse's attraction for the mystical Doctor caused some surprise. "One day, during her novitiate, Sister Thérèse of the Child Jesus spoke during recreation about the doctrine of St. John of the Cross with a former Mother, who had been prioress of the Carmel at Coutances [Mother Heart of Jesus]. The latter told me afterward: 'Is it possible that a child of seventeen

understands these things and speaks of them in such a way! It's admirable, I just can't get over it!'" (Mother Agnes of Jesus, NPPA, Reputation for Sanctity, p. 3). Thérèse's novice mistress spoke in the same way: "One day, I don't know if she was seventeen, she spoke to me of certain passages from his mystical teachings with an understanding so far above her age that I was totally astonished!" (Sister Marie of the Angels, PA, 1155.) We do not know in what order and in what editions Thérèse approached this reading. See LT 109, note 2.

LD *From Céline to Sister Agnes of Jesus, Sister Marie of the Sacred Heart, and Thérèse.*

July 22,
1890
→ LT 108

La Musse, July 22, 1890

My dear little Sisters,

Eight more days and we shall be returning, and what a joy! Our departure is set for Thursday a week from now, July 31. I long for the moment when I shall see you again, for you are my whole happiness.

Each day has its sharp thorns. Oh, dear little sisters, if you only knew what a heart, made like mine, suffers in a strange home. And it isn't the big things that wound my heart the most but little nothings: the bird fears the bullet less than the hunter's rifle.

All this serves to detach me from earth and to look upon what is taking place here as transitory and worthless. From my window, my eyes sweep out on the flat open countryside, and there I see fields and meadows, but how limited all this is! These fields are only narrow strips of land, cut very sharply; some are yellow, this is ripe corn; others are light green, dark green. They blend together, forming a striped carpet. I can see men tossing hay, and how tiny they are! I look with surprise on the haystacks, and these, though very large, appear to me only like mudpies shaped by the

hands of children. And yet both the happiness or the sadness of the workers consists in the odor and the color of this hay!

Among these workers, there are very few who love God. This morning, there was a civil burial. Ordinarily, this is rare in these country places; however, right here, the country places are worse than the towns, for they are populated by poorly educated people, who have not heard anyone speak of God except at their First Communion; since then, not a single word. They are absent from Church services, never receive Holy Communion. It is sad.

Oh! how necessary it is to pray for priests! I find they have a great responsibility; there is so much to do, and, in my opinion, they don't do all that is within their power. Never any sermons, never any paternal instructions, never any visits to their flock. Most of them don't know their parishioners. I would say, without judging the priests in particular, that I find the people much more excusable than the priests. They don't know their duties, how then would they carry them out? I don't think God expects anything from them.

It's true that in these parts there are only old priests, very aged and infirm, and they no longer have the zeal and strength of youth to lift up the crowds.

However, I will resume once again the chapter of my impressions of all that is around me . . . . I don't understand how they can seek to build up a human family when there is scarcely anyone who devotes himself to forming these people in spiritual matters. Earthly marriages form bodies, the soul produces souls, but how many souls without wings! Who, then, will engender souls for heaven? Oh, little sisters, this will be ourselves through our mystical union with Jesus and our soul . . . . And this union will not stop at tens but at a thousand million!

The world that doesn't understand us, that thinks us selfish, says we are living a useless life; it will see later on the ones who have worked the most. People will compare with astonishment the variety of vocations.

Dear little sisters, read into the whole soul of your little Céline. I'm thinking so much about these things!

And Thérèse! What should I tell you about your letter and the page you copied out for me? I commissioned my good angel with carrying my thanks to you. That letter is my *consolation*; I read it, read it again, and meditate on it endlessly . . . .

Monsieur La Néele[1] brought me some news about Papa. He did not see him, but Madame Costard told him that Papa is doing better than when we saw him last.[2] This helps me to bear up with this exile at La Musse.

Hug my dear Mother tightly for me. I was thinking very much about Mother Geneviève on her feast.[3] Had I been there, I would have treated you royally in her honor.

Your little Céline[4]

* Typewritten copy G..

1. Doctor Francis La Néele (1858-1916), was fiancé of Jeanne Guérin since the preceding June 8. Pharmacist (July 24, 1887) and medical doctor (January 8, 1888), he was living at Caen, 123, *rue Saint-Jean*, where he was running a pharmacy. In order to set up his medical practice, he had just bought, July 10, an old hotel (XVIIIth century) on 26, *rue de l'Oratoire*, Caen. This was his first visit to La Musse.
2. Probably June 28; see LC 128. That summer, M. Martin was able to take part in the annual outing by carriage into the countryside. This outing was organized by the Sisters at *Bon Sauveur* for the patients (judging by a letter from Sister Marie of the Sacred Heart to Céline, July 23, 1891).
3. On July 20, the Carmel of Lisieux had just celebrated the sixtieth anniversary of Mother Geneviève's reception of the Habit. She had received Extreme Unction for the second time, Good Friday, April 4; she was now definitively confined to bed in the infirmary where Thérèse was to die in 1897. It was because of the fear she would not live to celebrate her sixtieth anniversary of Profession that the nuns had solemnized the anniversary of her reception of the Habit on July 20.
4. This is the last letter from Céline to her sisters until the one she addressed to Thérèse, August 17, 1892 (LC 149). Apart from a short excerpt from a letter to Léonie (November 11, 1890), Sister Geneviève destroyed all her correspondence during these two years with her sisters.

LC 130 *From Marie Guérin to Thérèse.*

July 23-25, 1890

La Musse, July 23, '90

My dear little Thérèse,

I was very much touched by Pauline's tenderness in my regard; thank her for me, I beg you. How can I tell you how happy I was to receive this little poem[1] that corresponds so well with my sentiments!... I read it and read it again continually; in a word, I am relishing it. And you, my darling Thérèse, do you imagine that your few lines[2] did not do good to my soul? They supplied me with spiritual nourishment today. While Jeanne's fiancé[3] is here, the means of union with God are difficult to carry out, so meditation is often set aside. However, conversations with this poor human being cannot take its place for me!...

How can I tell you, dear little sister, all the temptations that I am experiencing since I am here; I am pursued by bad thoughts. Every moment is a struggle, and so I experience no joy in my Communions, and my thanksgivings after Communion are cold. I don't feel any love for God. Meditation, however, is a moment of delight for me; I could spend my days in this exercise. This is only one more proof that I'm not advancing in virtue, for prayer without mortification is like a body without a soul! I love to breathe in an air that is purer than the air of this earth, but as for drawing any fruit from this, there is nothing. It is true, nevertheless, that in my meditations I feel I am burning with love, but once I return to the combat, fortitude abandons me, and there can be no fruit without work. Very often, I ask myself this question: What do I have to offer to God today? Always nothing or next to nothing, a few times some little efforts. Dear Thérèse, you who have so much fervor in God's service,[4] teach your little sister to walk in it with courage. I am hardly born into the spiritual life; what have I done for the last twenty years?... I have allowed myself to live just as worldly people live, and God has been forgot-

ten. Now I have a great desire to love Him, but this desire has to bear fruit. I learned to make my first steps at Carmel, and will it be there that I'll make my last?... How I'd like it to be so![5]...

How can you expect God to call to Himself a child who is not seeking to procure His glory? If I had more will power, would not this single thought give me more fervor in overcoming myself? I must be, then, a tepid and cowardly soul? If you only knew the sorrow this thought gives me because I feel that I am this very weak soul.

This is the third time I've begun my letter, on three different days?[6] Today, in one of my walks, I came across an ant hill, and these little beasts gave me much to think about, furnishing me with a model. I saw their coming and going, with much fervor in their work, and I made this reflection: What is the goal and the reward of their efforts? They have none, and I who have a divine Master to love and serve, I remain inactive. The lesson from the ants was beneficial for me; I spent a blessed day, so this evening I am happy. Tell dear Mother that I have a little cell all to myself, and that I feel much at home there. First, I have a splendid view, and this does not harm the soul's ascensions. And then I love solitude so much; is it not there, more than anywhere else, that union of the soul with God becomes more intimate? Unfortunately, I am somewhat deprived in this matter, for I am not permitted to retire into my little room as much as I would like, a half hour at the most in the evening, and that is all.

Dear Thérèse, the four pages are filled, and this distresses me. If I were to listen to myself, I would talk with you indefinitely, but I have to fear Céline's wrath. She is already not pleased that I have taken up so much space. My darling's[7] green eyes are terrible to take in the evening.

Adieu, dear little sister. Kiss dear Mother for me, and tell her how much I love her; my heart feels it, but it cannot express it. I kiss you with my whole heart. We received the photographs, and Mamma's has to be done over again. I beg you to tell Pauline this.

Your little sister
Marie of the Blessed Sacrament

What do you think of my name?[8] It immerses me in deep meditation! As for myself, I see a divine inspiration in this, and I don't know another name that would give me more joy. What a beautiful title! However, *noblesse oblige*! . . . Let us console God's Heart; never before did I understand what outrages He is made the object of in the Sacrament of His love. You ought to come into these country places to see continual examples of these outrages.[9]

* Autograph.

1. Sister Agnes of Jesus had added a postscript to Thérèse's letter to Céline on July 18 (LT 108): "The little verses are for Marie; this is an answer to her letter, for our Mother does not dare write her. She was very pleased, however! . . . No worry over her scruples, Mother is taking charge of them. Don't let Aunt see the verses . . . ." This poem has not been found.
2. See the message with which Céline was entrusted for "Marie of the Blessed Sacrament" (LT 108, next to last paragraph).
3. Francis La Néele.
4. Thérèse took this sentence and rectified it: "You are mistaken, my darling, . . ." (See LT 109.)
5. See with reference to this LC 114, note 7.
6. July 25, consequently.
7. Céline had sea-green eyes.
8. As a matter of fact, this name was changed to "Marie of the Eucharist."
9. Céline had written in the same way just a few days earlier (LC 129).

LT 109 **From Thérèse to Marie Guérin.**

July 27-29, 1890 Approximate date; see note 1.
→ LC 130

J. M. J. T.

Jesus † Carmel, July '90[1]

My dear little Marie,

Thank God for all the graces He is giving you, and don't be so *ungrateful* as not to acknowledge them. You give me the impres-

sion of a little country girl to whom a powerful king should come and ask her to marry him, and she would not dare to accept under the pretext that she is not rich enough and schooled enough in the ways of the court, without realizing that her royal fiancé is aware of her poverty and weakness much better than she is herself . . . . Marie, if you are nothing, you must not forget that Jesus is *All*,[2] so you must lose your little nothingness in His *infinite All* and think only of this uniquely lovable *All* . . . . Neither ought you desire to see the fruit gathered from your efforts, for Jesus is pleased to keep for Himself alone these little nothings that console Him . . . . You are mistaken, my darling, if you believe that your little Thérèse walks always with fervor on the road of virtue. She is weak and very weak, and everyday she has a new experience of this weakness, but, Marie, Jesus is pleased to teach her, as He did St. Paul, the science of rejoicing in her infirmities.[3] This is a great grace, and I beg Jesus to teach it to you, for peace and quiet of heart are to be found there only. When we see ourselves as so miserable, then we no longer wish to consider ourselves, and we look only on the unique Beloved!. . .

Dear little Marie, as for myself, I know no other means of reaching perfection but (love). . . . Love, how well our heart is made for that!. . . Sometimes, I seek for another word to express love, but on this earth of exile words are powerless to express all the soul's vibrations, so we have to keep to this one word: (love!). . .

But upon whom will our poor heart hungry for love bestow it?. . . Ah, who will be big enough for this . . . will a human person be able to understand it . . . and, above all, will he know how to return it? Marie, there is only one Being who can understand the profundity of this word: Love!. . . It is only our Jesus who knows how to return infinitely more than we give Him . . . .

Marie of the Blessed Sacrament!. . . Your name speaks your mission . . . . Console Jesus, make Him *loved* by souls . . . . Jesus is sick,[4] and we must state that the sickness of love is healed only through love![5] . . . Marie, really give your whole heart to Jesus, He is thirsty for it, He is hungry for it. Your heart, that is what

He longs for, even to the point that to have it for Himself He consents to lodge under a dirty and hidden nook! . . . Ah! how not love a Friend who reduces Himself to such extreme indigence, and how does one dare speak of one's poverty when Jesus makes Himself like His fiancée . . . . He was rich and He made Himself poor[6] in order to unite His poverty to the poverty of Marie of the Blessed Sacrament . . . . What a mystery of love! . . .

All my love to the dear colony.

My heart is always with Marie of the Blessed Sacrament; the Tabernacle is the house of love where our two souls are enclosed . . . . Your little sister who begs you not to forget her in your prayers.

Sister Thérèse of the Child Jesus of the Holy Face
nov.carm.(ind.)[7]

* Autograph.

1. Completed on the evening of the 25th, Marie's letter must have been mailed on July 26. We may suppose that Thérèse answered on Sunday, the 27th; however, not later than the 29th, since she addressed her letter to *La Musse*, telling her cousin to give her love to "the dear colony," that returned to Lisieux on the 31st (ChrIG, p. 39).
2. See LC 120. Although the *all* of God and the *nothing* of the creature are common to all mystics, this teaching is especially emphasized in the Works of St. John of the Cross, especially in his *Ascent of Mount Carmel.* See Père Berthier: "Anyone who desires to profit from the Works of St. John of the Cross must begin by meditating on the *all* of God and the *nothing* of creatures." (Second letter to the Marquise de Créqui, p. 6, in the volume of the *Cantique Spirituel,* ed. 1875, a volume that Thérèse could use at her convenience, but we don't know from what date. The third letter of the same author, pp. 13-23, studies "the excellent doctrine of the Saint on the *all* of God as opposed to the *nothing* of creatures.") We don't know if Thérèse ever read the *Ascent of Mount Carmel* in its entirety, and if, then, the present letter to Marie Guérin was inspired by the spirit of this Work.
3. See 2 Corinthians 12:5.
4. Sister Geneviève (Céline) added: "d'amour" (with love).

5. See St. John of the Cross, *Spiritual Canticle,* explanation of stanza XI (pp. 200–202, according to the 1875 edition, translation of the Carmelites at Paris, to which we shall refer henceforth, unless otherwise indicated). We must note, with reference to this quotation, that Thérèse changed the roles. According to St. John of the Cross, it is the soul that is sick with love, and the soul's "sickness with love cannot be cured except by the presence and the figure of the object loved." According to Thérèse, it is Jesus who "is thirsty," "is hungry" for the love of His creatures.
6. See 2 Corinthians 8:9.
7. These three letters (abbreviation for "unworthy") are clearly enlarged.

"You, Jesus, be all! . . ." (*Letter of Profession.*)
(July–September 1890)
Age seventeen

"Thus flowed the time of my espousals . . . . The Blessed Virgin was aiding me in the preparation of the dress of my soul; as soon as it was completed, the obstacles went away of themselves" (Ms. A, pp. 160, 165). The major obstacle came from the superior, M. Delatroëtte, who considered the novice "too young to take on irrevocable promises" (LC 131). Without abdicating his judgment, he submitted to the favorable opinion of Monseigneur Hugonin.

The Profession day was set for September 8, 1890. Thérèse prepared for it by a retreat of ten full days, begun on the evening of Thursday, August 28. This retreat, she tells us, "was far from bringing me consolations; the most absolute aridity and abandonment were my lot . . . . However, God was showing me clearly, without my being aware of it, the means of pleasing Him and practicing the most sublime virtues" (Ms. A, p. 165). These lines find their full confirmation in the

seventeen contemporaneous documents, seven of which are from Thérèse's hand (LT 110 to 116).

The arrival on September 2 of Leo XIII's blessing for the professed and "for her venerable father, the holy old man, much tried through suffering" (LC 134bis) seemed to revive once more the memory of her father. Thérèse sought to have her father unite with her in this great event of her life, taking into consideration the lucidity of his mind at this time (LT 112 and 115; LD). In his favor, she disposed of the little money she had (about a hundred francs), and she had Masses offered for his consolation (CSG, p. 84). On September 8, "obliged" by her sisters to ask for his cure, she made this prayer: "My God, I beg You, may it be your will that Papa be cured!" (CJ 23.7.6.)

The four letters or inscribed holy pictures, dated September 8, are somewhat removed from the event. We must seek its deep meaning for her in the Autobiography (Ms. A, pp. 166–167), as well as in the touching little "billet de Profession," in which her handwriting reveals "the fright of a child and a warrior's determination" (J. Monnot, cited in Mss. II, p. 53). P. Pichon completes the description: "the simple confidence of a child, with the ardent love of a fiancée" (LC 132).

On the morning of her Profession, the novice, "inundated with a river of peace" (Ms. A, p. 166), consecrated herself to the Lord until death. In return, she asks from Jesus "only peace, and also love, infinite love without any limit other than Yourself! . . ." (billet de profession); and, too, the grace of saving "many souls" (ibid.), "especially the souls of apostles" (LT 201). In the evening, she was gazing at "the stars shining in the firmament" (Ms. A, p. 167). Could she have foreseen that one day "such will be her posterity" also (Genesis 15:5), just as it had been that of Abraham? It was in this

symbolic sense that Mother Agnes of Jesus, fifteen years later, interpreted this picturesque detail: "On the day of Thérèse's Profession, thousands of swallows were chirping from early morning on all our roofs. Never before had we seen such an army of these little emigrants. They had chosen, that year, our monastery as a point of departure for their flight to gentler climes" (Souvenirs intimes, 1905, p. 88).

The intimate ceremony of September 8 was completed on the 24th by the reception of the black Veil, in a public ceremony. It was a day "veiled in tears" (Ms. A, p. 167) because of a last minute disappointment, "a sorrow difficult to understand" (LC 120): the absence of M. Martin, whose blessing the little Queen had so much hoped to receive. Henceforth, there was no longer any other king for her but "the King of heaven." Sister Marie of the Sacred Heart speaks to her about this (LC 142) in terms which are a prelude to the spiritual exchanges they were to have in September 1896 (LC 169 and 170).

→Read Ms. A, pp. 157–167.

LC 131 *From Canon Delatroëtte to Thérèse.*

End of July - beginning of August (?), 1890 Approximate date; see note 1.

Good child and dear daughter
in Our Lord Jesus Christ,

Although, in my opinion, you are too young to take on irrevocable promises, I have no reason to oppose it; I place my faith entirely in Monseigneur's decision, and I gladly consent to your making your request to him.[1] I rejoice at the thought that you will be a worthy daughter of St. Teresa and a holy spouse of Our Lord Jesus Christ.

You may tell your little Sister Martha[2] that I gladly consent to her making her request to the Community.

I beg God to bless you both, and I bless you myself.

All in Our Lord Jesus Christ,
Delatroëtte
Canon of St. James
Superior of the Carmel

* Autograph.

1. Was the request made to Monseigneur Hugonin by writing? And was the answer granted in the same way? Thérèse writes: "*Monseigneur* sent me the permission I requested" (Ms A, p. 160). It is surprising that the bishop of Bayeux' letter was not preserved. Would Thérèse be confusing this with her former request for the reception of the Habit? (LC 89.) Had the novice presented her request *viva voce* on the occasion of a visit of Bishop Hugonin to Lisieux? (LD, following.) In spite of the research made regarding the matter, we can only conjecture.
2. Sister Martha of Jesus, who had received the Habit on May 2, 1889, made her Profession on September 23, 1890; see LT 119.

LD — *From Sister Agnes of Jesus to M. Guérin.* (Extracts.)

August 4 (?), 1890 — Conjectured date: see note 2.

J. M. J. T.

Jesus!

Dear Uncle,

Our good Mother permits me to tell you very secretly that she trusts our little angel will be accepted by the Community; her first Chapter[1] was held yesterday, as you know, and the last one will be held on Monday.[2] But because I think that this question won't

disturb you very much, I shall tell you immediately, as to a Father, that is, with the confidence of a child, the reason for this letter.

When writing our Father Superior about the result of the Chapter, we must also speak to him about the reception of the Veil,[3] and how can we dare to tell him to invite *Monseigneur* when he just had the bishop a very short time ago?[4] Besides, this Profession pleases him so little! . . . Dear Uncle, tell me if I am rash in hoping that, after the wedding of your older and loved daughter,[5] you will be willing to celebrate . . . at your home the spiritual wedding of your last child.[6] . . .

This celebration, without a doubt, will not be free from tears, and to console myself I have to think of the wedding at Cana in which Jesus changed water into wine.[7] This is what will take place later, I mean, at the Eternal Nuptials. It is then that the water of our tears will be changed into the wine of happiness . . . .

Dear Uncle, I think you'll understand me. Ah! you are so kind! It's true that this celebration at your home wouldn't have the atmosphere of sadness that it would have elsewhere, and it seems to me our dear Father would be less absent,[8] and we and Jesus' little Spouse less orphans! . . .

Now, dear Uncle, I'll give you a good kiss and leave you, for the hour of Matins is approaching. I'd be very happy to receive an answer *soon*, but whether the answer be "yes" or "no," I'd not love you less. However, should the answer be "yes," I just don't know if my heart could expand to love you more, in other words, *whether this is possible.*

As a matter of interest, Our good Mother doesn't expect to have the dowry immediately.[9] . . .

Your child and goddaughter,
Sister Agnes of Jesus
r.c.ind.

* Autograph.

1. A novice used to present her request of admission to Profession three times to the Community. The Community gatherings were spread

out over a space of eight days, and included one or two ordinary Chapters which were called "Chapters of faults" (these latter held preferably on Sunday).

2. At the latest, Monday, August 11, if it is true that Thérèse gives the "joyful news" to P. Pichon around August 14-17; see LC 132, note 1. The date for this letter is presented on the basis of August 11: August 4, the day after the first conventual Chapter, which could have been held on Sunday, the 3rd. It seems that Mother Agnes wrote M. Guérin after his return from *La Musse* (July 31).
3. A public ceremony, distinct from the pronouncing of the vows (see LT 43 B, note 2), and presided over, insofar as this was possible, by the bishop of the diocese. In fact, Bishop Hugonin was hindered, at the last moment, from presiding at Thérèse's taking of the Veil on September 24 (Ms. A, p. 167).
4. We have not been able to determine the date of this reception.
5. Jeanne's wedding took place on October 1, after Thérèse's reception of the Veil.
6. Thérèse was the youngest in age among the seven cousins in the Martin and Guérin families.
7. John 2:1-11.
8. M. Martin was still at the *Bon Sauveur* and could not be present at this celebration.
9. The "*Registre des Recettes et Dépenses Générales*" of the monastery for the year 1890 shows the payment of Sister Thérèse of the Child Jesus' dowry: 10,000 francs (*about* 20,000 francs in 1972).

LD *From Sister Agnes of Jesus to Céline.* (Extracts.)

August 20-25 (?), 1890 — Approximate date; see note 4.

My darling Céline .... What a good visit[1] recently!...

I told Sister Thérèse of the Child Jesus all.[2] Her eyes were shining, she was delighted .... She said to me: Ah! Céline, Céline ... how I love her.

She'd like the address of the Brother at Rome, whom Papa met

and to whom he spoke during your trip to Naples.[3] She wants to receive the Holy Father's blessing[4] on the day of her Profession.

Would you be able to bring to Papa the white crown of roses that she'll wear? She would like so much to have him bless it.[5]... Answer this so that we may know whether we should send it on Sunday.[6]

* Autograph.

1. It was only since July that Céline began again *to see* her sisters in the speakroom of the Carmel. From May 1889 to July 1890, because of the repairs being made on the Extern Sisters' house (see LD, end of January 1889, note 5), the visits took place in the Community's confessional, the curtains of which were doubled.
2. We do not know the subject of this conversation.
3. This was Brother Simeon: see LD, November 23, 1887 (Céline).
4. The blessing was dated August 29 (see LC 134). Since mail between Lisieux-Rome took two days, Thérèse wrote on August 26 at the latest (her letter is not preserved). This is our reason for setting August 25 as the latest date for the present letter.
5. September 5. Céline carried out this request; see LD for this date.
6. The 24th or the 31st, judging by the date of the writing of this note.

LC 132 *From P. Pichon to Thérèse.*

August 29,
1890
→ LT lost

† Rimouski
August 29,[1] '90

My very dear and blessed
Child in Our Lord,

The joyful news reached me yesterday, and I sang *Alleluia* with my whole heart. Oh! my *Alleluia* was filled with tears. Neither

one of your fathers will be there to offer you to Jesus.[2] Jesus has made a void around you in order that your whole and only self may be His alone and that you may center your love on Him.

Must I pity you very much here below when up above the angels congratulate you and the saints envy you? Your crown of thorns makes them jealous. Love, then, its stings as so many tokens of love from the divine Spouse.

Will you pray for me as much as I shall pray for you? Tomorrow, I will begin a novena for your intention. On September 8, the anniversary of my ordination, I will give you my Mass, which I ordinarily reserved for myself. In return, I count on your whole soul and your whole heart to plead with Jesus (who will be *so much yours* on September 8) the cause of my dear apostolate. As a true daughter of St. Teresa, ask, obtain for me souls, thousands of souls to save. On September 8, '73, during my ordination, I asked Our Lord for martyrdom.[3] Will you support my supplication? Finally, I recommend to you a very important special intention, particularly dear to my heart.

Look! I am so rushed that I can, at great pains, write you a word at an unreasonable hour, and I am so poor that I haven't even a little picture to send you. I hope to send you one from Montreal.

In spite of appearances, I shall be there, at the foot of the altar, consecrating you to Jesus.

Walk to the sacrifice with the simple confidence of a child, with the fervent love of a fiancée.

My tenderest blessings will shower your soul on September 8.

Almire Pichon

* Autograph.

1. This letter of August 29 reached Lisieux on September 12 (the postmark on the envelope), *via* London (date of the stamp is illegible). If Thérèse's letter took as long (two weeks), it could have been mailed around August 14. Reducing the time to ten days, the novice's letter would have had to be sent on August 18 at the latest, but this

assumption seems less probable. That is why Monday, August 11, has been suggested as the latest date of Thérèse's approval by the conventual Chapter (see LD, August 4, 1890, note 2).

2. This sentence and some others are quoted by Thérèse in a letter to Céline September 23, (LT 120).
3. In the note she carried on her person, September 8, "*billet de profession*," Thérèse likewise asked for the grace of martyrdom (see *Story of a Soul*, p. 275).

LT 110 **From Thérèse to Sister Agnes of Jesus.**

August 30-31, 1890
→ LC lost

J. M. J. T.

Jesus †

My own little Mamma, thank you, oh, thank you! . . . If you only knew what your letter[1] says to my soul! . . .

But the little hermit must tell you the itinerary of her trip and here it is. Before she left, her Fiancé seemed to ask her in what country she desired to travel, what route she desired to follow, etc., etc. . . . The little fiancée answered that she had but one desire, that of being taken to the summit of the *mountain of Love.*[2] To reach it many routes were offered to her, and there were so many perfect ones that she saw she was incapable of choosing. Then she said to her divine guide: "You know where I want to go, You know *for whom* I want to climb the mountain, for whom I want to reach the goal. You know the one whom I love and the one whom I want to please solely; it is for Him alone that I am undertaking this journey. Lead me, then, by the paths which He loves to travel. I shall be at the height of my joy provided that He is pleased. Then Jesus took me by the hand, and He made me

enter a subterranean passage where it is neither cold nor hot, where the sun does not shine, and in which the rain or the wind does not visit, a subterranean passage where I see nothing but a half-veiled light, the light which was diffused by the lowered eyes of my Fiancé's Face!...

My Fiancé says nothing to me, and I say nothing to Him either except that *I love Him more than myself*, and I feel at the bottom of my heart that it is true, for I am more His than my own!... I don't see that we are advancing towards the summit of the mountain since our journey is being made underground,[3] but it seems to me that we are approaching it without knowing how. The route on which I am has no consolation for me, and nevertheless it brings me all consolations since Jesus is the one who chose it, and I want to console Him alone, alone!... Ah, it's true that if I'm giving Him the wine from my heart, it is between the B and the A,[4] for I don't understand it myself.

Must I write to M. le Pelletier[5] and M. Révérony[6] that I am making Profession?...

Above all, don't forget to go into the cellar to take some of your wine,[7] and when you take it, think of your little daughter, who surely no longer drinks of the good, sweet wine of Engaddi.[8]... Ask that she be able to give some to her Spouse by saving souls, and she will be consoled ....

* Autograph.

1. Sister Agnes of Jesus, then, opened the dialogue, just as Sister Marie of the Sacred Heart will do also (LC 133).
2. See LT 105, in which the metaphor is no doubt called to mind by the context: Céline's trip to Lourdes. In the present note, as well as in LT 112 and in Ms. B, p. 187, does Thérèse have in mind the *Ascent of Mount Carmel* of St. John of the Cross? See LT 109, note 2.
3. This image of the subterranean passage could have brought back to Thérèse memories dating from the trip to Rome: when going there, the crossing from Saint-Gothard, which lasted from twenty to twenty-five minutes on the morning of November 8, 1887; and when returning, the numerous tunnels between Pisa and Genoa

(November 17), and between Genoa and Nice (November 28).

4. The words "it's true" suggest that Thérèse is taking an idea or an expression from Sister Agnes' letter. Not having the document, we are somewhat puzzled by the allusion.
5. L'abbé Lepelletier, curé of Lion-sur-mer, had been Thérèse's confessor from 1886 to 1888; see LD, November 28-29, 1887 (Sister Agnes of Jesus).
6. Regarding the latter, at least, Sister Agnes' response (now lost) must have been in the affirmative. The vicar general answered Thérèse on September 7 (LC 139).
7. Sister Agnes had access to the cellar as "refectorian" (see CJ 13.7.18). In an undated letter, no doubt written in August 1890, Sister Marie of the Sacred Heart wrote to Céline: "Little Céline, I'm returning the empty Cinchona bottles; you would be very kind if you were to send us two more. These will be the last we ask from you. They are for the little lamb and little Thérèse." Thérèse had her share of the medicinal wine (LT 112).
8. Canticle of Canticles 1:14. Here, again, Thérèse is, no doubt, taking an expression from Sister Agnes. The Office for the *Nativity of the Blessed Virgin*, September 8, had the whole of chapter 1 of the Canticle of Canticles at Matins.

LC 133 *From Sister Marie of the Sacred Heart to Thérèse.*

August 30 (?), 1890

Jesus!

In heaven, there is great jubilation .... All the angels are weaving crowns ... the cherubim gather flowers in the heavenly fields such as are not gathered here below .... Already their songs are heard, and the enraptured saints are wondering what new glory surrounds them. Let them ask the King of heaven, and He will say in His sweet voice: They are preparing for My wedding.

Over there ... over there ... on the earth of exile, there is a lit-

tle soul upon whom I have cast a glance of love. She has understood Me and has given herself to Me!... I am going to her... in no more than nine days,[1] we shall be one! Ah! if you only knew My joy! Yes, I am happy, I the Lord of lords, I who created heaven and earth by a single word and all of you, My angels and My saints... I who could create a million others still more beautiful... I am happy to have for *Myself alone* this heart that ravishes Me with love.... Little fiancée, My retinue is approaching. Can you hear the heavenly harmonies already singing about our divine union?... But let us leave them at a distance, and let us stay alone together....

* Autograph.

1. Although Sister Marie of the Sacred Heart was not too exact in her dates, we may deduce from this statement that she was writing on August 30.

LT 111 From Thérèse to Sister Marie of the Sacred Heart.

August 30-31, 1890
→LC 133

Dear little Godmother, if you only knew how your song from heaven delighted the soul of your little daughter!...

I assure you that she hardly hears the heavenly harmonies. Her wedding trip is very arid; it is true, her Fiancé is having her travel through fertile and magnificent countries, but the *night* prevents her from admiring anything and, especially, from enjoying all these marvels.

You're going to believe that she's saddened by this, but, no, on the contrary, she is happy to follow her Fiancé because of her love for *Himself alone* and not because of His gifts... He alone is so

beautiful, so ravishing!... even when He *is silent*... even when He *hides Himself*!...

Do you understand your little daughter?...

She is tired of earthly consolations; she wants only her Beloved alone.... Don't forget to pray very much for your little daughter whom you *have reared*[1] and who is yours.[2]

* Autograph.
1. See CJ 23.9.6.
2. Sister Marie of the Sacred Heart answered on September 1 (LC 135).

LC 134 *From Brother Simeon to Thérèse.*

August 31, 1890
→ LT lost

August 31, 1890

Collège Français
Saint-Joseph
des
Frères des Ecoles Chrétiennes
Place d'Espagne
ROME

My very dear Sister,

I just received the Apostolic Blessing which, upon your request, I asked for both you and Monsieur, your holy and Venerable Father.[1]

I have happy memories of him and yourself.[2] I thank God for having favored your very holy vocation.

I congratulate you on your wedding, September 8; heaven will ratify the Blessing that its representative here below is sending you for this great day in your life!

Pray for Our Holy Father, the Pope, so afflicted and humbled at Rome. His enemies persecute him in all ways, everything is per-

mitted here against him; they are assured of no retaliation. It is sad! Hell triumphs at Rome!!

Beg Monsieur, your Venerable Father, to accept my respectful wishes, and tell him how much I share in his sufferings. Heaven will be the reward for these!

Pray for me, dear Sister, and accept my respect and my congratulations.

Brother Simeon

* Autograph.

1. See LD, August 20-25, 1890. Thérèse's letter to Brother Simeon has not been found. With regard to the "Blessing," the Saint gave her reasons for seeking it: "I sought it through Brother Simeon for Papa and myself, and it was a great consolation for me to be able to return the favor my dear little Father granted me when taking me to Rome" (Ms. A, p. 165).
2. This statement does not permit us to say whether Thérèse met Brother Simeon personally in 1887, or whether the writer is just claiming acquaintance with her *ex auditu*. Asked on several occasions whether Thérèse ever met Brother Simeon, Sister Geneviève (Céline) was never certain about whether she did or not.

LC 134 bis *Text of the Apostolic Blessing.*

Most Holy Father,

Sister Thérèse of the Child Jesus, Carmelite religious of Lisieux, prostrate at the feet of Your Holiness, humbly begs Your Apostolic Blessing for her religious Profession; she begs it, too, for her venerable Father, the saintly old man, tried by suffering.

And may Your Holiness,[1] etc.

Romae e Secretaria Status, Die 29 Augusti 1890
SSmus D.N. Leo P.P.XIII benigne annuit pro gratia
† *Marius Mocenni Archiep. Aeliopolis*
Substitut. Secr. Stat.

* Autograph.

1. The letter for the request was evidently written by Brother Salutaire of the Christian Schools (see LC 176). The two lines following are written by a secretary from the Curia; then follows the autograph signature of Bishop Mocenni, archbishop of Heliopolis, substitute deputy of the Secretariat of State. The envelope for these two documents is addressed: "My very dear Thérèse of Jesus (*sic*) Carmelite Religious Lisieux Calvados France." The stamps from Rome and Lisieux are dated, respectively: August 31 and September 2, '90.

LC 135

From Sister Marie of the Sacred Heart to Thérèse.

September 1 (?), 1890
→LT 111

Jesus!

My dear little daughter, your short note pleased me. I was hungry for my little daughter.[1] . . . If it is night for her, it isn't night for her Spouse, and He is preparing her wedding gift in the sun of eternity. There are two weddings for His spouses, the spiritual wedding of this exile and the wedding of the homeland . . . . And all joys are reserved for the homeland . . . . On earth, Jesus is not generous with His joys, these would cause harm to celestial goods, and He who dreams of nothing but giving deprives us of them in order to enrich us. Ah! if only His little fiancée were to see His smile, if she were only to hear the sound of His voice! she would no longer live, she would die of love . . . . That is why *He hides Himself*, that is why *He is silent*.

But He hides for a SHORT time, He is silent FOR AN HOUR AT THE MOST! After the *dream* of this life, He will speak to His little spouse forever, He will give her nothing but caresses, her heaven will be the *eternal smile* of her Spouse!![2]

* Autograph.
1. This reflection suggests that Thérèse is ordinarily sparing of *words*. As far as *seeing* her was concerned, Sister Marie of the Sacred Heart was not deprived since she was living with her in the novitiate.
2. The note was folded in such a way as to reveal this address: "to my little daughter."

LT 112 From Thérèse to Sister Agnes of Jesus.

September 1, 1890

J. M. J. T.

Jesus † Monday

I am giving you the letter I wrote for Papa.[1] If you think it cannot go out, you will make me a little outline of a letter, but I believe he will not understand .... Ah! what a mystery is this love of Jesus for our family!... What a mystery the tears and the love of this Spouse of blood.[2]...

Tomorrow, I'll go and find M. Youf.[3] He told me to give him a little review[4] since I am in Carmel. Really pray in order that Jesus may leave me the *peace* which He HAS GIVEN ME.[5] I was happy to receive absolution on Saturday .... But I don't understand the retreat I am making; I think of nothing, in a word, I am in a very dark subterranean passage!... Oh! ask Jesus, you who are my light, that He not permit souls to be deprived of lights that they need because of me, but that my darkness serve to enlighten them .... Ask Him, too, that I make a good retreat and that He may be as pleased as He can be; then I, too, will be pleased, and I will consent, if this be His will, to walk all my life on the dark road on which I am, provided that one day I reach the summit of the mountain of Love.[6] But I believe this will not be here below.

(I'm going to take my little wine; I would have liked to do the same this morning, but I wasn't able to find Our Mother.)[7]

Must I write to Mme. Papinot?[8]. . . It seems to me that there is no point in doing so, she would not understand. It would be better perhaps to wait until the receiving of the Veil?[9]. . .

* Autograph.
1. This letter is not preserved.
2. See LT 82, note 1.
3. The chaplain of the Carmel (1842-1897), ordinary confessor of the Community since 1873.
4. That is, a general confession.
5. Her peace was still fragile, it seems; see LT 95, note 7; LC 117, note 4, and LT 114, note 9. The chaplain, "a priest and director, whose spirituality was rather austere" (P. Lemonnier, PO, 522), was not capable of setting the penitent at ease; nevertheless, he greatly esteemed Thérèse. Mother Agnes of Jesus stated: "One day, Thérèse admitted to the confessor 'her distress at suffering from exhaustion during the Mass even to the point of not being able to shake off sleep,' and he gave her a severe reprimand and told her that she was offending God." (NPPA, Prudence, Directors; undated episode in Thérèse's life.) The other religious were led along the same "energetic path": Thus, Sister Teresa of St. Augustine was dismissed from the confessional with these encouraging words: "My poor child, all I can tell you is that you already have one foot in hell and that, if you continue, you will soon put the second one there." (This religious' Circular, p. 5.) Mother Marie de Gonzague treated the matter with good humor: "Don't worry, I myself have both feet in it!" (DCL). See CJ 6.6.2.
6. See LT 110, note 2.
7. See LT 110, note 7. The version from the Process (CE II, p. 54) has this note written by Sister Marie of the Sacred Heart: "She was making a reference to the dinner for the celebration that her family had suggested for the day of her Profession. But she did not want to accept anything without having first asked permission from her Mother Prioress." We take this explanation with a certain amount of reservation; it is difficult to make a distinction between historical truth and the desire to edify on the part of the revisers of the "Writings."

8. Mme. Papinau, at whose home Thérèse took special lessons from 1886 to 1888.
9. We have not found Sister Agnes of Jesus' answer.

LC 136 *From Sister Marie of the Sacred Heart to Thérèse.*

September 2, 1890

According to the custom of the time, the novice went out of the cloister to the outside chapel in order to answer the ritual questions of the canonical examination. (See Ms. A, p. 149.) Leo XIII's blessing arrived on that same day, obtained through the intervention of Brother Simeon (LC 134).

Jesus! My dear little daughter, today, then, you bore witness to Jesus, today the angels of the Tabernacle listened enraptured, to your pledges . . . .

The Beloved couldn't remain silent. He willed to sow this day with holy joys, and the Sovereign Pontiff's hand was raised to bless the little fiancée of Jesus and her dear Father. Her aged Father who formerly held her by the hand with so much tenderness, who led her to the altar[1] . . . she, in her turn, is leading him and brings down all heaven's graces upon his venerable head . . . . Oh, little child, how mysterious life really is, and who will tell us what the Cross has in store for us? . . . This blessing from the Holy Father says much to my heart. It's like a letter from Jesus . . . . He cannot hold back . . . . He loves the one whom He is trying so much and *the dove which is His*[2] and which He made fly all the way to Rome in order to seek there *a word of His love*. "Oh, my beloved," He seems to be saying, "if you were to see my hidden treasures . . . . The patriarch's head already has its halo . . . and yours is a perfumed lily. Ah! I want to keep forever its perfume for MYSELF alone . . . ."

* Autograph.

1. For the reception of the Habit, January 10, 1889.
2. See Canticle of Canticles 6:9.

LT 113 From Thérèse to Sister Marie of the Sacred Heart.

September 2-3, 1890
→LC 136

J. M. J. T.

Jesus

If you only knew the good your little notes do me!... They are music from heaven for me, and it seems to me I am hearing an angel's voice....

But, then, are you not the angel who led me and guided me on the road of exile right up to my entrance into Carmel? And even now you are always for me the angel[1] who consoled me in my childhood, and I see in you what others cannot see, for you know so well how to hide what you are that on the day of eternity many persons will be surprised.

But your little daughter will not be surprised at anything, and as beautiful as your throne and your crown may be, she will not be surprised at what the love of the divine Spouse will give her who formed in her own heart the same love for the Spouse of virgins, and your little daughter hopes also to be a little flower in your crown, lending its humble splendor to the glory of its visible angel on earth.

* Autograph.

1. "Angel" had a special significance ever since April 1888; see LT 49, note 6.

LT 114 **From Thérèse to Sister Agnes of Jesus.**

September 3, 1890
→ LC lost

Date deduced from the content; see note 2

J. M. J. T.

Jesus †

Dear lamb, yes, joys are always mingled with suffering for us.[1] Yesterday's grace[2] demanded a crowning, and Jesus gave it to you and to me at the same time, too, for all that causes you to suffer wounds me deeply!... I'd like to know if Our Mother consoled you and if you are still sad? It seems to me that I should thank the saintly old man Simeon[3] and tell him his letter arrived, what do you think?... I'm giving you a note from Sister Thérèse of Jesus.[4] She gave it to me this morning. Must I do all this for her?[5]... I don't have any models, and, then, it seems to me, that the linen and the Blessed Virgin[6] are more important, but I'll do what you tell me.

Do you believe Céline is really going to die?... I promised her yesterday to make Profession for the both of us,[7] but I'll not have the courage to ask Jesus that He leave her on earth if this is not His will. It seems to me that love can make up for a long life.... Jesus does not look at time since there is no longer any time in heaven. He must look only at love. Ask Him to give me very much love too. I'm not asking for perceptible love, but a love felt only by Jesus. Oh! to love Him and make Him loved, how sweet this is!... Tell Him, too, to take me on the day of m, Profession if I must still offend Him afterward, for I'd like to carry to heaven the white robe of my second Baptism without any stain on it.[8] But, it seems to me, that Jesus can give me the grace of no longer offending Him or committing faults that DON'T OFFEND Him[9] but serve only to humble and to make love stronger. If you only knew the things I'd tell you if I had the words to express what I am thinking, or rather what *I am not thinking* but feeling!... Life is

very mysterious!... It is a desert and an exile ... but at the bottom of my soul I feel that there will be a day of DISTANCES, infinite DISTANCES that will make me forget forever the sorrows of the desert and the exile....

the little grain of sand[10]

M. l'abbé Domin[11] doesn't know I'm making Profession; must I tell him? It seems to me that if Our Mother hasn't yet written to the Abbey, she could tell these Sisters to inform him about it?

* Autograph.

1. This preamble suggests that Thérèse is answering a note from her sister; this has been lost. It would have informed us, no doubt, about the reason for Sister Agnes' sorrow.
2. Leo XIII's blessing which reached Lisieux on September 2.
3. Brother Simeon at Rome (LC 134).
4. Sister Thérèse of Jesus (1839-1918). Professed in 1875, she left the religious life in 1909. We do not have any of this Sister's letters.
5. Mother Agnes wrote in pencil on the autograph: "(This sister was asking for foolish things) Sister Agnes of Jesus." Thérèse frequently had occasion to practice charity with regard to this religious by carrying out, upon her request, various works of art. "Because this poor Sister was rather eccentric, she used to ask for subjects that were very grotesque ... really bizarre and in poor taste, such as painting a lion surrounded by flowers and birds. In 1897, the last year of her life, in the month of June, Sister Thérèse of the Child Jesus painted two little works for this Sister. This was the last time that she used her brushes." (Mother Agnes of Jesus, NPPA, Love for the neighbor, p. 6.)
6. Linen to be repaired and the statue of the Blessed Virgin to be decorated.
7. Thérèse could have kissed Céline the day before when she went out of the cloister for her canonical examination; see LC 136 and 137. Regarding Céline's "illness," see LT 104, note 2.
8. SeeThérèse's first request in her "*billet de profession*" (*Story of a Soul*, p. 275).
9. See LT 112, note 5. "Limit yourself ... to no longer offending God" P. Blino had advised her (see LT 107, note 8). Thérèse had to wait

for P. Alexis, in October 1891, to receive the assurance that her faults "*did not cause God any pain*" (Ms. A, p. 174); see, too, her "Act of Oblation to Merciful Love," June 9, 1895, and her peaceful request regarding her faults of weakness (*Story of a Soul*, p. 276).

10. This is the last time that Thérèse used this image in her correspondence; we find it, several days later, in her prayer of September 8 (*billet de profession*).
11. Chaplain at the Abbey at Lisieux, Thérèse's confessor from 1881 to 1886.

LC 137 *From Sister Agnes of Jesus to Thérèse.*

September 3, 1890 Date deduced from the content; see note 1.

→ LT 114

J. M. J. T.

Dear little grain of sand,

I don't believe that Céline is going to die immediately, but I would not be very much surprised. Ah! how blessed she would be.... What happiness to go and see that "unknown Face" about which Job was speaking to us this evening.[1] ... Let God do what He wills in our family, and let Him be under no constraint!... Is He not at home?... Formerly, Jesus complained at not having even a stone on which to lay His divine head,[2] and now it would be very bad to complain to Him, for our hearts want to be very soft and warm pillows for Him.

Céline was delighted to see you. She told me that you had very tender little cheeks and so fresh it was a pleasure to kiss them.[3] ... "I can see that they are not overheated by the world's atmosphere," she added.... Your fresh and tender little cheeks are going to be offered, then, on Monday, to the Bridegroom's kiss. Ah! what a moment. In the Office for the Nativity,[4] the first lesson begins by these words: "Let him kiss me with the kiss of his mouth"[5] ... and this is not surprising, for who is more worthy of

the divine kisses than the darling little Blessed Virgin of one day in her little cradle?

Prepare yourself, little grain of sand!... Prepare yourself *by not preparing yourself*, that is, by admitting that you are not capable of preparing and adorning yourself for this heavenly celebration.... If I were my little white dove, I know what I would do. I would go and rest my head on the Heart of Jesus, not the glorified Jesus but the suffering Jesus. There I would wait, without saying a word, until He allowed some brilliant pearls and precious rubies to fall on me....

The tears and the blood of Jesus: see, little dove, what will enrich your soul and make you so beautiful that the dazzled eyes of the angels will perhaps have trouble withstanding your brightness.... Then they will sing to you: "With your comeliness and your beauty set out, proceed prosperously, and reign!"[6]

Beloved little grain of sand, I am no longer distressed concerning yesterday evening's trifle.[7]... They have not spoken again about it, and I was careful not to say a word. My God! how everything passes here below! This gives us courage. Today, you are sad, the next day this sadness vanishes, and two days later the sky clouds over again. Oh! a thousand times blessed is the soul that lifts itself above all these vicissitudes.... It is difficult, but grace works marvels in the faithful heart....

Darling child... Thank your Fiancé, for He had made you follow this path of fidelity from your tender childhood.... He isn't giving you any consolation because you are in His arms, and you are not walking, He is carrying you.... Does the child in its Father's arms[8] need any other consolation?... And so I can picture Jesus carrying His little grain of sand, and, burdened with this light load, He is running in search of souls.... The little grain of sand stirs, it leaps when it sees some poor wounded lambs hidden in the bushes.... And Jesus is pleased with its desires. He saves the poor sinners with the help of His little grain of sand.... He uses it just as David used little stones from the brook in order to slay Goliath.[9]... With His little grain of sand, He sends the

ugly demon away. . . . He casts him to the ground, and, with His powerful hand,[10] He draws His sword in order to hurl him into the abyss.

See what Jesus' little grain of sand can do!. . . It does almost as much as Jesus!. . . Oh, Jesus, what would You do if You did not have Your little grain of sand![11]

* Autograph.

1. Job 4:16. They were reading this passage in the third lesson of Matins, the fifth ferial of the first week of September. This gives us a chronological reference: Sister Agnes of Jesus was writing on Wednesday evening, September 3.
2. Matthew 8:20.
3. A marginal note in pencil written by Mother Agnes of Jesus: "She had gone out into the outside chapel for her canonical examination." On this matter, see LC 136.
4. "Nativity of thc Blessed Virgin," addition in pencil by Mother Agnes of Jesus.
5. Canticle of Canticles 1:1.
6. Psalm 44:5. This text was used several times in the liturgical Office of September 8.
7. The "sadness" to which Thérèse refers (see LT 114, note 1), but we do not know the cause.
8. Should we see here an anticipated reference to the "elevator" (Ms. C, p. 207)? For Sister Agnes of Jesus and Sister Marie of the Sacred Heart (judging by a study of their correspondence) the "fatherly arms" of Jesus are considered a tender refuge in which the child abandons itself with confidence. This attitude was formed in their early education at the Visitation in Le Mans (influence of St. Francis de Sales and Blessed Margaret Mary). See the *Petit Bréviaire du Sacré-Coeur de Jésus*: "What have you to fear in the arms of the Almighty?" (p. 15); "Can a child who is loved as much as I love you perish in the arms of the Almighty?" This attitude (arms = abandonment) is to be found in Thérèse's writings; see, for example, LT 143 and 149 (1893) or Ms. C, p. 238. But she added to it, and this is proper to herself, a *dynamic* spirit which made "the arms of Jesus" an "elevator" instead of just a refuge. A study of all the Saint's writings would bring out the full meaning of this term.

9. See 1 Samuel 17:48-51.
10. Word omitted on the autograph.
11. The last use of this image to designate Thérèse by Sister Agnes of Jesus, at least in the notes that have been preserved. See LT 45, note 4.

LT 115 From Thérèse to Sister Agnes of Jesus.

September 4, 1890
→LC 137

Date deduced from the content; see note 3.

J. M. J. T.

I am giving you the letter from Rome[1] in order that you may give it to Céline if you so desire.[2] Perhaps Papa will not understand, but it is not difficult to bring it, and if sometime he were to understand, he would be happy. Should I also send him my vows so that he may bless them? If you think "yes," will you tell me tomorrow morning so that I may write them out very quickly.[3] They could be placed in the center of the crown, but it may be better to do nothing?. . .

Thank you for your little letter; if you only knew how much it pleased me!. . . My soul is always in the subterranean passage, but it is *very happy*, yes, happy to have no consolation whatsoever, for I find that then its love is not like the love of earthly fiancées who are always looking at the hands of their fiancés to see if they have brought them any gifts, or else at their faces to catch there a smile of love which delights them . . . .

But the poor little fiancée of Jesus feels that she loves Jesus for *Himself alone*, and she wants to look at her Beloved's face only to catch there the tears which flow from His eyes which have delighted her by their *hidden charms*!. . . She wishes to dry these tears in order to make her dress from them on the day of her wedding, a dress which *will be hidden* too but will be understood by her Beloved.[4]

* Autograph.
1. LC 134.
2. Céline was going to see M. Martin the next day, Tuesday; see the following LD.
3. Thérèse was writing, then, on Monday evening. The affirmative answer from Sister Agnes of Jesus was not preserved. We do not know precisely if it is a question of the same note, part of which is known to us through a letter from Céline; see LD, September 5, 1890.
4. This word must have been followed by two or three other words, but the line has been cut off from the autograph.

LD *From Sister Agnes of Jesus to Céline* .

September 5, 1890

My little Céline,

Be very careful of the crown; it's a relic. It was worn by Mother Geneviève on the day of her fiftieth anniversary, ten years ago, and for her diamond wedding this year.[1]

I am sending you the Crucifix[2] also in order that you may have Papa kiss it. Then the paper with the vows which our dear angel will hold in her hands when pronouncing them. She will carry this same paper in the tomb since this is a custom at Carmel.

We still do not know the hour of the Mass on Monday.[3] We shall let you know as soon as we hear Our Father's answer.

If Papa were to understand Brother's letter from Rome and the blessing of the Holy Father, he would be very happy. Aware of our little dove's desire that dear Papa understand all her little affairs just a little bit, I was unable to refrain this morning from asking this favor in my Communion, and I am only hoping.

Sister Agnes of Jesus
r.c.ind.

Thank Aunt for advancing her trip[4] and Uncle for having written to Monseigneur.[5] We are praying for all his intentions.

The Crucifix is not the one blessed by Père Pichon at Le Havre; it was so big that it was hurting her, and I took it and gave her mine.

* Autograph.

1. Mother Geneviève received the Habit on July 20, 1830 and made Profession on July 22, 1831. She celebrated her golden jubilee in 1881, and her sixty years of reception of the Habit on July 20, 1890 (see LD, July 22, 1890). She had worn the traditional crown of roses for these occasions. This crown was used also by Sister Agnes and Sister Marie of the Sacred Heart for their Professions respectively (judging by a statement of Mother Marie de Gonzague, September 8, 1890).
2. The Crucifix which the Carmelite wears on her breast, under the scapular, after she has made Profession. After having worn during her postulancy a "little Crucifix," a gift from Léonie (see LT 263 and DE, p. 464), Thérèse wore another, out of devotion, from the time of her reception of the Habit; at first, a "large" one which had been blessed by P. Pichon at Le Havre, November 3, 1888, at the time of his departure for Canada (see the P.S. of this present letter), and then, at the end of three weeks, a Crucifix of smaller size, one which Sister Agnes of Jesus had received for her Profession (May 8, 1884), and which Thérèse kept all through her religious life. This exchange of Crucifixes around February 1889 was confirmed by letters from Sister Marie of the Sacred Heart to Sister Françoise-Thérèse (Léonie), August 22, 1910 and September 10, 1911; and in a letter from Mother Agnes of Jesus to Léonie, September 11, 1911. See DE, pp. 463-465.
3. The precise time was given on September 7 (see following LD).
4. The trip to Paris, September 6, according to the ChrIG, p. 39.
5. To invite him to his home on the day of Thérèse's reception of the Veil; see LD, August 4, 1890.

LD *From Sister Agnes of Jesus to Céline.*

September 7, 1890 Date deduced from the content.

My dear little Céline,

The Mass will be tomorrow at 7:30.[1] I really fear this will spoil things,[2] but we must let it pass . . . .

The curtains of our little Communion grille will be from our little fiancée's dress of January 10, last year.[3] Take notice of them.

I believe we shall all receive Holy Communion at this Mass if Our Father does not say it.[4] If Marie really wants to come, you must take care to obtain permission for her.[5]

Our angel is perfectly prepared; if only we could see the celebration that is in preparation in heaven!... Ah! how all the magnificent weddings of this earth would pale before this spectacle!

My God, when will our eyes be opened?

I wrote our happy little hermit[6] that Papa, in a sense, would be hidden more in heaven than on earth.... It would take too long to explain what I am thinking.... May Jesus, then, have the two pretty boys of honor, namely, the two little Josephs, and she, the two darling little maids of honor, namely, little Hélène and little Thérèse.[7] And may the older ones, Joseph and Hélène, holding hands, take up the collection before God's throne from the Trinity itself, saying: "Lord, for our little exiled sisters on earth, if you please.... For our dear Father that he may come soon to be with us always," and may the purse of the heavenly and graceful collectors be filled immediately so that it may be emptied on us in a shower of mysterious and fruitful graces.

Aunt's oval photo is very good.... Thank you for the beautiful bouquet!!![8]

You cannot come twice tomorrow. Aunt wrote me that she will come.[9] What do you expect? Come together or, if the Profession does not last a long time, come a second time to the speakroom.

* Autograph.

1. "*et demie,*" is an addition made in pencil, but was, no doubt, done on September 7 just as the rest of the letter.
2. This allusion is not known to us.
3. Thérèse's wedding dress on the day she received the Habit, January 10, 1889.
4. The chaplain, l'abbé Youf, was probably better disposed than was Canon Delatroëtte in favor of frequent Communion.

5. Marie Guérin wanted to come with Céline to the outside chapel during Thérèse's Profession which took place within the cloister in the Chapter room after the Mass.
6. This note was lost; see LT 115, note 3.
7. The two little brothers and two little sisters who had died at an early age. In 1896, Sister Geneviève (Céline), on the occasion of her own Profession, asked Thérèse for an allegorical description of the celebration in heaven; these same four "charming angels" graced the occasion (LT 185, February 23, 1896).
8. Either for the Profession on the following day or for Sister Agnes of Jesus' twenty-ninth birthday (she was born on September 7, '61).
9. In the afternoon, according to LC 140.

LT 116 — From Thérèse to Sister Marie of the Sacred Heart.

September 7, 1890 — Date deduced from the content.

J. M. J. T.

I would really like the candles of little Jesus to be lighted when I go to the Chapter room,[1] so will you go and light them?. . . I beg you, don't forget. . . . I did not place the new pink candles there, for they say too much to my soul; they began to burn on the day of my reception of the Habit, and then they were pink and fresh. Papa (who gave them to me) was here and all was joy! But now the *pink* color has left them, and now are there still for the *orpheline de Bérésina*[2] joys of the color of *pink* here below?. . . Oh! no, there are no longer for her anything but heavenly joys . . . joys in which everything created, which is nothing, gives room for the uncreated, which is reality. . . .

Do you understand your little daughter?. . . Tomorrow, she will be the bride of Jesus; tomorrow, she will be the bride of Him whose Face was hidden and whom no one recognized![3] . . . What

an alliance and what a future!... Yes, I feel it, my wedding will be surrounded by angels;[4] there will be only heaven which will rejoice and also the little spouse and her dear sisters!...

* Autograph.

1. When going to the Chapter room, at the end of the Mass, the Community went in procession before the statue of the Child Jesus, under the outside cloister. Thérèse had decorated this statue according to her taste.
2. See LT 46, note 3; this is the last time that Thérèse uses this nickname in her letters. It appeared again only in Poem 8, "Prayer of the Child of a Saint," August 1894, and in the explanation of her coat of arms in January 1896.
3. Isaias 53:3. Among the twenty-eight uses of the verb "to recognize" in Thérèse's Letters, nine citations are in direct or indirect relationship to this text of Isaias since her discovery of it (see LT 108).
4. A probable reference to the Hymn for the Dedication of the Church (*Caelestis urbs Jerusalem*, first stanza: "You are escorted like a spouse by thousands upon thousands of angels"). On that Sunday, September 7, the Carmelite Order was celebrating the dedication of its churches.

LC 138 *From Sister Marie of the Sacred Heart to Thérèse.*

September 7, 1890 — Date deduced from the content.

→ LT 116

J. M. J. T.

Jesus!

My dear little daughter,

Your short note said very much to my soul.... How much Jesus made the *orpheline de Bérésina* grow in a few years! How He has loved with a privileged love this queen with the long blond

hair whom this poor little Father loved so much. She is still his joy, she is still his glory, bent over as he is under the trial, and, tomorrow, heaven will contemplate with delight the new crown which will shine on his venerable head.

Tomorrow, his queen will be truly a queen,[1] for she will have for her Bridegroom the King of kings.... The Face of her Jesus has not been hidden from her; she has recognized it in the shadows of this exile; she has recognized it[2] and has given herself to Him! Tomorrow.... What a day! No one can give it a name, no one can understand it ... the mystery of this day is written in letters of gold in eternity. On the day of your First Communion, Jesus made His first advances to you, and He gave Himself to you! And now you are giving yourself to Him!...

Pray for your little godmother so that she may become a saint and that she may answer also this grace with which she has been favored along with her little daughter. Blessed family! Family filled to overflowing by Jesus!...

Don't forget either to pray for the Father[3] who will pray so much for you tomorrow. Finally, give all our hearts with your own to your Spouse....

Marie of the Sacred Heart

* Autograph.

1. See Ms. A, p. 166, the account of September 8: "I really felt as the QUEEN." Thérèse used this title once more in her Autobiography, with reference to her reception of the Veil (Ms. A, p. 167). We find it very rarely in her correspondence (for example, LT 142). This sentence could bring back to mind a thought expressed in the hymn in LT 116, note 4; here, the second stanza: "Flooded with the Bridegroom's grace, very beautiful Queen, united to Christ, the Prince."
2. See Isaias 53:3.
3. P. Pichon in Canada. He wrote Thérèse on August 29, but she did not receive his letter until September 12 (LC 132).

LC 139 *From l'abbé Révérony to Thérèse.*

September 7, 1890

September 7, 1890

My Child,

When you receive these lines, all your desires, no doubt, will have been accomplished! You will belong to Jesus!... totally!... forever!... What a joy!... but what goodness on the part of Jesus!... what mercy!... Your life, your eternity will not be sufficient for acknowledging this grace and for thanking your Beloved!... Love and immolation: behold the program of your life henceforth![1]... Let it be fervent and it will please Jesus! and that is all. I am praying for you with my whole heart and for your dear father whom Our Lord loves and blesses.

M. Révérony
v.g.

* Autograph.

1. This is the program of the picture of Saint Teresa of Avila which was sent with this letter, commenting on the motto: "To suffer or to die."

LT 117 **From Thérèse to Sister Marie of the Sacred Heart.**

September 8, 1890

Inscription on the back of a picture representing the Nativity by Filippo Lippi.

Souvenir[1] of September 8, 1890.

Day of everlasting memory when your little daughter, like yourself, became the spouse of Him who said: "My kingdom is not of this world,"[2] and again: "Nevertheless, I say to you, hereafter you shall see the Son of man sitting on the right hand of the power of God, and coming in the clouds of heaven."[3] As for ourselves,

this is the day we are awaiting .... The day of the eternal nuptials when our Jesus will dry all the tears from our eyes,[4] when He will make us sit with Him[5] on His throne ....

Now His Face is as though hidden[6] from the eyes of mortals, but for us who understand His tears in this valley of exile, soon His resplendent Face will be shown to us in the fatherland and then this will be the ecstasy of the eternal union of glory with our Spouse .... Pray that she whom you instructed in the paths of virtue may one day be near you in the homeland!...

Your little daughter

* Autograph.

1. Thérèse wrote the first syllable in ink. Since the paper was slightly damp, she continued to write in pencil. Her handwriting is upright, and this reminds us of her copy of the text of Isaias, July 18, 1890 (see LT 108, note 1).
2. John 18:16.
3. Matthew 26:64.
4. Apocalypse 21:4.
5. Luke 22:30.
6. See Isaias 53:3.

Picture *From Sister Agnes of Jesus and Sister Marie of the Sacred Heart to Thérèse*

September 8, 1890

On the back of a holy picture representing the Presentation of the Blessed Virgin in the Temple, with these words calligraphied by Sister Agnes: "I am the spouse of Him whose Mother is a Virgin! (St. Agnes)." The text which follows is written by Sister Agnes. Sister Marie of the Sacred Heart was content to sign it.

J. M. J. T.

September 8, 1890

Beloved little Lily of Jesus. Remember forever this "beautiful Day of days!"[1] Remember Jesus' privileges given to your soul!

Remember that He said to you this morning: "Rise My Beloved, My Dove, My Sister, My Fiancée,[2] My Spouse, and come unite yourself to Me, for I have chosen you from eternity!"

And remember that soon you will hear for the second time these same words, this same call, no longer for immolation but for glory.

Between these two calls, dear Child, be faithful, remember that all passes,[3] excepting Love.

Your two former Mothers whose joy and crown you are.

Sister Marie of the Sacred Heart
r.c.ind.

Sister Agnes of Jesus
r.c.ind.

* Autograph.

1. See Ms. A, p. 77, where Thérèse uses this expression with regard to her First Communion. In her manuscript copy (*Carnet I*, p. 130), Mother Agnes of Jesus wrote: "This is a reference to a poem that Mamma used to love to repeat and which began in this way: '*Beau jour entre les jours, ton souvenir me reste, – Comme un fidèle ami dont rien n'a separé.*'"
2. See Canticle of Canticles 2:13-14 and 4:8-9.
3. See LT 81, note 7.

LC 140 — *From Mme. Guérin to Thérèse.*

September 8, 1890 — Date deduced from the content.

My dear little Thérèse,

I am sending you a basket of flowers. Jeanne and the doctor[1] arranged it for our family meal. I must tell you that yesterday we had a great reunion. I decided to send you this basket even though it was on our table. It seems to me that on this day of such a great celebration for you, my darling, it is going to delight your eyes. Are not flowers one of the joys of this exile, and on this day when Jesus willed to accept you as His spouse, is it not right that

everything around you should be joyful? I cannot write you any more this morning, dear little Thérèse; I hope to go and see you this afternoon. This morning, we were deprived of being able to assist at the Mass in Carmel,[2] and we went to Mass at St. Pierre's, and we thought of you, my darling.

We kiss you with our whole heart, and your sisters as well. Offer, I beg you, our respects to Mother Marie de Gonzague and Mother Geneviève.

Your very devoted aunt,[3]
C. Guérin

* Autograph.

1. Doctor La Néele, fiancé of Jeanne Guérin.
2. Perhaps because of the early hour? See LD, September 5, 1890.
3. On the fourth blank page of this letter, Thérèse wrote the draft of her "invitation" to her wedding; see LT 118.

LC 141 *From Sister Marie of the Angels to Thérèse.*
September 8, 1890

†J. M. J. T. September 8, 1890

To my heart's little Benjamin. May this little souvenir[1] always recall, along with the most beautiful day of your life, the tender affection of her poor mistress! Dear little child, you now belong to Jesus totally! . . . Taste, savor your great happiness envied by the angels of heaven!

Little virginal Spouse of Jesus, the Lamb, if you wish to follow Him one day with the virgins in the homeland, follow Him each day in the path which He traces out for you and which was His own! May the cross, suffering, humility, sublime poverty be your whole ambition, your joy!

Love little Jesus. The gentle little Child became today your Spouse, and for Him make yourself little, very little, too, so well hidden in His Heart that He alone, His Immaculate Mother, and the angels of heaven may find you.

Sister Thérèse of the Child Jesus, be truly His mother by bringing Him to birth in souls through your sacrifices of each day! and with Him save them and open heaven for them!

Your poor little mistress who wants you to be a saint, a great saint[2] and who loves you so tenderly.

Sister Marie of the Angels of the Sacred Heart
r.c.ind.

* Autograph.

1. Perhaps a picture, not identified? Unless it is a reference to the copy of verses composed by the mistress of novices and sung in the Community during the evening recreation. This copy ends with these words: "Souvenir of the poor mistress for her beloved little Benjamin. Sister Marie of the Angels of the Sacred Heart." The last couplet recalls "this morning's sweet tears." See the following LD.
2. See LT 107, note 8.

LD *From Mother Marie de Gonzague to the prioress of the Tours Carmel.* (Extract.)

September 9, 1890

The remainder of this letter deals with the death of Mother Thérèse of St. Joseph, former prioress of Tours, which took place on September 8.

Venerable Mother Geneviève is changing and she has been very tired for a week. However, (God)[1] permitted her to witness the joy of a child whom I offered yesterday. This angelic child is seventeen and a half, and she has the judgment of one of thirty, the religious perfection of an old perfected novice, and possession of herself; she is a perfect religious. Yesterday, not an eye remained dry at the sight of her great and entire immolation.[2]

Sister Marie de Gonzague
R.c.i.

* Copy of the autograph.

1. Word absent from the autograph, and inserted according to the meaning of the sentence.
2. The concluding couplet of the Community's song composed by Sister Marie of the Angels (see LC 141, note 1) began by these verses addressed to Mother Marie de Gonzague: "*Votre parole, ô Mère bien-aimée, - A fait couler de doux pleurs ce matin; - Quand vous avez uni la fiancée - Toute joyeuse à son Epoux divin*!" (Your words, oh, beloved Mother, - Made sweet tears flow this morning; - When you united the all-joyful fiancée to her divine Spouse.) See, too, in the Appendix, the picture inscribed by Mother Marie de Gonzague for Thérèse, September 8, 1890.

LT 118 "Letter of Invitation to the Wedding of Sister Thérèse of the Child Jesus of the Holy Face."

September 8-20 (?), 1890

This is the title which Thérèse gave to her symbolic invitation in her Autobiography (Ms. A, p. 168). It was inspired by the invitation to the marriage of her cousin Jeanne Guérin to Doctor La Néele, October 1, 1890. Approximate date; see notes 1 and 2.

THÉRÈSE'S DRAFT[1]	SISTER AGNES' COPY[2]
J. M. J. T.	J T
Almighty God, creator of Heaven and earth, sovereign ruler of the world, and the most glorious Virgin Mary, Queen and princess of the heavenly court, come down to invite you to the wedding of their son Jesus, King of Kings and Lord of Lords, to Mademoiselle Thérèse Martin, now lady and princess of the kingdoms brought as dowry by her spouse, namely, the childhood of Jesus and His Passion, her titles	Almighty God, Creator of Heaven and earth, Sovereign Ruler of the World, and the Most Glorious Virgin Mary, Queen and Princess of the heavenly Court, wish to invite you to the wedding of their Divine Son Jesus, King of Kings and Lord of Lords, to Mademoiselle Thérèse Martin, now Lady and Princess of the kingdoms brought as dowry by her Divine Spouse, namely, the Childhood of Jesus and His Passion,

of nobility being the Child Jesus and the Holy Face.

Monsieur Louis Martin, proprietor and owner of the domains of suffering and humiliation, and Madame Martin, princess and lady of honor of the heavenly court, wish to invite you to the wedding of their daughter Thérèse to Jesus, the Word of God, second person of the Blessed Trinity, who, through the operation of the Holy Spirit, became man and was born of the Virgin Mary.

Being unable to invite you to assist at the nuptial blessing which was bestowed on them on the mountain of Carmel (the heavenly court being alone admitted there), they beg you, nonetheless, to be present at the return from the wedding which will take place tomorrow, on the day of Eternity, to which Jesus, the Son of God, will come on the clouds of Heaven to judge the living and the dead. (The hour being still uncertain, you are invited to hold yourselves in readiness and to watch.)

her titles of nobility being: of the Child Jesus and of the Holy Face.

Monsieur Louis Martin, Proprietor and Owner of the Domains of Suffering and humiliation, and Madame Martin, Princess and Lady of honor of the Heavenly Court, wish to invite you to the wedding of their Daughter Thérèse to Jesus, the Word of God, Second Person of the Adorable Trinity, who, through the Operation of the Holy Spirit, was made Man and Son of Mary, the Queen of Heaven.

Unable to invite you to the nuptial blessing given on the mountain of Carmel (the heavenly Court alone was admitted), they beg you, nonetheless, to be present at the return from the Wedding which will take place tomorrow, on the Day of Eternity, to which Day Jesus, the Son of God, will come on the clouds of Heaven to judge the Living and the Dead.

The hour is uncertain as yet, so you are invited to hold yourselves in readiness and to watch.

* Autograph.

1. This was written on the back of a letter from her aunt, received on September 8 (LC 140). In her account, in 1895 (Ms. A, p. 168), Thérèse recalls this "amusement" after having spoken of her

cousin's wedding. But perhaps it was written at the time of receiving the invitation (the Carmel archives have not preserved any trace of this), two or three weeks before the ceremony. It is difficult to imagine Thérèse doing this after the experience of her own sorrow at the reception of the Veil (see LT 120). It could still be placed in the first two weeks of October, but it is strange that Thérèse would have used a letter from Mme. Guérin on September 8. CMG I, pp. 55-56, states that it was written for September 24, 1890, giving it the title chosen by Thérèse in her manuscript. This version in the Autobiography is identical with that of Sister Agnes. The *Story of a Soul* has this interpolation: "Having seen the letter of the invitation to the wedding, I amused myself by composing the following which I read to the novices in order to show them what struck me: how the glory of earthly unions is little when compared with the titles of a spouse of Jesus." (*Story of a Soul*, 1907, p. 135.)

2. The copy was made on two separate sheets of paper, each ornamented with a vignette of the Holy Face of Tours. The second paragraph, relative to M. Martin, takes up the second page. Sister Agnes gave this "invitation" to Céline, along with a note in pencil: "These letters are addressed to the whole Universe. What do you think of it?. . " The back of the note has the beginning of a letter written by Sister Agnes: "J.M.J.T. Jésus Mesdam . . . Nous vous p . . . ." *Perhaps* this was an invitation to certain people in the town to Thérèse's reception of the Veil (September 24)? We notice the proximity of the version of Ms. A, p. 168 to Sister Agnes of Jesus' copy, the copy that Sister Geneviève (Céline) kept until her death. Thérèse could have read it over again in 1895 when she was writing her manuscript A. A copy seems to have been sent to P. Pichon, no doubt by Sister Marie of the Sacred Heart; see his answer of February 15, 1891: "I enjoyed the letter of the invitation from the dear little Lamb." (To Sist_r Marie of the Sacred Heart.) There is a reference to this in P. Pichon's letter to Thérèse (LC 146).

LT 119 **From Thérèse to Sister Martha of Jesus.**

September 23, 1890

Lines in pencil, on the back of a lace picture entitled: "Two inseparable devotions: the Holy Face and the Sacred Heart."

To my dear little Companion. Souvenir of the most beautiful day of your life,[1] unique day on which you were consecrated to Jesus.

Together, let us console Jesus for all the ingratitude of souls, and, through our love, let us make Him forget His sorrows.

Your unworthy little Sister
Thérèse of the Child Jesus and of the Holy Face
rel.carm.ind.[2]

* Autograph.

1. Thérèse wrote "*de votre jour*" instead of "*de votre vie.*" This was the day of Sister Martha's Profession. There was no outside ceremony of the reception of the Veil for the lay Sisters; they retained the white veil throughout their life. Sister Martha offered Thérèse a picture also; see Appendix, Pictures.
2. Abbreviation for "*religieuse carmélite indigne*" (unworthy Carmelite religious), a title used at this time, which we shall find henceforth in Thérèse's signature.

LT 120 **From Thérèse to Céline.**

September 23, 1890

Indications of a slight improvement in M. Martin's health (see LD, July 22, 1890), gave rise in Céline and Thérèse to a somewhat foolish hope: that of a visit of their father to Lisieux. "Naturally, Céline thought immediately that we should choose the day of my reception of the Veil" (Ms. A, p. 160). It seems, judging by a letter from Sister Agnes (undated; around September 20?), that Céline was to go to Caen on Monday, the 22nd, to offer Thérèse's black veils for M. Martin's blessing just as she had done for the Profession crown. On Tuesday morning, in the speakroom, Céline and Thérèse made their plans concerning the visit of their patient on the next day: "In order not to tire him," [said Céline], "I will not have him assist at the whole ceremony; at the end of the ceremony, I will go and get him, and I will bring him quietly up to the grille so that Thérèse may receive his blessing" (Ms. A, p. 160). The plan defied all "human prudence!" (ibid.). Uncle Guérin came to the speakroom, no doubt in the afternoon of the same day, to express his formal refusal to share in these plans.

J. M. J. T.

Jesus †

Oh! Céline, how can I tell you what is taking place in my soul? . . . It is torn apart, but I feel that this wound is made by a friendly hand, by a *divinely jealous hand*! . . .

All was ready for my wedding, but don't you find that there was one thing lacking for the celebration? It is true that Jesus had already placed many jewels in my basket, but there was one of incomparable beauty missing, no doubt, and this precious diamond Jesus gave me today . . . . Céline . . . when receiving it, my tears flowed . . . they are still flowing, and I would almost reproach myself for them if I did not know "That there is a love

the only proof of which is tears."[1] It is Jesus alone who is conducting this affair, it is He, and I recognized His touch *of love* . . . .

You know the extent to which I wanted to see our dear Father again this morning; and now I see very clearly that it's God's will that he not be here. God has permitted this simply to test my love . . . . Jesus wants me as an *orphan*, He wants me to be alone with Him alone in order to unite Himself more intimately with me, and He wills to give me in the homeland the very *legitimate* joys that He has refused me in the exile! . . . Céline, be consoled, for our Spouse is a spouse of tears and not smiles. Let us give Him our tears in order to console Him, and one day these tears will be changed into smiles of an ineffable sweetness! . . .

Céline, I don't know if you are going to understand my letter, for I can hardly hold my pen . . . and so another should give you many explanations concerning Uncle's visit. But your Thérèse can speak only the language of heaven. Céline, understand your Thérèse! . . .

Today's trial is a difficult sorrow to understand. We see a joy which is offered to us; it's possible, natural. We extend our hand . . . and we cannot grasp this consolation so much desired . . . . But, Céline, how mysterious all this is! . . . We no longer have a home here below,[2] or, at least, you can say just as the Blessed Virgin did: "What a home." Yes, what a home . . . but it's not a human hand that has done this, it's Jesus. It is His veiled look that has fallen upon us! . . . I received a letter from our exiled Father,[3] and here is one passage from it: "Oh! my *alleluia* is filled with tears. Neither one of your Fathers will be there to offer you to Jesus. Must you complain very much here below when the angels up above congratulate you and the saints envy you. It's your crown of thorns that makes them jealous. Love, then, its stings as so many proofs of love from the divine Spouse."

Céline, let us accept with a good heart the thorn that Jesus is offering us. Tomorrow's celebration will be a celebration of tears for us,[4] but I feel that Jesus will be consoled! . . . I would like to say

more to you, but words fail me! . . . I was put in charge of writing you in order to console you, but no doubt I have carried out this duty very poorly. . . . Ah! if I were able to convey to you the peace Jesus placed in my soul at the height of my tears, this is what I am asking Him for you who are myself! . . .

Céline! . . . The shadows are falling[5] and the image of this world is passing away;[6] soon, yes, soon, we shall see the unknown and beloved Face which ravishes us through its tears.

Sister Thérèse of the Child Jesus of the Holy Face
rel.carm.ind.

* Autograph.

1. A quotation from Céline's poem, "The Divine Charm" (see LC 128, note 1). We read there: "Here below, there is a love Whose smile is its language; But there exists another love, Whose only proof is tears."
2. See LT 91, note 4.
3. P. Pichon's letter reached Lisieux on September 12 (LC 132).
4. Thérèse's tears flowed, in fact, the next day. Commenting on Ms. A, p. 167, Mother Agnes wrote in her testimony at the beatification process: "She said that her tears were not understood, and it's true. Instead of consoling her, I said, almost at the moment of entering the chapel, 'I can't understand your crying! How can you hope to have our Father at your ceremony? If he were here, we would be exposed to much greater distress than the sorrow of his absence.' Mother Geneviève, who was sick, having heard Thérèse was crying, sent her, too, a very severe reprimand" (NPPA, Fortitude, Proofs that she was not spoiled, p. 3).

   It is within this context that we should read V. Lahaye's account, March 19, 1923, in which he described the ceremony of September 24, 1890. He had assisted at it "in the sanctuary, next to the grille where Thérèse was." He wrote, "Her eyes had a light tempered by candor and purity, but on this moving and decisive occasion, their natural gentleness gave way to a certain seriousness." (*Souvenirs d'un témoin aux cérémonies de Vêture et de Profession.*)

There were more tears in the afternoon of the 24th in the speak-room. This time, Céline received Sister Agnes of Jesus' reprimand: "It seems to me that you have cried very much with Sister Thérèse of the Child Jesus on the day of her reception of the Veil. This has caused me much distress . . . . Sadness and tears are good for nothing and they destroy one's strength. Our little Mother, who is now in heaven, did not cry often on earth, and, nevertheless, she suffered! We can shed tears of the heart all our life but not tears of the eyes, unless we receive the gift of tears!" (Letter to Céline, undated; September 26, 1890.)

5. See Canticle of Canticles 4:6.
6. 1 Corinthians 7:31.

LC 142 *From Sister Marie of the Sacred Heart to Thérèse.*

September 23, 1890

Jesus! Tuesday evening, 8:00 o'clock

My dear little daughter, I am thinking so much about you that I can't fall asleep. I have to speak a little word from heaven to you. You know better than I all that you are to your Spouse, but allow me, nonetheless, to repeat it to you. You cannot grow tired of hearing such a song. You are, beloved little child, His privileged one *among all others*, and when I hear you sing: "He has set His seal on my forehead,[1] and He has adorned me," I cannot express what music this will be for me, a music made a thousand times more melodious through today's trial. Ah! what, then, are you to Jesus? He alone could tell . . . .

This is His own secret which He will one day reveal to us. Tomorrow, darling little child, the angels will be able to say in all truth: "Who is this that comes up from the desert, leaning on her

Beloved?"[2] Will you not, in fact, be coming up from the desert of all earthly joys? And your Beloved, is He not your sole support! But what a support! He, your heart's beloved, who will answer the astonished angels: "My dove is unique,[3] chosen from among a thousand, she who has ravished my Heart by one of her glances."

Ah! how blessed you are to be able to give your Jesus so much. If He is rich, you too are rich, you are competing with the King of heaven . . . . Ah! in His very Heart, He has gathered your tears; they are mingled with His own, for you are one with your Spouse.

* Autograph.

1. The third antiphon of Matins for the Office of St. Agnes, taken from the ceremonial for the reception of the Veil.
2. Canticle of Canticles 8:5. Perhaps Sister Marie of the Sacred Heart was recalling, at this hour, her own Profession, on May 22, 1888, and also the letter she had written the day before to P. Pichon, commenting on this same verse from the Canticle of Canticles.
3. Canticle of Canticles 6:9.

About Us

ICS Publications, based in Washington, D.C., is the publishing house of the Institute of Carmelite Studies (ICS) and a ministry of the Discalced Carmelite Friars of the Washington Province (U.S.A.). The Institute of Carmelite Studies promotes research and publication in the field of Carmelite spirituality, especially about Carmelite saints and related topics. Its members are friars of the Washington Province.

The Discalced Carmelites are a worldwide Roman Catholic religious order comprised of friars, nuns, and laity—men and women who are heirs to the teaching and way of life of Teresa of Avila and John of the Cross, dedicated to contemplation and to ministry in the church and the world.

Information about their way of life is available through local diocesan vocation offices, or from the Discalced Carmelite Friars vocation directors at the following addresses:

Washington Province:
1525 Carmel Road, Hubertus, WI 53033

California-Arizona Province:
P.O. Box 3420, San Jose, CA 95156

Oklahoma Province:
5151 Marylake Drive, Little Rock, AR 72206

Visit our websites at:

www.icspublications.org and *http://ocdfriarsvocation.org*